Language Behavior in Infancy and Early Childhood

Language Behavior in Infancy and Early Childhood

Proceedings of a Pediatric Round Table held at the Santa Barbara Biltmore Hotel, Santa Barbara, California, October 10–13, 1979.

Editor:
RACHEL E. STARK
Ph.D., Associate Professor of Neurology, Johns Hopkins University, Director, Division of Hearing and Speech, John F. Kennedy Institute, Baltimore, Maryland, U.S.A.

Sponsored by:

Johnson & Johnson

BABY PRODUCTS COMPANY

ELSEVIER/NORTH-HOLLAND
NEW YORK • AMSTERDAM • OXFORD

©1981 by 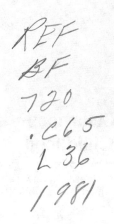 *Johnson & Johnson* Baby Products Company

Published by:

Elsevier North Holland, Inc.
52 Vanderbilt Avenue, New York, New York 10017

Sole distributors outside USA and Canada:

Elsevier Science Publishers B.V.
P.O. Box 211
1000AE Amsterdam, The Netherlands

Library of Congress Cataloging in Publication Data:
Main entry under title:

Language behavior in infancy and early childhood.

Bibliography: p.
Includes index.
1. Interpersonal communication in children—Congresses.
2. Children—Language—Congresses.   3. Infant psychology
—Congresses.   4. Verbal ability in children—Congresses.
I. Stark, Rachel E.   II. Johnson & Johnson Baby
Products Company.
BF720.C65L36   155.4'22   81-9745
ISBN 0-444-00627-3   AACR2

Manufactured in the United States of America

To the children who taught us

Contents

Preface

The conference on which this text was based was the fourth in the series of Pediatric Round Tables sponsored by the Johnson and Johnson Baby Products Company. In fostering this series, the company has sought to provide support for a scholarly undertaking that will benefit the scientific community as well as bringing new information to parents and health-care professionals.

The plan for the conference on "Language Behavior in Infancy and Early Childhood," initially proposed by myself, was developed with the help of a team of consultants made up of the following individuals: Lois Bloom, Rebecca Eilers, Catherine Garvey, David Ingram, and Daniel Stern. All of these individuals became participants except Catherine Garvey, who felt that, because her work is primarily with older children, she might have less to contribute to a conference concentrating upon the first two years of life. The planning team were much indebted to her for her encouragement and helpful suggestions.

The conference was motivated in part by the model of language development and language disorders proposed by Bloom and Lahey (1978). In this model three dimensions of language are dealt with, namely, those of content, form, and use. The model has important implications for the understanding of language disorders as well as language development.

Although the form of language has been emphasized both in structural linquistics (Bloomfield, 1933) and in theories of transformational grammar (Chomsky, 1965), very little account was taken until recently of communicative uses of language, except in Skinner's system of mands and tacts (1957). Neither the form nor the use of language was described in relation to its content or meaning until the 1970's.

These three dimensions of language may be described as follows:

1. The content of language has to do with the meaning that is encoded in messages. Meaning is conveyed by means of words or signs and by the relations among objects, between objects and events, and among events, that are expressed. Thus, all children learn to talk about objects and actions and about relations such as possession and location, whatever their particular interests or particular experience of objects and activities may be. The development of content in language relates to the child's experience of the world but more importantly it relates to the concepts he acquires as a result of those experiences.

2. The forms of spoken language comprise phonetic and semantic units and the syntactic structure of an utterance. These forms may be represented in terms of the articulatory and phonatory events of speech and of the physical, acoustic characteristics of the speech signal thus generated. They may also be represented in terms of the perceived auditory features of individual segments of speech and of its intonation contour and rhythmic pattern. The relationship among these different aspects of form is complex and at each level, phonetic, semantic, and syntactic, it is highly encoded. So, too, are the signs of sign language. The forms of language specify the relation between sounds (or signs) and meaning in any given language. Their use is governed by rules which must be learned by the child.

3. The use of language is considered to have two major aspects, one having to do with the goals or functions of language that motivate its users; the other having to do with the selection of forms based upon the social context of an exchange. This selection depends upon the participants; who they are, and the knowledge they are expected to have about the prevailing communicative situation. Modes of address and the ability to link one utterance with another in discourse are important in relation to this aspect of language.

Bloom and Lahey define language competence as a plan for speaking and understanding which rests upon the integration of content, form, and use. Thus, the child must develop "cognitive-linguistic rules for pairing sound (or movement) with meaning in messages and social rules for sound/meaning or movement/meaning connections with different situations." These authors further point out that children induce the integration of content, form, and use from their experience of language, that is, the language they hear and the language they use.

It was decided by the planning team that the conference should address ways in which content, form and use might become integrated in the language of children. The participants were asked to consider this question and also to describe their most recent findings in relation to two major themes that were selected for the conference by the team. These were: (1) the nature of individual differences among children; and (2) continuity or connectivity as opposed to discontinuity or disconnectedness of development. The participants were also asked to deal with methodological problems in their respective fields. It was hoped that new insights might be afforded into the processes of normal language development and their disruption in language disorders in children as a result of this approach.

In the first section of the resulting text, current research in the areas of social interaction and communicative behavior in infancy is discussed and the question is asked, What is the importance, if any, of these aspects of development for language? Are they important for the development of content or form of language? or for the later use of language? In the second section of the text, current research into aspects of development that *are* considered to be important for language development, namely, the development of speech production and speech perception abilities, is reviewed. By definition, these abilities should provide the substrate for the development of the forms of language, yet little is known about the processes by which they are acquired in infants and young children. In the third section, the relevance of cognitive sensorimotor development to the early development of language is re-examined. The development of object permanence, in particular, is discussed in relation to the early development of the content and form of language.

Finally, the implications of the material discussed in the first three sections of the text for language handicaps in children are considered in the last section. Early detection of such handicaps is stressed. Different kinds of language handicaps in children are described, and, in a summary chapter, patterns of disability which may place the young child at risk for these handicaps are suggested.

The participants have reviewed and edited all of the discussions included in the text. However, the editor must assume sole responsibility for the brief introduction to each section. The introductory statements are intended to provide some background for the reader who may be less familiar with any one topic area, and to reference research that is relevant to the topics covered but that could not be represented at the original conference. The summary chapter also reflects the views and biases of the editor, which are not necessarily those of the other participants.

I would like to express my personal indebtedness to the conference participants for their contributions to the conference and for their support in the preparation of this text. Their support was expressed in encouraging songs made up for the occasion as well as the more mundane tasks of editing and referencing. I would also like to thank Robert B. Rock, Jr., Director of Professional Relations at Johnson and Johnson. He and his staff not only worked on the conference arrangements and facilitated the preparation of the text but also gratified us by becoming interested in the content of our discussion.

xiv

References

Bloom, L. and Lahey, M.A. (1978) *Language Development and Language Disorders*. New York: Wiley.

Bloomfield, L. (1933) *Language*. New York: Holt, Rinehart and Winston.

Chomsky, N. (1965) *Aspects of the Theory of Syntax*. Cambridge: MIT Press.

Skinner, B.F. (1957) *Verbal Behavior*. New York, Appleton Century Crofts.

Rachel E. Stark

Foreword

I am the only contributor to this book that did not attend the conference at Santa Barbara on Language Behavior in Infancy and Early Childhood. Consequently, my role should be somewhat different from the other's. Logically I should look at the manuscripts, not as one of the illustrious group of participants, but rather as an observer after-the-fact. I should not so much try to contribute to the message as to provide perspectives about the message.

The planners have chosen their topics and participants with obvious care. The combination of developmental topics on social, cognitive, and psycholinguistic competence provide for a broad organized coverage of a complex and difficult literature.

This extensive coverage provides for a book that is especially timely, I think, because we are still struggling to get a comprehensive grasp of the combined area of normal and abnormal language acquisition. This information is essential as a basis of language intervention.

The interventionists have an especially difficult task at this time. The research literature tells us that we should approach the delayed and disordered child as early as possible. We are told also that functional language is extremely important in early childhood, that cognitive, syntactical, social, and functional features of language are interrelated at all stages of development, and that early transactional experiences provide the bases for communication competence. The excitement we find in reading about these and many other relevant issues may impel us to undertake new professional ventures. However, it is likely that most of us will not easily derive an organized approach for our individual professional purposes. We must each strive to organize the available literature. In undertaking this effort, we are each of us fortunate to have a comprehensive book on early language. The book is especially valuable for its organized design of information. The format is apparent from the table of content. The three sections relate to the early development of (1) social and communicative behavior, (2) the forms of language, and (3) cognitive development. Each of these sections includes an introduction (by the editor), three or more papers dealing with subtopics, and discussant paper.

This format provides the reader with a remarkable amount of assistance in thinking through the content. Also, this format assures the reader of up-to-date coverage and thoughtful critiques to supplement the impressions gained from individual manuscripts.

I feel privileged to have this ''sneak preview'' of the book's content. In much the same way I have been privileged for years in knowing many of the contributors to this volume and to have drawn from them in supplementing my own ideas.

The issues of early detection, early planning, and early intervention for infants and small children at-risk for speech, for language, and for communication are strikingly important. However, the importance is purely theoretical until the research is done and the reports are compiled and analyzed. Then we are able to assess the feasibility of these early operational approaches. Our efforts in this regard should receive a great impetus from this book.

Undoubtedly the designs for early assessment and early intervention need to be assessed for feasibility, but they also must be refined and subjected to clinical practicality. Beyond these stages will be also the further refinements and individualized applications that good clinicians devise. These efforts will require years of additional research and application. This book should signal the beginning of that work.

For now, we should assess our knowledge base for current designs that will help all infants and small children to play the *communication game*.

Richard L. Schiefelbusch

Participants

Lois Bloom, Ph.D.
Department of Psychology, Teachers College, Columbia University, New York, NY 10027

Arnold J. Capute, M.D., F.A.A.P.
Deputy Medical Director, The John F. Kennedy Institute, 707 North Broadway, Baltimore, MD 21205

Robin S. Chapman, Ph.D.
Department of Communicative Disorders, University of Wisconsin, 1975 Willow Drive, Madison, WI 53706

James T. Dettre
Director of Marketing Services, Johnson & Johnson Baby Products Company, 220 Centennial Avenue, Piscataway, NJ 08854

Rebecca E. Eilers, Ph.D.
Associate Professor of Pediatrics and Psychology, Mailman Center for Child Development, University of Miami, P.O. Box 016820, Miami, FL 33101

Alan Fogel, Ph.D.
Department of Child Development and Family Studies, Purdue University, West Lafayette, IN 47907

Kurt W. Fischer, Ph.D.
Department of Psychology, University of Denver, University Park, Denver, CO 80208

Thomas F. Gorman
Director of Consumer Research, Johnson & Johnson Baby Products Company, 220 Centennial Avenue, Piscataway, NJ 08854

Gerald Gratch, Ph.D.
Department of Psychology, University of Houston, Houston, TX 77004

Janet B. Hardy, M.D.
Professor of Pediatrics, The Johns Hopkins University, School of Medicine, 720 Rutland Avenue, Baltimore, MD 21205

David Ingram, Ph.D.
Department of Linguistics, The University of British Columbia, 2075 Westbrook Mall, Vancouver, B.C., Canada V6T IW5

Jerome Kagan, Ph.D.
Professor of Psychology, Department of Psychology and Social Relations, Harvard University, William James Hall, 33 Kirkland Street, Cambridge, MA 02138

Raymond D. Kent, Ph.D.
Senior Research Associate, Human Communication Laboratories, The Boys Town Institute, 555 North 30th Street, Omaha, NE 68131

Patricia K. Kuhl, Ph.D.
Associate Professor, Department of Speech and Hearing Science, Child Development and Mental Retardation Center, WJ-10, University of Washington, Seattle, WA 98195

Lewis A. Leavitt, M.D.
Department of Pediatrics, Waisman Center for Mental Retardation and Human Development, University of Wisconsin, 1500 Highland Avenue, Madison, WI 53706

Karin Lifter, M. Phil.
Department of Psychology, Teachers College, Columbia University, Box 5, New York, NY 10027

Ronald W. Netsell, Ph.D.
Human Communication Laboratories, The Boys Town Institute, 555 North 30th Street, Omaha, NE 68131

D. Kimbrough Oller, Ph.D.
Associate Professor of Pediatrics and Psychology, Mailman Center for Child Development, University of Miami, P.O. Box 016820, Miami, FL 33101

D. R. Petterson, Ph.D.
Vice President and General Manager Professional Products, Johnson & Johnson Baby Products Company, 220 Centennial Avenue, Piscataway, NJ 08854

Diane J. Powell, R.N., M.A.
Manager of Professional Relations, Johnson & Johnson, 501 George Street, New Brunswick, NJ 08903

Abigail Peterson Reilly, Ph.D.
Science Writer, 43 Fern Street, Hartford, CT 06105

Robert B. Rock, Jr., M.A., M.P.A.
Director of Professional Relations, Johnson & Johnson Baby Products Company, 501 George Street, New Brunswick, NJ 08903

Steven Sawchuk, M.D.
Director, Medical Services and Chairman, Institute for Pediatric Service, Johnson & Johnson Baby Products Company, 220 Centennial Avenue, Piscataway, NJ 08854

Rachel E. Stark, Ph.D.
Director, Hearing, and Speech Division, The John F. Kennedy Institute, 707 North Broadway, Baltimore, MD 21205

Daniel N. Stern, M.D.
Department of Psychiatry, The New York Hospital, Cornell Medical Center, 525 East 68th Street, New York, NY 10021

Edward Tronick, Ph.D.
Department of Psychology, The Commonwealth of Massachusetts, University of Massachusetts, Amherst, MA 01003

Peter H. Wolff, M.D.
The Children's Hospital Medical Center, Enders Research Laboratory, 300 Longwood Avenue, Boston, MA 02115

Language Behavior in Infancy
and Early Childhood

SECTION I:
Social Development and Communicative Behavior in Infancy

Introduction

In the 1960's, studies of child language were dominated by Chomsky's theory of transformational grammar. This theory, deriving from the work of de Saussure (1959) and Jakobson (1972) dealt with the formal nature of adult language and made it possible to apply powerful mathematical techniques to the study of language. It was believed that the formal aspects of syntax must be acquired by the child by virtue of the innate knowledge of universal aspects of language that he possessed, and the innate capacity to observe regularities of structure and grammatical relations in the corpus of data available to him in adult speech. In the 1970's, it was realized, however, that, just as the Rosetta Stone hieroglyphics could not be deciphered until a glossary became available in the form of a translation in a known language (Hockett, 1961), so too, language could not be comprehended by the child unless it occurred within a familiar context and in relation to familiar objects and events. Only with the support of that context could the child figure out what was being said (Macnamara, 1972). Accordingly, the focus in studies of child language shifted from formal grammatical relations to the word meanings and semantic relations that were learned by the child (Brown, 1973).

In addition, it began to be realized that language derived its significance from its communicative function. Thus, language learning demanded knowledge about the roles of the speaker and the listener as well as knowledge about the world. The social setting was important as well as the physical setting (Bruner, 1975; Bates, 1976). A comprehensive description of language acquisition, therefore, had to include an account of the learning of language forms in relation to the context of utterances and also in relation to the social aspects of communication.

A number of somewhat different accounts of language development (Halliday, 1973; Dore 1974; Bruner, 1978) agree upon a basic inventory of social communicative functions which motivate the child to learn language. These are: making contact, establishing and maintaining social exchanges, controlling others, influencing others to act in a desired way, labeling and indicating, and making reference to objects and events.

The work of Halliday (1973) and Bates and her colleagues (1977) suggests a close relation between level of perceptual and cognitive development and the ability to express such communicative intentions. Bates et al. (1977), in a detailed longitudinal study of Italian and American infants, have described the nonverbal behaviors of establishing eye contact, pointing, reaching, and showing and offering of objects, which young children use to obtain the attention of adults and to get adults to assist them in obtaining objects. Bates et al. have identified protodeclarative and protoimperative types of utterances and have related these to stages of cognitive development in the sensorimotor period.

Halliday has described the functions of language in the order in which they are mastered by the young child as follows:

1. Instrumental. "I want" function; satisfaction of need and desires.
2. Regulatory. "Do as I tell you" function; controlling the behavior of others.
3. Interactional. "Me and you" function; greetings and establishing mutual attention to familiar objects.
4. Personal. "Here I come" function; expressing personal feelings and awareness of self—ultimately expressing of individuality, personality.
5. Heuristic. "Tell me why" function; exploring the environment, categorizing objects, asking questions.
6. Imaginative. "Let's pretend" function; making believe, creating interesting effects with words.
7. Informational. "I've got something to tell you" function; communicating information.

This system is probably the most comprehensive one for description of communicative function thus far proposed. However, it requires further testing.

Other aspects of communication which have social importance are those of:

1. Modifying a message to suit different speech contexts. Children learn to distinguish contexts which are more and less formal and also how to address adults as opposed to their peers. Modifications in the form of intonation and different uses of gesture with different postures are present even preverbally (Bates, 1976; Ervin-Tripp, 1976). Children learn how to

indicate politeness and emphasis by linguistic forms of expression as well as by intonation and gesture very early in the preschool years (Garvey, 1975).

2. Linking utterances in a systematic way with antecedent utterances in order to sustain a topic and to maintain the flow of meaning in a conversational exchange. Linkages are accomplished in a functional manner in an answer to a question or a request for clarification. Formal linkages are also employed to provide cohesiveness, for example, ellipsis and conjunctive devices. The child who has single words only at his command is limited in the number and type of cohesive devices he can use. However, he can use intonational cues and he can also make choices as to the part of a message he will encode, depending upon whether what he wants to say is new information or old (Greenfield and Smith, 1976).

Bruner (1975) has suggested that development of such communication skills may be fostered by the nature of social interaction between mother and infant. He has shown that, in the joint enterprises of mothers and babies at play, the baby learns to pay attention to the same objects as the mother; he also learns segments of joint actions in play routines and how to put them together in various ways. In the course of this play, roles are shifted and routines substituted for one another according to increasingly complex rules. Initially the mother provides support and interpretation, but over time the infant takes a more active role in the joint regulation of activity.

From such exchanges the infant acquires the ability to initiate and maintain exchanges, and also acquires rules for turn-taking and for action and attention in an interactive situation. Bruner believes that grammatical rules as well as rules of discourse may be learned by analogy from the regulation of joint action and attention.

These studies indicate that the development of the skills required for mutual play exchanges may be as important to language acquisition as the development of object concepts. Werner and Kaplan (1963) have suggested that social, interactive behaviors and manipulation of objects may be learned separately at first, and later combined. Thus, social schemes and object schemes are coordinated in schemes for social play involving objects, probably toward the latter part of the first year.

There is some indication from recent studies (Stern, this volume Chapter 3; Tronick, this volume Chapter 1) that the acquisition of social interactive schemes occurs earlier in life than the learning of object play schemes. In the earliest months, in fact, the infant's social activity may contrast quite sharply with his physical immaturity—that is, with his poor head control and lack of ability to grasp or to sit without support. In the early social interactive phase as well as in the later, the mother provides support or "frames" for interaction by adapting to the infant's behavior. She also interprets his contributions to the interaction quite liberally. The infant, who is never really passive but reciprocates from the beginning to some extent, takes an increasingly active role. He also has a very powerful effect on the behavior of the mother throughout.

Mother-infant interaction in the earliest months of life has not traditionally been considered as having importance for language development. Some aspects of that interaction have importance for survival, for example, crying and the mother's responsiveness to crying (Dunn and Richards, 1977; Wolff, 1969) and interaction in feeding (Kaye, 1977). Others also have importance for emotional development and mother-infant bonding, for example, eye contact and smiling. It is noteworthy that visual behaviors, and the control of gaze and facial expression, are much better developed and more mature in the very young infant than other behaviors. Thus, infants are able to express affective states from birth. Their earliest expressions are reactive, reflections of state rather than intentional communications; or, as Bates would term it, they are perlocutionary acts. Vocal expressions of affect develop until, at 5 to 6 months of age, the infant is capable of expressing delight and amusement as well as distress. These forms of expression, however, are probably universal. They are not tied to conventional forms of any language and, as Stern points out (this volume), they are not encoded verbally by the young child when he begins to speak. Yet they are an essential part of communication in adult life.

In this section of the text, early social-interactive behaviors of the infant are considered in relation to the later development of communication. The question is asked, do these nonverbal behaviors influence later language development? And, if so, (1) do they contribute to the acquisition of language content, form or use; (2) in what manner do they contribute to these dimensions of language? These questions are asked in relation to those communicative behaviors that are later encoded verbally and those that are not.

Published 1981 by Elsevier North Holland, Inc.
Stark, ed.
Language Behavior in Infancy and Early Childhood

Infant Communicative Intent: The Infant's Reference to Social Interaction

Ed Tronick

Department of Psychology, University of Massachusetts, Amherst, Massachusetts

Communicative intentions are generally not ascribed to an infant prior to the age of seven or eight months by most linguistically oriented researchers and cognitive theorists (Bruner, 1975; Bates et al., 1977). The criteria used for making this ascription generally require or imply reference to an object, and varied or indirect means persistently applied until the partner acts on the referenced object. That is, the infant's actions are directed toward an end state, are varied in order to achieve that state, and are persistent and stimulus specific. However, this object-based view fails to index the infant's communicative competence properly, not because of the criteria per se but because of the requirement for an outside object. For when the infant's acts are seen as performed with reference to interaction with a partner or the actions of infant's partner, the communicative intent of the infant becomes evident long before there is reference to objects.

Sander (1969) has characterized a sequence of tasks that the infant and its caretaking environment regulate during early ontogenesis. The stage generally focused on in linguistically oriented research is the stage of initiative, beginning at seven to nine months. It is the period when the infant has preferred activities, initiates social exchanges, and shows frustration and anger when goals are not accomplished. Most researchers agree that by this time the infant is communicating intentionally. But, there are two earlier stages.

During the newborn period, the infant's task is one of regulation of sleeping, feeding, quieting, and arousing. Much of this regulation is achieved through the process of entrainment, the coordination of endogenous processes of the infant to the timing of exogenous environmental events, such as caretaking. Wolff, (1968) in his classic work on sucking rhythms and state organization in the infant, was the first to make clear to us just how organized the infant is. He found that infants lacking in or showing poor endogenous organization were often developmentally deviant in other respects. Wolff emphasized that the development of complexly organized performances was dependent on the endogenous timing mechanisms that also make the initial rhythmicities possible. Sander (1977) has examined how these rhythmicities become entrained to environmental events during early postnatal development. For example, infant diurnal cycling is influenced by the caretaking routine and the particular person performing it. When either is changed, diurnal cycling changes. In one experiment, masking of the caretaker at seven days of age produced a marked immediate reaction in the infant and a continuing reaction over the next 24 hr (Cassell and Sander, 1976). Sander argued that it is the self-regulated rhythmic organization and the receptivity to highly specific environmental cues that makes the regulation of endogenous processes possible. Sander (1977), reviewing the evidence on early successful regulations, summarizes by saying that the infant is capable of goal-directed action adapted to a specific configuration within an assimilated context. One need only think of the directed quality of a rooting reflex when an infant is in an appropriate state and in an appropriate temporal and physical environment to have another illustration of Sander's statement.

The next developmental task beginning at two months is the regulation of reciprocal exchanges, typically between the mother and infant around caretaking activities and affective vocal and motor play. It is on this stage that I would like to concentrate because when one defines the *interaction* as that which is regulated or referenced by the infant's actions, the communicative capacities of the infant become clarified, as does the question of how the regulation is achieved.

The regulation of reciprocal interchanges can be viewed as a form of skilled performance. Bruner (1971) sees the skillful regulation of joint activities as being on a par with skillful performance on objects and both skills as the major accomplishments of the first year. Indeed, joint regulation is the more complex; it requires a sharing of time, content, and intent (Tronick, 1980). Successful joint regulation of behavior presents to the communicators the task of understanding the communicative acts of his/her partner and modifying his/her own communicative acts in accordance with the other's expressed intent while fulfilling his/her own intent. Thus, when trying to understand the communicative capacities of the infant and the prerequisites of language, one must concentrate on the extent to which the infant is able to modify his/her communicative acts and how or according to what rules his/her acts are organized.

It is clear that these two questions are sensible when one examines how well coordinated the interaction is in infants of three to four months of age. Wolff (1968) demonstrated that the basis for coordination was present even in the newborn; that the newborn was rhythmically organized. He showed that sucking and crying were organized into "temporal sequences of high frequency" which were relatively unaffected by external events. He further explained them as originating in "intrinsic regulators of serial order. . .central mechanisms that cannot be reduced to experience alone" (Wolff, 1967). This endogenous organization allows for the occurrence of coordinated actions between adult and infant, although in and of itself it does not imply how the coordination takes place or who is responsible for successful coordination.

At the time that Wolff made these observations he felt that there were few other observations to "prejudice his hypotheses." This is no longer the case. There are now multiple demonstrations of coordinated interchanges between mothers and infants at two to four months of age and even prior to that during the newborn period. These coordinations take place at different temporal levels and have been looked at in terms of different forms of behavioral organization.

Condon and Sander (1974), in probably the most dramatic and to some extent most controversial set of findings, demonstrated synchrony of neonatal movement and speech. They argued that changes in direction of the infant's movement were coordinated with the phoneme boundaries of adult speech. Such coordination would require regulation on the order of tenths of a second. At the present time, there is no explanation of how such coordination could possibly take place, although one important suggestion (Dowd, 1979) is that *if* such coordination takes place, it must be in relation to longer duration qualities of speech such as stress marks, rhythm, or tempo. Certainly these results require replication and they alone are not strong enough to support an argument for coordination between infant and adult interactions. Fortunately, there are several other far less controversial demonstrations of coordinated interchanges between adults and infants.

Brazelton, Koslowski, and Main (1974), in their important pioneering study, demonstrated that there were rhythmic cycles of attention and non-attention in the infant during face-to-face interactive exchanges. Studying these cycles in great detail they demonstrated that mothers and infants were able to fit these cycles together such that the interaction took on the form of a regulated homeostatic system. Stern (1974a) focused on the positive segments of face-to-face interactions, segments he refered to as games, and found that mothers and infants are typically able to coordinate both gaze and vocalization. Tronick, Als, and Brazelton (1980a) analyzed five interactions of infants at approximately 100 days of age, and showed that the largest proportion of transitions between different behavioral interactive states were simultaneous transitions. That is, transitions did not typically occur with one partner leading and the other partner following, but rather with both partners changing to similar behavioral and affective states at the same time. Additionally, in examining interactions between infants and mothers at three, six, and nine months of age, Ricks, Krafchuk, and Tronick (1979) demonstrated that infant and mother spend respectively 18%, 23%, and 41% of the total time of the interaction in the same interactive behavior state.

A complementary or dialogic structure has also been described for face-to-face exchanges. The prototypical demonstration comes from Kaye and Brazelton (1971). They showed that during nursing, mother and infant fit their behavior together in a complementary fashion. That is, when the infant was nursing with a burst of sucks the mother would pause, and when the infant paused between bursts, the mother jiggled the infant. Mothers typically interpreted the jiggling as leading to a resumption of sucking on the part of the infant. However, careful analyses showed that the pause between bursts of sucking was actually lengthened when the mother jiggled the infant. Kaye and Brazelton (1971) then argued that the lengthened pause allowed for a communicative interchange between mother and infant.

A similiar structure of one partner active and the other inactive has been described for other aspects of face-to-face exchanges between mothers and infants. Bateson (1979), Tronick (Tronick, Als, Brazelton, 1980a,b), and Fogel (1977) have demonstrated at two months an alternating sequence of maternal vocalizations to infant pauses and maternal pauses to infant vocalizations. This meshing resulted in a typical conversation-like structure between mother and infant. Stern (1974a), in his description of games, found alternating patterns of activity: one partner playing one part of a game while the other reciprocated, followed by a switch in roles.

This research demonstrates that the interaction can be seen as a coordinated time-locked sequence of joint behaviors. It is organized at several temporal levels ranging from tenths of a second to several seconds, and the different levels appear to be hierarchically embedded and related to one another. This can be seen, at the very least, as a process of entrainment of phase synchronization in which the endogenous rhythmical organization of the infant is coordinated to the exogenous rhythmicity of the caretaker's behavior. However, such a characterization leaves open the question as to whether or not the infant is able to adjust and modify his/her behavior in response to his/her caretaker's behavior.

A first approach to answering this question is to show that the infant's behavior is specific to specific situations and that the behavior is appropriate to that stimulus context. Such a demonstration is analagous to the investigations by Gibson and Walk (1960) of the infant's capacity to perceive depth at a visual cliff. Gibson and Walk have argued convincingly that the infant was able to perceive depth rather than just proximal changes in the simulation because the infant's behavior at the visual cliff was appropriate to the perception of depth. That is, infants avoided the cliff and showed signs of fear when they were close to it. A similar finding of appropriate behaviors by the infant to different stimulus configurations during social interaction would be a first indication of the infant's capacity to regulate his/her actions with communicative intent.

Indeed, several studies have shown that the infant is able not only to discriminate, but also to act appropriately in social and non-social situations. Bullowa (1975) observed and contrasted the infant's behavior alone and with a person. She summarized her observation as follows:

"The most striking feature is the contrast between this four-month-old infant's behavior alone and during interaction. I have watched the mother pat the infant's open mouth rhythmically and heard the infant vocalize producing between them an undulating sound. The infant's vocalization starts and stops with the mother's patting. . .and as evidence in other activities it can be seen that she is able to go along with her mother in complicated interactional sequences. But, when put in her crib she has a small repertoire. She can raise her head and chest in prone. She can turn from prone to supine, but not the reverse. She can watch and reach for objects. She can go to sleep. These activities follow one another like beads on a string. Naked eye observation does not detect any embedded units. . .one might propose that during communicative activity she is participating in some aspects of her mother's hierarchically structured behavior."

This observation quite strikingly shows the differences in the kinds and qualities of behavior that the infant engages in when alone and in social interaction. When combined with the following observations by Brazelton and his colleagues (Brazelton, Koslowski and Main, 1974) on the infant's behavior with objects as contrasted to people, a convincing case begins to be made for the specificity of the infant's actions.

Brazelton (Brazelton, Kowlowski and Main, 1974) observed infants as young as two months of age as they interacted with a small object dangling from a string and contrasted it to the infant's interaction with people. They observed that the infant's attention, posture, and facial expression as well as the rhythmicity and smoothness of the infant's movement were different in the two situations. When interacting with an object, the infant focused his attention on the object for periods of time up to two minutes without a shift in gaze. The infant would pounce at the object: raise his shoulders, stretch out his arms and with a sudden burst of activity strike or swipe at the object, generally unsuccessfully. Facial expressions were intense. Movements were jerky. After a large flurry of activity, the infant would turn away briefly and then look back at the object for an extended period of engagement that culminated once again in a flurry of activity directed at the object.

In contrast, during social interaction, they described the infant as having a cyclic pattern of attention with gaze shifting toward and away from the partner 4 or 5 times per minute. Movements were smooth and gestural in quality. Facial expressions varied and often culminated in large and broad smiles (see also Trevarthen, 1974; Bower, 1974). Furthermore, when one looks at the development of interactions over the first 9 months of life, one can see the elaboration of these different aspects of the infant behavioral repertoire, (Ricks, Krafchuck, and Tronick, 1979). At 3 months of age, during an interaction the infant spends the greatest proportion of time in social engagement with only small amounts of time devoted to actions on objects.

However, at 6 months more than 40% of the interaction is spent focused on objects, even if the objects are rather uninteresting ones in the context of the interaction, and a somewhat smaller proportion of time is spent in social engagement. At nine months of age, the interaction is made up of elaborated sequences that simultaneously combine objects with social interactions.

.However, although the contrast between the infant's behaviors with objects, people, and being alone is quite striking, one could argue about the significance of the infant's differential behavior since these stimuli are so different in terms of the complexity, quantity, and mobility that they present to the infant. And even though such stimulus differences do not explain the differences in the quality and form of the infant's behavior with each, it still seems necessary to examine those studies which have shown differences in the infant's performance in different types of social interactions in order to assess the infant's capacity to regulate the interaction.

Gottman (1979) reanalyzed data presented by Tronick, Als, and Brazelton (1977) using spectral analysis to determine whether or not the infant's behavior was influenced by the behavior of the mother. He analyzed three interactions of infants varying in age from 88 to 103 days. In each interaction, he found strong evidence that the mother's behavior was influenced by the infant's behavior. In two of the three interactions he found no evidence that the infant's behavior was influenced by the mother's behavior. That is, these infants' patterns of behavior could be predicted from their own previous behavior. Adding information about the mother's behavior did not increase that prediction. However, in the third interaction, Gottman found that the infant's behavior was best predicted by a combination of his own behavior and his mother's behavior. In this case, there was clear evidence that the infant was adjusting and modifying his own behavior in relationship to the mother's behavior during the interaction. Unfortunately, there have been few other comparable analyses on normal interactions, although several studies have examined and found changes in the form of the infant's response to different partners.

Winn and Tronick (1980), in a study of changes in infant behavior in response to five exposures to an initially unfamiliar adult, demonstrated that from the first exposure to the last, the infants showed modifications and adjustment in their behavior appropriate to the quality and kind of behavior presented to them by the stranger. There was an increase in positive affective displays and in the meshing of infant behavior with adult behavior. Similarly, Yogman et al. (1976) have shown that the infant at three months of age interacts differently with his/her mother, father, and stranger. Indeed, in one analysis, Yogman et al. showed that the patterning of an infant's behavior was different in interaction with the father than with the mother. He found that infants showed larger and more abrupt affective changes during interaction with their fathers as contrasted to more modulated and smaller changes during interaction with their mothers (see also Field, 1978).

More direct demonstrations of infant modifications in behavior to specific interactive sequences are found in studies where the behavior of the adult partner has been experimentally altered. Bloom (1975) showed that the adult's pattern of gaze did not affect the amount of infant vocalization, but did result in a modification of the infant's pattern of vocalizations. In a series of studies, Tronick (Tronick et al., 1978; Tronick, Als, and Adamson, 1979) has demonstrated the effects of more dramatic changes in the infant's behavior. In one study, (Tronick et al., 1978) the mother was asked to interact with the infant in a normal fashion followed by a three-minute period in which the mother remained still-faced. The infant's reaction to the still-faced mother was dramatic and specific. The infant first gave the mother the normal greeting. When she failed to return the infant's greeting, the infant stilled, stared, and looked away. This sequence was usually followed by a second but foreshortened greeting. Following this second greeting, the infant again would stare, look at the mother in a wary fashion, and glance off to the side. With the adult's continued non-response, the infant's body, face, and gaze would tend to shift away from the mother such that the infant began to look at the mother out of the corner of his or her eye, making use of peripheral vision. This looking away was punctuated by brief elicitations directed at the mother. However, when these failed to produce the normal maternal response, the infants slumped away from the mother. They lost postural control and they often engaged in self-comforting behaviors. Cohn and Tronick (1980) have extended this work and asked mothers to act in an affectless fashion. That is, the mothers were to eliminate the slowed down and exaggerated pattern of facial and vocal behaviors they normally engaged in with their infants but to continue to move and change their behavior. Observing infants three months of age, the investigators found that the infants reacted to this pattern on the mother's part with initial wariness and elicitations that were eventually followed by crying. In another study, Tronick, Als, and Brazelton (1980a) demonstrated that when the mother sits in profile with her infant, the infant reaches out toward her and makes calling vocalizations.

Other changes do not produce elicitations but do produce modifications in the infant's behavior. For example, when mothers are asked to slow down even further their already slow pace of interaction, the infant actually shows more positive affect during this interaction than during the normal interaction (Tronick, Als, and Adamson, 1979). Or when mothers are asked to act somewhat like puppets, that is, in a jerky, noncontingent fashion to their infant's displays, infants stare at this display for long periods of time as if the mother was object-like rather than person-like (Tronick, Als, and Brazelton, 1980b). This set of studies makes it clear that a simple discrepancy model or an arousal model is inadequate to account for these findings, since such models contain neither behavioral nor stimulus specificity.

Other demonstrations of similar effects have come from more naturalistic observations. Brazelton, Koslowski, and Main (1974) showed that mothers who overload their infants during an interaction by engaging in too many behaviors, too fast, thereby not allowing the infant to take his or her turn, produce looking away on the part of the infant. Moreover, they showed that this pattern of looking away actually increased over the early months of development and eventually developed into interactions with a rigidly complementary structure: the mother overloading and the infant looking away for long periods of time with mutual gaze seldom being established. Stern (1971), in his study of twins, described a similar pattern in which the mother and one of her twins were unable to achieve mutual gaze. Massie (1975), using home movies parents had taken of their infants prior to the diagnosis of a childhood psychosis at three or four years of age, also found similar distorted patterns of interaction. He showed that mothers would often fail to respond to the infant's signals in an appropriate fashion and the infant would react to this inappropriateness on the mother's part by first attempting to elicit the mother's behavior and then give up, become wary, and turn away.

Two other studies are relevant in this context, one the study of a sighted infant of blind parents (Adamson et al., 1977) and the second, a study of a blind but neurologically intact infant of sighted parents (Als, Tronick, and Brazelton, 1980). In the first instance, we have an infant who is exposed to apparently extremely distorted rearing conditions. The parents, because of their blindness, obviously missed the visual signals emitted by the infant and they showed few appropriate "visual" behaviors in relationship to the infant. For example, the mother although having some idea as to what vision is, seldom presented objects to the infant in the midline but rather, away out to the side in her peripheral field. The mother also had a characteristically immobile face. The infant responded to this distortion in her mother's communicative behavior by turning away and seldom making visual contact with the mother's face. This looking away characterized her behavior in the first 4 to 5 months of her development. It wasn't until the normal developmental step of incorporating objects into social interaction that the infant began to make face-to-face contact with the mother. Nonetheless, despite this distortion, the infant not only developed normally, but mother, father, and infant were able to interact successfully even during the first half year of life. They established interactions similar in structure to normal interactions which did not employ face-to-face posturing. The infant would look off to one side while cooing and moving with her parent's playful talk, songs, and touches. Importantly, in this context, the infant was able to make this adjustment in her normal pattern of behavior by distorting one modality, gaze, so as to employ other modalities. Furthermore, with sighted adults the infant interacted in a typical face-to-face fashion.

In the second case (Als et al., 1980), the blind infant also developed normally. She obviously was deprived of the visual input presented by her parents. The infant was able to use auditory and tactile stimulation to gain information from the social environment and use it to control her own interactive behaviors. Fraiberg's (1977) observations of the gestural signaling of blind infants, signals that in the normal case are not used for communication, are also relevant here. These naturalistic situations emphasize that no particular modalities are of unique importance to the infant during this developmental period nor to the capacity of the infant to generate communicative signals in establishing an interaction.

These studies suggest several things about the infant's communicative competence. First, they indicate that the infant is able to modify his/her behavior in an appropriate fashion during social interaction. Second, that when the interaction is distorted the infant engages in behaviors that are aimed at reinstating the normal interaction. Third, particularly from the studies of the blind infant and the study of the sighted infant with blind parents, it would seem that the infant's goal is to establish mutuality and that such mutuality is not necessarily tied to specific modalities or specific content in the interaction. Additionally, from the study of the blind infant it seems that certain rules or formats of the interaction are built into the infant. That is, this infant was unable to learn that her mother's pattern of behavior was the normal pattern of behavior, despite the fact that it was the pattern the infant was always exposed to.

The infant during social interaction is demonstrating capacities that will not be manifested in interactions with objects until later in development. The infant regulates the interactions; his/her actions are referenced to the current state of the interaction. This referencing is most evident during distorted interactions, when the infant enacts behaviors aimed at changing that current state. During such aberrant situations, the infant flexibly and persistently varies behaviors directed at establishing mutuality. Data and implication make it likely that this occurs during the normal interaction as well.

This capacity for reference to the interaction rather than to objects develops first because it is a prerequisite skill. The infant must develop the capacity to regulate another's behavior to fit in with his or her own behavior before he or she can coordinate another's behavior both to his or her own behavior and to an outside event. Thus, initially, the interaction is what is regulated; it is the referent of the infant's behavior. Successful regulation of the interaction is followed developmentally by simultaneous regulation of interaction and object. In transition to that accomplishment, at six months of age the infant either interacts socially or exercises his/her newly emerging object skills, but he/she seldom combines both into a joint format.

As in the case of language, there is a strong indication that the initial competence for imposition of a social relationship is not learned. In the normal interaction, there are too many complicated patterns of interaction between mothers and infants, and between infants and other adults, for the infant to have learned each of those patterns in so short a span of time. In the case of the infant with blind parents, the infant was unable to learn that the mother's unresponsive face was appropriate. In the case of the blind infant with sighted parents, we have an example of the underlying competence when a major modality of perception was eliminated. Lastly, it is also clear from looking at interactions that they are unique, not quite in the infinite varietal sense of linguistic utterance, but nonetheless in a sense that implies that they are created at the time of occurrence, and therefore contain a generative component.

Such characteristics suggest the following model for the joint regulation of behavior (Tronick, 1980). The infant has a goal to interact in a particular fashion and this goal must be communicated to and then shared with a partner. The communication employs expressive modalities as a means of signalling one's interactive intent. No receptive or expressive modality is necessarily required, although some information carrying and conveying channels must be functional. The sequencing of the infant's and the partner's communicative behavior is governed by a set of rules that has a format specifying each interactant's own behavior and the expected behavior of his/her partner. For example, when I talk, you will listen, or when I greet, you will greet. They are rules of simultaneous actions. The infant possesses these rules implicitly and innately. Some of the rules are specified, witness the infant's reaction to blind parents, and the normal simultaneous occurrence of greetings. Some will be elaborated or filled in by particular experience with particular individuals, for example, interactive sequences unique to father and mother. These rules permit the elaboration of patterns while specifying the permissibility of a pattern. They govern each partner's typical interactive behavior as he or she tries to fulfill his or her interactive goal. They also are operative when one partner modifies his or her own behavior in order to get the second partner to act differently and conform to his or her own goal, as for example when the infant uses elicitations to reestablish the normal interaction.

The model suggests how joint regulation is accomplished. The data suggest that infants have a referential capacity prior to their ability to reference objects during social interaction. However, it is clear that these are developmentally distinct accomplishments. Moreover, the approach emphasizes the view that examination of development solely in terms of a later-coming end state will distort the nature and the richness of earlier developmental events.

Discussion

Fogel, in commenting on Tronick's paper, indicated that he was having trouble with the concept of shared meaning on the part of mother and infant. Shared meaning, according to George Herbert Mead, implies that the mother and infant always understand the same gestures as conveying the same concepts. At the same time, Tronick's conclusions seemed to imply that behavioral programs were inherent in the infant, but that the infant could not respond according to these programs unless certain facilitating conditions in the environment were present. The difficulty of the normally sighted child with a blind mother would be an example in point. The two notions, that is, of inherent programs and shared meaning, appeared to be contradictory. If there is an internalized pattern of responding in the infant, that argues against the notion of shared meaning.

Fogel added that he had struggled with contradictory hypotheses also. The finding with the "still-faced" mother, for example, could be explained on the basis only of the infant's preference for one pattern of stimulation as opposed to another. The preference might be along an activity dimension, or some other purely physical characteristic of the stimuli.

With respect to the problem of shared meaning and inherent programs, Tronick did not see a contradiction but rather a problem in terminology, at least in part. Meaning could be shared because the infant possessed programs that permitted the decoding and generation of affective signals. These programs were not simply sets of responses but something more analogous to a lexicon with rules governing the sequencing of the signals. If they were just responses, then there would be no explanation for the behavior of the normally sighted infant with the blind mother.

Tronick agreed that preference for one pattern of stimulation was a possible alternative explanation. However, he was inclined to reject it on the basis of two primary pieces of evidence. One was the quality of the infant's reaction to some of the distorted behaviors on the part of the mother. The infant tried to re-elicit the behavior which the mother previously emitted. According to one interpretation, the infant is merely trying to reinstate the level of stimulus input that the mother previously provided. Sroufe would certainly agree with this interpretation and Stern might also. But, the interpretation did not account for the variety of behaviors, both positive and negative, in which the infant engaged.

Secondly, in the studies of Stern (1971) and Massie (1975), and of the infant of the blind mother, it was not sufficient to evoke the explanation of level of arousal to explain the infant's avoidance of the mother's face. The infant could have adjusted to the "still-face" of those naturalistic studies, paying attention instead to the level of intensity of the mother's behavior in some other respect. Instead, it seemed that the mother's inexpressive face violated an expectancy about the mother's behavior on the part of the infant when he/she was engaged in a positive social behavior and was abhorrent to the infant, causing him/her to look away. The "still-face" experience was certainly one in which the stimulation received by the infant was reduced, but it was not clear why it should be so distressing to the infant. Why didn't it merely bore him? Why didn't he just focus on something more interesting or show a disinterested attitude? He did not show these reactions, he did not get bored, he looked distressed. Tronick felt that the notion of attempting to modulate level of arousal was not sufficient to explain this reaction on the part of the infant.

Chapman asked if there were cross-cultural studies of mother-child interaction and if variations in level of arousal in different cultures had been reported. Tronick replied that there were all too few such studies, at least until recently. Tronick himself had carried out studies of mother-infant interaction in Kenya, where normally mother and infant engage in very little face-to-face contact. He found that when asked to engage in face-to-face interaction, the Kenyan mothers failed to show the rhythmic build up of intensity followed by reduction in intensity of interaction. Instead, the mothers acted at a high level of intensity throughout. The infants watched in a fascinated way, as if examining an object. They did not become distressed, they were not overloaded or overwhelmed. Perhaps, however, the very fact that there was so little face-to-face contact between mother and infant in that culture was more interesting than the infant's reaction to the mothers when the mothers were forced to engage in it.

Published 1981 by Elsevier North Holland, Inc.
Stark, ed.
Language Behavior in Infancy and Early Childhood

The Ontogeny of Gestural Communication: The First Six Months

Alan Fogel

Department of Child Development and Family Studies, Purdue University

Investigators of infant behavior have found all of the adult's basic repertoire of facial expressions in newborns or in infants only a few months of age (Darwin, 1972; Charlesworth and Kreutzer, 1973). Oster and Ekman (1977) report that by 18 to 29 weeks of gestation the differentiation and innervation of facial muscles is complete. Newborns appear to have all of the elementary muscle action units possessed by the adult, even though the surface cues produced by these actions may not appear the same due to differences between adult and infant facial morphology. Facial expression becomes mature and differentiated prior to speech. Articulated movements of the hands and fingers, many of which resemble the adult gestures of pointing, waving, grasping, clenching, and finger-thumb closing, have also been observed in infants during the first few months of life (Trevarthen, 1979).

This "too early" appearance of certain movement patterns occurs in a number of different species and in a wide variety of contexts (Beach, 1974; Harper, 1978). The occurrence of a movement pattern, at a developmental age which is considerably earlier than seems necessary to perform mature functions, constitutes one of the most intriguing, and as yet unsolved, problems in the study of development. Part of our ignorance of these processes is the result of gaps in the natural history of these phenomena: there have been few ontogenetic studies of individual development which have been detailed enough to capture a variety of individual expressions or gestures. Another reason for our failure to understand these processes is due to the fact that developmental psychologists have not provided a useful theoretical framework with which to test specific hypotheses.

This paper presents a working model of the ontogeny of expression which is based on embryological models of development. I will also present some descriptive data on the early develoment of facial expressions and hand movements based on weekly observations of two infants as they interacted with their mothers in a free play situation.

Theoretical Considerations

The early emergence of adult-like patterns of movement have the appearance of long-term developmental continuities, but since the contexts in which these movements occur and the functions which they serve for the infant are likely to be very different than for the adult, these phenomena fit under the rubric of *heterotypic continuity* (Kagan, 1971; Lewis and Starr, 1979). Heterotypic continuity is adequate as a description of the phenomenon, but it offers little explanation for the important issues which need to be addressed: issues such as the adaptive function of these movements for infants (why are they developed so early?), the ontogenetic course of changes in function and organization of the movements (what are the developmental processes and sequences which regulate the observed changes?), the role of contextual and environmental factors in that process (what are the relevant features of the environment which facilitate changes in function and organization?).

In his studies of embryological development, Anokhin (1964) found few cross-species similarities in the timing of the emergence of particular organ systems or neurological functions. For any particular species, however, Anokhin discovered that a mature level of functioning emerged only when each of its components had reached maturity. Rather than developing at the same rate, each component of the mature constellation was characterized by a different rate of maturation. As a result, the appearance of mature elements in the early stages of ontogenesis was not only possible, but quite common. As I have already suggested, the ontogeny of human communication is characterized by different rates of development for each of the communicative components: facial expression, gestures of the hands and fingers, and speech.

Anokhin offered an evolutionary explanation for what he called "heterochronic maturation." Since selection operates on the entire life cycle, it acts to conserve resources and energy by allowing a small number of components to serve multiple functions over the life span. Each species has evolved its own particular pattern of change, its own heterochronic sequence of development. Since this sequence has been determined largely by selection pressures which operate on an evolutionary time scale, it is unlikely that the causal links between one phase of development and the next could be explained simply by circumstances in the ontogeny of individuals.

Kagan, Kearsley, and Zelazo (1978) have argued that there may be little connectivity between one phase of development and the next. They reach this conclusion from data showing that there is little cross-age stability on most measures of cognition and social development during the first few years of life. Stroufe and Waters (1977), on the other hand, have argued that this lack of stability is the result of focusing on measures of discrete behaviors. They argue that when the investigator considers the organization of all the behaviors taken together, that one can find reliability and stability.

The outcome of this controversy may have to await the collection of more data, but it is likely that there will be discontinuous jumps in development which cannot be explained by antecedent and concurrent conditions alone. In such cases, the connectivity between one stage and the next might better be understood using an evolutionary approach.

No matter what the ultimate explanation of the particular timing and sequence of development, the heterochronic model suggests that the behavior which seems to appear "too early" probably serves some adaptive function for the infant at the time when it first appears. Harper (1978) has shown that certain components of adult sexual behavior—purring and lordosis—which are present in the newborn guinea pig may function to elicit maternal solicitude of the infant.

Because the heterochronic model predicts that early appearing components are likely to serve different functions than the same components which later become integrated into the mature system, there is little reason to suspect that early exercise, practice or stimulation of the early forms will have a direct influence over the mature functioning. Thus the early stimulation and practice of the neonatal walking and reaching reflexes in humans has not appreciably improved or hastened the acquisition of mature reaching and walking in older infants (Bower, 1974).

Descriptive Studies of the Development of Face-to-Face Communication Between Mother and Infant in the First Six Months of Life

Study 1

Although many studies have been done on early mother-infant face-to-face interaction (Brazelton et al., 1974, 1975; Stern, 1974b; Stern et al., 1977; Trevarthen, 1977, 1979; Field, 1979a and b), most have been cross-sectional in design and few have systematically followed up on the changes in the infant's behavior over time. The two studies presented here grew out of a need to have normative-descriptive information on the developmental course of face-to-face interaction, as well as more detailed descriptive findings on developmental changes in each infant's use of expressive movements.

In the first study, Kenneth Kaye and I observed fifty-two primarily white, blue-collar, Chicago mothers and their infants in face-to-face interaction at 6, 13, and 26 weeks (Kaye and Fogel, submitted). Infants were videotaped while on their mother's laps in the infant's home. We independently coded infant's attentiveness to mother (eyes alert and looking at mother vs. eyes closed or looking away), infant's expressiveness (smile, wide open mouth, vocalization or laugh), mother's expressiveness (smile, exaggerated facial movement or head bobbing), and mother's touching, bouncing, and posture changing. We were interested, simply, in the way in which attention was regulated in the interaction. In an earlier case study (Fogel, 1977), I had found that there was a relationship between mother's *expressiveness* and infant's *attention*. The mother was more successful at *attracting* the infant's attention if she was relatively non-expressive, but once the infant was gazing at her she was more successful at holding the infant's attention by means of increasing her rate of facial and vocal expressiveness, which in turn released a series of facial expressions and vocalizations from the infant. Since Stern and his colleagues had studied the mother's expressiveness in great detail (Stern et al., 1977), we felt justified in making a rather crude classification of maternal and infant behavior into periods of expressive vs. non-expressive. Each of these categories was coded continuously in time using a Datamyte event recorder and a computer program which mixes independently coded streams of behavior into a single session and then derives latencies, frequencies, and contingencies for later analysis (Kaye and Fogel, submitted).

Our findings show that infants spent increasingly less time attending to mother over the six months of observation (infants were attentive to mother about 50% of the session at six weeks, 40% at 13 weeks, and 30% at 26 weeks). If, however, one looks at the amount of co-occurrence between infant attentiveness and mother expressiveness, it remains relatively constant over time (about 20% of the session). Thus the drop in the overall proportion of time infants attended to mothers' faces seemed to be accounted for by a drop in the proportion of time infants spent watching their mothers' non-expressive faces. In a reciprocal manner, mothers increased the amount of expressive activity as the infant got older, but only during the periods when the infant was attentive. Even though they spent less time interacting at six months, the mother and infant appear to be more enmeshed in their interaction. A further finding of interest is that there was a change in the patterns of initiative taking over the six-month period. At six weeks the infant usually waited until his mother made some expressive gesture before he would respond. By six months infants were seen to initiate just as many mutual exchanges as their mothers: a shift from mere responsiveness to spontaneous, reciprocal communication.

Study 2

The Kaye and Fogel study contributes to our understanding of the development of the global categories of attentiveness and expressiveness. It does not, however, provide any of the details relating to the kinds of expressive movements which have been described by Trevarthen. For this purpose it is necessary to code the infant's behavior in great detail (1977) and at more frequent intervals. Since this extra work of coding implies a sacrifice in the number of subjects, I turned to a case-study design. Four infants were videotaped at weekly intervals from birth to one year in various types of social interaction with their mother's. All of the observations took place in the laboratory where we could control lighting and camera angle in order to increase the visibility of fine details of movement. In this paper, I will report some initial findings on two of these infants, a girl (H.) and a boy (J.), observed while engaged in face-to-face interaction on their mother's lap during the first six months. This lap situation is comparable to the Kaye and Fogel study, but done in the laboratory with fewer subjects, more observations per subject, and with a considerably more detailed coding catalogue.

In the course of this work, my students and I have categorized over 100 reliable patterns of face and body movements displayed by infants between the ages of birth and six months. In order to facilitate the observation and coding of these patterns, we divided the infant's body up into mutually exclusive regions of movement. What is reported here is a first analysis of each body region independent of the others. Future work will allow us to put the pieces back together into a more coherent picture of the whole infant.

Table 1 lists a subset of these categories and a brief description. The photographs and drawings on the next few pages document a few of these expressions. All of the infants shown in these photographs were between one and three months of age, and they were sitting in an infant seat. The expressions are identical to those observed in the lap interactions.

Coding was done by a team of observers who coded each body region independently. They were free to stop the videotape and discuss their judgments, thus increasing the accuracy of the coding. A digital clock (accurate to 0.01 seconds) was superimposed on the screen. The observers stopped the tape when they observed a category change and they recorded the time and the category. Any particular category change had to be held by the infant for at least 0.5 seconds, or it was not recorded.

Since there were four coding teams (two for each infant), reliability was assessed by having the second coding team independently code a subset of the total number of sessions which were coded originally by the first team. Five sessions (about 25% of the total) were randomly slected for each infant. In each of the 10 five-minute sessions, a two-minute interval was randomly

Table 1. Coding Categories Used in Case-Study Analysis.

Body region	Category	Description
Mouth	Smile	Lips retracted, mouth corners raised
	Mouthing	Movements of the mouth which resemble speech movements
	Cry 1	Frown and lip movements or tremors
	Cry 2	Frown plus whimper
	Cry 3	Burst-pause crying with face cycling between eyes closed with frowning and eyes open, with pouting
	Cry 4	"Full-blown" crying: Cry is loud and continuous, eyes closed and mouth open wide
	Laugh	No definition needed
	Yawn	No definition needed
	Mouth open	Exaggerated mouth opening with lips forming a vertically aligned oval shape
	Object in mouth	Infant or mother places object in infant's mouth
	Hand in mouth	No definition needed
Arms	Shield	Arm or arms crossed over in front of the infant's body or face as if to cover self
	Reach	Arm extended with hand open, palm out
	Object reach	Reaching directed at a specific inanimate object
	Stretch	Arms extended completely with minimal lateral movement or Flexion
Hands and fingers	Finger curling	Rapid alternation of flexing fingers
	Curled fingers	Fingers relaxed and loosely bend inwards
	Point at mother	Other fingers curled, index finger extended in direction of mother
	Point at other	Index finger extension in a direction other than that of mother
	Finger spread	Sustained extension of all fingers and the thumb; can be static or dynamic (bye-bye movements)
	Finger to thumb	Tip of any finger (usually the index finger) touches the tip of the thumb forming a circle
	Fist	Fingers tightly curled, thumb behind fingers with knuckles standing out
	Hand clasp	Both hands touching, either by one clasping the other, with fingers interwoven, or with palms touching (clapping movement)
	Grasp	Clasping of any object including clothing, other parts of body, mother, seat or toy
Gaze	Visual engagement	Looking at mother's face, body or at an object which she is holding

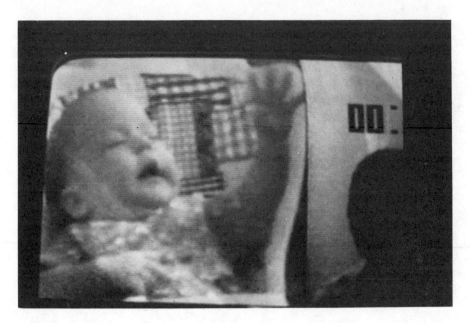

Figure 1. Photograph of *finger spread* movement. All photographs were made from video recordings of mother-infant interaction.

Figure 2. Photograph of *hand clasp*.

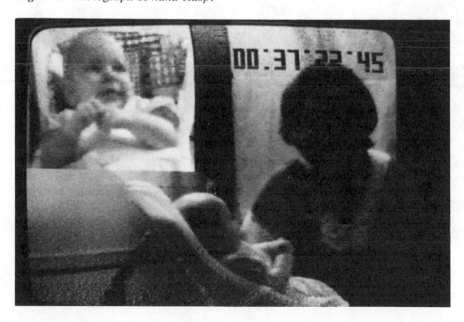

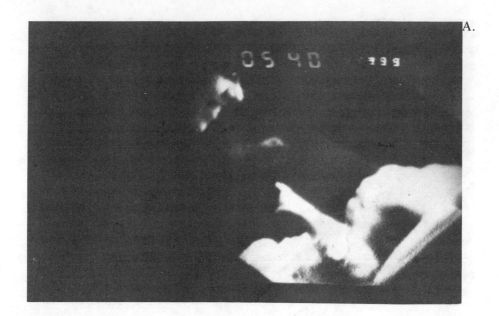

Figure 3. (a) and (b). Photographs showing two instances of *point at mother*.

selected, thus giving reliability assessments over the 6-month age range and across the beginning middle and end of the sessions. For each subject the total duration of reliability codings is about 10% of the total duration of the sessions. The second team was not aware that their codings would be compared to those of the first team. They were told that the first team's work was inaccurate in places and needed to be re-done. For the body regions listed in Table 1, the proportion of agreements were: mouth, .83; arms, .87; hands and fingers, .83; gaze, .88.

In this type of intensive coding, one tries to balance the amount of detail required to preserve the identity of individual expressions, with the time required to code such a large number of categories per session. Our compromise has been to stop the videotape when we see a change and record the time on the screen, rather than replaying the tape over the change in order to find the exact frame number in which the change first began. This process introduces a certain amount of lag-time error: two different coders will be likely to record the change at different times. The differences are due to individual variation in coder response time, the rise time of the change itself (some categories have clear-cut changes, others are slow to manifest change) and the clarity of the video image.

In judgments about agreements between coding teams, we decided that if the difference between the time that team A recorded a change was greater than 3 seconds from the time that team B recorded a change, then this would count as a disagreement. Change time differences less than 3 seconds, either preceding or following the original coding, were counted as agreements, provided the teams both coded the same category. By tabulating the values of these time differences, we can get an assessment of the precision with which time is recorded. Since we expect the error, if it is random, to be a Poisson distribution, the best estimate of the time error is the median, rather than the mean (cf. Cox and Lewis, 1966). The median between team time error for each body region was: mouth, 0.5; arms, 0.6; hands and fingers, 0.6; gaze, 0.4 (in seconds).

Results

The results presented here will be limited to an analysis of the rates of occurrence of each of the categories listed in Table 1. Two questions will be addressed using these rate measures: (a) Taking each category independently (an obvious oversimplification, but a necessary first step in understanding the data), are there any systematic age trends in a category's rate of occurrence? (b) Is there any tendency for a particular category to be more likely to occur during the infant's *visual engagement* with the mother, rather than during periods of *visual non-engagement?*

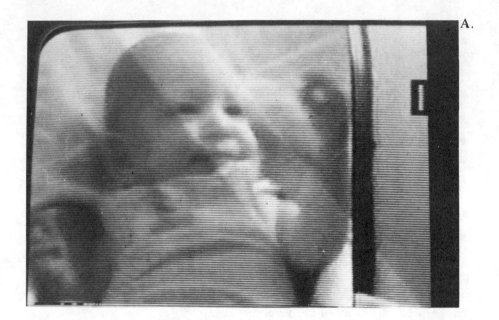

A.

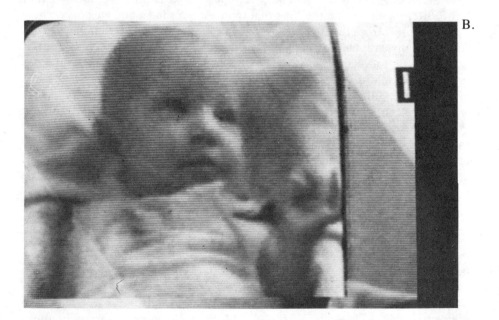

B.

Figure 4. (a) and (b). Photographs showing two instances of *finger to thumb*.

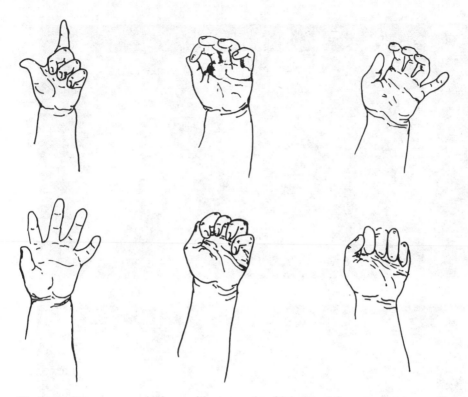

Figure 5. Drawings made from video records of hand and finger movements. From upper left: *point, finger to thumb, finger curling, finger spread, curled finger, fist*.

The rate of occurrence of a category in any session was measured as the frequency of category onsets per minute during the session. Each session typically lasted five minutes An episode of *visual engagement* was counted if the infant was gazing at his mother's face or body, gazing at the mother's hand or at an object which she was holding. *Non-engagement* included periods of eyes closed, or periods in which the infant was gazing away from the mother's face, body or hands. There are some difficulties with this definition of *visual engagement*. It is unclear whether looking at an object the mother is holding should count as a social act, or as non-social engagement. Another ambiguous situation arises when the mother puts the infant on her shoulder or face down on her lap. In these cases the infant maintains full body contact with the mother, but since he is looking over her knee or shoulder, these periods are counted as instances of *non-engagement*. If the infant is fully engaged looking around the room from this vantage, the situation is relatively unambiguous. Often, however, the mother will nuzzle

A.

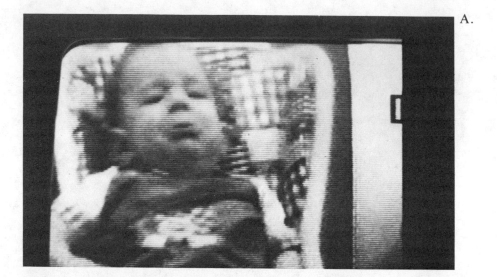

B.

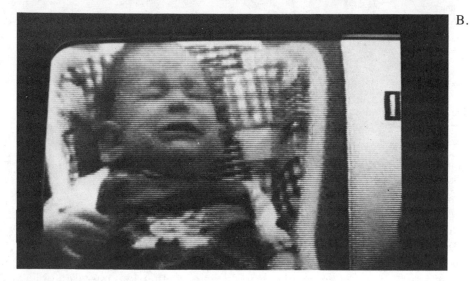

Figure 6. Photograph of two variations on *cry* face: (a) pout with open eyes, (b) audible cry with eyes closed and frown.

and kiss the infant's neck or shoulder, or pat his back, evoking *smiling* and other expressive movements. Since we did not take account of these special cases, the definition of engagement, therefore, provides nothing more than a rough parsing out of the organization of the infant's expressive movements in relation to his gazing. A more complete analysis would have to consider the specific postures and contexts of maternal behavior in relation to the gaze direction.

In order to determine whether the infant's rate of occurrence of a category is higher during *visual engagement* or during *non-engagement,* a measure of co-occurrence is derived in the following manner. The total duration of *visual engagement* divided by the total duration of the session is equivalent to the proportion of category onsets which would be expected to occur during *visual engagement* purely by chance (P_{exp}). The *co-occurrence ratio* is equal to $(P_{obs} - P_{exp})/P_{exp}$ (see Fogel, 1977), where P_{obs} is the proportion of onsets which actually occurred during *visual engagement.* If this ratio is positive it means that during *visual engagement,* more category onsets occurred than would be expected by chance. If the ratio is negative more category onsets occurred during *non-engagement* than chance would predict.

Tables 2 and 3 list the main findings. Note that the rate of occurrence is tested for age trends using a correlation coefficient; the co-occurrence ratio is tested both for age trends and for the extent to which it tended to be mostly positive or mostly negative across sessions. The fractions listed in the final column represent the proportion of sessions in which the co-occurrence ratio had a positive or a negative sign (whichever was the largest) taking only those sessions in which there was at least one occurrence of the category. Thus the denominator represents the number of sessions in which a category was observed at least once. Any tendency for the co-occurrence ratio to be predominantly negative or positive over sessions was tested using a binomial sign test (two-tailed).

The most frequently occurring category was *finger spread,* at the rate of about five times per minute for H. and three times per minute for J. *Curled fingers,* the hand rest position, occurred next most frequently: between three and four times per minute for both infants. *Visual engagement* and *mouth open* occurred at the rate of between one and two times per minute for both infants. It should be mentioned that the overall rate for most of the categories was fairly low: most things happened every two or three minutes on the average. There was also a relatively high standard deviation in these measures across sessions. This suggests that the display of most of these behaviors is a highly variable affair, even within individuals on repeated occasions.

A considerable number of categories had significant age trends in rate of occurrence. In order to simplify the discussion of these trends, Table 4 summarizes the trends by grouping categories into type of trend profile. Most of the categories were present throughout the six-month period. For these categories, the rates remained relatively constant or slowly increasing over time in spite of sometimes large fluctuations from one session to the next. This suggests that many of the movement patterns which were in the infant's repertoire from the early weeks of life were articulated (rather than diffuse) such as *mouthing* and *mouth open, finger spread, hand clasp, grasp, point,* and *finger to thumb.* In addition some of the more primitive, non-articulated movement patterns did not drop out of the repertoire during the six-month period, for example, *curled fingers, finger curling, fist,* and *shield.*

Table 2. Descriptive Statistics for H. (N = 18 Sessions; Age Range = 18 to 188 Days).

	Rate of occurrence (Frequency per minute)			Co-occurence ratio	
Category	Mean	Standard deviation	Correlation with age	Correlation with age	Binomial sign test (two-tailed)
Mouth					
Smile	0.70	0.91	.55[b]	.35	+10/10[b]
Mouthing	0.54	0.73	.24	−.17	+7/12
Cry 1	0.06	0.13	−.44	.25	−3/4
Cry 2	0.23	0.35	−.64	.32	−5/8
Cry 3	0.11	0.20	−.56[b]	−.50	−5/7
Cry 4	0.16	0.34	−.41[a]	.25	−3/4
Laugh	.00	.00	—	—	—
Yawn	0.03	0.07	−.33	.87	−3/4
Mouth open	1.53	1.37	.65[b]	−.63[b]	+12/14[b]
Object in mouth	0.27	0.52	.72[b]	−.73	+4/5
Hand in mouth	0.38	0.73	.20	−.11	−4/8
Arm					
Shield	1.08	1.15	−0.3	.09	−8/14
Reach	0.51	1.00	.58[b]	.75[b]	+6/9
Object reach	0.07	0.19	.71[c]	−.78	−2/3
Stretch	0.08	0.02	.60[b]	−.15	+2/4
Hand and fingers					
Finger curling	1.02	0.75	−.62[b]	−.13	+10/18
Curled fingers	3.89	1.27	−24	.01	+10/18
Point at mother	0.64	0.54	−.03	−.28	+13/18[a]
Point at other	0.98	0.98	.10	−.13	−11/16
Finger spread	5.17	2.58	.71[c]	−.20	+13/18[a]
Finger to thumb	0.46	0.55	−.05	.32	−8/14
Fist	0.28	0.42	−.37	.73[b]	−7/10
Hand clasp	0.72	0.91	.14	−.37	+8/10
Grasp	1.61	1.96	.87[c]	−.23	+9/16
Gaze					
Visual engagement	1.94	1.89	.37		

[a] $p < .05$.
[b] $p < .01$.
[c] $p < .001$.

Very few of the patterns which were coded actually declined over time. *Finger curling* declined slowly for H. and *cry* abruptly declined at about 60 days. For J., *yawn* declined sharply at 60 days. The coincident declines, as well as the coincident rising trends at approximately 60, 100, and 140 days for both infants (see Table 4) may reflect underlying developmental pro-

Table 3. Descriptive Statistics for J. (N = 20 Sessions, Age Range = 9 to 150 Days).

| Category | Rate of occurrence (Frequency per minute) | | | Co-occurrence ratio | |
	Mean	Standard deviation	Correlation with age	Correlation with age	Binomial Sign test (two-tailed)
Mouth					
Smile	0.53	0.65	.42[a]	−.24	+11/13[a]
Mouthing	0.27	0.37	−.22	−.22	−8/12
Cry 1	0.33	0.45	−.27	−.14	+6/11
Cry 2	0.44	0.60	.05	−.17	−7/11
Cry 3	0.13	0.37	.15	.31	−3/4
Cry 4	0.03	0.13	.13	—	−1/1
Laugh	0.19	0.53	.49[b]	.87	+2/4
Yawn	0.11	0.21	−.54[b]	−.44	−6/7
Mouth open	1.27	1.06	.74[c]	.25	+9/14
Object in mouth	0.03	0.12	.46[a]	—	+1/2
Hand in mouth	0.53	0.67	.67[c]	−.39	−7/12
Arm					
Shield	0.51	0.61	.74[c]	−.23	−10/14
Reach	0.81	1.82	.35	−.22	−5/10
Object reach	0.20	0.46	.48[b]	−.38	−3/5
Stretch	0.59	1.06	.51[b]	.56	+6/7
Hand and fingers					
Finger curling	0.45	1.04	.34	.56[a]	−6/11
Curled fingers	3.25	1.08	.26	.07	+13/20
Point at mother	0.21	0.30	.61[b]	−.01	+4/8
Point at other	0.35	0.53	.45[a]	−.39	−10/12[a]
Finger spread	2.59	1.45	.26	−.05	+14/20
Finger to thumb	.00	.00	—	—	−0/0
Fist	0.25	0.57	.29	.82[a]	+3/6
Hand clasp	1.37	1.31	−.33	−.03	+10/15
Grasp	0.90	1.13	.05	.33	−10/14
Gaze					
Visual engagement	1.15	1.13	.76[a]		

[a] $p < .05$.
[b] $p < .01$.
[c] $p < .001$.

cesses. Figure 7 depicts representative categories which typify these age trends.

Most of the categories which showed sharp increases in rate for J., showed sharp increases for H. at approximately the same age. This is true for *smile* (60 days), *object reach* and *stretch* (100 days), and *object in mouth* (140

Table 4. Summary of Category Changes over Time.

	H.	Body region	J.
Present in most sessions with no systematic change in rate or with a slowly increasing age trend in rate	*Mouthing* *Mouth open* *Yawn* *Hand in mouth*	Mouth	*Mouthing* *Mouth open* *Cry*
	Shield *Reach*	Arms	*Shield* *Reach*
	Curled fingers *Finger spread* *Fist* *Hand clasp* *Finger curling*[a] *Finger to thumb* *Point at mother* *Point at other*	Hands and fingers	*Curled fingers* *Finger spread* *Fist* *Hand clasp* *Finger curling* *Grasp*
	Visual engagement	Eyes	*Visual engagement*
Present in early sessions with abrupt decrease at about 60 days	*Cry*	Mouth	*Yawn*
Absent in early sessions with abrupt increase at about 60 days	*Smile*	Mouth	*Smile* *Hand in mouth*
Absent in early sessions with abrupt increase at about 100 days	*Object reach* *Stretch* *Grasp*	Arms Hands and fingers	*Object reach* *Stretch* *Point at mother* *Point at other*
Absent in early sessions with abrupt increase at about 140 days	*Object in mouth*	Mouth	*Object in mouth* *Laugh*

[a]Shows a slowly decreasing trend in rate.

days). There were some variations reflecting individual differences in patterns of development. *Point,* for example, was displayed by H. continuously over the six-month period, whereas *point* only begins to be displayed by J. at about 100 days. The opposite pattern holds for *grasp:* continuously present for J., but appearing for H. only at 100 days.

It is not clear from these case studies alone whether these individual variations belie any organized patterns of development. We can, however, conclude that there seems to be no clear developmental progression from diffuse to articulated expression, nor from proximal to distal activity. Nevertheless, both infants show some developmental changes which correspond to other studies which have been done in this period. There is a reduction of diffuse expressions of anxiety, distress or fatigue (*cry* and *yawn*) at about eight weeks with a corresponding increase in the social *smile* at that age. There was also an increasing number of categories related to object involvement which began to appear between three and five months such as *object reach* and *object in mouth*. The appearance of *laugh* for J. in the fifth month signals a new phase of cognitive sophistication. It is important to note that these behaviors, which have been used in the past as developmental milestones, are only a small fraction of the total behavioral repertoire of the young infant.

The second issue to be dealt with in this analysis is the extent to which the independent patterns of movement co-occur either with *visual engagement* or with *visual non-engagement*. These results can be found in Tables 2 and 3. Binomial sign tests revealed very few systematic co-occurrences across sessions. For H., *smile, mouth open, point at mother*, and *finger spread* were all associated with *visual engagement*. For J., only *smile* was systematically coincident with *visual engagement; point at other* was associated with visual *non-engagement*. From Tables 2 and 3 it can be seen that J. maintained *visual engagement* with his mother fewer times and for briefer periods than H. This fact does not account for the greater number of co-occurrences shown by H., since the co-occurrence ratio was constructed to be independent of the duration of *visual engagement* or any other category.

It is important to note that these results obscure some of the details of the use of these movements in interaction. For example, in five out of H.'s 18 sessions, *point at mother* did not co-occur with *visual engagement*, and furthermore there were a few instances of *point* in every session which occurred during periods of *non-engagement*. A more complete analysis of the behavioral and temporal context is the only way to find general regularities which may govern the display of these movement patterns.

Point at other occurs during *non-engagement* for J. and a similar tendency exists in the data for H. Could this be suggestive of some protoreference activity? Older infants never point at their mothers and they never look at their mothers when pointing at an object (Anderson, 1972). It may be that the early mother-directed *pointing* during *visual engagement* drops out after six months of age when the infant can cognitively differentiate the mother from other people and from inanimate objects. If the young infant is referencing the mother as an interesting object, it would be important to know whether the infant displayed social engagement behavior such as *smile* or *laugh* at the same time as *pointing*. This would suggest a lack of functional differentiation between social and non-social objects in the infant under six months.

Very few of the co-occurrence ratios were related systematically with age. Since only those sessions in which there was at least one instance of a category were counted, some relatively high correlation coefficients were not significant due to the small number of sessions on which they were

34

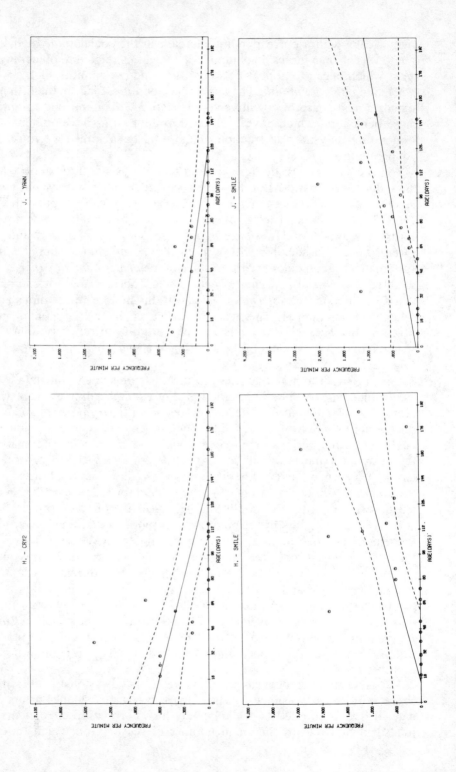

35

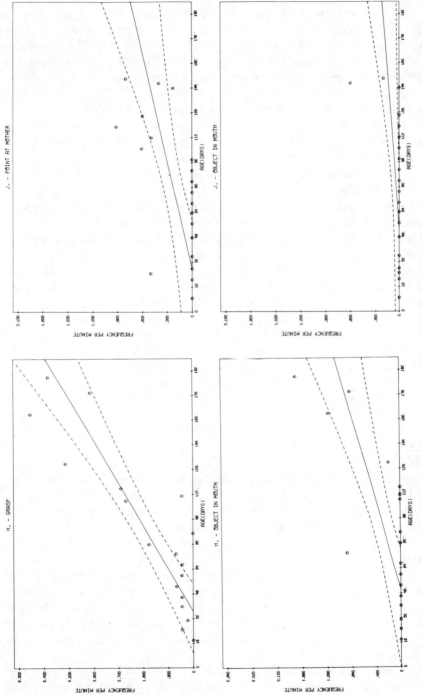

Figure 7. Age profiles for rate of occurrence in selected categories: first row shows decrease in rate of about 60 days, second row shows increase in rate at 60 days, third row shows increase in rate at 100 days, fourth row shows increase in rate at about 140 days. The regression line with 95% confidence is superimposed on each graph.

computed. Although the findings of a case study can never be conclusive, they do reveal some of the processes which may be operating in a single individual. Out of the six categories whose co-occurrence ratio changed significantly with age (four for H. and two for J.), *fist* and *reach* for H. showed sharp changes at about 60 days (see Figure 8); the other categories had slowly increasing or decreasing age trends.

If one divides age into two categories—less than or equal to 64 days and greater than 64 days—a 2 × 2 table can be formed with age as one dimension and co-occurrence ratio less than zero vs. greater than zero as the other dimension. For both *fist* and *reach* for H., there is a significant tendency for values of the co-occurrence ratio less than zero to occur before 64 days, and values greater than zero to occur after 64 days ($\chi^2 = 4.28$(d.f. $= 1$), p $<$ .05 for *fist*; $\chi^2 = 9.00$ (d.f. $= 1$), p $<$ .01 for *reach*). So even though the sign test based on all the sessions was not significant for these two categories, it appears that there was a systematic shift at about nine weeks from entirely negative to an entirely positive co-occurrence with *visual engagement*.

This reaching behavior, like *pointing at mother*, is mother-directed as opposed to object directed. *Point at mother* was also associated with *visual engagement* for H. for all the sessions taken together. A recent study of year-old infants has shown that reaching for *objects* (which begins about 4 months) and pointing at *objects* (which begins about one year) were responded to in similar ways by the mother: they looked where the infants directed the gesture and verbally acknowledged the gesture. The infants also displayed very similar accompanying behavior with both *reach* and *point*, vocalizing and looking at the mother as they directed their limbs at the object (Leung and Rheingold, 1977).

Conclusions

A number of conclusions emerge from the data presented in this paper. The first is that even very young infants have a rich repertoire of expressions which are organized and differentiated. This conclusion is not original; it replicates the findings of other investigators such as Darwin (1972), Charlesworth and Kreutzer (1973), and Trevarthen (1977, 1979).

Second, infants seem to differ in the degree to which any particular expression is displayed and in the timing of the display in relation to other activity. The same kind of communicative variability has been observed in studies of blind infants who develop non-typical signals to express their intentions (Fraiberg, 1974). The large number of early appearing movement patterns suggests that human infants are able to develop alternative pathways to mature communicative competence.

Perhaps the single most important conclusion from these data is that many communicative achievements of older children are based on movement patterns which appear early in infancy and remain active in the infant's rep-

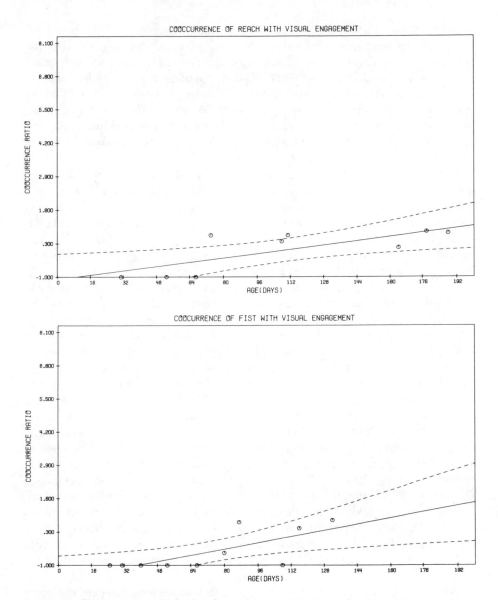

Figure 8. Co-occurrence ratio for *fist* and *reach* in H. as a function of age.

ertoire. Rather than indicating a direct relationship between early and later behavior, the findings suggest that the same movement patterns serve functions early in life which may be very different from how they are used later. This result, which fits the model of development proposed by Anokhin (1964), is not readily explained by the models of development to which psychologists usually attend. Rather than suggesting a steady accretion of competence, the heterochronic model proposes that early movement patterns become recycled by undergoing changes in organization and integration with other behavior. This is akin to Piaget's (1952) concept of decalage, which at present remains unexplained. The heterochronic model, at least as formulated by Anokhin, suggests that decalage shifts may not be explained by ontogenetic processes; they could be the result of selection pressures which have operated on a phylogenetic time scale, and for which the life span must be understood as an organized whole.

The issue is far from being conclusive; in fact there are a number of questions which can be investigated if one accepts the possibility that such a model might account for developmental changes. One group of questions relates to the early usage of these movements—an area in which our knowledge is particularly tentative and incomplete: what use do they serve and why do they appear so early in life? Another question relates to the developmental continuities between early and later gestures: to what extent do early uses of the same movement patterns pre-figure later movements?

Questions relating to the early use of these movements have been the topic of a number of research studies which my colleagues and I have been doing. Although we consider the findings incomplete, there are a number of consistencies which can be noted. The most salient result is that 2-month-old infants (the age at which we have done these studies) are capable of displaying different movement patterns and different organizations of the same movement patterns as a function of contextual factors. Thus we have found that infants behave differently when with their mother than with another infant: to the mother there were more fine motor movements such as *grasp* and *point at mother* which was displayed in a smooth progression, while to the peer there were more gross motor movements such as arm thrust, straining the body forward as well as very long and intense gazing (Fogel, 1979). In another study, the 2-month-old's response to maternal vs. stranger's leave-taking was compared. When mothers left the room infants were more likely to *cry*, to *reach*, and to look back toward the door from which the mother left. After the departure of the stranger, we observed more diffuse signs of anxiety such as yawning and stereotypic movement of the mouth (Fogel, in press).

We found that infants will display different movements depending upon the nature of the mother's behavior. After the mother interacted normally with her infant for several minutes she was asked to assume a "still-face" posture in which she continued to look at the infant but refrained from moving or talking. Brazelton et al. (1975) and Trevarthen (1977) report marked changes in infant behavior under such conditions. We found that there was a reduction in the amount of *gazing at* the mother and *smiling* during the "still-face" condition, but an increase in *point at mother* during "still-face" (Fogel et al., in press). Such findings are inconclusive with respect to the question about what function these gestures are serving, since we do not have a clear enough understanding of the salient dimensions of the contextual differences to which the infant may be responding. The results do indicate, however, that there may be some specific relation between gesture and environment which cannot be accounted for by simple models of diffuse excitement with regard to infant responses.

Another possible early function of these movements may be related to the effect the behavior has on the adult (Bell and Harper, 1977). This may indeed be the case for the more salient movements such as *smile* and *cry*, but it has been our experience that mothers do not seem to specifically notice the more subtle movements of the hands and fingers. We know very little about the role of these movements in the mother-infant interaction.

The ontogeny of the early repertoire of expressions is virtually uncharted territory. In Table 5, I have provided an abbreviated listing of the later use of the same movement patterns which we have observed in infants under 6 months of age. We have no idea whether the apparent continuity of form of expression is coincident with an underlying continuity of psychological and/or physiological functioning.

Table 5. Functional Significance of Hand and Finger Movement Patterns at Different Ages.

Movement pattern as seen in the first months of life	Movement pattern as seen later in life
Point at mother	Point at objects in relation to mother or another person, (referencing or requesting begins at approximately 1 year).
Grasp—fortuitous grasping at infant's clothing, or at small objects placed in or near the infant's palm	Integrated reaching, grasping, handling of objects, requesting (begins at approximately 4 months). Can also be used for holding, hair pulling, caressing.
Finger to thumb	Fine prehension of small objects having no known social function (beginning at about 5 months). Non-verbal linguistic sign meaning completion or satisfaction (begins only in later childhood).
Finger spread *Curled fingers* *Hand clasp*	Can be used later as non-verbal signs. For example, finger spread, palm out means wait or stop; curled fingers or fist means determination; hand clasp may become part of clapping or a sign meaning reverence. Each of these movements are also used as gestures accompanying speech (it is not known when children acquire these particular usages).

A particularly intriguing developmental change is that of *reach* and *point* over the first year of life. It appears that these expressions are directed primarily at mother during the first half year, and then at objects while looking at mother in the second half year. What does this say about the later development of attachment and cognition in the first year? Do babies have to point at their mothers before they can point at objects? Do all infants progress in this manner? What does this suggest about the role of social interaction vis-a-vis the development of non-social competencies?

The question becomes even more complex when we realize that there is no simple transition from mother-oriented to object-oriented behavior. In fact the use of the expressions of *reach* and *point* in the latter half of the first year and beyond would make no sense without another person to whom the object can be referred. One hypothesis then is that *reach* and *point* are at first simple mechanisms by which the infant expresses a primitive attraction for other people, after which the psychological experience in relation to the same expression becomes differentiated to include physical objects and other people, but always in relation to the original social bond. In this view, the infant's contacts with the world, and later with language, facilitated a system of gestural communication which develops from early, perhaps reflex-like, responses to people, into reciprocal, conventionalized patterns of non-verbal social exchange.

This hypothesis is in agreement with the ideas of Kaye (1977, 1979) and Bruner (1975), among others, who postulate that the basis for language learning is the prior establishment of a system of rules for social interaction and dialogue. These models do not relate to the amount of expressiveness by which infants may differ, nor to the use of any particular expression rather than another: there is no reason to believe that individual differences on these dimensions will have anything to do with the acquisition of language. Language development probably is related to the ability of the infant and mother to develop a communicative exchange in which some of these expressions will be the basic components.

ACKNOWLEDGEMENTS
  The study was funded, in part, by a grant to Purdue University (BNS-77-14524) from the National Science Foundation. I would like to express my appreciation to the subjects and coders who participated in this study. The contributions of Glenn Diamond and Thomas Hannan were invaluable in all phases of this work. I appreciate the help of Beth Langhorst (who read an earlier draft of this paper) and Jacqueline Fogel (who made the drawings).

Discussion

Capute first pointed out that there is an array of primitive reflexes or automatic responses in the first months of life which are present *in utero*, demonstrated at birth, and usually "disappear" between three and six months of age. As a result of these reflexes, the head controls the posture of the upper and lower extremities. There are several primitive reflexes; one common reflex is the Asymmetrical Tonic Neck Reflex (ATNR). If the infant's head is turned to one side or if the infant looks to one side, one sees "chin" extension manifested by extension of the upper and lower extremities; occiput flexion is noted with flexion of the upper and lower extremities on the occiput side. Thus, the infant assumes a "fencing" position.

In addition, extremity tone and posture can be influenced by head extension or flexion, in addition to turning to one side or the other. Thus, it is essential that one know the positioning of the head when examining the extremities of infants, particularly in the first six months of life. It is preferable to keep the head in the midline position because this equalizes the tone in the four extremities.

A second example of primitive reflexes is the Moro Reflex. When one studies the movements of the extremities, including the hands and fingers, it is essential that neither a noise be produced nor the head extended since these stimuli may produce a Moro Reflex. This reflex produces an extension and abduction of the upper extremities with subsequent adduction with semiflexion of the elbows, wrists, and fingers with the index finger and second finger assuming a "C" positioning. This positioning of the fingers is quite different from the prehensile movement of the fingers which is voluntary and later becomes quite functional in grasp. It is also different from the overhand pincer movement which emerges at 10 to 11 months of age.

Capute added that the infant would have more free movement if his head is controlled in the midline. Then the infant is not locked into these automatic responses. He offered these descriptions of primitive reflexes as word of caution. It was important that in any study of arm and hand gestures, spontaneous movement should be differentiated from reflex or automatic responses. Capute had not seen finger pointing at mother as early as one month of age and he did not see how it could occur if the infant were looking to one side. He would find such a gesture very surprising. The infant was likely to be locked into a position of flexion or extension in this case. Fogel said that some of his observations of the pointing gesture were made at two months of age. But Capute answered that the reflexes he was referring to reached their maximum expression between one and two months of age and then began to disappear. A similiar confusion, he suggested, could arise if alternating movements of the extremities made by the infant at four to six months of age on the bases of involuntary automated responses were to be equated to crawling, an eight-month voluntary activity.

Capute mentioned these reflexes to emphasize the effect of head movements upon automated responses of the extremities. He offered these descriptions of primitive reflexes as word of caution for investigators studying arm and hand gestures in infants. Voluntary hand and finger movements should be differentiated from reflex or automatic responses.

Fogel said some of his observations of pointing movements were made at two months of age. Capute answered this point by stating that the primitive reflexes reach their maximum expression between two and three months of age before they begin to "disappear." A similar confusion, he suggested, could arise if the reflexive "walking or stepping" responses seen at 4 to 6 weeks were interpreted as voluntary reciprocal walking. The latter did not occur until about 12 months of age.

Capute also pointed out that smiling is considered medically to be a developmental marker with this onset at 44–46 weeks of postconceptual age depending upon the accuracy of the historian. In this sense the social smile was not environmentally produced, but was viewed as a maturational event.

Bloom remarked that the major participants in this section were responding as if they had never thought about primitive reflexes. She did not believe that this was true. What were their comments upon the effects of these reflexes upon the gestures of very young infants? Stern replied on behalf of himself and his colleagues to the effect that some of the behaviors of the infant they had presented might well be reflexive in nature. This possibility did not at all change the essence of their presentation. It did not really matter what the origins of the gestural behavior might be. In addition, reflexes as described in the medical literature were usually elicited under conditions that were maximally favorable for their appearance.

Indeed, it is only then that they can be reliably assessed. These are not always the conditions under which reflexes find their expression and in which their expression evolves in real life. Occasionally, extreme conditions, for example, a loud noise, may occur, giving rise to a full-fledged Moro reflex. There are, however, many intermediate situations which reflexologists and the medical profession generally have ignored. The behaviors that Fogel described, at least their earliest manifestations, might be the expresions of reflexes under everday social situations. Their expression might be variable under these conditions, so that they were not reliable and not of interest to the physician, but they might be extremely important as far the life of the infant was concerned. Even though they were reflexes and were controlled by different neurological mechanisms than other behaviors, for example, responses to ethologically salient stimuli, they might eventually come under voluntary control and be used communicatively or meaningfully at a later time. A behavior should not be dismissed merely because it was reflexive in nature at some developmental point in the infant (the smile was a good example). It might have a different origin and a different relationship to biological protection of the organism from other behaviors. That did not mean that it would not become part of a useful communicative system.

Eilers asked how long a hand position had to be held before it was recognized as a specific gestural entity. Fogel said the duration was variable. Eilers and Stark wanted to know if there was a criterion for their duration before the gestures would be considered as an endpoint; or alternatively if they were formed merely in transition from one movement or position to another. Fogel replied that, at least after one month of age, the gestures were steady states, not transitional phenomena, and they lasted a second or two at least.

Hardy asked about the significance of the pointing gesture in the young infant. Fogel said that this was the most interesting question from his point of view. He thought that the gesture had something to do with specifying a figure in a ground, or a way of recognizing a specifiable, localized phenomenon. But that was only a guess. However, he reiterated that the possible functional significance could only be examined in experimental studies where infants were placed in different contexts to see if they then preferred to display certain expresions or gestures in one context as opposed to another. One example of such an experiment was that in which an infant was placed in proximity to another infant, an age-matched peer, instead of his mother. As Fogel had indicated, the infants' responses to a peer were more like those made in the presence of an interesting object than in the presence of their mothers. Infants directed pointing at their mothers but not at their age-matched peers. Also, as he had indicated in his paper, infants directed more pointing to the mother during a "still-face" condition than during a normal interaction. Already it seemed that infants used these gestures in specified contexts. It was not yet possible however, to identify the dimensions that were common to those contexts and thus make the gestures more understandable. But it was certain that gestures had a different frequency of occurrence in different contexts. For example, during the "still-face" condition when pointing increased, it was not found that other gestures increased also. The pointing increase appeared to be specific to that context.

Oller raised the issue of the ethological significance of the gestures Fogel had described. It seemed to him that Fogel was assuming that the hand positions of the infant were, if not of ethological significance, then at least culturally universal in having some specifiable, universal "meaning." Oller thought, on the whole, that there might be universality of meaning in the gesture of pointing to an object for mutual reference, but the same sorts of shared meanings would not obtain gestures Fogel had described with respect to the other hand. However, he pointed out that, interestingly, these hand positions were in fact among the core hand positions that had been identified as occurring earliest by investigators studying the acquistion of American Sign Language (ASL). Among the first hand configurations that occur (McIntire, 1977) are those that correspond to the letters "A," "S," "O," "G," and "C," and the number "5," all having configurations very like those identified by Fogel. They were used by the young child as substitutions for other (possibly more difficult) hand configurations when they were beginning to acquire sign language. The remarkable thing about them in relation to their occurrence in the infant was that their use by adults was independent of ethological factors (that is, they were attached to meanings arbitrarily).

Consequently, the gestures which the infants in Fogel's studies systematically manipulate have the potential for arbitrary pairing with meaning. Fogel did not see why that fact made the hand gestures non-ethological or non-biological in nature. Oller replied that he did not think they were non-biological, only that they were not ethologically tied to a particular meaning. Tronick, however, cited Fraiberg's work on the communication gestures of blind infants. She had indicated that certain hand gestures were used in common by all blind infants to convey certain meanings. She gave them a somewhat constant interpretation. The blind infants, in other words, had certain meaningful gestures to which their parents did not normally attend. But when parents were made aware of these gestures they were able to respond to them. It might well be that the hand configurations Fogel described were not without significance when they first appeared.

Oller added that the hand configurations used in sign language may be assumed in different positions in relation to the body. The ASL significance of the O.K. ("fine") sign, for example, is only apparent if the sign is executed in a certain position in relation to head and the trunk. Fogel replied that each of the two infant subjects that he had studied had used similar gestures in very different ways. This finding added emphasis to the issue which Oller had raised about arbitrariness. Fogel thought that infants had a very small repertoire of distinctly defined gestures and expressions which they could use in a number of different ways. He thought, in fact, that social interaction in the first two years of life was idiosyncratic, and that rules of social interchange were local rather than having generally accepted conventions. Thus, different sets of games, of expressions and gestures, were characteristic of different mother-infant pairs. Generally speaking, social skills developed during the first two years of life. But when the specifics of this development were examined, there was a great deal of individual variation and arbitrary assignment of meanings. Stark objected that when the infant is two months of age, the mother, according to Fogel, was not yet aware of the infant's hand gestures. How was it, then, that these gestures were incorporated into games? Fogel said that gestures were not incorporated into games until they had clear functional significance for the mother. So, even though the baby at two months was grasping and reaching out to the mother, the mother did not pay attention to these gestures, that is, not until the infant began to grasp objects or to catch hold of her finger. The same was true of pointing. The mothers might notice pointing but they did not comment on it or respond to it specifically until the infant started to point at objects or pictures in a book. Fogel himself found this perplexing.

Published 1981 by Elsevier North Holland, Inc.
Stark, ed.
Language Behavior in Infancy and Early Childhood

The Development of Biologically Determined Signals of Readiness to Communicate, which are Language "Resistant"

Daniel N. Stern

Department of Psychiatry, Cornell University Medical Center, New York Hospital, New York, New York

This chapter will focus on the development, during infancy, of a set of nonverbal behaviors which largely determine whether any communication can begin or proceed, and to a lesser extent, what kinds of communications can occur. This set of behaviors consists of: gaze, head orientation, upper and lower body orientation, spatial positioning, and assumption of posture and distance. These behaviors will be discussed from several different perspectives. We shall first address the issue of intention and degrees of readiness to interact as a prerequisite context regarding communication or language. We shall then examine the orientational and postural signals which establish this context, from an ethological and developmental viewpoint. Finally, we shall speculate on why these behaviors remain nonverbal, appearing, in fact, to be language resistant, rather than becoming part of the formal language.

The Degree of Intention and Readiness to Communicate as a Context

Successful communication requires much shared knowledge about behavior. It has often been observed that this knowledge is generally taken for granted and rarely made explicit (Garfinkel, 1972; Shegeloff, 1976; Bates, 1976; Goffman, 1974; Watson, 1979; Sachs, Shegeloff and Jefferson, 1974; Searle, 1975; Bloom, 1973; Greenfield and Smith, 1976; Zukow, Reilly and Greenfield, 1979). Most of this shared nonverbal knowledge concerns: world knowledge about people and objects, the nature of interactions, and some rules and methods for negotiating certain activities between people, and between people and objects.

Orientational and postural behaviors have been identified as prerequisite conditions for successful communication. It has been noted that for certain communications, the participants must be visually attending to one another, sharing focus upon a third point in space, or that they must be oriented or maintaining a postural configuration in space relative to an object or person or both, in order that the propositional content of a communicative act, e.g., requesting or offering, can be accomplished (Kennan, Schieffelen, and Platt, 1977; Sachs et al., 1974; Bates, 1976; Shegeloff, 1971).

In this chapter we shall not attempt to examine the orientational and positional behaviors which help to establish propositional context. Rather, our major focus will be on the development and use of orientational and positional signals to indicate the degree of readiness or intention to interact and communicate with a partner. Interactive readiness is a prior context to propositional contexts which usually make no assumptions about the motivational state pertaining to the act of communicating itself. By communicative readiness, we do not simply mean that there is inattentiveness of one partner requiring attention-getting behaviors by the other, and then that there is mutually focused attention permitting the exchange of propositions. These two situations occupy opposite ends of a spectrum along which there are many distinct and important divisions. It is this spectrum, and the points along it, that we refer to in speaking of the degree of readiness to communicate.

One impelling reason to examine interactive readiness is that, in reality, so much of the time between mother and infant is spent in adjusting or negotiating their separate and joint readiness so that various planned propositional contexts can be established and specific communicative acts can be conducted. Pre-linguistic and linguistic behaviors that are studied must also be examined in the spatial interpersonal context in which they occur, since the meaning of a communicative behavior is dependent on whether it is intended to convey semantic information or to readjust, negotiate or manipulate the spatial interpersonal context with regard to communicative readiness. As we shall illustrate below with an example, much of the time, the infant is unready to a greater or lesser degree to interact. By unready, I do not mean simply attending elsewhere. Rather, the infant appears not to wish to interact, his agenda does not include communication and he will ignore or refuse attempts at communication, or partially accept them in various ways, or if pushed far enough, will protest or make some compromises with mother about his level of readiness to interact. The main point I wish to highlight is that when the mother executes a communicative act, the function of that act will differ depending upon the infant's relative state of readiness to interact. The relative degree of readiness-nonreadiness will determine the extent to which the act is taken for its propositional content and/or as a manuever to influence or manipulate the infant's current state of readiness. It is for this reason that readiness to interact is such an important context. It alters what is meant. (It may be that readiness is only a special form of context or a special case of sincerity conditions [Searle, 1969].) However, mother-infant interactions provide a special case of communication in the sense that mutual manipulation of one another's readiness to interact is a predominant rather than a rare and special feature of their communication. This is an inevitable result of the many large asymmetries betwen the two partners.

Orientational and Postural Signals of Readiness or Intention to Interact

Ethological Perspective

Gaze, head orientation, body orientation, posture, and distance are all suggested to be biologically determined species-specific behaviors regulating the momentary relationship between the participants and providing information mainly about: status, motivational state, affective state, and immediate intentions. In the case of gaze, head orientation, body orientation, and distance, much of the signal value of these behaviors derives from the fact that among humans and many non-human primates, mutual gaze, and the vis-a-vis position assume such importance as intraspecific signals (Chance, 1962; Eibl-Eibesfeldt, 1970; Hinde, 1974; Schaller, 1963; Sparks, 1967). At the most general level, mutual gaze and the vis-a-vis position of head and body, plus close distance indicate a heightened state of readiness to interact, and are experienced as arousing and activating. The nature of the intended interaction and the valence of the arousal can be either positive or negative, or it can rest at almost any point in between, depending on the general context, the exact nature of each of the signals and the addition of other signals (e.g., facial displays, etc.). Accordingly, prototype displays or intention movements involving aggression, sex, or affiliation involve this set of behaviors, and signal a high readiness to engage or interact (or communicate).

The intention movements which indicate the opposite, i.e., various degrees of *nonreadiness* to interact, are behaviors which, so to speak, dismantle the full readiness display. These are: gaze aversion, turning the head aside or down, angling the body away from the "squared off" postion, and moving backwards. These behaviors not only "undo" the full readiness signal but taken together are, in fact, steps in a flight or avoidance sequence, just as the full-readiness-to-engage signal is part of the aggressive or affiliative sequence. Chance (1962) has observed such behaviors as partial head aversions in many species, and has called these "cut-off signals." He points out that they achieve the function of mitigating the full impact of the interaction, while permitting the interactant to remain in position and at a distance to continue the interaction as modified, i.e., they allow a compromise between complete termination through flight and full engagement (as do some displacement behaviors). Except for complete physical withdrawals, these compromises are largely what we deal with in most interactions.

From a conceptual point of view, there is a problem with positioning general signals indicating readiness to interact or communicate. The problem arises from the question of toward what specific goal the interaction or communication is directed. In ethological inquiries, it has generally proven more productive to think of signals to interact in terms of the specific goal they are intended for, i.e., aggression, affiliation, sex, etc. More progress has generally been made by considering the specifics of behavioral readiness to engage in aggression versus affiliating, for instance, rather than to focus on whatever set of features the two signals may have in common. In this chapter, we are considering a situation in which a major goal of certainly the mother, and often both partners, appears to be to "communicate." In ethological terms, the next question would be communicating in the service of what biological goal(s) or motivational system(s). In our mother-infant play situation, we can rarely answer that question (even with the help of speech-act analysis) but are left with the impression that the major biological goal is to communicate per se or to teach communication. Accordingly, if we assign to communication per se the status of a biological motivation or goal, then we can perhaps feel more comfortable considering signals of readiness to communicate from a biological perspective. In doing so, it seems reasonable to search for the common features of signals of readiness to interact toward a variety of goals with conspecifics. Among these, certainly the most salient, as it may apply to readiness to communicate, is the readiness position consisting of full "sensory address," i.e., eyes upon, face toward, ears equidistant from, body facing, position close to, the communicative target. In other words, it seems probable that signals of readiness to communicate per se (to the extent that such truly exist) have evolved or emerged from the common features of signals of readiness to interact towards other goals involving conspecifics.

Developmental Perspective

Developmental issues are often more clearly viewed after some picture of the developmental end piont has been sketched. To this end, the literature on the spatial and orientational relationships among adults that prevail during various interactional projects, involvements or agendas will be briefly and selectively summarized (Birdwhistell, 1970; Goffman, 1963, 1974; Kendon, 1977; Scheflen, 1965). Several major points which are crucial to the developmental view follow: (1) Particular interactional agendas or involvements require specific spatial and orientational configurations. For instance, for two partners to belong to, or be "properly accredited participants" in a "focused encounter" as labeled by Goffman or a "jointly focused encounter" as labeled by Kendon, the interactants must establish periodic eye contact, must maintain a roughly face-to-face orientation, remain at a normal speaking distance, and their upper body (shoulders) and lower body (pelvis) cannot be oriented too far away from a position facing the other person. In this position the participants may perform interpersonal exchanges pertaining to the nature or status of their relationship. If any of these spatial or orientational constraints are not adhered to, the agenda of the ongoing interaction cannot proceed. In contrast to this "face-to-face" encounter just described, a second configuration is relevant to us here. Kendon has described an "L"-shaped spatial and orientational configuration (Kendon, 1977). In this position, the upper and lower bodies of both participants are roughly at right angles to each other in that they point at or cover a transactional space ("segment") which is common to both but which does not include the other person's body. Their faces are free to engage and disengage from the vis-a-vis position; however, their upper and especially lower bodies must maintain directional focus at or encompass an overlapping shared transitional space which does not include the other's body. In this position the interpersonal agenda most generally concerns an external topic, i.e., one outside of the relationship between the participants per se. (2) Any major shift in topic or change in interactional agenda is generally accompanied by a major positional shift by both partners. This is accomplished by a shift in the weight-bearing axis of the body, not simply a broad gesture. This marks off process boundaries roughly analagous to paragraphs. (3) Within an established interactional spatial and orientational configuration, such as face-to-face, minor kinesic modification can "fine tune" the interpersonal context. For instance, crossing the upper body with one or both arms reduces the physical openness of the presentation and acts to reduce the psychological availability of that partner. Crossing the legs will accomplish a similar function but with altered meanings, depending on context. Similarly, different degrees of head aversion to the side and down or up introduce important modification in the interpersonal context while still maintaining the larger context, which is established through the spatial and orientational configuration of the pelvic and shoulder axes. (4) Posture sharing, in the form of imitating or mirror imaging another's posture, is generally a sign of "being with" the other. This "being with" can refer to an empathic tie or to an intellectual agreement; or it can refer to the feeling of being a member of a sub-group to which the mimicked partner belongs.

When can infants perform the individual behaviors that make up the signals which regulate degrees of readiness to communicate? There is a widely held contention that, upon their first appearance, infant abilities are immediately available for interactional use (they are, in fact, readied for use in the service of interaction with people). This appears to be very much the case with the orientational and postural behaviors under question. As soon as an infant can walk, walking towards and away in order to regulate the interpersonal physical distance appears to function. The infant does not appear to learn to walk first and later apply this mobility to the problem of interpersonal proxemics. The two occur hand in hand. A similar situation seems to prevail with all of the orienting and spatial behaviors under discussion.

Gaze. Because of the precocity of the visual and oculomotor system the infant has essentially mature voluntary control of gaze behaviors by the fourth month of life (White, Castle, and Held, 1964). At roughly the same time that this functional maturity is achieved, the infant clearly begins to use gaze behavior to initiate, maintain, terminate, and avoid interactions with caregivers (Stern, 1971, 1974b). The potency of mutual visual regard as a highly salient and arousing stimulus situation by this age is well known (Robson, 1967; Wolff, 1963).

Head orientation. The neck muscles controlling head orientation are, along with the striated muscles involved in sucking and oculomotor control, among the first to come under voluntary control. Instrumental head turning is observable during the neonatal period (Papoušek, 1967; Siqueland and Lipsitt, 1966). From the third to sixth month, the infant seeks, and greatly enjoys, his first extended period of social interaction involving largely visual and auditory channels. This occurs in what is usually called "face-to-face" play. The infant is positioned on knee, lap, infant seat, etc., anywhere comfortable so that face-to-face interaction can occur. At this point in development, the infant has relatively poor control over the upper and lower extremities and weight bearing muscle systems. Accordingly, even if the infant's body were not held or contained in this first face-to-face interaction, gaze and face orientation are the major signals of readiness available for his own use. This apparently simple system has more subtleties than first meet the eye. Several distinct spatial and orientational behaviors can be delineated and seem to have different signal functions: gaze and head aversion to the side with head lowering is interpreted as a definitive termination signal; gaze and head aversion to the side with raising the head and looking up is interpreted as a "hold" signal; head aversion past 100 degrees away from the target (where all visual contact is lost) is interpreted as an escape or withdrawal signal; head aversion that loses foveal vision (form perception) but maintains peripheral vision (motion perception) is seen as a form of monitoring in a partial cut-off position; full enface head orientation can occur with a glazed look, this is a different form of unreadiness to interact (see Beebe and Stern, 1977; Stern, 1977). The central point is that a suprisingly mature signal system (given the few behaviors involved) is already "in place" by six months.

Upper body. Between roughly 5 months and 12 months the following motor landmarks have been achieved: control of sitting postures is good; coordination and voluntary control of the upper extremities is excellent; and crawling and cruising are developed. Used together, these give the child control over the spatial orientation of his body and in particular his upper body (shoulder axis). During this same period the infant's preferred stimuli and forms of activity shift from the human face, voice, and touch, and purely social interactions, to objects and object play on the floor, with mother filling in the third point of the triangle. The infant can now control shoulder or upper body positions of: oriented towards mother, (the "face-to-face" position); the "L" position, each seated at right angles but oriented to the same interactional space; or oriented away, back to mother. These three positions occupy points on a continuum, different shadings of which come to have different signal value. With these additional developments, the infant now has more control over indicating his degree of readiness to interact, but additionally, he has control over what kind of interactions with mother may proceed, object oriented or purely interpersonal. Object-oriented interactions can occur in the face-to-face position or the "L" position. Interpersonal interactions occur mainly in the face-to-face. Add to this system the previously gained gaze and head control and the richness of the infant's signal repertoire concerning readiness and intent is considerable.

Lower body. With the advent of walking, at around one year, the infant can better control lower body orientation and proxemics. The full set of nonverbal readines signals available to the adult is then available to him. There have been almost no systematic quantitative studies of infants' use of these behaviors in controlled or semi-controlled interpersonal situations. A few exceptions exist. Stern and Bender (1974) asked children aged 3-5 years to walk up to three different stimuli: a standing strange adult, a seated strange adult, and an empty chair. The children were asked to "stop when you get there." At the end of the approach they measured: approach distance, degree of orientation of lower body (angular distance), horizontal head orientation, and vertical head orientation. In addition, facial expression and hand gestures while approaching were scored. All behaviors were different in the different stimulus situations. The important findings from the point of view of this chapter, however, were that the major signals of readiness to interact were functioning in a predictable way by the age of 3 and changed little over the next two years. The basic signal system was early maturing in this sense. Several other researchers working with pre-schoolers in natural but structured situations have observed that, while many changes occur from ages 2 to 5, it is striking how much of the basic nonverbal signalling system is developed by 2 to 3 years of age, and perhaps earlier (Brannigan and Humphries, 1972; Jones, 1972; McGrew, 1972).

An Illustrative Sample of Free Play at 12 Months

The constant, moment-by-moment use of these postural and orientational behaviors as signals to negotiate mutual intentions to communicate and readiness to communicate is illustrated in the following sample of free play between a mother and a one-year-old infant in a playroom full of different objects. The situation was skewed to produce a large number of verbal and "proto-linguistic" exchanges between mother and infant. In fact, it was designed to maximize language behaviors and object play of both mother and infant. The sample interaction to follow consists of 1 minute and 40 seconds of fairly ordinary object-oriented free floor play. A microanalysis of this section is presented to show that during this short section the infant produces at least 12 distinct orienting and/or positioning shifts to establish or adjust the context as it concerns intention or readiness to communicate. The interaction is presented in a dialogic format below, in which the behaviors of each are described and an interpretation of the likely intention and probable signal effect of the behavior is placed in parentheses.

1. Mother: She tugs on infants' shorts from behind. He is facing away, back to her, scanning the toys. Both are sitting on the floor. As she tugs she says, "All the toys, ah! Look at all the stuff you have." (An attempt to attract his attention to her and alter his position to include her or share his interactional space.)

2. Infant: Swings upper body around, turns face to her and gazes at her. Vocalizes. (He responds to her bid for attention. He does not, however, swing his lower body around and thus is not sharing his main interactional space.)

3. Mother: As he gazes at her she says, "What?" (She acts as if his head turn to her and gaze at her were a request on his part, rather than a response to her bid for attention.)

4. Infant: Immediately breaks gaze, looks away and turns away to his original position after she says "What?" (He rejects her attempt to engage him and firmly indicates his nonreadiness to communicate at that moment.)

5. Mother: "You have a lot of toys." (Can be interpreted as either a commentary, or a reiteration of her bid for attention and shared space as in 1 and 3 above.)

6. Infant: Continues to play with puzzle with his back to her. He shows no orienting to her statement in 5. (He ignores her reiterated bid. We know from previous and subsequent behaviors that he hears her and can respond. He is maintaining the nonreadiness signal.)

7. Mother: Reaches over into his area of play and takes a piece of the puzzle that he was not playing with. She turns it over in her hand to show it to him, while saying, "That's a bird." (A bid to focus his attention this time on a specific object. Mother does this by invading his unshared interactional space and forcing an interaction with her in that space.)

8. Infant: Swings his shoulders and head towards mother, stopping at a point about midway between his starting position and a direct line towards her. He looks at the puzzle piece in her hand but not at her face. (He appears to partially accept her bid, i.e., he responds to her indirect request to attend to the bird, he repositions to create a shared interpersonal space, but he does not accept her implied request to share focus with her about it because he does not glance at her face also. A mixed message.)

9. Mother: Moves her head and upper body closer to the infant, continues to show the piece and says "See, that's a bird." (She has indirectly requested that the bird become a focus of joint attention or actions, i.e., she reiterates the implied request that he did not freely accept in 8; she is also intensifying proxemically her signal of intention to interact.)

10. Infant: Turns fairly sharply away from her and the bird and resumes play with back to her. (He does not accept her above bid and returns to the full nonreadiness position.)

11. Mother: Reaches out to the space in front of infant to give him the bird-piece and says, "Here, put this back." (A variant of strategy seen in 7 above. However, her manner of acting is deintensified.)

12. Infant: He takes object while orienting to her only very slightly. He smiles, pronates hand and throws the object down. He then turns further away to play. (An apparent response to, then protest and refusal of her bid and a reiteration of nonreadiness.)

13. Mother: She moves her upper body and head back and away from the infant thus creating a large *positional shift*. (She "pulls out of" the interaction at least momentarily. She has performed a major positional shift indicating a change in agenda, namely, to leave him alone.)

14. Infant: He turns his head and shoulders to her without establishing eye contact and reaches out his hand and touches her by laying his hand on her lower arm. (He responds to her major positional shift and new agenda of withdrawal by making his first initiative toward her with a gesture of readiness.)

15. Mother: She turns her hand over palm up—to his touch—and says, "You wanna give me the bird?" (She appears to accept his signal as if it were an implied request not to withdraw. She then reiterates her attempt to achieve focused attention or shared transactional space as before.)

16. Infant: He quickly scans the room, smiles and puts his hand to his mouth, and vocalizes. (He appears to be mildly in conflict or confused. He produces no clear signal of readiness to indicate his imminent trend.)

17. Mother: Picks up a doll and stands it on the floor to show him, saying, "What? Dolly?" (A reattempt on her part to establish communication about an object in a shared interactional space.)

18. Infant: Looks at doll and smiles. (He responds to the object and shared space but does not share gaze with her about it.)

19. Mother: She wiggles the doll a bit and says "It's Dressy Bessy." (A reiteration of the attempt to achieve acknowledged joint focus.)

20. Infant: He smiles weakly and performs an aborted reach for the doll which stops midway. (Incomplete acceptance or response to her repeated attempts. Again he partially goes for object but does not include her with referencing gaze.)
21. Mother: Wiggles doll more forcefully and says, "See—a dolly!" (An intensified attempt on her part for engagement with joint focus.)
22. Infant: Turns head and upper body away from her and dolly—back to puzzle. (Refusal of her intensified attempt. He signals unreadiness with head and upper body.)
23. Mother: Picks up and tosses a puzzle piece to the side. (She appears frustrated. A questionable attempt to recapture his attention.)
24. Infant: Notices the tossed piece, scans the surround and starts to move off crawling away from mother to a new part of the room. (He now initiates the second major positional shift indicating a change in agenda. In this case his intention to withdraw from the interaction.)
25. Mother: She fondles his head by ruffling his hair as he starts to move off. (She appears to accept his altered agenda to withdraw and so signals.)

In this example the agendas being negotiated by both partners are in partial conflict. Their states of intention and readiness to communicate with one another are different. Accordingly, the semantics of the mother's verbal statements or the infant's proto-linguistic behaviors are secondary to their function of negotiating or establishing the interpersonal context, as it concerns intention and readiness to interact. A major reason to stress this state of affairs is that there are also interpersonal contexts of mutual readiness to communicate with shared attentional focus in which information about objects is exchanged. It is these situtations that are mainly isolated for study in inquiries about language acquisition. However, in ongoing natural interactions, the interpersonal communicative-readiness context constantly shifts. At times, the context permits the communication of information about objects and agents to be primary, in which case verbal and proto-linguistic behaviors play the major role with nonverbal, orienting and positioning behaviors supporting them. At other times, the negotiation of the readiness to communicate context itself is the primary issue (because of asymmetries of agendas). When this is so, the nonverbal orientational and positional behavior play the predominant role and the verbal and proto-linguistic behaviors become ancillary. The study of language acquisition must include language behaviors in these multiple interpersonal contexts.

Why Signals of Readiness to Communicate Are and Remain Nonverbal?

"Proto-lingusitic" vs. Language "Resistant" Behaviors

Some nonverbal behaviors performed by pre-linguistic infants are labeled "proto-linguistic" (or linguistic precursors) because they later become linguistically encoded. Such nonverbal behaviors and their semantic functions became very closely mapped onto or transformed into the formal language system. The transition from sensorimotor to linguistic communication has been described for various behaviors such as pointing or reaching for an object with gaze shifting between object and caregiver. After that transformation has occurred, the original nonverbal behaviors may drop out or remain as ancillary signals which perform modifying functions for the central verbal message. This line of approach to the study of language acquisition and the assumptions that underlie it have proven and are still proving productive for understanding the cognitive and linguistic developmental processes involved (Antinucci and Parisi, 1973; Bates, 1976; Bruner, 1975; Bloom, 1973; Dore, 1975; Greenfield and Smith, 1976; Zukow, Reilly and Greenfield, 1980).

The central thrust of this section, however, will flow in the opposite direction. We will ask why many pre-linguistic nonverbal behaviors never become part of the formal language system. In part, they appear to be "resistant" to linguisitc encoding in the sense that the transition from sensorimotor interaction to language loses much, perhaps the essence, of the impact of the original nonverbal behavior.

If we take a prospective point of view, all nonverbal behaviors during the first year or so of life might be fair game to be "proto-linguistic" in the manner that reaching for an object, with opening and closing hand and gaze shifting back and forth between object and adult is a "proto-imperative" which fairly rapidly transforms into "gimme. . . . . .etc" (Bates, 1976). On the other hand a behavior such as: stepping back a half step from an interactant, averting gaze to the side, and lowering the head, will never undergo an analogous transformation. A first task, then, would be to consider what would be likely criteria to delineate communicative nonverbal behaviors which will be amenable or resistant to linguistic coding. Hopefully such a delineation would help us better know what language is and is not.

Possible Criteria of Ease of or Resistance to Linguistic Encoding

The following tentative list is intended to take into account the biological needs of a communicating species that needs to and can exchange information about: external events, ideas, and objects; internal events; and dyadic or interpersonal events. The list is not intended to compare linguistic and non-linguistic systems per se but rather to question the advantages of an already present nonverbal behavior acquiring linguistic encoding for verbal use. Comparing, then, a communicative behavior in its nonverbal and potentially verbal form, the following questions comprise some of the basic comparisons:

1. How much overlap is there in semantic meaning?
2. How much overlap is there in denoting another's affective state?
3. How much overlap is there in ability to empathize with another's affective state? (Empathy here is meant as a vicarious affective response to the other, as against simply denoting the other's affective state.)

4. How much overlap is there in the ability to generate or regulate different levels of arousal in another?
5. How much overlap is there in the power to activate various motivational systems: sex, aggression, flight, etc.
6. Relative speed of transmission and decoding.
7. Effective range of signal transmission.
8. Advantages and disadvantages of having the signal be silent or not and vice versa.

Those pre-linguistic behaviors that appear to be resistant to linguistic encoding are those that as nonverbal behaviors have important advantages in comparisons 3, 4, and 5 (and sometimes 6, 7, and 8).

Why Resistance to Linguistic Encoding?

We shall discuss four reasons why these behaviors signalling readiness to communicate may be resistant to linguistic encoding:

(1) They involve biologically determined species-specific signals regulating interpersonal behavior rather than object-related behavior. These nonverbal behaviors are generally considered to be ethologically salient signals in the sense that they are species-specific signals communicating information about the nature of the momentary relationship between the participants, information largely about: status, motivational state, affective state, and immediate intentions. They are not sign stimuli releasing invariant fixed-action patterns; rather they are intention movements, in which biological constraints limit, but not completely, the arbitrariness of the signal. The phylogenetic similarities in form and function of these behaviors mentioned above argue that their antogenic course is heavily biologically determined. In these intention movements, then, we are dealing with partially built-in perceptual and response tendencies which operate (certainly with the need of much experience) through visual and proprioceptive cues. In addition, these behaviors have as their "reference" the immediate interpersonal state between the partners and operate through visual cues of other's behavior. They are not designed for referencing external objects, events, or locations. It appears that pre-verbal behaviors, developmentally speaking, which are object, event or location referencing are the ones that are "proto-linguistic."

One might conclude, as has often been done, that the basic signal system to regulate interpersonal state evolved in our non-human ancestors as a nonverbal system and remained so, while the advent of tool use and the subsequent greatly increased interaction with the object world represented an adaptive need that was "responded" to through natural selection with the emergence of speech. While there is no evidence to counter this conclusion and much to recommend its general outlines, it leaves several important questions unanswered. First, well after the assumed onset of tool use, the anatomical features of the face, in particular, continued to undergo evolutionary changes permitting a much richer and more subtle repertoire of facial expressions and combinations thereof (Ekman, 1973.) Since these evolutionary events were roughly concomitant with the explosion in tool use and language emergence, why were not some of the new interpersonal signalling features embraced by the emerging language system as we presume the new object phenomena were?

Even if the interpersonal signalling system at issue did evolve in an already established form phylogenetically prior to speech, a second question remains. Why did the formal language system never replace or provide a full substitute for the nonverbal system, thus providing a redundant channel? Of course language can describe the nonverbal signalling system. A revealing example is the word "supercilious" derived from the Latin and freely translated as "(raising the eyebrow) hairs over and above." It is a good description of the display of hauteur and disdain but, as a word, has nothing of the effect of the actual behavior as performed for, or at, a viewer.

We are left with the fact that our responses to these nonverbal behaviors, but not the words that describe them, appear on biological grounds to involve immediately and directly the level of arousal, the activation of motivational sets, and in the case of affect displays, vicarious affective responses. In spite of the biological constraints, there remains much room for these general purpose behaviors to be used in different degrees and combinations so as to provide very precise information about the exact state and intention of the organism. This leads to the second feature of these behaviors which may make them language resistant, the fact that they are ideally designed to communicate gradient or dimensional information rather than categorical information.

(2) Dimensional versus categorical information: The difference between dimensional (gradient) information and categorical information about a signal is best illustrated with an example. The presence or absence of a smile is categorical information indicating whether a positive affective display exists or not. The dimensional information about that smile concerns how positive the smile is. Is it a weak or strong smile? The two main dimensions along which there is general agreement that all signals are distributed are intensity or potency, and activity.

The signal display features that convey the gradient information about the signal are, for visually received signals: the fullness of display, and the speed and timing of performance; and for aurally received signals: loudness, pitch, stress (a timing feature), and speed. The behaviors of interest, namely head and body orientation and distance, are performed so as to provide precise information concerning which point along a dimension the communication in question occupies. This ability of certain nonverbal behaviors to cover all points along a gradient is in contrast to linguistically encoded signals which in their essence concern categories, and not dimensional information (Marler, 1965; Scherer, 1979). An attempt to convey dimensional information in a verbal form is instructive. For instance Labov and Fanshel (1977) describe how the force of a sentence can be aggravated (going down the list) or mitigated (going up the list):

Would you please dust the room?
Would you dust the room?
Please dust the room.
Dust the room.
Dust the God-damn room.

By "aggravated," the authors mean progression along the dimension of intensity or urgency. However, because of the nature of language, the above progression is more of a stepwise or staircase increase along the dimension, rather than a sliding along the gradient to occupy any possible position as in fact one could do with the very first sentence "Would you please dust the room" by varying in gradient fashion the various paralinguistic features that convey the dimensional information.

The transmission of gradient information about signals which mainly concern the current, momentary level of intentions, motivations, and affects is crucial, and the nonverbal behaviors under focus have several advantages over verbal behaviors in conveying this aspect of communication.

First, as suggested above, the nonverbal signals transmit more precise gradient information than verbal ones. In actual adult discourse, what usually occurs is that a general "ball park" level is indicated by the verbal message and the fine tuning accomplished by the nonverbal behaviors, i.e., one might say "Dust the room" and leave to the paraverbal and nonverbal channels the important information of how close that statement is to "Please dust the room" as against "Dust the God-damn room." In fact, with very conventionalized verbal messages such as "Hello," or "Oh really!" once the convention has been observed, virtually all of the information resides in how it is said, i.e., the dimensional aspect. In fact, the effective stimulus in such conventionalized events, is the degree to which the gradient signal is discrepant from the anticipated gradient signal on that occasion. The actual verbalization in these cases becomes simply a vehicle for this interplay.

A second advantage of these nonverbal behaviors over their verbal counterparts concerns speed of transmission of gradient information. For intraspecific issues of such great biological consequence as territorial fights, courtship, etc., most often instant-by-instant feedback of transmitted information is required. The outcome of a potential fight, for instance, is dependent on the rapid transmission of slight shifts in levels of intensity of threat or readiness to perform in a certain way. Orienting and positional behaviors can transmit this gradient information in split-seconds. Such a negotiation, if carried on only verbally (without nonverbal cues) would take forever by comparison.

(3) Accountability versus deniability of message: Language "resistant" behaviors involve signals for which explicit accountability is disadvantageous. Several authors such as Scherer (1977) and Labov and Fanshel (1977) have argued that for a large array of interpersonal exchanges, communication is a multimodal phenomenon in which the greatest flexibility and maneuverability of communication provide simultaneous information which differs not only to the extent that it is categorical or dimensional but also, relatedly, to the extent that the sender can and will or will not be held accountable for information in the various channels. Labov and Fanshel (1977) describe this very well in discussing intonational signals. In the following quote, for our purposes, we can freely substitute other nonverbal behaviors for intonational signals: ". . . .the lack of clarity or discreteness in the intonational signal is not an unfortunate limitation of this channel, but an essential and important aspect of it. Speakers need a form of communication which is deniable. It is advantageous for them to express hostility, challenge the competence of others, or express friendliness and affection in a way that can be denied if they are explicitly held to account for it. If there were not such a deniable channel of communication and intonation contours become so well recognized and explicit that people were accountable for their intonations, then some other mode of deniable communication would undoubtedly develop." The surest way to keep a behavior "deniable,"or such that one cannot be held explicitly accountable for it, is to prevent it from becoming part of the formal language system.

This line of argument suggests that in a multi-channel communicative system there will exist constant environmental or cultural pressure to keep same signals resistant to linguistic encoding so that they will remain "deniable." We are adding to this argument that biological considerations help to explain which behaviors those are likely to be.

(4) Accumulating evidence from split-brain studies and related neurological experiments and clinical findings (Gazzaniga and LeDoux, 1978) suggest that different "mental systems" dealing with different forms of sensory-motor-cognitive experience are encoded differently, some as language and others non-linguistically (as well as being primarily registered in different parts of the brain). These experiments suggest that such tasks as appreciation of spatial relations of objects; body spatial relations; recognition of nonverbal forms and face recognition tasks are all performed better in the right hemisphere, are more severely affected after right-brain injury, and most telling, appear to be encoded non-linguistically. Reaction-time experiments to various nonverbal spatial stimuli support this view. The behaviors of central interest to us here, namely, gaze, head and body orientation and distance, all fall into those categories of spatial, body-environment mapping and form-perception tasks that appear to be non-linguistically encoded.

As we have pointed out, the signal behaviors of interest appear to be almost fully developed by age two. Further maturation will bring relatively minor elaborations or inhibitions to an established system. These communicative behaviors clearly were encoded prior to the developmental advent of language, and from the above experiments there appears to be no reason to suggest that their mode of encoding ever becomes linguistic, or was ever under any adaptive pressure to become encoded into formal language systems.

Conclusions

We have examined some of the nonverbal behaviors used by pre-linguistic infants to signal their degree of readiness to engage in communication. The writing of this chapter has largely been stimulated by several perceived lacks in our current approaches to and understanding of language behavior in infancy, and has been written with the hope of drawing more research attention to certain areas. The first such area is the nature of the communicative contexts established by the infant's orientation, position, and postural configuration. While attention has been paid to these nonverbal events in creating appropriate propositional contexts, insufficient attention has been paid to their special and subtle signal role in establishing the larger context of readiness to communicate. Further, we feel that readiness to communicate can not simply be treated as an issue of getting and maintaining attention, but constitutes a high order interpersonal context which influences the meaning of language as used.

A second area of relative neglect concerns the need for accurate developmental descriptive accounts of pre-linguistic infant's nonverbal communication repertoires. Our emphasis concerning these behaviors has been selectively focused on those that are obvious candidates as language precursors, yet these occupy only a small proportion of the behaviors from which we interpret infant communications, intentions, and affects. An additional point about this "over emphasis" on obvious language precursors concerns a clinical issue. Many children who will develop disturbed language will also develop disturbances in all communicative modes. By focusing more sharply on the entire repertoire of communicative nonverbal behaviors, regardless of their apparent fate as regards language, we may be in a better position to identify and intervene earlier in cases of deviant development.

Finally, there remains the intriguing question of which mental operations and registerings become encoded into formal language systems, and which do not. Our understanding of thought and language will ultimatley depend on answers to these questions. By examining more closely, in the pre-linguistic infant, which communicative nonverbal behaviors are candidates as language precursors and which are not, we may be in a better position to approach some of these larger questions.

ACKNOWLEDGMENTS
This Research was supported by The Jane Hilder Harris Foundation. I wish to acknowledge the contribution of suggestions and criticisms of Drs. Roanne Barnett, Susan Speiker, and Gail Wasserman. In addition, I would like to acknowledge the exchange of ideas about these issues afforded by the Society for Research in Child Development Summer Institute on the Origins of Communication, led by Dr. Cathrine Garvey, Delaware, 1979, and by a Seminar on Human Ethology, conducted at Rockefeller University, by Dr. Peter Marler, 1979.

Discussion

Leavitt was concerned about the concept expressed in Stern's paper, of innate behaviors that automatically take on a shared meaning. He accepted the concept of a sequence of behaviors emerging in the infant but was disturbed by the assignment of shared meaning to those behaviors. He cited the example of proxemics. It was known from studies of rapidly approaching objects and studies of the visual cliff phenomenon in infants that there are rather profound differences in what could be called the meaning of depth for infants having these experiences. What was the nature of the progression from the infant, who regards looming objects with interest rather than arousal and fear, to the behavior of the infant who can crawl or walk and has acquired a personal space? If there was such a progression, then the whole notion of early establishment of shared meaning seemed to crumble. Perhaps this progression had to be regarded in a different way.

Stern thought that this was a very broad issue. Leavitt had given an example of progression from reflexive behavior that might provide a basis for later development, to later-developing behaviors. But the later behaviors might include species-specific responses to ethologically salient signals and also behaviors that are learned in the more usual sense of that term. These two aspects of development, he thought, were different. Leavitt said it bothered him when species-specific behaviors were discussed or thought of in terms of fixed action patterns. Stern said that he did not confuse fixed action patterns with species-specific behaviors. He thought that this confusion could be avoided if one's terminology and concepts were sufficiently precise. When Stern referred to a set of behaviors as having ethological and biological salience, he did not at all mean that they were pre-wired behavioral programs in the sense that fixed action patterns are pre-wried. There may be a built-in biological bias for a variety of behaviors to acquire certain cognitive meanings once they have emerged, given the average expected environment in which infants are reared. Other behaviors might, however, be much more likely to acquire an arbitrary meaning. He believed these general statements would be acceptable to most workers in the area.

Bloom stated that there appeared to be some confusion with respect to innate behaviors. It appeared to her that certain framing behaviors had been referred to as fixed at two years of age and certain gaze behaviors had been referred to as being fixed at three to four months of age. Stern replied that the utilization of a basic behavior in a given social context seemed to change very little. It was essentially a fully developed behavior. However, it became associated with other behaviors and thereby more complex behavioral patterns were built up and developed as the infant became able to respond in a greater variety of social contexts. For example, gaze aversion was present very early in certain social contexts. But, as the child became older, different facial expressions became attached to it. The same gaze behavior of aversion could later be modified in extent and accompanied by a smile, raising of the eyebrows, and intermittent glances at the partner of the exchange, and thus be incorporated into coy behavior.

Bloom was interested in the meshing of gaze behavior with what people were actually saying, that is, the units of an utterance. She and her colleagues had data to show that there were marked changes in the manner in which gaze and utterance units were coordinated in the second year of life. Stern said that this was a very good example of what he had been talking about. Bloom added that the context was also important in this development. Stern was sure that this was true. The increases in complexity of the child's behavior should be based on how complicated or difficult it was for the child to process content in addition to the exchange signals he was receiving and using to mark the turn-taking of the interaction. He felt that a good deal of variance would be related to those factors. The more complicated the content of an exchange, the less the child would gaze at his partner. His gaze might be fixed at some distant part of the environment of it might wander, but it would not be fixed on the partner in the exchange.

Bloom said that the patterns of gaze in her examples depended on the communicative nature of the exchange, not so much on the complexity of the content. For example, if the child was talking about what she/he was doing, taking a car and pushing it under a bridge, gaze behavior would be different from that in the case where she/he expressed the desire to have the mother put a doll in a cup to "give it a bath." In the first case the child might say "car, bridge, ride," looking only briefly at the mother and then away. In the second example, the child would more likely pick up the doll, walk to the mother, and say "baby, cup" looking at the mother throughout the whole exchange. There would be different gaze patterns in these two communication situations. Bloom found it difficult to reconcile these patterns, which might also change with development, and the notion of patterns which were already fully developed and not subject to change at three months of age. Stern said that these developmental changes represented the intergration of two behaviors, one relating to interpersonal aspects, the other to communicative content.

Published 1981 by Elsevier North Holland, Inc.
Stark, ed.
Language Behavior in Infancy and Early Childhood

Discussion of Social Development and Communicative Behavior in Infancy

Peter H. Wolff

The Children's Hospital Medical Center
Boston, Massachusetts

In her introduction to this section, Stark posed the important theoretical questions: whether nonverbal communication between infant and parent during the first year of life influences the child's language development; how nonverbal communication might contribute to language acquisition; and what kind of evidence can be adduced in support of either a causal or functional relationship. From a clinical-etiological perspective, for example, one might assume that nonverbal social transactions provide the necessary baseline of experiences that awakens the infant's awareness of the social partner as an independent agent, motivates it to make gestural communications, and establishes primitive strategies for nonverbal conversation. The hypothesis does not hold that such experiences are the structural basis for language performance but it implies that impoverished social interaction may affect language development adversely. An adequate test of this "weaker" etiological hypothesis requires knowledge about the normal variations of nonverbal interaction between infant and partner in different famlies, social classes, culture, etc., because white middle class American expectations about mother-infant interaction are probably not a universal standard for the basic requirements of healthy socialization during infancy. An adequate test of the hypothesis also requires some knowledge about the normal range of variations in language performance of children and adults since white middle class English is also not a valid standard for language competence.

On the other hand, from a structural-linguistic perspective, one might assume that the formal rules of interpersonal communication elaborated in the course of early nonverbal transaction become the structural matrix for later verbal interchange. An adequate test of this "stronger" structural hypothesis requires a formal notation system that can be applied to represent both social nonverbal communication and linguistic discourse; it requires decision rules for determining when patterns of nonverbal and verbal communication are or are not similar; and it requires transformation rules for predicting how particular forms of nonverbal communication are represented in the use of language for conversations.

Unlike psycholinguists, students of formal linguistics might consider it absurd to expect that we can learn anything of value about language competence or performance by observing either manual gestures, or rhythms of eye-to-eye contact and mutual head alignment in young infants and their parents. Yet the inclusion of papers by Fogel, Tronick, and Stern at a conference on language acquisition, as well as the many empirical and theoretical studies on human nonverbal communication, attest to a strong interest in the possibility that communicative intent and conversational skills are developed long before the onset of language, and that they may be essential prerequisites for verbal communications (Bates, 1976; Bullowa, 1977; Waterson and Snow, 1978).

On common sense grounds it seems reasonable to assume that nonverbal social interchanges establish some of the basic techniques for sharing knowledge, taking turns and nonverbal conversational skills which will later be utilized in verbal discourse. Detailed observations on infants alone and with their mothers clearly demonstrate that babies are remarkably sensitive to their immediate social environment; whereas the pattern of their nonverbal gestures seem to imply "communicative intent." However, when common sense expectations are hypostatized as established knowledge, and then used to justify intervention programs for "socially at risk" families that intend to prevent impaired language development by enhancing the social communication skills of infants and parents, we are, I believe, obliged to examine what is the evidence on which such intrusions into familiy life are predicated.

The papers presented by Fogel and Tronick contribute to our understanding about the process of preverbal socialization, and identify some of the behavioral means by which infants actualize their "communicative intent;" their relevance for language acquisitions, however, is neither evident nor is it a major goal of the presentations. Stern's paper makes an explicit distinction between social communicative acts that can be encoded linguistically and those which are language resistant; but the main emphasis of his presentation is again on language resistant social signals. Since the three papers do not directly address Stark's questions, I will draw on clinical or experimental evidence from other sources, organizing my remarks around the arbitrary distinctions between an etiological and structural hypothesis on the developmental relation between nonverbal communication and language performance.

For obvious ethical reasons, animal experiments in total social isolation cannot be utilized for investigating the social prerequisites of human language acquisition. Human experiments of "nature" may however bring indirect clues about the potential contributors of nonverbal social interaction to normal language development. For example, the clinical case histories of Kaspar Hauser (von Feurerbach, 1831), The Wild Boy of Aveyron (Itard, 1962), and the wolf children of India (Singh and Zingg, 1945) indicate that gross social neglect during the formative years causes severe language impairment. However these case histories are inadequate tests of the etiological hypothesis. For one thing, the severity of social isolation was usually not documented but inferred after the children had been rescued, so that the feral children might have been raised in a stimulating social environment. For another thing, the feral children may have suffered from brain damage, mental retardation or autism before their extrusion from society. Finally, according to the case histories, most of the children were linguistically as well as socially isolated, and the lack of exposure to a language environment could adequately explain their language retardation independent of social isolation in the preverbal period of development. On the other hand, if the anecdotal case histories have any scientific validity, the fact that at least some of the children acquired a working knowledge of their language, argues for the robust human capacity to acquire language even under degraded social conditions, rather than for the criticality of nonverbal communication as a precondition for language development.

The detailed psycholinguistic study of "Genie" (Curtiss, 1977), provides more substantial data for testing the merits of the etiological hypothesis. This young woman was presumably raised in total social isolation between her twentieth month and her thirteenth year, and was then rehabilitated in a normal foster home but was given no explicit language training. At the end of her seclusion, she was mute, could understand only a few words and simple commands, and revealed no comprehension of English grammar. After seven years of exposure to a normal language environment, Genie had made remarkable strides in acquiring standard English. Her progress in acquiring a first language is similar to that of normal children, although her comprehension and usage of conversational English remain deficient in specific areas. Since Genie's use of English is more like, than different from, that of normally reared children, despite near total social and linguistic deprivation from infancy in puberty, the case history argues strongly against any critical period hypothesis which holds that a child must acquire a first language before puberty; or that nonverbal social transactions are an essential prerequisite for the communicative use of language.

Again, however, the evidence is not unassailable. Genie was probably reared in a more or less adequate social environment until her twentieth month of life; she was visited several times a day by her mother who presumably spoke to her since she was able to understand isolated words. While she showed no gross evidence of developmental retardation or impaired brain function as an infant, the possibility cannot be excluded that she was organically impaired even before her seclusion, whereas her nearly complete physical immobilization and severe malnutrition probably contributed materially to her developmental retardation.

Less dramatic instances of social isolation due to family disruptions or institutionalization provide little evidence which would support the etiological hypothesis. From a review of the literature, Rutter (1972), for example, concludes that the amount of nonverbal social stimulation in early childhood has no detectable effect on subsequent verbal development, whereas the quantity of non-social verbal stimulation can materially influence the course of language development.

In summary, the available clinical evidence is not a satisfactory test of the hypothesis that major degradation in the social interchanges between infant and parent, short of total isolation, influence the course of language acquisition. Although a moderately degraded social environment during the first year may have measurable effects on the syntactic, semantic, phonological or pragmatic features of language acquisition during childhood, such effects have to date not been demonstrated. A linguistic perspective on early socialization therefore, constitutes no basis which would justify enrichment programs for families whose social communications with their infants do not meet conventional middle class standards. Some degree of social interchange in the early years is obviously essential for language development, but the same minimum is essential for the development of other mental processes and probably for physical growth and survival.

Of greater theoretical interest for understanding the process of early language acquisition, may be the "structural" hypothesis that has served as the major impetus for contemporary studies of early social communication. Most generally this hypothesis holds that the rules of nonverbal reciprocity, turn taking, mirroring, etc. are the structural foundations for verbal interchange, although the causal relation between the two domains of communication are usually not specified. In a trivial sense the proposition must be true that the rules of nonverbal and verbal communication are similar. However, investigators concerned with structural continuities between nonverbal communication and verbal interchange are usually concerned with more specific versions of the hypothesis. They assume, for example, that particular forms of nonverbal communication are isomorphic correlates of specific forms in language pragmatics; or that the developmentally earlier rules of communication functionally determine forms of verbal discourse.

Apparent similarities between the communicative acts of nonverbal infants and the verbal interchanges of competent speakers do not test the functional relationship, but may simply be an artifact of the ways in which verbal and nonverbal communication are coded. Thus, Bates et al. (1976) comment: "There is a strong structural resemblance between the final forms of sensory motor performative procedures and the componential analysis of adult performances . . . This resemblance may of course be quite coincidental. Most formal notational systems can be used to describe a variety of events and relationships; this does not necessarily mean that all events so described bear some relationship to one another.'' Similarly, Fogel (this volume) calls attention to the fact that the communicative gestures of the young infant may serve very different functions from those for which the same gestures or rules of transaction are used in verbal discourse, even when the gestures appear similar by some formal criterion. Any test of the structural hypothesis must specify the relationship of form to function in rules of communication and it must state such a relationship in operational terms. Otherwise one observer may discover ''homologies'' that are not apparent to a second observer who in turn, however, may discover his own set of homologies. Where the two sets do not overlap, both observers must then appeal to self evidence inviting the reader to share their own untested convictions.

Not only does a test of the structural hypothesis require *a priori* definitions of the formal categories for describing rules of nonverbal communication, as well as decision procedures for determining when a nonverbal communication is similar to verbal conversation. The categories and procedures must also be constructed with reference to a model that distinguishes between form and function in a verbal and a nonverbal communication. Yet a review of the literature on human infant behavior suggests that at present no such model exists for nonverbal communication.

The counting of word frequencies and transitional probabilities between strings of words was probably useful in establishing the taxonomic categories that were once the principal preoccupation of descriptive linguistics. However, such computational methods and the linear models of language performance on which they are based, proved inadequate for explaining the ability of native speakers to generate all the grammatical sentences of a natural language, and to comprehend such sentences when produced by another native speaker. Chomsky has presented strong arguments against any probabilistic model of grammar (1957), pointing out that transitional probabilities between words in a string of words (i.e., the probability with which one word may follow another) have no relation whatever to whether the string of words is a grammatically correct or semantically meaningful sentence. Lashley (1951) anticipated many of the later developments in linguistics by presenting strong arguments against an associative chain theory to explain the learning of any complex behavior. For example, he argued that the temporal sequence of words in a sentence, or of movement components in a directed action, are determined by an underlying schema or ''determining tendency'' which is extrinsic to the elements whose sequence is regulated by that schema. To illustrate the need for assuming a determining tendency, Lashley gave the following sentence: ''Rapid righting with his uninjured hand saved from loss the contents of the capsized canoe.'' To a person listening to the sentence rather than reading it, the meaning of the word ''righting'' is not disclosed until the end of the sentence. Yet the speaker knows exactly what he intends to say before starting to speak; and it is this intent rather than any transitional probability which determines the order of the words.

More generally in the case of language performance, there are many instances when the choice of one element is determined by elements occurring much earlier in the sentence. The position of this element is ultimately determined by the structure of the sentence (and the order of movement components in an action and by the goal that organizes the action). Whereas the meaning of the sentence depends on the order of its words, it is probably impossible in most cases to infer the speaker's communicative intent by counting co-occurrences or transitional probabilities between words in the word string. All these issues are thoroughly familiar, and there would be little reason to restate them here, if it were not for the fact that the same issues are raised by contemporary efforts to test the structural hypothesis of developmental continuities between rules of nonverbal and verbal communication.

The empirical literature of the social transactions of nonverbal infants suggests that most of the studies are carried out under a model which implicity or explicitly assumes that each gesture-act by one member of a social dyad is the stimulus for a gestural response by the interactive partner; and that the essential features of nonverbal communication can be adequately represented by frequencies of isolated gestures, by frequencies of co-occurrence of gestures by infant and parent, and by Markov transition matrices derived from linear chain theories of social interaction (Lewis and Lee-Painter, 1974). Yet knowledge about the "determining tendencies" of social interaction may be as important in disclosing the communicative intent of a gesture as they are in disclosing the meaning of a word in a sentence. Thus, a mother may have an end state in mind when she initiates a "conversation" with her nonverbal infant. However, the end state may not be apparent to the infant or to the investigator until the conversation is completed. Thus, the gestural response of the infant that immediately follows the mother's initial gesture, may be an irrelevant datum whereas motor patterns occurring many steps later in the "conversation" may be the critical event which reveals the communicative intent. If this assumption is correct, frequency counts and the analysis of co-occurrences or other statistical procedures based on linear chain models could not hope to reveal the structure of a gestural conversation between infant and parent. At the same time the coding of social behavior for the purpose of later analyzing social transactions in terms of linear statistical models may so distort the actual conversation that communicative intent can no longer be reconstructed from the data.

In summary, I am suggesting that hierarchic models are required for representing nonverbal communications between infants and parents, especially when the goal is to demonstrate structural similarities between "rules" of nonverbal and linguistic communications. Application of a conceptual model of social transactions based on Markov processes makes it theoretically unlikely that the "structural" hypothesis can be tested or that the formal relation between variations in early transactions and language development can be demonstrated to be either true or false.

Discussion of Wolff's Presentation

Capute referred to Wolff's suggestion that there are strong and weak hypotheses with respect to the influence of early social interaction on language acquisition. Capute suggested that there might be times in an infant's life, perhaps the first year, where the weak hypothesis would be appropriate. At later stages of language acquisition the strong hypotheses might be invoked. He asked Wolff why he suggested an all-or-none situation. Wolff replied that he did so for heuristic or rhetorical purposes only, and to examine what might be the questions of principal interest in future empirical studies.

Capute pointed out that the Wild Boy of Aveyron had been shown by a psychiatrist to be mentally defective to begin with, probably in the trainable range of retardation. Thus, the work of Itard and Seguin in enhancing the boy's self-help skills was quite monumental. Capute also believed that this boy was defective to begin with. Wolff replied that similar questions had been raised about why Genie had been locked up in a closet in the first place. Thus, Wolff said, such cases might not be a useful test of the deprivation hypothesis. Bettelheim (1959), for example, believed that all feral children might in fact have been autistic or neurologically impaired.

Leavitt pointed out that even if one were to adopt a hierarchical model of mother-infant interactions, its use would presuppose a knowledge of more simple aspects of interaction. Thus, one would have to create a taxonomy for basic gestural behaviors or other actions. Hierarchical models were interesting to build, but the mathematics of clustering and modeling presented difficulties that were at least equalled by the difficulties inherent in the statistics of conditional probabilities. A major difficulty with clustering models was the lack of common decision rules that all statisticians could agree to. Methods for describing basic behavioral elements needed to be incorporated into studies which made assumptions about goals. Leavitt had chosen to do this, for example, in studying infant feeding behavior. In feeding, there were clearly defined goals about which infant, mother, and experimenter could all agree. Leavitt suggested that models of complex and varied behavioral patterns might be needed, but they must rest upon descriptions of more basic units of behavior.

Wolff esentially agreed. Conventional statistical procedures and the models on which these procedures were based, were obviously useful for establishing taxonomies in many domains of behavior and development, including language acquisition and comparative linguistics. Therefore it would be foolish to abandon them, especially during the formative phase of a new discipline such as psycholinguistics. At the same time, however, it seemed important to emphasize that such statistics could only take us so far, that they were useful only for the descriptive phases of our inquiry. Endless elaboration on essentially the same linear chain model, by substituting second for first order Markov processes, or flow models of interaction borrowed from ''systems theory'' for ''simple element'' models would not get us much closer to stating or testing causal propositions about the relation between nonverbal and verbal communication, or structural propositions about similarities of function and form in nonverbal and verbal discourse.

Bloom asked what kind of evidence was required to show that a hierarchical model was, indeed, the proper model for describing language acquisition. She wanted to know if Wolff was offering arguments based upon such evidence, or arguments dealing only with the level of classification or representation. In other words, she had understood Wolff to say that frequency counts and taxonomic descriptions were not enough, that it was necessary to think more in terms in hierarchies of behavior. Would such models presuppose a very different kind of evidence than that offered by frequency counts?

Wolff thought they would, but conceded that this was a generally troublesome issue. At present there was no direct evidence either for the kinds of "determining tendencies" of which Lashley spoke with reference to motor behavior, or for the innate acquisition devices which Chomsky postulated to explain the development of generative grammars. Instead, we must for the present assume, for example, that "open loop" motor programs regulate the goal-directed actions of a skilled tennis player or skier, mental schemes that control the logical procedures used in solving a series of problems in three independent variables. We cannot locate, measure, manipulate or videotape such programs, schemes and acquisition devices. In each case, the "proof" is negative and comes from a demonstration that other extant explanations are simply inadequate to account for the phenomena of constructive intelligence, generative grammatical competence, or skilled motor performance across a wide range of physically dissimilar elements. Therefore, the "evidence" is limited to arguments of logical necessity from critical examples like Lashley's sentence, the motor performance of animals who have been deprived of all sensory feedback information, the operational logic of adolescents, etc. Wolff further conceded that it was not easy to apply the same strategy to demonstrate the logical need for hierarchic models to represent social nonverbal transactions, because the critical examples did not exist. However, critical examples might simply be lacking because we have looked at the phenomenology from much too empiricist a perspective.

Leavitt insisted that the same kind of data sequences as were used in classifying behavior might also be used to build hierarchical models. He presented an example of subjects performing an outlandish task, such as wrapping a baby buggy in paper. If many kinds of paper are available, the first sequence they engage in is to decide upon the best paper to use. Data points are derived from this sequence, and the sequence is also part of a hierarchy of behaviors. Wolff clarified his argument by stating that the behaviors in question were clearly the same, but by transforming the data, deriving proportions or ratios based upon specific time intervals, the most important aspects of a behavioral sequence might be distorted, and one's ability to gain fresh insights disrupted. In some cases it might no longer be possible to return to the raw data.

Published 1981 by Elsevier North Holland, Inc.
Stark, ed.
Language Behavior in Infancy and Early Childhood

Bibliography:
Section I

Adamson, L., Als, H., Tronick, E., and Brazelton, T.B. (1977). The development of social reciprocity between a sighted infant and her blind parents, *Journal of the American Academy of Child Psychiatry,* 16:194–207.

Als, H., Tronick, E., and Brazelton, T.B. (1980). Affective reciprocity and the development of autonomy: The study of a blind infant. *Journal of the American Academy of Child Psychiatry,* 19:22–40.

Anderson, J.W. (1972). Attachment behavior out-of-doors. In N. Blurton Jones (Ed.), *Ethological Studies of Child Behavior.* Cambridge: Cambridge University Press.

Anokhin, P. (1964). Systemogenesis as a general regulator of brain development. *Progress in Brain Research,* 9:54–86.

Antinucci, F. and Parisi, D. (1973). Early language acquisition: A model and some data. In C. Ferguson and D. Slobin (Eds.), *Studies of Child Language Development.* New York: Holt, Rinehart & Winston.

Bates, E. (1976). *Language and Context: The Acquisition of Pragmatics.* New York: Academic Press.

Bates, E., Benigni, L., Bretherton, I., Camaioni, L., and Volterra, V (1977). From gesture to first word: On cognitive and social prerequisites. In M. Lewis and L. Rosenblum (Eds.), *Interaction, Conversation, and the Development of Language.* New York: Wiley Press.

Bateson, M.C. (1979). Mother-infant face-to-face interaction at 3, 6, 9 months of age. Paper presented at Society for Research in Child Development, San Francisco.

Beach, F.A. (1974). Human sexuality and evolution. In W.A. Montague and W.A. Sadler (Eds.), *Reproductive Behavior.* New York: Plenum Press.

Beebe, B. and Stern, D.N. (1977). Engagement-disengagement and early object experiences. In N. Freedman and S. Grand (Eds.), *Communicative Structures and Psychic Structures.* New York: Plenum Press.

Bell, R.Q. and Harper, L.V. (1977). *Child Effects on Adults.* Hillsdale, N.J.: Erlbaum.

Bettelheim, B.R. (1959). *Amer. J. Sociology,* 64:455–467.

Birdwhistell, R.L. (1970). *Kinesics and Context.* Philadelphia: University of Pennsylvania Press.

Bloom, K. (1975). Social elicitation of infant vocal behavior, *Journal of Experimental Child Psychology,* 20:51–58.

Bloom. L. (1973). *One Word at a Time: The Use of Single Word Utterances Before Syntax.* The Hague: Mouton.

Bower, T.G.R. (1974). *Development in Infancy.* San Francisco: W.H. Freeman.

Brannigan, C.R. and Humphries, D.A. (1972). Human nonverbal behavior, a means of communication. In N.B. Jones (Ed.), *Ethological Studies of Child Behavior.* Cambridge: Cambridge University Press.

Brazelton, T.B., Koslowski, B., and Main, M. (1974). The origins of reciprocity. In M. Lewis and L. Rosenblum, (Eds.) *The Effect of the Infant on its Caregiver.* New York: Wiley.

Brazelton, T.B., Tronick, E., Adamson, L., Als, H., and Weiss, S. (1975). Early mother-infant reciprocity. In *Parent-Infant Interaction.* Ciba Foundation Symposium, *33*, New York: Elsevier.

Brown, R. (1973) *A First Language: The Early Stages.* Cambridge, Mass.: Harvard University Press.

Bruner, J. (1971). The growth and structure of skill. In K.J. Connolly (Ed.), *Motor Skills.* London: Academic Press.

Bruner, J. (1975). The ontogenesis of speech acts. *Journal of Child Language.* 2:1–19.

Bruner, J. (1978). From communication to language: A psychological perspective. In I. Markova (Ed.), *The Social Context of Language.* New York: Wiley Press.

Bullowa, M. (1975). When infant and adult communicate, how do they synchronize their behaviors? In A. Kendon, R.M. Harris, M.R. Key (Eds.), *Organization of Behavior in Face-to-Face Interaction.* The Hague: Mouton.

Bullowa, M., (1977). *Before Speech: The Beginnings of Human Communication.* Cambridge: Cambridge University Press.

Cassell, T.Z.K. and Sander, L. (1976). Neonatal recognition processes and attachment: effects of masking mother's face at 7 days. Unpublished manuscript.

Chance, M. (1962). Cut-off behavior. *Symposium Zoological Society of London,* 8:71.

Charlesworth, W. and Kreutzer, M. (1973). Facial expressions of infants and children. In P. Ekman (Ed.), *Darwin and Facial Expression.* New York: Academic Press.

Chomsky, N. (1957). *Syntactic Structures.* The Hague: Mouton.

Cohn, J. and Tronick, E. (1980). The infant's response to affectless displays during social interaction. Unpublished manuscript.

Condon, W.S. and Sander, L. (1974). Synchrony demonstrated between movements of the infant and adult speech. *Child Development,* 45:456–462.

Cox, D.R. and Lewis, P.A. (1966). *Statistical Analysis of Series of Events.* New York: Halsted Press.

Curtiss, S. (1977). *Genie: A Psycholinguistic Study of a Modern-day "Wild Child."* New York: Academic Press.

Darwin, C. (1972). *The Expression of the Emotions in Man and Animals.* New York: Appleton.

de Saussure, F. (1959). *Course in General Linguistics.* New York: Philosophical Library.

Dore, J. (1974). A pragmatic description of early language development. *Journal of Psycholinguistic Research,* 3:343–350.

Dore, J. (1975). Holophrases, speech acts, and language universals. *Journal of Child Language,* 2:21–40.

Dowd, J. (1979). A developmental study of neonatal movement and adult speech. Unpublished manuscript.

Dunn, J. and Richards, M. (1977). Observations on the developing relationship between mother and baby in the neonatal period. In H.R. Schaffer (Ed.). *Studies in Mother-Infant Interaction.* London: Academic Press.

Eibl-Eibesfeldt, I. (Ed.) (1970). *Ethology, the Biology of Behavior*. New York: Holt, Rinehart & Winston.

Ekman, P. (Ed.) (1973). *Darwin and Facial Expression*. New York: Academic Press.

Ervin-Tripp, S. (1976). Is Sybil there: The structure of American English directive. *Language in Society*, 5:25–66.

Feuerbach, A. von (1831). Beispiel eines Verbrechens am Seelenleben des Menschen. Germany: Ansbach.

Field, T. (1978). Interaction behaviors of primary versus secondary caretaker fathers. *Developmental Psychology*, 14:183–184.

Field, T. (1979a). Visual and cardiac responses to an animate and inanimate faces by young term and preterm infants. *Child Development*, 50:188–194.

Field, T. (1979b). Differential behavioral and cardiac responses of 3-month-old infants to mirror and peer. *Infant Behavior and Development*, 2:179–184.

Fogel, A. (1977). Temporal organization in mother-infant, face-to-face interaction. In H.R. Schaffer (Ed.), *Studies in Mother-Infant Interaction*. London: Academic Press.

Fogel, A. (1979). Peer vs. mother directed behavior in one- to three-month-old infants. *Infant Behavior and Development*, 2:215–226.

Fogel, A. The effect of brief separations on two-month-old infants. *Infant Behavior and Development*, in press.

Fogel, A., Diamond, G., Langhorst, B., and Demos, V. Affective and cognitive aspects of the 2-month-old's participation in face-to-face interaction with its mother. In E. Tronick (Ed.) *Joint Regulation of Behavior*, in press.

Fraiberg, S. (1974). Blind infants and their mothers: An examination of the sign system. In M. Lewis and L. Rosenblum (Eds.), *The Effect of the Infant on its Caregiver*. New York: Wiley Press.

Fraiberg, S. (1977). *Insights from the Blind: Comparative Studies of Blind and Sighted Infants*. New York: Basic Books.

Garvey, C. (1975) Requests and responses in children's speech. *Journal of Child Language*, 2:41–63.

Garfinkel, H. (1972). Remarks on ethnomethodology. In J.J. Gumperz and D. Hymes (Eds.), *Directions in Sociolinguistics*. New York: Holt, Rinehart & Winston.

Gazzaniga, M.S. and LeDoux, J.E. (1978). *The Integrated Mind*. New York: Plenum Press.

Gibson, E. and Walk, R.D. (1960). The "visual cliff." *Scientific American*, 202:64–71.

Goffman, E. (1963). *Behavior in Public Places*. New York: The Free Press.

Goffman, E. (1974). *Frame Analysis*. New York: Harper-Row.

Gottman, J. (1979). Spectral analysis of interactive data. Unpublished manuscript.

Greenfield, P.M. and Smith, J. (1976). *The Structure of Communication in Early Language Development*. New York: Academic Press.

Halliday, M.A.K. (1973). *Explorations in the Functions of Language*. London: Edward Arnold.

Harper, L.V. (1978). Toward a general model of behavioral ontogeny: The heterochronous maturation of functional systems. Paper presented at Animal Behavior Society, Seattle.

Hinde, R.A. (1974). *Biological Bases of Human Social Behavior*. New York: McGraw-Hill.

Hockett, C.F. (1961). Linguistic elements and their relations. *Language, 37*, 29–53.

Itard, J.M.G. (1801, 1962) *The Wild Boy of Aveyron*. New York: Appleton Century Crofts.

Jakobson, R., (1972) *Collected Papers*. The Hague: Mouton.

Jones, N.B. (1972). Categories of child-child interaction. In N.B. Jones (Ed.), *Ethological Studies of Child Behavior*. Cambridge: Cambridge University Press.

Kagan, J. (1971). *Change and Continuity in Infancy*. New York: Wiley Press.

Kagan, J., Kearsley, R., and Zelazo, P. (1978). *Infancy: Its Place in Human Development*. Cambridge: Harvard University Press.

Kaye, K. (1977). Toward the origin of dialogue. In H.R. Schaffer (Ed.), *Studies in Mother-Infant Interaction*. London: Academic Press.

Kaye, K. (1979). Thickening thin data: The maternal role in developing communication and language. In M. Bullowa (Ed.), *Before Speech*. Cambridge: Cambridge University Press.

Kaye, K. and Brazelton, T.B. (1971). Mother-infant interaction in the organization of sucking. Paper presented to the Society for Research in Child Development, Minneapolis.

Kaye, K. and Fogel, A. (Submitted) The temporal structure of face-to-face communication between mothers and infants.

Kendon, A. (1977). *Studies in the Behavior of Social Interaction*. Lisse, Netherlands: Peter de Riller Press.

Kennan, E.O., Schieffelin, B., and Platt, M. (1977). Propositions across utterances and speakers. Paper presented at Stanford Child Language Research Forum, Stanford University.

Labov, W. and Fanshel, D. (1977). *Therapeutic Discourse*. New York: Academic Press.

Lashley, K. (1951). The problem of serial order in behavior. In L.E. Jeffries (Ed.), *Cerebral Mechanisms in Behavior*. New York: Wiley.

Leung, E. and Rheingold, H. (1977). The development of pointing as a social gesture. Paper presented at society for Research in Child Development, New Orleans.

Lewis, M. and Starr, M. (1979). Developmental continuity. In J. Osofsky (Ed.), *Handbook of Infant Development*. New York: Wiley Press.

Lewis, M. and Lee-Painter, S., (1974). Interactional approach to the mother-infant dyad. In M. Lewis and L.A. Rosenblum (Eds.). *The Effect of the Infant on its Caregiver*. New York: Wiley.

McGrew, W.C. (1972). Aspects of social development in nursery school children, with emphasis on introduction to the group. In N.B. Jones (Ed.), *Ethological Studies of Child Behavior*. Cambridge: Cambridge University Press .

McIntire, M.L. (1977). The acquisition of American Sign Language hand configurations. *Sign Language Studies*, 16:247–266.

Macnamara, J. (1972). Cognitive basis of language learning in infants. *Psychological Review*, 79:1–13.

Marler, P. (1965). Communication in monkeys and apes. In I. DeVore (Ed.). *Primate Behavior: Field Studies of Monkeys and Apes*. New York: Holt, Rinehart & Winston.

Massie, H. (1975). The early natural history of childhood psychosis. *Journal of the American Academy of Child Psychiatry, 14*, 683–707.

Oster, H. and Ekman, P. (1977): Facial behavior in child development. In A. Collins (Ed.), *Minnesota Symposium of Child Psychology* (Vol. 11), Hillsdale, N.J.: Erlbaum.

Papoušek, H. (1967). Conditioning during early postnatal development. In Y. Brackbill and G.G. Thompson (Eds.), *Behavior in Infancy and Early Childhood*. New York: The Free Press.

Piaget, J. (1952). *The Origins of Intelligence in Children*. New York: Norton, 1952.

Ricks, M., Krafchuk, E., and Tronick, E. (1979). A descriptive study of mother-infant face-to-face interaction at 3, 6, 9 months of age. Paper presented at Society for Research in Child Development, San Francisco.

Robson, K.S. (1967). The role of eye-to-eye contact in maternal-infant attachment. *Journal of Child Psychology and Psychiatry*, 8:13–25.

Rutter, M. (1972). *Maternal Deprivation Reassessed*. London: Penguin.

Sachs, H., Shegeloff, E., and Jefferson, G. (1974). A simplest systematics for the organization of turn taking in conversation. *Language*, 50:696–735.

Sander, L. (1969). Regulation and organization in the early infant-caretaker system. In R. Robinson (Ed.), *Brain and Early Behavior*. London: Academic Press.

Sander, L. (1977). The regulation of exchange in the infant-caretaker system and some aspects of the context-content relationship. In M. Lewis and L. Rosenblum (Eds.), *Interaction, Conversation and the Development of Language*. New York: Wiley Press.

Schaller, G.B. (1963). *The Mountain Gorilla*. Chicago: University of Chicago Press.

Scheflen, A.E. (1965). Quasi-courtship behavior in psychotherapy. *Psychiatry*, 28:245–257.

Shegeloff, E. (1976). Lectures. University of California, Los Angeles.

Shegeloff, E. (1971). Notes on a conversational practice: Formulating place. In D. Sudnow (Ed.), *Studies in Social Interaction*. New York: The Free Press.

Scherer, K.R. (1979). Non-linguistic indicators of emotion and psychopathology. In C.E. Izard (Ed.), *Emotions in Personality and Psychopathology*. New York: Plenum Press.

Searle, J.R. (1969). *Speech acts*. London: Cambridge University Press.

Searle, J.R. (1975). Indirect speech acts. In P. Cole and J. Morgan (Eds.), *Syntax and Semantics III: Speech Acts*. New York: Academic Press.

Singh, J.A. and Zingg, R.M., (1945). Wolf Children and Feral Man (IV). Contributions of the University of Denver. New York.

Siqueland, E.R. and Lipsitt, L.P. (1966). Conditioned head-turning in human newborns. *Journal of Experimental Child Psychology*, 3:356–376.

Sparks, J. (1967). Allogrooming in primates: A review. In D. Morris (Ed.), *Primate Ethology*. London: Weidenfeld and Nicolson.

Sroufe, L.A. and Waters, E. (1977). Attachment as an organizational construct. *Child Development*, 48:1184–1199.

Stern, D.N. (1971). A micro-analysis of mother-infant interaction. *Journal of the American Academy of Child Psychiatry*, 10:501–517.

Stern, D.N. (1974a). The goal and structure of mother-infant play. *Journal American Academy of Child Psychiatry*, 13:402–422.

Stern, D.N. (1974b). Mother and infant at play: The dyadic interaction involving facial, vocal, and gaze behaviors. In M. Lewis and L. Rosenblum (Eds.), *The Effect of the Infant on Its Caregiver*. New York: Wiley Press.

Stern, D.N. (1977). *The First Relationship: Mother and Infant*. Cambridge: Harvard University Press.

Stern, D., Beebe, B., Jaffe, J., and Bennett, S. (1977). The infants stimulus world during social interaction. In H.R. Schaffer (Ed.), *Studies in Mother-Infant Interaction*. London: Academic Press.

Stern, D.N. and Bender, E.P. (1974). An ethological study of children approaching a strange adult: Sex differences. In R.C. Freedman, R.M. Richart, and R.L. Vanderwiele (Eds.), *Sex Differences in Behavior*. New York: Wiley Press.

Trevarthen, C. (1974). Conversations with a two-month-old. *New Scientist*, 62:230–235.

Trevarthen, C. (1977). Descriptive analysis of infant communicative behavior. In H.R. Schaffer (Ed.), *Studies in Mother-Infant Interaction*. London: Academic Press.

Trevarthen, C. (1979). Communication and cooperation in early infancy: A description of primary inter-subjectivity. In M. Bullowa (Ed.), *Before Speech*. New York: Cambridge University Press.

Tronick, E. (1980). On the primacy of social skills. In D.B. Sawin, R.C. Hawkins, L.O. Walker, and J.H. Penticuff (Eds.), *Exceptional Infant, Vol. 4, Psychosocial Risks in Infant Environment Transactions*. New York: Bruner/Mazel.

Tronick, E., Als, H., and Adamson, L. (1979). The structure of face-to-face communicative interactions. In M. Bullowa (Ed.), *Before Speech*. New York: Cambridge University Press.

Tronick, E., Als, H., Adamson, L., Wise, S., and Brazelton, T.B. (1978). The infant's response to entrapment between contradictory messages in face-to-face interaction. *Journal American Academy of Child Psychiatry*, 17:1–13.

Tronick, E., Als, H., and Brazelton, T.B. (1980a): Monadic phases: A structural descriptive analysis of infant-mother face-to-face interaction. *Merrill Palmer Quarterly*, 26:3–24.

Tronick, E., Als, H., and Brazelton, T.B. (1980a): Monadic phases: A structural descriptive analysis of infant-mother face to face interaction. *Merrill Palmer Quarterly*, 26:3–24.

Tronick, E., Als, H., and Brazelton, T.B. (1980b). The infant's communicative competencies and the achievement of intersubjectivity, In. M.R. Key (Ed.), *Verbal and Nonverbal Communication*. The Hague: Mouton, in press.

Waterson, N. and Snow, C. (1978). *The Development of Communications*. New York: Wiley.

Watson, J.S. (1979). Perception of contingency as a determinant of social responsiveness. In E.B. Thoman (Ed.), *The Origins of the Infant's Social Responsiveness*. Hillsdale, N.J.: Erlbaum.

Werner, H. and Kaplan, B. (1963). *Symbol Formation*. New York: Wiley Press.

White, B.L., Castle, P., and Held, R. (1964). Observations on the development of visually directed reaching. *Child Development*, 35:349–364.

Winn, S. and Tronick, E. (1980). Changes in infant's behavior during repeated interactions with an initially unfamiliar adult. Unpublished manuscript.

Wolff, P.H. (1963). Observations on the early development of smiling. In B.M. Foss (Ed.), *Determinants of Infant Behavior*. New York: Wiley Press.

Wolff, P.H. (1967). The role of biological rhythms in early psychological development. *Bulletin of the Menninger Clinic*, 31:197–218.

Wolff, P.H. (1968). The serial organization of sucking in the young infant, *Pediatrics*, 42:943–956.

Wolff, P.H. (1969). The natural history of crying and other vocalizations in early infancy. In B.M. Foss (Ed.), *Determinants of Infant Behavior, Volume IV*. London: Methuen.

Yogman, M,. Dixon, S., Tronick, E., Adamson, L., Als, H., and Brazelton, T.B. (1976). Development of social interaction with fathers. Paper presented at Eastern Psychological Association meeting, New York, April.

Zukow, P.G., Reilly, J., and Greenfield, P.M. Making the absent present: Facilitating the transition from sensorimotor to linguistic communication. To appear in K. Nelson (Ed.), *Children's Language. Volume 3*. New York: Gardner Press.

Early Development of the Forms of Language

Introduction

It may be a truism to say that, in order to understand the language spoken in his environment, the child must first be able to discriminate and identify the sounds of that language in linguistic contexts; and that, in order to make himself understood, the child must be able to produce the sounds of that language in various combinations with one another, that is, in syllables, words, and phrases. Nevertheless, in spite of many years of research, it is still not clear how the young child arrives at the required level of skill in speech production, or how he puts that skill to use in learning to talk. And research in infant speech perception is still of such recent origin that the questions asked have dealt almost entirely with speech perception capabilities known to be important for adults. Questions about the properties of speech which are salient for the infant and the ways in which the infant segments speech have been approached hardly at all.

Somewhat different approaches have been taken in accounts of developmental processes in production and perception. It is easier to observe the sounds made by the infant than to observe his responses to sound. Even so, there were few detailed studies of infant sound production until recently. Perhaps because most observations were superficial, it was believed for many years that there was no lawful sequence in the development of pre-speech sound making. Most writers followed Jakobson (1968) who stated, "The question of the prelanguage babbling period proves to be . . . one of external phonetics, predominantly articulatory in nature, and it is significant that here one cannot establish any general sequence of acquisitions." The belief that babbling merely reflected the range of sounds possible to the human speaker continued to be expressed until recently (Osgood, 1953; Lenneberg, 1967; Rees, 1972). Infants were also believed to produce sounds in a completely random fashion until 12–14 months of age, when they began to realize the need to make clear speech sound distinctions in order to produce a number of discriminable words. At this point, Jakobson held, phonological development became orderly and systematic and followed universal patterns or rules.

Speech perception in infants, on the other hand, was studied very little until the 1970's, when new and more sophisticated methods became available for this purpose. It was found that, even in very young infants, speech perception capabilities were quite remarkable. Newborn infants showed a clear preference for vocal as opposed to instrumental music (Butterfield and Siperstein, 1972). They were thought to be highly responsive to the rhythms of speech in their own body movements (Condon and Sander, 1974). They were able to show discrimination of speech sounds in syllables such as /ba/ and /pa/ in their sucking behaviors as early as one month of age (Eimas et al., 1971). It was thought that these examples of precocity revealed the presence of innate linguistic feature detectors in the auditory system of the human infant.

Thus, it came to be thought that speech production skills did not develop but were merely practiced until the infant was ready to make use of them in word production; and that speech perception skills did not emerge gradually but were in place early in life, merely waiting to be made use of in language comprehension. These notions, although they were not stated explicitly, influenced intervention approaches to language delay in children. They have been dispelled by more recent research. It has been shown that the sounds produced by young infants are quite unlike those of speech in their temporal patterning, overall resonance, and spectral characteristics (Zlatin, 1975; Stark, Rose, and McLagen, 1975; Stark, Heinz, and Wright-Wilson, 1976; Stark, 1978; Oller, 1978; Buhr, 1980). Speech production skills do develop in a coherent way until true babbling emerges, and there appears to be a logical relationship between the structure of babbled sounds produced in the first year of life and the phonetic forms which are found in the child's production of words in the second year (Menyuk, 1968; Dore, 1975; Oller et al., 1976; Cruttenden, 1970).

It has also been shown that the speech perception abilities of infants need not require a higher level linguistic interpretation. The infant's responses to speech-like stimuli may be evoked by the basic psychophysical properties of the signal, at a sensory level (Pisoni, 1977; Jusczyk et al., 1980; Walley, Pisoni, and Aslin, in press). They may reflect constraints operating upon the mammalian auditory system generally and do not appear to be peculiarly human (Kuhl and Miller, 1975, 1978). The processes underlying development of speech perception and production skills in the first two years of life, however, are not yet well understood.

A number of stages of development of speech production have been proposed by different investigators working independently of one another (Zlatin, 1975; Stark, 1980; Oller, 1980). The descriptions of the stages provided by these different investigators are quite similar, and this similarity has provided some assurance that the descriptions are not peculiar to a few individual infants only, but may apply to the majority of infants. These stages are:

Stage 1. Reflexive sound making; cry, discomfort, vegetative sounds.

Stage 2. Cooing and laughter.

Stage 3. Exploratory vocal play.

Stage 4. Reduplicated babbling.

Stage 5. Nonreduplicated babbling; jargon; protowords.

Stage 6. Referential words.

It has been observed that most, if not all, of these stages have a relatively clear onset. At each onset, new vocal behaviors can be recognized by parents and other family members quite readily. It could be argued that these are milestone behaviors only, and that the stages are merely step functions marked by the addition of a new milestone. There is some evidence, however, that vocal development is cyclical in nature, with the most rapid rate of development being found immediately after a milestone behavior appears, and a slower rate of development succeeding that spurt as the next milestone is approached (see Bever's [1961] reanalysis of the data of Irwin and his colleagues [1946; 1947; 1948]). New behaviors are elaborated and combined with old behaviors in each developmental stage (Stark, 1980). It is not yet known, however, whether the proposed stages are always found in the normal infant's speech sound development, whether they are always set off from one another by particular characteristics and whether, if so, they occur in invariant order. Also, if there are such stages, then it must be asked what motivates the infant's shift from one stage to the next? In the first months of life, extensive changes in vocal tract structure and increasing neurophysiological control may make a significant contribution to change, as described in this volume (Chapters 5 and 6). These changes may be sufficient to account for the stages of vocal development.

Other accounts of the progression from one stage to another are provided by Oller (1980; this volume, Chapter 4) and Stark (1980, 1981). Oller proposes that the infant has a metaphonological system of sound making which has some of the characteristics of speech from the very beginning. Significant new characteristics are added progressively in each stage of development of speech production, as the infant's output shows finer and finer approximations to adult-like speech patterns. Oller hypothesizes that the infant may be trying to produce speech-like utterances systematically and consciously throughout the first year of life. He suggests that the infant may constantly be asking himself "What am I supposed to sound like?"

Stark, on the other hand, suggests that changes in infant speech production reflect successive recombinations of phonatory skills. She proposes that two very different types of vocal behavior are present from the beginning, namely cry-discomfort sounds and vegetative sounds. Cry-discomfort sounds are vowel-like, produced on an outgoing breath, and are often prolonged so that they may show variations in pitch and loudness. Vegetative sounds are consonant-like, brief, faint, and may be produced on an outgoing or an ingoing breath. All of the features of speech are present in these two classes of sounds, but in the newborn infant they form primitive segments that are quite unlike those of speech. It may be as a result of the combining and coordinating of these features with one another that more speech-like segments begin to be formed. In this process, prosodic features may be successively imposed upon segments of prespeech vocalization. Crystal (1980) suggests that there are stages of acquisition of prosodic features of speech also. The integration of segmental and prosodic features may also be cyclical in nature. The successive integration of features of speech appears to be related to increasing neurophysiological maturity as well as to experience of vocalizing in different situational contexts.

Little is known at present about developmental changes in speech perception in the first year of life, but it has been found that some speech sounds may be discriminated and categorized earlier than others (Eilers, Wilson, and Moore, 1979). Certain contrasts may be more salient and may thus be attended to earlier. On the other hand, even difficult contrasts may be responded to within an effective training paradigm (Holmberg, Morgan, and Kuhl, 1977). In addition, infants may be able to respond to a given speech sound contrast, for example, /fa/ versus /tha/, at 12 months of age in a discrimination procedure involving turning of the head to one sound and not another, but may not be able to respond to that same contrast at 18 months of age when they are asked to find toy objects labeled, for example, as /fa/ and /tha/ (Eilers, personal communication). Thus, the infant's ability to respond to speech sound contrasts may depend upon the nature of the task he is expected to carry out, as well as upon the inherent ease or difficulty of discrimination of the contrastive features themselves.

Aslin and Pisoni (1980) and Walley, Pisoni, and Aslin (in press) have proposed a number of different mechanisms that may underlie the development of speech perception. These are:

1. *The Universal Theory* which states that at birth infants are capable of discriminating all possible phonetic contrasts; early experience functions to maintain the ability to discriminate those contrasts that are phonologically relevant for the language spoken in the infant's environment, while those that are not relevant to that language are selectively lost as a result of neural mechanisms (of degradation) or attentional mechanisms or both.

2. *The Attunement Theory* which assumes that at birth infants are capable of discriminating at least some of the possible phonetic contrasts; early experience functions to align or sharpen these partially developed discriminative abilities, so that contrasts phonologically relevant to the infant's language environment become more finely tuned, and those that are not relevant remain less sharp or become attenuated.
3. *Perceptual Learning Theory* which holds that the ability to discriminate particular phonetic contrasts is entirely dependent upon early experience with those contrasts in the language-learning environment; the rate of development of this ability would then depend upon the frequency of occurrence of the phonetic contrasts to be learned, the relative psychophysical discriminability of each contrast, and the attentional state of the infant.
4. *Maturational Theory* which assumes that the ability to discriminate a particular phonetic contrast is independent of early linguistic experience and unfolds according to a predetermined developmental schedule; the language environment would thus have little influence upon the infant's discriminative abilities and the age at which discrimination of specific phonetic contrasts might be acquired would depend upon the developmental level of the underlying auditory system.

These authors stress the complexity of processes of perceptual development. They do not suggest that one or other of the above theories will uniquely account for the development of all speech contrasts. As in the development of visual perception, it may well be that a number of different, parallel processes must be invoked to account for development of speech perception. Discrimination of different classes of speech sound, for example, of voiced, voiced unaspirated and voiceless stops, of stops with different place of articulation features (labial, apical, and velar), of fricatives with differing voice and place features, and of vowels might be mediated differently within the auditory system. Different processes may also be involved at different developmental levels with respect to the same phonetic contrasts; for example, memory (Pisoni, 1977), concept formation (Kuhl and Hillenbrand, 1979) and ability to form categories (Pisoni and Lazarns, 1974; Pastore 1976; Kuhl, 1978).

In the development of speech perception also, recognition of two very different aspects of speech, the segmental or phonetic aspects and the suprasegmental or prosodic aspects, must be acquired. It has sometimes been suggested that perception of the prosodic aspects may precede perception of phonemic aspects (Crystal, 1973). Current research does not support this notion (see Kuhl, this volume Chapter 8). It is possible that the development of speech perception also is cyclical, and that within each cycle the infant learns to respond to old segments within a new prosodic framework, or to insert new segments perceptually into more familiar prosodic patterns. There is some evidence, for example, that contrastive pitch contours are more readily perceived in stressed than in unstressed syllables at 4 months of age (Kaplan, 1969); and that recognition of phonemic contrasts embedded in a series of syllables (ba*da* vs. ba*ka*, or pada*ta* vs. pada*ka*) may depend upon the duration of the contrastive syllable (the final syllable in the above examples) (Trehub, 1976). Mothers' speech to infants may be very important in this respect. It is highly repetitive in content and shows increased syllable duration and, phrases that are produced many times over with only slight changes in wording, in timing, and intonation (Stern, 1977).

In this section of the text, anatomic and neurophysiologic influences on the early development of vocal behavior are examined. Questions are asked as to whether the infant is making an active effort to talk throughout the ''prelinguistic'' period, and if not, about the forces which may motivate change in his output. In addition, recent work in infant speech perception research is presented. Methodological problems are addressed and some higher level capacities of the infant, perceptual constancy, and perceptual generalization, are considered in relation to the speech that the infant hears and to the speech that is addressed particularly to him.

A. Speech Production: Acoustic, Anatomic and Neurophysiologic Considerations

Published 1981 by Elsevier North Holland, Inc.
Stark, ed.
Language Behavior in Infancy and Early Childhood

Infant Vocalizations: Exploration and Reflexivity

D. Kimbrough Oller

Mailman Center for Child Development, University of Miami, Florida

The purpose of this paper is to address the possibility that the vocalizations of infancy are a manifestation of exploratory intellect as opposed to instinctiveness-reflexivity. The evidence to be reviewed provides a variety of useful indications about the sense in which infant sounds show intellect and/or reflexivity. However, the data are sparse in a number of areas. A secondary goal of this treatment, consequently, is to highlight and differentiate areas of relative need for empirical work.

Prelude: Infant Vocalizations and Speech

Before addressing the evidence on reflexivity and exploration, it is necessary to offer a brief statement concerning the relationships between infant vocalizations and speech. Infant vocalizations are highly structured and a large proportion are clearly phonetically related to speech. This conclusion, however contrary to a commonly held belief, is easily verified upon empirical examination. For example, toward the end of the first year (8–12 months of age) syllabic babbling sounds (e.g., baba, dede, ma, etc.) of infants have much in common with the sounds found in children's first words (Cruttenden, 1970; Lewis, 1963; Menyuk, 1968; Oller et al., 1976). Furthermore, the babbling sounds consist primarily of phonetic elements which are remarkably like the most commonly occurring phonetic elements of the world's languages. In addition the babbling sounds include very low proportions of sounds that are uncommon in mature phonologies. While it has not been shown that there are *no* phonetic differences between babbling and speech, certain similarities have been documented unequivocally and the data leave no reasonable doubt that babbling is a speech-related behavior.

From a phonetic standpoint, a number of other infant sound types have less in common with speech than babbling does. Obviously, pain cries, coughs, sneezes, hiccoughs, and the like are phonetically different from speech in definable ways. Similar sounds occur in adult vocalizations, and for similar reasons. In addition there are a variety of non-babbling infant sound types that do not occur (except as "baby talk" or some other special usage) in adult vocalizations, e.g., gooing, raspberries, squealing, etc. In previous work (Oller, 1978, and in press), justifications have been presented for viewing these sound types as important manifestations of an emerging speech capacity. Each major sound type (excluding cries, grunts, etc.) occurring commonly in infancy can be thought to represent the incorporation into the child's vocal repertoire of the ability to control some crucial phonetic speech parameter (e.g., pitch, resonance, etc.). Stark, Rose, and McLagen (1975) and Stark (1981) have argued further that even the vegetative sounds (i.e., artifacts of such vegetative functions as swallowing, sucking, etc.) of early infancy are related to early speech-like "comfort" sounds since phonetic characteristics of comfort sounds first appear in vegetative sounds.

It appears possible, then, to trace the phonetic relationship of infant vocalizations and speech starting from the first month of life. In considering the roles of reflexivity and exploration, it is not, however, purely *phonetic* relationships that are of interest. The *usage* of infant sounds (independent of their phonetic character) is also relevant. Consider, for example, the fact that infants commonly produce "coughs" imitatively. Although such a cough remains phonetically distant from speech, its occurrence has other features in common with speech—social responsiveness and imitativeness. These non-phonetic speech features might be called "linguistic-pragmatic" or "speech-usage" features and have been discussed with regard to infant sounds in Peters (1974) and Oller (1978). Of course, sound types that are important for language acquisition need to be mastered to allow their usage in any speech-relevant manner or situation. In general, as the infant becomes capable of using speech-like sounds in more complex pragmatic settings (i.e., incorporating a larger number of pragmatic features), she/he comes closer to producing real speech and shows in vocalization a correspondingly higher level of intellect.

Empirical Studies on Exploration and Reflexivity

Given that later infant vocalizations manifest greater intellect than earlier ones, can it be said that infant sounds in the early stages are purely passive or reflexive? Fenton (1925) believed so, saying that early sounds "are uttered without intent." Two points may appear to support this view for vocalizations of infants in the first half year of life: (1) a large proportion of early sounds seem to be artifacts of vegetative or patently reflexive sounds (cf. Stark, Rose, and McLagen, 1975); and (2) even the sounds that are not clearly artifactual often seem to be produced in response to vocal stimulation (see Anderson, Vietze, and Dokecki, 1977; Stern et al., 1975; Zlatin and Whitman, 1976). One might be tempted to interpret these sounds as reflexes to social interaction. But, in fact, various authors have intended the terms "reflexive" and "passive" in a variety of ways in discussing infant sounds. In order to place these interpretations in perspective so that they can be addressed empirically, it is necessary to specify various notions of reflexivity and address them individually. What these views have in common is that they do not attribute to the child an active intelligent approach to vocalization.

Passive Response to Mechanical Forces

McCarthy (1952) suggests that the form of infant vocalizations is influenced by the force of gravity. She speculates that the characteristic supine position of babyhood would result in vocalization types that are affected by passive response of soft tissues, e.g., the soft palate would fall back, closing off the velopharyngeal port and result in non-nasal sounds. Similarly, in an upright position, the port would open by the force of gravity on the soft tissues and the baby would be able (indeed would be obliged) to produce nasal sounds whenever phonating.

McCarthy's specific suggestion about nasality as a result of passive response to gravity is inconsistent with the well-documented fact that infants are nasal breathers primarily, even in the supine position (cf. Bosma, 1972). Stark and Nathanson (1974) have also provided indications that infant crying includes nasality regardless of infant posture. If an infant can control his soft palate for breathing and crying, it seems unreasonable to assume that it would be impossible to control the palate for vocalization. Furthermore, nasal sounds are observable in the supine position in very early infancy and non-nasal sounds are observable in the upright position.

In spite of the incorrectness of McCarthy's specific prediction, the suggestion that infant sounds are affected by gravity is provocative. The high proportion of velar and uvular (i.e., soft palatel) articulations (sometimes called gooing) in early vocalizations (cf. Irwin, 1947) has long been a mystery. Such sounds are perplexing since, as Jakobson (1968) notes, young children often *fail* to produce velar consonants in early meaningful speech.

Recent anatomical evidence may be instructive with regard to the mystery and may offer insight into a possible role for gravity in the occurrence of gooing. The infant larynx is positioned very high during the first few months of life. The dorsum of the tongue and the epiglottis are similarly high and are consequently either in contact or in near contact with the soft palate under most circumstances (Sasaki et al., 1977; Stark, 1981 ; see Kent, this volume, Chapter 5, for illustrations). Possible effects of posture on this anatomical arrangement are worthy of consideration. For example, in the supine position, a vocalizing infant might produce gooing sounds because the tongue might fall back against the soft palate, which itself might be restrained from falling back and obstructing the airway. In the upright position the same force presumably would not result in articulation of soft palate and tongue. Consequently one would expect to see a greater proportion of gooing in the supine than in the upright position.

In fact, it is not certain precisely what effect gravity should be expected to have on articulations with the soft palate in early infancy. Kent (this volume, Chapter 5) has drawn our attention to the work of Sasaki et al. (1977), focusing on the proximity of the lingual surface of the epiglottis and the posterior surface of the soft palate during the first four months of life. If the epiglottis is the primary articulator with the palate in gooing (and current evidence cannot rule out that possibility), then a supine position might result in less gooing rather than more, since the epiglottis might fall back *away* from the palate. Furthermore, since the palate is positioned *between* tongue and epiglottis, there is yet another possibility: namely, that gravity might favor epiglotto-palatal contact in one position and lingua-palatal contact in the other. In such a case the proportion of gooing could be equal in the two positions, even though the system were basically a passive one, responding to gravity in both cases.

Thus, a test of the proportion of infant gooing in two body positions can be conclusive in showing an effect of gravity only if a significant difference between the gooing proportions in the two positions is obtained. A failure to find differences in proportion of gooing in the two positions could mean either that the infant very effectively compensates for gravitational forces in different positions, or that gravity causes passive gooing in two positions by producing two different articulations (one epiglottal and one lingual).

Given these interpretive cautions, we may now consider a study (Oller and Gavin, forthcoming) which tested the proportion of gooing in two body positions. At the point of this writing, vocalizations of thirty normal infants (in the height of the gooing stage, that is, at 1–4 months of age) have been recorded in both the supine and upright positions. Each infant was recorded in each position at least twice per recording session (all orders counterbalanced) with an equal number of upright and supine recording segments for each child. The duration of each recording segment was also rigorously matched. The experimental setting included a high quality sound-proof anechoic chamber and an adjacent control room. E_1 was with the baby in the sound chamber, while E_2 was in the control room monitoring the procedure and passing instructions to E_1.

At 10 second intervals, E_2 instructed E_1 (through headphones) to produce one of three infant-like sounds as a model to the baby (a vowel, a goo sound, or a labially articulated "front" sound). In each recording segment, E_1 was instructed to produce each of the three models three times. E_1, in addition to presenting models to the baby, engaged the baby with facial and vocal communication. When an articulated infant utterance occurred, E_1 offered a verbal "on-line" description concerning visible place of articulation features. Such a description was given for the vast majority of articulated infant utterances in the sample. The great bulk of the data as transcribed could thus be based on the relatively reliable visual, rather than purely auditory, judgments.

The largest proportion of the recording sessions have resulted in unusable data. Often the babies simply failed to vocalize. Other times they cried or fussed. Data from 10 babies, so far, have met the minimal criteria for a useful sample: (1) at least 30 utterances occurred in the goo, front, and vowel categories, (2) no indication of inordinate stress in one position (upright or supine) occurred (i.e., the baby did not vocalize in one position and cry in the other), and (3) at least two upright and two supine recording segments were available.

Results of the study up to this point are shown in Figure 1. The strongest possible prediction of a gravity hypothesis would be that goo-type sounds should occur exclusively in one of the positions. The data are obviously inconsistent with this view. A weaker form of a gravity hypothesis would predict that the greater *proportion* of goo-type sounds would occur in one of the positions. This prediction also fails, as the figure indicates. Three methods of computing a ratio of goo-sounds to other speech-like sounds are presented. All three computation methods show a slightly greater proportion of goo-sounds in the upright than in the supine position. The small effect was statistically nonsignificant. The effect of gravity, then, appears in these data to have little, if any, effect on proportion of gooing sounds produced.

Perhaps more importantly, the data in the figure also indicate an extremely large range of ratios across the 10 subjects. In fact, data from some subjects showed a greater gooing proportion in the upright position while data from others show a greater proportion in the supine. Infants often adopted a particular vocalization pattern and maintained it for a while, sometimes for the length of the recording session, and sometimes for 30 seconds or less. These patterns did not seem to be position-determined, but appeared to be a manifestation of a tendency to repeat whatever sound type the child was focused on at the time. A change in position of the baby often had the effect of breaking the pattern. Thus the infant might begin the next segment vocalizing in a way that differed from the previous one and again the tendency for repetition might be seen. Consistent with this interpretation, the results showed large discrepancies between the proportions of goos in the upright and supine positions from sample to sample within subject. For example, across five sessions S_{10} gave a 19% goo/goo + vowel ratio in the upright position and a 22% ratio in the supine. However, across the five sessions there were substantial differences in gooing proportions for this child. In session 2 (N = 66), there were 25% supine goos to only 9% upright goos.

90

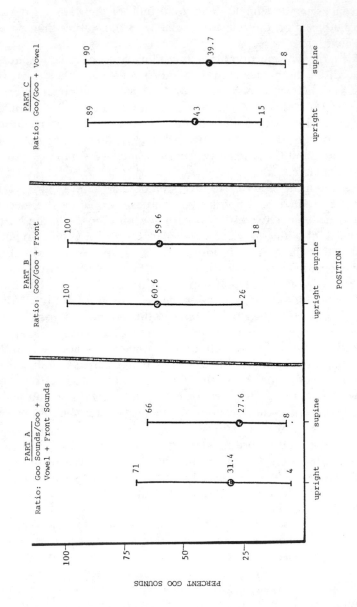

Figure 1. Preliminary data (mean and range) on the effect of gravity on goo sounds for ten subjects (N = 897 utterances).

In session 5 (N = 52), the pattern was reversed (7% supine goos to 20% upright goos). Such intersession effects cancelled each other in the mean data.

The large intersession within-subject variations in gooing proportions, occurring independent of body position, provide evidence against the possibility that the primary determinant of infant sound types could be passive response to gravitational force. Because of the magnitude of the intersession variations, it appears that any possible effect of gravity on gooing proportions would have to be relatively small.

While these individual subject data only provide a preliminary indication concerning infant vocal tendencies, they are provocative contradictory evidence with respect to the reflexivity or passivity of infant sounds. In contrast to the predictions of the reflexivity hypothesis, babies seem to structure their vocal output actively, compensating for whatever constraints are imposed by a physical organismic factor like posture. This point may be a key to understanding the intelligent nature of infant vocal behavior, and we shall return to it later.

Reflexivity and Vocalizations: The Strict Definition

A strict behavioral/biological definition of a reflex includes the following components: (1) the reflexive behavior can be elicited on every occasion by any threshold level presentation of some definable physical stimulus, (2) the behavior can be elicited equally well by any elicitor in the class meeting the criteria of definition, and (3) the reflexive response does not grossly change its physical form across time (although it may simply disappear).

In asking whether or not some infant vocalizations are reflexive in this strict sense, we should address ourselves especially to sound-types that do not pertain to patently reflexive categories (i.e., pain cries, gags, etc.). The question is, are some of the more speech-like sounds (gooing, quasi-resonant vowel-like sounds) reflexive in the first months and if so what are the elicitors that produce them? My answer to this question is based at present on only casual observation for babies under one month of age, and a variety of studies of babies beyond one month of age (K. Bloom, 1977; Oller and Gavin, forthcoming; Smith and Oller, in press; Zlatin, 1975).

Considering part one of the definition of reflexive behavior, it would appear that there is *no* environmental stimulus which reliably elicits speech-like sounds. Vocalizing, smiling, and touching are elicitors that are effective only a relatively small proportion of the time they are used. Thus the first requirement of the definition does not seem to be met.

The second requirement may also be violated (at least beyond the first month) since some individuals (e.g., the mother or father) may under some circumstances be more effective as elicitors than others. When eliciting a knee jerk reflex, the knee responds equally to an extremely wide variety of hammers. Babies, however, may not respond equally to different people attempting to elicit vocalizations from them. This question deserves investigation in a situation where proper controls are exercised over how various individuals act in attempting to elicit sounds and over degree of familiarity of the elicitors.

The third requirement of the definition is clearly violated in the case of speech-like sounds, since even across the first six months of life, vocal types produced by infants in response to elicitation attempts change dramatically from month to month, and in some cases from day to day (cf. Oller, 1978, in press; Stark, 1981; Zlatin, 1975; Zlatin-Laufer and Horii, 1977).

Thus, even though some aspects of the issue have not been resolved in formal experimentation, it appears that speech-like vocalizations of infants are not reflexive in the strict biological sense. However, in referring to the sounds of infancy as "reflexive," previous authors have probably not commonly intended this strict usage but rather a weaker one.

Reflexivity of Infant Sounds: The Weaker Definition

To my knowledge no formal definition of "reflexive" other than the strict one has been given. However, it seems reasonable to formulate a plausible weak form which is as far as possible consistent with implications of other writers who have used the term weakly. In general, a speech-like vocalization is said to be reflexive if it can be elicited at least sometimes by presentation of some definable stimulus (normally by adult vocal, facial, and tactile stimulation). However, in order to differentiate the activity from clearly non-reflexive behaviors, the notion "sometimes" must be restricted—either (1) it must be said that the probability of successful elicitations is stable across time (discounting changes in situation or infant state) or (2) it must be said that simple conditioning principles are at work and the frequency of elicitation is a function of the reinforcing properties of the elicitation paradigm. The latter restriction proposes a sort of positive feedback system which, in principle, should result in increasing infant vocalization with contingent adult stimulation and decreasing vocalization without contingent stimulation.

The broad literature on infant vocal conditioning may offer insight into the possible weak reflexiveness of infant speech-like sounds. Early studies (Rheingold, Gewirtz, and Ross, 1959; Todd and Palmer, 1968) suggested that the probability of vocalization was *not* stable across time in response to adult social stimulation. Indeed the writers interpreted their findings to indicate that rates of speech-like vocalization could be increased from unstimulated baseline levels, maintained by social reinforcement (i.e., contingent adult stimulation) and decreased in an unstimulated extinction period. In order to tie down the results of these studies to indicate that reinforcement per se was operative, Weisberg's (1963) experiment included one condition in which contingent stimulation was presented and one in which noncontingent stimulation was presented. He reported that only in the case of contingent stimulation did the vocalization rate increase above baseline.

Weisberg's result was widely interpreted as proof that social stimulation is a reinforcer of infant vocalizations. From the perspective of the weak notion of reflexivity, it could be said that Weisberg's result suggested that social stimulation is not an *elicitor* of vocal sounds but is rather a reinforcer that increases their probability of occurrence. In terms of the weak reflexivity hypothesis, the result might be said to be consistent with alternative two above, that "simple conditioning principles are at work and the frequency of elicitation is a function of the reinforcing properties of the elicitation paradigm." However, this interpretation of infant vocal patterns is called into question by subsequent results.

Bloom and Esposito (1975) and Bloom (1977, 1979) provide a substantially different picture. They, like Weisberg, presented infants with both contingent and noncontingent stimulation. However, their results were radically different from Weisberg's, since they found substantial increases in vocalization in both conditions. Furthermore, Bloom (1977) presented another group of infants with equal amounts of social stimulation in two experimental conditions. In both conditions the stimulation was presented noncontingently; but in the second condition a brief silence was presented contingent on the infant's vocalization. The results were surprising in that infants significantly increased vocalizations above baseline in both conditions and no significant differences were found between conditions. Bloom (1979) and Bloom and Esposito (1975) argue that Weisberg's result may not be representative of normal behavior, since the infants in his study vocalized at very low frequency levels in all conditions.

These results offer a dramatically different picture from the traditional one. Since babies were shown to vocalize in response to social stimulation whether or not stimulation was presented contingently and even when stimulation was contingently halted, Bloom argued that the results indicated social stimulation is an elicitor, but not a reinforcer of vocalizations.

Other results of Bloom refute the weak reflexivity hypothesis directly by showing that probability of elicitation varies in a way not predicted by conditioning theory. Bloom and Esposito (1975) and Bloom (1977) reported that while contingent stimulation or contingent silence did not have a reinforcing effect increasing the overall rate of vocalization, the treatments did yield a pattern of response that differed importantly from the pattern resulting from noncontingent stimulation. For brief periods after contingent stimulation or contingent silence, the babies tended to halt as if waiting for something, before they continued vocalizing. Noncontingent vocalization did not produce the halt. This pattern of infant response appears to be based on far more complex mechanisms than postulated in the weak reflexivity hypothesis. The probability of elicited vocalization changes for a brief interval when there is a contingent event present. However, the nature of the contingency (e.g., silence vs. contingent vocalization) seems unimportant.

Bloom interprets these results to mean that when babies vocalize they are engaged in a relatively high level activity not very unlike conversation. Their hesitations during both contingent stimulation and contingent silence might represent some attempt on their part to determine whose turn it is to talk or simply to figure out why the adult is doing something consistently in response to infant sounds. Such a cognitive activity is at a relatively higher level than a simple or passive/reflexive level. Further research in this area is highly desirable since to my knowledge no other researchers have yet replicated the findings of Bloom, and more in-depth analysis of contingencies across time might reveal further patterns in infant response.

Randomness or Selectivity in Vocalization Type

Since even one-month-old infants commonly have more than one speech-like vocal type in their repertoire, and interesting issue concerns their possible choice of particular vocal types for particular situations. If the infant's vocal patterns are highly selective for different situations, it would rule out their being passive-reflexive in any simple sense. That such a pattern of selectivity might occur was not supported by earlier writers (e.g., Jakobson, 1941; Osgood, 1953) who claimed that the sounds in the infant repertoire are produced at random, suggesting either a lack of phonetic control or a lack of interest in controlling sound types on the infant's part. However, there are four research areas that have provided evidence contradicting this view. All the areas are relatively young.

Selective Elicitation of Different Vocal Types

Routh (1967) found that by stimulating ("reinforcing") 2–7-month-old infants with either vowel or consonant-like sounds, he could selectively increase the vowels or consonants produced by the infant. This result suggests that the infants engaged in an imitative (or quasi-imitative) activity like that described in an anecdote by Piaget (1952). Surprisingly, Webster (1969) reported effects in which stimulation with vowel sounds resulted, perversely, in an increase in the proportion of infant consonant sounds while stimulation with consonant-vowel syllables resulted in an increase in the proportion of infant vowels. Webster's infants differed from Routh's in that they were older (six-month-olds), and Webster employed recorded speech samples rather than face-to-face stimulation. Perhaps these differences in procedure could help account for the differing results.

Assuming that both these results are replicable, it appears that infants during the first half-year of life are sensitive to the vocal-type of stimulation, and that they are capable of responding vocally by either matching (in quasi-imitation) or dissimilating (producing sounds that systematically differ from the model) depending on the circumstances. Such an ability suggests an intelligent activity in which higher-level cognitive processes of recognition and vocal planning must be operative.

Selective Vocal Imitation in Infancy

Piaget (1952) believed that two-month-olds could engage in quasi-imitation (i.e., adult says "goo" and baby may respond by beginning a gooing sequence) but not in selective imitation (i.e., baby is not capable of switching from gooing to pure vowels under the influence of selective stimulation). McCarthy (1929) reviews the literature, concluding that "most writers report a tendency to imitation occurring during the second six months of life."

Recent results showing gestural imitation in two-week-olds from Meltzoff and Moore (1977) have inspired an attempt to reveal delicate, though observable vocal imitative tendencies in very young infants. Kessen, Levine, and Wendrich (1979) presented 3–6-month-old infants with high-pitched and low-pitched vowel models and tones and monitored infant vocal pitch in response to these presentations. They found a definite selective imitative tendency. These results, like those of Meltzoff and Moore, seem to require a sensitive experimental procedure, since imitation in early infancy is often not immediate, lagging many seconds after the model (Moore, personal communication), since extreme control over variables of infant state are necessary to elicit the limitations, and since the imitative behaviors may in fact differ substantially from the models. Further studies of infant vocal imitation are underway and hopefully the interest in this area will continue, because infant selective vocal imitation sheds further light on the apparent ability of infants to vocalize with substantial control. As yet selective imitation of vocal sounds has not been shown with infants under three months of age and imitation of articulated sounds has not been investigated at all with sensitive procedures for babies in the first half year.

Selectivity as Manifest in Early Communicative Vocal Behavior

Another area of research need is communicative (instrumental) behavior. Infants appear to learn fairly early that certain vocal-types can be used to elicit desired behaviors from adults. For example, infants may learn to cry for attention. Bell and Ainsworth (1972) have shown that very early in life infants cry when in proximity, but not when in contact, with the parent. It is possible that infants employ a discernibly different cry (acoustically speaking) in requesting attention than the one produced reflexively to pain (say by three months). Whining likewise appears to be instrumentally employed from a fairly young age (probably by three months). Furthermore, as the child becomes older (say, by five months of age) vocal game playing with adults may occur—the child may produce a non-reflexive cough, for instance, expecting to elicit laughter or imitative behavior from adults. Thus, it seems that infants vocalize selectively in order to achieve pragmatically complex ends. These issues deserve further investigation.

Müller, Hollien, and Murry (1974) have failed to demonstrate parental identification of infant cry for 3–5 month-olds for pain, hunger, and startle. However, in these studies the operational definitions of "hunger," "pain," and "startle" appear to have left uncertainty as to whether they represented the categories of common usage. The "hunger cry" for instance was elicited by withdrawing food from a feeding infant. Such a cry might well be considered an "anger or startle cry" by a different investigator. These studies do not, then, seem adequately to address the possible instrumental (and conscious) nature of cries, since important cry types may not have been represented at all and those that were represented may have had too much in common with each other. Further investigation of auditory or acoustic characteristics of various cries may be desirable in the attempt to determine to what extent early infant vocal behavior may be consciously differentiated for communicative purposes.

Selectivity by Repetition and Systematic Alternation in Monologue

Zlatin (1975), Zlatin-Laufer, and Horii (1977), Stark (1981) and Oller (1978) have recently focused on the infant's tendency to produce repetitive sequences of vocalizations during the vocal play or expansion stage (variously set between 2 and 7 months of age). For example, the infant may, in monologue, begin to produce a particular sound type and continue with it for a substantial time frame, switching to a different sound type rather suddenly. The concentrated period may last for days in some cases or for less than a minute. Even in cases of stimulated vocalization (as in Oller and Gavin, described above), repetitive tendencies occur that cannot be accounted for by the nature of the stimulation. It seems worthwhile to consider the possibility that this repetitive behavior is a kind of practice.

Later in the first year of life, babies may engage in an even more complex systematic behavior. Toward the end of his first year, the author's son was observed producing a repetitive sequence of [a]'s, then a sequence of [ʊ]'s, then a sequence of [aʊ]'s, all within one minute. Such a systematic alternation behavior suggests that the child is literally engaged in *practice* of phonetic contrasts and of combinatorial possibilities of an emerging vocalic system.

The possibility that infants do practice speech-like sounds suggests that, in addition to controlling the production of various sound types, they are (even if only occasionally) actively engaged in a process of learning to talk. This possibility suggests that systematic investigation of infant monologue repetition and alternation employing time series analysis may be among the most important avenues of potential work on infant vocalizations and, indeed, on infant intellect.

The "Exploration" Hypothesis and the "Active-Language-Learner" Hypothesis

The evidence on infant vocalizations suggests that there is no reasonable sense in which infant speech-like sounds of the first six months or even the first three months are purely reflexive or passive. The infant engages instead in complex activities in vocalizing and the cognitive nature of the process is at least partly revealed in an analysis of patterns of selective production of different sound-types as well as patterns of pragmatic usage of the sound type in practice, conversation, imitation, and communication.

Beyond the reflexivity hypothesis are two alternative views that attribute to the infant a good deal more than reflexivity. Both views take the infant vocalizer to be an explorer (Oller, 1981, 1978; Stark, 1981; Zlatin, 1975) who investigates the production of various dimensions of vocal sounds (e.g., pitch, airstream mechanism, articulation and resonance possibilities, etc.). The notion of exploration can help explain why repetitive and systematically alternating monologues occur and why infants seem to focus on particular dimensions of vocal activity in apparent practice.

The two cognitively oriented views of infant sounds differ in that one assumes that the exploration is due to an interest in the vocal activity and its parameters (Stark, in press; Zlatin, 1975) but not to an attempt to learn to talk. The other view which I have proposed tentatively (Oller, 1981) suggests that the infant may have an overall strategy for learning to talk and that vocalization practice may be at least partly motivated by the desire to learn speech. It is important to clarify here that the latter view assumes the child's concept of speech to be grossly different from the adult's. Presumably, by two or three months of age the infant has an understanding of "conversation" or at least of reciprocity in comfortable interactive vocalization (Anderson, Vietze, and Dokecki, 1977). Further, the infant may have come to understand that talking is a natural aspect of being human. In exploring vocal sounds, then, the infant may at least occasionally be spurred on by the desire to act like a human being talking and to provide him/herself with tools for conversation.

It may not be easy to provide empirical tests of the exploration vs. active-language-learner hypotheses—the two views have a great deal in common. It is surely the case that at some point many children do become active language-learners. The question is, how soon? The author's belief is that it occurs sporadically during the first half year of life in most normal infants (if not during the first quarter). It seems to have been established that the 3–5-month-old understands and engages in reciprocity in talking, that she/he can and does interactively vocalize with selective matching of modeled sounds, that she/he "communicates" in interaction by making non-reflexive vocal requests, and she/he practices in monologue sound types along a number of vocal dimensions selectively. The infant might have some grasp of the relationship between vocal practice in monologue and interactive vocalization. Indeed, the practice could be motivated by the desire to advance in interactive vocalization.

Yet the exploration and active learner hypotheses may remain undifferentiable because it will be difficult to extract infant desire to *learn* to "talk" from infant desire simply to *engage* in talking.

Evidence Limiting Cognitive Interpretations of Infant Vocal Sounds

Whether we subscribe to either of these views, there are important empirical areas providing evidence for the placing of limits on the extent of "active" phonetic exploration or language learning behavior in infancy. Perhaps the most important of these areas concerns vocalizations of deaf infants. If the normal infant is engaged in an active exploration of sounds as *acoustic* entities, then we would expect very different vocalization tendencies in the deaf infant. What does occur is impossible to evaluate with certainty from sparse existing evidence. With caution, then, let us approach general conclusions of authors who have indirectly or directly observed or recorded vocalizations of deaf infants: (1) deaf infants produce sounds that are phonetically like those of hearing infants up until about six months of age (Fry, 1966; Lenneberg, Rebelsky, and Nichols, 1965; Mavilya, 1972), (2) in the second half-year differences can be seen (Fry, 1966; Lenneberg, Rebelsky, and Nichols, 1965; Murai, 1961), and (3) deaf and normal infants differ in pragmatic uses of vocalizations, the deaf being limited to utilitarian and face-to-face usage while the hearing often vocalize for pure pleasure (Fry, 1966; Mykelbust, 1957).

In order to shed further light on these issues Oller, Eilers, and Carney (forthcoming) have investigated vocalizations of a profoundly deaf baby, a victim of Waardenburg's syndrome. This baby is a particularly interesting case since her syndrome is associated with hearing loss but not with cognitive, speech-motor or other sensory impairments. The baby was seen between 8 and 12 months of age for four formal vocalization recordings. In part, the studies' results are consistent with previous literature because the deaf baby at 12 months was clearly different from normal babies in vocalization categories produced. Specifically, canonical (or syllabic) babbling was absent. Not a single one of 20 normal babies that have been seen in longitudinal studies at the Mailman Center (University of Miami) and at the University of Washington (Smith and Oller, in press) failed to show evidence of canonical babbling by 12 months. Further, the vocalizations produced by the deaf infants seemed to have high proportions of uncommon sound types for this age (e.g., velar fricatives, quasi-resonant sounds). At the same time, it should be emphasized that a full complement of normally expected pre-canonical sounds did seem to occur (e.g., vowel-like fully resonant sounds, raspberries, squeals) even as early as eight months.

It is important to realize that few deaf infants have been studied and those have only been studied in a cursory manner. Conclusions concerning deaf vocal patterns should remain tentative. Especially little is known concerning patterns of pragmatic vocal interaction in deaf infants, about possible practice, and even about possible phonetic differences from hearing babies early in the first year (cf. Stanley, 1976, for one study suggesting differences).

With these cautions in mind, and assuming that the traditional views of deaf vocalizations are correct, let us offer a preliminary statement of what impact information about deaf vocal behavior might have on the exploration and language-learner hypotheses. First of all, the information suggests that babies in the first half-year do *not* require acoustic information from the outside world in order to develop some (if not all) common precanonical sounds. At the same time the normal pragmatic usage of these sounds may be dependent on acoustic information—monologue practice may be uncommon in the deaf, and they may *require* eye contact for dialogue to an even greater extent than normals. Because of the tentativeness and ambiguity of the data, it is too soon to say whether they support or refute the hypotheses under discussion, but it is certain that evidence from this realm is relevant to proper specification of a theory of exploration in infant sounds.

Another area that has potential significance for such a theory is cross-linguistic studies of vocalization. Nakazima (1962) has described vocalizations of English and Japanese-learning infants and found remarkable similarities. At the Mailman Center, we are engaged in a broad longitudinal study of English and Spanish learners and have observed similarities much like those reported by Nakazima. Instrumental acoustic studies by Preston, Yeni-Komshian, and Stark (1967) have also revealed similarities in voice onset time of consonant-like sounds produced by English and Arabic-learning babies. In two major studies, adult listeners have failed to identify differences in vocalizations of babies from widely different language environments (Atkinson, McWhinney, and Stoel, 1970; Olney and Scholnick, 1976).

While these studies do not show that infants vocalize exactly alike regardless of language environment, they *do* indicate gross similarity in vocalization across cultures. It would, therefore, seem that in exploring vocal possibilities, infants have a tendency to restrict themselves (or to be restricted) to development of a relatively universal core of sound types at least by the canonical stage. Earlier, precanonical vocalizations of infants in a variety of cultures may also be similar across cultures (as Stark, 1981, points out). However, some of the precanonical sounds do not commonly occur in adult phonetic systems (e.g., ingressive vowels).

Stark interprets these not-very-language-like phonetic explorations of infants to mean that infants are not really trying to learn to talk but rather to explore vocal capacities per se. However, such explorations could be an extension of practice with a linguistic-phonetic (metaphonological) parameter (airstream mechanism) that *is* controlled in all languages even though its control does not always result in ingressive sounds employed contrastively. That the child explores extremes of continua is not unique to the airstream parameter. Squealing and growling (which I interpret as pitch exploration by infants) also represent extremes not represented with high frequency of occurrence in adult speech. Similarly yelling and whispering (which represent amplitude extremes) are not the usual modes of adult speech.

Infants, then, in my view produce vocalizations in patterns of exploration that are consistent with (though they do not necessarily demand) an interpretation as *speech* exploration and active *vocal communication* development. Whether evidence ultimately supports these interpretations or requires the somewhat more conservative view that infant sounds represent exploration of a vocal capacity independent of speech, we shall have come a long way from the belief that infant sounds are purely passive or reflexive.

Discussion

In the discussion of Oller's paper, Kagan questioned the value of approaching the ontogeny of infant vocalization by asking what motivated the infant to vocalize. He drew a parallel between the study of infant vocalization and a study of movement in a plasmodium. One would not ask "Why does the plasmodium move?" but rather "What are the occasions of its moving?" Similarly one should not ask "Why does the baby of six months make a raspberry sound?" but rather "What are the occasions for the raspberry?" Kagan again said that the first question should be "What are the occasions for this behavior?" Oller agreed that this was a part of the question he had asked, but felt that more could be done with such results. He thought that by examining the occasions on which vocal behavior was observed, it might, in some cases, be possible to figure out what motivated the infant to produce it. In other cases, the motivation might not be inherent in the child, but rather inherent in the tasks that the human infant must undertake in his development.

Capute emphasized the importance of studying the vocalizations of deaf infants with reference to this possible motivational factor. Oller agreed that such studies were crucial. Since profoundly deaf infants receive no auditory feedback, but only kinesthetic feedback from their own vocalization, their exploratory behavior should be more limited. Thus, if the profoundly deaf infant in the first six months of life produces sounds like those of normal infants, and, in addition, used them under similar circumstances and conditions, it would severely weaken the position he, Oller, had taken. In other words, if the deaf infant produced vocalizations in the same kind of practice patterns and also showed similar patterns of vocal responses especially in face-to-face interaction with the parent to the parents imitations of these vocalizations, then he would have to revise his hypothesis about the normal infant's motivation and desire to learn to talk. However, the available information on the vocal behavior of deaf infants was not very trustworthy.

Hardy pointed out that it was a very rare child who had total loss of hearing. The child with a sensory neural loss was likely to have greater limitation of hearing in the higher than the lower frequencies, but seldom had a loss of hearing across all frequencies. Stark pointed out that profound hearing loss might not be present, except in a very few cases, at birth. It might be acquired in many children over a period of several months postnatally. Oller believed that it was possible, however, to find infants who were profoundly deaf from birth yet were normal in other respects in order to carry out the appropriate study.

Ingram described observations he had made on one of his own infant subjects, D., a boy of ten months. He described how this infant was recorded playing with the vowels "i," "a," "u," and at this age, going from one vowel to the other in the same order "i'', "a," "u," over and over again and in the manner that suggested purposeful exploration. Ingram did not think this babbling was motivated by a desire to learn to talk. Unlike a second infant subject, K., who was a rapid speech learner but showed very little babbling, D. did not talk early. Indeed, in the second year of life, he showed more interest in babbling than in talking. An example was provided in a later tape recording session in which D. requested a banana by saying "nana." During the time in which the banana was taken from a bundle and offered to him, D. babbled "nana, nana," ten to fifteen times over and over without paying attention to the adults as if he had lost interest in the banana and in his previous communicative intent. Suddenly D. realized that he still did not have the banana, caught sight of it and said "nana" again in a quite different imperative manner. During this sequence, the exploratory sound-making appeared to be of more interest to D. than the banana and was not motivated by the need to communicate.

Oller said that he was not talking about motivation to communicate on the part of the infant as adults understand verbal communicating, but rather motivation to prepare the skills for communication as he or she, the child, understands those skills. He was not sure that Ingram's example provided evidence one way or the other for his hypothesis, although Ingram was clearly talking about an infant who was beyond the first six months of life.

Stark agreed that the process of development of speech was not a reflexive or passive one. She was not, however, convinced that it was always motivated by an interest in communication. She referred to Kagan's comment on the occasions for vocalizing. It was true that cooing sounds at the time of their emergence were most often, if not solely, produced in face-to-face interaction with an adult. However, in a very few weeks these sounds began to be produced when the infant was alone, often when he was examining interesting visual patterns and visual displays as well as in face-to-face interaction. Furthermore, although the exploratory behaviors of squealing and raspberrying were produced in many different social contexts, reduplicated babbling, when it first emerged, was much more likely to be produced in the context of play-with-objects than in adult-infant interaction. These observations might not provide evidence one way or the other but should be considered in developing hypotheses about motivation.

Oller replied that he did not doubt that infants found sound making to be fun for its own sake. But he believed that, at least part of the time, infants of six months were aware that the sounds they were producing were like those of speech. Infants produced these sounds not just as play but as an activity that was more like work.

Leavitt contributed an observation from his own studies. He had been interested in the context in which infants of four months vocalized in the home. In one study, Verhoeve, Stevenson, and Leavitt (1979) found that the mothers talked a great deal. The speech of the mother had a powerful effect on the vocalizing of the infant. It caused him to stop vocalizing. However, a direct response from the mother was always elicited by vocalization on the part of the infant. Thus, the baby is interested in the mother's speech and also learns that his own vocalizations are very important in soliciting attention and vocalization from the mother.

Bloom asked Oller how the experimenter presented stimuli to a supine infant in the study of the effect of gravity upon vocal behavior. Oller replied that the experimenter leaned over so that he was about three hand's distance from the infant's face and his head was at the same angle as the infant's. The distance was held appropriately constant. The activity was very like that observed in the face-to-face interaction study described by Fogel and Tronick (this volume, Chapters 1 and 2). Bloom wondered about the effect of the angle of the experimenter's head when the baby was in the upright as opposed to supine position. Oller replied that the question of position was a methodologically important one. Infants have very strong preferences for particular positions, indeed for certain angles of position, and there were marked individual differences with respect to these preferences. Certain criteria for positioning had been employed. The supine position was defined as a cephalocaudal axis with an angle of incidence of 0 to 40 degrees to the ground while the upright position was defined as a cephalocaudal axis with an angle of incidence of 90 to 110 degrees. Some infants would not accept any position within the range of supine positions at all, but would only accept an upright position, and vice versa. Their data could not be used since their response in one position or the other was distress. The positions were achieved by having the mother hold the child or by use of an adjustable infant seat. The study would have been prohibitively difficult without this degree of flexibility, since infants often have strong individual preferences for or against body contact.

Stern asked if there was a difference in the total amount of vocalizing produced in the upright position versus the supine position. Oller said that there was more vocalizing in the supine than in the upright position. Stark asked if this effect was related to age. Oller replied that as the babies grew older they would in general tolerate the upright position more readily, and thus might vocalize more in this position than formerly. However, even some very young infants preferred the upright position.

Bloom asked about the imitative contingencies in this study. Oller replied that he had not yet studied the data from this point of view but thought it unlikely that the data would provide evidence for or against the finding that imitation was occurring. Bloom asked if the interval between one stimulus and the next had been too short to permit the baby to respond. Oller said he felt that that was not the case, the problem was more one of the infant's state. In order to elicit imitation, one had to have the infant in a highly attentive state. The control over infant attentiveness had been much less complete in his study than, for example, in the Meltzoff and Moore (1977) study of imitation of facial and hand gestures.

Published 1981 by Elsevier North Holland, Inc.
Stark, ed.
Language Behavior in Infancy and Early Childhood

Articulatory-Acoustic Perspectives on Speech Development

R. D. Kent

Human Communication Laboratories, Boys Town Institute, 555 North 30th Street, Omaha, Nebraska

Introduction

Recent investigations of speech development tell us that this process is only grossly described by the order of acquisition of sound units such as phonemes. Order of acquisition is important, but theoretical and clinical demands require a more refined, multidimensional analysis, one that recognizes speech production as a highly precise and practiced motor skill. This paper focuses on the interactions among three aspects of the process of speech development: changes in vocal tract anatomy, motor control of speech articulation, and the articulatory-acoustic conversion. These three topics are cast against some major issues of speech-language development, including babbling, early syllable formation, order of acquisition of speech sounds, and phonologic universals.

One major thesis is developed for each of the three topics. The theses are:

1. Vocal tract anatomy: During infancy and childhood, the vocal tract not only lengthens but changes in its relative anatomical relationships. These changes predispose the organism to certain sound-producing patterns and require persistent modification of the motor organization of speech.
2. Motor control of speech articulation: Speech motor control, often subsumed without explicit mention in accounts of speech development, has a complex acquisition in its own right. This acquisition should be considered in the light of developmental reflexology and theories of motor skill learning.

3. Articulatory-acoustic conversion: The essential property of speech is the conversion from articulatory configuration to acoustic product. The acoustic signal is the unifying link between the partly separate processes of speech production and speech perception. There is some evidence that the articulatory-acoustic conversion is not simple and may in fact be highly nonlinear. Possibly, these nonlinearities are seed to the development of categorical speech motor control; that is, motor regulation that reflects phonetic categories.

Anatomy of the Vocal Tract: Phylogenetic and Ontogenetic Considerations

Du Brul (1977) described three primary forces in the evolutionary remodeling of human head form: erect bipedalism, modification of the oral apparatus, and enlargement of the brain. These factors are considered to have contributed significantly to the emergence of a "vocal tract." This tract is critically shaped by the evolutionary forces to have the features illustrated in Figure 1: (1) a short, broad oral cavity; (2) a nearly right-angle bend of the oropharyngeal channels; (3) a relatively posterior tongue mass; (4) a considerable separation of epiglottis and soft palate; (5) a long pharyngeal cavity; and (6) a larynx deeply recessed in the neck.

Whereas in the general mammalian anatomy of the head, exhaled air normally does not have access to the oropharyngeal channel, such access is readily accommodated by the human anatomy. This difference is distinctive of the human vocal tract. As the sketches in Figure 2 show, most animals have epiglottic-velar contact, but man does not. The anatomical differences are of interest not only for evolutionary study but because the changes observed across mammalian species often are recapitulated in human ontogeny.

Bosma (1975), in his review of the developmental anatomy and physiology of the speech apparatus, observed that in this system, as in the limbs, "motor functions generate their performance anatomy by stimulating the growth of muscle and the growth and structural adaptation of the fascia, tendons, bones, and articulations upon which the muscles act" (p. 489). Bosma emphasizes the differential chamber enlargements of the larynx, pharynx, and mouth during childhood and puberty as being strategic for speech maturation. These enlargements are not thought to result from the small forces generated during speech but from the more substantial forces produced during continuous positional actions and feeding. The enlargements of the laryngeal, pharyngeal, and oral cavities are shown in Figure 3, which contrasts the vocal tract dimensions of an adult with those of an infant.

Using a static articulatory model with growth parameters, Goldstein (1979) concluded that the infant's vocal tract differs from that of an adult in four major respects: (1) the infant's tract is appreciably shorter, (2) the pharynx

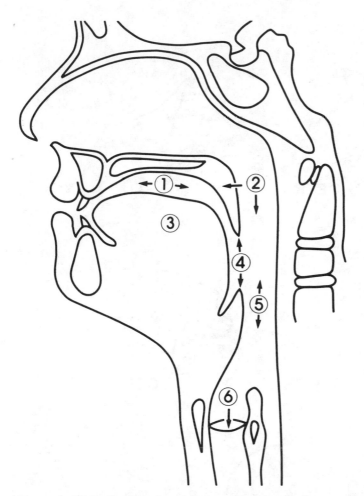

Figure 1. Midsagittal-section drawing of human vocal tract, showing the important anatomic features (no. 1–6) discussed in the text.

is relatively shorter in the infant, (3) the infant's tract is wider in relation to its length, and (4) because the infant does not have erupted dentition, the oral cavity is flatter than in the adult. Many of these features are consistent with the phylogenetic and ontogenetic changes described by Du Brul (1976, 1977), Bosma and Showacre (1975), and George (in press).

The differences in oropharyngeal anatomy between primates and man—and between infant and adult—are important considerations in the potential for speech sound production (Lieberman, Harris, Wolff, and Russell, 1971; Lieberman, Crelin, and Klatt, 1972). Of interest here are differences in the geometry of the system as an acoustic resonator and differences in orientation, and therefore function, of the oropharyngeal muscles.

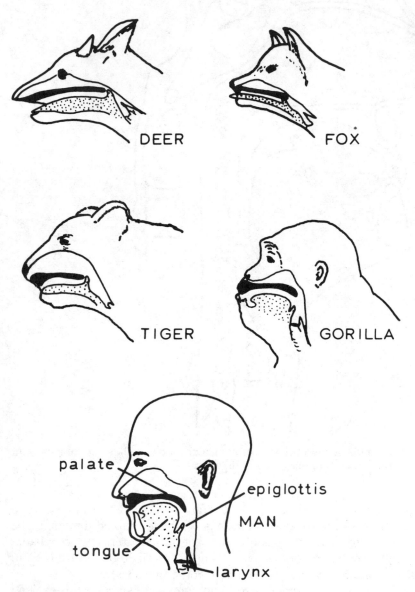

Figure 2. Comparisons of the head anatomy of different species. Note uniqueness of the human vocal tract.

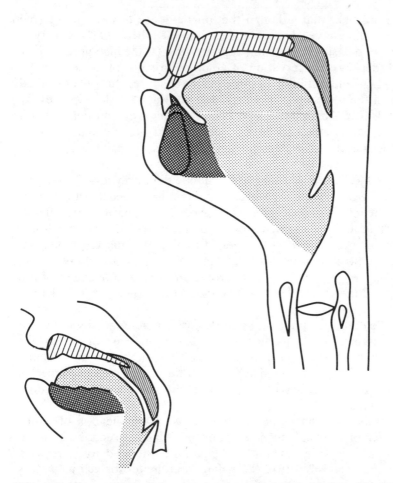

Figure 3. Comparison of the vocal tracts of adult and infant. Note the differences described in the text.

Functional Implications of Anatomic Changes

The anatomic differences between infant and adult have some important motoric implications. The tongue of the infant is especially adapted to two motions, thrusting and rocking, both of which aid in prehension, suckling, and swallowing (Fletcher, 1973). Tongue motion is restricted not only by the limited sensorimotor development of the organ but also by the fact that the tongue almost fills the oral cavity. Fletcher (1973) likened the tongue of the infant to a piston that is driven back and forth within the oral cavity by the extrinsic tongue muscles. Many writers regard the intrinsic muscles of the tongue to be less important than the extrinsics in the infant's lingual functioning. In considering the role of these two major sets of muscles, it is important to remember that although the tongue does not have an internal bony skeleton, it does have a hydrostatic skeleton (Du Brul, 1977). This type of skeleton has two basic biomechanical properties: (1) the incompressibility of water (and therefore conservation of volume during displacement or deformation), and (2) contractibility in three planes of space. Du Brul described the tongue as a fluid-filled bag of water that contracts in three planes by action of its intrinsic longitudinal, vertical, and transverse muscular fibers. This fluid-filled bag is attached directly or indirectly to the skull by four paired extrinsic muscles, the genioglossus, hypoglossus, palatoglossus and styloglossus.

Some writers have proposed that in the adult, the intrinsic and extrinsic muscles of the tongue have quite different functions in speech articulation. For example, the intrinsic musculature is regarded as primarily a consonant-producing system and the extrinsic musculature as primarily a vowel-producing system (Perkell, 1969). However attractive this muscular dualism may be, its generalization runs considerable risk of error, for many consonants, including / k g η ∫ 3 t∫ j r w / involve substantial movement of the tongue body, and therefore, a strong likelihood of extrinsic muscle activation.

Generally, the earliest sounds of the infant are characterized by large and relatively undifferentiated tongue movements, as in the case of the vowels and the velar consonants / k g /. More refined adjustments of tongue shape and position apparently await the maturation of the intrinsic tongue muscles and a reshaping of the oral cavity to permit additional degrees of freedom of tongue movement.

Another example of a changing anatomy causing modification of motor control is the velopharyngeal mechanism, or the valve between the oral and nasal cavities. The infant's levator veli palatini is situated to serve as a tensor, rather than an elevator, of the palate, and the tensor veli palatini is situated to function more as a depressor, rather than tensor, of the palate (Bosma and Fletcher, 1962). Thus, these two muscles undergo a change in function as the oropharyngeal anatomy is modified. Given these anatomical differences, it is not surprising that nasalization frequently has been reported as a characteristic of infants' vocalizations. With the appearance of the distinctively human craniovertebral angle, the direction of palatal movement changes from cephalic in the infant, to cephalodorsal in the adult. In addition, Fletcher (1973) described a change in palato-pharyngeal approximation, which is broad and "somewhat indiscriminate" (p. 167) in the infant but more focal in the adult. Because nasalization carries a large information load in adult speech, developmental changes in the velopharyngeal region are highly significant.

The approximation of epiglottis to palate accomplishes an interlocking of larynx and nasopharynx that may have life-preserving value to the infant. With this arrangement, food can be swallowed on either side of the engaged larynx and nasopharynx to pass through the pyriform fossae into the esophagus, thereby minimizing risk of choking or aspiration of food particles. The separation of epiglottis and palate, and with it a transition from obligate nasal breathing to the possibility of oral breathing, occurs between 4–6 months of life (Sasaki et al., 1977). Interestingly, babbling commences at about the same time. Perhaps disengagement of larynx and nasopharynx is an important anatomic condition for the appearance of babbling. Oller (in press) calls this period of 4–6 months *the expansion stage* of phonetic development, a stage that is characterized by a frequent appearance of "fully resonant nuclei" and a diversification of place of consonant production. Before this period, most consonants appear to have a velar to uvular constriction, which might be explained by the engagement of larynx and nasopharynx.

Other anatomic-physiologic changes occurring at about the same time further prepare the child for speech acquisition. For example, Wilder and Baken (1978) determined from a pneumographic study that over the first eight months of life, an increase in the mean duration of respiratory cycles was explained entirely by an increase in the duration of the expiratory phase. Lengthening of this phase was viewed as preparatory for two requirements of speech production: rapid inspiration at appropriate intervals and prolonged, primarily voiced, expiration.

There appear to be parallels between changes in vocalization during the first year of life and changes in the anatomy and physiology of the speech apparatus. Some of these parallels are summarized in Table 1, which shows for the major periods of phonetic development described by Oller (in press) corresponding or related changes in anatomy and physiology. Although a causal relationship has not been firmly established, the evidence certainly invites the tentative conclusion that major discontinuities in vocal behavior in the first year are related to significant remodeling of the oropharyngeal anatomy. This is not to argue for a physiologic-anatomic determinism of early vocalization, but merely to stress the importance of physiologic and anatomic factors in evaluating early vocal behavior.

From the standpoint of motor organization, the child must contend not only with a changing vocal tract anatomy but also with a maturing nervous system. Neuromotor control of the speech apparatus changes considerably during the first years of life and more gradually thereafter up to puberty (Moyers, 1971; Kent, 1976; Kent and Forner, in press). A basic question about the early stage of development is whether changes in reflexes, the basic level of motor organization, precede and prepare the way for various motor developments in speech. Some recent theories about motor control stress the concept that reflexes are orchestrated into functional sets or systems to accomplish the motor control of complex learned behavior (see Easton, 1972). It may be that normal development of speech motor control is based on reflexes that are organized into functional units. Although the

Table 1. Parallels Between Stages of Phonetic Development (After Oller, in press) and Significant Anatomic-Physiologic Changes in Speech Apparatus.

Age of infant	Phonetic development	Anatomic-physiologic correlate
0-1 month Phonation stage	Quasi-resonant nucleus	Nasal breathing and nasalized vocalization because of engagement of larynx and nasopharynx. Tongue has mostly back-and-forth motions and nearly fills the oral cavity.
2-3 months Gooing stage	Quasi-resonant nucleus plus velar or uvular constrictions	Some change in shape of oral cavity and an increase in mobility of tongue; but tongue motion is still contrained by larynx-nasopharynx engagement.
4-6 months Expansion stage	Fully resonant nuclei	Disengagement of larynx and nasopharynx allows increased separation of oral and nasal cavities, so that non-nasal vowels are readily produced.
	Raspberry (labial)	The intraoral air pressure necessary for fricative-like productions can be developed with some regularity because of larynx-nasopharynx disengagement. Raspberry results from forcing air through lips, which close after each air burst because of natural restoring forces.
	Squeal and growl	Contrasts in vocal pitch are heightened perhaps because descent of larynx into neck makes the vocal folds more vulnerable to forces of supralaryngeal muscles.
	Yelling	Better coordination of respiratory system and larynx, together with prolonged oral radiation of sound, permit loud voice.
	Marginal babble	Alternation of full opening and closure of vocal tract is enhanced by larynx-nasopharynx disengagement.

reflexology of the developing speech apparatus (or the mature apparatus, for that matter) is far from well understood, there is abundant evidence of extensive reflex interactions in the respiratory, laryngeal, oral, and perioral regions. The possibility of neural interactions between various structures of the speech apparatus has both anatomic and functional evidence behind it (Dubner and Kawamura, 1971; Bratzlavsky, 1976; Sessle, 1977; Netsell and

Abbs, 1975; Larson et al., 1978). Zimmerman (in press) has summarized many of the neural interactions pertinent to speech. It is clear that stimulation of oral receptor sites can alter the input to the motoneuron pools that activate brainstem structures and that the activity of oral and perioral reflex pathways can be modulated. Knowledge about the normal development of such reflexes might explain certain aspects of speech motor control, such as constraints on the timing and coordination of movements.

Perspective on Babbling

The so-called babbling stage of speech development is not easily defined, although most writers on speech development acknowledge its occurrence beginning somewhere between the sixth and sixteenth week of life (Lewis, 1963; McCarthy, 1970; Oller, 1981). Wood (1957) noted that the babbling stage is a time at which the infant engages in "vocal play." Siegel (1969, p. 4) commented that "the speech of the child who is said to be babbling is marked by a diversity of sounds, repetitions, and adult-like intonation patterns." From a functional point of view, babbling is a stage that (1) precedes the emergence of a language-specific phonetic system, and (2) offers considerable exercise of the organs of speech. It appears that babbling is not dependent on normal hearing, for children born deaf apparently produce babbling vocalizations similar to those of normal children (Lenneberg, 1967; Mavilya, 1972). Therefore, babbling is not necessarily an integrated auditory-motor behavior in the same sense as imitation and vocal exchanges between child and parent.

As far as normal infants are concerned, it commonly is assumed that babbling gives the child a sensorimotor awareness of his speech production capabilities. Osgood (1953, p. 688) spoke to this issue as follows: "The elaborate practice provided by babbling serves both to develop and stabilize those complex skill sequences that are required for speech and to associate auditory sounds (self-produced) with the motor reactions that produce them." The association of auditory and motor events during babbling may ready the child for the act of imitation. This idea is expressed by Fry (1968, p. 18): "The auditory-motor links once established through babbling, the child is in a position to profit to the full from the repeated imitations of the speech models provided in the first instance by his mother, for *imitation is the major factor in the learning of the articulations which normally accompany the development of the phonemic system*. When a mother speaks to her baby, she is giving him material for discriminating one sound from another, for developing the acoustic cues which enable him to sort sounds into phonemic categories and at the same time a model for imitation on the motor side, where the same acoustic cues are used in controlling and modifying articulation." (Emphasis added).

Articulatory-Acoustic Relationships as Universal Determinants of Speech Development

Articulatory-Acoustic Boundaries

If categories of speech production begin to emerge during babbling, one might hypothesize that the infant, like natural languages, would employ the principles of maximal opposition (Schane, 1973) to derive the point vowels /i/, /u/, and /a/. If nothing else, the extreme articulatory adjustments for these vowels might insure stability of production, which is one criterion of categorical control. Lindblom and Sundberg (1969) reached essentially this conclusion from experiments on an articulatory model consisting of "a mandible, a tongue, a quasi-muscular and jaw-independent 'labialization' parameter and larynx height" (p. 18). Lindblom and Sundberg put the model through a "babbling stage" by manipulating the various articulatory components and by observing the corresponding changes in the acoustic signal.

The articulatory model produced only certain combinations of formant frequency values, with movement of the jaw having a primary effect on the first formant frequency (F_1) and movements of the tongue having a primary effect on the second formant frequency (F_2). In addition, it was established that the two-dimensional area corresponding to the first and second formant frequency ranges of the model was roughly triangular in shape, with vertices that corresponded to the vowels /i/, /u/ and /a/ (Figure 4). These extreme vowels were judged to be important insofar as they exhibited *"a unique relation between articulation and acoustic result"* (p. 20, emphasis in the original). For example, the acoustic properties corresponding to the vowel /i/ could be produced only with a small jaw opening, spread lips, and a high-front tongue position. The extreme vowels on the triangular acoustic surface appear to mark the boundaries of the infant's articulatory-acoustic potential; therefore, it might be expected that these vowels would assume a special significance in the child's evolving sound system. However, these vowels do not appear to be the most frequently used vowels in early infant vocalizations. Irwin and Curry (1941) and Irwin (1948) reported that the front vowels constitute the great majority of a baby's vowel productions (see also Mavilya, 1972; Buhr, 1980). In view of the overwhelming preference for front vowels, Irwin and Curry concluded, "It is evident that a fundamental process of development in early speech consists of the mastery of the back vowels" (p. 82; cf. Irwin, 1948, p. 31).

The weak representation of back vowels such as /u/ and /a/ in an infant's early vocalizations might be explained by a closer look at a simplifying assumption that Lindblom and Sundberg made about tongue-jaw interaction for vowel production. Radiographs revealed that the front vowels have similar tongue shapes so long as the lingual contours are compared with reference to the mandible. Hence, one basic tongue shape, *relative to the mandible,* suffices for the production of seven front vowels. If a similar

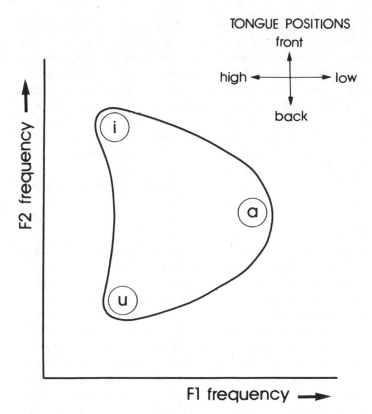

Figure 4. The two-dimensional area of vowel production defined by the first (F_1) and second (F_2) formant frequencies (based loosely on the results of Lindblom and Sundberg, 1969).

principle applies to an infant's early vowel productions, he may produce almost all of his vowels with a fixed relationship between the tongue and the jaw. Different front vowels are produced by variations in jaw position. The reason for the front vowel preference is not clear, although it might be encouraged by the peculiar oropharyngeal anatomy of the infant (Sloan, 1967; Lieberman et al., 1971; Fletcher, 1973; Bosma, 1975), or by activities such as sucking. Given this reasoning, the back vowels may be more difficult to produce because the infant has to learn a different tongue-jaw relationship from that employed for the front vowels. But it should be remembered that many back vowels of English are rounded vowels (/u ʊ o ɔ /), which means that their production requires coordinated gestures of the tongue-jaw-lip complex. The importance of tongue-jaw relationship in explaining the early vowel usage could be tested by examining the order of acquisition of vowels in languages with both front and back rounded vowels.

Lindblom and Sundberg's work underscores the importance of babbling as the child's self-discovery of his potential for speech production. In this view, the fundamental lessons that a child derives from babbling are (1) generalizations about articulatory-acoustic relationships, and (2) the related discovery of articulatory and acoustic bounded continua. But another lesson, implicit in Lindblom and Sundberg's modeling work, is that the infant discovers articulatory synergy, like that between tongue and jaw. Many adult speakers seem to have a small number of basic tongue shapes, which, when properly matched with a jaw position, yield a diversity of vowel productions. Tongue shapes derived from x-ray tracings for two adults are shown in Figures 5a and b. For these two speakers, the tongue shapes can be arranged into a small number of groups or families.

Articulatory-Acoustic Nonlinearities

The articulatory-acoustic relationships described by Stevens (1968, 1969, 1972) in his quantal theory of speech production carry the implication that a babbling infant might discover natural categories of sound production. Stevens (1972, p. 65) posited that a "talker manipulates his speech generating mechanism to select sounds with well-defined acoustic attributes that are relatively insensitive to small perturbations in articulation." That is, in the case of some articulatory configurations, even a slight change in a given articulatory characteristic may result in a relatively large change in the acoustic output. But for other articulatory configurations, large changes in certain articulatory characteristics have very little effect on the acoustic signal. Hence, the relationship between articulatory and acoustic dimensions may be discontinuous, and the possibility of discontinuities holds the promise of categorical speech behavior. This quantal theory of speech production has some evidence behind it: using a tubelike vocal tract model, Stevens demonstrated that articulatory-acoustic relationships are characterized by a quantal nature that depends upon variations in the stability of the conversion between vocal tract shape and the acoustic signal.

If this theory is correct, then the infant may be predisposed to certain consonants and vowels. These propensities could simplify the task of learning speech because crude articulatory-acoustic categories could be acquired on the basis of babbling experience. (It might not be too far-fetched to think that some of the ambiguous sounds that characterize early babbling are formed in regions that have an unstable articulatory-acoustic relationship, so that their phonetic description is exceedingly difficult given the supposed exclusion of such articulation points from language systems.)

The quantal theory allows the hypothesis that the motor control of an infant's earliest vocalizations might be essentially continuous in nature, but such continuous motor control gradually would give way to a crudely categorized control that reflects the discontinuous nature of articulatory-acoustic conversions. Babbling drift based on this principle should exhibit language-universal properties, as the early changes in babbling content would

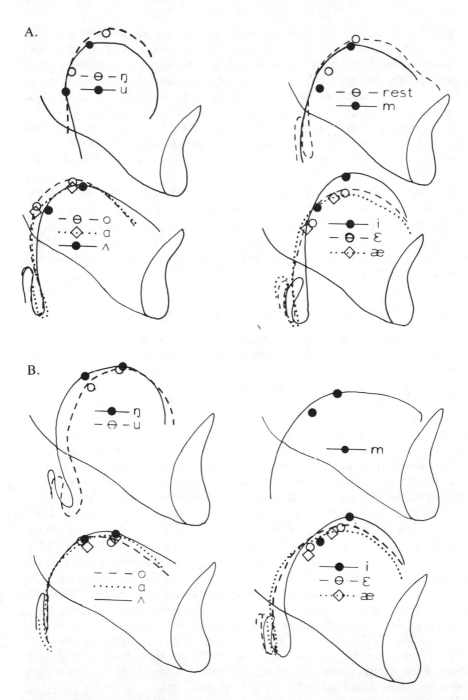

Figure 5. Families of tongue shapes derived from x-ray studies of two adult speakers (a and b). Shapes are shown for different vowels, the dorsal nasal consonant /ɔ/, and the rest position of the tongue.

be dictated largely by physical relationships that are common to the vocal tracts of all infants. If, on the other hand, the initial stages of babbling drift do not have common trends among different language communities, then sociolinguistic factors would seem to be paramount. Of course, because sociolinguistic factors inevitably exert an influence on speech development, the prediction based on the quantal theory should be tested only against the earliest trends in babbling content. Unfortunately, very few cross-language studies of infants' babbling have been reported. Jakobson (1968) proposed a universal order of acquisition of sound classes, but the available data are not sufficient to test his theory (however, see Olmsted, 1971). Ferguson (1964, 1975) discussed "baby talk" in various languages, but his remarks apply to stages of development that are strongly influenced by linguistic factors. In 1962 and 1966, Nakazima reported comparative studies of speech development in American and Japanese children. The latter study did not reveal spectrographic differences between the utterances of American and Japanese infants until as late as the twelfth month of life.

Syllables, Segments and Motor Organization of Speech

The CV syllable frequently has been touted as the most natural syllable shape and the earliest phonetic combination to appear with regularity. Branigan (1976) concluded that all consonants appear first in initial position, presumably because this position is the most stable environment and serves as a kind of "testing ground" for acquisition. He speculated that the advantage of the initial position derives from the fact that consonants in this position receive the first neural commands and therefore are minimally affected by earlier articulatory requirements. Branigan also notes that, "with CV syllables, there would be no effects of backward assimilation" (p. 130).

However, the evidence for superiority of the initial position is mixed. Although an initial-position advantage does seem to accrue to stops, fricatives may have a position-final advantage. Children frequently substitute fricatives and affricates for position-final stops and final fricatives outnumber final stops in early speech (Olmsted, 1971; Ferguson, 1973; Oller, 1973, 1976). This stop-spirant asymmetry argues against the primacy of CV syllables for all consonants. Furthermore, data on coarticulation (reviewed by Kent and Minifie, 1977) indicate that consonants in the initial position do not necessarily receive either the first or uncontaminated neural commands, as anticipatory coarticulation of later segments is common.

Nonetheless, CVs do constitute a majority of the syllable shapes in childrens' speech and many sounds do appear to be mastered first in CV shapes. Some of the advantage of CV syllables might be motoric, perhaps reflecting a special neuromotor integrity or cohesiveness (Stetson, 1951; MacKay, 1976). The initial-position advantage for stops could be motorically based in the sense that the stop release gesture is tightly integrated with the vocal tract opening for the following vowel, being expressed acoustically as a highly distinctive formant transition. The release gesture and accompanying formant transition are not as critical for fricatives, which require instead a sufficiently long interval of turbulence noise, generated by a high-velocity airstream moving through a narrow articulatory constriction. One way in which syllables could offer a motoric advantage is if the syllable is a basic organizational unit of speech motor control. For example, the stop-vowel transition in a CV syllable might be a functional organization of early-developing oral reflexes, somewhat along the line of Easton's (1972) coordinative structure.

If speech is viewed as a special case of the general area of skilled motor behavior, some useful ideas about speech control might be gained from recent work on motor behavior in general. A *skill* may be defined as an organization of movements in space and time, in the context of a program of action (Connolly, 1977). Thus, a child learning a motor skill such as speech has to learn an organization of movements that is purposeful. Bruner (1973) viewed the development of a motor skill as the construction of serially-ordered acts, the performance of which is modified to achieve diminishing variability, increased anticipation, and improved economy. One of the few models of motor control to address the problem of learning is Schmidt's (1975) *schema theory*. In addition to the problem of learning, schema theory attempts to answer the storage problem and the novelty problem in motor control. The former problem refers to the large number of motor programs that would have to be stored to account for a behavior such as speech. For example, MacNeilage and MacNeilage (1973) calculated that some 100,000 sound units are needed to produce English speech with appropriate intonation and accent. The novelty problem arises from the fact that two apparently identical movements are never really the same. But then how does a subject generate these novel programs and evaluate their correctness? Schema theory proposes an answer to this question and the storage problem as well.

The schema theory incorporates two types of memory: (1) *recall memory,* which is essential to the generation of motor commands, and (2) *recognition memory,* which is needed to evaluate response-produced feedback to obtain error information. A *recall schema* is an acquired relationship among past initial conditions, past response specifications, and past actual outcomes. In making a movement on different occasions, a subject pairs response specifications and actual outcomes, until he eventually acquires a well-established schema. The critical test of an adequate schema lies in its ability to generate a novel response suited to a particular set of initial conditions and a particular desired outcome. The novel response can be "interpolated" from past outcomes, taking into account the applicable initial conditions. Storage of fixed motor programs is not required. A *recognition schema* is an acquired relationship among initial conditions, sensory consequences, and actual outcomes. By means of this relationship, a subject can predict the sensory consequences of a movement. Error information is obtained by comparing the expected feedback with the actual feedback. Thus, the subject has information about his performance even when he is not given actual knowledge of results (KR).

Schema theory applied to speech development offers several useful principles. For example, schema theory can explain how a child acquires motor control of speech even as the speech organs grow in size and change in relative configuration. As these changes occur, the recall and recognition schema are adjusted as required. Another advantage of considering speech development within the framework of schema theory is that the theory allows for different kinds of feedback to be used at different times in skill learning, depending upon the need for and availability of feedback. Thus, proprioceptive or auditory feedback can be used preferentially, depending in part on the degree to which a particular feedback is suited to a particular motor goal. But schema theory also allows for the integration of different forms of feedback and for the individual's ability to predict the sensory consequences of movements. In learning a skill such as speech, a child has to learn not only the response specifications (motor instructions to the articulators) but also the expected sensory consequences, so that errors can be detected and the schema refined. For an application of this idea to the acquisition of speech in cerebral palsy, see Kent and Netsell (1978).

Schema theory can explain several aspects of response novelty in speech, including the imitation of new patterns and the remarkable variability in articulation of a given sound (see the different vocal-tract shapes for sounds with r-coloring in Figure 6). Imitation of new patterns is basically a problem of interpolation by the recall schema. Articulatory variance for a given phoneme is the result of highly flexible response specifications, adapted to particular initial conditions and particular desired outcomes. As another example of schema theory's application to problems of speech motor control, the syllable-position advantages noted above might be explained by considerations of recall and recognition memory in the control and modification of motor programs. When movements are rapid, as for syllable-initial stops, the movement is executed under control of recall memory, meaning that all details of the movement are prepared in advance (Schmidt, 1975, p. 46). When movements are slow, or when articulations can be sustained, as is the case for final fricatives, performance is governed primarily by the comparison of expected and actual feedback (recognition memory). Stops have a syllable-initial advantage because this position gives them a priority in response specification (and recall memory). Fricatives tend to have a syllable-final advantage because this position enhances feedback, especially proprioceptive feedback, and the use of recognition memory.

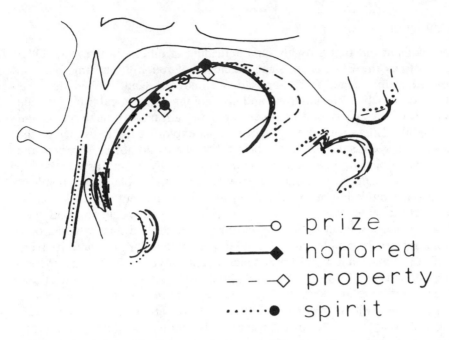

Figure 6. Vocal-tract shapes for different sounds with r-coloring (retroflexion or bunching). Note the variability in tongue, lip, and jaw positions for sounds having a similar phonetic quality. The shapes were obtained from productions of the words identified in the legend.

Summary

The changes in vocalization during the first year or so of life cannot be understood without careful consideration of anatomic development, maturation of neuromotor control and properties of the articulatory-acoustic conversion. Just as the speech apparatus and its motor control are gradually reshaped by developmental processes, so is the acoustical signal generated by this apparatus. Various changes in anatomy and neuromotor control could lead to developmental discontinuities, that is, periods of relatively rapid and marked modification of function. The same processes may explain in part individual differences in development. Certainly, a variety of factors inevitably influence speech and language development. Anatomic remodeling, articulatory-acoustic relations, and neuromotor development are just a few of these factors, but their collective impact on early vocal behavior probably has been more often under-emphasized than over-emphasized.

Discussion

Eilers pointed out that growling and squealing of infants in the stage Oller referred to as the Expansion Stage, occurred at roughly the same point in time within that stage. They opposed one another. Kent replied that was entirely reasonable. The anatomy and kinesiology of the vocal tract changed so much within that period of time that the infant had to make significant adjustments. Eilers said she thought of it as exploring the extremes of the vocal range. Kent said that might be so, but one could not be sure that the infant was employing a deliberate exploratory strategy. It was just as possible that marked changes in phonatory activity were taking place as a result of the drastic remodeling of the vocal system. Eilers did not see an inconsistency between the two positions. Two changes were occurring and they appear to be contingent upon one another. Kent replied that it would be a difficult inferential problem to separate intentional exploratory activity from the effect of anatomic conditions which might move the infant toward extremes of activity. Although bimodal phonatory activity was present, it did not necessarily follow that that activity was exploratory. The forces of change in the system might move the infant toward extremes of activity without it being necessary to hypothesize that he was exploring.

Stark said that she had always been convinced of the importance of the marked changes taking place in the anatomy of the infant vocal tract. Nevertheless, she was struck by the fact that some older, severely retarded children, who had shown normal growth of the vocal tract, were, at three to four years of age, still producing primitive sounds of the kind that she and Oller had described as characteristic of the first six months of life. Kent asked how she knew that these children had a normal vocal tract. Children with Down syndrome, for example, did not. Stark replied that she was not thinking of children with Down syndrome. In fact, these children often had relatively normal vocal development in the first year of life even though the growth of the facial skeleton was not normal in their case (Smith and Oller, in press). She was thinking instead of children with cytomegalic inclusion disease, children with porencephalic cysts and severe maldevelopment of the central nervous system. Leavitt pointed out that the overall motor control of these children had not been studied. Stark agreed. She felt that differences in development of motor control might be more important in accounting for the vocal production of some retarded children than differences in vocal tract configuration. Kent said that clearly the vocal tract did not determine output completely, and the presence of a normal vocal tract did not guarantee the development of normal speech.

Ingram and Oller both raised questions about the chronology of changes in vocal tract structure in relation to vowel production. Oller believed that the infant might be 12 months of age before he could produce a clearly definable /i/, /a/, and /u/. Kent believed that it would earlier than that (Buhr,

1980). However, he pointed out that, although the infant's vowel productions could be characterized phonetically and acoustic confirmation of the phonetic data might be obtained, one could not make assumptions about the mechanisms by which sounds were being produced. The anatomic data were still sketchy but they had to be considered in accounting for vocal behavior.

Tronick suggested that there were parallels between the development of vocalization behavior and development of hand-eye coordination. The relationship between hand and eye changed radically over the first six years of life. The distance between the eyes changed rapidly and also the length of the arm, yet the infant became a fairly skillful reacher early in life. Tronick felt that the argument that the infant is not learning skills merely because he is changing anatomically was not a very strong one. Kent replied that the importance of auditory feedback had to be kept in mind. The highly nasalized signal produced by the infant in the first three months of life was very different from adult speech. The infant indeed was confronted with a very difficult problem in speech learning which might not be parallel to the development of hand-eye coordination. He could not produce exact physical replicas of the vowels produced by adults because he had a much shorter vocal tract in which all of the resonances were shifted in comparison with those of the adults. The situation was very different from that of learning bird song. As Gottlieb (1971) had shown, chicks are capable of producing essentially veridical replicas of the adult call. Unlike the human infant, they do not have the problem of establishing acoustic equivalence classes for their own and the adult vocal calls.

Stern commented that questions about the infant's perception of speech sound contrasts now appeared much more interesting to him than previously. Kent agreed that they were of great interest. However, it was clear that infants were capable of discriminating some contrasts that they were not capable of producing. Auditory self-stimulation by the child was tied to his speech production capabilities. For that reason it was very important to know the vocal tract configuration of the infant and the articulatory-acoustic transformation.

Oller asked Kent if he felt that the schema theory he had presented accounted well for adult speech motor control but not for the vocalizations of infants whose vocal tract was changing rapidly. Kent said that he did not believe that the infant of less than three months acquired speech motor skills. There would be little point in doing so because this system was changing so drastically. Also, at this time when the musculoskeletal system was ill-adapted for speech the infant speech motor cortex had not yet developed sufficiently to undertake speech motor control. Oller agreed that these factors had to be taken into account in any attempt to explain the infant's vocal behavior, but he felt that infants were producing complex vocal behaviors even before three months of age; complex vocal behaviors that could not be predicted by Kent's system. These vocal behaviors could not be regarded as reflexive. They were not, to use Stern's term, ethologically tied and did not have obvious biological significance. Oller felt most comfortable interpreting them as having significance for speech development per se.

Kent said that he had not used the term reflexive in referring to these early vocalizations. However, he did not believe that they presented learning of a complex motor skill. Oller asked Kent to characterize these early vocalizations in terms of motor skill. Kent replied that the parallels between early vocal behavior and speech in his view simply reflected the differential neuromuscular maturation of the speech apparatus. Stark said that in one sense the foundations for skill acquisition *were* laid down in the first three months of life. Kent and Oller had referred to the quasi-resonant nasalized vowel nuclei in the vocal output of the very young infant. But, it had to be remembered that in the first three months of life, the infant gave up the obligate nasal respiration during cry. Vowel-like sounds produced during cry were fully resonant, sustained, and characterized by certain temporal rhythms quite unlike those of the vowel sounds produced in cooing. Some of these aspects of cry sounds began to be imposed upon non-cry sounds even in the first three or four months of life. This imposition appeared to occur first as the infant moved from one state to another, for example, from a comfort to a discomfort state.

Kent objected that skill acquisition could not be inferred merely from changes in behavior. He had a rather stringent definition of speech motor skill. Stark replied that she was describing a cyclical change in vocalization behavior which could be viewed as a combination and recombination of elements of behavior. It was cyclical because it occurred many times over and at different developmental levels in the first year of life. Kent said that, if cyclical or repetitive changes in behavior were to be demonstrated, one might have good reason to question their being described in terms of motor skill. Rather, these cyclicals should be viewed as reflecting the basic periodicities of the nervous system.

Kagan again said he could not understand why there was so much interest in the notion of purposiveness in early infant babbling. The neonate had erections. Were we to believe that these erections were essentially a form of practice for his heterosexual life? He noted that everyone smiled at that notion because there was clearly no basis for it. Kent's argument seemed entirely reasonable to him and there were no data to support the notion of purposiveness. Why were some of the participants entertaining, on a presuppositional basis, the notion that early behaviors were practical or useful or helpful? That was such an old-fashioned 16th century view of development—that everything had a purpose, everything had a function, nothing was wasted.

Oller replied that he did not take the view that nothing was wasted. But he had found that infants' behaviors, at least from three to six months of age, were hard to explain without assuming that infants were actively involved in their own productions. They produced sounds in ways that suggested very subtle control over their behavior, for example, in repetitive monologues or in systematically alternating sequences. Infants also made subtle responses to their environment as in imitation. They initiated interactions with adults through vocal behavior obviously to create an effect, to show off. Infants saw, for example, that when they coughed, they created amusement among adults, so they pretended to cough once again. There was often a systematic alternation, from production of a particular type of vocal behavior over and over to silence for five seconds or so during which time the infant observed the effect he had created. The silence might then be followed by a long series of productions of a different type of sound. These behaviors, taken together, seemed more complex than an erection. Kagan asked, so what did Oller want to attribute to the infant? Oller answered that he attributed involvement in the activity and selective responsiveness to outside stimulation which could not be explained merely as a simple innate propensity to make sounds. There had to be an interest in the sounds and their effects, a willingness to explore the range of possible sounds, and to adapt them for use in particular situations.

Kagan retorted that the vocal behaviors of the infant under six months of age were no more complicated than the dances of Von Frisch's bees. Did we want to attribute to Von Frisch's bees all these extra characteristics of involvement and interest and exploration that Oller was attributing to the six-month-old infant?

Oller said that he had never studied bees and did not know if they showed imitation or playful interaction. But if they did, he would agree that bees were similar to children.

Kuhl suggested that it might be appropriate to consider the song bird in terms of an appropriate animal model. The manner in which certain song birds learned their song was intriguing. There were many constraints upon its learning. For example, some, like the white crown sparrow, had to be exposed to the song of their species early in life in order to learn it. According to the characteristic time line, there were about fifty days during which the fledgling was silent. Then he began to engage in subsong, a kind of babbling. Syllables from many different dialects were produced in this babbling or subsong and finally the real song was crystallized.

What was the purpose of this subsong? Was it a form of motor practice or something that is part of a reflexive behavior? Because the white crown sparrow sings from memory one can make some interesting manipulations. Experiments by Marler (1970) and Konishi (1965) have shown that a bird deafened before exposure to the song will not sing normally. The bird can also be deafened after initial exposure so that he now has an engram or schema. These experiments have shown that the later-deafened bird does not sing in a normal way. However, he sings in a slightly more normal way than if he had been deafened at birth. The bird therefore, can be deafened at progressive times during the subsong period and it can be determined to what extent subsong is necessary for the development of the full song. In this way one can show that the more practice of song the fledgling has in this period the more the song becomes like the song of the adult white crown sparrow.

Kuhl mentioned that Nottebohm was working on a method of preventing motor practice of subsong that could be reversed. He had tried inserting small rubber sponges in the bird's syringes. The sponges may be inserted and taken out at different times, thus delaying practice or controlling specific amounts of practice. She believed these experiments would produce some very interesting findings.

Published 1981 by Elsevier North Holland, Inc.
Stark, ed.
Language Behavior in Infancy and Early Childhood

The Acquisition of Speech Motor Control: A Perspective With Directions for Research

Ronald Netsell

Human Communication Laboratories, Boys Town Institute, 555 North 30th Street, Omaha, Nebraska

Introduction

The content of this chapter will focus on *speech* production as a *motor control system,* hence the term "speech motor control" in the title. The term "acquisition" is used to designate speech production as a *motor skill.* This speech motor skill undergoes a long period of acquisition (perhaps to early adolescence), has several developmental prerequisites (especially neuroanatomic/physiologic and musculoskeletal), and is paralleled as a motor skill perhaps only by the unusual person who plays the piano entirely "by ear."

Almost all the declarative statements made in this chapter should be stated as hypotheses. However, as a convenience, the hypothetical form will be avoided for the most part. As a neophyte in the subject matter of this conference, perhaps I can be allowed to ask some of the old questions again that most of you have dealt with for years. In return, I might provide some information on speech motor control that will enhance the interpretation of existing data, condition somewhat the collection of new data, and provide the theory and model builders in language development with anatomic and physiological hypotheses to account for much of the speech behavior seen in infancy and early childhood.

In reviewing several theories of phonologic development, Ferguson and Garnica (1975) suggest that a more cohesive and unifying theory probably could be pieced together from parts of the existing ones. More important, these authors state that:

"the development of more satisfying theories of children's acquisition of phonology will come not from elaborate speculation, no matter how sophisticated linguistically, nor from large-scale data collection without reference to particular problems, but from principled investigations focused on specific hypotheses and questions of fact." (p. 176).

A corollary thesis of the present chapter is that these developmental theories would be strongly served by a solid base of *descriptive physiologic* data that underlies the speech acoustic patterns of the infant and young child. With an eye toward stimulating research in this area, the remainder of this chapter will focus on: (1) understanding *adult speech* motor control in relation to *speech acquisition;* (2) a review of *neural maturation* and *motor control* processes believed to operate in the prenatal and two-year postnatal periods; (3) speculations regarding the *neural origins* of *speech movements;* and will (4) introduce the concept of a *speech motor age;* and (5) form *hypotheses* about the *acquisition* of *speech motor control* that are both testable and requisite to a more complete theory of language development.

Adult Models and Speech Acquisition

The physical act of speaking can be viewed as a series of transformations beginning with a set of neural effector commands that control more than 100 muscle contractions. These muscle contractions move the various peripheral structures depicted in Figure 1. The movements of these structures (bones, cartilages, and muscles) in turn generate the time-continuous acoustic waveform that we perceive as speech. The primary interest of speech motor control research is to characterize the muscle forces and structure movements in terms that ultimately allow inferences about the nature of the underlying neural control mechanisms. To both the casual and long-term observer of these procedures, these are very difficult problems to solve. Figure 1 shows the representation of the peripheral speech mechanism as a set of ten functional components.[1] The movements of these semi-independent parts act to generate air pressures and air flows. The points of aerodynamic measurement, also shown in Figure 1, become valuable indices of the speech movements as well as partial sources for the generation of the speech acoustics. Together with the actual component part movements, the aerodynamic and acoustic-phonetic information probably hold the greatest promise for describing the acquisition of speech control. Undoubtedly, the age and cooperation of the particular subject will condition which types of measurement are feasible. Ideally, of course, measurements would be taken simultaneously from all levels of the speech production process.

Adult Speech Motor Control

This section is designed to acquaint the naive reader with certain properties and capabilities of the adult speech motor control system. The adult system

---

[1] A *functional component* is defined as a structure, or set of structures, used to generate or valve the speech air stream.

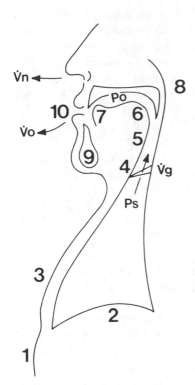

STRUCTURES

1 - abdominal muscles
2 - diaphragm
3 - ribcage
4 - larynx
5 - tongue/pharynx
6 - posterior tongue
7 - anterior tongue
8 - velopharynx
9 - jaw
10- lips

AERODYNAMICS

Ps - subglottal air pressure
Po - intraoral air pressure
V̇g - glottal air flow
V̇o - oral air flow
V̇n - nasal air flow

Figure 1. A drawing of the vocal tract that shows functional components and aerodynamic variables involved in speech production.

is of interest when considering skill acquisition because it represents the end point of the developmental continuum and, as such, contains the elegance to which the developing system aspires and can be compared. All the data on adult speech motor control are far from being in. The "hard facts" about the system properties and function are really very few. The greatest range of movement in the system is seen for the lips, tongue, and jaw and this is about 1 to 1.5 cm. Typical velocities of movement for these structures are around 10–15 cm/sec, with maximum speeds approaching 25 cm/sec. The maximum rate of syllable repetition for the adult speaker is around six per second. For example, in trying to say *pa pa pa pa* at a rate faster than about 6 cm sec, most adults will begin to fuse the lip and laryngeal movements together such that the voiceless *p* consonant becomes voiced. The physical limitation appears to be the rate at which the vocal folds can be adducted/abducted across the outgoing air stream. The laryngeal muscles have one of the few clearly reciprocal muscle arrangements in the speech mechanism; this is the muscle system used to rapidly position the folds in and out of the air stream for contrasts such as voiced/voiceless consonants. In conversational speech, these in and out motions of the folds to the midline are accomplished in about 75–100 ms. In effect, then, certain laryngeal muscles are behaving as an "articulator" in the same way as do the lips, tongue, and velopharynx. This point is emphasized here because many earlier phonologic accounts emphasized the larynx as a sound source for voicing and a frequency generator for pitch. When viewed also as an "articulation," the coordinative role of the vocal folds with the lips, tongue, etc., becomes critical, as reflected in the voice onset time (VOT) measure. Interestingly, the VOT does not reach adult-like precision until around age 11 (Kent, 1976). However, the VOT does not represent the time minima of coordination between two articulators in the adult system. For example, for various *sp* consonant strings the tongue-alveolus constriction for the *s* is never released prior to the complete lip closure for *p,* and never delays more than 10 ms in releasing after the bilabial lip seal has been completed (Kent and Moll, 1975). Thus, the adult speech system has a time minima for such coordinations as fine as 10 ms.

Another intriguing feature of the adult speech motor system is the "subconscious" manner with which speech movements are made. If normal adults hold rigid pieces between their teeth and produce the vowel *i,* their tongues will assume almost identical positions in the high-front regions of the oral cavity and they will produce nearly identical acoustic-perceptual *i* vowels without any "conscious" repositioning of the tongue. The summary of preliminary data from one such experiment is shown in Figure 2 (from Netsell, Kent, and Abbs, 1978). The left side of the figure shows superimpositions of tongue shapes for three speakers; solid lines are with the jaw free to move and dashed lines are with the upper and lower incisors separated by a 16 mm spacer. The tongue shapes on the right side of Figure 2 are referenced to the mandible and show the extent to which each subject "subconsciously" repositioned the tongue to produce the vowel *i* when the jaw was in a fixed position. An even more striking feature of this "subconscious" motor control of speech is shown in Figure 3. The same three subjects repeated the sentence "you heap my hay high happy" with the jaw free to vary and in three fixed positions. The use of this more natural language production revealed additional remarkable capabilities of the adult speech motor control system. Figure 3 contrasts upper and lower lip movements, with and without the jaw fixed, for the "heap my" segments of the test sentence. With the upper and lower incisors separated by the 16 mm spacer, the lips moved a greater distance to make the lip closure for *p.* Interestingly, they moved this distance at a greater velocity (especially the lower lip) such that the moment of lip closure was achieved in the same time interval as the control (jaw free) condition. The point of lip contact was made 5 mm lower for the jaw fixed condition. Moreover, the lip seal for the *mp* segments was maintained for the same period of time in both speaking conditions. As in

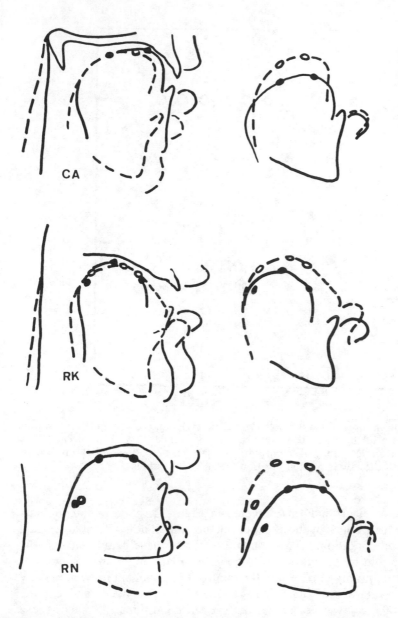

Figure 2. Mid-sagittal line drawings of the upper airway for (i) vowel productions by three adult speakers. *Left side:* superimpositions of lips, tongue, and pharynx when the jaw was free to move (solid lines) and held in a fixed position (dashed lines). *Right side:* superimpositions of tongue shapes referenced to the jaw which shows the extent of adjustment made with the tongue to achieve the similar tongue positions on the left.

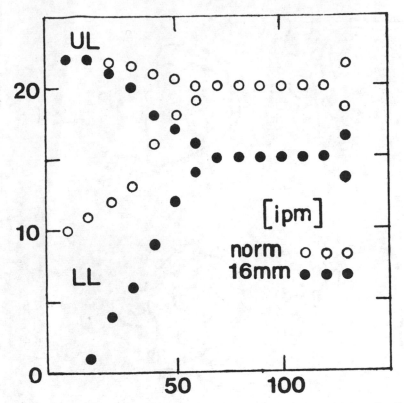

Figure 3. Time-motion displays for the upper lip (UL) and lower lip (LL) resulting from production of the *ea,* and *m* sounds in the sentence "You h*eap my* hay high happy." Open circles: lip movement with the jaw participating. Filled circles: lip movement with the jaw in a fixed position (see text for details).

the isolated vowel productions depicted in Figure 2, none of the subjects reported any awareness of these temporal and spatial adjustments recorded in the jaw fixed conditions. Further examination of these data, which is now underway, should reveal particular temporal/spatial minima in the jaw fixed conditions, i.e., points in time that the controller may deem most necessary to bring the vocal tract into a particular shape to yield the necessary acoustic equivalents of the jaw free, or normal speech conditions. As such, these temporal/spatial minima may reflect something about the motor goals of the neural control system.[2] Clearly, it would be of considerable interest to learn when children develop this level of "subconscious" control of their speech motor output. Rutherford (1967) and Hardy (1970) among others have spec-

---

[2]Further analyses of these data are currently underway in collaboration with Jerry Zimmerman of the University of Iowa.

ulated that children place their emerging speech movements under a rather direct afferent monitoring system, in which auditory and movement cues are used to help refine the positional and temporal control of the developing speech movements. At some unknown time, these more overt monitoring systems fade into a background where the child no longer "uses" them. Whether or not the children really "use" afferent cues in a "conscious" or "semiconscious" manner also is not known. If they do, it is not at all clear when they begin to produce speech unconsciously, as we adults too often do.

Speech Acquisition

The above relationships that may be used in the acquisition of speech are diagrammed in Figure 4. It is hypothesized that the normal child learns to talk by listening, watching, and imitating an external model (e.g., a parent caretaker, or another child). The model provides both auditory and visual afferent cues (AFFa and AFFv) which the child attempts to imitate with his own movements and vocalizations (shown as EFF, efferent). This EFF has two important consequences.

First, it generates the auditory patterns that return to the ears of the model and to the child himself. The latter auditory feedback closes the important motor-auditory loop shown as (1) in Figure 4. Second, EFF creates feedback associated with the speech movements and postures (AFFm + p) that the child pairs with his own auditory patterns. In essence, he hears and "feels" his speech movements as they are being developed. This right sensorimotor-auditory coupling presumably is the key to his refinement of output (EFF) to approximate the external model. By this process, the child eventually develops internal representation in his nervous system of these sensorimotor-auditory patterns.

Figure 4. A block diagram of elements hypothesized to function in the acquisition of speech motor control (see text for details).

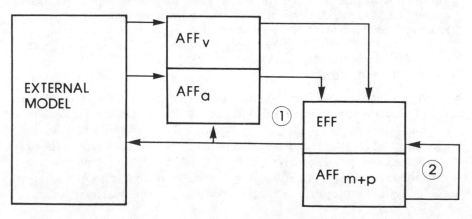

Speech as a Motor Control System

We seem no closer today than we were ten years ago to understanding or even conceptualizing the nature of speech as a motor control system (MacNeilage and Ladefoged, 1976; Kent and Minifie, 1977; Lindblom, Lubker, and Gay, 1979). Whether the system is under "open or closed loop control" or both, or whether it is "preprogrammed" and playing out a "motor tape" while oblivious to its "senses" remain matters of essential conjecture. Many researchers seem stymied as to the critical experiments to perform, but the multidisciplinary research at the Speech Motor Control Laboratories at the University of Wisconsin holds considerable promise (Abbs, Muller, Hassul, and Netsell, 1977; Abbs, 1979). Researchers of speech motor acquisition should watch closely the outcome of the above-mentioned adult experiments for cues to useful paradigms. A similar watchful eye should be kept on the "shadowing paradigms" at the Louisiana State University Medical Center (Porter, 1978; Porter and Lubker, submitted; Porter and Castellanos, submitted).

Neural Maturation and Motor Control

The temporal courses and eventual attainment of adult speech motor control seem most dependent upon the individual's nervous system maturation. The study of neural maturation is by no means a straightforward matter, and Yakovlev's (1962) distinctions between *development, growth,* and *maturation* will be used here in forming a working definition of *neural maturation.*

Definitions and Perspectives

Yakovlev depicted growth and maturation as subordinate and additive to his concept of development:

> "The development of the nervous system follows a sequence of morphological events which reflect and correlate with the changes in the internal state, outward form and dynamic relations of the organism to the environment. All these changes are subsumed in the conceptions of growth and maturation of the biological action systems. The conception of *maturation*, however, has a broader connotation of an exponential process of the progressive organization of functions and of their morphological substrata which go on through the life span of the individual . . . " (p. 3, emphasis not in the original).

Yakovlev's definition of *neural maturation* above contains both morphologic and functional components, i.e., a process of "progressive organization of functions and their morphological substrata." This definition fits well with the concept of "systemogenesis" (Anokhin, 1964). Anokhin hypothesized that motor behavior was governed by a number of "functional systems" within the nervous system. A functional system was made up of a group of nervous system structures that developed an "action-system specificity."

For example, the neuroanatomy and neurophysiology subserving swallowing would be one such functional system and that subserving speech production would be a second functional system. Given this scheme, swallowing and speech could share certain neuroanatomic structures while maintaining separate neural functional systems. These systems are said to develop on different schedules, according to the needs of the organism. Therefore, the functional system for swallowing is developed *in utero* in order that it be ready for use at birth. The functional system for speech motor control, on the other hand, is not present at birth. Indeed, as will be indicated in more detail later, it appears the neural functional system for speech is not in place until near the end of the second year of life.

Criteria for Neural and Motor Maturation

The five criteria used here in a discussion of neural maturation are myelination, axonal-dendritic growth, nerve cell proliferation, synaptogenesis, and changes in the electroencephalogram (EEG). These criteria are emphasized because of their frequent appearance in the speech and language literature. Myelination is used with the caution that many neurons may be quite functional in a given system without a myelin sheath. The more judicious use of the myelin criterion is to regard *full* myelination of a given set of neurons as evidence of full, or nearly complete maturation of that part of a "functional system." The two criteria used in this chapter to reflect motor maturation are status of the primitive reflexes (after Capute et al. 1978) and movements associated with vegetation (sucking, swallowing, chewing, etc.), sound production (crying, vocalization, verbalization, etc.), and walking.

"Critical" and "Sensitive" Periods

Clearly, embryogenesis and other fetal developments represent "critical periods" in the infant's maturation. As Ferry et al. (1979) point out:

"The concept of various critical periods in neurologic development has been proposed to indicate finite items in which specific events must occur to provide the substrate for subsequent developmental achievements. This "now-or-never" hypothesis is based upon imprinting studies in animals and psychologic studies of sensorimotor development leading to cognitive skills in children.

More recently, however, the concept has been challenged. Wolff, in 1970, suggested that child behavior depends upon the complex interaction of many biologic and environmental factors. The concept of "sensitive" periods has been proposed as an alternative, referring to periods when a child may learn particular skills more easily than others.

Based on the early precocity of brain development and the highly complex interaction between neurogenesis, synaptogenesis, and myelination as described, all phases of early brain development are critical. The most important (if not critical) period of neurologic development is the first 10 weeks of intra-uterine life, when the anatomic, physiologic, and biochemical substrates of future developmental progress are being formed." (p. 15).

One of the theses to be developed in this chapter is that the acquisition of speech motor control is a continuous but nonlinear process. "Sensitive" periods of nonlinearity occur when certain neural, musculoskeletal, environmental, and cognitive changes combine (or "get together") in the individual organism. The points in time at which a particular number of these factors combine can result in "jumps in performance" that appear incremental, if not placed on a conceptually broader map of sensorimotor and cognitive development.

Since the environmental impact upon the natural course of neural and motor maturation probably will eternally blur the "innate vs. acquired" distinction, we're basically left with the construction of "milestone maps" that chart the age ranges at which particular neuroanatomic, sensory, motor, and cognitive functions presumably are available. The paragraphs below will draw attention to particular "periods" of change in motor control in general (and speech motor control in particular) and corresponding changes in the maturation of the nervous system. Obviously no cause-effect relationships can be drawn from the temporal coincidence of reported motor control and neural maturation changes. Nevertheless, the correspondence of these neural and musculoskeletal developments will lead to a number of hypotheses that are in need of investigation.

Prenatal Period

Neural maturation. In the period of 4–10 fetal months, several basic neural structures apparently undergo considerable or nearly complete myelination including the lower motor neurons, *pre*-thalamic auditory pathways, the pre- and post-thalamic exteroceptive and proprioceptive routes, and portions of the inferior cerebellar peduncle (Figure 5).[3] Parenthetically, it should be noted that the *post*-thalamic auditory pathways do not fully myelinate until around the fourth or fifth year!

Motor control. The fetus during this time is developing a number of movement routines, some of which will be called into action as he moves at birth from the medium of water to air. Anokhin (1964) points out that the neural

[3]Figure 5 is a reproduction of LeCours (1975) "Myelogenetic" chart (taken in part from Yakovlev and Lecours, 1967). Mindful of the caution given earlier, it is assumed that the extent of myelination of the various nervous system regions is a reasonable first approximation of their functional maturation. Concurrent and subsequent accounts provide important details on other maturational criteria, but they do not result in major revisions of the Yakovlev-Lecours myelin map (Sloan, 1967; Milner, 1976; Jacobson, 1975; Lecours, 1975; Whitaker, 1976; Scheibel and Scheibel, 1976). Myelination functions are shown for 10 nervous system regions believed to play some role in the acquisition of speech motor control. The functions span the time period from the 4-month-old fetus through 15 postnatal years. Related developments are shown for certain speech and language variables (rows A–F in Figure 5).

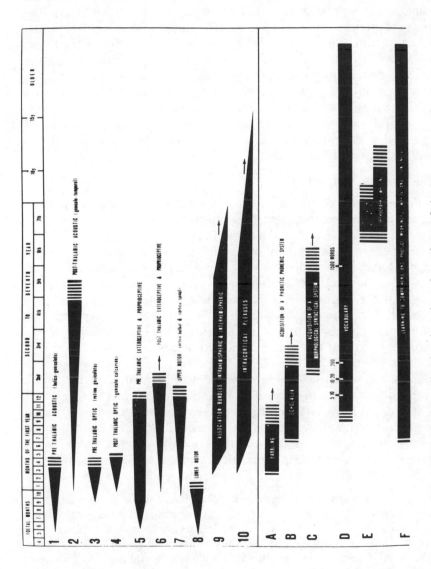

Figure 5. Table of myelination in selected portions of the nervous system (rows 1–10) and related development of certain speech and language variables (rows A–F). Reprinted from Lecours, 1975 (see text for details).

"functional systems" to support survival at birth (namely, breathing, sucking, and swallowing) are developed and fully practiced in this period. Indeed, at birth, the facial nerve connections to the lips are complete while those to other muscles of facial expression are not. The most cited studies of fetal movements are those of Hooker and Humphrey (see review in Humphrey, 1971) where responses of aborted fetuses to tactile stimuli were documented with motion picture film. Evoked fetal movements ranged from total body reactions to orofacial responses; including a sucking, swallowing, gagging, and jaw extension, among others. In this stimulus-response paradigm, even independence of lip and jaw movement was reported for the 25-week-old fetus. Although the young aborted fetus often initiates breathing, implying sufficient neural innervation of the diaphragm, it is estimated that full innervation of the respiratory system is not complete until approximately 8 months after birth (Bouhuys, 1971).

The Neonate (0–3 Months)

Neural maturation. According to the myelination charts, the major neural connections being formed and nearly completed in this period are the pre- and post-thalamic optic tracts. An important myelination with respect to sensorimotor control that begins at or near birth is of the upper motor neuron (corticospinal and corticobulbar) tracts, and post-thalamic auditory and somatosensory pathways. First evidences of myelination are also reported in this period for the middle cerebellar péduncle, corpus striatum, and frontopontine pathway. The inner cell layers of cerebral cortex (especially the primary motor and sensory areas) are fairly well developed in this period, suggesting that some of the observed newborn movement patterns are utilizing the cortical levels (Milner, 1976). However, the secondary and association areas are regarded as nonfunctional at this point, as evidenced in both axonal-dendritic connections and EEG activity (Milner, 1976; Woodruff, 1978). For the most part, primitive reflexes are obligatory in this period, and the general assumption is that they remain so until the cortical mechanisms begin to inhibit them at about three months (Capute et al., 1978). The consensus seems to be that subcortical neural mechanisms dominate in this period. Woodruff's (1978) statement is representative of this view:

> "The parallels between human and monkey development and the similar concordance between EEG alpha onset and the disappearance of primitive reflexes in both species provide evidence that normal infants are functionally subcortical organisms (Lindsley and Wicks, 1974). These authors find additional evidence for subcortical dominance in neonates in the developmental parallels between normal infants and anencephalic monsters in the first 2 months of life. Born without a cerebral cortex, anencephalic monsters do not survive more than 2 months, but while they live they show reflex development similar to the patterns of normal human infants of the same age." (p. 125).

Motor control. Corresponding to its neuroanatomic status, the visual motor system of the newborn is quite highly developed. Oculomotor control for object following and object and person recognition (implying higher levels of function) is seen within the first few weeks following birth (Wolff, 1969). The most notable motor act of the newborn for the listener is crying. The cry has its own developmental course (Wolff, 1969; Bosma, Truby, and Lind, 1965; Stark and Nathanson, 1973). It is debatable that the respiratory-laryngeal mechanics, muscle forces, and aerodynamics developed in crying are prerequisites or co-requisites to the development of respiratory-laryngeal controls used for speaking[4] (see Moyers, 1971). The forceful cries associated with pain or other distress can be generated with subglottal air pressures in excess of 60 cmH$_2$O (where values of 5–10 cmH$_2$O are used for child and adult speech) and both the rib cage and abdominal muscles contract vigorously (Bosma et al., 1965; Hixon, 1979). Acoustic-physiologic studies of infant vocalizations in "non-distress" modes probably are considerably closer to the respiratory laryngeal controls used for speech development (Wilder and Baken, 1974; Langlois and Baken, 1976; Wilder and Baken, 1978). It is not surprising that the speech-like vocalizations toward the end of this first 90 days of life are largely vocalic, nasalized, and of short duration (Wolff, 1969; Nakazima, 1975; Oller, 1978). Preliminary observations suggest the respiratory contributions to these vocalizations are made entirely in the expiratory phase of tidal breathing and without opposition of rib cage and abdominal movements (Baken, 1979; Hixon, 1979).

All sound productions of the infant indicate a rather simple function for the larynx. In terms of upper airway movements, (1) there is no indication the velopharynx is alternately opening and closing for speech, (2) the tongue and jaw move as a single piece to effect velar-like stops (with the infant reclining or on his back) or apicals (viz., da-da-da or na-na-na), (3) lip-jaw independence seldom is seen for front-of-the-mouth speech movements in this period. This lack of tongue or lip independence from jaw movements during speech-like vocalizations of this period stands in contrast to lip-jaw independence in smiling (Wolff, 1969) or tongue-lip responses independent of jaw movement in response to tactile stimuli (Weiffenbach and Thach, 1973).

In summary, the neonate appears as a rather unsophisticated sound generator (by adult standards) who may occasionally surprise himself and his other listeners with "speech" by simply opening and closing his mouth while phonating.

The Babbler (3–12 months)

As is suggested below from the review of neural and motor correlates, this may be the single most *sensitive postnatal period* with respect to the eventual acquisition of *normal speech motor control*.[5] Delays or other abnormalities that appear or remain in this period would seem to have extremely serious

---

[4]This potentially-provoking statement is discussed in a later section dealing with the neurogenics of speech production and vegetative movements (sucking, swallowing, chewing, etc.).

[5]See earlier distinction between "sensitive" and "critical" periods on page 135.

consequences in terms of building in the fundamental speech movement routines that are later refined in the overall coordination of the speech mechanism. In addition, it is a period of rather dramatic changes in the musculoskeletal system (see Kent, this volume, Chapter 5). As a consequence, the morphologic and functional plasticity of the maturing nervous system is put to test in this early period and neurological abnormalities detected here would seem to have high clinical value. Speech motor control descriptions of individual functional components (see Figure 1) and their developing coordination may prove to be a rather sensitive index of neuromotor maturation and, as such, provide diagnostic and prognostic additions to the clinical neurologic examination.

Neural maturation. Major developments occur here in pyramidal tract (corticospinal and corticobulbar) myelination as well as post-thalamic somatosensory pathways. The major development in "hard-wiring" of the middle cerebellar peduncle is formed in this period, and, the input-output at this level of the cerebellum is generally regarded as the key neural component for cerebellar function in speech motor control. In addition, the beginnings and completion of corpus striatum myelination occur in this nine-month period (see Yakovlev and Lecours, 1967) and this seems a reasonable neuroanatomic correlate for the postural and movement developments that are outlined below. Taken together, these motor corticofugal-striatal-cerebellar-thalamic-sensorimotor cortical connections are forming a network of "loops" or "circuits" that are most strongly implicated in more recent theories of fine motor control (see Desmedt, 1978, for review). Also of major importance to the development of speech motor control is the considerable myelination seen in the *post*-thalamic auditory projections. Assuming the child is forming critical "auditory-motor linkages" at this time (see Ladefoged, DeClerk, Lindau, and Papcun, 1972; MacNeilage and Ladefoged, 1976), the above neuroanatomic developments of the motor, somatosensory, and auditory systems are quite timely.

As the primitive reflex patterns remit, presumably due to cortical inhibition, clear organization in EEG activity appears (Milner, 1976; Woodruff, 1978). Using the visual system development in illustration, Bronson (quoted by Woodruff) suggests a secondary, subcortical and phylogeneteically older visual system regulates visual behavior in the first three months and is superseded by a cortically-controlled system thereafter:

"In a recent review of the literature on neonatal visual behavior, Bronson (1974) argued that newborns rely on a phylogenetically older 'subcortical' 'second visual system' in the first months of life, and it is only in the third month that the newer (cortical) 'primary visual system' dominates. Bronson (1974) contended that rather than conceiving postnatal changes in visual behavior as indicative of general improvement in the efficiency of the total system, changes in visual behavior in infancy can be interpreted in terms of underlying neural changes corresponding to the progressive development of increasingly sophisticated neural networks. Specifically, the progression involves first a subcortical system located in the superior colliculus and pulvinar, which is involved in processing stimulation falling on the more peripheral areas of the retina. This system functions to transmit information about direction of salient peripherally-located stimuli and is not capable of analyzing patterns. As development progresses, another system takes precedence. This is the primary visual system, the geniculostriate system involving foveal vision and pattern detection." (p. 125–126 in Woodruff, 1979).

In review of work by Hecox (1975), Woodruff (1978) points to parallels in development for the visual and auditory evoked potentials, VER and AER, respectively:

"Hecox presented evidence that both peripheral and central mechanisms are responsible for higher thresholds to auditory stimuli in infancy. The neurophysiological data indicated that the human infant is more sensitive to auditory stimuli at a brain stem level than had been indicated by the behavioral data. The more rostral the response is processed in the auditory system, the higher the threshold. Thus, Hecox presented new electrophysiological evidence that in the auditory system, brainstem or subcortical mechanisms mature earlier than cortical mechanisms. This provides evidence for parallel developmental patterns in auditory and visual systems and suggests that neonates operate at subcortical levels early in life." (p. 144).

Comparisons of waveform shape and peak delays for the VER, AER, and SER (somatosensory evoked response) in the infant and child would seem to hold considerable promise developing sensory maturation profiles.

Motor control. There may be a transition between the periods of the neonate and babbler that marks the onset of emergence for movement subroutines that will eventually form the efferent-afferent (auditory-movement-somatosensory feedback) substrata of adult speech motor control. We'll call this period that of the *Ya*bbler in recognition of the *yeah* sound the infant can produce by simply raising and lowering the jaw fast enough to blend the /i/ and /ae/ vowels together. The early period of the Babbler also marks the infant's initial struggle with gravity in terms of probable effects on speech production. In beginning to speak while sitting up or semi-reclining, the 3-month-old infant almost spontaneously assumes adult-like usage of rib cage and abdominal movements (Hixon, 1979). The partitions of lung volume and inspiratory/expiratory ratios used in speaking at 7 months are essentially adult-like (Baken, 1979). Baken also reports the adult-like respiratory patterns for speech are formed shortly after the child assumes the vertical alignments of the head, neck, and torso. Gravity effects are also posited to affect mandibular function, downward-forward growth of the mandible is more rapid than other craniofacial expansions (Moyers, 1971), the larynx moves markedly downward (around 4–6 months) as the mandible-hyoid-laryngeal suspension system develops, and the upper airway assumes more adult-like dimensions (see Kent, this volume, Chapter 5). The immature swallow pattern of the infant (with tongue fronting and single piece, plunger-like action of the jaw and lips) is giving way to a more mature swallow with tongue retraction and more independence of lip and jaw movement. The appearance of front teeth increases tongue retraction and lip, tongue, and jaw movements become more independent in the early stages of chewing (Fletcher, 1971; Moyers, 1971). No study was found in the literature that examined the correspondence of orofacial movements developed in feeding (and especially chewing) and the emergence of speech movement. A motion picture study of infant feeding and speech movements is in progress (Morris, 1979a).

Against this background of neural maturation, musculoskeletal growth, and vegetative orofacial development is the emergence of movements in the same peripheral structures for the motor control of speech.

In a later section of this chapter, the hypothesis is developed that the vegetative and speech movements emerge in parallel, and are not sequentially dependent. Various accounts of the acoustic-phonetic sound pattern changes in this period give clues as to the increases in speech motor skill (Nakazima, 1975; Oller, 1978; Morris, 1979b). Two to four syllables appear in a single expiration and the more typical shapes are consonant-vowel (CV), vowel-consonant (VC), and vowel-consonant-vowel (VCV). In terms of motor complexity, it should be noted that this requires only that the child start with the oral tract constricted and open it (CV), start with it open and close it (VC), or open-close-open (VCV). A parsimonious hypothesis is that through the *ya*bbling period the infant begins generating these basic syllable types by simply lowering and elevating the jaw while phonating. Somewhere between 3–9 months jaw independence from lower lip and tongue movements emerge for most normal children as inferred from reports of consonant productions such as *r, s, z, th,* and *w.* A full range of vowels and diphthongs also are developed in this period, implicating shifts and shaping of the entire tongue body. The voiced-voiceless contrast is established routinely by six months and this suggests the adductor-abductor muscles of the larynx have at least the beginnings of reciprocal action. Finer gradations of voice fundamental frequency for pitch variations in phrases of declaration and question indicate more precise control of muscle contraction (viz., *cricothyroideus*) in a non-reciprocal situation. Finally, the appearance of nasal-non-nasal contrasts /m/b/ and /n/d/ in this period signals the probability that at least gross contractions of the *palatal levator* take place. It seems reasonable to predict from the adult physiology also that the nasal contrast would developmentally precede the voicing contrast since complete or nearly complete velopharyngeal closure accompanies the voiceless consonant productions.

The Toddler (12–24 Months)

Reference to other motor milestones shows that most 12-month-olds are beginning to walk at about the time of their "first words" (Shirley, 1959). The practice of walking *or* talking seems sufficient to "tie up" all the available sensorimotor circuitry because the Toddler seldom, if ever, undertakes both activities at once. As will be developed below, this period is marked by considerable practice and refinement of speech motor skills acquired in the previous period as well as the acquisition of more and more complex speech movement patterns.

Neural maturation. A close look at Figure 5 reveals that full myelination of the *post*-thalamic somesthetic pathways is not complete for most normal children until about 18 months, also a point at which most children walk unaided. From a speech motor perspective, this final "hard wiring" of the somatosensory pathway puts the child in touch with his cerebral cortex, and motor cortex in particular, such that the emerging speech movement patterns can be practiced using the full range of the fast acting cortico-cerebellar-somatosensory-thalamo-cortico loops.[6] Myelination of the *post*-thalamic auditory pathways are continuing at a moderate rate. Considerable growth occurs in cerebral neocortex during the 12–24-month period, especially in the middle and anterior sections (Milner, 1976). Most of the layers of the cortex are vertically connected with respect to the neuraxis, and horizontal connections between association areas are just getting underway. Myelination of the cerebral commissures, which was initiated in the previous period, shows a rather marked growth in the second year, but does not near completion until about the end of the seventh year (see Yakovlev and Lecours, 1967; Milner, 1976). The rather sparse connections of the cortical association areas coupled with the myelination rate of the hemispheric connecting commissures may have been part of the rationale for Gazzaniga's hypothesis that infants are functionally "split-brained" with good interhemispheric function not being realized until age 2–3 years (Gazzaniga, 1970).

Motor control. The emergence of "words" in this period coincides nicely with (1) the completion of "hard wiring" in the major sensorimotor pathways believed to operate in speech motor control, and (2) a period of stabilization

[6]This so-called "hard-wiring" refers to the longer, larger axons that connect various centers of the nervous system; Jacobson's Class I neurons (Jacobson, 1975). Class II neurons have shorter, smaller diameter axons with less myelin and serve mainly to interconnect neurons within a particular brain region, e.g., the cerebral cortex. The "soft-wiring" of the nervous system via the Class II neurons may have innate and performance aspects; where certain synapses are genetically predetermined and others will be conditioned by particular sensory and motor experience (also see Anokhin, 1964). The full maturation of the "soft-wiring" for the speech motor control system may extend to the close of puberty.

in musculoskeletal growth. In puzzling over how the child might generate speech movement patterns for new words, the inescapable question arises as to what size of "movement units" are being developed and practiced.

Some theorists argue it is the syllable that is the basic programming unit of the speech motor command structure, others maintain these units are smaller than the syllable, while some imagine command structures as large as a phrase or sentence (see review in MacNeilage and Ladefoged, 1976). Regardless of the size of programming unit the child eventually uses in his adult nervous system, the "basic units of practice" (especially in the second year of life) appear to be words (mainly nouns) of rather motorically simple syllable structure. If locomotion practice in the early part of this period is that of the Toddler, the speech motor skill might be characterized as that of the Wobbler. By the end of this period, most normal children will have produced and practiced many times almost all of the single consonant and vowel combinations of their "mother" tongue, including some consonant blends and most diphthongs as well. The movements are slower than adults and the durations of consonant and vowel segments are more variable than the adults. This also seems a reasonable time for the child to be learning some of the *gross coordinations* between the functional components. Because the velopharynx, larynx, lips-tongue-jaw, etc., are now moving in concert, it becomes increasingly difficult to infer the functional motor skill of the individual parts by simply listening to the word productions and making some perceptual-phonetic interpretation of the acoustic output. Acoustic studies of this period will help immeasurably, but aerodynamic and movement data should prove to be even more illuminating. If some components develop skill more quickly than others, it may be that the overall coordination of the movements is timed to the less skilled members of the system.

Refinement Period (2–14 Years)

If the first 24 months of vocalization and verbalizations are thought of as a Speech Emergence Period, the time span of 2–14 years might be termed the Speech Refinement Period in terms of speech motor control. Whereas the adult listener may consider most seven-year-olds to be adult-like talkers, even the most general studies of speech acoustics show the voice onset times, formant frequencies, and fundamental frequency control are far from adult-like at this time (see review in Kent, 1976).

Neural maturation. The middle cerebral peduncle is fully myelinated around 3–4 years of age and the post-thalamic acoustic pathways at 4–5 years. The cerebral commissures complete their myelination at about 7 years while the secondary association areas continue until the third decade of life, if not longer (Milner, 1976; Yakovlev and Lecours, 1967).

Motor control. The child begins to adjust consonant and vowel durations to the number of syllables and stressed elements in a phrase or sentence at around 3–4 years of age (Kent, 1976). That is, he may be beginning to make durational adjustments of the overall motor command structure at about the time the *spatial-temporal coordination* of his speech motor control system is nearing full maturation. The term *spatial-temporal coordination* refers here to the ability to bring the individual component parts to a particular vocal tract *place or shape* at a particular point in *time* to effect critical acoustic events. For example, in producing the syllable *pa,* several structures have to be spatially coordinated at particular *points in time.* Just a few milliseconds prior to lip release for aspiration of the *p,* the velopharynx has to be sealed and the vocal folds have to be abducting, if not fully abducted. The lips, velopharynx, and larynx have to spatially coordinate at this particular time point in order for the aspirated, voiceless *p* to be acoustically realized. The thesis is that the child's earlier speech motor tasks are to build in these spatial-temporal coordinations of the vocal tract. The spatial-temporal coordination of these fundamental movement routines are made with little regard to the total time it takes to execute them or the overall length of the phrase/sentence being produced. As the child increases this spatial-temporal coordination skill, he begins to increase the overall execution speech of the motor programs, where the spatial coordination can still be maintained and the various segment durations become conditioned by the linguistic content of the productions. Partial support for this notion is found in the data and interpretation of Gilbert and Purves (1977) for consonant durations in 5- and 7-year-old children. They posit an early "articulation dominant" system followed by a "timing dominant" system (after Ohala, 1970).

Neural Origins of Speech Movements

The earlier discussion of speech motor control placed it in a unique category of human movement. The search for a particular neuroanatomy that subserves speech movements has remained essentially at the armchair level. The thesis developed in the present chapter is that the neural controls for speech movements are unique to the human and it is hypothesized that an equally particular microneuroanatomy has evolved to control those movements. A corollary to this hypothesis is that speech movements are *not* differentiations, elaborations, or any other form of refinement of more primitive or vegetative processes such as sucking, biting, chewing, or swallowing. This matter has more than theoretical interest since a number of speech therapists reportedly require their clients to practice vegetative movements as necessary prerequisites for the eventual practice of speech production (see reviews in Hixon and Hardy, 1964; Fawcus, 1969; Crickmay, 1977).

One of the central rationales for using "vegetative therapy" is that these nonspeech movements are ontogenic predecessors of speech movements. According to this notion speech is an "overlaid function" on these earlier movement patterns that are the "building blocks" from which speech movements emerge. Several lines of evidence are developed below to hypothesize that speech and vegetative movements are: (1) developed *in parallel;* and (2) subserved at least in part by *different* neuronal structures.

Embryonic Differentiation

Yakovlev (1962) uses the "principal of the three-layered structure" in his discussion of human embryologic development. The body representation in the two-week embryo is in three layers: from inside out, these are labeled the *endoderm, mesoderm,* and *ectoderm.* The internal organs and viscera will grow from the *endoderm,* the musculoskeletal system from the *mesoderm,* and the skin, sense organs, and nervous system from the *ectoderm.*

"The development of the nervous system recapitulates the three-layered plan of the body in the differentiation of neuron aggregates in the three germinal layers of the wall of hollow neuraxis, the innermost or *matrix,* the intermediate or *mantle* and the outermost or *marginal* layers, and anticipates the development of behavior in three space-referred spheres of motility from within out. The matrix layer, nearest the central hollow of the neuraxis, becomes the substratum of the homeostatic regulation of the physiological processes (changes of states) in the internal environment through a diffuse network of neurons that pervade the body and form the short reflex arcs with the peripheral ends sunk deeply in the tissues and organs of the body. The mantle or nuclear layer becomes the substratum of the postural adjustments of the body and its parts to the body itself (changes of form) in all motility of outward (overt) expression of internal states ('emotions') through the nucleated aggregates of neurons which make up longer reflex arcs with the peripheral ends buried in the body wall. The marginal or *cortical* layer, facing the world of objects and of public events about the body, becomes the substratum of translation of the private experience of living into increasing public motility-experience of effective transaction with the external environment (changes of adaptive relations) mainly through the strati-laminate neuronal aggregates of cerebral cortex making up the central ends of long reflex arcs with the peripheral ends cast out into the external environment." (Yakovlev, pp. 4–5, 1962).

From these embryologic hypotheses, it seems reasonable to surmise that the neural and musculoskeletal elements that eventually comprise the speech mechanism had their *body* origins in the ectoderm, mesoderm, and entoderm. The vegetative movements are hypothesized to have their musculoskeletal origins in the mesoderm and endoderm. The *neural* controls for speech movements are hypothesized to arise from the mantle (nuclear) and marginal (cortical) layers, whereas the neural mechanisms that eventually serve vegetative movements originate primarily in the matrix and mantle layers. In short, although the speech and vegetative movements may share certain embryonic origins (e.g., the mesoderm and entoderm of the body, and the mantle or nuclear layer of the nervous system), they also have separate body and nervous system origins in the embryo.

Myelination

There is a centrifugal growth pattern of the myelin (beginning *in utero* in the brainstem) that progresses headward and footward, mostly along a vertical axis (Milner, 1976; Whitaker, 1976). Life begins with subcortical substrate for the vegetative survival functions (i.e., breathing, sucking, and swallowing). As myelination proceeds to the head and feet, the beginnings of talking and walking, respectively, appear around the end of the first year of life.

Growth and maturation of the cerebral cortex proceeds in a centrifugal pattern and at different rates in particular areas (Milner, 1976; Yakovlev and Lecours, 1967). The primary areas of the visual, motor, somatosensory, and auditory cortices myelinate in that approximate order to complete a *vertical* "hard wiring" of the long loop, fast-acting pathways toward the end of the first year. Secondary areas and association areas myelinate in a *horizontal* direction as zones around these primary centers. These later horizontal developments are regarded as critical to the eventual development of speech and language and have no known role in the regulation of vegetative movements.

Dendritic Growth

Dendritic bundles have been recommended as storage sites for motor programs or routines (Scheibel and Scheibel, 1976; Scheibel, 1979). These bundles are clustered about cortical motoneurons as well as lower motoneurons. Scheibel and Scheibel point out that:

> "The development of these bundles appears, in some cases, to be temporarily correlated with the appearance of certain types of motor output of a stereotyped or repetitive nature, and a putative relationship has been suggested between the two. . . . The dendrite bundle appears to offer a relatively sheltered, and probably specialized, milieu where fragments or whole sequences of stereotyped or repetitive output programs may be coded along the facing membranes of dendrites sprung from the neurons supplying the muscle masses involved." (pp. 242–243).

It is hypothesized that these functional bundles appear as part of the "soft wiring" established for the explicit motor routines of speech. This "plastic" aspect of neural development for speech becomes less flexible as the particular speech movement pattern becomes ingrained. Such inflexibility to speech motor control appears toward the end of the first decade of life when the learning of a second language becomes more difficult and motor patterns of the "mother tongue" become rather fixed. The "fixing" of these speech motor patterns thus occurs at a time of "fixing" of the microneuroanatomy that subserves them.

There is an obvious chicken and egg problem here in determining if the neuroanatomy development leads the emergence of the speech movements or if the speech motor practice evoked the dendritic and axonal growth. A reasonable third hypothesis is that both genetically-determined growth and practice of the speech motor skill influence the final "hard wiring" of the speech motor control system.

The Nature of Speech and Vegetative Movements

As with the embryologic and postnatal neural development, there are certain commonalities and differences in speech and vegetative movement patterns. One common feature of both types of movement is that they are highly stereotyped and automated. This has led some people to categorize both activities as "reflexive" and this raises the issue as to whether reflexes are used in speech movements.[7] Others might contend that reflexes must be inhibited or suppressed in order for normal speech movements to occur. Again, there is a middle ground thesis to suggest we use some "reflexive" motor patterns that would be competitive with the speech movements. For example, consider the diagram in Figure 6. Stimulation to the afferent (trigeminal) nerve evokes two responses (R1 and R2) from the lip muscle (orbicularis oris). The first response is ipsilateral and occurs around 12 ms post-stimulus and runs a short peripheral loop through the lower brainstem. R1 is modulated during speech movements but the central vs. peripheral contributions to these modulations have yet to be determined (Netsell and Abbs, 1975; McClean, 1977). The second response (R2) is bilateral and has a latency of around 30–40 ms and its pathway is less certain. Some contend it runs as high as motor cortex while others maintain the longer delay reflects multiple synapses at the subcortical level (Ekbom, Jernelius, and Kugelberg, 1952).[8] In persons with certain central nervous system pathologies, R2 does not habituate to repeated stimulation and is accompanied by "reflexive" muscle contractions. Such a contraction is clearly deleterious to speech movements although some might argue that part or all of the circuitry for R2 is used for speech movements by the neurologically-normal talker.

Even though the neural commands for speech and vegetative movements might share certain elements of the schematic circuits shown in Figure 6, it is clear that the command centers have different origins *at some place* in the nervous system. From preceding discussions, it is generally assumed that the speech commands originate in the cerebral cortex and the vegetative

---

[7]*Reflex* is defined here as a highly-stereotyped response to an adequate stimulus that may or may not be modulated by repeated stimulation.

[8]The eye has R1 and R2 counterparts, with R2 being associated with the eye blink.

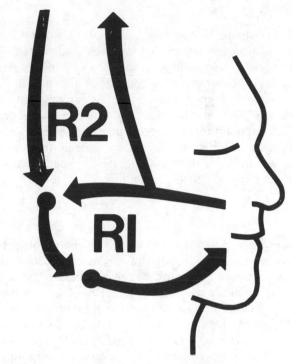

right side stimulation

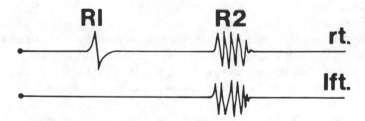

Figure 6. Schematic representation of perioral reflex circuits and the origins of their first and second responses (R1 and R2, respectively).

commands are triggered from external stimuli or subcortical neurons. Regardless of their loci, the speech and vegetative neural commands are conceived as *parallel* inputs and that would *compete* at some level of the neuraxis for the "final" effector neurons if issued *simultaneously*. It follows that the vegetative command neurons might be "inhibited" or otherwise "quieted" during speech activity.

Summing Up

Given the embryologic and postnatal neural development reviewed here, the existence of a microneuroanatomy for speech movements seems entirely plausible. Assuming there are motor analogs to the loss of sensory nerve cells due to disuse, the establishment and maintenance of the speech neuroanatomy would seem dependent upon the emergence, refinement, and practice of speech movements. The establishment and practice of vegetative movements as prerequisites or facilitators of speech movements seems counterintuitive to the hypotheses developed in this section. Indeed, the practice of vegetative movements would serve only to facilitate the vegetative synapses that must be inhibited during speech production.

Speech Motor Age

It may prove useful to develop a measure of the child's Speech Motor Age, SMA.[9] Figure 7 shows one way to represent such an age, where the individual functional components (as depicted in Figure 1) are assigned a particular month-level based upon the child's performance of selected speech motor acts. The acts were selected as a minimal set to represent increasing control of the particular part. Moreover, the speech acts or behaviors shown here are a very preliminary set, and were drawn from the existing literature which (for the most part) is based upon phonetic transcriptions. Descriptions of and criteria for these particular speech behaviors will be published elsewhere (Miller, Netsell, and Rosin, in preparation). A more comprehensive chart is being developed by Morris (1979b) that includes developmental aspects of pre-speech activities and feeding as well as vocalizations and verbalizations of the first 24 months.

A more complete Speech Motor Age chart would extend to perhaps 14 years and the long-term goal would be to include speech motor acts that captured the essence of minimal change or development in both the Speech Emergence and Speech Refinement Period. It is implicit that the "Final Chart" will be built from a large body of perceptual, acoustic, and physiologic data taken from normally-developing children. Given these data, it may be possible to assign a fairly well-defined Speech Motor Age to a child. He may show a rather uniform delay in motor development across the component parts, or he may show differential problems in controlling the parts for speech. Regardless, these speech motor profiles should prove quite useful in implicating or ruling out a neurologic component to the speech motor output, especially when coupled with electrophysiologic data on afferent system maturation and the developmental age of other motor systems.

[9]The author thanks Pamela Boren and Amy Grothman for their assistance in developing this particular chart. It appeared initially in a related representation (Miller, Rosin, and Netsell, 1979).

SPEECH MOTOR AGE

Inferences Derived from Vocal/Verbal Production

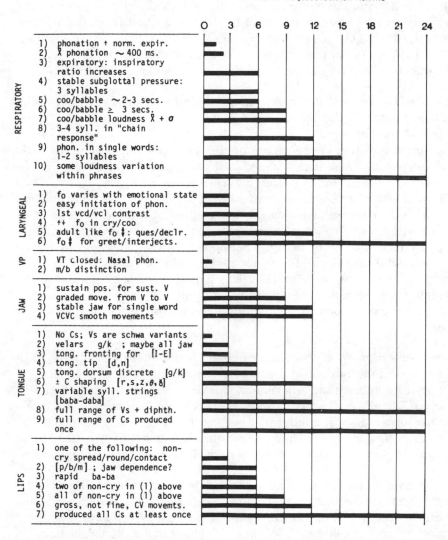

Figure 7. A preliminary chart of speech motor milestones in the first two years. Selected speech behaviors are listed for each functional component of the speech mechanism (e.g., 10 behaviors are listed for the respiratory component, six for the laryngeal component, etc.). Descriptions of each behavior and associated criteria will appear in Miller, Netsell, and Rosin (in preparation).

Hypotheses About the Acquisition of Speech Motor Control

Throughout this chapter there has been a number of implicit hypotheses about how the skill of speech motor control might be acquired. It may bore the reader and over extend the writer to summarize all those notions at this point. Considering the above, a few of the more central themes that were developed will be abstracted below. In each case, the hypothesis and any corollaries are largely unsupported by data as are hypotheses to the contrary. As such, I believe they represent important issues around which to build experiments to further our understanding of human language development.

Speech is a motor skill. *Speech* motor control is an *acquired* motor *skill.* It is *learned* through the *imitation* of *acoustic* patterns provided by an "adult *model*" of the language.

Normal acquisition of speech motor control is dependent upon the early establishment of "auditory linkages" and the somatic afferent patterns associated with the emerging speech movements and postures.

Functionally, the neonate is nearly a "subcortical, split-brain organism" in terms of the neural and movement substrate that will serve the acquisition of speech motor control. Accordingly, the vegetative sensorimotor routines used and developed in the neonatal period are *not* the "building blocks" or "neuromotor foundations" from which speech movements will emerge, differentiate, or otherwise be refined. This hypothesis does not exclude the possibility that speech motor control may not use many of the neonatal nervous system circuits or incorporate elements of certain neonatal "reflexes."

"Sensitive period." A "sensitive period" for the eventual acquisition of normal speech motor control appears in the postnatal span of 3–12 months. This period combines the crucial anatomic developments of the neural and musculoskeletal systems that subserve speech production with the emergence of discrete speech movements along the vocal tract. Failure of the infant to mature at near normal rates in this period will likely place him at risk with respect to delays or other abnormalities in speech motor control.

From spatial to temporal control. Speech motor control developed in the first 24 months is dominated by "spatial" goals in that the child is practicing placement, shaping, or movements of the component parts that yield acoustic patterns to approximate his model(s). "Spatial-temporal coordination," a "bringing together of selected structures at critical points in time", is dominant in speech motor control over a period of, perhaps, 1 to 6 years. As the child increases this spatial-temporal coordination skill, he begins to increase the overall execution speed of the motor programs, in which the spatial coordination can still be maintained and the various segment durations become conditioned by the linguistic content of the productions. This latter "temporal" period undoubtedly overlaps the "spatial-temporal" period, ranging perhaps from 3 to 11 years of chronological age.

A continuous process. The acquisition of speech motor skills is a continuous, but nonlinear process. Periods of nonlinearity occur when certain neural, musculoskeletal, environmental, and cognitive changes combine in the individual organism. One such nonlinearity occurs around 1 year of age when marked developments in speech motor control occur with the completion of "hard wiring" of the sensorimotor pathways and a stabilization of musculoskeletal growth.

Optimal behavioral intervention. It is problematic that the child uses "conscious" control of speech movements in learning to talk. He may "unconsciously" develop control of speech movements in a manner similar to the way in which adults "unconsciously" generate their speech movements. Intervention strategies that bring speech movement routines to a level of visual or kinesthetic awareness may be contrary to these more natural control processes. Optimal behavioral interventions will treat the speech motor control problem at the "level" it was learned.

From physiology to phonology. The "naturalness" of fundamental phonetic units (e.g., syllables of CV, VC, and VCV shape) are "physiologic artifacts" of the infant's speech motor capability. The speech motor capability of the first 12 months is influenced most strongly by the status of his neurosensorimotor maturation and musculoskeletal system. Similar physiologic influences on phonologic development should be sought for parsimonious explanations of language development in the second year of life. As stated by Peterson and Shoup (1966): "There is considerable reason to believe that the phonological aspects of speech are primarily organized in terms of the possibilities and constraints of the motor mechanism with which speech is produced" (p. 7).

ACKNOWLEDGMENT
The author wishes to thank Ms. Jan Jensen of the Boys Town Institute Research staff for editing the manuscript and providing many of the references cited herein. Dr. Josephine Moore (Department of Anatomy, School of Medicine at the University of South Dakota in Vermillion) provided valuable comments on an earlier draft, but is in no way responsible for any inaccuracies of this final form.

Discussion

Kuhl opened the discussion by asking for the formant structure of vowel sounds produced by adults in the bite block experiments that Netsell had described. Netsell replied that, as in a similar experiment by Abbs et al. (1977), at least the first three formants were identical for vowels produced by the subject with and without the bite block. Thus, the bite block did not introduce shortening of the vocal tract, but a movement adaptation only.

Kuhl asked what would constitute evidence refuting or supporting the practice of working to improve vegetative activity or feeding as a means of facilitating speech motor activity in the developmentally disabled child? Would it be neurophysiological data, neuroanatomic data, or behavioral data? Netsell replied that all of these classes of data would be important to consider as evidence. Kuhl then asked if there were not instances of impaired children who had paralysis or other types of malfunction of the vocal tract and, for that reason, had to be fed by some artificial means in earliest infancy. Netsell indicated that he was, himself, interested in investigating the speech motor development of such children. For example, it would be important to study the speech development of children fed from birth by a gastric tube and children who did not experience the supposed prerequisite behaviors of sucking and swallowing. Leavitt pointed out that Scott Dowling had carried out such studies. His investigation had not dealt with speech motor gestures, but, it had been found that those children who did not have normal experiences of feeding in infancy showed later abnormalities of sucking, swallowing, and other vegetative functions. The trouble with such evidence was that these children had had an extraordinarily distorted experience early in life. Generally, they were children with tracheoesophageal fistulae who had been fed by tube for many months. Other supporting evidence for a "vulnerable period" in the development of sucking and swallowing came from the infant studies of Illingworth and Lister (1964).

Stark asked about the evidence from anencephalic children. Netsell said that the data suggested that these children showed a normal course of development of vegetative functioning and primitive oral reflexes until about two months of age, if they survived that long. Oller wanted to know if their vegetative sound making activity was considered normal. Leavitt replied that he and his colleagues (Graham et al., 1977) did have some evidence from their studies of anencephalic and normal infants suggesting that the cortex did function in the first weeks of life and in an inhibitory fashion. Specifically, they found precocious responses to auditory speech-like stimuli in anencephalic infants, suggesting that processing of such stimuli takes place at lower brainstem levels. However, from very early in life the cortex interacts with lower brainstem levels in a highly complex manner.

Netsell said he believed that it was dangerous to apply such data to consideration of the motor system. He was sure that the cortex did function from very early in life in normal infancy, but to argue from that that it had a role in development of speech motor skills in the first weeks of life was, in his opinion, questionable. Stark said that in her studies of infant vocal behavior in the first eight to 15 weeks of life (Stark, 1978) she had compared the auditory (descriptive) features of vegetative sounds, cry sounds, and comfort sounds—the equivalent of gooing in Oller's system. She had found that comfort sounds, emerging between six and eight weeks of age, had some of the features of cry sounds (they were primarily voiced and were almost always produced on an outgoing breath) and some of the features of vegetative sounds (consonantal friction sounds and stops). A greater degree of control over the larynx was indicated in comfort sounds by the ability to produce voice when not under stress, that is, in a state of pleasure instead of discomfort. The primitive vegetative sounds were imposed upon comfort sounds and did not at all resemble those found in the adult (sneezing, yawning, coughing), but included brief ingressive clicks and egressive noises. Stark had always considered vegetative sounds to be reflexive, indicating neuromuscular immaturity of the vocal tract. The sounds also appeared to be related, however, to the anatomy of the infant vocal tract as described by Kent, that is, to the size of the tongue in relation to the oral cavity and to the relative size and the angle of the epiglottis. It was noteworthy that these vegetative sounds decreased in frequency of occurrence at about three months of age, that is, at the time when the downward and forward growth of the face and change in the height of the larynx was greatest. The sounds however, had a high frequency of occurrence in the infant of less than three months and appeared to be associated with protection of the upper airway. They probably reflected release and resumption of tongue-palate and tongue-epiglottic contact. If making and breaking of the contact coincided with pleasure voicing, then friction noises and stops were superimposed upon voicing in comfort sounds. These consonantal noises occurred at the initiation of comfort sounds, in the middle of comfort sounds, or at their termination.

Stark did not regard these data as offering support for the practice of training vegetative (feeding) behavior as a prerequisite for facilitation of speech development. She felt that this therapeutic practice was not well founded.

in competition with one another for access to the final common path in the motor system, so that one must be inhibited if the other was to find the expression, then it was interesting that the adult was able to speak and eat the same time (in defiance of polite custom).

He believed that the ability to chew and to talk simultaneously was learned and was not found in the infant. Instead, the infant was preoccupied with chewing or talking, just as he did not walk and talk at the same time in the first year of life. Stark indicated that, while it was generally true that infants did not produce the more advanced vocal behaviors of which they were capable while feeding, they *did* produce partially voiced sounds at six to seven months of age during bottle feeding and, if the spoon or the nipple were withheld during feeding, they would make protest noises upon which anticipatory feeding movements were again imposed.

Kent suggested that these issues be considered in relation to the development of myelination. There were two arguments with respect to this development: (1) that it was effected in accordance with a genetic plan; (2) it was to some extent responsive to the frequency of neurotransmission along a nerve fiber. If that were true, then there was a sense in which vegetative actions might contribute to later voluntary motor control. That is, there might be preferential myelination of nerve fibers along those pathways that were used in early reflexive vocalizations. This preferential myelination might explain some of the apparent phonetic or motor continuities of vocal activity. It might then be that early sucking or chewing activities predisposed the infant to motor control of a different type as applied to the same musculature.

Netsell replied that if Scheibel and Scheibel were correct in their description of the development of dendritic bundles as a consequence of particular types of motor activity, then vegetative circuits were integrated as vegetative activities developed and speech motor circuits were developed as speech motor skills were practiced. Kent said he was referring to the peripheral nervous system. Netsell said that the development of peripheral hardwiring which both motor systems shared was facilitated by swallowing even *in utero*. To the extent that the peripheral circuitry was shared by both systems, then, vegetative activity might be considered as providing a basis for later speech acquisition.

Published 1981 by Elsevier North Holland, Inc.
Stark, ed.
Language Behavior in Infancy and Early Childhood

Primitive Reflexes: A Factor in Nonverbal Language in Early Infancy

Arnold J. Capute, Bruce K. Shapiro, Frederick B. Palmer, Pasquale J. Accardo, and Renee C. Wachtel

The Johns Hopkins University School of Medicine, The John F. Kennedy Institute, Baltimore, Maryland

Primitive reflexes are movement patterns which initially develop during gestation, are present in the newborn, and are readily elicited during the first half year of life. They gradually diminish during the second six months as cerebral maturation progresses.

Abnormalities of primitive reflexes, either in degree or rate of disappearance, may result in failure of normal motor development. Abnormalities of degree/duration may inhibit the appearance of righting and equilibrium responses which normally develop in the second six months. In cerebral palsied patients, reflexes persist to an excessive degree and far beyond the normal time of disappearance. This phenomenon is quite familiar to physical therapists treating cerebral palsied children with neurodevelopmental techniques.

There is confusion about primitive reflexes in the cerebral palsy literature. Various authors define reflexes differently; many authors only consider reflexes in isolation. Despite this confusion, there is a need to define primitive reflexes in a clinically useful fashion. Several preliminary studies (Paine et al. 1964; Bleck, 1975) have attempted to relate primitive reflexes to later motor outcome. Little is known about those with minor deviations and less is known about the interplay of reflexes in determining motor function in children. Thus, a more refined quantitation is required not only to predict motor outcome in the handicapped, but also as a means of monitoring normal motor development.

*Supported by Grant No. MC-R-240392-01-0, Maternal and Child Health Service, U.S. Department of Health, Education, and Welfare.

The Clinical Research Unit of the John F. Kennedy Institute for Handicapped Children is presently studying the development of seven primitive reflexes and their interrelationships. Our study group felt that these reflexes were very influential in the motor development of cerebral palsied children. A profile of seven reflexes are being graded on a five-point scale (0–4+) (Capute, Accardo, Vining, Rubenstein, and Harryman, 1978) in an effort to develop a standardized instrument which can be used with children from birth until two years of age. With such a tool, we hope to accomplish the early detection of several groups of children, namely:

1. Children whose profile is not normal and who are thus at "high risk" for motor involvement.
2. Children who demonstrate a constellation of reflexes which may preclude a specific motor act.
3. Children who have cerebral palsy.
4. Children who may have mild brain damage which manifests itself as cerebral dysfunction and perceptual problems without necessarily having significant motor difficulty.

A well standardized Primitive Reflex Profile will give therapists and physicians a much needed rating system; such a quantitative scale will also be of use when classifying cerebral palsy. The constellation of reflexes and equilibrium reactions necessary to perform specific tasks has even greater import for the motor handicapped children than the normal, for such a profile may be used to define reasonable goals of therapy.

The seven primitive reflexes being studied are:

1. The Moro Reflex (M).
2. The Galant Reflex (G).
3. The Tonic Labyrinthine Reflex (Supine) (TLS) and (Prone) (TLP).
4. The Asymmetrical Tonic Neck Reflex (ATNR).
5. The Symmetric Tonic Neck Reflex (STNR).
6. The Positive Supporting Reflex (PS).
7. Segmental Rolling (SR).

Thus far, over 400 infants have been enrolled in the project from birth and are being followed for a two- to three-year period. During this time, a developmental pediatrician is scoring a Primitive Reflex Profile examination at each well-baby visit. At one year of age, the Bayley Scales of Infant Development are administered, and if normal, these children are followed another year. If the Bayley is abnormal or suspect, it is repeated at two years and if it is again abnormal or if the infant has a motor deficit, the children are followed until age three years.

The initial findings on the first 120 children are restricted to the area of walking. As Figure 1 shows, there is a correlation between the primitive reflex profile and walking in normal children. One will note that children

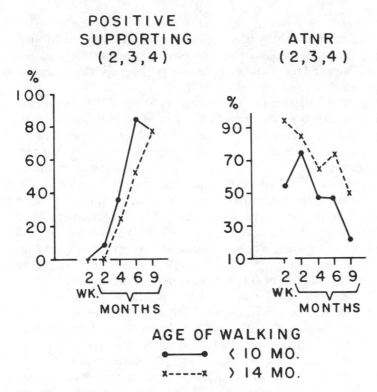

Figure 1. The correlation of primitive reflexes and walking (normal children). This figure shows the cumulative percentages of visible (2, 3, 4) Primitive Reflexes in an early walking group (≤10 months) vs. a later walking group (≥14 months).

who are walking earlier have primitive reflexes that disappear sooner. Those who are late walkers have primitive reflexes which persist. Further analysis of the total group will be undertaken to weigh the contribution of individual reflexes to walking, and thereby, define the profile necessary for achievement of walking. Similar analysis will also attempt to correlate subgroups of reflexes with specific motor actions such as rolling, crawling, sitting, etc.

Since it is believed that early intervention may alter oral-motor patterns thereby resulting in better articulation and speech production, speech pathologists have become interested in primitive reflexes (particularly oropharyngeal reflexes). Thus far, it appears as though none of the above noted reflexes significantly affect oral-motor movements or positioning with one possible exception, the Tonic Labyrinthine Reflex in supine position (TLS). In the TLS, head extension to 45° stimulates the otoliths resulting in a mild tongue thrust which is short lived. However, in the cerebral palsied child, this maneuver may result in grossly exaggerated adder-like movements of the tongue which interfere with suckling and swallowing. The tongue thrust is significantly reduced by bringing the head to neutral (or flexing the neck to 45°) thereby placing the otoliths in a neutral position. Occupational therapists and some speech pathologists believe that by overcoming this response and enhancing suckling and feeding, better speech production will ultimately result. This is presently unproven.

Nonverbal or gesture language of early infancy is being studied in relation to maternal-child interaction. A complete knowledge of primitive reflexes is essential to prevent misinterpretations of upper extremity motion. Professionals studying gesture language of early infancy need to be cognizant that the extremity responses are greatly influenced by the position of the head. At this age, the infant is "locked into" automatic responses. That this is true is well demonstrated by two primitive reflexes, the asymmetrical tonic neck (ATNR), and the tonic labyrinthine (TLS). The asymmetrical tonic neck reflex, or fencing reflex, is determined by the baby's head position with extension of the two extremities on the chin side and flexion of the extremities on the occipital side. One can easily misinterpret a visible ATNR for willful pushing away of the mother. The TLS also determines the position of the extremities; with extension of the neck stimulating the otoliths, there is retraction of the shoulders and extension of the trunk and legs. In some babies, it may be associated with arching of the back away from the mother and difficult feeding because of tongue thrusting. A damaged baby with excessive reflexes may be seen as "rejecting" if the true nature of the movement is not appreciated. If finger, hand, or arm movements are being observed during the first three months of life, the head should be in the neutral midline position to minimize the effects of primitive reflexes. The baby's state is also of importance in assessing early gestures; a sudden noise may well stimulate the Moro response with extension and abduction of the upper extremities along with semi-flexion of the elbows, wrists, and fingers with each thumb and second finger forming a "C" position. This has been felt to represent an attempt to embrace the mother in response to a frightening stimulus: the volitional aspect of the embrace is questionable (Mitchell, 1960). Early gesture language must be interpreted within the context of overall motor development, proceeding in a cephalocaudal direction: voluntary control of head and eye movements being followed by head movements in combination with upper extremities and finally involving trunk and lower extremities.

The study of the language development of infants has become respectable. Much remains to be learned about mechanisms of neural control and the implications for speech development. Even more remains to be learned about therapeutic implications for abnormally functioning neural mechanisms. It is essential that those studying such mechanisms remember that speech and language development of early infancy is intimately tied to other aspects of development and cannot be viewed in isolation.

ACKNOWLEDGMENTS
The participation of Harvey P. Katz, M.D., the staff of the Columbia Medical Plan, and Leroy Bernstein, M.D. is gratefully acknowledged. This paper was supported by Grant No. MC-R-240392-01-0, Maternal and Child Health Service, U.S. Department of Health, Education, and Welfare.

Discussion

Netsell referred to a theory of motor control proposed by Easton (1972), who worked with the activity of walking as his model. Easton suggested that in walking the individual used his central nervous system as a means of controlling lower-level postural reflexes, such that in walking the individual was like a puppeteer managing strings of reflexes. Netsell wanted to know whether or not the primitive and postural reflexes might reappear in adult patients with head trauma. Capute answered that many of the reflexes were protective in nature. Some people believed that these reflexes found expression in the postures assumed by athletes. That might or might not be the case, but certainly the reflexes were under inhibitory control in a normal adult. They did reappear in cases of head trauma and acquired neurological diseases. Netsell asked if the character of these reflexes was the same in the adult with head trauma and in the normally developing infant. Capute answered that that was essentially true. The cerebrum was largely an inhibitory organ controlling the brainstem where many of the reflexes he had discussed were mediated. It was believed that, in cases of injury to the cerebrum, the brainstem might be released from inhibitory control and that primitive reflexes would then reappear. These reflexes might also disappear again as the individual recovered from head trauma. They were the same reflexes as were found in very young infants.

Capute added that oral and pharyngeal reflexes were less well understood, partly because it was very difficult for different observers to agree about the exact nature and manifestation of these reflexes or about how best to elicit them. Because of this lack of agreement, these oral and pharyngeal reflexes could not yet be subjected to ratings or other forms of measurement.

B. Speech Perception: Developmental and Methodological Considerations

Published 1981 by Elsevier North Holland, Inc.
Stark, ed.
Language Behavior in Infancy and Early Childhood

Auditory Category Formation and Developmental Speech Perception

Patricia K. Kuhl

Department of Speech and Hearing Sciences and Child Development and Mental Retardation Center, University of Washington, Seattle, Washington

Historical Perspectives

There are many reasons why extensive research in the 70's centered on the young infant's auditory abilities. Clinical concerns have led to attempts to determine auditory thresholds for very young infants (see Wilson, 1978, for recent review), although, other than threshold measurement, we have little data describing basic psychoacoustic abilities such as acuity measures for frequency and intensity.

Another set of concerns, largely theoretical as opposed to clinical, led to the extensive study of speech-sound discrimination in young infants. Begun only a decade ago with the publication of the Eimas et al. (1971) classic paper on categorical perception, the field has produced some 40 studies that are either abstracted or published in the archival literature (see Kuhl, 1979a, for a current listing of studies and that paper as well as Morse, 1978, and Eilers, in press, for general reviews of the literature). Based largely on the high-amplitude sucking technique (Eimas et al., 1971), the data demonstrate that very young normal infants (4 to 16 weeks of age) discriminate many of the acoustic cues underlying speech-sound distinctions. That is, infants discriminate consonants that differ with respect to voicing (Eimas et al., 1971) and place of articulation (Morse, 1972; Eimas, 1974a); they discriminate among fricatives (Eilers and Minifie, 1975) and liquids (Eimas, 1975a). The tempo of spectral change, which for the adult is sufficient to cue a change in the manner of articulation, say from plosive to semi-vowel (Liberman et al., 1956), is also discriminable by the young infant (Hillenbrand, Minifie, and Edwards, 1977). Some of these contrasts have also been tested in the medial and final positions of syllables (Jusczyk, 1977; Jusczyk and Thompson, 1978; Jusczyk, Copan, and Thompson, 1978). Trehub (1973) demonstrated that infants discriminate between spectrally-dissimilar (/a/ vs. /i/; /i/ vs. /u/) vowels; Swoboda, Morse, and Leavitt (1976) demonstrated that infants also discriminate between spectrally-similar vowels (/i/ vs. /I/). The list of negative findings is relatively short. Other than for certain fricatives (Eilers 1977) and stimuli in which the discriminable contrast is embedded within the syllable (/atapa/ vs. /ataba/; /mapa/ vs. /pama/) (Trehub, 1973), no negative findings for speech-sound contrasts that are phonemic in English have been reported, and no studies which attempt to replicate the above-mentioned failures have been published.

One could summarize these data, then, as providing strong evidence that very young infants (1 to 4 months of age) have sufficient auditory acuity to discriminate the acoustic differences which distinguish many, perhaps all, of the phonemic categories of English when they are represented by canonical consonant-vowel (CV) syllables. This is an important conclusion because, if the infant's auditory capabilities were not sufficiently good to perceive the appropriate differences among stimuli, the infant would have an extremely difficult time attempting to learn language.

In addition to the ability to perceive the relevant *differences* between stimuli, however, the infant's attempts to learn language would be aided by the perception of *similarity* or *equivalence* between certain stimuli. To explain why the perception of similarity may be of interest, we have to develop a perspective on the formation of auditory categories.

Current Issues: Formation of Auditory Categories

Category Centers and Category Boundaries

A central theme in perceptual psychology relates to the study of perceptual groupings. Just as the field of vision has attempted to explain the perceptual recognition of patterns or of size and shape constancy, the field of audition has attempted to explain auditory pattern perception and speech-sound constancy. Each discipline has examined the extent to which changes in the physical parameters of a stimulus can be related to a change, or a lack of change, in its perceived attributes. Similarly, each field has been impressed (and baffled) by the difficulty involved in the identification of the critical stimulus information that underlies perceptual groupings, largely because of the extreme variation in the physical parameters of objects or events in the world that look or sound similar to a viewer or listener.

The study of categorization for speech sounds has focused on two rather different phenomena (Kuhl, 1978). One approach has been the extensive work on the perception of the *boundaries* between categories indicative of studies on categorical perception. Studies of categorical perception involve a highly restricted and narrowly defined set of conditions for testing the discrimination and identification of stimuli (Studdert-Kennedy et al., 1970). They involve the use of computer-synthesized stimuli in which one set of acoustic cues considered to be sufficient to distinguish between two phonetic categories are varied in step-wise fashion to create a continuum of sounds; all other non-criterial dimensions, such as fundamental frequency, intensity, and duration, are held constant. The evidence for categorical perception derives from the fact that, under these testing conditions, a listener's ability to discriminate among variants along the continuum is considerably better for any two stimuli that straddle the boundary between the two categories than it is for any two stimuli that are equally distant on the continuum but that both form part of a single phonetic category (see Kuhl, in press, for a current discussion).

The other approach has been to attempt to define the set of acoustic cues that underlie the perception of similarities (constancy) for any group of exemplars, all belonging to the same phonetic category. These studies involve the acoustic analysis of many different naturally produced or synthetically produced exemplars representing a category. In this approach, the non-criterial acoustic dimensions, such as the phonetic context and the position in an utterance or the talker who utters the token, are allowed to vary, thus producing wide variation in the physical representations of the acoustic cues that are considered to be critical to a particular phonetic distinction.

Both of these approaches tap a listener's proclivity to form acoustic categories: categorical perception studies assess the perceived discontinuities or boundaries between categories; perceptual constancy studies are aimed more at defining the category centers, the prototypes which best fit the description of the category. Categorical perception has been widely studied, but the study of constancy has been discouraged largely by a set of early descriptive studies which failed to identify invariant acoustic correlates to perceived categories (Liberman et al., 1967). Recent studies (see review in Kuhl, in press), however, represent renewed interest in this approach, adopting the position that much of the difficulty that has been experienced in identifying invariant acoustic cues for phonetic categories stems from a lack of information concerning the way in which the peripheral auditory system transforms complex signals like speech. Thus, more recent approaches have relied on psychoacoustic data to create speech-analysis programs which mimic peripheral auditory processing. These cochlear-modeling approaches (Blumstein and Stevens, 1979; Searle, Jacobson, and Rayment, 1979) have been more successful at identifying invariant acoustic cues for speech sounds.

Infant Data Categorical Perception Experiments

While infant listeners cannot provide labels for stimuli in an experiment, they can be tested in a discrimination paradigm such as that provided by the high-amplitude sucking technique. Studies in which pairs of stimuli were drawn from a synthetic speech-sound continuum demonstrated that infants discriminated two stimuli when they were labeled differently by adult listeners, but did not discriminate between stimuli that were labeled similarly by adult listeners. These data were taken as support for the notion that infants perceived the synthetic speech stimuli in ways that resembled the categorical perception demonstrated in adult listeners. These findings were first shown for a voiced-voiceless (/ba-pa/) continuum (Eimas et al., 1971); subsequently the same results were demonstrated for a place of articulation (/dae-gae/) continuum (Eimas, 1974a) and a liquid (/ra-la/) continuum (Eimas, 1975a).

These studies led to the conclusion that, like adult listeners, infant listeners are particularly sensitive to small differences between sound stimuli, particularly when those differences serve to separate adult-defined phonetic categories. That infants should do so is extremely relevant to their linguistic development, since the infant appears to perceive a natural perceptual discontinuity between acoustic events that will come to signal significant (meaningful) differences between words.

One of the important questions not answered sufficiently by the data is whether the human infant at some early age demonstrates these perceptual discontinuities for *all* phonetic distinctions, even those not relevant to the linguistic environment in which the infant is being raised. If it were the case that the infant demonstrated the effect for a universal set of phonetic distinctions, then one would argue that due to the lack of exposure to certain phonetic units (those phonetic units not utilized by the language) during development, the infant loses the ability to distinguish them as contrasting phonetic elements (Eimas, 1975b). In other words, this line of inquiry suggests that infants have innate mechanisms enabling them to perceive all the possible phonetic distinctions of natural languages. In the course of development, however, they lose the ability to perceive contrasts not relevant to their language community while maintaining the ability to distinguish among those that are relevant to the language they eventually will learn.

This is a complex issue because it requires, first, the demonstration that very young infants, regardless of their linguistic environments, behave similarly—demonstrating these boundary effects for contrasts that are used in their linguistic environments and for other contrasts that are not used in their environments. Second, this theoretical posture requires the demonstration that infants from different linguistic environments behave differently at some point in time, demonstrating an effect of linguistic exposure. The data gathered to date loosely support such claims, but the data are not without contradiction. The evidence is fairly convincing that infants under four months of age, reared in non-English-speaking environments, are capable of discriminating at least one phonetic contrast (voiceless unaspirated /pa/ from voiceless aspirated /pʰa/) that is phonemic in English but not in the infant's native language. Streeter (1976) demonstrated that 2-month-old African Kikuyu infants discriminated the English contrast, in addition to discriminating a voicing contrast that is phonemic in the Kikuyu language but not in English (prevoiced /ba/ from voiceless unaspirated /pa/). Lasky, Syrdal-Lasky, and Klein (1975) demonstrated similar results for Spanish infants using a heart-rate technique to measure responses.

However, the case for discrimination of the prevoiced /ba/ from the voiceless unaspirated /pa/ by American infants under four months of age is not quite as clear. Eimas (1975b) failed to provide evidence that American infants discriminated pairs of stimuli that are as close on the continuum as those discriminated by the Spanish and Kikuyu infants. As Kuhl and Miller (1978) note, however, there are a number of problems with these cross-language comparisons. First, the stimuli are synthesized to manipulate an acoustic cue that is acoustically fragile, and is likely to be subject to variation due to the differences in acoustic calibration across laboratories. A recent set of studies applied this approach to the study of older infants. Using the head-turn technique, Eilers, Wilson, and Moore (1979) and Eilers, Gavin, and Wilson (1979) tested 6-month-old American and Spanish infants in the same laboratory and demonstrated that while both groups perceived the English contrast, only the Spanish infants discriminated the Spanish contrast.

Eilers, Gavin, and Wilson (1979) would attribute the superiority of the Spanish infants on the Spanish contrast at 6 months of age to linguistic exposure, but, in the absence of data demonstrating that American infants do discriminate the contrast at an earlier age (say, under 4 months of age), the story is far from complete. Using a more sensitive technique, Aslin et al. (1979 showed that 6-month-old American infants are capable of discriminating the Spanish contrast using a tracking procedure. But, these authors have not to date tested Spanish infants to see if the Spanish infants would in some way demonstrate a superior ability to do so by 6 months of age.

In summary, both the demonstrations of similar perceptual tendencies by very young infants from different linguistic environments, and the demonstrations of increasingly dissimilar perceptual tendencies by older infants from different linguistic environments (presumably due to linguistic exposure), are incomplete. These areas will remain important target areas of research in the future.

Perceptual Constancy: The Study of Perceptual Similarity

General Considerations

However extensive the data on speech-sound perception by infants may be, we have little information concerning an infant's perception of phonetic similarity for phonemes which appear in different phonetic contexts, different positions in a syllable, or are spoken by different talkers. We might expect this kind of task to present quite a different set of problems for the infant than the typical discrimination task.

Gibson (1969) describes perceptual constancy as involving at least two processes. First, a listener must discover and focus on the acoustic dimension relevant to the particular phonetic distinction. This may be relatively easy when the phonetic context and the talker are held constant as in the typical experiments described above in which single tokens from each of two phonetic categories are to be discriminated (Eimas et al., 1971; Morse, 1972; Eimas, 1974a; Eilers and Minifie, 1975; Swoboda, Morse, and Leavitt, 1976; Eilers, Wilson, and Moore, 1977). But when a variety of tokens representing a phonetic distinction are used, the critical cues vary and the listener must abstract a cue that is common to the set. One would predict from this that the discovery of a set of abstract configurational properties or attributes that typify a phonetic category would depend upon the appropriate or sufficient exposure to a set of exemplars of that phonetic category, exemplars that differ with respect to phonetic context and talker.

The second process related to the perception of constancy is a concomitant of the first. When the phonetic context and the talker are varied, acoustically-prominent but phonetically irrelevant acoustic dimensions are introduced. For the infant to recognize that /di/ and /du/ are somehow similar, she/he must ignore the most prominent difference between them, that is, the vowel. The fundamental frequency and timbre differences between the voices of different talkers, and the pitch contour of the utterances, are other prominent acoustic characteristics that a listener must ignore when categorizing phonetically since these dimensions do not provide critical information concerning the phonetic identification of the stimulus.

These two processes—abstracting the critical dimensions that typify a phonetic category and, at the same time, ignoring other prominent but irrelevant dimensions—have been discussed in the literature on visual perception. There is some evidence in this literature to suggest that some aspects of these two processes improve with age. It has been shown, for example, that infants become increasingly adept at focusing their attention on the critical aspects of a stimulus array. A study of eye movements directed at an unfamiliar design that must be remembered demonstrated that 3-year-olds keep their eyes fixed on a single spot longer and do not systematically explore figures, while 6-year-olds orient to the distinctive features employing brief and frequent gazes and systematically exploring the figure (Zinchenko, van Chzhi-Tsin, and Tarakonov, 1963). Vurpillot (1968) studied the eye movements of children between 5 and 9 years of age in a same-different comparison task. The data from the study supported the notion that skill in scanning systematically and in sampling the relevant features increases with age.

The notion that infants become increasingly selective in their visual attention carries with it the implication that infants become more adept at filtering out irrelevant information. Evidence from experiments on incidental learning support this notion. Gibson (1969) reported experiments run by herself and colleagues on form identification in 5-year-old preschoolers. The task was simply to learn the names of nine Roman capital letters of the alphabet. When presented during the learning sessions, the letters were colored—3 were red, 3 blue, and 3 yellow; these colors, of course, did not differentiate the letters uniquely, but served as an irrelevant dimension. After practice sessions, the children were asked to identify the same 9 forms that were now colored black. In addition, they were tested for recall of the color of each of the forms. Gibson reported that the children remembered correctly as many, or more, colors than they did the names of the letters, even though color was an irrelevant dimension in this experiment. The experiment was repeated with 9-year-olds using artificial graphemes rather than letters. The task was identical. For these children, recall of the names of the graphemes had improved slightly; but more importantly, color was recalled at a level no better than chance. Some children did not even remember what colors had been presented. In a related experiment, Maccoby and Hagen (1965) presented 6 picture cards, each with a distinctively colored background, to first through seventh grade children. Subjects were instructed to remember the order of the colors presented. After repeated trials on color identification, the subjects were asked to recall the picture that had appeared on each one of the colors. The results demonstrated that recall on the main task increases steadily with age, but that first through fifth graders recalled the correct picture significantly more often than seventh graders, even though it was an irrelevant dimension.

In summary, Gibson concludes that there is evidence to suggest that the ability to seek out the invariant information in a stimulus array is a developmental phenomenon. Both the tendency for greater efficiency at picking up the invariant information in a stimulus array, as well as the increasing tendency to filter out irrelevant information, contributes to this gradual approach to perceptual economy.

Two Early Studies

Only recently have researchers attempted to find out whether infants are capable of recognizing the similarity among sounds that have the same phonetic label when the sounds occur in different phonetic contexts, in different positions in a syllable, or when they are spoken by different talkers. Fodor, Garrett, and Brill (1975) examined the acquisition of a head-turn response for visual reinforcement in 14- to 18-week-old infants under two stimulus conditions. In both conditions, three syllables were randomly presented (/pi/, /ka/, /pu/) but only two of the three were reinforced. In one condition, the stimuli being reinforced were phonetically related (/pi/ and /pu/); in the other condition, the stimuli being reinforced were not phonetically related (/pi/ and /ka/). The hypothesis tested was as follows: if infants tend to hear the similarity between two syllables that begin with the same consonant, in spite of the differences in the acoustic cues for that consonant and in spite of the irrelevant differences between the two syllables that must be ignored (like their vowels), then their tendencies to learn the association ought to differ in the two conditions. The results showed that the proportion of head turns obtained from the infants when phonetically similar sounds were reinforced was significantly greater than the proportion of head turns obtained when phonetically dissimilar sounds were reinforced.

These data demonstrated that the infants group the syllables beginning with /p/ more readily than they grouped the syllables that did not share a phonetic feature. But the data also demonstrated that neither task was accomplished very accurately. Two factors may have made the task inordinately difficult. First, observations in our own laboratory on the audiometric testing of infants has demonstrated to us that until 5½ months of age, a large percentage of infants do not make volitional head-turn responses for a visual reinforcer with ease. At 5½ months, or older, infants make head-turn responses easily and 90–95% of the infants are conditionable when an easy contrast is tested. Second, the task was very difficult; it involved a two-response differentiation. That is, a head turn either to the right or to the left was required (two different responses) depending on the loudspeaker from which the reinforced stimulus was presented.

Kuhl and Miller (1975a) began a systematic exploration of the infant's predispositions to form acoustic categories that were based on shared phonetic features. The perception of vowel categories seemed an appropriate place to begin. The earliest descriptions of the acoustic cues which govern vowel identity were relatively straightforward. Vowel perception is directly related to the location of formants on the frequency axis, and two or three formants are sufficient to computer-synthesize the full complement of English vowels (Delattre, Liberman, and Cooper, 1951). However, in natural speech, the vowel nucleus is coarticulated with one or more consonants and, in rapid speech, a steady-state value is rarely achieved (Lindblom, 1963). In addition, the acoustic properties of the vowel nucleus are influenced by the coarticulated consonants (House and Fairbanks, 1953; Stevens and House, 1963). Assuming a constant vocal-tract length, the formant frequencies directly reflect the resonances created as the configuration of the vocal tract changes for different vowels (Stevens and House, 1961). But most importantly, a dramatic variation in formant frequency occurs when the overall dimensions of the vocal tract are changed. Thus, when the identical vowel is produced by a male, a female, and a child, the formant frequencies are quite different (Peterson and Barney, 1952). Furthermore, these changes in overall vocal-tract dimensions, such as vocal-tract length, are not proportional (Fant, 1960), so that the resulting formant frequencies are not related in a multiplicative way such as in the transposition of a melody (Ward, 1970). Fant (1973) has demonstrated that the scale factor relating the formants produced by a male, a female, and a child is not constant across vowels or across formants within a particular vowel. In other words, there is no constant relationship between the formants spoken by different talkers. Still, formant locations can be described as the invariant cues which allow the adult listener to perceive the similarity among vowels.

These facts led a number of theorists to hypothesize that listeners perceive vowel identity by calibrating or normalizing each utterance, that is, by referencing it to a coordinate system based on that talker's extreme articulations (Joos, 1948; Gerstman, 1968; Lieberman, 1973). Experimental tests of the notion that listeners require exposure to a talker's "calibrating vowels" in order to correctly identify other vowels spoken by that talker have not been supported (Shankweiler, Strange, and Verbrugge, 1977). In fact, there is no evidence that the identification of vowels can be improved by presenting the calibrating vowels prior to the target vowel (Verbrugge, Strange, and Shankweiler, 1974). Our understanding of how vowels are perceived remains unclear.

As a preliminary step toward testing perceptual constancy in infants, Kuhl and Miller (1975a) asked whether 4- to 16-week-old infants could detect a change in a target dimension if an irrelevant dimension was randomly varied throughout the experiment serving as a kind of distracting stimulus. The high-amplitude-sucking paradigm was employed. A change in the target dimension occurred at the shift-point, but the irrelevant dimension was randomly varied throughout both the pre- and post-shift periods.

In one condition, the target dimension was a phonemic change in the vowel and the irrelevant dimension was the pitch contour of the vowel; in a second condition, the target dimension was the pitch contour of the vowel and the irrelevant dimension was the vowel color. The choice of pitch contour as a distracting acoustic dimension is particularly appropriate given that the literature is replete with suggestions that suprasegmental dimensions such as pitch contour, loudness, and stress pattern are more salient than segmental (phonetic) dimensions at this young age (Crystal, 1973). The stimuli were two /a/'s and two /i/'s synthesized such that one /a/ and one /i/ had identical monotone pitch contours, and one /a/ and one /i/ had identical rise-fall pitch contours. Discrimination of vowel color and pitch contour targets was tested *with* and *without* irrelevant variation (distracting stimulus) in the other dimension.

The data demonstrated that infants detected a vowel change, that is, discriminated the two vowels, regardless of the distraction imposed by the random changes in the pitch contour of the vowels. In contrast, infants detected a change in the pitch contour of the vowel only when all other dimensions were held constant; they failed to respond to a pitch contour change when the vowel color was randomly changed. In addition, infants responded for a significantly longer period of time before habituating (pre-shift) when the vowel color was constantly changing, than when the pitch contour was constantly changing. Using these stimuli, it would appear that the vowel-color dimension captured the infant's attention more readily than the pitch contour, both when pitch contour was the target and when it served as the distractor. This research demonstrated the infant's ability to tolerate some degree of distraction and still make the phonetic discrimination, but it did not demonstrate the infant's ability to recognize the phonetic similarity among vowel tokens when the talker producing the vowels was varied. Furthermore, this study did not support the notion that suprasegmental dimensions are more salient at this age.

In order to extend these results to a situation in which the infant had to contend with variation in both the critical and noncritical dimensions of the signals, Kuhl (1979b) combined the use of a head-turn technique for visual reinforcement with an experimental format that required the infant to recognize the similarity among tokens in a category. Research using this format is described below.

Methods for Testing Auditory Category Formation with Infants: The Head-Turn Technique

Many laboratories have attempted to develop a head-turn technique for use in speech-sound discrimination testing but, until recently, no one had described a technique that had been extensively tested and found to work with a large number of infants. This technique was originally developed for assessing auditory thresholds by a team of clinical audiologists at the University of Washington in Seattle (Wilson, Moore, and Thompson, 1976). Later, the technique was adapted by Eilers, Wilson, and Moore (1977) to study speech-sound discrimination. In the Eilers, Wilson, and Moore study, infants were trained to make a head turn whenever a speech sound, repeated once every second as a background stimulus, was changed to a comparison speech sound. A head turn which occurred during the presentation of the comparison stimulus was rewarded with the presentation of a visual stimulus, for example, a toy monkey that would clap cymbals when activated.

Two types of trials, change trials and control trials, are run. During a change trial, the stimulus is actually changed from one speech sound to another speech sound for the duration of the observation interval (typically 4–6 seconds). During control trials of the same length, the sound is not changed. For both types of trials, the experimenter and the assistant report whether or not a head turn has occurred during the specified observation interval. If both judges report that a head turn has occurred on a change trial, the trial is scored as correct; if one or neither reports a head turn, an error is scored. During a control trial, if either judge reports a head turn, the trial is scored as an error; if neither reports a head turn, the trial is scored as correct. Eilers, Wilson, and Moore accepted a criterion of at least 5 out of 6 correct responses in 6 consecutive trials, half of which were change trials and half of which were control trials, as evidence that the infant discriminated the comparison stimulus from the background.

The experimental-control suite is shown in Figure 1. The infant is held by a parent so that she/he faces an Assistant. The Assistant maintains the infant's attention at midline or directly in front of the Assistant by manipulating a variety of silent toys. A loudspeaker is located at a 90° azimuth to the Assistant; the visual reinforcer is placed directly in front of the loudspeaker. A toy animal is housed in a dark plexiglass box so that the animal is not visible until the lights mounted inside the box are illuminated. The Experimenter is housed in an adjoining control room which contains a tape deck and a logic device. The two speech sounds being tested are stored on two separate channels and on each channel the sound repeats once every 1–2 sec, depending on the specific experiment.

Figure 1. Experimental/control suite for the head-turn experiments. The reinforcer is located 90° to the left of the Assistant, approximately 5 feet from the infant. (Reprinted from Kuhl, 1979b.)

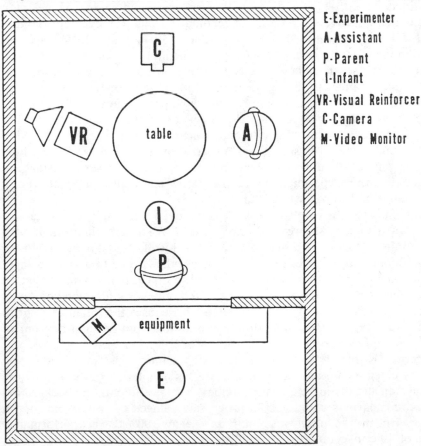

E-Experimenter
A-Assistant
P-Parent
I-Infant
VR-Visual Reinforcer
C-Camera
M-Video Monitor

The basic technique has been improved in two ways since it was originally described (Eilers, Wilson, and Moore, 1977). First, the logic device controlling the experiment is more sophisticated. In a recent modification of the technique (Kuhl, 1979b), the logic device contains a probability generator; the state of the probability generator determines whether a change trial or a control trial will be run. In this way, when the Experimenter begins a trial by depressing a start button, she/he has no control over the type of trial that will be run. This ensures that the Experimenter cannot inadvertently (or otherwise) start change trials when the infant is visually engaged by the toys. The logic device also times the trial interval, records both the Experimenter's and the Assistant's votes, scores the trial, activates the reinforcer when it is appropriate, records the latency of the infant's head-turn response, and prints all of the above data for each trial. This automatic recording system allows one to assess the agreement of the two judges.

The second improvement in the technique consists of a number of added experimental controls, in addition to those necessitated by the change in the logic, which improve the validity of technique. This improvement (Hillenbrand, Minifie, and Edwards, 1977; Aslin et al., 1979; Kuhl, 1979b) requires that both the mother and the Assistant wear headphones and listen to music throughout the session; the intensity level of the music is adjusted to mask the stimulus change. In this way, neither the mother nor the Assistant can differentially change their behavior during change or control trials. Mothers do not know when trials occur. The Assistant is informed that a trial is occurring by a small vibrating pin that is located on the vote button held in the Assistant's hand, but she/he is unaware of the type of trial. These added controls achieve a situation in which both the mother and the Assistant are "blind," and the Experimenter does not know ahead of time what type of trial, change or control, will be run.

The technique has been successfully employed with infants as young as 5½ months (Wilson, Moore, and Thompson, 1976) and as old as 18 months of age (Eilers, Wilson, and Moore, 1977). It is ideally suited to infants in the 5½ to 10-month age range. Beyond this age, infants tend to be increasingly restless, and they become wise with regard to object permanence. That is, the 10-month-old appears to realize that the monkey is still in the box, even if the lights are out and it cannot be seen; this causes the infant to want to peer in the box. For a six-month-old, the notion "out of sight and out of mind" still appears to hold.

Recently, Kuhl (1979b) adapted the basic technique just described to test auditory category formation in infants. In this adaptation of the technique, Kuhl systematically increased the number of tokens in both the background and the comparison categories in progressive stages of an experiment. In this experiment, the infant was required to achieve 90% correct performance (9 out of 10 consecutive trials, half of which are change trials and half of which are control trials) at each stage before advancing to the next stage.

The extent to which the infant's learned responses to single tokens from a phonetic category generalized to novel tokens from the same phonetic category, was evidence that the infant recognizes the similarity among speech tokens sharing a common phonetic feature despite the many ways in which the tokens differ acoustically.

Table 1 describes the stimuli in the background category and in the comparison category for each of five stages in the /a/ vs. /i/ category formation experiment (Kuhl, 1979b). In each category, the number of vowels is increased until the two ensembles include six different tokens spoken by three different talkers (male, female, and child) each with two different pitch contours (rise and rise-fall). In the initial training stage of the experiment, each of the two categories is represented by a single token; these two tokens are matched in every detail except for the critical cues which differentiate the two categories. In stage two, the pitch contour of the vowels in both categories is randomly changed from rise to rise-fall. The pitch-contour variation stage was included for two reasons: first, this stage could provide the infant with a cognitive set regarding the rules of this experimental "game." That is, category formation requires a certain mental set, the infant has to recognize that she/he is to group stimuli together based on their similarities, even though the stimuli differ in acoustically prominent ways. The pitch-contour variation ought to provide this mental set, and also serve as proof that the infant is capable of auditory category formation. A failure

Table 1. The Stimulus Ensembles for the Background and Comparison Categories for All Five Stages of the /a/ vs. /i/ Experiment. The Talker and Pitch Contour Values for Each Stimulus Are Given in Parentheses (from Kuhl, 1979b).

Experimtental Stages	Background	Comparison
Conditioning	/a/ (Male, fall)	/i/ (Male, fall)
Initial training	/a/ (Male, fall)	/i/ (Male, fall)
Pitch variation	/a/ (Male, fall)	/i/ (Male, fall)
	/a/ (Male, rise)	/i/ (Male, rise)
Talker variation	/a/ (Male, fall)	/i/ (Male, fall)
	/a/ (Female, fall)	/i/ (Female, fall)
Talker × pitch variation	/a/ (Male, fall)	/i/ (Male, fall)
	/a/ (Male, rise)	/i/ (Male, rise)
	/a/ (Female, fall)	/i/ (Female, fall)
	/a/ (Female, rise)	/i/ (Female, rise)
Entire ensemble	/a/ (Male, fall)	/i/ (Male, fall)
	/a/ (Male, rise)	/i/ (Male, rise)
	/a/ (Female, fall)	/i/ (Female, fall)
	/a/ (Female, rise)	/i/ (Female, rise)
	/a/ (Child, fall)	/i/ (Child, fall)
	/a/ (Child, rise)	/i/ (Child, rise)

to generalize to new talkers, then, could not be attributed to an inability to form auditory categories.

In stage three, the talker producing the vowels is randomly varied between the male voice and the female voice. In stage four, both talkers produce the vowels with a randomly-changing pitch contour. In the final stage, the child's voice (computer synthesized), also with pitch-contour variations, is added to the ensemble bringing the total number of tokens in each category to six (3 talkers × 2 pitch contours).

The criterion for progressing from one stage of the experiment to the next is 9 out of 10 consecutive trials correct, 5 of which are change trials and 5 of which are control trials. No more than 3 trials of one kind (either change or control) are allowed to occur consecutively. Typically, 25 trials are run each day in a 20-minute session. However, sessions were always terminated when an infant began to fuss or not attend to the Assistant's toys. If, on the other hand, an infant was doing well, the session was extended. Infants were tested on consecutive days whenever that was possible.

The data resulting from this /a/ vs. /i/ category-formation task (Kuhl, 1979b) can be seen in Table 2. The number of trials to reach criterion performance is shown for 4 subjects. The data demonstrate that fairly rapid acquisition of the head-turning response occurred; all 4 subjects met the conditioning criterion within the first 22 trials. Second, and more importantly, the infants demonstrated rapid transfer-of-learning from the training token to the novel exemplars of /a/ and /i/, and the conditions of pitch, talker, and pitch × talker variation.

In a second experiment reported by Kuhl (1979b), six-month-old infants were trained on the /a/ and /i/ tokens produced by the male talker, and then immediately presented with each of the novel tokens in the category. These data are shown for 8 subjects in Figure 2. The histograms represent the percentage of head-turn responses that were made to each of the tokens in

Table 2. Trials to Criterion for Each Condition of the /a/ vs. /i/ Experiment for Each Subject. The Session in Which the Criterion Was Met is Listed in Parentheses (from Kuhl, 1979b).

Condition	S_1	S_2	S_3	S_4	$\bar{X}$
Conditioning	12 (1)	13 (1)	5 (1)	9 (1)	9.75
Initial training	23 (2)	14 (1)	32 (2)	13 (1)	20.5
Pitch variation	11 (2)	11 (2)	10 (2)	15 (1)	11.75
Talker variation	10 (3)	10 (2)	10 (2)	14 (2)	11.0
Talker × pitch variation	10 (4)	29 (3)	10 (3)	18 (2)	16.75
Entire ensemble	10 (4)	29 (4)	22 (4)	19 (3)	20.0
Total trials to complete	76	106	89	88	89.75
Total days to complete	4	4	4	3	3.75

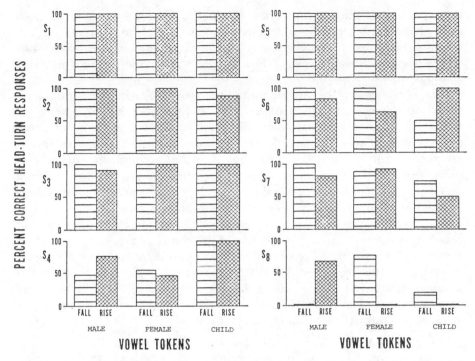

Figure 2. Individual-subject data representing the percentage of correct head-turn responses which occurred during all change trials for each of the six stimuli presented during the /a/ vs. /i/ category-formation experiment. (Reprinted from Kuhl, 1979b.)

the reinforced category (either /a/ or /i/). The data demonstrate that the infants produced reliable head-turn responses that were made to each of the tokens in the reinforced category (either /a/ or /i/). The data also demonstrate that the infants produced reliable head-turn responses to each of the novel tokens in these categories.

Other examples of category-formation for phonetic categories include the studies of fricative categories, such as /sa/ vs. /ʃa/ (Holmberg, Morgan, and Kuhl, 1977), and categories based on a suprasegmental acoustic cue, pitch contour (Kuhl and Hillenbrand, 1979).

Conclusion

General Comments

These results on the perception of constancy by young normal infants demonstrate their capability to recognize the abstract dimensions of sound in a task that has a considerable cognitive load. In order to complete the task, the infant must be capable of abstracting a criterial dimension that allows the separation of the two categories. In order to do so, the infant must ignore very prominent but irrelevant dimensions such as pitch contour, talkers, and vowel context, as well as constantly monitor the signal and recall the rules of the game (something like, "turn to see the monkey when the sound changes from /a/ to /i/, no matter who says it or how it is said").

The advantages of this testing format are obvious. Since the multi-dimensional stimulus sets can be grouped according to a number of dimensions, including segmental (vowel color, for example) as well as suprasegmental (intonation contour, for example) features, one can test the relative ease or efficiency an infant displays at forming acoustic categories based on these dimensions; in this way, one can assess their relative acoustic salience, and determine whether an infant's auditory proclivities to form categories change with maturation and/or exposure to a particular language.

These techniques may provide valuable information concerning the theoretical issues most critical to the field of developmental speech perception. But there is an additional reason why these experiments may be of interest. If run properly, they allow the infant to tell us how they choose to cut up auditory space. In essence, this technique for studying category formation allows one to identify the infant's "sorting rules" for the separation of auditory stimuli. An illustration may explain:

> In order to convince ourselves that the infants in the category-formation experiments were doing what we thought they were doing (i.e., "sorting" the sounds into two perceptual categories) rather than something else (like simply memorizing the set of stimuli that were reinforced), we began running what we called "random-category" experiments. In these studies, the stimulus ensembles were randomly assigned to one of two categories, one reinforced category and a second non-reinforced category. Since no criterial dimension predicted the set of stimuli to be reinforced, we expected that infants could only succeed by memorizing the set of stimuli that were reinforced and the set that were not reinforced, producing head-turn responses accordingly. We expected infants to fail at this task and they did, but in doing so they gave evidence of attempting to formulate a rule which predicted the occurrence of the reinforcer. For example, if the first stimulus that was reinforced happened to be produced by a female talker, and the first non-reinforced sound by a male talker, the infants demonstrated the tendency to produce head-turn responses to all stimuli produced by female talkers. In other words, they demonstrated the tendency to generalize their learning to novel stimuli that shared a single property with the reinforced stimulus. In so doing, these infants provide additional evidence concerning the dimensions of sound that are most easily used as sorting rules. In addition, the data add credibility to the general argument that infants are "natural" sorters. The fact that they are should make coping with the world an easier task. For example, we know that infants at this age can also use pitch contour as a sorting rule (Kuhl and Hillenbrand, 1979). The pitch contours we used were typical of those used by adult talkers producing interrogative vs. declarative statements to other adults. One would predict, then, that infants could use the more extensive pitch contours typical of "motherese" (Fernald

and Simon, 1977) as a sorting rule to separate the caretaker's utterances from the utterances of other speakers. Experiments testing such a premise are now underway.

This particular orientation is appealing because, despite the extensive effort by a large number of individuals, one cannot help but feel when reviewing the infant perception literature, that the field of infant auditory perception has somehow failed to capture the essence of audition from the infant's point of view. That is, no one has concentrated on how the infant uses his/her auditory abilities to cope with living. The approach that has been missing is the one taken by ethologists, who ask how the infant of a species uses its sensory capabilities to survive. These questions are not "better" than those addressed in the past, but they are different, and they might lead to the formation of a theory of developmental auditory perception, one which integrates how evolution has provided the infant with solutions to communicating in the world.

Discussion

Questions about the signal salience of particular acoustic dimensions arose in the discussion of Kuhl's paper as well as Eilers'. In discussing these questions, Kuhl referred to signal salience with different species of mammal and within different human cultures. With respect to species-specific capabilities, she referred first to the Japanese macaque monkey. The vocalization of these monkeys had been categorized by Green (1975) who developed a taxonomy of ten different categories as well as within-category variation. In experiments at the Kresge Hearing Research Laboratory (Petersen et al., 1978; Zoloth et al., 1979), the monkeys were trained to "port" these stimuli perceptually by using certain features, such as the localization of pitch peaks in what Green called "smooth early highs" and "smooth late highs." It was found that after the animal was trained to respond to natural tokens from each of these classes, they were able to transfer their learning experience, that is, to generalize to other tokens within that class with great ease. However, if they were required to respond to the same stimuli on the basis of some other dimension, such as the average pitch, then the Japanese monkeys did very poorly indeed. Another monkey, the Nemestrena, did very well in the average pitch classification experiment.

Bloom asked how well the human infant was likely to do in responding to the stimuli appropriate for Japanese macaque monkeys. Kuhl said she had not tried that experiment, but thought that since infants had good reason to pay attention to pitch contour, they would do very well on such a task. She pointed out that there might be basic guidelines that would be applicable to all mammalian species, and others that would be specific only to certain species. As Leavitt had pointed out, there were great similarities with respect to the auditory system across mammalian species.

With respect to human cultural differences, voicing contrast for Spanish- and English-learning infants had already been mentioned. Another example was provided by infants exposed to a tone language, such as Mandarin Chinese. This dimension might become more salient for the infant learning a tone language than an infant learning a language such as English. Kuhl also mentioned the relevance to the question of signal salience of the work of one of her students, James Hillenbrand. Hillenbrand had shown that normal infants were able to differentiate, within the VRISD paradigm, between plosives and nasals. However, when the reinforcement contingencies were changed, such that no rule governed the formation of perceptual categories which were random, the infants were unable to sort stimuli into these categories. It was presumed that the infants, in order to succeed, would have to memorize the entries belonging in each arbitrarily formed category, a task that would be beyond them. In fact, their performance indicated that they did sometimes attempt to develop strategies for dealing with the task or to discover a rule for responding. For example, infants always turned to a stimulus for which a head turn was first reinforced in the experiment. They might also, however, turn to another stimulus that was not reinforced because it shared an acoustic dimension with the first stimulus that *was* reinforced. Kuhl thought that experiments such as these might be very valuable in indicating those features which the infants noticed most, those that had most salience for them. Kuhl thought that an approach based upon this finding might be even more revealing than the original memory experiment that had been designed.

Oller suggested another possible interpretation of the results of Hillenbrand's experiment. It might be that it is easier for the baby to handle a simple test than a more complicated one. In other words, it is easier for him to find a feature and use it to form a class than to memorize a group of complex stimuli. Oller suggested an alternative follow up study in which, instead of setting up random categories following the phonetic discrimination task (of nasals vs. plosives), a task based upon differences in nasal murmur characteristics or other within-class differences that are not used contrastively in the English language might be employed. The nasal murmur difference might then be of a kind considered salient from an acoustic structure point of view. It would provide another approach to the question of signal salience. Kuhl thought that Oller's suggested variant of the experiment was a sensible one to try. The approach might be to construct synthetic speech exemplars along certain dimensions in order to find out the criteria that infants employed when sorting them into groups. She thought that some exemplars were inherently better than others, that they were better representatives of a category or better prototypes, and therefore formed a category center. She thought, for example, that there must be an ideal stimulus that characterized the alveolar stop. Although stops vary with vowel context as well as other features, such as the sex of the speaker, she thought that there was a natural prototypic alveolar stop. She would like to find out if it was one single dimension or a group of dimensions that provided essential descriptors for the category center. She believed that, from a speech perception theory standpoint, this was a really important question.

Leavitt thought that perception in infants must be multi-dimensional. Kuhl referred to Marler's work (Marler and Peters, in press) and to his argument that simple dimensions were important earlier in development. She cited the example of the red spot on the herring gull's beak that the chick responded to first, thus setting in motion the development of an entire schema. Stern reminded her that reanalysis of these data had suggested that the chick was responding first to the movement of an object in the visual field in a certain orientation and contrasting it with the background in certain ways. This movement later became associated with the red spot on the beak which in itself constituted a later-acquired schema. He thought that if Kuhl could examine the infant's capabilities earlier in life, which of course was not possible with the VRISD paradigm, then she might find more atomistic responses. Kuhl said that she and her colleagues had thought of using evoked potential measures, specifically measures of the late components of the averaged evoked potential waveform, to auditory stimuli as a means of studying the importance of stimulus dimensions in infants. Components which were thought to be sensitive to habituation could then be studied early in life. Examples of features which might be presented to the infant in single dimension experiments were rise time characteristics, stop bursts, and nasal murmurs.

Kagan recalled a paper by Kearsley (1973) in which responses of neonates were studied. Kearsley had found that certain combinations of auditory features, for example, pitch rise time and dB level, were more effective in eliciting responses than either feature presented alone. This finding suggested that a single dimension was unlikely to be as powerful in eliciting a response as a multi-dimensional stimulus. Kuhl thought that this argument was certainly worth considering, especially since dimensions did not occur singly in the natural world, but rather in combination with one another. However, she felt that in some signals, for example, motherese, something simple like the very large excursions of fundamental frequency contour might first separate perceptually mother's speech to the infant from mother's speech not addressed to the infant. Once the fundamental dichotomy was formed, mother's speech-to-infant versus mother's speech-to-adult, then the mother's speech might begin to be associated perceptually with many other properties. Kagan thought that this simple guideline certainly offered a very good starting point.

Published 1981 by Elsevier North Holland, Inc.
Stark, ed.
Language Behavior in Infancy and Early Childhood

The Evaluation of Infant Speech Perception Skills: Statistical Techniques and Theory Development

Rebecca E. Eilers and William J. Gavin

Mailman Center for Child Development, University of Miami, Florida

Introduction

The area of infant speech perception is undoubtedly deeply involved in its own infancy. Although there has been a proliferation of data and progress has been made in the area of paradigm development, we are still relatively naive concerning normal development and even more so about abnormal development. In the areas with which this text is most concerned, that is, individual differences, continuities, and discontinuities of development and deviant development, little is known. Consequently this paper is organized in two parts; the first is a review of a decade of research, selecting work which bears most heavily on issues of development and which individual differences and differences between children and age groups to a theoretical view of infant perception; the second is a reevaluation of methodological issues which have clouded interpretation of infant perception data. The first section will include the presentation of an interactive-pragmatic model of infant speech perception. The second section will address some recurring statistical issues which have interfered with attempts to interpret cross-study data. Finally, a method of analysis will be provided within which individual differences and differences between children and age groups can be evaluated.

Section I: Theory Development
The bulk of research in infant speech perception involves testing of discriminability to phonemic contrasts. Rather than beginning this review with a listing of discriminable contrasts (the reader is referred to other reviews which provide information on the breadth of research, including Morse, in

press; Trehub, Bull, and Schneider, in press; and Eilers, in press), it would seem more fruitful to examine infant skills from the perspective of more general theoretical considerations. Some of the theoretical work reviewed in this paper is landmark in nature and naturally interpretations of results have changed somewhat with the benefit of hindsight.

A. The "Phonetic Innateness" Theory

The phonetic innateness theory of infant speech perception proposed by Eimas (1975a) has opened several important areas of investigation of speech perceptual abilities in infancy. In part, the importance of the theory resides in the fact that it can be directly tested. The following axioms, although not stated by Eimas exactly as shown below, may be derived from the phonetic innateness model:

1. Infants are able, at birth or shortly after, to discriminate between minimally different classes of phonetic elements which represent common phonemic categories in the languages of the world.
2. Infant speech perception approximates categorical perception.
3. Listening experience is not an important factor in determining whether or not phonetic elements can be discriminated from one another.
4. Categorical perception is a result of the functioning of physiological feature detectors similar to those found in the human visual systems (Blakemore and Campbell, 1969; McCollough, 1965).
5. Categorical perception occurs in a linguistic mode.

These points will be addressed one at a time.

Initial support for the phonetic innateness model was presented by Eimas et al. (1971), who demonstrated that very young infants discriminate voicing contrasts in a manner thought to be analogous to categorical perception in adults (see Liberman et al., 1967; Mattingly et al., 1971; Abramson and Lisker, 1970). Eimas et al. (1971) found that infants were able to discriminate voicing contrasts (/ba/ and /pa/) which are contrastive in English but did not provide evidence of discrimination of other pairs, equally distant along the voicing dimension but non-phonemic in English. Further support for the phonetic innateness view was provided by evidence of categorical-like discrimination of place of articulation contrasts (Eimas, 1974a; Miller and Morse, 1976; Till, 1976) and liquid (/r/ and /l/) contrasts (Eimas, 1975c).

Although the data mentioned have proven extremely reliable and replicable using a variety of experimental paradigms, several more recent works have thrown a different light on the interpretation of innateness theory, the role of listening experience, phonetic feature detectors, the phenomenon of categorical perception and its relationship to linguistic processing.

The first area of evidence which contradicts an axiom of the phonetic innateness hypothesis is evidence concerning difficult-to-discriminate contrasts. The phonetic innateness theory predicts (axiom one) that infants should be able to discriminate common phonetic contrasts. While it is difficult if not impossible to gather evidence which "proves" that infants *cannot* discriminate a given contrast, it is possible to show that some contrasts are more difficult to discriminate than others. Butterfield and Cairns (1974) and and Morse (1974) review data from the heart rate and sucking paradigms (see below for description) citing evidence from Eimas (1975) and Moffitt (personal communication) and note that little if any evidence of discrimination was found in English-learning one-to-four month-olds in the prevoiced (that is, lead) region of the voice onset time (VOT) continuum despite the fact that stimuli from a wide range of VOT values were employed. Similar results for six-month-olds using a head-turning procedure (VRISD) (in which 6 trials were presented per subject and 5 out of 6 correct was accepted as evidence of discrimination) were reported by Eilers, Wilson, and Moore (1979) for a variety of prevoiced labial contrasts. Further, with a contrast differing only in voice-onset time, computer synthesized /du/ vs. /tu/, Eilers et al. (1980), failed to demonstrate evidence of discrimination by six-month-olds using a version of the VRISD paradigm. These same infants did provide evidence of discrimination of synthetically and naturally produced /ba/ vs. /pa/ and naturally produced /du/ vs. /tu/. These synthetic /du/ and /tu/ stimuli were similar to lead boundary stimuli in that only voice onset time differed within the stimulus pair.

In a preliminary report using a head-turn procedure, Aslin et al. (1979) suggest that some infants may provide evidence of discrimination of a lead VOT contrast. Two things are noteworthy of this last result: (1) a technique was employed that is rather rigorous for an infant, typically demanding 50 to 75 trials, so that only a small number were tested along the lead VOT range; (2) the authors themselves note "discrimination in the voicing lead region is more difficult than discrimination in the voicing lag region" for these infants. Thus, the majority of evidence suggests that one major phonemic contrast, foreign to English, is discriminated by English-learning infants only with great difficulty, if at all.

In addition to stimuli differing in voice onset time, the presentation of other stimuli to infants has resulted in failure to show evidence of discrimination. Eilers and Minifie (1975) failed to obtain evidence of discrimination of /sa/ vs. /za/ while obtaining evidence of discrimination of /sa/ vs. /va/ and /sa/ vs. /ʃa/ in one- to four-month-olds. Further, Eilers (1977) demonstrated that some aspects of perception are context-sensitive (evidence of discrimination was not found for /sa/ − /za/ but was found for /as/ − /a:z/). Eilers, Wilson, and Moore (1977), using the head-turn paradigm and a five out of six criterion for 6- to 8- and 12- to 14-month-old infants, found developmental changes in discrimination. Even the oldest infants had difficulty demonstrating discrimination of the English contrast /fa/ − /θa/. In a later study using similar /fa/ − / θa/ stimuli, Holmberg, Morgan, and Kuhl (1977), using a floating criterion of 8 out of 10 correct responses, found infants met initial training criterion within 68 trials on the average. These data have often been interpreted to suggest that the /fa/ − /θa/ contrast is difficult, but discriminable given enough trials (see Jusczyk, in press).

Further perceptual difficulties of infants were reported by Trehub (1976) who found that infants' perception was limited by the temporal frame in which syllables were embedded. Infants failed to provide evidence of discrimination of multisyllabic utterances when syllable length was less than 500 ms.

These empirical findings, then, taken together do not provide support for the first axiom of the innateness theory, that all important phonemic categories are discriminable by infants. At the very least the theory requires modification to account for wide discrepancies in degree of difficulty of various contrasts. At the same time the data do seem to support the second axiom, that infant speech discrimination is categorical-like.

The third axiom of the phonetic innateness theory, that linguistic listening experience is not an important aspect of the infant's ability to discriminate speech sounds, has also been brought under recent scrutiny. Several cross-linguistic studies provide evidence that infants exposed to prevoiced stop contrasts discriminate these contrasts (Eilers, Gavin, and Wilson, 1979; Lasky, Syrdal-Lasky, and Klein, 1975; Streeter, 1976), while as mentioned above, results of other studies suggest that in the majority of infants from linguistic environments whose native language does not include the contrast there is no evidence of discrimination (Butterfield and Cairns, 1974; Eilers, Wilson, and Moore, 1977; Eimas, 1975a).

Lasky, Syrdal-Lasky, and Klein (1975) tested Spanish-learning Guatemalan infants with three pairs of labial stimuli differing along the VOT dimension. They found that infants provided evidence of discriminating two boundary values, one associated with the English-like pair and one associated with a prevoiced pair (− 20 ms vs. − 60 ms). While the prevoiced pair was not precisely the one occurring in Spanish, these Spanish-learning infants were able to provide evidence of discrimination of the prevoiced contrast, a feat which had not been demonstrable with English-learning infants. Likewise, Streeter (1976) demonstrated that Kikuyu-learning infants were able to discriminate a labial prevoiced contrast despite the fact that there is only one category for the labial stop, a prevoiced category, in Kikuyu. However, the language did have oppositions between prevoiced stops and voiceless unaspirated stops at both the alveolar and velar places of articulation. These data suggest that in order for language experience to be influential, exposure to prevoicing need not be specific at a given place of articulation.

In a later study, Eilers, Gavin, and Wilson (1979) presented a native Spanish contrast (/ba/ vs. /pa/) and a native English contrast (/pa/ vs. /pʰa/) to both Spanish and English-learning infants. Performance of Spanish-learning infants was significantly different from that of English-learning infants on the Spanish contrast. Both groups of infants did well on the English pair. Thus in a single study, using two language groups and identical stimuli, differences between infants' performance were demonstrated. These data should not be taken to suggest that all English-learning infants would fail to discriminate the Spanish boundary and all Spanish infants would succeed. Rather this study suggests an asymmetry in performance which can be accounted for by differing linguistic histories. The data to be accounted for in this study do not concern whether individuals can discriminate a given contrast, but whether groups of babies whose linguistic backgrounds differ show different performance on native and non-native contrasts. To date the data suggest that the latter may be the case for stimuli in the prevoiced region of the VOT continuum.

However, not all VOT stimuli show the effects of linguistic experience on perception. Stimuli in the voicing lag (or English-like) region have been shown to be discriminable by both Spanish infants (Eilers, Gavin, and Wilson, 1979; Lasky, Syrdal-Lasky, and Klein, 1975) and Kikuyu infants (Streeter, 1976). Likewise, discrimination of an English-like boundary (as well as the Spanish boundary) has been shown for Spanish adults (Lisker and Abramson, 1970) as well as Kikuyu adults (Streeter, 1974). Part of the explanation of the asymmetry in ease of perception at the English boundary rests on the notion that VOT is not a single continuum. The English boundary may be especially salient in an acoustic sense, incorporating cues from more than one continuum. Stevens and Klatt (1974) argue that the English boundary includes an additional cue beyond VOT, the presence or absence of first formant transitions. Formant transition cutback is not available as a cue in the prevoiced region. Thus, the relative discriminability of lag versus lead contrasts may be in part independent of infant language experience, and may be due to relative salience of the lag region boundary.

Other studies from the 70's examining the effects of linguistic experience on speech discrimination have yielded seemingly conflicting results. Studies have involved vowel, fricative, and liquid contrasts. Trehub (1973), using HAS, demonstrated that 5- to 17-week-old English-learning infants discriminated a French nasal-oral vowel distinction (/pa/ vs. /pã/). Similar results were reported (Trehub, 1976) for a Czech contrast (/řa/ vs. /ža/). In a cross-linguistic study, Eilers, Oller, and Gavin (1978) presented 16 six- to eight-month-old English and Spanish-learning infants with four pairs of stimuli, two phonemic in Spanish (/be/ vs. /bej/) and (/alá/ vs. /aɫá/) and two phonemic in English (/bit/) vs. /bɪt/) and (/awá/ vs. /ará/). In this individual subject design, all of the infants provided evidence of discrimination of the English pairs and one of the two Spanish pairs (/alá/ vs. /aɫá/). Both of the groups of infants found the remaining Spanish pair (/be/ vs. /bej/) fairly difficult, with only 11 infants reaching criterion (9 out of 10 successful trials). Six of the 11 successful infants were English-learners while the remaining

5 were Spanish-learners. In this study no obvious differences were found between performance of Spanish and English-learning infants. Failure to demonstrate group differences in discriminability may have been a function of the relatively insensitive individual subject design used in the study.

A recent Spanish-English study (Eilers, Gavin, and Oller, in preparation) has yielded different results. Fourteen Spanish-learning and 14 English-learning infants were tested on three contrasts, one phonemic in Spanish (/ará/ vs. /a£á/, a trill vs. tap distinction), one phonemic in English (/asá/ vs. /azá/) and a Czech contrast (/řa/ vs. /ža/). In this group study Spanish-learning infants provided evidence of discrimination of all contrasts while the English-learning infants failed to provide evidence of discrimination of the Spanish contrast. In addition, the Spanish-learning infants differed significantly from the English-learning infants in their ability to discriminate the Spanish contrast and the Czech contrast. The English-learning infants and Spanish-learning infants did not differ significantly on the English contrast.

We are left, then, with a fairly puzzling picture of the role of linguistic experience in speech perception in infancy. Axiom 3 of an innateness model does not seem to be valid: some studies show clear effects of linguistic experience while others do not. Clearly, a model of infant speech perception will have to include rules governing the role of linguistic experience. Such a model will be presented in Section B.

The fourth axiom of the innateness theory concerns the role of feature detectors in categorical perception.[1] Debate is ongoing in the literature (see Simon and Studdert-Kennedy, 1978, for a review) concerning the possible role and/or existence of feature detectors. Eimas (1974b, 1975a) postulated physiological phonetic feature detectors which were thought to be activated automatically in the presence of appropriate acoustic information. These feature detectors were used to explain the phenomenon of categorical perception of speech stimuli. Detectors were thought to be tuned to particular points along acoustic continua so that perception would be enhanced in some regions and depressed in others.

The feature detector model has been primarily tested in adaptation experiments wherein phonetic category boundaries are shifted by repeatedly presenting one member of a stimulus continuum (usually an endpoint stimulus). Adaptation with a /pa/ stimulus results in a shift in identification of the /pa/ − /ba/ (voicing) boundary such that more tokens on the voicing continuum come to be labeled as /ba/ (the boundary is shifted toward /pa/). The proposed explanation for this shift includes two feature detectors for voicing, a voiced detector (sensitive to /ba/-like stimuli), and a voiceless detector (sensitive to /pa/-like stimuli). In this case the shift marks the fatiguing of the adapted detector for the voiceless feature /pa/.

---

[1]Categorical perception describes perceptual discontinuities along physical continua. Differences across category boundaries are relatively easy to detect while differences within categories are more difficult.

Recent research has cast doubt upon the level in the auditory system within which feature detectors could be thought to operate. For instance, Ades (1974) has shown that adaptation effects predicted by the phonetic feature detector model were not observed when phonetic contexts were varied. This result suggests that the "feature detectors" involved are not phonetic/phonemic but simply auditory. Carney (1977) also found in a dichotic listening study of VOT results that could not be explained by phonetic/ phonemic detectors.

Further, Sawusch and Nusbaum (1979) suggest that phonetic feature detector fatigue is not adequate to account for adaptation results with vowels. The authors employed an "anchoring" technique wherein there were very few presentations of the adaptor, spaced widely across time, ruling out the possibility of fatigue. Using this technique, Sawusch and Nusbaum found shifts similar to those found after traditional adaptation. Adults, then, seem to shift boundaries (especially for vowels) in response to hearing an asymmetry in frequency of occurrence independent of fatigue. These results suggest that some type of frequency analysis and consequent boundary adjustment may be inherent in auditory perception—a concept that has broad implications for the developing organism (this point will be returned to in the next section).

The phenomenon of categorical perception thus has not been tied tightly to innate physiological phonetic detectors. Furthermore, little if any direct data exist examining the effects of anchoring on speech perception in infancy. This is a particularly serious problem since most infant paradigms present repeated tokens of the stimuli in question. With regard to category formation, the neonate may in fact exhibit plasticity resulting from some form of frequency analysis. If infant boundaries can be shifted by anchoring techniques, it would suggest that at least some aspects of speech perception might be influenced by specific linguistic environments. Further, one might predict that minimal contrasts which occur relatively infrequently might be perceptually unstable at early stages of development.

Finally, the relevance of the concept of categorical perception to linguistic processing (axiom five) has been called into question. For instance, the assumption that only speech-like stimuli can be perceived categorically has been challenged by Cutting and Rosner (1974), who have shown that a variety of nonspeech musical stimuli can be perceived categorically, by Miller et al. (1976), and by Jusczyk et al. (1977), who have shown that two-month-olds demonstrate categorical perception of music-like stimuli. Similarly, Kuhl and Miller (1975) have shown that categorical perception of speech is not limited to humans or even primates (see Morse, in press, for a review). They have shown that the South American chinchilla perceives speech-like stimuli differing in VOT in a manner analogous to adult humans. If chinchillas perceive speech-like stimuli categorically, it seems unreasonable to assume any direct or exclusive relationship between categorical perception and specialized innate specifically linguistic capacities.

Where does this leave us with respect to the innateness model? It seems clear that speculations about innateness were premature: (1) infants have not provided evidence of discrimination of some speech contrasts, (2) infants from different linguistic environments show differences in discrimination patterns, (3) while some aspects of speech perception can be thought of as categorical, "phonetic" detectors do not seem to underlie categorical perception, and (4) categorical perception does not bear a direct relationship to perception of linguistic stimuli.

What are we left with? Despite the fact that innateness theory was tied to a number of constructs and assertions which have not held up over time, it is clear that from an early age infants are able to discriminate among a wide variety of speech and speech-like stimuli. The mechanism or mechanisms responsible for discrimination are little understood, although it seems parsimonious to assume that the infant is at least in part constructed to decipher the acoustic events of speech. The next section provides a model taking account of prewiring and the course of learning.

B. An Interactive-Pragmatic Model

In some measure, part of the usefulness of the innateness model rested on the possibility of empirical validation. A pure experience model could also be validated since it would predict that infants should always be superior on native as opposed to foreign contrasts and that comparisons between infant groups should always favor the group whose language contains the contrast. But such a model is only a straw man and it is clear that the data do not support this simplistic view.

Any workable model of infant speech perception must be multifaceted and must take into account non-linguistic pragmatic factors. The proposed interactive-pragmatic model includes at least three such factors. One of these factors is the physiological maturity of the infant's auditory system. A second factor includes acoustic salience and a third is environmental/experiential. All three will be discussed in the following section.

1. The developing auditory system. Although some details are known about the developmental anatomy of the auditory system little is known about structural-functional aspects of development. From the structural point of view, Hecox (1975) points out that much of the auditory system is virtually mature at birth. The stapedial footplate reaches adult size by birth as do the middle ear ossicles. However, the external auditory canal, tympanic membrane, and middle ear cavity reach adult dimensions by about one year. Cochlear development is nearly complete at birth with the possible exception of the extreme basalward portion of the cochlea and the outermost layer of hair cells. Myelination of the auditory nerve is complete though myelination from the inferior colliculus through the cortex is less mature. Behavioral and physiological correlates of these infant structures are rather hard to predict.

It seems likely that increased middle ear compliance in the neonate coupled with different resonance patterns associated with differing middle ear volume and canal size could account for some conductive loss, perhaps as much as 10 dB (Hecox, 1975), but at the same time these anatomical differences might enhance higher frequency hearing. Predictions concerning the effects of hair cell development are less clear, especially since the immature area is also thought to affect high frequency hearing.

Contrary to expectations expressed by Hecox concerning threshold based on tentative cochlear anatomical findings, Trehub, Bull, and Schneider (in press) have found, using a sensitive variation of Visual Reinforcement Audiometry and psychophysical testing procedures, that infants' high frequency hearing (between 4 and 10 KHz) was more sensitive than low frequency hearing (below 4 KHz). In fact, infant thresholds at 19 KHz seemed indistinguishable from adult thresholds. It is not clear whether this overlap is a function of heightened sensitivity on the part of the infant or diminished sensitivity on the part of the adults tested. In any event, developmental changes in sensitivity amount to continued threshold improvement primarily at the lower frequencies.

At the physiological level, infant auditory-evoked potentials exhibit prolonged latencies, lowered amplitudes, and elevated thresholds as compared to adults. In general, the more caudally located structures generate the lowest threshold while the most cephalad structures (cortical-evoked response) generate the highest thresholds. Electrophysiological measures yield lower estimates of auditory thresholds than do most behavioral measures (Hecox, 1975).

From a gross anatomical perspective, Witelson and Pallie (1973) have demonstrated differences in size between the right and left hemispheres of the planum temporale (a language mediating area) of both adults and neonates. While Witelson and Pallie suggest that this "asymmetry indicates that the infant is born with a pre-programmed biological capacity to process speech sounds," it is clear that such a judgment awaits at least investigation of other mammalian species. The finding, however, does suggest that differential function of the hemispheres is likely. In fact, in a recent study by Molfese and Molfese (1979) in which an electrophysiological measure of hemispheric cortical activity was obtained, adults, 2- to 3-month-olds and newborns showed left hemisphere responses to place of articulation differences. The right hemisphere of adults, preschoolers, and 2- to 5-month-olds, on the other hand, responded differently to voice onset time differences in English-like stop consonants. (Interestingly, this effect was not found in neonates.) This finding is surprising in light of the results of dichotic listening studies in adults (Shankweiler and Studdert-Kennedy, 1967) and infants (Entus, 1977) in which right ear advantage is commonly reported. Traditionally, the right ear advantage in dichotic listening tasks was considered primary evidence for the belief that the left hemisphere was responsible for processing speech information. Molfese and Molfese's (1979) findings suggest that both hemispheres are involved in speech processing, and that the left hemisphere may process place contrasts, while the right is involved in categorical perception of voice onset time.

In conclusion, several anatomical and physiological differences and similarities between the adult and infant auditory processing systems have been discussed. Little is known about the relationship between structural and functional components, but it is clear that changes occur across at least the first years of life as measured by physiological and behavioral procedures. Until the maturational-structural contribution to the developing auditory system is understood, it will be impossible to disambiguate environmental/ experiential vs. maturational processes. In fact, there is a possibility that some aspects of physical maturation may be dependent on environmental factors. Any discussion of the role of linguistic experience in infant speech perception must be viewed within the perspective of an anatomical and physiological backdrop, and against the possibility that the neonatal perceptual system is limited by biological constraints.

2. Acoustic salience. The second pragmatic factor which contributes to discriminability is the relative salience of the stimuli in question, a factor which is assumed to consist of an interaction of innate auditory endowment and acoustic difference (the acoustic nature of the cue or cues which differentiate the members of the stimulus pair). If one were to construct a scale for acoustic salience on intuitive grounds one might rate citation-form vowel contrasts as relatively high in salience. These contrasts include spectral changes which occur over relatively long periods of time. Acoustic cues related to stop consonant voicing differences in the lag region (English-like phonemes) might be thought of as less salient than vowel cues since they occur over a shorter window. However, these contrasts are still relatively salient since multiple cues are operative, including differences in presence or absence of formant transitions, voice onset time, and aspiration. Lead contrasts (Spanish-like), on the other hand, can be thought of as less salient than vowel and lag contrasts, since the critical cue differentiating lag from short-lead contrasts is relatively brief and low in amplitude. Similar judgments could be made concerning other types of acoustic cues. Such a rating scale for salience at this point in time assumes that traditional instrumental acoustic analyses yield results on acoustic saliency that would differ little from results obtained by analysis through the intact auditory system, that is, the innate endowment of the listener. Independent verification of these acoustic difficulty assignments could, in principle, be made by having a variety of foreign speakers evaluate contrasts in both discrimination and labeling tests.

3. Linguistic experience. The third pragmatic factor in the model concerns the nature of the linguistic environment/experience. The environmental factor has at least two components. The first depends on how analogous the contrast to be discriminated is to any other contrast to which the listener has been exposed; the second depends on how frequently the infant listener has heard the analogous contrast, that is, does the analogous contrast have a relatively high frequency of occurrence or a relatively low frequency of occurrence in the native language?

4. Predictions of the model based on interactions of pragmatic factors. The contribution of sensory development toward discrimination of specific contrasts is difficult to specify. Predictions can be made, however, concerning the interaction of factors 2 and 3, acoustic salience, and linguistic experience. In listening to a relatively difficult-to-discriminate contrast (one which has low acoustic salience), the interactive-pragmatic model predicts that foreign contrasts which might be thought of as analogous to frequently-occurring native contrasts are more discriminable than those that are analogous to contrasts with a low frequency of occurrence in the native language. Given a foreign contrast which has high acoustic salience, differences in discriminability associated with linguistic experience would not be predicted (that is, it would be an easy contrast regardless of experience).

In order for the model to be useful, the notion of acoustic salience must be rigorously defined in terms of empirical data. Likewise, the notion of analogy between acoustic events must be better understood, and frequency of occurrence information must be carefully gathered. The interactive-pragmatic model was constructed on the basis of available data. In the following pages, we describe how the model accounts for results of cross-linguistic studies. We intend the model to be robust enough to apply to results of future studies.

To date the largest discrepancy in performance between Spanish and English-learning infants has been found for the pre-voiced stop consonants. As mentioned earlier, this contrast can be thought of as relatively low in acoustic salience. (For instance, even Spanish-learning infants have higher mean scores on the English contrast than on the Spanish contrast [Eilers, Gavin, and Wilson, 1979, Aslin et al. 1979]; also note this asymmetry for English-learning infants with the two types of contrasts.) Secondly, since both voiced and voiceless stop consonants have a high frequency of occurrence in Spanish, Spanish-learning infants have a great deal of listening experience with these contrasts. Whether an analogous contrast is present in English is harder to evaluate. Although English does not have prevocalic lead stop contrasts which are phonemic, it does have lead fricative contrasts like /sa/ vs. /za/ which may be discriminated on the basis of the onset of voicing. However, as Minifie (1973) points out, the primary cues for adults in discriminating /sa/ and /za/ are spectral, that is, they are differences between the spectrum and amplitude of the frication noise. In fact, Eilers and Minifie (1975) found that minimizing the spectral and amplitude differences in the frication noise of test stimuli rendered /sa/ − /za/ stimuli difficult to discriminate for 2- to

3-month-old infants. Thus, since the prevoiced contrast has low salience, has high frequency of occurrence in Spanish, and may not be directly analogous to an English acoustic event, the model is consistent with the obtained linguistic experience effects for VOT in the lead region with Spanish and English babies.

On the basis of relative acoustic salience alone, English-like VOT contrasts would not be expected to show linguistic experience effects. (For example, these contrasts are discriminable by all adults tested, whether or not their language contains the contrast [Eilers, Wilson, and Moore, 1979; Lisker and Abramson, 1970; Streeter, 1976] and by all infants tested [Eilers, Gavin, and Wilson, 1979; Eilers, Wilson, and Moore, 1979; Lasky, Syrdal-Lasky and Klein, 1975; Streeter, 1976; Eimas et al., 1971].) The outcome of experiments with infants concerning voicing contrasts agree with these predictions.

A second contrast of interest is the tap /ɾ/ vs. /r/ trill distinction found in Spanish. The distinction tested was one tap (manifested as silence of approximately 20 msec) vs. two taps (each of which are approximately 14 msec). The event is relatively difficult from an acoustic perspective since the perceiver must count or judge duration of relatively short, similar and closely spaced acoustic events to discriminate between the tap and trill. Taps and trills occur with relatively high frequency in Spanish and no similar or analogous contrast is present in English. The model predicts that the obtained differences in perception (that is, Spanish-learning infants discriminated this contrast significantly better than English-learning infants) would be found.

The /sa/ − /za/ English contrast was shown to be moderately difficult for English-learning infants (Eilers and Minifie, 1975; Eilers, Wilson, and Moore, 1977). Eilers, Gavin, and Oller (in preparation) tested discrimination of /asá/ vs. /azá/ with both Spanish and English-learning infants. Both Spanish and English-learning infants showed significant evidence of discrimination (p < .001). Despite the fact that mean performance scores favored the English-learning infants, performance on this contrast did not differ significantly between language groups. This similarity in performance can be explained in several ways. First, there are analogous acoustic contrasts of fricative voicing in Spanish, for example,´ /abá/ vs. /asá/ or /aβá/ vs. /afá/. Thus, Spanish-learning infants have what appear to be fairly good models, by analogy, for the non-native /asá/ − /azá/ contrast, and these models occur with relatively high frequency in Spanish. The interactive-pragmatic model would, therefore, not predict large differences between English and Spanish-learning infants on /asá/ − /azá/.

Linguistic experience effects have not been found for vowel contrasts presumably because vowel differences are relatively acoustically salient as compared to consonant differences (Eilers, Gavin and Oller in preparation). An apparent exception to this general point is the data on contrasts between Spanish vowels and Spanish diphthongs (/be/ vs. /bej/). In Spanish, unlike English, vowels and their corresponding diphthongs have the same starting formant frequencies so that discrimination is accomplished on relatively small changes in formant slope for the diphthong. English vowels and diphthongs, on the other hand, have multiple cues including different starting and ending formant frequencies. The fact that these Spanish pairs are difficult to discriminate was reflected by poor infant performance in both English and Spanish babies. About half of the infants tested from each language group on this pair failed to provide evidence of discrimination. On the surface these data might seem to contradict the model since these particular stimuli seemed acoustically non-salient and no linguistic experience effects were observed. However, it must be kept in mind that (1) English does not contrast vowels and diphthongs which have the same starting formant frequency, so that no close analogies are available, and (2) the frequency of occurrence of the contrast is low in Spanish as well as in English, so that Spanish babies also have relatively little exposure to the contrasts. Thus, the model does not provide an unequivocal prediction in this case.

The ultimate utility of the interactive-pragmatic model will rest on our ability to independently verify and scale factors such as acoustic salience and acoustic analogy. While much more infant-based evidence also needs to be collected before the model can be adequately tested and revised, the present framework seems to be a reasonable starting point for viewing speech perceptual development.

Section II: Paradigms and Procedures

In order to understand both the nature of the evidence concerning speech perception by infants and the possible range of questions which might be addressed using current techniques, it is helpful to describe briefly presently available procedures. To date three general methodologies are available: the High Amplitude Sucking (HAS), Heart Rate (HR), and Visually Reinforced Infant Speech Discrimination (VRISD) paradigms. A brief description of each follows. The discussion of statistical analysis techniques will be limited to VRISD for reasons outlined below.

A. High Amplitude Sucking Procedure (HAS)

In HAS, first successfully employed by Eimas et al. (1971), infants are presented with a repeating speech stimulus contingent on high amplitude sucking: the more sucks emitted, the greater the number of syllables heard. During the acquisition stage, the number of high amplitude sucks typically increases over baseline until an asymptote is reached and, finally, decline in sucking is obtained. When the sucking rate declines to some arbitrary criterion (for example, 80% of the prehabituation rate for two minutes) the infant is assumed to have habituated to the stimulus and one of two conditions is applied. Half of the babies are presented with a new speech stimulus (experimental group) and half are maintained on the original stimulus (control group). A significant increase in sucking in the experimental group relative to the control group is accepted as evidence of discrimination. HAS has undergone modification (see Spring and Dale, 1977) which seems to highlight the change from stimulus 1 to stimulus 2 for infants. HAS procedures are applicable to infants between about one and four months of age. They typically can be used for group data only. In addition, in a given group of infants usually only a single discriminative pair can be tested. Further, HAS has not been useful for looking at *relative* ease of discrimination. All-or-nothing effects are typically obtained.

B. Heart Rate Procedure (HR)

The HR procedure (Moffitt, 1971) differs from HAS in that the infant does not control stimulus presentation. Stimuli are presented in fixed blocked trials, during which infant heart rate typically decelerates from baseline. (Heart rate deceleration is an index of the orienting response in infants). Each block is followed by a relatively long inter-trial interval in which the infant HR returns to normal. After several blocks are presented and orienting no longer occurs, a new stimulus is introduced. If recovery of the orienting response (that is, renewed deceleration) is found, discrimination is inferred. Modifications have also been applied to the HR procedure (Leavitt et al., 1976), which seem to make the procedure more sensitive. HR procedures in principle can be used throughout the life span. However, in practice, it is difficult to obtain HR measures beyond 5 to 6 months of age because of the prevalance of confounding state changes in older infants. HR procedures are most often applied to groups but can be adapted for single subject designs.

C. Visually Reinforced Infant Speech Discrimination Paradigm (VRISD)

The visually reinforced head turn paradigm (Eilers, Wilson, and Moore, 1976) involves the presentation of a repeating background stimulus (S_B) which is (at an appropriate point) changed to some contrastive stimulus (S_Δ) for a fixed interval (for example, four seconds) and then returned to the original background (S_B). During the presentation of S_Δ, a head turn toward the sound source is reinforced by the activation of a lighted animated toy placed at the sound source. The outcome of any given trial in the VRISD paradigm can be described as a combination of two events: trial type (experimental or control) and head turn (presence of absence) (see Table 1). The measure of discrimination depends on the comparison of head turns to S_Δ vs. head turns during equivalent control intervals (during which S_B is maintained and no change occurs). The VRISD paradigm has been successfully modified by Kuhl (1976) for multiple-token testing and by Trehub, Bull, and Schneider (in press) for use in auditory sensitivity testing.

The VRISD paradigm is applicable to infants between 6 and 18 months of age and offers a number of advantages for developmental studies over both HR and HAS paradigms. First, it is possible to use VRISD to assess

Table 1. Matrix of Possible Outcomes For Any Given Trial.

| | | Factor 2: turning behavior | |
		Head turn = p_H	No head turn = $p_{\bar H}$
Factor 1: trial type	Exp. = p_E	$P(E_S) = p_E p_H$	$P(E_F) = p_E p_{\bar H}$
	Control = $p_{\bar E}$	$P(C_F) = p_{\bar E} p_H$	$P(C_S) = p_{\bar E} p_{\bar H}$

S = success; F = failure; E = Experimental; H = Head turn; $\bar{}$ = NOT.

a broader age range than HAS or HR (though the latter two procedures can be used with infants below 6 months while VRISD cannot). Secondly, VRISD can be used to assess a number of contrasts in either a cross-sectional or longitudinal design. Third, since the reinforcement in VRISD is not the speech signal itself, as in the HAS procedure, no assumptions need be made concerning the reinforcing value of the speech signal; therefore reinforcers can be chosen which maximize individual performance. Thus, it would seem that in order to answer questions concerning a broad range of speech perception skills which are developmental or deal with individual differences, VRISD or one of its modifications appears for now to be the method of choice.

One experimental question commonly asked in using the VRISD paradigm is whether infants can discriminate a given contrast. A second set of questions involves not absolute discrimination but rather the ease of discrimination among contrasts and relative level of discrimination between groups of infants. Often these questions are not considered separately, and various criteria have been used to answer one or another or both. To date, little work has addressed the issue of the relative merits of the analyses commonly employed. Comparison between studies that have used different analysis techniques has proven difficult, since there has not been adequate development or clarification of procedural analysis requirements. Some studies concerned with the first question (that is, can infants discriminate the tested contrast?) report data by listing the frequency with which subjects meet an arbitrary criterion for discrimination, for example, 5 correct responses out of 6 trials, or 6 out of 8 trials (Eilers, Wilson, and Moore, 1977, 1979; Hillenbrand, Minifie, and Edwards, 1977). A second measure commonly used is number of trials to reach an arbitrary criterion level. The criteria used in these studies have typically been either 8 correct out of any 10 consecutive trials (Holmberg, Morgan, and Kuhl, 1977; Aslin et al., 1979) or 9 correct out of any 10 consecutive trials (Kuhl and Hillenbrand, 1979).

A third method of analysis, aimed primarily at answering the second set of questions (that is, with respect to relative discriminability of contrasts and relative discrimination by groups), involves the use of parametric statistics such as the F-test of analysis of variance procedures (Eilers, Gavin, and Wilson, 1979; Eilers and Oller, in press). In these studies, each subject is scored for the proportion of correct trials achieved in a test session. Mean performance across all subjects tested on each contrast is then determined. Comparisons of the mean performances using analysis of variance techniques are made to determine if significant differences between contrasts exist and to determine possible order of the contrasts in terms of difficulty.

The further development of statistical techniques to analyze data from VRISD studies has been prompted by the desire to answer rigorously the first commonly asked question: Can infants discriminate a given contrast? This question must be addressed indirectly, however, since statistical inferences can only be drawn by comparing a test sample to a population whose parameters are known. While we do not have the tools for describing the parameters of head turn performance in VRISD for populations of infants who can discriminate contrasts, we can describe the population of infants whose head turning performance is random. Once we determine parameters for random performance, we can compare the infant's test performance on a given contrast to random performance. If the likelihood of the observed performance occurring in a randomly operating population is very small (say, $p < .05$), the observed performance on the test contrast can be accepted as evidence of discrimination. The following arguments describe a procedure used to determine the distribution of expected performance scores obtainable in the VRISD paradigm when the head turning performance is *random;* that is, not motivated by detection of differences in auditory cues. A simple statistical procedure for comparing performance levels obtained in experimental testing to performance levels expected from random behavior is also discussed.

D. Statistical Procedures for use with the VRISD Paradigm

Before any statistical procedure can be developed for VRISD, two basic questions about the nature of the data derived from the procedure should be considered. These are: (1) how can we ascertain the form of the distribution of possible performance scores obtainable from the VRISD paradigm and (2) does the probability of a head turn for a given trial affect the distribution of possible performance scores?

To answer the first question, we must consider the number of possible outcomes for each test trial. During the testing phase of VRISD, a trial may be either experimental (a trial where S_B is changed to S_A) or a control (a trial where S_B continues to be presented). Behavior is scored as correct (successful behavior) if the infant turns his/her head during an experimental trial or does not turn his/her head during control trial. Behavior is scored as incorrect (failure) if the infant does not turn his/her head during an experimental trial or does turn his/her head during a control trial. Scoring test trials as being either correct (successes) or incorrect (failures) results in data that is dichotomous in nature; hence, the test trial data can be considered to be samples from a Bernoulli distribution. To determine the probability of getting r successes out of N trials (when the sequence of successes is not important), one applies the following formula:

$$p(r \text{ success}/N,p) = \frac{(N!)}{r! \, (N-r)!} \, p^r q^{N-r}$$

where p = probability of success for a given trial
q = 1 − p.

When a sample of N trials is taken from a Bernoulli distribution and for each possible number of successes the probability is calculated, the resultant distribution is binomial. Therefore, the distribution of possible performance scores resulting from the VRISD paradigm is binomial in nature.

However, before one can derive the appropriate binomial distribution for N trials, the probability of a successful trial, P(S), must be determined. On any given trial, two factors interact (trial type and turning behavior). A trial is specified as either experimental or a control, and a head turn may or may not occur. The combination of these two factors leads to four possible outcomes as shown in Table 1. The probability of occurrence of each outcome can be stated as the crossproduct of the marginal probability of each factor. If the head turning behavior is not motivated by detection of acoustic differences between tokens (that is, it is "random" head turning) then these factors are independent of one another. The probability of a successful trial, P(S), could then be described as the sum of the two crossproducts which define a successful trial:

$$P(S) = P(E_S) + P(C_S)$$

where $P(E_S)$ is the probability of success for an experimental trial and $P(C_S)$ is the probability of success for a control trial.

The probability of success on an experimental trial, $P(E_S)$, is the joint probability of an experimental trial occurring and a head turn occurring. This could be formalized as follows:

$$P(E_S) = P_E * P_H$$

where P_H = probability of a head turn occurring and
P_E = probability of an experimental trial occurring.

Similarly, the probability of success on a control trial, $P(C_S)$, is the joint probability of the occurrence of a control trial and a head turn not occurring. This could be formalized as follows:

$$P(C_S) = P_{\bar{E}} * P_{\bar{H}}$$

where $P_{\bar{E}} = 1 - P_E$, the probability of a control trial occurring and
$P_{\bar{H}} = 1 - P_H$, the probability of a head turn not occurring.

Expressing the probability of success, P(S), as the sum of the two joint probability statements, the following formula is obtained:

$$P(S) = (P_E * P_H) + (P_{\bar{E}} * P_{\bar{H}}).$$

Since the VRISD procedure generally sets the probability of an experimental trial at .50, P_E and P_E become constants and the above formula can be further reduced as shown below:

$$P(S) = (.50 * P_H) + (.50 * P_{\bar{H}})$$
$$= .50 (p_H + P_{\bar{H}}).$$

And since $P_H + P_{\bar{H}}$ equals 1 by definition,

$$P(S) = .50.$$

In determining the probability of successful behavior on any given test trial, the second basic question, "Does the probability of a head turn on any given trial affect the distribution of possible performance scores?," is answered. If the probability of an experimental test trial is paradigmatically set at .50, then the probability of success, P(S), will always be .50, and this value is independent of the probability of a head turn for any trial. *Since the probability of success is a known constant from trial to trial for random performance, a binomial distribution of a sample of N trials can be determined without knowing the probability of a head turn for any given trial.*

In addition, the population parameters, μ and σ, can be determined for the distribution of random performance in the VRISD paradigm. For proportional data, the population mean (μ) of a binomial distribution is defined as:

$$\mu = \frac{Np}{N} = p \text{ (see Hays, 1966, p. 169)}$$

where   p = the probability of successful (correct) behavior.

Applying the formula to the distribution of random head turning where P(S) = .50:

$\mu = P(S) = .50.$

The second population parameter, σ, can also be formulated from the binomial distribution where the standard deviation of a binomial distribution is given as:

$$\sigma = \sqrt{\frac{pq}{N}}$$

where p = probability of success, q = 1 − p, and N = number of trials. Remembering that P(S) is the sum of the two crossproducts of the marginal probabilities of two independent factors (P(S) = $P_E P_H + P_{\bar{E}} P_{\bar{H}}$), to determine σ for random performance one must pool the variance of successful experimental trials and successful control trials. When the probability of experimental trials is set at .50, P_E is constant (hence, no variance is attributable to the factor of trial type). Therefore, σ for N trials of random performance can be calculated by substitution as below:

$$\sigma_{pooled} = .5 \sqrt{\frac{P_H P_{\bar{H}}}{N}} + .5 \sqrt{\frac{P_H P_{\bar{H}}}{N}} = \sqrt{\frac{P_H P_{\bar{H}}}{N}}.$$

This formula shows that the *variance* of the distribution of random performance *is directly related to the probability of a head turn which,* as mentioned earlier, cannot be predicted for any given trial. However, by substituting various probability values for P_H, one can determine the distribution of possible standard deviations (see Figure 1). This distribution shows that maximum dispersion for random performance occurs when $p_H = .50$.

While one can mathematically derive parameters for a population of infants whose head turning performance is random (that is, not due to discrimination of acoustic differences in contrasting tokens), the empirical verification of these population parameters is useful, given that trials are actually presented in pseudorandom rather than random order. Empirically, verification has been obtained through the use of simulation techniques employing a DECLAB 11/03 computer. The particular program used in the simulation was an adaptation of the program used to control the VRISD testing procedure within our laboratory. The adaptations allowed control over the number of trials given per subject and also control over the probability of a head turn on any given trial.

Specifically, within a simulation, each of 10,000 pseudosubjects (random performers) were given N blocks of 10 test trials (N varied for each simulation where N = 3, 4, and 5). The order of presentation of either experimental trials or control trials was controlled by the computer random number generator, with constraints resulting in three possible combinations of trial types per block of 10 trials: 6 experimental and 4 control, 4 experimental and 6 control and 5 experimental and 5 control. A random number between 0 and 99 was obtained from a random number generator subroutine supplied in the Fortran compiler of the RT-11 operating system (Digital Equipment Corporation). An experimental trial occurred if the random number was less than 50 and no other constraints applied; otherwise a control trial occurred. For each experimental or control trial, a simulated head turn response was determined by again obtaining a random number between 0 and 99. Numbers less than 50 were considered as head turns while numbers greater than or equal to 50 were considered as absence of head turns. When all test trials were completed, the proportion of correct responses was calculated for each block of 10 trials and for the entire session. These data were entered into frequency distributions, which were printed after all pseudosubjects had been "tested." The mean performances and standard deviations of the simulated conditions are shown in Tables 2 and 3, respectively.

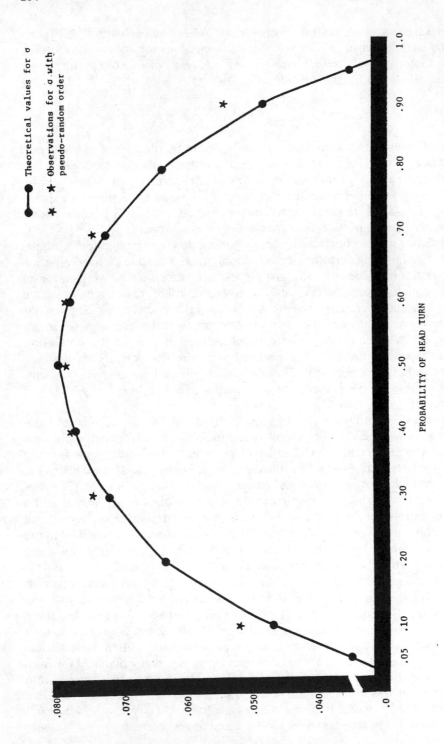

Figure 1. Theoretical and obtained σ for 40 trials/session. •→• theoretical values for σ ; ✶✶ observations for σ with pseudorandom order.

Table 2. Means of Simulated Populations as Function of the Probability of Head Turn and the Number of Trials Run per Subject.

		Number of Trials		
		30	40	50
	.10	.50	.50	.50
	.30	.50	.50	.50
Probability of Headturn	.50	.50	.50	.50
	.70	.50	.50	.50
	.90	.50	.50	.50

Table 3. Standard Deviations of Simulated Populations as Function of the Probability of Head Turn and the Number of Trials Run Per Subject.

		Number of Trials		
		30	40	50
	.10	.061	.053	.047
	.30	.085	.074	.066
Probability of Headturn	.50	.092	.078	.070
	.70	.084	.074	.064
	.90	.060	.053	.046

As shown in Table 2, the mean performance for the simulation of randomly performing subjects is .50 regardless of the specified probability of a head turn or the number of trials tested. This is exactly as predicted by the binomial distribution. Table 3 lists the values of σ also as a function of the number of trials run and the probability of a head turn. As the equations derived from the binomial distribution predicted, for a given number of trials the standard deviation of the population decreases as the probability of a head turn departs from .50. Figure 1 shows the values of σ as a function of P_H obtained from both the binomial distribution and the simulated populations for 40 trials.

As the data from the computer simulation of infants performing randomly in the VRISD paradigm demonstrates, the population parameters derived from equations for binomial distributions are appropriate for a population when head turning behavior is non-cued (random). In a further investigation of parameters of random performance, 24 six-month-old infants were given 40 trials using the VRISD procedure employing a pseudocontrast (Eilers, Morse, Gavin and Oller, in press; Morse, Eilers, and Gavin, in preparation). During testing with a pseudocontrast, the same stimulus is presented during experimental and control trials. In other words, S_B is maintained throughout the experiment. Head turns are counted and reinforcement is administered as in the usual paradigm. As in minimal-pair testing, the number of head turns during experimental trials and control trials is compared. Performance on this pseudocontrast provides a measure of random performance, since infants do not have changes in acoustic cues to respond to. Mean performance was found to be .4958, nearly identical to the theoretically predicted μ and the computer simulated μ (.50).

The standard deviation (s) of the performance scores for those subjects tested of the pseudocontrast was .055. Estimating the standard deviation of the population of random performance from this sample we obtain the value, = .056. These values (s and σ) are slighly lower than the maximum value for the standard deviation obtained mathematically (.079) and through simulation techniques (.078) when the probability of head turn was .5. However, since many infants failed to continue responding throughout the session when the pseudocontrast was employed, the probability of head turn was proabaly less than .5. This may account for the small discrepancy between the obtained and predicted standard deviations. Thus, three sources of data, mathematical predictions, computer simulation outcomes and empirical findings using infant data, all predict nearly identical random population values for μ. Further, both computer simulation and pseudocontrast testing support the idea that the mathematically derived value for σ is conservative.

Knowledge of the values of random population parameters allows the use of the Z-test of means. With this test the probability that a sample of experimental performance is a subset of the population of random performance can be determined. Z_m is defined as:

$$\frac{\mu - X}{\sigma_m}$$

where m is the standard error of the mean for the population, defined as

$$\sigma_m = \frac{\sigma}{n}$$

where n = number of subjects in the sample. Obtained values from the Z-test of means are in terms of standard deviation units; hence, p values can be found by referring to a Z-table for area under a normal curve.

In addition to p values for the mean performance of infants tested in VRISD, performance levels for individual subjects can also be evaluated for discrimination using the Z-score transformation techniques and the Z-table.

1. An example of the use of Z-tests for VRISD data. Recently, Eilers, Gavin, and Oller (in preparation) have been pursuing work on the possible role of linguistic experience for phonetic perception in infancy. In this study, 14 Spanish-learning and 14 English-learning infants were presented with three natural speech contrasts: /ará/ − /aɾá/ (a trilled r vs. a tapped r, which are phonemic in Spanish), /asá/ − /azá/ (/s/ and /z/ are phonemic in English), and a Czech contrast, /řa/ vs. /ža/. Infants received 40 trials per contrast, approximately half of which were experimental and half of which were control. An analysis of variance performed on the data yielded only a significant contrast effect. Comparisons between language groups on the three contrasts yielded significant differences favoring the Spanish-learning infants on both the Spanish and Czech contrasts. Using a Z-test of the means, we found that both infant groups were able to discriminate all contrasts with the exception of the English-learning infants on the Spanish contrast. The example illustrates the richness of interpretations possible using a combination of two statistical tools. The Z-tests based on mathematical and simulated derivations of random population parameters can be used as a sensitive measure of discrimination, while analysis of variance procedures can be used to test for significant differences between contrasts by groups. These two analyses together suggest that although most contrasts prove discriminable by infant groups, significant differences in performance between groups can still be found which may be attributed to linguistic experience.

2. Comparison with previous VRISD studies' analyses. With the present understanding of the factors determining population parameters in the VRISD paradigm, we can now examine, with the benefit of hindsight, analysis techniques used to date. The first operationalizations of the VRISD paradigm used a small number of trials, six (Eilers, Wilson, and Moore, 1977) or six to eight (Hillenbrand, Minifie, and Edwards, 1977). These studies reported using criteria of 5 correct out of 6, in the first study, and either 5 out of 6 or 6 correct out of 8 in the second. Evaluating these criteria in light of the binomial distribution, 5 out of 6 trials barely fails to meet standard α values (p < .051) as does 6 correct out of 8 (p < .08). Using a 6 out of 8 criterion (p < .08), after infants fail to provide evidence with a 5 out of 6 criterion, inflates estimates of discriminability. (An 8 or 9 out of 10 criterion yields significance (p < .029, p < .006, respectively). However, often the 8 or 9 out of 10 criterion itself is too rigid to be useful with infants. In order to extract discriminative behavior from fussing, momentary loss of attention, and other competing behaviors, a more flexible analysis procedure is preferable to help minimize Type II errors.

Running infants in designs in which data are reported as trials to an arbitrary criterion is in part an attempt to incorporate more flexibility in testing. Studies which use these procedures (Holmberg, Morgan, and Kuhl, 1977; Aslin et al, 1979; Eilers and Oller, in press) assume implicitly or explicitly that subjects who can *eventually* meet the criterion can discriminate the contrast. Judgments as to the relative difficulty of the contrasts can then be made by subjective comparisons or formal analysis of group performance for one contrast versus another. In some cases, the assumption that meeting criterion indicates evidence of discrimination may be misleading. If subjects are run to criterion, one needs to determine how many trials are necessary for subjects to meet criterion by chance alone. Using a floating criterion (for example, 8 out of any 10 consecutive trials) rather than a blocked criterion (for example, 8 out of the first 10 or second 10 or third 10, etc.) greatly inflates the probability of meeting criterion by chance alone. Figure 2 shows data derived through computer simulation for trials necessary to reach a floating criterion of 8 or 9 correct out of 10 consecutive trials. After 20 trials, using an 8 out of 10 criterion, 20.21% of subjects meet criterion by chance. By 50 trials, 50.89% of subjects meet criterion by chance alone. Using a 9 out of 10 criterion greatly lowers the probability of meeting criterion by chance.

Failure to address the problems inherent in floating criteria has led to a number of possible misinterpretations in the recent literature. For instance, Eilers, Wilson, and Moore (1977) report lack of evidence of discrimination of /θ/ − /f/ contrasts for individual six-month-olds using a 5 correct out of 6 criterion. Holmberg, Morgan, and Kuhl (1977), using a floating 8 out of 10 criterion for these pairs, found infants reached criterion with a mean performance of 68 trials. In a recent chapter, Jusczyk (in press) suggests that "failure" on the Eilers, Wilson, and Moore /θ/ − /f/ contrast may have been mediated by the small number of trials. (Recall that 5 out of 6 has a p < .051). Jusczyk states that "these contrasts may have been difficult ones for infants and a greater number of observations may have been necessary to obtain reliable evidence for discrimination." Jusczyk failed to note that when using an 8 out of 10 criterion and presenting a large number of test trials, most babies can reach criterion while performing randomly. In fact.

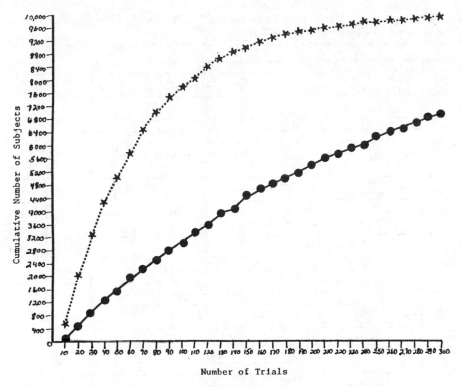

Figure 2. Trials needed to reach criterion by chance alone. 8 out of 10 = *....*.
9 out of 10 = •—•.

the use of a fixed criterion of 5 out of 6 trials (as in Eilers, Wilson and Moore,
1977) leads to fewer Type II errors than the use of a floating criterion of 8
out of 10 when more than 10 trials are given (see Table 4). Thus, the use of
large numbers of trials is not necessarily important, as Jusczyk has suggested.
Rather one must consider the appropriate procedures for determining the
probability of discrimination (either with groups or individuals) for any given
sequence of trials.

Analysis of variance techniques have been used to demonstrate differences
between contrasts and between groups. Their shortcoming lies in the fact
that ANOVA techniques are not designed to answer the questions of whether
infants do in fact discriminate a contrast, except in cases where an appropriate control group is incorporated into the experiment. Unfortunately,
running control conditions (for example, employing a pseudocontrast) is
costly in terms of time involved in testing an extra contrast, but more importantly, subject attrition may increase. If contrasts are tested in random
order, presenting a pseudocontrast before a real contrast affects the infant's
performance on the real contrast, since infants become confused about the

Table 4. Relative and Cumulative Percentage of Pseudosubjects Reaching Floating Criteria of 8 or 9 Correct Out of 10 Trials.

	80%			90%	
# of Trials	Relative	Cumulative	# of Trials	Relative	Cumulative
10	.0565	.0565	10	.0098	.0098
20	.1456	.2021	20	.0413	.0511
30	.1258	.3279	30	.0375	.0886
40	.1009	.4288	40	.0374	.1260
50	.0801	.5089	50	.0338	.1598
60	.0775	.5864	60	.0317	.1915
70	.0640	.6504	70	.0288	.2203
80	.0543	.7047	80	.0303	.2506
90	.0395	.7442	90	.0312	.2818
100	.0384	.7826	100	.0294	.3112
110	.0326	.8152	110	.0266	.3378
120	.0286	.8438	120	.0306	.3684
130	.0257	.8695	130	.0242	.3926
140	.0201	.8896	140	.0257	.4183
150	.0179	.9075	150	.0251	.4434
160	.0137	.9212	160	.0215	.4649
170	.0113	.9325	170	.0198	.4847
180	.0109	.9434	180	.0212	.5059
190	.0075	.9509	190	.0200	.5259
200	.0071	.9580	200	.0190	.5449
210	.0053	.9633	210	.0162	.5611
220	.0062	.9695	220	.0165	.5776
230	.0054	.9749	230	.0192	.5968
240	.0040	.9789	240	.0169	.6137
250	.0033	.9822	250	.0167	.6304
260	.0022	.9844	260	.0157	.6461
270	.0016	.9860	270	.0122	.6583
280	.0026	.9886	280	.0116	.6699
290	.0024	.9910	290	.0140	.6839
300	.0018	.9928	300	.0132	.6971

contingency relationships between detecting auditory changes and receiving reinforcement. During the pseudocontrast testing, infants are reinforced whenever they turn during experimental trials despite the fact that they never hear a change from S_B to S_Δ.

Babies seem to function as if in an extinction phase of an operant conditioning paradigm. We can only assume that their expectations concerning contingency relationships in the paradigm are violated and this in itself is aversive. Therefore, it is simply more convenient and practicable to use Z_m statistics, eliminating the need for controls, rather than the analysis of variance when asking whether individual contrasts are discriminable.

In conclusion, the number of trials employed in the VRISD paradigm is not in itself important in the sense that any number of trials which meets minimal constraints of the binomial theorem is adequate. Rather than choosing trial number on purely statistical grounds, practical factors such as infant attention span and possible learning effects should be taken into account. In addition, care must be given to interpretations of studies employing a floating criterion, especially when large numbers of trials are necessary before infants meet criterion. Computer simulation can assist in this interpretation by estimating the probability of reaching criterion by chance for any given number of trials.

Summary

This paper has presented evidence which suggests that the phonetic innateness hypothesis is not adequate to account for various kinds of evidence, including data from cross-linguistic infant studies, developmental studies and studies concerning the relationship between categorical perception, speech detectors, and linguistic modes of processing. An alternative model is presented which has three main components, one which is thought to be innately determined, one which is a function of the nature of the speech code, and one which is environmentally specified. Finally, nagging methodological issues relating to data analysis from one of the major infant speech perception paradigms (VRISD) were addressed, and a framework for statistically analyzing data and comparing across studies was presented. We look forward to the continued exploration of the infant's capacity for language learning using new methods and procedures, especially as this exploration probes the role of linguistic experience in language development.

Discussion

There was some discussion led by Kagan, of the manner in which the statistical model presented by Eilers was being used. In other words, it was asked was the model used (1) to ask questions about the infant's ability to discriminate particular contrasts or (2) to ask questions about the relative discriminability of the contrast, given the different linguistic environments of the infants. Eilers considered both of these questions to be interesting. She and her colleagues had approached the first question by means of Z-tests, based upon mathematical and simulated derivations of random population parameters, and were approaching the second question by means of analyses of variance procedures.

Bloom then asked if habituation, while it was not a response variable in the VRISD paradigm might, nevertheless, affect the infant's response. In other words, the more stimuli were presented, the less likely the infant might be to give a head turn response after habituation levels were reached. Clearly, one could not continue to test an infant indefinitely during one session, there must be response attrition. Eilers said that that sort of habituation did not take place within the time period in which the infant was capable of responding satisfactorily. Probe trials were frequently given to insure that the baby was attending. Bloom accepted that statement, but said she still wanted to know if there was not some ceiling beyond which the baby could no longer attend. Eilers said that it was obvious that there was such a ceiling, but it varied across infants. The aim was to avoid reaching it. Very often the infant was tested over a number of sessions so that fussiness and fatigue would be avoided.

Stern said that he was impressed with the model Eilers had presented but he was concerned about the issue of signal salience. Did that have to do with innate feature detection abilities? Eilers replied that the notion of innate propensity for discriminating certain kinds of acoustic events was an essential component of any model of infant speech perception. The baby at birth had an easier time discriminating certain kinds of acoustic events than others. These abilities might be thought of as innate, but she would not be comfortable in saying that speech perception was innate.

Kent asked if signal salience, then, was to be interpreted as her intuitive notion of auditory perceptual salience. Eilers replied that in part it was intuitive. The notion of salience was also, however, based upon examination of instrumental acoustic analyses. Judgment of brevity of a cue or lack of change in formant trajectory might be taken into account, together with discrimination data, suggesting that certain contrasts were more difficult for babies to discriminate than others. Eilers was the first to admit that, in order to support these notions, it would be necessary to scale stimuli along a continuum from easy to difficult. Kuhl's reaction was that this could be very hard to do. This spectrum did not as yet provide a very good analog for the ear. It captured some of the features that were important for the listener but in other cases could lead the investigator completely astray. Another problem was that discrimination of some of the phonetic contrasts had been tested only with synthetic stimuli. Kuhl did not believe that anyone had synthesized a really satisfactory prevoiced versus voiceless unaspirated stop contrast. She had found that monkeys also had a harder time discriminating the Spanish voicing contrast than the English voicing contrast. She believed it might be because the Spanish contrast was not being synthesized by Spanish speakers and therefore lacked some of the appropriate acoustic cues.

Eilers agreed that there was stimulus dimension problem. She had found in her cross-linguistic studies that Spanish infants did better in discriminating English than Spanish voicing in contrasts. However, the asymmetry notwithstanding, the Spanish infants still did better on the Spanish contrast than the English infants.

Kuhl also pointed out that prevoicing of stops did occur in the speech output of some speakers of English, even though it was not used contrastively by English speakers. Eilers acknowledged that this was true. Some speakers of English prevoiced in initial stops while others did not. Also, stops were sometimes prevoiced in the medial position in a word. Did the infant equate that prevoicing with prevoicing of initial stops? Perhaps the two situations could not be considered analogous. The fact remained, however, that the Spanish-learning infant was exposed a great deal more often to the prevoiced vs. voiceless unaspirated stop contrast than the English-learning infant.

Tronick asked if the computer simulation data suggested that after several hundred subjects had been run, one would begin to get significance by chance alone from these studies. Eilers explained that concern for distortion of significance had to do more with the number of trials presented to any one subject or any one group of subjects. After a large number of trials using floating criteria were run, it was very likely that infants would meet criteria levels by chance alone. Kuhl pointed out that in all fairness, in many infant studies where such criteria were applied, a transfer-of-learning design was employed. Thus, the infant was required to learn one contrast, and when he met the criterion level for that contrast he was transferred to different sets of stimuli in a generalization experiment. In these studies, the investigators did not interpret the data as showing that after so many trials the baby finally achieved discrimination, but rather, their aim was to get the baby to behave in a particular way and then to see what happened. Eilers agreed. She felt, however, that she and her colleagues now had a statistical technique that would enable them to examine cross-linguistic data in a manner that was not possible before. She believed the technique would enable them to develop and test more complex and interesting models of speech perception in the infant. She viewed it as an exciting prospect.

Published 1981 by Elsevier North Holland, Inc.
Stark, ed.
Language Behavior in Infancy and Early Childhood

Discussion of Early Development of the Forms of Language

Lewis Leavitt

*Department of Pediatrics, Waisman Center for Mental Retardation and Human
Development, University of Wisconsin, 1500 Highland Avenue, Madison,
Wisconsin*

My aim will be, in commenting on the 6 papers presented in this section,
to try to integrate their content with the materials presented in the section
on social development and communicative behavior. I will also try to integrate the papers on speech perception and production with the topic area
of cognitive development. Finally, I will try to glean some information of
an applied sort that may be of particular interest to the clinician whose
concerns we are, in the end, addressing.

With respect to the papers from the present section, which might be
considered under the overall heading of biology, I believe it is important to
begin with a cautionary statement. It is natural for investigators in any one
field to try to make use of interesting data from other fields, and to relate
that data to their own. There is a tendency, in doing so, to simplify and
perhaps to glorify the data from these other fields. I found the use of myelination data and neuroanatomic data in Netsell's paper very interesting.
However, it is important to point out that the myelination data of Yakovlev
(1962) provides only a crude index of developmental changes in the nervous
system. Furthermore, they are derived from very small number of speci-
mens. Our current understanding of the neurobiology of animals is limited,
of humans even more so. But there are other, more interesting indices of
development that we may wish to use. One must keep in mind that, in
biology much as in psychology, today's dogma is tomorrow's heresy. Nevertheless, the work of Scheibel and Scheibel (1976) to which Netsell referred,
and the studies of Purpura (1975) in which he examined neural budding and
some of the neuronal interactions, is most exciting. There appears to be
evidence of a lawful course of development in the nervous system, albeit

complex, as well as effects on that development of particular metabolic and environmental events. Eventually, we may want to make use of these newer indices in studies of development of the nervous system. Unfortunately, at the present time, the indices have not been used in studies of human development so that we may only make inferences from animal studies. Nevertheless, myelination as an index is a poor substitute and must be regarded with caution.

A second caution must be that the prevalent view of the human neonate as a subcortical organism is quite false. My own data (Graham et al., 1977) and that of others have demonstrated that interactions of cortical and subcortical structures are already taking place in the first week of life.

In spite of these cautions I believe that we should pay attention to what is known about neuroanatomy, and about the anatomy of the structures involved in speaking, as we consider other aspects of the development of production and comprehension of speech. The papers of Kent and Netsell are very important in helping us to take into account the constraints under which the infant and young child must operate in acquiring both speech production and speech comprehension skills. The data on the anatomy of the newborn and young infant is not exactly voluminous. Some of it derives from very elegant dissections (Crelin, 1973; Bosma, 1975) and also from a limited number of cineradiographic studies (Bosma, Truby, and Lind, 1966). But these studies are limited with respect to the information about developmental changes in the anatomy of the human infant's head and neck which they provide. We do not have a good estimate of the variance of anatomical measures at different ages of the child. We do not even have very good developmental landmarks. And we have no clear idea at the present time as to the effects of environment, nutrition or individual aspects of metabolism on development. Although we must take our knowledge of anatomical constraints into account as best we can, and although we must remain aware of new developments in the fields of anatomy and biology, we ought not to regard existing data as fixed or immutable. Having said all this, I want to compliment Kent and Netsell for their well integrated presentations of existing data.

Also pertinent to our discussion is the tendency in other fields, such as psychology, to resurrect theories from biology and to apply them, by analogy, to the study of behavior. An example is the theory of critical periods which is always reviving in spite of our efforts to put it down. Biologists, too, have had to deal with the periodic resurgence of this theory. Current hypotheses about critical periods in the growth of the human brain which have been offered for some years now by Winick (1976) and Dobbing and Sands (1973) have recently been called into question by Dobbing himself. Dobbing and his colleagues (Sands, Dobbing, and Gratrix, 1979) have presented evidence that the notion of critical periods in early organ development may be misleading. It may derive from methodological problems in estimating cell size and number. Brain vulnerability may, after all, not be quite so dependent on critical periods. This example indicates that, although the paradigms used in other fields, such as biology, may be productive when used in relation to behavior, we must remember that these fields are changing as rapidly as our own. Theories motivating experimental work in our own field have changed for example, the motor theory of speech perception, which enjoyed vogue for a time, fell into disuse, and then more recently was revived. In addition, the glamour attached to advanced technology in the fields of biology or biochemistry should not cause us to accept without question the theories generated in these fields. We have to be particularly careful when we try to draw analogies from another field to explain data in our own.

Another set of concerns that we might dwell upon have to do with methodology. Both Kuhl and Eilers have presented some fascinating data in their discussions of methodology. Many of us are still talking about innateness, about hardwiring and softwiring of the system. Yet when we try to explore the earliest perceptual abilities of young infants, we have to realize that we are constrained a great deal by the experimental interventions that can be used with such young infants. Much of the information we have about infant speech perception derives, not from newborns, but from significantly older infants. There are good reasons for that bias in terms of methodological problems. I would like to point out some of these problems as we examine the literature on infant speech perception.

In general, at least in the last decade, there have been three, more or less popular, methods for examining issues in speech perception or speech discrimination in infants. Each of these methods has had interesting and exciting properties but also at the same time certain drawbacks. The HAS paradigm used by Eimas and his colleagues (1971), and also by Eilers (this volume, chapter 9) and myself, makes use of ongoing sucking behavior of the young infant. It is a useful and powerful methodology but it has a major problem. Because infants have varieties of experience with materials to be sucked, from the human breast to the Nuke-Sauger nipple, they are comfortable to a greater or lesser degree with any particular experimental apparatus. Even when a cafeteria of nipples is offered to the infant, as in our own experiments, not every infant is willing to partake. Secondly, because of the maturational course of sucking behavior, infants beyond the age of 4 or 5 months simply will not take to these experimental nipples. Thus, this experimental method has not had utility beyond that age.

Heart rate methodology is very easy to use; however, many data analysis problems arise in dealing with heart rate measures and it is not always as simple as it seems to discover what has happened when a change is observed. There are many serious statistical considerations involved which have not always received proper attention in experimental work. Even when these problems are attended to, they are difficult to deal with. The heart rate response has been used to examine the maturational course of perception. Heart rate measures have the advantage of being differentially sensitive to different stimuli. Some people have used the measures to ask questions as to how easily heart rate changes are elicited by different stimuli at different ages. The problem is a complex one, however, and it is difficult to know which data from these experiments to trust. Suffice it to say that below the age of 2 months the use of heart rate is fraught with difficulties although above that age it can be used fairly readily.

The head turning VRISD paradigm that has been discussed here by Eilers and Kuhl is a very promising one. Before I dwell upon its advantages, however, let me mention its drawbacks. For some of us, including myself, the most interesting age of the infant in terms of experience, be it social, cognitive, or physiological, is the first 4 or 5 months of life. This may seem a very short period to those who are concerned with 6-year-olds, but to investigators who study infants, the first 4 months are an infinity of time.

This is also a period, however, during which the head turning procedure cannot be used. Many of us have tried to modify the existing head turning paradigm for use with the very young infant, but we have found it extremely difficult to do so. Perhaps a satisfactory modification of the procedure will ultimately be devised, but meantime a number of very fine investigators (for example, Clifton, Meyers, and Solomons, 1972; Clifton, Siqueland, and Lipsitt, 1972) have found the attempt frustrating and difficult. The head turning paradigm also has an upper limit to its use. Kuhl has said it is at 10 months of age, and Morse has also found that infants as young as 10 months may no longer respond when presented with this procedure. Thus, there is a valuable but only limited time window over which this powerful paradigm may be used.

The most promising and exciting aspect of the VRISD paradigm is its ability to tell us something about the individual infant. All of the studies reported prior to the development of this procedure dealt with group data only. When it was reported that infants could discriminate /ba/ from /ga/ and /di/ from /du/, that meant that a group of 10, 12 or 14 infants were able to do so with one or two of the sharpest pulling the group up to a satisfactory significance level. What clinicians typically need to know, however, is not so much what the group can do, but what the individual infant can do in comparison with his peers. Can a particular infant discriminate between /na/ and /ga/, for example? The VRISD paradigm holds out great promise for clinical use and may prove to have predictive value also with respect to later language development.

I would like to point out, however, that it is also possible to use various combinations of paradigms to probe the process of speech perception in infants. In my own work, I have used the heart rate paradigm and sucking paradigms under different conditions of stimulus presentation. For example, in one study (Leavitt et al., 1976), cardiac responses were obtained upon presentation of different stimulus trains and different stimulus variables. In these studies both intermittent and continuous trains of syllables were employed. We first presented a train of /ba/ syllables followed by a silent interval of 30 seconds duration and then a train of /ga/ syllables. Under this condition the 6-week-old infant has to hold the /ba/ syllable in short-term memory, later retrieve it, and compare it with /ga/. We later presented a train of /ba/ syllables followed immediately by a train of /ga/ syllables. Different results were obtained with very young infants under these two conditions, depending upon the nature of the dependent variables being measured.

In another group of studies (Swoboda, Morse, and Leavitt, 1976; Swoboda et al., 1978), vowel stimuli along the /i/ − /I/ continuum were presented to infants in a high amplitude sucking paradigm in order to examine their short-term memory capabilities. Vowels of very brief duration (60 ms) and of longer duration (240 ms) were presented. It was found that normal 8-week-old infants were able to discriminate the 240 ms vowel pairs /i/ and /I/ continuously, that is, equally well between and within-vowel categories. When the same vowels were presented with a 60 ms duration only, however, the results revealed reliable between-category but not within-category discrimination. A silent interval between the last vowel of the first, now familiar, series and the first vowel of the second novel series, was also varied. The magnitude of response recovery in the between-category shift was found to be inversely related to the duration of this interval. Interestingly, significant differences were observed in this experiment in the initial attention to, and discrimination of, the stimuli and in memory for short vowels, between a group of normal infants and a group of at-risk infants who were also studied. While this test may not provide a definitive clinical tool, it does indicate that ultimately it may be possible to derive clinical procedures from basic research aimed at the investigation of normal processes. Even so, there is still much to learn about the methodology of such studies, as was shown by Eilers' discussion of the statistical procedures being used by herself and her colleagues. Our understanding of the capability of infants depends upon the efficacy and appropriateness of the procedures we use.

I believe that it is important for us to try to integrate these studies of speech perception and speech production with what we know about cognitive development and the development of attachment and of social behavior. In the attempt to do so, I feel that I am reifying distinctions which I do not really like to make, such as the distinction between physiology and behavior, or cognition and language. Perhaps these distinctions do exist. I tend to think they are an artifact of our formal desire to systematize and classify phenomena. I would like to present some data from my own laboratory which may help us to integrate these diverse areas.

Oller has been questioned not only about the motivation for infant vocalizations but also about their occasions (this volume, Chapter 4). In a study of 4-month-old infants, my colleagues and I (VerHoeve, Stevenson, and

Leavitt, 1979) examined the contexts in the home in which infants vocalized. Although mothers talked a lot and a number of outcome events appeared to depend upon what the mother said, the effects of infant vocalization upon the mother were much more impressive. The vocalizations influenced her behavior in lawful ways. A cascade of behaviors was shown by means of lag sequential analysis to follow them. We were not simply examining the conditional probability of one event following another, but the entire sequence of following events. The mother stopped talking, smiled, and then engaged in a whole series of other behaviors when the infant vocalized. The consequences were complex and contained a strong affective component. These findings suggest that infant vocal behavior not only provides a basis for later development of spoken language, it also acts as a powerful determinant of behavior on the part of the caretaker.

In another series of studies, we did not ask how infants process the signals emitted by adults, but rather how adults process infants' signals? I have been very interested in the question: Are there special infant signals? Smiling, crying, and gaze behaviors have all been identified as important signals emitted by the infant. In a series of studies (Leavitt and Donovan, 1979; Frodi et al., 1978a; Frodi et al., 1978b; Donovan and Leavitt, 1978; Donovan, Leavitt, and Balling, 1978), we examined the physiologic responses, for example, heart rate, skin conductance, and blood pressure, of both fathers and mothers to infant signals. We found, as one might expect, that the smiles and cries of infants were powerful elicitors of physiologic responses in the mother. More interestingly, we found that these responses were correlated with the mother's perception of her own infant as determined by a questionnaire. It was possible on the basis of this questionnaire to divide the mothers into two groups according to whether they perceived their own infants as easy or difficult to care for. It was found that mothers who labeled their infant as "difficult" were physiologically less sensitive to changes in the signals emitted by infants, specifically in gaze behaviors, than those who labeled their infants as "easy."

My colleagues and I wanted to know what the implications of this finding might be, if any, for the mother's behavior towards her own infant. We therefore studied these same mothers in relation to their infants in a feeding situation. We chose the feeding situation because in it, the goal is agreed upon by all the participants and measures of behavioral responsiveness to the infant on the part of the mother can be made reliably. The index of behavioral responsiveness that was used, was a ratio of rate of maternal responding during infant gaze at mother/to rate of maternal responding during the times when the infant was looking away. It was found that mothers who were physiologically less sensitive to infant gaze behaviors (those who had labeled their own infants as difficult to care for) could also be differentiated behaviorally in the feeding situation from the mothers who were physiologically more sensitive (those who had labeled their infants as easy to care for). Thus, the physiologic measures were correlated significantly with, and were predictive of, maternal responsiveness to the infant in the feeding situation. It is not clear at this time how these measures are related to one another or which measure, the behavioral or the physiologic, should be considered as a primary one. It is our belief, however, that the mental set and perception of the mothers was very important in determining their behavior towards their own infants.

This labeling was specifically tested in a further study of responsiveness of both fathers and mothers (Frodi et al., 1978a). In this study the fathers and mothers watched a videotape of either a crying or a smiling infant. Physiologic measures were obtained from the parents during this viewing. The babies, who were 3 months of age, were labeled as "normal" or "difficult and premature" in equal proportions of the sample viewings. The results showed that the smiling infant triggered positive behavioral responses and negligible autonomic arousal. The crying infant was perceived as aversive and elicited blood pressure and skin conductance increases. The latter increases were even more apparent when the infant was described as "premature." These results suggested that the labeling effect was an important one in this experiment. We have hypothesized that it determines the mother's overall responsiveness towards her own infant.

In a follow-up study of the mothers previously described as participating in the feeding situation experiment, their infants were tested at 18 to 20 months of age by means of the Uzgiris-Hunt Object Permanence Scales (Donovan and Leavitt, 1978). It was found that the infants whose mothers, both behaviorally and physiologically, were less sensitive to them, performed at a significantly lower level on these scales than the infants whose mothers, by both measures, were found to be more sensitive. These results suggest that the interactions taking place between mother and infant, which later cascade into great complexities of human behavior and reactions to family relationships, may be related in many ways to language development. It may, therefore, be of value to consider the quality and nature of mother-infant interaction as one of the determinants of language behavior in the child.

Discussion of Leavitt's paper

Kent referred to a new body of data on the anatomy of the infant vocal tract (George, in press). He believed that this work might help to fill the existing gaps in our understanding of the development of the vocal tract, which Leavitt had rightfully pointed out.

Reilly (scientific editor, *The Communication Game*) asked if Leavitt had any independent measures indicating whether the infants labeled as "difficult" to care for really were difficult babies. Leavitt replied that he did not have such independent measures for that particular group of infants. For other groups, he and his co-workers had found, with few exceptions, that the babies' responses to caregiving matched the parents' perceptions. Ease of management was a relative matter. Fortunately most babies were more or less readily cared for. Leavitt was interested in defining problems in caregiving, but he was even more interested in the mental set of the mother as caregiver. He believed that the labeling effect, that is, the mother's labeling of the infant, on the basis of her perceptions, as easy or difficult to care for, was very important. All individuals, he believed, carried expectations around with them because of what they read or heard about the behavior of infants. These expectations as well as the labeling effect had clinical implications. Clinicians were constantly applying labels to both children and adults and it was very important to examine the effect of that labeling.

Reilly responded that she was sure there were sickly babies or colicky babies who really were difficult to care for. She thought there might be mothers who labeled their babies as difficult to care for because their babies *were* sickly or colicky and mothers who labeled their babies as difficult because they themselves were less adept at managing a baby with a particular temperament.

Leavitt agreed that there might in some cases be a chicken-and-egg phenomenon. He had attempted to ask questions about the nature of signals emitted by the infants themselves (Frodi et al., 1978b). Parents had been asked to listen to a cry signal from a premature infant dubbed onto a videotape of the cry of a normal infant and vice versa, that is, to a cry signal from a normal infant dubbed onto a videotape of a crying premature infant. The auditory cry signal turned out to have important effects upon the adult, independent of the face with which it was paired. Frodi had gone on to study responses of this kind in mothers who had been termed neglectful or abusive or who had other psychiatric conditions. Even in these mothers, differential responses to stimuli emitted by normal or premature infants had been found. The findings suggested, as others had proposed, that infants who are neglected or abused may be difficult to manage from the beginning. Stark added that some infants appeared to be poor or inconsistent emitters of signals and it might be difficult for normal mothers to respond to them.

Leavitt stated that there were marked variations among mothers, for example, in the density of their vocalizations. Such population differences needed to be taken into account. Great care needed to be exercised in applying data from studies such as those he described. Methodological variables, population differences, and statistical problems all had to be examined critically before such findings were applied clinically. These cautions were particularly important for clinical assessment and prediction. Even sophisticated clinicians were anxious to find ready answers to the problems of early diagnosis. The problem was especially acute when at-risk populations of infants were being considered. There was no test that could allow the clinician to predict, on the basis of the capabilities of the one-month-old infant, what his overall status was likely to be in later childhood, adolescence, or adulthood. There were too many complex discontinuities in human behavior, and too many developmental changes taking place in the first year of life, much less the first 10 years. Errors of prediction and the resulting inaccuracy of labeling of the child or creation of faulty expectations could be harmful to the child.

Bibliography:
Section II

Abbs, J., Muller, E., Hassul, M., and Netsell, R. (1977) A systems analysis of possible afferent contributions to lip movement control. Paper presented to American Speech and Hearing Association, Chicago, Illinois.

Abbs, J. (1979). Personal communication.

Abramson, A.S. and Lisker, L. (1970) Discriminability along the voicing continuum: Cross-language tests. *Proceedings of the Sixth International Congress of Phonetic Sciences, Prague, 1967.* Prague: Academia.

Ades, A. (1974) How phonetic is selective adaption? Experiments on syllable position and vowel environment. *Perception and Psychophysics* 16:61–66.

Anderson, B.J., Vietze, P., and Dokecki, P.R. (1977) Reciprocity in vocal interactions of mothers and infants. *Child Development* 48:1676–1681.

Anokhin, P. (1964) Systemogenesis as a general regulator of brain development. In W. Himwich and H. Himwich (Eds.), *The Developing Brain.* New York: Elsevier.

Aslin, R.N., Hennessy, B., Pisoni, D., and Perez, A. (1979) Individual infants' discrimination of voice onset time: Evidence for three modes of voicing. Paper presented at the Biennial Meeting of the Society for Research in Child Development, San Francisco (March).

Aslin, R.N. and Pisoni, D.B. (1980) Some developmental processes in speech perception. In G. Yenikomshian, C. Ferguson, and J. Kavanagh (Eds.). *Child Phonology: Perception, Production and Deviation.* New York: Academic Press.

Atkinson, K.B., McWhinney, B., and Stoel, C. (1970) An experiment in the recognition of babbling. *Papers and Reports on Child Language Development* (Stanford University) 1:71–76.

Baken, R. (1979) Personal communication.

Bell, S.M. and Ainsworth, M.S. (1972) Infant crying and maternal responsiveness. *Child Development* 43:1171–1190.

Bever, T.G. (1961) Prelinguistic behavior: A systematic analysis and comparison of early vocal and general development. Honors thesis, Cambridge: Harvard University.

Bell, S.M. and Salter Ainsworth, M.D. (1972) Infant crying and maternal responsiveness. *Child Development* 43:1171–1190.

Blakemore, C. and Campbell, F. (1969) On the existence of neurons in the human visual system selectively sensitive to the orientation and size of retinal images. *Journal of Physiology* 203:237–360.

Bleck, E.E. (1975) Locomotor prognosis in cerebral palsy. *Developmental Medicine Child Neurology* 17:18.

Bloom, K. (1977) Patterning of infant vocal responses. *Journal of Experimental Child Psychology* 23:367–377.

Bloom, K. (1979) Evaluation of infant vocal conditioning. *Journal of Experimental Child Psychology* 27:60–70.

Bloom, K. and Esposito, A. (1975) Social conditioning and its proper control procedures. *Journal of Experimental Child Psychology* 19:209–222.

Blumstein, S.E. and Stevens, K.N. (1979) Acoustic invariance in speech production: Evidence from measurements of the spectral characteristics of stop consonants. *Journal of the Acoustical Society of America* 66:1001–1017.

Bosma, J.F. (1972) Form and function of the infant's mouth and pharynx. In J.F. Bosma (Ed.), *Third Symposium on Oral Sensation and Perception: The Mouth of the Infant.* Springfield, Illinois: C.C. Thomas.

Bosma, J.F. (1975) Anatomic and physiologic development of the speech apparatus. In D.B. Tower (Ed.), *The Nervous System. Vol. 3: Human Communication and its Disorders.* New York: Raven Press.

Bosma, J.F. and Showacre, J. (Eds.) (1975) Symposium on the development of upper respiratory anatomy and function. Washington, D.C.: U.S. Government Printing Office.

Bosma, J.F. and Fletcher, S.G. (1962) The upper pharynx. *Journal of Otology, Rhinology and Laryngology* 71:134–157.

Bosma, J., Truby, H., and Lind, J. (1965) Cry motions of the newborn infant. In J. Lind (Ed.), *Newborn Infant Cry.* Uppsala: Almqvist and Wiksells.

Bosma, J.F., Truby, H.M., and Lind, J. (1966) Studies of neonatal transition: Correlated cineradiographic and visual acoustic observations. *Acta Paediatrica Scandinavica* 49, Supplem. 163:93–109.

Bouhuys, A. (1971) Respiration: growth and development. In *Patterns of Orofacial Growth and Development,* ASHA Reports No. 6:96–105.

Branigan, G. (1976) Syllabic structure and the acquisition of consonants: The great conspiracy in word formation. *Journal of Psycholinguistic Research* 5:117–133.

Bratzlavsky, M. (1976) Human brainstem reflexes. In M. Shahan (Ed.), *The Motor Systems: Neurophysiology and Muscle Mechanisms.* New York: Elsevier.

Bruner, J. (1973) Organization of early skilled action. *Child Development* 44:1–11.

Bruner, J. (1978) From communication to language: A psychological perspective. In I. Markova (Ed.), *The Social Context of Language.* New York: Wiley Press.

Buhr, R.D. (1980) The emergence of vowels in an infant. *Journal of Speech and Hearing Research* 23:73–94.

Butterfield, E. and Cairns, G. (1974) Whether infants perceive linguistically is uncertain, and if they did its practical importance would be equivocal. In R. Schiefelbusch and L. Lloyd (Eds.), *Language Perspectives: Acquisition, Retardation and Intervention.* Baltimore: University Park Press.

Butterfield and Siperstein, G.N. (1972) In J.F. Bosma (Ed.) Third Symposium on Oral Sensation and Perception: The Mouth of the Infant. Springfield, Illinois: C.C. Thomas.

Capute, A., Accardo, P., Vining, E., Rubenstein, J., and Harryman, S. (1978) *Primitive Reflex Profile: Monographs in Developmental Pediatrics, Volume 1*. Baltimore: University Park Press.

Carney, A.E., Widen, G.P., and Viemeister, N.F. (1977) Noncategorical perception of stop consonants differing in VOT. *Journal of the Acoustical Society of America* 62:960–970.

Clifton, R.K., Meyers, W.J., and Solomons, G. (1972) Methodological problems in conditioning the head turning response of newborn infants. *Journal of Experimental Child Psychology* 13:29–42.

Clifton, R.K., Siqueland, E.R., and Lipsitt, L.P. (1972) Conditioned head turning in human newborns as a function of conditioned response requirements and states of wakefulness. *Journal of Experimental Child Psychology* 13:43–52.

Condon, W.S. and Sander, L. (1974) Synchrony demonstrated between movements of the infant and adult speech. *Child Development*, 45:456–462.

Connolly, K. (1977) The nature of motor skill development. *Journal of Human Movement Studies* 3: 123-43.

Crelin, E.S. (1973) *Functional Anatomy of the Newborn*. New Haven: Yale University Press.

Crickmay, M. (1977) *Speech Therapy and the Bobath Approach to Cerebral Palsy*. Springfield, Illinois: C.C. Thomas.

Cruttenden, A. (1970) A phonetic study of babbling. *British Journal of Disorders of Communication* 5:110–118.

Crystal, D. (1973) Non-segmental phonology in language acquisition: A review of the issues. *Lingua* 32:1–45.

Crystal, D. (1980) Prosodic development. In P. Fletcher and M. Garman (Eds.) *Language Acquisitions*. Cambridge: Cambridge University Press.

Cutting, J.E. and Rosner, B.S. (1974) Categories and boundaries in speech and music. *Perception and Psychophysics* 16:564–571.

Delattre, P.C., Liberman, A.M., and Cooper, F.S. (1951) Voyelles synthetiques a deux formantes et voyelles cardinales. *Maitre Phonetique* 96:30–36.

Desmedt, J. (1978) *Cerebral Motor Control in Man: Long Loop Mechanism*. New York: S. Karger.

Dobbing, J. and Sands, J. (1973) Quantitative growth and development of human brain. *Arch. Dis. Child* 48:757.

Donovan, W.L. and Leavitt, L.A. (1978) Early cognitive development as a function of maternal behavioral and physiologic responsiveness. *Child Development* 44:1251–1254.

Donovan, W.L., Leavitt, L.A. and Balling, J.D. (1978) Maternal physiologic response to infant signals. *Psychophysiology* 15:68–74.

Dore, J. (1975) Holophrases, speech acts and language universals. *Journal of Child Language* 2:21–40.

Dubner, R. and Kawamura, Y. (1971) *Oral-Facial Sensory and Motor Mechanisms*. New York: Appleton-Century-Croft.

DuBrul, E.L. (1976) Biomechanics of speech sounds. *Annals of the New York Academy of Sciences* 280:631–642.

DuBrul, E.L. (1977) Origin of the speech apparatus and its reconstruction in fossils. *Brain and Language* 4:365–381.

Easton, T. (1972) On the normal uses of reflexes. *American Scientist* 60:591–594.

Eilers, R.E. (1977) Context-sensitive perception of naturally produced stop and fricative consonants by infants. *Journal of the Acoustical Society of America* 61:1321–1336.

Eilers, R.E. (in press) Infant speech perception: History and mystery. In G. Yeni-Komshian, C. Kavanagh, and C. Ferguson (Eds.), *Child Phonology: Perception, and Deviation*. New York: Academic Press.

Eilers, R.E., Gavin, W.J., and Wilson, W.R. (1979) Linguistic experience and phonemic perception in infancy: A cross linguistic study. *Child Development* 50:14–18.

Eilers, R.E., Morse, P.A., Gavin, W.J., and Oller, D.K. (in press) Discrimination of VOT in infancy. *Journal of the Acoustical Society of America*.

Eilers, R.E. and Minifie, F.D. (1975) Fricative discrimination in early infancy. *Journal of Speech and Hearing Research* 18:158–169.

Eilers, R.E., Morse, P.A., and Gavin, W.J. (in preparation) Exploring the perception of the "sound of silence" in infancy.

Eilers, R.E. and Oller, D.K. (in press) A comparative study of speech perception in young severely retarded children and normal infants. *Journal of Speech and Hearing Research*.

Eilers, R.E., Wilson, W.R., and Moore, J.M. (1976) Discrimination of synthetic prevoiced labial stops by infants and adults. *Journal of the Acoustical Society of America* 60, Supplement 1:S91. (Abstract).

Eilers, R.E., Wilson, W.R., and Moore, J.M. (1977) Developmental changes in speech discrimination. *Journal of Speech and Hearing Research* 20:766–780.

Eilers, R.E., Wilson, W.R., and Moore, J.M. (1979) Speech discrimination in the language-innocent and the language-wise: A study in the perception of voice-onset-time. *Journal of Child Language* 6:1–18.

Eimas, P.D. (1974a) Auditory and linguistic processing of cues for place of articulation by infants. *Perception and Psychophysics* 16:513–521.

Eimas, P.D. (1974b) Linguistic processing of speech by young infants. In R.L. Schiefelbusch and L.L. Lloyd (Eds.), *Language Perspectives: Acquisition, Retardation and Intervention*. Baltimore: University Park Press.

Eimas, P.D. (1975a) Speech perception in early infancy. In L.B. Cohen and P. Salapatek (Eds.), *Infant Perception*. New York: Academic Press.

Eimas, P.D. (1975b) Developmental studies of speech perception. In L.B. Cohen and P. Salapatek (Eds.), *Infant Perception*. New York: Academic Press.

Eimas, P.D. (1975c) Auditory and phonetic coding of the cues for speech: Discrimination of the (r-1) distinction of young infants. *Perception and Psychophysics* 18:341–347.

Eimas, P.D., Siqueland, E., Jusczyk, P.W., and Vigorito, J. (1971) Speech perception in infants. *Science* 171:303–306.

Ekbom, K., Jernelius M., and Kugelberg, E. (1952) Perioral reflexes. *Neurology* 2:103–111.

Entus, A.K. (1977) Hemispheric asymmetry in processing of dichotically presented speech and nonspeech stimuli by infants. In S. Segalowitz and F. Gruber (Eds.), *Language Development and Neurological Theory*. New York: Academic Press.

Fant, G. (1960) *Acoustic Theory of Speech Production*. The Hague: Mouton.

Fant, G. (1973) *Speech Sounds and Features*. Cambridge: M.I.T. Press.

Fawcus, R. (1952) Oropharyngeal function in relation to speech. *Developing Med. Child Neurology* 11:556–560.

Fenton, J.C. (1925) *A Practical Psychology of Babyhood*. Boston: Houghton Mifflin.

Ferguson, C.A. (1964) Baby talk in six languages. *American Anthropologist* 66, Part II:103–256.

Ferguson, C.A. (1973) The acquisition of fricatives. *Papers and Reports on Child Language Development*. Stanford University 6:61–86.

Ferguson, C.A. (1975) Baby talk as a simplified register. *Papers and Reports on Child Language Development*. Stanford University 9:1–27.

Ferguson, C. and Garnica, O. (1975) Theories of phonological development. In E. Lenneberg and E. Lenneberg. (Eds.), *Foundations of Language Development: A Multidisciplinary Approach, Volume 1*. New York: Academic Press.

Fernald, A. and Simon, T. (1977) Analyse van grundfrequenz und sprach segmentlange bei der Kommunikation von Muttern mit neugeborenen. Torschungsberichte: Institut fur Phonetik und Sprachliche Kommunikation der Universitat Munchen 7:19–37.

Ferry, P., Culbertson, J., Fitzgibbons, P., and Netzky, M. (1979) Brain function and language disabilities. *Journal of Pediatric Otorhinolaryngology* 1:13–24.

Fletcher, S. (1971) Deglutition. In *Patterns of Orofacial Growth and Development*. ASHA Reports No. 6:66–78.

Fletcher, S.G. (1973) Maturation of the speech mechanism. *Folia Phoniatrica* 25:161–172.

Fodor, J.A., Garrett, M.F., and Brill, S.L. (1975) Pi ka pu: The perception of speech sounds by pre-linguistic infants. *Perception and Psychophysics* 18:74–78.

Frodi, A.M., Lamb, M.E., Leavitt, L.A., and Donovan, W.L. (1978a) Fathers' and mothers' responses to infant smiles and cries. *Infant Behavior and Development* 1:187–198.

Frodi, A.M., Lamb, M.E., Donovan, W.L., Leavitt, L.A., Neff, C., and Sherry, O. (1978b) Fathers' and mothers' responses to the faces and cries of normal and premature infants. *Developmental Psychology* 14:490–498.

Fry, D.B. (1966) The development of the phonological system in the normal and deaf child. In F. Smith and G. Miller (Eds.), *The Genesis of Language*. Cambridge: MIT Press.

Fry, D.B. (1968) The phonemic system in childrens' speech. *British Journal of Disorders of Communication* 3:13–19.

Gazzaniga, M. (1970) *The Bisected Brain*. New York: Appleton-Century-Crofts.

George, S. (in press) A longitudinal and cross-sectional analysis of early cranial base growth change. *American Journal of Physiological Anthropology*.

Gerstman, L.H. (1968) Classification of self-normalized vowels. *IEEE Transactions on Audio and Electroacoustics* AU-16:78–80.

Gibson, E.J. (1969) *Principles of Perceptual Learning and Development*. New York: Appleton-Century-Crofts.

Gilbert, J. and Purves, B. (1977) Temporal constraints on consonant clusters in child production. *Journal Child Language* 4:417–432.

Goldstein, U. (1979) Modeling childrens' vocal tracts. Paper presented at 97th Meeting of the Acoustical Society of America, Cambridge, Massachusetts, June 12–16.

Gottlieb, G. (1971) *Development of Species Identification in Birds*. Chicago: University of Chicago Press.

Graham, F.K., Leavitt, L.A., Strock, B.D., and Brown, J.W. (1977) Precocious cardiac orienting in a human encephalic infant. Science 199:322–324.

Green, S. (1975) Communication by a graded vocal system in Japanese monkeys. In L.A. Rosenblum (Ed.), *Primate Behavior, Vol 4*. New York: Academic Press.

Hardy, J. (1970) Development of neuromuscular systems underlying speech production. In *Speech and the Dentofacial Complex: The State of the Art*. ASHA Reports No. 5:49–68.

Hays, W.L. (1966) *Statistics for Psychologists*. New York: Holt, Rinehart, and Winston.

Hecox, K. (1975) Electrophysiological correlates of human auditory development. In L.B. Cohen and P. Salapatek (Eds.), *Infant Perception: From Sensation to Cognition*. New York: Academic Press.

Hillenbrand, J., Minifie, F.D., and Edwards, T.J. (1977) Tempo of frequency change as a cue in speech sound discrimination by infants. Paper presented at the Biennial Meeting of the Society for Research in Child Development, New Orleans (March).

Hixon, T. (1979) Personal communications

Hixon, T. and Hardy, J. (1964) Restricted motility of the speech articulators in cerebral palsy. *Journal Speech and Hearing Disorders* 29:293–306.

Holmberg, T.L., Morgan, K.A., and Kuhl, P.A. (1977) Speech perception in early infancy: Discrimination of fricative consonants. *Journal of the Acoustical Society of America* 62 Supplement 1:S99 (Abstract).

House, A.S. and Fairbanks, G. (1953) The influence of consonant environment upon the secondary acoustical characteristics of vowels. *Journal of the Acoustical Society of America* 25:105–113.

Humphrey, T. (1971) Human prenatal activity sequences in the facial region and their relationship to postnatal development. In *Patterns of Orofacial Growth and Development*. ASHA Reports, No. 6:19–37.

Illingworth, R.S. and Lister, J. (1964) The critical or sensitive period with special reference to certain feeding problems in infants and children. *Journal of Pediatrics* 65:839–848.

Irwin, O.C. (1947) Infant speech: Consonantal sounds according to place of articulation. *Journal of Speech and Hearing Disorders* 12:397–401.

Irwin, O.C. (1948) Infants' speech: Development of vowel sounds. *Journal of Speech and Hearing Research* 13:31–34.

Irwin, O.C. and Chen, H.P. (1946) Infant speech: Vowel and consonant frequency. *Journal of Speech Disorders* 11:123–125.

Irwin, O.V. and Curry, T. (1941) Vowel elements in the crying vocalizations of infants under ten days of age. *Child Development* 12:99–109.

Jacobson, M. (1975) Brain development in relation to language. In E. Lenneberg and E. Lenneberg (Eds.), *Foundations of Language Development: A Multidisciplinary Approach, Volume 1*. New York: Academic Press.

Jakobson, R. (1968) *Kindersprache, Aphasie, und allgemeine Lautgesetze* (1941). Translated by A.R. Keller, *Child Language, Aphasia, and Phonological Universals*. The Hague: Mouton.

Joos, M.A. (1948) Acoustic phonetics. *Language Supplement* 24:1–136.

Jusczyk, P.W. (1977) Perception of syllable-final stop consonants by two-month-old infants. *Perception and Psychophysics* 21:45–454.

Jusczyk, P.W. (in press) Infant speech perception: A critical appraisal. In P.D. Eimas and J.L. Miller (Eds.), *Perspectives on the Study of Speech*. New Jersey: Lawrence Erlbaum Associates.

Jusczyk, P.W., Copan, H., and Thompson, E. (1978) Perception by 2-month-old infants of glide contrasts in multisyllabic utterances. *Perception and Psychophysics* 24:515–520.

Jusczyk, P.W., Pisoni, D.B., Walley, A.C., and Murray, J. (1980) Discrimination of relative onset time of two-component tones by infants. *Journal Acoustical Society America* 67 (1):262–270.

Jusczyk, P.W., Rosner, B.S., Cutting, J.E., Foard, C.F., and Smith, L.B. (1977) Categorical perception of nonspeech sounds by two-month-old infants. *Perception and Psychophysics* 21:50–54.

Jusczyk, P. and Thompson, E. (1978) Perception of a phonetic contrast in multi-syllabic utterances by two-month-old infants. *Perception and Psychophysics* 23:105–109.

Kaplan, E. (1969) The role of intonation in the acquisition of language. Unpublished Doctoral Dissertation, Cornell University.

Kearsley, R.B. (1973) The newborn's response to auditory stimulation. *Child Development* 44:582–590.

Kent, R.D. (1976) Anatomical and neuromuscular maturation of the speech mechanism: Evidence from acoustic studies. *Journal Speech and Hearing Research* 19:421–447.

Kent, R.D. (this volume) Articulatory and acoustic perspectives on speech development.

Kent, R.D. and Forner, L.L. (in press) Speech segment durations in sentence recitations by children and adults. *Journal of Phonetics*.

Kent, R.D. and Minifie, F.D. (1977) Coarticulation in recent speech production models. *Journal of Phonetics* 5:115–133.

Kent, R. and Moll, K. (1975) Articulatory timing in selected consonant sequences. *Brain and Language* 2:304–323.

Kent, R.D. and Netsell, R. (1978) Articulatory abnormalities in athetoid cerebral palsy. *Journal of Speech and Hearing Disorders* 43:353–373.

Kessen, W., Levine, J., and Wendrich, K. (1979) The imitation of pitch in infants. *Infant Behavior and Development* 2:93–100.

Konishi, M. (1965) The role of auditory feedback in the control of vocalization in the white-crowned sparrow. *Zeitschrift für Tier psychologie* 22:770–783.

Kuhl, P.K. (1976) Speech perception in early infancy: Perceptual constancy for vowel categories. *Journal of the Accoustical Society of America* 60 Supplement 1:S90 (Abstract).

Kuhl, P.K. (1978) Predispositions for the preception of speech-sound categories: A species-specific phenomenon? In F.D. Minifie and L.L. Lloyd (Eds.), *Communicative and Cognitive Abilities—Early Behavioral Assessment*. Baltimore: University Park Press.

Kuhl, P.K. (1979a) The perception of speech in early infancy. In N.J. Lass (Ed.), *Speech and Language: Advances in Basic Research and Practice, Volume I*. New York: Academic Press.

Kuhl, P.K. (1979b) Speech perception in early infancy: Perceptual constancy for spectrally dissimilar vowel categories. *Journal of the Acoustical Society of America* 66:1668–1679.

Kuhl, P.K. (in press) Speech perception. In N.J. Lass, J.L. Northern, D.E. Yoder, and L.V. McReynolds (Ed.), *Speech, Language and Hearing*. W.B. Saunders: Philadelphia.

Kuhl, P.K. and Miller, J.D. (1975a) Speech perception in early infancy: Discrimination of speech-sound categories. *J. Acoust. Soc. Am.* Suppl. 1:58, S56(A).

Kuhl, P.K. and Miller, J.D. (1975b) Speech perception by the chinchilla: Voiced-voiceless distinction in alveolar-plosive consonants. *Science* 190:69–72.

Kuhl, P.K. and Miller, J.D. (1978) Speech perception by the chinchilla: Identification for synthetic VOT stimuli. *Journal of the Acoustical Society of America* 63:905–917.

Kuhl, P.K. and Hillenbrand, J. (1979) Speech perception in early infancy: Perception constancy for categories based on pitch contour. Paper presented at the Biennial Meeting of the Society for Research on Child Development (March).

Ladefoged, P., DeClerk, J., Lindau, M., and Papcum, G. (1972) An auditory-motor theory of speech production. *UCLA Working Papers on Phonetics* No. 22:48–75.

Langlois, A. and Baken, R. (1976) Development of respiratory time-factors in infant cry. *Developmental Medicine and Child Neurology* 18:732–737.

Larson, C.R., Folkins, J.W., McClean, M., and Muller, E.W. (1978) Sensitivity of the human perioral reflex to parameters of mechanical stretch.. *Brain Research* 146:159–164.

Lasky, R.E., Syrdal-Lasky, A., and Klein, R.E. (1975) VOT discrimination by four- to six-and-a-half-month-old infants from Spanish environments. *Journal of Experimental Child Psychology* 20:215–225.

Leavitt, L.A., Brown, J.W., Morse, P.A., and Graham, F.K. (1976) Cardiac orienting and auditory discrimination in six-week-old infants. *Developmental Psychology* 12:514–523.

Leavitt, L.A. and Donovan, W. (1979) Perceived infant temperament, locus of control, and maternal physiological response to infant gaze. *Journal of Research in Personality* 13:267–278.

Lecours, A. (1975) Myelogenetic correlates of the development of speech and language. In E. Lenneberg and E. Lenneberg (Eds.), *Foundations of Language Development. A Multidisciplinary Approach, Volume 1.* New York: Academic Press.

Lenneberg, E.H., Rebelsky, F.G., and Nichols, I.A. (1965) The vocalizations of infants born to deaf and hearing parents. *Human Development* 8:23–37.

Lenneberg, E.H. (1967) *Biological Foundations of Language.* New York: Wiley Press.

Lewis, M.M. (1963) *Language, Thought and Personality in Infancy and Childhood.* New York: Basic Books.

Liberman, A.M., Cooper, F.S., Shankweiler, D.P., and Studdert-Kennedy M. (1967) Perception of the speech code. *Psychological Review* 74: 74:431–461.

Liberman, A.M., Delattre, P.C., Gerstman, L.J., and Cooper, F.S. (1956) Tempo of frequency change as a cue for distinguishing classes of speech sounds. *Journal of Experimental Psychology* 52:127–137.

Lieberman, P. (1973) On the evolution of language: A unified view. *Cognition* 2:59–94.

Lieberman, P., Harris, K.S., Wolff, P., and Russell, L.H. (1971). Newborn infant cry and nonhuman primate vocalization. *Journal of Speech and Hearing Research* 14:718–727.

Lieberman, P., Crelin, E.S., and Klatt, D.M. (1972). Phonetic ability and related anatomy of the newborn, adult human, Neanderthal man, and the chimpanzee. *American Anthropologist* 74:287–307.

Lindblom, B.E.F. (1963) Spectrographic study of vowel reduction. *Journal of the Acoustical Society of America* 35:1773–1781.

Lindblom, B., Lubker, J., and Gay, T. (1979) Formant frequencies of some fixed-mandible vowels and a model of speech motor programming by predictive simulation. *Journal of Phonetics* 2:147–161.

Lindblom, B. and Sundberg, J. (1969) A quantitative model of vowel production and the distinctive features of Swedish vowels. *Quarterly Progress Status Report, Speech Transmission Laboratory, Royal Institute of Technology, Stockholm, Sweden* No. 1:14–32.

Lisker, L. and Abramson, A.S. (1970) The voicing dimension: Some experiments in comparative phonetics. In *Proceedings of the 6th International Congress of Phonetic Sciences.* Prague: Academia.

McCarthy, D. (1929) The vocalizations of infants. *Psychological Bulletin* 26:625–651.

McCarthy, D. (1952) Organismic interpretation of infant vocalization. *Child Development* 23:273–280.

McCarthy, D. (1970) Language development in children. In P.H. Mussen (Ed.), *Carmichael's Manual of Child Psychology,* Third Edition. New York: Wiley.

Marler, P. (1970) A comparative approach to vocal learning: Song development in white-crowned sparrows. *Journal of Comparative and Physiological Psychiatry.* 7:1–25.

Marler, P. and Peters, S. (in press) Birdsong and speech: Evidence for special processing. In P. Eimas and J.D. Miller (Eds.), *Perspectives on the Study of Speech.*

McClean, M. (1978) Variation in perioral reflex amplitude prior to lip muscle contraction for speech. *Journal of Speech and Hearing Research* 21:276–284.

Maccoby, E.E. and Hagen, J.W. (1965) Effects of distraction upon central versus incidental recall: Developmental trends. *Journal of Experimental Child Psychology* 2:28–289.

McCollough, C. (1965) Color adaption of edge-detectors in the human visual system. *Science* 149:1115–1116.

MacKay, D.G. (1974) Aspects of the syntax of behavior: Syllable structure and speech rate. *Quarterly Journal of Experimental Psychology* 26:642–657.

MacNeilage, P. and Ladefoged, P. (1976) The production of speech and language. In E. Carterette and M. Friedman (Eds.), *Handbook of Perception, Volume VII: Language and Speech*. New York: Academic Press.

MacNeilage, P.F. and MacNeilage, L.A. (1973) Central processes controlling speech production during sleep and waking. In F.J. McGuigan and R.A. Schoonover (Eds.), *The Psychophysiology of Thinking*. New York: Academic Press.

Mattingly, I., Liberman, A., Syrdal, A., and Hawles, T. (1971) Discrimination in speech and nonspeech modes. *Cognitive Psychology* 2:131–157.

Mavilya, M. (1972) Spontaneous vocalization and babbling in hearing-impaired infants. In G. Fant (Ed.), *International Symposium on Speech Communication Ability and Profound Deafness*. Washington, D.C.: Alexander Graham Bell Association for the Deaf.

Meltzoff, A.N. and Moore, M.K. (1977) Imitation of facial and manual gestures by human neonates. *Science* 198:75–78.

Menyuk, P. (1968) The role of distinctive features in children's acquisition of phonology. *Journal of Speech and Hearing Research* 11:138–146.

Miller, C. and Morse, P.A. (1976) The "heart" of categorical speech discrimination in young infants. *Journal of Speech and Hearing Research* 19:578–589.

Miller, J., Netsell, R., and Rosin P. (in preparation) *Assessing Speech Motor Control in Children*. Baltimore: University Park Press.

Miller, J., Rosin, P., and Netsell, R. (1979) Differentiating productive language deficits and speech motor control problems in children. Paper presented at the meeting of the Wisconsin Speech and Hearing association. Madison, Wisconsin.

Miller, J., Wier, C., Pastore, R., Kelley, W., and Dooling, R. (1976) Discrimination and labeling of noise-buzz sequences with varying noise-lead times: An example of categorical perception. *Journal of Acoustical Society of America* 60:410–417.

Milner, E. (1976) CNS maturation and language acquisition. In H. Whitaker and H.A. Whitaker (Eds.), *Studies in Neurolinguistics, Volume 1*. New York: Academic Press.

Minifie, F.D. (1973) Speech acoustics. In F.D. Minifie, T.J. Hixon, and F. Williams (Eds.), *Normal Aspects of Speech, Hearing and Language*. New Jersey: Prentice Hall.

Mitchell, R.G. (1960) The moro reflex. *Cerebral Palsy Bulletin* 2:135.

Moffitt, A.R. (1971) Consonant cue perception by 22 twenty-four-week-old infants. *Child Development* 42:717–732.

Molfese, D.L. and Molfese, V.J. (1979) VOT distinctions in infants: Learned or innate? In H.A. Whitaker and H. Whitaker (Eds.), *Studies in Neurolinguistics, Volume 4*. New York: Academic Press.

Morris, S. (1979a) Personal communication.

Morris S. (1979b) *Pre-Speech Assessment Scale: A Rating Scale for the Measurement of the Pre-Speech Behaviors from Birth Through Two Years*. Experimental Edition.

Morse, P.A. (1972) The discrimination of speech and nonspeech stimuli in early infancy. *Journal of Experimental Child Psychology* 14:477–492.

Morse, P.A. (1974) Infant speech perception: A preliminary model and review of the literature. In R.L. Schiefelbusch and L.L. Lloyd (Eds.), *Language Perspectives: Acquisition, Retardation and Intervention*. Baltimore: University Park Press.

Morse, P.A. (1978) Infant speech perception: Origins, processes, and alpha centauri. In F.D. Minifie and L.L. Lloyd (Eds.), *Communicative and Cognitive Abilities—Early Behavior Assessment*. Baltimore: University Park Press.

Morse, P.A. (in press) The infancy of infant perception: The first decade of research. *Brain Behavior and Evolution*.

Morse, P.A., Eilers, R.E., and Gavin, W.J. (in preparation) /tu/-/du/ or not /tu/-/du/: A critical study in infant speech perception.

Moyers, R. (1971) Postnatal development of the orofacial musculature. In *Patterns of Orofacial Growth and Development*, ASHA Reports No. 6:38–47.

Müller, E., Hollien, H., and Murry, T. (1974) Perceptual response to infant crying: Identification of cry types. *Journal of Child Language* 1:89–95.

Murai, J. (1961) Speech development of a child suffering from a central language disorder. *Studia Phonologica* 1:58–69.

Mykelbust, H.R. (1957) Babbling and echolalia in language theory. *Journal of Speech and Hearing Disorders* 22:356–360.

Nakazima, S. (1962) A comparative study of the speech developments of Japanese and American English in childhood: (I) A comparison of the developments of voices at the prelinguistic period. *Studia Phonologica* 2:27–39.

Nakazima, S. (1966) A comparative study of the speech developments of Japanese and American English in childhood: (II) The acquisition of speech. *Studia Phonologica* 4:28–55.

Nakazima, S. (1975) Phonemicization and symbolization in language development. In E. Lenneberg and E. Lenneberg (Eds.), *Foundations of Language Development: A Multidisciplinary Approach, Volume 1*. New York: Academic Press.

Netsell, R. and Abbs, J. (1975) Modulation of perioral reflex sensitivity during speech movements. *Journal of the Acoustical Society of America* Supplement 58:541.

Netsell, R., Kent, R., and Abbs, J. (1978) Adjustments of the tongue and lips to fixed jaw positions during speech: A preliminary report. Paper presented to the Conference on Speech Motor Control, University of Wisconsin, Madison, Wisconsin.

Ohala, J. (1970) Aspects of the control and production of speech. *UCLA Working Papers on Phonetics*, No. 15.

Oller, D.K. (1973) Regularities in abnormal child psychology. *Journal of Speech and Hearing Disorders* 38:36–47.

Oller, D.K. (1978) Infant vocalizations and the development of speech. *Allied Health and Behavioral Sciences* 1:523–549.

Oller, D.K. (1981) The emergence of the sounds of speech in infancy. In G. Yeni-Komshian, C.A. Ferguson, and J. Kavanagh (Eds.), *Child Phonology: Vol. I: Production*. New York: Academic Press.

Oller, D.K., Eilers, R.E., and Carney, A.E. (forthcoming) Speech-like vocalizations of a deaf infant. University of Miami, Mailman Center for Child Development.

Oller, D.K. and Gavin, W.J. (forthcoming) The effect of posture on infant vocal sounds. University of Miami, Mailman Center for Child Development.

Oller, D.K., Wieman, L.A., Doyle, W., and Ross, C. (1976) Infant babbling and speech. *Journal of Child Language* 3:1–11.

Oller, D.K. (1978) Infant vocalizations and the development of speech. *Allied Health and Behavior Sciences* 1:523–549.

Olmsted, D.L. (1971) *Out of the Mouths of Babes*. The Hague: Mouton.

Olney, R.L. and Scholnick, E.K. (1978) Adult judgments of age and linguistic differences in infant vocalization. *Journal of Child Language* 3:145–156.

Osgood, C.E. (1953) *Method and Theory in Experimental Psychology*. New York: Oxford Press.

Paine, R.S., Brazelton, T.B., Donovan, D.E., Drorbaugh, J.E., Hubbell, J.P., and Sears, G.M. (1964) Evolution of postural reflexes in normal infants and in the presence of chronic brain syndromes. *Neurology* 14:1036.

Pastore, R.E. (1976) Categorical perception: A critical re-evaluation. In S.K. Hirsh, D.H. Eldredge, I.J. Hirsh and S.R. Silverman (Eds.), *Hearing and Davis: Essays Honoring Hallowell Davis*. St. Louis: Washington University Press.

Perkell, J.S. (1969) *Physiology of Speech Production: Results and Implications of a Quantitative Study. Research Monograph No. 53*. Cambridge, Mass: MIT Press.

Peters, A.M. (1974) The beginnings of speech. *Papers and Reports on Child Language Development* (Stanford University) 8:26–32.

Petersen, M.R., Beecher, M.D., Zoloth, S.R., Moody, D.B., and Stebbins, W.C. (1978) Neural lateralization of species-specific vocalizations by Japanese macaques (macaca fuscata). *Science* 202:324–327.

Peterson, G.E. and Barney, H.L. (1952) Control methods used in a study of the vowels. *Journal of the Acoustical Society of America* 24:175–184.

Peterson, G.E. and Shoup, J. (1966) A physiologic theory of phonetics. *Journal of Speech and Hearing Research* 9:5–67.

Piaget, J. (1952) *The Origins of Intelligence in Children*. New York: Norton.

Pisoni, D.B. (1973) Auditory and phonetic memory codes in the discrimination of consonants and vowels. *Perception and Psychophysics* 13:253–260.

Pisoni, D.B. (1977) Identification and discrimination of the relative onset time of two-consonant tones: Implications for voicing perception in stops. *Journal of the Acoustical Society of America* 61:1352–1361.

Pisoni, D.B. and Lazarus, J.H. (1974) Categorical and noncategorical modes of speech perception along the voicing continuum. *Journal of the Acoustical Society of America* 55:328–333.

Porter, R. (1978) Rapid shadowing of syllables: Evidence for symmetry of speech perceptual and motor systems, Presented at the 19th Annual Meeting of the Psychonomic Society, San Antonio, Texas, November 9–11.

Porter, R. and Castellanos, F. (submitted) Speech production measures of speech perception: Rapid shadowing of VCV syllables.

Porter, R. and Lubker, J. (submitted) Rapid reproduction of vowel-vowel sequences: Evidence for a fast direct acoustic-motoric linkage in speech.

Preston, M.S., Yeni Komshian, G.H., and Stark, R.E. (1967) Voicing in initial stop consonants produced by children in the prelinguistic period from different language communities. *The Johns Hopkins University School of Medicine, Annual Report of Neurocommunications Laboratory* 2:305–323.

Purpura, D.P. (1975) Dendritic differentiation in human cerebral cortex: Normal and aberrant developmental patterns. In Kreutzberg, G. (Ed.), *Advances in Neurology*. New York: Raven Press.

Rheingold, H.L., Gerwirtz, J.L., and Ross, B.G. (1959) Social conditioning of vocalizations in the infant. *Journal of Comparative Physiological Psychology* 52:68–73.

Rees, N. (1972) The role of babbling in the child's acquisition of language. *British Journal of Disorders of Communication* 7:17–23.

Routh, D.K. (1967) The conditioning of vocal response differentiation in infants. Doctoral dissertation, University of Pittsburgh.

Rutherford, D. (1967) Auditory-motor learning and the acquisition of speech. *American Journal of Physical Medicine* 46:245–251.

Sands, J., Dobbing, J., and Gratrix, C. (1979) Cell number and cell size: Organ growth and development and the control of catch-up growth in rats. *Lancet* 2:503–505.

Sasaki, C.T., Levine, P.A., Laitman, J.T., and Crelin, E.S. (1977) Postnatal descent of the epiglottis in man. *Archives of Otolaryngology* 103:169–171.

Sawusch, J.R. and Nusbaum, H.C. (1979) Contextual effects in vowel perception I: Anchor-induced contrast effect. *Perception and Psychophysics* 25:292–302.

Schane, S.A. (1973) *Generative Phonology*. Englewood Cliffs, N.J.: Prentice Hall.

Scheibel, A. (1979) Development of axonal and dendritic neuropil as a function of evolving behavior. In F.O. Schmitt and G.G. Worden (Eds.), *The Neurosciences Fourth Study Program*. MIT Press.

Scheibel, M. and Scheibel, A. (1976) Some thoughts on the ontogeny of memory and learning. In Rosenzweig, M. and Bennett, E. (Eds.), *Neural Mechanisms of Learning and Memory*. Cambridge, Mass.: MIT Press.

Schmidt, R.A. (1975) A schema theory of discrete motor skill learning. *Psychological Review* 82:225–260.

Searle, C.L., Jacobson, Z., and Rayment, S.G. (1979) Stop consonant discrimination bases of human audition. *Journal of the Acoustical Society of America* 799–809.

Sessle, B. (1977) Modulation of alpha and gamma trigeminal motoneurons by various peripheral stimuli. *Experimental Neurology* 54: 323–339.

Shankweiler, D., Strange, W., and Verbrugge, R. (1977) Speech and the problem of perceptual constancy. In R. Shaw and J. Bransford (Eds.), *Perceiving, Acting, and Knowing: Toward an Ecological Psychology*. New York: Lawrence Erlbaum.

Shankweiler, D.P. and Studdert-Kennedy, M. (1967) Identification of consonants and vowels presented to the left and right ears. *Quarterly Journal of Experimental Psychology* 19:59–63.

Shirley, M. (1959) *The First Two Years. Volume 1: Postural and Locomotor Developments*. Minneapolis: University of Minnesota Press.

Siegel, G.M. (1969) Vocal conditioning in infants. *Journal of Speech Hearing Disorders* 34:3–19.

Simon, H.J. and Studdert-Kennedy, M. (1978) Selective anchoring and adaption of phonetic and nonphonetic continua. *Journal of the Acoustical Society of America* 64:1338–1357.

Sloan, R.F. (1967) Neuronal histogenesis, maturation and organization related to speech development. *Journal of Communication Disorders* 1:1–15.

Siqueland, E.R. and DeLucia, C.A. (1969) Visual reinforcement of non-nutritive sucking in human infants. *Science* 1144–1146.

Smith, B.L. and Oller, D.K. (in press) A comparative study of premeaningful vocalizations produced by normal and Down syndrome infants. *Journal of Speech and Hearing Disorders*.

Spring, D. and Dale, P. (1977) The discrimination of linguistic stress in early infancy. *Journal of Speech and Hearing Research* 20:224–231.

Stanley, C.J. (1976) Spectrographic analysis of pre-linguistic vocalizations: A comparative study of deaf and normal-hearing infants' stop consonant production. Paper presented at the convention of the American Speech and Hearing Association, November.

Stark, R.E. (1978) Features of infant vocalization: The emergence of cooing. *Journal of Child Language* 3:379–390.

Stark, R.E. (1980) Prespeech sequential feature development. In P. Fletcher and M. Garman (Eds.) *Language Acquisition* Cambridge: Cambridge University Press.

Stark, R.E. (1981) Stages of speech development in the first year of life. In G.H. YeniKomshian, C.A. Ferguson, and J. Kavanagh (Eds.), *Child Phonology: Vol. I: Production*. New York: Academic Press.

Stark, R.E. and Nathanson, S.N. (1973) Spontaneous cry in the newborn infant: Sounds and facial gestures. In J.F. Bosma (Ed.), *Fourth Symposium on Oral Sensation and Perception: Development in the Fetus and Infant*. Bethesda, Maryland: U.S. Government Printing Press.

Stark, R.E., Rose, S.N., and McLagen, M. (1975) Features of infant sounds: The first eight weeks of life. *Journal of Child Language* 2:205–222.

Stark, R.E., Heinz, J.M. and Wright-Wilson, C. (1976) Vowel utterances of young infants. *Journal Acoustical Society America* S.43 (A).

Stern, D.N., Beebe, B., Jaffe, J., and Bennett, S.L. (1977) The infant's stimulus world during social interaction: A study of caregiver behaviors with particular reference to repetition and timing. In H.R. Schaffer (Ed.), *Studies in Mother-Infant Interaction*. New York: Academic Press.

Stern, D.N., Jaffe, J., Beebe, B., and Bennett, S.L. (1975) Vocalizing in unison and in alternation: Two modes of communication within the mother-infant dyad. *Annals of the New York Academy of Sciences* 263:89–100.

Stetson, R.H. (1951) *Motor Phonetics*. Amsterdam: North Holland.

Stevens, K.N. (1968) Acoustic correlates of place of production for stop and fricative consonants. *Quarterly Progress Report, Research Laboratory in Electronics, M.I.T.*, No. 89:199–205.

Stevens, K.N. (1969) Evidence for quantal vowel articulations. *Journal of the Acoustical Society of America* 46:110 (A).

Stevens, K.N. (1972) The quantal nature of speech. In P.B. Denes and E.E. David (Eds.), *Human Communication: A Unified View*. New York: McGraw-Hill.

Stevens, K.N. and House, A.S. (1961) An acoustical theory of vowel production and some of its implications. *Journal of Speech and Hearing Research* 4:303–320.

Stevens, K.N. and House, A.S. (1963) Perturbation of vowel articulations by consonantal context: An acoustical study. *Journal of Speech and Hearing Research* 6:111–128.

Stevens, K. and Klatt, D. (1974) Role of formant transitions in the voiced voiceless distinction for stops. *Journal of the Acoustical Society of America* 55:653–659.

Streeter, L. (1974) The effects of linguistic experience on phonetic perception. Unpublished doctoral dissertation, Columbia University.

Streeter, L. (1976) Language perception of two-month-old infants shows effects of both innate mechanisms and experience. *Nature* 259:39–41.

Studdert-Kennedy, M., Liberman, A.M., Harris, K.S., and Cooper, F.S. (1970) The motor theory of speech perception: A reply to Lane's critical review. *Psychological Review* 77:234–249.

Swoboda, P.J., Morse, P.A., and Leavitt, L.A. (1976) Continuous vowel discrimination in normal and at-risk infants. *Child Development* 47:459–465.

Swoboda, P., Kass, J.E., Morse, P.A., and Leavitt, L.A. (1978) Memory factors in vowel discrimination of normal and at-risk infants. *Child Development* 49:332–339.

Till, J. (1976) Infants' discrimination of speech and nonspeech stimuli. Unpublished doctoral dissertation, University of Iowa.

Todd, G.A. and Palmer, B. (1968) Social reinforcement of infant babbling. *Child Development* 39:591–596.

Trehub, S.E. (1973) Infants' sensitivity to vowel and tonal contrasts. *Developmental Psychology* 9:91–96.

Trehub, S.E. (1976) Infants' discrimination of multisyllabic stimuli: The role of temporal factors. Paper presented at the annual convention of the American Speech and Hearing Association, Houston (November).

Trehub, S.E., Bull, D., and Schneider, B. (in press) Infant speech and nonspeech perception: A review and reevaluation.

Trehub, S.E. and Chang, H.W. (1972) Speech as reinforcing stimulation for infants. *Developmental Psychology* 6:74–77.

VerHoeve, J.N., Stevenson, M.B., and Leavitt, L.A. (1979) The contexts of infant vocalization and the beginnings of conversation. Paper presented at the Fourth Annual Boston University Conference on Language Development.

Verbrugge, R., Strange, W., and Shankweiler, D.P. (1974) What information enables a listener to map a talker's vowel space? *Haskins Laboratories Status Reports on Speech Research* SR-37/38:199–208.

Vurpillot, E. (1968) The development of scanning strategies and their relation to visual differentiation. *Journal of Experimental Child Psychology* 6:622–650.

Walley, A.C., Pisoni, D.B., and Aslin, R.N. (in press) The role of early experience in the development of speech perception. In R.N. Aslin, J. Alberts, and M.R. Petersen (Eds.), *Sensory and Perceptual Development*. New York: Academic Press.

Ward, W.D. (1970) Musical perception. In J.V. Tobias (Ed.), *Foundations of Modern Auditory Theory, Volume 1*. New York: Academic Press.

Webster, R.L. (1969) Selective suppression of infant's vocal responses by classes of phonemic stimulation. *Developmental Psychology* 1:410–414.

Weiffenbach, J. and Thach, B. (1973) Elicited tongue movements: Touch and tests in the newborn human. In J. Bosma (Ed.), *Fourth Symposium on Oral Sensation and Perception: Development in the Fetus and Infant*. Washington, D.C.: Report DHEW (NIH) 73-546, Superintendent of Documents.

Weisberg, P. (1963) Social and non-social conditioning of infant vocalization. *Child Development* 34:377–388.

Whitaker, H. (1976) Neurobiology of Language. In E. Carterette and M. Friedman (Eds.), *Handbook of Perception, Volume VII: Language and Speech*. New York: Academic Press.

Wilder, C. and Baken, R. (1974) Respiratory patterns in infant cry. *Human Communication* Winter issue: 18–34.

Wilder, C.N. and Baken, R.J. (1978) Some developmental aspects of infant cry. *Journal of Genetic Psychology* 132:225–230.

Wilson, W.R. (1978) Behavioral assessment of auditory function in infants. In F.D. Minifie and L.L. Lloyd (Eds.), *Communicative and Cognitive Abilities—Early Behavioral Assessment*. Baltimore: University Park Press.

Wilson, W.R., Moore, J.M., and Thompson, G. (1976) Auditory thresholds of infants utilizing Visual Reinforcement Audiometry (VRA). Paper presented at the American Speech and Hearing Association Convention, Houston.

Winick, M. (1976) *Malnutrition and Brain Development*. New York: Oxford University Press.

Witelson, S. and Pallie, W. (1973) Left hemisphere specialization for language in the newborn: Neuroanatomical evidence of asymmetry. *Brain* 96:641–646.

Wolff, P. (1969) The natural history of crying and other vocalizations in early infancy. In B.F. Foss (Ed.), *Determinants of Infant Behavior, Volume IV*. London: Methuen & Co.

Wood, K.S. (1957) Terminology and nomenclature. In Travis, L.E. (Ed.), *Handbook of Speech Pathology*. New York: Appleton-Century-Crofts.

Woodruff, D. (1978) Brain electrical activity and behavior relationships over the life span. In Bates, P. (Ed.), *Life Span Development and Behavior, Volume I*. New York: Academic Press.

Yakovlev, P. (1962) Morphological criteria of growth and maturation of the nervous system in man. In Kolb, L., Masland, R., and Cooke, R. (Eds.), *Mental Retardation, Research Publications in Nervous and Mental Disease, Volume XXXIX*.

Yakovlev, P. and Lecours, A. (1967) The myelogenetic cycles of regional maturation of the brain. In A. Minkowski (Ed.), *Regional Development of the Brain in Early Life*. Oxford: Blackwell Scientific Publications.

Zimmerman, G.N. (in press) Stuttering: a disorder of movement. *Journal of Speech Hearing Research*.

Zinchenko, V.P., van Chzhi-Tsin, and Tarakonov, V.V. (1963) The formation and development of perceptual activity. *Soviet Psychology and Psychiatry* 2:3–12.

Zlatin, M.A. (1975) Explorative mapping of the vocal tract and primitive syllabification in infancy: The first six months. *Purdue University Contributed Papers* Fall:58–73.

Zlatin, M.A. and Whitman, I.A. (1976) Parent-infant interactive utterances: An examination of silent pause intervals. In *Final Report, Grant No. NE-G-00-3-0077*, N.I.E.

Zlatin-Laufer, M. and Horii, Y. (1977) Fundamental frequency characteristics of infant nondistress vocalization during the first 24 weeks. *Journal of Child Language* 4:171–184.

Zoloth, S.R., Petersen, M.R., Beecher, M.D., Green, S. Marler, P., Moody, D.B., and Stebbins, W. (1979) Species-specific perceptual processing of vocal sounds by monkeys. *Science* 204:870–873.

Cognitive Development and Language Behavior in Early Childhood

Introduction

The integration of the three dimensions of language, content, form, and use has been examined most frequently within the context of debate about the relationship of language and thought. It has been observed by a number of investigators that there is a significant relationship between level of cognitive development and the content of language in young children (Bloom, 1970, 1973; Sinclair, 1970; Brown, 1973). These observations may be summarized as follows: In the second year of life, children reflect their knowledge of categories or classes of objects and events by the names they give them, sometimes overextended in meaning, and by their ability to look at or reach for objects named. They first talk about objects and respond to requests for objects that are physically present (Chapman, 1978). If they are asked to carry out actions with objects named or offered to them, they may adopt the strategy of "doing what one usually does" with that object. Thus, they will eat a cookie or throw a ball, but not throw a cookie. As they learn to imitate activities, they may talk into the telephone or sweep with a broom when these objects are named for them in a request.

As the young child learns to solve problems through reflection and by anticipating events, he also becomes able to store many words rather than just imitating them directly. He acquires words enabling him to express relations, for example, "no," "up," "more," or "this." Some verbs that are acquired early may have this function, for example, "put" and "go." Also, as object relations begin to be understood a number of object names and function (relational) words may enter into a simple relationship with one another in two word utterances. Objects can be located in another room when they are requested, especially if it is a familiar room. However, words expressing simple relations may only be comprehended if these relations are evident to the child in a normal situation. He needs to know the probable relation between the objects and the persons named before he will understand their verbal expression (Chapman, 1978).

Still later, as object permanence is more fully grasped, the child becomes capable of referring to objects that are not immediately present and visible to him. He is beginning to put words together in such a way as to express a number of different meaning relations involving objects and actions, for example, "Daddy car" (location or possession). In these utterances the meaning is greater than the sum of the meanings of the individual words standing alone. The words have entered into a hierarchical relationship with one another and their order within an utterance has become important. In comprehending an utterance, the child may shift from a strategy of guessing about the probable relation between objects and people named. He may instead begin to use grammatical rules to get at the meaning of a sentence. He may overgeneralize from these rules and make errors of a kind he would have avoided if he had continued to rely on his old guessing strategy.

In observations such as these, however, the relation between level of cognitive development and language form has clearly been introduced as well as that between level of cognitive development and language content. Superficially at least, it makes sense that the ability to deal with the relations between objects and events cognitively, and the ability to express and to comprehend these relations verbally would develop together. Observations of normal children has suggested that indeed they do. The first attempts to test the extent of this relationship experimentally yielded results that were consistent with the general observations. Greenfield, Nelson and Saltzman (1972), for example, demonstrated that children of one to three years developed consistent strategies for combining seriated cups, that were parallel in form and order of acquisition to the types of grammatical structures appearing in multiword utterances. It was suggested that children learning to talk may reacquire the representation of objects and events as they map these concepts onto the structured forms of spoken language (Beilin, 1975).

These notions have been challenged in the last few years. It has been suggested that cognitive development and language development may not be as highly correlated in young normal children as was previously supposed. The nature of cognitive development is at the same time being reexamined. In this Section of the text, therefore, new approaches to the study of early cognitive development are first described; secondly, recent and ongoing studies of early language and cognitive development are presented. Questions are asked about the content and form of language in spontaneous utterances and in comprehension, and how these aspects of language relate to stages of development of cognition in the sensorimotor period.

A. Cognitive Development in Relation to Language

A Skill Approach to Language Development

Kurt W. Fischer[1] and Roberta Corrigan[2]

[1]*Department of Psychology, University of Denver, Denver, Colorado, and*
[2]*University of Wisconsin, Milwaukee, Wisconsin*

Most modern approaches to language development assume that the rules or schemes that the child develops have a very broad generality. By age 2 or so, children are said to use rules involving abstract categories like nouns and verbs or agents and actions. The Piagetian approach to cognitive development makes the same general assumption: Children develop schemes of very broad applicability, such as object permanence, causality, means-end relations, class inclusion, and conservation.

In the past decade, a number of investigators have challenged this assumed generality and have begun to build models of language development and cognitive development that assume much more specificity: Language rules begin as fairly specific, limited behaviors, and only gradually does the child build them into the generalized rules that so many linguists and psycholinguists have previously assumed (see, Ingram, this volume, Chapter 13; Maratsos and Chalkley, 1980; Shatz, 1977; MacWhinney, 1978). Likewise in cognitive development, schemes or skills are assumed to be relatively situation-specific, with particular processes specified for generalization (e.g., Cole and Bruner, 1971; Carey, 1973; Case, 1978; Gratch, this volume, Chapter 11).

In this paper, we begin from a theory of cognitive development called skill theory (Fischer, in press), which assumes that in all domains the child acquires skills that are situation-specific. Building upon that assumption, the theory aims to provide a set of tools that will explain and predict the development of specific skills in any domain, including language. Language is viewed as a large set of diverse, partially overlapping skills. Although language skills do seem to have some distinctive properties, their general developmental course should be essentially the same in outline and process as that of other sets of skills. Broadly, language involves pragmatic, semantic, and syntactic skills, as well as certain skills involved in other types of cognitive activity.

In much of the developmental literature, the term "cognition" is used to refer to concepts of the physical world or concepts as measured by Piagetian tasks. Developments in this "cognition" are frequently assumed to be prerequisites for language development. In our approach, on the other hand, there is no meaningful sense in which cognition in general can be a prerequisite for language in general, or vice versa. Piagetian cognition, like language, comprises diverse sets of skills. In any skill, the person controls sources of variation in what she thinks or does, and psychological development involves changes in the structure and scope of this control. Language skills, social skills, emotional skills, and skills involved in traditional Piagetian "cognitive" tasks all require that the individual control sources of variation in her own behavior in a particular context. The central processing characteristics of the child seem to be the only legitimate candidates for prerequisites, and no single type of skill can be singled out *a priori* as a superior measure of these processing characteristics.

The first section of this paper sketches some of the general postulates of skill theory—including, on the one hand, the assumption of specificity and, on the other hand, the general levels through which all skills are hypothesized to develop. The second section presents some of the most important methodological implications of approaches that assume specificity in development. The final section illustrates how skill theory can be used to explain certain language acquisitions.

Skill Theory

A skill is, of course, the basic psychological unit in skill theory. Skill development is analyzed in terms of a set of skill structures together with a set of transformation rules that relate those structures to each other. In development, skills in a given domain change through a series of cognitive levels, with the particular steps in the sequence specified by the transformation rules

What Is a Skill?

A skill is an organized ability that is composed of one or more components under the control of an individual. The components can be sensorimotor actions, representations, or abstractions. In using a skill, a person controls sources of variation in what she does or thinks. These sources of variation are determined jointly by the person's actions and by the particular environment that supports those actions. The skills under an individual's control will change systematically as she develops. For example, a 3-month-old may have the ability to grasp her rattle. By 7 months, she has combined the grasping skill with a listening skill to form a single, more complex skill—grasping the rattle to hear it.

Because a skill is jointly determined by the person's actions and the environment that supports those actions, skills must be relatively specific. The essential contribution of the environment dictates that children master particular skills rather than developing uniformly across the entire range of skills. A skill is thus markedly different from a Piagetian scheme or schema, which is assumed to have a high degree of generality resulting from a *structure d'ensemble* (Piaget and Grize, 1971). While Piagetian theory and most other cognitive-developmental theories characterize a *person* as being at a particular developmental stage, skill theory characterizes a *skill* as being at a particular level. Each child has many different skills at different levels.

The concept of skill thus requires unevenness across developing skill domains. Changes in the environmental context of skills produce changes in the skills, and therefore skills in different domains seldom show precise synchrony in developmental level (Jackson, Campos, and Fischer, 1978). Unevenness—what Piaget (1941) calls *décalage horizontal*—is consequently the rule or norm in development (see Fischer, 1974 and in press, for a more complete discussion).

Not only does each person exhibit skills at a number of different levels at the same time, but different people exhibit behaviors that look the same but involve different skills. Behavior is intrinsically ambiguous. The "same" act can be carried out via a number of different strategies and therefore via ·different skills. These different skills often involve grossly different developmental levels. For example, the same two-word utterance—"yellow bird"—could be produced as a single-word productive formula ("yellow + x"), a narrow semantic-category formula (color + x), or a broad semantic-category formula (attribute + entity) (MacWhinney, in press; Maratsos and Chalkley, in press). The key to analyzing the development of language behavior is not the utterance itself but the particular skill or skills that an individual controls in producing the utterance.

For most purposes, a straightforward rule—the *minimal-task rule*—proves to be useful in moving beyond the ambiguity of behavior to an analysis of development: In predicting or explaining developmental sequences, find the simplest possible skill that could produce a particular behavior. This principle is probably most useful in structured assessments, where the investigator designs the simplest task that she can think of for testing each step in a predicted developmental sequence. This assumption will allow her to predict the earliest possible level at which that behavior can appear (Fischer, in press).

Skill Levels

Because different skills will be at different levels in the same child at the same time, there is no such thing as a developmental stage in the strong sense of the term. Even if analysis is limited to one area, such as language, children will not show the same level of performance across skills. However, major statistical shifts in population of skills do occur, both within and across children (Feldman and Toulmin, 1975; McCall, Eichorn, and Hogarty, 1977).

Skill theory explains these shifts through the construct of *optimal level*. That is, on a developmental scale, the child has an upper limit to her abilities—a highest skill level beyond which she cannot go. Consequently the skills that she practices frequently will be at this highest level, but other skills will not. Operationally, optimal level is defined as the most developmentally advanced performance that a child shows across a wide range of skills.

Optimal level increases with age, of course, and the population of language skills gradually shifts upward in a statistical fashion as the child develops a higher optimal level. The increase in optimal level does not seem to be constant, however: It seems to show cyclical periods of relatively faster change and relatively slower change, and so in a probabilistic sense, levels or stages of skill development can be differentiated and measured precisely (Fischer, 1979; McCall et al., 1977). These changes in speed mean that children at a given level should be able to master more complex steps within that level but should have difficulty performing even the simplest step at the next level.

Optimal level thus accounts for the broad course of development in all skills, including language skills. Indeed, language skills are at least as good a measure of this processing limit as Piagetian skills or any other cognitive skills.

Skill theory defines ten successive optimal levels through which a person develops from infancy to adulthood (Fischer, in press).[1] The levels specify skills of gradually increasing complexity, with a skill at one level built directly upon skills from the preceding level through a process of combination of the lower-level skills into a new unit. The existence of these levels has been supported by other investigators for the period of infancy (McCall et al., 1977; Uzgiris, 1976). Strong tests of the levels beyond infancy have not yet been performed.

The progression of skills through the levels shows a repetitive cycle such that the structures of Levels 1 to 4 parallel the structures of Levels 4 to 7 and Levels 7 to 10, as shown in Table 1. Each of the cycles, called a tier, specifies skills of a different types: sensorimotor, representational, or abstract. But for each of these general types of skills, the four successive levels have similar structures. Levels 1, 4, and 7 involve single units: The child can control single sources of variation but cannot yet coordinate such sources with each other. At Levels 2, 5, and 8, the characteristic structure is a mapping, in which variations in one component are systematically related to variations in a second. That is, the child maps one component onto another. At Levels 3, 6, and 9, the child can control a relation between at least two different aspects of each of two components, thus forming a system.

---

[1]If very early infancy is included, the theory predicts three additional levels, involving the combination of pre-adapted species—specific components to form actions. However, because of the dearth of research on skill development in the first few months, it is difficult to evaluate the plausibility of these three initial levels.

Table 1. The Ten Developmental Levels Described by Skill Theory.

Tier		Level	Structure
Sensorimotor	1	1	Single sensorimotor action
	2	2	Sensorimotor mapping
	3	3	Sensorimotor system
Representational	1 4	4	System of sensorimotor systems = single representation
	2	5	Representational mapping
	3	6	Representational system
Abstract	1 4	7	System of representational systems = single abstraction
	2	8	Abstract mapping
	3	9	Abstract system
	4	10	System of abstract systems

In this system, the ability to relate several distinct aspects of each component allows the child to understand complex relations between the components. Levels 4, 7, and 10 are the culmination of development within each tier: The child can coordinate two or more systems into a single skill, which allows her to use one system to cognitively control another system. This ability generates the new type of skill for the next tier, and therefore the fourth level of one tier is also the first level of the next tier.

In the first tier, Levels 1 to 4, the child's skills are sensorimotor. She understands only sensorimotor actions—what she can do or perceive—and the direct relations among her actions. At Levels 1 to 3, she gradually increases the complexity of the actions that she can control, moving from single sensorimotor actions to sensorimotor mappings to sensorimotor systems. Level 4 moves the child beyond sensorimotor skills to representations. The characteristic structure is a system of sensorimotor systems, which is the same as a single representation. In skill theory, "representation" is not defined either as a copy of an event or as a symbol, because (among other things) rudimentary memories and symbols can occur at Levels 1 to 3. Instead, representation is defined as the use of one sensorimotor system to cognitively evoke another, thus allowing the representation of properties of objects, events, or people independently of any one action system. Beginning with Level 4, therefore, the child can understand in a strong sense that objects, events, and people can act or have characteristics independently of her own sensorimotor actions.

In the second tier, Levels 4 to 7, the child's skills are representational. She moves from the ability to use only one representation at a time at Level 4 to the ability to relate representations at Level 5, and then to the ability to control systems of representations at Level 6. At Level 7, she coordinates two or more representational systems into one skill and thus constructs a single abstraction.

The abstract tier involves the abstraction of intangible attributes that characterize broad categories of objects, events, or people. Language development continues beyond Level 6 into adolescence and adulthood (Fischer and Lazerson, in press), but little research has been conducted in this area of skill development and it is not the focus of this paper.

Transformation Rules

The levels allow predictions of the general types of skills, including those for language, that should emerge during a given age period. In addition, four microdevelopmental transformation rules prescribe how skills can be made more complex within a level and thus allow detailed prediction of micro-developmental sequences. One of the rules, for example, is compounding, in which an additional component is added to a skill: The simplest Level 5 representational mapping, for instance, relates two different representations; by compounding, the system can be expanded to include a third representation. In our research on the development of social roles (Watson and Fischer, 1979a), a simple mapping involves relating a representation for a doctor to a representation for a patient (see Table 2). A compounded mapping adds a representation for a nurse, so that the child relates doctor, nurse, and patient in a single skill. The microdevelopmental rules are important for understanding most of the language-acquisition research, since it concentrates primarily on three levels—numbers 3, 4, and 5—and therefore many of the phenomena studied are microdevelopmental.

Experimental Evidence

Skill theory has been used successfully to predict a number of developmental sequences and other developmental phenomena, involving such diverse behaviors as a self-recognition (Bertenthal and Fischer, 1978), classification skills (Fischer and Roberts, 1979), skills for social interactions (Hand, 1979), object permanence (Jackson, Campos, and Fischer, 1978; Bertenthal and Fischer, in press), agent use (Watson and Fischer, 1977), social roles (Watson and Fischer, 1979a), and spontaneous play (Watson and Fischer, 1979b).

Table 2 shows a detailed social-cognitive sequence of the development of agent use and social roles; most of the steps in this sequence have been tested and supported in the experiments by Watson and Fischer. An even larger number of differentiated steps could be predicted from the transformation rules. According to skill theory, the number of steps within a level can be so numerous and involve such small differences that the scale is virtually continuous.

The number of steps that a child actually shows in a given domain, however, is a function of the child's environment in that domain. By testing her on a finely graded sequence, the researcher intervenes in her environment and in a sense *produces* the finely graded, continuous scale. Without this intervention, she would almost always show a different set of microsteps in her spontaneous behavior—typically a smaller number. The effects of measurement techniques on developmental sequences and synchronies have been ignored by many researchers; skill theory is intended to provide a vehicle for analyzing them and taking them into account.

Table 2. A Developmental Sequence of Agent Use and Social Roles in Pretend Play.

Step	Cognitive level	Type of skill	Example of behavior
1		Self as agent	Child pretends to go to sleep.
2		Passive other agent	Child pretends to put doll to sleep.
3		Passive substitute agent	Child pretends to put a toy block to sleep.
4	4: Single representations	Active other agent	Child pretends that a doll goes to sleep, acting on its own.
5		Active substitute agent	Child pretends that a toy block goes to sleep, acting on its own.
6		Behavioral role	Child makes a doll carry out several actions appropriate for a doctor, like taking a patient's temperature and putting the patient in bed.
7		Shifting behavioral roles	Child makes one doll carry out several actions appropriate for a patient, like saying it is sick and going to bed, and then makes a second doll carry out several doctor actions.
8	5: Representational mappings	Social role	Child makes a patient doll and a doctor doll interact, showing several appropriate behaviors similar to those in steps 6 and 7.
9		Shifting social roles with one common agent	Child makes two dolls interact as doctor and patient and then makes the patient doll interact with a nurse doll.
10		Social role with three agents	Child makes three dolls interact as doctor, patient, and nurse.
11		Shifting social roles for the same agents	Child makes two dolls interact as doctor-patient and then makes them interact as father-daughter.
12	6: Representational systems	Social-role intersection	Child makes two dolls interact simultaneously as doctor-patient and father-daughter.
13		Shifting social-role intersections with one common agent	Child makes two dolls interact simultaneously as doctor-patient and father-daughter and then makes the man-doll interact with another doll as doctor-mother of patient and husband-wife.
14		Social-role intersection with three agents	Child makes three dolls interact simultaneously as doctor-patient-mother of patient and father-daughter-wife.

Note: This sequence is based on research reported in Watson (1978) and Watson and Fischer (1977, 1979a).

Analysis of Skill Development: Methods and Their Implications

A common assumption in research on language development and cognitive development is that all children—or at least most children—show the same developmental sequence in a given domain. But for virtually any theory that grants essential importance to the molding effect of the environment, this uniformity in developmental sequences cannot hold. Even if all human children were genetically identical, they would necessarily show important individual differences in the development of language or any other type of skill. To understand both developmental commonalities and individual differences, it seems to be important to build the analysis starting from two important phenomena: (1) Context has a powerful effect on skill development, and (2) a given behavior can be performed via a number of different strategies or skills.

The Effect of Context

One of the best documented facts in developmental psychology is that environmental factors of many kinds have a major effect on skill development (Flavell, 1972; Fischer, in press). This effect is so pervasive that it has wreaked havoc on the testing of all kinds of developmental hypotheses. It is not merely that practice affects the developmental maturity of a skill, but all kinds of contextual factors—task, procedure, seemingly minor details of the stimuli—affect developmental step. In a study of person permanence and object permanence, for example, Jackson, Campos and Fischer (1978) tested the effects of three different environmental variables—practice, task, and stimulus. All three variables affected developmental step, and two of the variables had substantial effects. With environmental variations producing such powerful effects, research that does not deal with the variations is inevitably plagued with a huge quantity of noise in its results.

To try to deal with this problem, skill theory starts with the assumption that context is essential and must be taken into account from the very beginning in developmental research. Methods need to be built upon the assumption that context is centrally important. For predicting and testing developmental sequences and synchronies, the most direct way of dealing with context is to design the assessment tools so that the context for different tasks is as nearly identical as possible. For every developmental step the same basic task and procedure are used; the task is changed only the minimum amount necessary to assess the differences between steps.

With the sequence in Table 2, for example, each step is assessed with a pretend-play procedure in which the experimenter models a story and the child then tells her own story based on the experimenter's. Also, as much as possible, the same dolls and actions are used from one step to the next. In both steps 7 and 8, for instance, the experimenter makes the patient-doll say it is sick and go to bed, and he makes the doctor-doll take the patient's temperature and put the patient to bed. The difference between the two steps is that in step 7 each doll acts alone, treating the other as no more than a passive object, while in step 8 the dolls interact.

For most purposes, we also follow another methodological rule, which adds greatly to the power of developmental measures. For every step predicted in a developmental sequence, we devise a separate assessment. With this strong scalogram method, outlined in Table 3, developmental sequences and synchronies can be tested precisely without any need for troublesome assumptions about development. For example, Piagetian researchers commonly assume that errors on a given task, such as conservation of liquid or class inclusion, reflect the child's actual competence. Language researchers commonly assume that spontaneous utterances likewise reflect the child's actual competence. With the method proposed, these questionable assumptions can be investigated and no longer merely assumed (Fischer, 1979).

The Necessity of Task Analysis

In addition to the problem of context, one of the other most pervasive and troublesome problems for developmental research is that behavior is ambiguous. Children may use very different strategies to produce superficially identical behaviors, as we pointed out earlier for two-word utterances. Different strategies will involve different skills, and consequently the development of the behavior will show a different course.

To analyze or predict development precisely, it is necessary to perform a task analysis, determining the particular skills required to perform a task. Wherever possible, the experimenter should employ tasks and procedures which reduce the range of strategies that can be used to solve each task and

Table 3. The Strong Scalogram Method: Profiles Predicted for a 7-Step Developmental Sequence.

Developmental Step	Tasks						
	A	B	C	D	E	F	G
0	−	−	−	−	−	−	−
1	+	−	−	−	−	−	−
2	+	+	−	−	−	−	−
3	+	+	+	−	−	−	−
4	+	+	+	+	−	−	−
5	+	+	+	+	+	−	−
6	+	+	+	+	+	+	−
7	+	+	+	+	+	+	+

Note: The tasks for assessing the predicted developmental steps are devised from *a priori* skill analyses. They are not merely taken inductively from a wide range of tasks, most of which do not scale.

thus reduce the ambiguity of the behavior. For example, Bertenthal and Fischer (in press) performed a task analysis of Piaget's object-permanence task involving invisible displacements, which is commonly used as a measure of representation. These authors have shown that the task can be performed easily with a strategy that does not require representation, as defined by Piaget (1937/1954). It can be solved with a pre-representational sensorimotor skill, and many children seem to solve it that way.

The task used to assess a language skill is a factor that needs to be controlled in language research, because it is a major determinant of both the age at which the skill is first detected and the sequence in which it develops. This difficulty is not eliminated by examining spontaneous language, because lack of experimental control does not eliminate the ambiguity of behavior; indeed, it often increases the ambiguity. In uncontrolled situations, the child is still faced with specific tasks to be accomplished or problems to be solved.

In addition, controlling for context in language research simplifies task analysis. For example, when the developmental relation between two distinct skills is being investigated, the failure to control for context typically makes task analysis of the two skills very difficult. The most straightforward solution is to measure the two skills with tasks that are as nearly identical as possible. Research relating language and "cognitive" abilities has almost always used dissimilar tasks, however. It is not surprising, then, that studies designed to assess the same two abilities, such as object permanence and single-word use, have produced contradictory results. Neglect of task and context typically produces chaotic results (see Corrigan, 1979, for a detailed examination of this problem for object permanence and language).

Effects of Methods on Developmental Phenomena

When context and task analysis are taken into account, then the developmental researcher can more effectively search for both developmental commonalities and systematic individual differences in development. In this search, however, the contributions of different methods must be considered. The choice of structured or spontaneous assessments and cross-sectional or longitudinal designs will have an important effect on the types of developmental phenomena that will be found.

For example, the Piagetian cognitive-developmental literature demonstrates developmental commonalities repeatedly—sequences that most children share, even across diverse social groups (e.g., Dasen et al., 1978; Elkind, 1978; Inhelder and Piaget, 1959/1964). The data almost never seem to show individual differences in developmental sequences. The language-development literature, on the other hand, shows a number of individual differences in development, as well as important commonalities (e.g., Nelson, 1973; Bloom, Lightbown, and Hood, 1975; Bowerman, 1976; Braine, 1976; Peters, 1977; Corrigan, in press; Maratsos and Chalkley, 1980). One reason for this difference between cognitive-developmental findings and language-development findings is undoubtedly that the Piagetian approach predicts commonalities in developmental sequences across all people but says little about individual differences in sequences. Researchers in the Piagetian tradition therefore tend to search for commonalities and to neglect individual differences.

More important, the difference between the findings in the two research literatures also seems to stem from differences in the sensitivity of various methods to developmental commonalities and differences. Researchers in the Piagetian tradition tend to use structured assessments and cross-sectional designs, which are normally more sensitive to commonalities. Researchers in language development tend to use spontaneous assessments and longitudinal designs, which are normally more sensitive to individual differences.

Before elaborating this argument, it may be useful to say a word about level of analysis and how it relates to commonalities and individual differences. With molecular analysis, focusing on individual behaviors, every child develops differently from every other. For example, one must look far to find two children whose first two-word utterances are the same; each child produces what is virtually a unique first "sentence." With global analysis, focusing on highly general categories of behavior, on the other hand, virtually every child follows what seems to be the same developmental progression. For example, most children first coo, then babble, then utter single words, and finally utter productive two-word utterances. Where the issue of commonalities and differences becomes interesting is in the middle ground between these two extremes. And it is in this middle ground that most developmental researchers have sought to make generalizations about commonalities and individual differences.

Structured versus spontaneous assessment. Assessments that provide structured tests of developmental sequences tend to produce different kinds of results than assessments that measure the child's spontaneous behavior. Structured assessments tend to demonstrate commonalities in development, while spontaneous assessments are more likely to uncover individual differences.[2]

With structured assessments, every child performs the same or nearly the same tasks, and therefore every child is exposed to the same contexts. These common contexts will tend to evoke common developmental steps. Common steps will be most easily detected when strong scalogram analysis is used—with a separate task for assessing each predicted developmental step. According to skill theory, some of these same steps will not appear in the

---

[2]This difference in sensitivity is not a necessary characteristic of the two types of assessment, however. A researcher can build structured assessments that are sensitive to particular hypothesized individual differences, or she can focus on commonalities across children in spontaneous behavior.

spontaneous behavior of many children, because the common contexts are missing; but the steps nevertheless accurately reflect the common developmental sequences and synchronies that children show when exposed to these contexts. In addition, structured assessments generally reduce the problem of measurement error, which can substantially affect findings from spontaneous assessments, often producing erroneous conclusions.

Structured assessments do seem sometimes to lead to a major error of inference about commonalities, however. When a single structured-assessment test is used by a large number of investigators, for example, Piagetian object permanence which has come to dominate research on cognition and early language development (Corrigan, 1979), the behaviors assessed in the instrument tend to become reified. Investigators begin to assume that most children actually produce those specific behaviors in their spontaneous activities, and consequently the behaviors are treated as if they were universal. Yet just as every infant spontaneously produces unique, early two-word utterances, so every infant spontaneously carries out unique patterns of search behaviors for finding hidden objects (except when she is tested with the structured object-permanence assessment).

The virtues and limitations of spontaneous assessments are very different from those of structured assessments. In spontaneous assessments, the child is allowed to act, with little or no intervention; and her behavior is recorded and scored in some way. This type of assessment leads to substantial error in measuring the child's competence, because of the vagaries of the contexts to which different children happen to be exposed. A language behavior appears in one child and does not appear in another simply because of the occurrence of a particular contextual event at the time of assessment for the first child.

Because of this same property, spontaneous assessments maximize the detection of certain kinds of legitimate individual differences. The common contexts supplied by structured assessments produce behaviors that many children never normally demonstrate. Spontaneous assessments, on the other hand, reflect the genuine developmental differences that occur in children as a result of normal contextual variations (when the above-mentioned assessment errors are controlled for).

For some developmental issues—perhaps many—the best procedure seems to be to use both structured and spontaneous assessments. In studies of motivation, for example, a spontaneous assessment can detect the child's motivational pattern, while a structured assessment can evaluate her competence. Using this procedure in a series of studies of pretend play, Watson and Fischer (1977, 1979b) have found that in spontaneous play, early preschool children (1- to 3-year-olds) usually demonstrate the highest step that they are capable of, but older children do not.

Longitudinal and cross-sectional designs. Like structured and spontaneous assessments, longitudinal and cross-sectional methods also tend to produce different kinds of results. Contrary to common beliefs, longitudinal studies are not generally superior to cross-sectional ones; on the contrary, longitudinal studies seem to be subject to more sources of error than cross-sectional ones (see Horn and Donaldson, 1976). Nevertheless, both types of designs have their virtues: for example, longitudinal studies seem to be superior for detecting certain kinds of individual differences, and cross-sectional studies seem to be better for analyzing commonalities.

One of the most serious flaws of longitudinal designs stems from the very fact of repeated assessment. The child is exposed to the same or similar tasks or situations each time that the assessment is repeated. This repeated exposure gives the child practice with the skills being measured. Such practice effects can influence many diverse developmental phenomena. One of the most problematic influences is that practice effects can produce misleading evidence for developmental sequences. When a child practices skills repeatedly, she usually can perform them at or near her optimal level (Case, 1978; Fischer, in press), and consequently skills in different practiced domains show a high degree of synchrony in developmental step. As a result, they seem to form developmental sequences as if they were in the same domain. If the practice is eliminated, the sequences no longer hold, because the skills are in fact in distinct domains.

Longitudinal designs do have some special virtues, however. They allow direct assessment of certain types of individual differences that are difficult to assess with cross-sectional studies. For example, to test for consistency in individual differences over time, longitudinal designs are the method of choice. Likewise, to examine individual differences in microdevelopment, longitudinal designs are often superior, as when a given child tends to develop adjacent microsteps in clusters instead of in the usual sequence.

In cross-sectional designs, many individual differences cannot be detected as easily, but the most important errors and biases from longitudinal designs are not a problem. Consequently, cross-sectional designs are superior for testing most kinds of developmental commonalities. For developmental sequences in particular, they provide a rigorous unbiased test. (Of course, a combination of longitudinal and cross-sectional methods will still be best for many purposes; e.g., Schaie and Parham, 1977.)

Also, with use of the strong scalogram method, many of the alleged limitations of cross-sectional designs can be overcome, and important developmental phenomena can be studied directly. For example, the existence of developmental levels or stages can be tested with cross-sectional designs (Fischer, 1979). The design must have the following three properties: Every step must be assessed independently; there must be at least two or three steps for each level (as in the sequence in Table 2); and subjects must be distributed evenly as a function of age—for instance, one infant for every week over a given age range. Then, if levels exist, the distribution of subjects will show clustering at each developmental level, as illustrated in Figure 1. This kind of clustering for one finely-graded sequence for a language skill

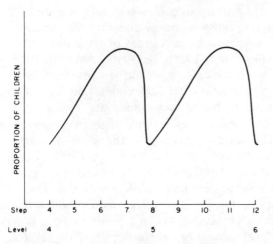

Figure 1. An idealized example of clustering as a result of developmental levels.

will also predict where spurts will occur in the acquisition of closely related language skills, according to skill theory.

Studies of language development typically use longitudinal designs and assess spontaneous language behaviors, while studies of cognitive development (especially within the Piagetian tradition) typically use cross-sectional designs and structured assessments. Because of the biases built into these methods, researchers in the two areas naturally find different phenomena. Most obviously, language researchers report many individual differences in the sequences of language acquisitions (as well as commonalities), while Piagetian researchers report virtually nothing but commonalities in the sequences of cognitive acquisitions. These different patterns of findings cannot be attributed to differences between language and cognition.

In conclusion, methods have pervasive implications for all aspects of research on psychological development. If psychologists are to achieve an adequate understanding of commonalities and differences in development, they must build methods that take account of the pervasive effects of context. They must deal with the ambiguity of behavior by analyzing how children perform specific tasks. And they must recognize that their assessments are essentially interventions that contribute to the results that are obtained.

Language Levels

For any skills, including language, it is important to realize that there is no one true developmental sequence that all children will show (Fischer and Roberts, 1979). As the previous section argues, the language sequences that a child demonstrates will be determined in large part by his individual language environment and by the tasks and methods used in the assessment. (Genetic biases will also play an important role, of course.)

These many differences do not in any way preclude commonalities, however. Indeed, the cognitive levels of skill theory can be used to predict the general kinds of skills that children can construct when they are at a certain optimal level. In this section, we will sketch some of the skills that emerge at Levels 3 through 5, encompassing roughly the ages of 10 months through 4½ or 5 years. These levels were chosen because they cover the ages at which most research on language development has concentrated. The language skills discussed are meant to be illustrative rather than comprehensive. Based on the general analyses given, it should be possible to devise specific tasks that allow more precise task analyses and that thereby allow the use of skill theory to predict detailed developmental sequences and synchronies of language development.

A thorough analysis of language acquisition is no easy endeavor, however. Language involves many different sets of skills, including vocalization (articulation, motor control, intonation, etc.), hearing, concepts to be talked about, social interactions, and much more. A skill analysis of language development in general would require an analysis of the many sets of skills in each of these domains and a determination of how the skills in each domain are combined with each other and with skills from other domains. A more reasonable goal at this point is probably a general sketch of the types of abilities possible at each level and a more detailed skill analysis of a few particular skills.

In the discussion of language behaviors at each level, it should be remembered that task and context factors can cause a general category of behavior, such as two-word utterances, to develop over several skill levels. Nevertheless, with use of the minimal-task rule, we can predict the first level at which an instance of that category could develop, and we can also predict the level at which the first great burst of behaviors in that category will emerge.

Level 3: Sensory-Motor Systems

Early speech is not representational, according to the meaning of representation in skill theory. That is, it requires the coordination only of sensorimotor actions, such as vocalization and hearing—not the coordination of sensorimotor systems into a representation. The first words and even the first, simple, two-word utterances require only sensorimotor skills.

Even beyond infancy, "speech is a form of motor activity dominated and coordinated by thought processes" (McNeill, 1978, p. 177). Thought, which is made up of representations or abstractions, develops out of sensorimotor actions. Recall that the first single representation is actually a coordination of two or more sensorimotor systems. By means of this coordination, thought can control sensorimotor actions. The representational skills of language involve, of course, several distinct sensorimotor components, including speech and gesture.

Before the emergence of representation, the child develops a number of sensorimotor skills related to language. Besides vocalization and gesture, there are communication and conceptual skills that are sometimes coordinated into a linguistic output and sometimes used independently. All these sensorimotor skills develop through the four levels of the sensorimotor tier. Before Level 3, little happens that can be called language, because the child cannot deal simultaneously with multiple variations in several actions. A wide range of skills emerge at Level 3 (starting towards the end of the first year) that clearly involve language or communication. In a Level 3 system, the child is able for the first time to control subtle variations in sensorimotor actions, because he can control several aspects of two or more actions at the same time. As a result, he can systematically vary his actions to observe how one type of action relates to another. Consequently, he can—for example—imitate some new sounds, including simple words, as we will demonstrate. Examples of Level 3 language skills include certain types of intonation, communication, comprehension of single words, and production of single-word and two-word utterances.

Intonation. One of the variations in sounds that the child can imitate is intonation contours of utterances in his native language. Without the use of any words, the child can mimic many of the simple contours that the adult uses. This expressive jargon, consisting of well intoned, prosodically isolable patterns of meaningless syllables, has been described as appearing between babbling and single words by some investigators (Dore, et al. 1976; Peters, 1977). It requires the ability to control the contour of utterances in order to produce the shape of adult speech, but the child needs to control little or no phonological variation. For example, through a closed door, one of the authors overheard a one-year-old friend carry on a telephone conversation. Although there was no one on the other end of the phone and the child was not using words, the intonation and phrasing were so good that it sounded like a real conversation. All children may not be so adept at using intonation at Level 3, however. Weir (1962) noted that even some 2-year-olds do not reliably use intonation. Dore (1974) described two different styles of language and intonation use in two children: One used more words, while the other used fewer words but controlled a larger number of intonation patterns, which he used "mainly to manipulate people" (p. 350). Peters (1977) described two different strategies in early speech production—a global strategy that emphasized intonation of whole "sentences" and an analytic strategy that emphasized single words.

Communication. Unlike certain other cognitive skills involving inanimate objects, language ultimately requires *social* skills. The child must be able to decipher others' intentions and communicate his own, although the skills involved in producing language may develop somewhat independently of the skills involved in social interaction. In any case, communication can certainly occur without language, and several researchers have argued that skills for nonverbal communication are laid down during infancy and then used later in communication involving language (Bruner, 1975; 1978; Dore, 1978; Sugarman-Bell, 1978).

In communication situations before Level 3 (at Level 2), the infant can only relate simple variations in one aspect of one of his actions to simple variations in one aspect of what he sees or hears or feels (from another person). But the Level 3 ability to relate variations in several aspects of his own actions with several aspects of what he perceives in the other, makes possible a great advance in communication skills. The result is that the child begins to relate multiple aspects of the other's behavior and his own, and thus starts actually to communicate. Many of the early communicative behaviors described in the literature seem to involve Level 3 systems, such as the ability to use a gesture to signal the mother in order to get help in obtaining an object (Bates, Camaioni, and Volterra, 1975; Sugarman-Bell, 1978). In all but the crudest of such behaviors, the child must relate several aspects of what he perceives in his mother to several aspects of his own action.

Comprehension. In young children, speech-comprehension tasks typically involve elementary communication of some sort, but the degree to which the communication actually depends on comprehension of speech seems to have been exaggerated. The common observation that the child's speech comprehension is far in advance of his speech production is called into question by a more careful task analysis. In most assessments of comprehension, the child has a high degree of contextual support that he can use to help him understand what is being communicated. The degree of this support is illustrated by an incident observed by one of the authors with four children ranging in age from 2 to 5 years. English-speaking Christopher and Steven were playing with French-speaking Anne-Beatrice and Jerome. They all played together for several days, each speaking his or her own language and generally making appropriate responses to what the others said. It was only after several days of playing that each of the older children (Christopher and Jerome) remarked to his parents that the other children "talked funny." At first, the context and vocal contours provided so many cues for appropriate responses that the children simply did not notice that they really did not comprehend what was said.

Chapman (1978, this volume, Chapter 14) points out similarly that the one-year-old may appear to comprehend entire sentences, but really does not understand them. He is simply "doing what he usually does in the situation." What he can do is to attend to the individual object that is named, but his actions on that object are determined not by the utterance he hears but by what he normally does with it in this context. These results provide an excellent example of the importance of task analysis for determining the actual skill that a child is controlling. He need only coordinate hearing a single word with a familiar sensorimotor action on an object.

Production. Skills for language comprehension and production seem to be only partially overlapping, but the kinds of utterances that are actually understood or produced should not be very different, since they all involve control of the same types and relations of words. Because of the differences in ease of data collection and task analysis, however, research on production seems to be far advanced over that on comprehension, for the most part. According to skill theory, both single words and certain kinds of limited two-word utterances can be produced or understood through Level 3 skills. On the other hand, at Level 4 both of them can be learned more efficiently and used in more complex tasks and in more productive ways.

At Level 3, single simple words can be produced as direct imitations of adult utterances. This task requires the child to relate variations in his own vocalizations to variations in what he hears. A Level 3 sensorimotor system allows the child to experiment with variations in his vocalizations and thus to discover how to produce a sound equivalent to what he has just heard.[3] After extensive practice, the word can be spoken without any need to listen carefully to the sound produced; and consequently to utter the word, the child now needs to control only one action (vocalizing). In this way, one action in a Level 3 system is freed up, so to speak, and the word can therefore be combined with more nonspeech actions than before.

At Level 3, this process is not a quick one, however, and even after production of the sound of the word has been mastered, use of the word remains closely tied to the child's sensorimotor actions. For example, Corrigan (1977) reported an example where a mother said "light" every time her infant pulled a cord to turn on a light. As the infant began to imitate adult words, he began to imitate his mother when she said "light" and then to produce the word "light" when he was pulling the cord. The word thus became associated with the child's skill of pulling the cord independently of the mother's utterance. In other words, the child's sensorimotor skill was broadened to include a vocalization, but the word was not yet independent of the child's immediate actions.

Once the words acquired through imitation become automatized, they can be produced without the direct support of the adult utterance, although they

---

[3]According to skill theory, the child's phonological productions at this level will still have severe limitations, however, which will gradually be overcome at later levels.

still require a host of environmental, contextual supports. The ways that the newly acquired words may then be attached to other sensorimotor systems are predicted by the microdevelopmental transformation rules. These rules require that the process of acquisition of the first words and extension of them to new contexts is laborious, time-consuming, and not easy and automatic. Just as an ape must be carefully taught step by step to use a word (Savage-Rumbaugh, 1979), a child too must construct the skill for the word gradually, step by step. The child has some important advantages over the ape, however, including the help of adults who provide a contextual scaffolding that helps the child to learn each word more efficiently (Bullock, 1979).

These Level 3 words are not referential in any strong sense. Dore (1978) argues that the linguistic criteria for reference include the ability to use words across situations and detached from particular actions. Referential word use thus includes the use of the same word for more than one function and the use of different words to perform the same functions. At Level 3, there is no general relation between a sign and its referent; instead, words are simply parts of systems of sensorimotor actions. The following description of primate language also applies to the Level 3 child: "When an ape initially uses a word . . . , it may be showing that it has learned when to use the word, not what the word represents. Symbol production in this case may merely be a set of behaviors emitted in a given context to produce a desired set of events" (Savage-Rumbaugh, 1979, p. 3).

Two-word utterances have traditionally been thought to be sharply distinct from single words, in that they are rule-governed linguistic constructions. However, skill theory predicts that non-rule-governed two-word utterances can be learned at Level 3. Several investigators have reported the production of such early two-word utterances (Corrigan, 1977, in press; Ingram, 1975; this volume, Chapter 13). The children producing these utterances seem to be using a highly imitative strategy of language acquisition; and so by imitation, they can build complex Level 3 skills that subsume two words. Children may also produce two-term utterances containing consistent, non-conventional, "meaningless" terms, such as Allison Bloom's "widə" (Bloom, 1973). Finally, multi-word utterances can be produced, of course, as unanalyzed units rather than word combinations (Dore et al., 1976; Nelson, 1973; Peters, 1977). These rote productions contain individual words that do not occur in combination with other single words.

All of these various Level 3 skills involving language or communication—skills of intonation, communication, comprehension, or production—are still sensorimotor: They involve the coordination of a number of aspects of several actions into a single skill, a sensorimotor system; but they do not yet involve the coordination of more than one system into a single skill. That coordination awaits the onset of Level 4.

Level 4: Systems of Sensorimotor Systems, Which Are Single Representations

In a Level 4 skill, the child coordinates two or more separate sensorimotor systems into an integrated, higher-level unit. This combination of sensorimotor systems into a single unit provides the child with the ability to represent, because while he is actually carrying out one system, he can be thinking about the other one. The capacity to relate sensorimotor systems allows the child to begin to integrate the many diverse skills that he constructed at Level 3; for instance, he can integrate an intonation pattern with a word or a production system with a comprehension system. In this way, the separate components of language are integrated to form genuine speech. Any two Level 3 systems can be combined into a Level 4 representation, so long as the environment will support the combination.

Although our previous research has not focused on Level 4 skills for speech, we have investigated a fairly broad range of Level 4 skills in general. We will give just two examples here to illustrate the point that Level 4 skills are defined by their structure—the combination of two or more sensorimotor systems—not by their symbolic nature. This fact is important for understanding some of our predictions about Level 4 language skills.

One kind of symbolic behavior that emerges at Level 4 is the ability to use independent agents in pretend play (Watson and Fischer, 1977). When a 2-year-old makes a doll eat off a plate, he is using one sensorimotor system for manipulating the doll and coordinating that system with a second one for eating off a plate. The system for eating guides the ways in which he manipulates the doll so that he can pretend that the doll is eating. Thus, his manipulation of the doll is the symbol, and the system for eating is what it symbolizes.

A second kind of Level 4 skill does not involve any obvious symbolic behavior, but it does fit the structure for Level 4. When children sort a pile of toy blocks into several homogeneous categories (e.g., triangles and circles, with all blocks within each category identical), they must coordinate a sensorimotor system for sorting triangles with a sensorimotor system for sorting circles. This coordination of two systems requires a Level 4 skill—a representation—even though no clear-cut symbol is involved. Like the Level 4 pretend-play skill, the Level 4 classification skill develops at about 2 years of age, as predicted (Fischer and Roberts, 1979). (For a Level 4 skill involving self-recognition, see step 5 in Bertenthal and Fischer, 1978.)

Many new skills involving speech, language, or communication should develop at Level 4, but in this paper we will concentrate on speech-production skills involving single words and multi-word utterances, because they provide some interesting results. The skill structure for learning single words seems superficially to differ in complexity from the skill structure for speaking two-word utterances productively, but careful task analysis indicates, to the contrary, that the two behaviors require virtually the same type of skill structure.

Single words. For a child to be able to learn appropriate use of a large number of single concrete words, he must coordinate two sensorimotor systems. With one system, he relates variations in his vocalizations to variations in what he hears; thus he learns to say the word. With the other system he carries out the set of actions and perceptions that the word refers to; this system provides the meaning of the word. This Level 4 ability to coordinate the two systems allows him to relate the new word directly to its meaning in a single skill, in contrast to a slow, laborious process of imitation and extension required at Level 3. Consequently the efficiency of his ability to learn words rises sharply; and he shows a spurt in vocabulary growth (Smith, 1926; Bloom, 1973; Ramsay, 1977; Corrigan, 1977, 1978).

Although we have not directly investigated such Level 4 skills for acquiring new words, the Level 4 pretend-play skill is similar in certain ways. The system for manipulation of the doll is the symbol for eating and therefore is roughly analogous to the system for producing the word. If the child did not have to manipulate the doll actively, then pretending to eat could be performed with a less complex skill; a Level 4 skill would not be required. For example, if he himself were pretending to cat or if he were pretending that the doll was eating without making the doll actually carry out an action, then only a complex Level 3 skill would be required, since there would be no need for two separate sensorimotor systems (Watson and Fischer, 1977). Similarly with single words, a word can be learned at Level 3 in situations that do not require two separate systems, as described earlier.

At Level 4 as at Level 3, the skill required for use of a single word also becomes less complex after the vocalization for the word has been mastered. The separate sensorimotor system for uttering the word is initially necessary because to learn to say the word correctly, the child must relate variations in vocalization to variations in hearing. But once the word has been learned, it can usually be performed by rote without any need for careful coordination of the two kinds of variations. Consequently, uttering the mastered word requires only a single sensorimotor action rather than an entire system. This single action can then be added to the sensorimotor system that the word refers to. In other words, mastery of the word and its meaning is greatly facilitated by a Level 4 skill, but use of the word once it is mastered requires only a complex Level 3 skill.

Multi-word utterances. This change in the skill required for a single word explains how a child can use his Level 4 capacity for both learning new single concrete words and learning to speak two-word utterances productively. A productive two-word utterance requires a Level 4 single representation in which each word is attached to one sensorimotor system in the representation. The relation between the systems is the basis for the production rule. In the same way, when the child makes a doll act independently in pretend play, one could say that he has a production rule for agent and action in play. (But according to skill theory, the production rule or rules would actually be much more narrow and specific than is implied by the use of general terms like "agent" and "action.")

This likeness in the structure required for the "productive" acquisition of new single words and the productive use of two-word utterances explains why the vocabulary spurt and the spurt in two-word utterances occur at about the same age. Many different investigators have demonstrated that even by conservative behavioral criteria, children begin to use some two-word utterances productively by age 2 (e.g., Bloom, 1970; Bloom et al., 1975; Bowerman, 1976; Braine, 1976; Corrigan, 1977; Ingram, this volume, Chapter 13; Maratsos and Chalkley, 1980). For example, the child says "more X" to indicate recurrence of X, "X all gone" to indicate disappearance of X, and similar productive combinations, such as "small X" and "X out." In some productive two-word utterances, the relation signified may be less explicit. For example, "Mommy sock" and similar two-word utterances are used to indicate possession, and "sweater chair" and similar utterances are used to indicate location. Note, however, that the implicit nature of the relation does not mean that the rules are more general than in the more explicit cases. According to skill theory, the relations remain relatively specific and local and cannot, therefore, be likened to the general categories for possession or location used by adult speakers.

According to this skill analysis, the developmental shift from one-word utterances to productive two-word utterances should be much more striking and sudden than the development from two words to three or more. Although a few two-word utterances will appear before Level 4, the emergence of the new level will produce a major spurt in two-word utterances because of the child's ability to construct productive relations between words. Productive three-word utterances, on the other hand, should follow closely on the heels of productive two-word utterances.

This difference in developmental pattern results from the fact that productive two-word utterances require a Level 4 skill, and productive three- or four-word utterances require a skill of the same level—albeit one that is slightly more complex. In utterances like "sweater chair," all that is required is the addition of another word to one of the two sensorimotor systems to elaborate its meaning—"sweater on chair." In utterances like "Johnny want candy," the skill would seem to involve the addition of a third sensorimotor system to the single representation, because "want" seems to involve the addition of a new category of meaning to the sentence. Elementary inflections could be acquired by the same processes of making Level 4 skills more complex by microdevelopmental changes in the skills. In utterances like

"Johnny's candy," for example, the addition of the possessive inflection would require some simple elaboration of the representational skill used for "Johnny candy," where possession is implied.

Level 5 and Beyond: Combining Representations

The child builds more and more complex Level 4 language skills for at least a year after he has first reached Level 4. Then he moves beyond single representations to coordinating two or more representations into a Level 5 representational mapping. This change should produce another quantum leap in the child's development. In language, the child should begin to be able to construct skills for producing much more complex utterances—for example, tag questions where one representation has to be transformed into another, as in "You want a piece of pie, don't you?" The modal age at which this general shift takes place is open to question, with some cognitive research placing it as early as 3 years (Epstein, 1974a,b; McCall et al., 1977) and other research seeming to place it as late as 4½ or 5 years (e.g., Piaget, Grize, Szeminska, and Vinh Bang, 1968). In order both to pin down the ages and to determine exactly which types of rules emerge at this point, research based on careful task analyses will be required.

The development of language skills does not stop at Level 5, although researchers have neglected developments beyond 4 or 5 years of age. Within Level 5, the child can use microdevelopmental processes to build more complex rules, and then at later levels he can move beyond coordinating single representations to coordinating multiple aspects of representations at Level 6 and then to building abstractions at Levels 7 and above (Fischer and Lazerson, in press). At each of these later levels, language skills change in diverse ways. Not only can the individual utter more complex sentences, but he can also produce more complex sounds, understand more complex messages, monitor his own production better, take others' perspectives more successfully, and eventually he may be able to write prose or give speeches.

Conclusions

The approach to language development that we have proposed is opposed to many of the traditional approaches in that it assumes that the child develops language skills that show specificity rather than a high degree of generality. The skill approach has much in common with recent revisionist and pragmatic analyses of language development, which tie their constructs much more closely to the child's actual behavior than many traditional approaches. Here are our main conclusions about the nature of language development:

1. Language is comprised of a large set of specific skills. Although these skills have some properties that are distinctive to language, their de-

velopmental course is similar in outline and process to that of other sets of skills.

2. So-called "cognition" likewise comprises a large number of skills. It is *not* a single coherent entity separate from language, and there is no meaningful sense in which cognition in general can be said to be a prerequisite for language in general, or vice versa.

3. Unevenness, or *décalage,* is the rule in language development as in the development of other skills. That is, for different language skills, the same child frequently functions at different developmental steps.

4. General processing limits of the child or adult account for the overall course of development in all skills, including language skills and cognitive skills. As the child develops higher processing limits, the population of language skills gradually shifts upward in a statistical fashion; but the skills always continue to be distributed across a wide range of steps. The statistical shifts seem to show cyclical periods of relatively faster change followed by relatively slower change, and so in a probabilistic sense, levels or stages of language development can be discriminated.

5. Environmental factors exert important influences on the sequence and speed of development of language skills. Therefore, even if all children were genetically identical, individual children would show different developmental paths in the acquisition of specific skills.

6. The task used to assess a language skill is an environmental factor that needs to be controlled in language research. It is a major determinant of both the age at which the skill is first detected and the sequence in which the skill develops. Most behaviors are ambiguous; that is, they can be performed by any of a number of different strategies and so cannot be used to provide a clear assessment of developmental step. Task analysis is therefore essential to predicting and explaining development. In spontaneous language, the task that is posed by the interaction of child and situation has the same importance.

7. A developmental assessment is an intervention in the child's behavior, and the exact nature of this intervention will help to determine the kinds of results that will be obtained. For example, steps that appear in a structured assessment will frequently not appear in the child's spontaneous behavior. Much recent language research has used methods that are especially sensitive to individual differences in development. Most Piagetian research, on the other hand, has used methods that are more sensitive to commonalities in development than to individual differences.

8. Early speech is sensorimotor, not representational. That is, it involves the coordination of two or more sensorimotor actions (including vocalization and hearing) into a single sensorimotor system. The first words, and even the first, simplest two-word utterances involve such sensorimotor systems.

9. The general capacity termed representation requires the coordination of at least two sensorimotor systems into a higher-order skill called a single representation. The capacity for single representations, which first appears in most middle-class children at age 1½ to 2 years, allows the child to begin to use large numbers of words referentially. The same capacity allows the child to begin to utter simple sentences productively, because the coordination of two or more sensorimotor systems can generate simple language rules.

10. At about age 3 to 4, the child starts to relate representations to each other. Only with this capacity can the child use language rules that begin to approximate the rules of adult grammars. Language development does not cease at age 4 or 5, however, but continues to higher levels as the child, adolescent, and adult come to control more complex forms of language representations and ultimately language abstractions.

ACKNOWLEDGMENTS
The work on which this paper is based was supported by grants from the Spencer Foundation to each author. The authors would like to thank Brian MacWhinney for helpful comments on an earlier draft.

Discussion

In the discussion of the Fischer-Corrigan paper, the participants first wrestled with the notion of different developmental sequences appearing in different children. They wanted to know if Fischer really meant that different stages were present or if he meant that different steps were followed within each stage. Fischer explained that some of the differences he had talked about were attributable to the different methodologies employed in different studies. However, he thought that if stages were defined abstractly enough, that is, in sufficiently general terms, then one might arrive at a universal sequence. For example, the developmental levels proposed in skill theory specify such a sequence. In research, however, one is always dealing with a much more *task-specific* approach. When specific tasks are considered, individual children show quite different developmental sequences. In this connection, Gratch referred to the work of Nelson (1973) and her identification of two possible groups of language-learning children, the referential and the expressive.

Chapman then asked if Fischer had any evidence of discontinuities in development as a function of the level that was realized. Fischer said that the notion was a theoretical one and that the evidence for it was scattered and not yet sufficiently strong. He felt that the best evidence thus far was from the work of McCall, Eichorn, and Hogarty (1977), to which he had referred, with respect to their use of correlational analysis. These authors had shown stage-like shifts in populations of skills by means of their correlational analyses.

Chapman then asked, what was the explanation for the changes in level that Fischer had proposed? Fischer said that there were two ways in which one might think about these levels. One, which did not require a strong hypothesis, was that the child simply could not go above some upper limit set upon his overall processing capacity. The other, more interesting way, was that development was not monotonic in nature but cyclical. Changes in level were manifested by changes in the rate of development of capacities. The child, in moving from one level to another, showed massive amounts of change in all respects. He then consolidated his skills at that new level, and the rate of change slowed down until a new major shift occurred. This view of development was an empirically testable one and provided very different definition of stage from the Piagetian one. Bloom asked, what was the nature of the constraints upon level of skill? Fischer replied that they had to do with central processing capabilities. Chapman pressed Fischer to explain the nature of the transition from one level to the next. Fischer said he could not provide a deep explanation but could only attempt to give a good descriptive explanation of the nature of the change from one set of behavioral structures to a discontinuously higher set. Kagan referred to the transition as an "eternal mystery."

Lifter then challenged Fischer's claim, that there were no developmental sequences occurring across all children in language development. Fischer replied that he had not made that claim exactly. He had merely pointed out that individual differences had been identified with respect to language development much more often than with respect to cognitive development. Lifter suggested that it was important to keep clear in such discussion the differences between form and content of language. She referred to the work of Bloom, Lightbown, and Hood (1975), whose longitudinal studies of spontaneous language behavior had shown great regularity in the content of utterances in children but also great variation in form. The same authors had also identified differences with respect to the amount of imitation used by different children.

Fischer again said that he would predict commonalities at the time of marked developmental change from one level to another, but not within levels, with respect to the details of behavior. Lifter maintained that there were regularities with respect to the detailed analyses of the content of child utterances—for example, with respect to categories of content relations. Lifter felt that it was not only methodology that gave rise to different accounts of developmental sequence, but also different interpretations of data. Thus, as language does map cognitive development with respect to content, language was subject to a developmental sequence in that respect. However, the development of language forms might show great variability in relation to content.

Fischer argued that language development and cognitive development were not different with respect to the amount of individual variation that might be observed among children. He merely wished to show that certain experimental methods were better suited to the examination of individual differences while others were better suited to the discovery of commonalities.

This exchange lead to some semantic confusion. Wolff asked that Fischer clarify some points. Wolff particularly wished to know in what ways skills differed from schemes. Fischer replied that the notion of skill was a much more specific one, that of scheme much more general. Wolff then asked, in what sense were skills more predictive of sequences of behavior than schemes and at what level were they predictive? If, for example, the child had acquired a skill with respect to the passive voice, did Fischer wish to predict the child's choice of agent, say, between grandmother and grandfather, or did he wish to predict the child's choice of the object of the action of playing by the child, for example, playing with cherries as opposed to apples. Wolff thought that, at that level, individual differences would obviously be present, universal, and trivial just as at the opposite end of the generalitics-specificity continuum it would be obvious and trivial to say that all normal children develop language. Fischer said that that was exactly the point he was making. The level of analyses employed, together with the methods used, determined whether one found commonalities or differences. Wolff said that, nevertheless, when one was trying to construct a theory, it was best to move away from apples and cherries and to get to some underlying structures, albeit equally ambiguous ones. He thought Fischer's idea of skills referred to already underlying structures. Fischer agreed and added that he was trying to make them less ambiguous than in Piagetian theory. He had tried for 8 years to predict developmental sequences from Piagetian theory and had failed. In particular, he thought that Piagetian theory was wrong because it did not deal with context. Wolff persisted in asking, was a skill simply a subscheme, a finer detail of the scheme, or was it something else. Fischer replied that Piaget used the word scheme to refer to very general logical structures sometimes called structures d'ensemble. They were supposed to be very powerful phenomena. Piaget did admit that there was décalage, a phenomenon that he could not explain. In Fischer's view, décalage was so central a phenomenon as to render the schemes much less general. Fischer believed there was a lot in common in the terms skill, scheme, and operant. The differences he had intended to convey with the term "skill" were that the skill was much less general than the scheme. He did not see general schemes except in adolescents and adults. He argued that adult schemes were being projected onto the behaviors of the one-month-old and the one-year-old infant, but they had no basis in reality. In adults there also was specificity of behaviors but, in addition, a more general basis could be found for a concept such as the scheme.

Oller remarked that if there was anything especially new about the Fischer-Corrigan formulation, it was the emphasis placed upon the notion of complexity. As Oller understood this idea of complexity, it was built up in much the same way as he had been attempting to view it in the development of a "natural logic of speech and speech-like acts." In Oller's logic, there were components of behavior which he thought resembled Fischer's notion of skills. When Fischer referred to new behaviors as more complex, he was saying that the more complex activity involved at least one more component or skill than the earlier, less complex, activity. Fischer amended that statement to read, one more component or a change in one component.

Oller then commented that the primary limitation he had encountered in his own attempts to work with such a model was that each complexity comparison based upon it assumes a *ceteris paribus* principle (that is, an "all other things being equal" principle). One could say that X was more simple than X + Y, just so long as one could be sure that the X skill or behavior was the same in both cases. The fact of the matter was that, in practice, there were relatively few cases where the X's were identical. Thus, while Oller thought the approach had a lot of merit and he was engaged in something very similar himself, he saw it as having severe limitations that could only be addressed empirically by testing the relative complexity of the various forms of a particular behavior or skill. It was impossible to know the significance of the differences in terms of complexity.

Fischer replied that he was trying to build a system for defining the psychological complexity of skills. The developmental transformation rules in skill theory might be seen at their simplest as nothing but a system for predicting complexity. It was not always easy to decide when something had been added. His model, however, was designed in such a way that if something was added, it was predicted that that something would make a difference; it would represent a later development. He had tried to develop a set of transformation rules that would allow one to predict the manner in which generalization would proceed. He and Corrigan had also suggested specific methods that would allow the researcher to deal with the measurement and assessment problems that Oller had raised. Also, if an infant developed two skills that had the same general structure (skill level), but different individual components, and if those skills had been practiced by the infant, then they should emerge at approximately the same time, at the time of a quantal leap to a new skill level, that is, within a matter of days.

Oller still did not understand how, at the level of microscopic skill or lowest units of behavior, one skill could be equated in terms of complexity with another purely on the basis of logic and without empirical support. Fischer said that that was his assumption—not that the skills were identical, but that they had some degree of commonality. That commonality had to do with the general processing characteristics involved in their expression and ultimately with the general processing characteristics involved in human behavior whether it was in language, in operating an automobile, or writing a paper. Oller said that he had not made such an assumption and saw many reasons for not making it. The skills at a microscopic level that one had to pose were extremely different, he thought, in terms of the demand that they placed on the infant organism. Fischer said, then they had made a different choice. His theory was bound to be proven wrong ultimately, he thought. The question was, would the strong hypothesis (of levels and cycles of development) prove correct or would the weaker hypothesis (of upper limits of capability which merely changed over time) prove correct.

Hardy suggested that one kind of structure which should be taken into account had to do with the perceptual processing capabilities for dealing with speech stimuli. She believed that there might be marked individual differences with respect to this ability. There might be neurological or bio-chemical reasons for such differences. Fischer said that the problems of blind or deaf children might provide a stronger example. Most infants did not show such large differences in perceptual processing capabilities. Also, individual differences in perceptual processing capabilities might tend to increase with age.

Wolff then pointed out that it might depend upon the kind of skill one chose to demonstrate whether or not there would be individual differences. Fischer said that that was certainly true, but he was asking for the best generalization that could be made from existing data and for psychological development in general?

Bloom indicated that she could not understand, if all behaviors were to be reduced to the same level of components and those were to be called skills, how real capacities could be accounted for. She did not believe that the reduction of development to the acquisition of skills could be considered an explanatory theory. Fischer suggested that the attempt to account for language development in terms of Piagetian concepts was equally problem-atic. Piaget made similar assumptions about schemes. Fischer felt that by applying these assumptions to skills, he had not eliminated the problem, but he had provided a framework that, if it was successful, would explain and predict the development of specific capabilities in all domains in child lan-guage.

Some Thoughts on Object Permanence and Language Development

Gerald Gratch

Department of Psychology, University of Houston, Houston, Texas

In brief, this paper begins with some generalities about language and thought and then examines Piaget's ideas about the development of object permanence. Through consideration of the tasks he used, a claim is made that there is a good aspect to Piaget and a bad one. The good Piaget is an extraordinarily acute observer who shows us in surprising ways that the infant orients to the world very differently than do children and adults. The bad Piaget gives us an infant in the second year of life who has a well formed mind that some have interpreted as a base for the meaningful use of language. To close the paper, alternative approaches to understanding how thought and language come together are considered.

The focus of the paper is on some general ideas about the manner in which infants come to think and talk. The paper dwells primarily on the general level because there is reason to think that we need to reflect on the metaphors that guide our investigations. Despite innumerable studies, it is not clear that we have gone beyond a few long-known observations and ideas. Somewhere during the second year, infants put out words relatively often and provide relatively clear evidence of thought in the imaginal sense, e.g., they recall and pretend. Before that time, they perform in ways that are, at best, pale shadows of such activities, and they live in a fashion that is highly dependent upon their caretakers.

One very general way of trying to order these observations has been to make a distinction between an animal and a human nature. Animals are not human because they don't talk and think, and infants are not human or intelligent or capable of sentiment or object relations before they think and talk. This distinction has been used to emphasize the uniqueness of man in

Christian dogma, and it has figured in attempts to account for the evolution of higher forms from lower ones (Nisbett, 1969). The resurgence of interest in chimpanzees stems in part from their equivocal status relative to this distinction. The special issue of *The Behavioral and Brain Sciences* on "Cognition and consciousness in nonhuman species" highlights this point. There, Premack and Woodruff (1978) state that the upshot of chimpanzee studies is that they are clever creatures, that they may even be able to reflect on their thoughts as well as their activities—that is, to engage in "metacognition"—but they are not linguistic creatures in the communicative sense. Savage-Rumbaugh, Rumbaugh, and Boysen (1978), on the other hand, believe that they have shown that chimpanzees communicate about ideas. They believe that the key to the development of language lies in the actors acquiring it in a shared pragmatic framework. That issue of the journal contains an almost countless number of commentaries by others on the limits of concluding that chimpanzees do or don't talk, do or don't think.

In this paper, the focus will be on a somewhat more particular version of the animal-human idea. It contains the premise that before you can talk about something meaningfully you must have an idea of it. Further, it is assumed that one can diagnose the presence of ideas by studying action on non-present objects. According to this view, the infant first comes to perceive objects. Then he becomes "human" in that he comes to re-present objects when they are absent. During this time, the infant comes to label these objects and then comes to use these labels to think about the objects even when they are absent. Usually, labeling is thought to come about through a process of point-and-name (Brown, 1958; Vygotsky, 1962).

The approach is not unreasonable, but some of its limitations lie in its manner of dealing with the notion of reference. One of the major achievements of recent research on the nature and development of language has been its dramatization of the fact that words and sentences do not refer to events in an unequivocal way. While no one can quarrel with the admonition that we speak clearly and precisely, twentieth century psychology was long dominated by the logical-positivist tradition that held that we could state meanings unequivocally. In particular, the point-and-name program rests on the assumption that the infant and the tutor share a common referent. The work of investigators in the speech-act tradition has provided much evidence that ostensive definitions have to be augmented by pragmatic considerations (e.g., Bruner, 1978), a point argued cogently by such philosophers as Dewey, G.H. Mead, Polanyi, Popper, and Wittgenstein. What is emphasized here is that the force of this criticism applies to non-linguistic ideas as well.

Many have felt that they could understand how infants come to think and talk by combining a pragmatic view of linguistic meaning with Piaget's ideas about the achievements of the sensorimotor infant (e.g., Bates, et al., 1977; Bloom, 1975; Bloom, Lifter, and Broughton, this volume, Chapter 12). There is a sense in which this notion is justified. Both sets of ideas lead to attempts to discover which of many possible events the child has in mind when he focuses with adults on a common situation. But the two sets of ideas diverge when Piaget's view of the structure of the child's mind and how it develops is considered.

The particular facet of Piaget's theory of the development of thoughtfulness in infancy that fits within the line of reasoning sketched above is his account of the development of the object concept, the idea of object permanence (Piaget, 1954). Piaget's empirical work is keyed to the notion that the presence or absence of ideas can be inferred from the infant's manner of dealing with non-present objects. This view has a long history in American psychology, the tradition being identified early with the work of Walter S. Hunter (1913). Work along these lines has tried to distinguish between search mediated by motor sets and search governed by non-motor, thoughtful means. Generations of researchers have sought to determine which species can think, at what point in their ontogenesis the ability appears, how such representational activity is tied to neural development, and so on (Schrier, Harlow, and Stollnitz, 1965).

Piaget introduced some major innovations into the approach. One was to emphasize that hidden object problems may be solved in thoughtless as well as thoughtful ways, that the thoughtless solutions involve more than motor sets, and that there is a developmental order among the various solutions. Another was to focus not upon *whether* the infant could remember the missing object but rather upon describing *what* aspects of the situation the infant has in mind. In taking this tack, Piaget was influenced highly by the Gestalt approach to problem-solving. Wertheimer (1959) and others argued that how one defines the problem determines the solution. They emphasized that objects exist in contexts and how one sees the relation between the focal object and its surround, determines the meanings of the figure. The fundamental issue in perception and thought was organization, organization of the mind, of the environment, and of the manner in which they come together.

Piaget basically described the development of the object concept as occurring in three steps. In the first, stages 1–3, "out of sight was out of mind." Young infants might continue to orient to hidden objects like Hunter's pointing dogs, but Piaget argued that such orientations were continuations of actions initiated while the object was in view. In the third step, stage 6, the infant shows true intelligence, is able to re-present the missing object and its possible locations. The infant can solve invisible displacement problems, problems where the infant can only see that the object is in one of several possible places and must figure out the correct one.

The second step, a prelinguistic one, will now be dwelled upon because it illustrates the virtue of Piaget's emphasis on *what* rather than *whether*. In this step, the infant is able to find the hidden object in a way that does not merely involve the continuation of an already initiated action. To get the toy, the infant must suspend his act of reaching, and must keep his "eye" on the goal while focusing on the obstacle of the occluder. By 8 or 9 months, infants do this in a relatively skilled way, and one might conclude that the infant guides his search by an image of the missing toy. Piaget reasoned differently and took the observation one step further. In plain view of the infant, he proceeded to hide the object in a second well-marked place. The infant watched the covering and then went directly to the first place. Piaget reported that the success and the error occurred together in development and identified stage 4 in terms of this concordance. He concluded that infants in this phase of development still see objects in space in terms of their own egocentric action schemes and do not represent missing objects. Clearly the observation can be interpreted differently.

Before taking up alternative interpretations, it is important to consider in detail the behavior of 9-month-old infants confronted with this displacement problem. A study of videotapes of two 9-month-old infants revealed the following:

> The infants who alertly watched the toy disappear at site A, kept their eye on the A-cover while reaching for it during a three-second delay, and then directly removed the cover and secured the toy. They then alertly watched the toy being hidden at site B and reached toward it as it was being hidden. When the toy disappeared, they immediately turned to and reached for the A-cover and removed it when the delay-period was over. They repeated the performance on a second trial. The surprising thing about the phenomenon was how undistracted the infants were, how quickly they changed the direction of their reach, and how certain they appeared to be about where to search. It was as if they did not believe their eyes.

If like some investigators, one doesn't focus on the possibility that infants and adults perceive different facets of the event, then one may try to account for the phenomenon in terms of forgetting. Kagan, Kearsley, and Zelazo (1978) have explained Piaget's developmental sequence in terms of 3 types of memory processes: recognition memory for infants who cannot search; recall memory for infants who *can* solve invisible displacement problems; and some kind of intermediate process in which the recognition schemes can be retrieved and combined but which is still tied to perceptually-present phenomena, such as the cover. Such explanations do not take all the facts into account. It is not that memory is not involved. Variations in the delay interval do affect both the likelihood of error and the way in which it occurs (Gratch, et al., 1974; Harris, 1973). But such accounts are oriented to the question of whether the creature keeps the focal event in mind and ignores the fact that the event has been observed in a context. Unless the lights go out, the context does not disappear, and as Michotte (1955) and E.J. and J.J. Gibson (1969, 1979) have pointed out, such a disappearance specifies a very different event than a disappearance in which something covers a stationary object or a moving object goes behind a stationary surface.

Piaget has an uncanny ability to surprise us about how children view events differently than adults. Just as in his conservation tasks, Piaget leads one to believe that the child understands the focal event, the mutual topic in the same manner as adults. But a seemingly trivial and transparent change—one row of pennies is spread and not the other, the object is hidden in a second place—is treated as an important variation by the child. Piaget's ability to surprise us stems, at least in part, from his functional approach to knowing about some domain such as number or space. He takes the prevailing theoretical conception of the domain as the model of what it means to know the domain. This provides him with a basis for identifying essential factors and irrelevant factors. He then tries to distinguish child from adult in terms of whether they can key their conduct to the "essential" as opposed to the "variable" appearances, and he models their minds in terms of structures that incorporate these different notions of what is "essential." One need not accept Piaget's structural explanations, but the problem is one of conceptualizing these surprising events without destroying the fact that they lead us to be surprised. Memory explanations that do not account for what is seen are unsatisfactory as well as accounts that reduce the phenomena to procedural issues, like the wording of instructions or the nature of the covers and their surrounds.

There are various ways to describe what the infants have in mind when they make the error of searching under the wrong cover. One is in terms of the rule of the game, namely that the toy is in the place where it disappeared. Gratch and Landers (1971) played the game bi-weekly with some infants and found that the path to this rule generally took a couple of months and was marked by the infants' learning about each place separately and then confounding them. For example, the infants initially would not try to correct themselves by searching at the second place. Later they did, and still later they would search correctly but only after looking at or touching the first hiding place. During this latter period, the object was again hidden at the first place after the infants had found it at the second place. The infants would then err by searching at the second place. How little understanding of the structure of the situation such infants possess can be indicated by yet another of Piaget's observations. When infants would reliably search only where he hid the toy, introduction of a third place led them once again into error.

Another approach is to focus on the features of the hiding situation. Making the covers and their backgrounds more distinctive decreases the likelihood of error (e.g., Butterworth, 1979; Lucas and Uzgiris, 1977). Varying where the hiding places are situated in relation to the infant also affects the error (e.g., Bremner, 1978; Butterworth, 1975). In particular, Butterworth has shown that infants are less likely to err if the toy is hidden first off to the infant's side and then at the midline, than when the sequence is reversed. This observation is akin to those made by Köhler (1959) and other Gestaltists with regard to tool use. When the desired object is at the midline and is attached to a string or rests on a support, then the infant is more likely to use the intermediary than when the object is off to one side. But as Piaget (1952) and, more recently, Bower (1977) have shown, the infant also is likely to use the intermediary located at the midline even when it "clearly" is not attached to the object. These examples should bring out two points. One is the importance of what the infant is perceiving. The other is that the adult can so structure the situation that it will be easier for the infant to act appropriately. However, it is not clear that the infant shares the adult's view of the situation.

In the second step of keeping track of hidden objects, Piaget's stages 4 and 5, Piaget does not attribute ideas to the infant. While his account of the period involves the attribution of structures to the infant, the creature he conjures up is very akin to one that S-R learning theorists can be comfortable with. Piaget views the infant as coming to keep his "eye" on hidden objects by associating them with their places of disappearance, and he sees the infant as gradually groping his way to a perceptually larger space through a process of trial and error.

In the third step, Piaget's stage 6, the infant frees himself from the sensorimotor stream. The upshot of his groping with an ambiguous environment, in terms of ill-formed and ill-coordinated schemes, is the emergence of a coherent organization of schemes that permits him to distinguish self from object, to locate them in a system of possible places, to recall events, and to plan about non-present events. Piaget now attributes concepts to the infant, believes he is intelligent. It is this view of the infant in the second year of life, a creature who now really has a definite mind, that has attracted many investigators as they sought a base on which they could build an account of language as a symbolic system. There is no question that the infant at this time is a far more resourceful creature than he was earlier and that he has in mind a far more detailed and widely spanning sense of events. But how clearly organized a mind is it? Consider the invisible displacement task. One of its widely used forms was standardized by Uzgiris and Hunt (1975). The infant sits midway between two covers. The examiner shows the infant a toy, occludes it by enclosing it in his hand (or an opaque container) and then proceeds to place his hand under one of the covers, leaving the toy there. Then he presents his closed hand to the infant at the midline. The task can be complicated by hiding at the second place as well, by adding more locations, and so on. Piaget describes a sequence of development for the invisible displacement task that he feels parallels that described for step 2.

Piaget argues that an infant who has a stage 6 mind will, at least after the first trial, see that the examiner moves his hand through a path that involves several possible locations. His understanding that the object must be in one of several locations will lead him to persist in a systematic program of search, a program involving inferential reasoning.

Piaget is well aware of how little of the world the stage 6 infant understands and symbolizes, and his idea of décalage indicates he is fully cognizant of the fact that such a child will show many limitations in his handling of invisible displacement situations. In his model, he is trying to capture the system that underlies the variable appearances. But how much "essence" is there and where does it lie? In the child, in the environment, or in their transaction? Some examples will now be presented which hopefully make the point that there is more variety than system in the child's mind and that one must seek a model of the developing mind that is more "loosely coupled" and transactional than the kind of embryological model that Piaget offers us.

First, consider two anecdotes from an invisible displacement game that was played with children aged 2 to 8 years (Gratch, 1964). The study was an attempt to get at how children come to understand the structure of that common two-person, zero-sum game, "guess which hand I'm hiding the marble in?" One usually plays the game by hiding the marble behind one's back. Eighteen- to 24-month-olds cannot play the game in that form, and an attempt was made to shape them by starting the hiding with hands in front. The children enjoyed that, but when the shift to hands behind the back was made—which also involved turning around so they could see the hands—they became disoriented. The failures can be accounted for by possible limitations in the shaping procedures, but the point is that the children have little understanding of this not very complicated change in the spatial layout of the game. Even more to the point was the behavior of a two-year-old, Bobby. He played the game on a couch in his own home with the hiding being done hands-in-front. About 15 trials were run in which the hand containing the marble was regularly alternated, and Bobby quickly began a run of successes. He would squeal with delight each time the examiner introduced a turn by pushing his hands together vigorously and saying in an ominous tone "You won't find it this time." Finally the examiner did not alternate. Bobby opened the empty hand, was dismayed, and then immediately searched in and around the couch, ignoring the other hand entirely. It is not clear what Bobby would have done on Piaget's tasks, but he certainly was not engaged in a systematic analysis of the display. His search had much in common with the earlier description of the solution course of 9-month-olds in the stage 4 two-place hiding game.

Consider another example. LeCompte and Gratch (1972) explored what infants understand about finding an object hidden in a single place by hiding the same toy three times and then tricking the infants by having a different toy appear under the cover. The behavior of 9-, 12-, and 18-month olds was quite compatible with Piaget's ideas. Only the older infants seemed to have a well-formed idea of what was going on. They tended to react to the trick with a sudden onset of surprise, ignored the toy in view, and then repeatedly searched in and around the box. This pattern seemed to indicate that they had an image of what was supposed to be in the box and an idea that the missing toy must be somewhere, that it had been invisibly displaced.

Ramsay and Campos (1978) chose to repeat the general procedure and find out how it related to invisible displacement tasks. In one study, involving 11-month-olds, they reported a strong concordance. Infants who solved the invisible displacement task described earlier responded to the trick by ceasing smiling and showing some kind of evidence of search for the missing toy. However, that pattern did not appear for infants who failed the invisible displacement task. Recently, LaBasse and Turner, two of my students, informally repeated this procedure with 15-month-olds. To their surprise, the infants failed the invisible displacement task but they *did* search for the missing toy in the trick game. These investigators then examined Ramsay and Campos' description of their procedure more carefully and found an ambiguity in their description of the way in which the examiner moved the container. When the examiner finished putting the container under one of the two covers, he could have placed it in front of the baby at midline, or in front of the cover. LaBasse and Turner had followed Uzgiris and Hunt's procedure and placed the container at the midline. When they subsequently placed it in front of the cover, 15-month-olds easily solved the invisible displacement task. The results should bring to mind the earlier mentioned string and support problems.

In this same pilot study, we also tried a simple version of the old "shell game" that Bower (1977) reports he has played with 11-month-olds. There are two covers. The examiner places the toy under one cover. Then in full view of the infant, he exchanges the places of the covers on the table. Many of our 15-month-olds did not solve this simple version of the "invisible displacement" problem.

Hopefully, the drift of these examples is clear. Just as in the discussion of step 2, there are many ways in which the older infant fails to keep track of the covered object even though he seems to have a relatively clear idea about the relation of the object to the cover. Further, it is easy to imagine ways in which one could spotlight features of the display and thus help the infant solve the problems. Further, there is much merit in Piaget's or Fischer and Corrigan's (this volume, Chapter 10) attempts to find a kind of developmental order that would help one account for the many variations in task variables and infant responses. This author's quarrel is with Piaget's conceptualization of the process.

Piaget rightly sought to find a way to describe both change and continuity, process and organization. He sought a middle ground between the sensation-based inductivism of the associationists and the event-keyed *a priori* categories of the Kantians. In his view, the neonate begins with small segmental schemes that order sensations in a small way, and the results of such active orderings finally lead to an organization of the schemes, a logic of action which permits symbolic conduct in stage 6. In line with his Kantian sympathies, Piaget's primary focus was on identifying the schemes that ordered the sensory array rather than in seeking order in the sensory array.

During the time Piaget was trying to go beyond the notion of egocentrism as a way of conceptualizing the nature of the organization of the individual, he found "Bourbaki." Under that pseudonym, a group of French algebraicists were attempting to structure the diversity of mathematical activities into a hierarchically ordered series of logically coherent forms. In particular, Piaget (1954) was captured by one form, the Abelian group, in terms of which one can describe transformations on various spaces. Such a form can be used to describe the movements of an infant who knows his way around a territory populated with well-known objects, or the actions of an infant who understands the spatial relations among the many facets of a three-dimensional object. Piaget has had an ambiguous romance with these mathematical forms (Feldman and Toulmin, 1975; Rotman, 1978). Sometimes he used them simply to describe the set of actions he observed and to characterize the actor *as if* he were such an organization. At other times he used them to describe the mind of the actor. But at all times, he was trying to describe an organization that has a definite form in each stage of development; that underlies the various specific actions observed in the child; that orders the various lessons that caretakers and nature offer and impose on the child; and that alters its form as a consequence of its operations. In Piaget's account of development, external events are the occasions for forms to work and change, but in his view, they, like food, are simply aliments, not basic stuff. Herein lies the disagreement with him. He sees too much internal order, and he gives the environment too secondary a role in the development of thoughtful action and talk.

What are the alternatives? One is that proposed by E.J. and J.J. Gibson (Gibson, 1977, 1979), namely, ecological optics. Ecological optics is a description of event structures and of infants learning to act in terms of these structures rather than in terms of bits and pieces of the event. The Gestalt psychologists tried to describe awareness and event structures in terms of the ambiguous notion of prägnanz, principles of figural organization such as closure and good continuation. The Gibsons have made a signal advance by providing physical descriptions of the objects and layouts of perception. They have done so in a context which takes account of the perceiver's action, that may or may not facilitate his tuning in on the event structure. The act of perceiving is not conceived of as a series of snapshots which are assembled into a percept and perhaps augmented by a thought. Rather, the Gibsons present a time-lined environment and an actor who, over time, can extract invariant information from the flux. The metaphor for knowledge is perceiving, and the Gibsons are so bold as to talk about perceiving symbolic as well as non-symbolic events and to deny the validity of classical distinctions between perceptual, memorial, and thoughtful performances.

In this presentation, it has been suggested that much of the value of Piaget's work lies in his use of the Gestalt-perceptual metaphor. However, along with Neisser (1976), this author hesitates to join the Gibsons in what

Eleanor Gibson (1977) has called the "third revolution," ecological optics, as opposed to information processing or as opposed to S-R learning theory. There is a need for a more fully elaborated model of the knower than the metaphor of a tuner which they propose. There is also a need for a view of what is known about events that involves more of a "trial and error of imperfect 'internal' orders" quality (Campbell, 1973, 1977, personal communication) than the Gibsons offer. While events like flow patterns and occlusions, and even presence of the self, do seem describable in Gibsonian terms, what of notions like "cat," let alone family terms like "son" or social roles like "scientist?" As Wittgensteinians point out, these are "fuzzy" terms and are where talk leads to. Attempts to conjure their original meanings as prototypical perceptual forms (Rosch, 1973) dissolve into functional analysis (Brown, 1979).

The seeds of a proper metaphor may lie in the recent revival of interest in Vygotsky's (1962, 1978) ideas (e.g., Stone and Day, in press; Wertsch, 1979). He attempted to understand the development of thought and language in functionalist terms. He saw thought and language as a process of coming together, the former from the inside out, the latter from the outside in. The joining of culture and the individual was seen as a transactional process whose results could not be analyzed solely in terms of thought or of language. He traced a process of outer to inner speech, wherein the latter notion attempted to capture the idea that we think with words and images in the light of the audience we want to share our ideas with. The thinking individual is a particularly familiar audience with whom much of the message can be left implicit because of many shared meanings.

A decade ago, David Ausubel (1968) tried to popularize one facet of Vygotsky's thought through the concept of "advance organizers." The point was that the tutor and nature put frames around our activities which constrain them and lead to an accommodation to these frames. Along with Piaget, this view holds that what one knows and learns within these frames is a function of the ideas one brings to them. But Piaget's particular embryological metaphor involved only tacit descriptions of the "ecology," the frames, and scripts. It emphasized that the ecology exists in the mind only insofar as it is assimilated into the organism. His aim was to capture the activity of reasoning in terms of a mind that is structured logically and to chart its metamorphosis from a series of lesser logical structures. The environment is necessary for development, but the sequence of stages is highly "canalized." As such, his account of the development of intelligence has a teleological quality which has rightly led some (e.g., Beilin, 1971) to refer to Piaget as a maturationist instead of focusing on Piaget, the functionalist, who gave us the surprises inherent in his conservation and object permanence observations.

The idea of "advance organizer" brings out the limitation of the notion that the learning of language is based on what the child knows. Words, ideas, and natural events that the child ill understands both are reduced by the child into his own terms and lead him to act and know in those terms. When one puts on "airs" in adolescence and childhood, there is a sense in which one does what one doesn't know, one acts artificially or out of constraint, but there also is a sense in which such "phoniness" is the necessary step toward becoming what one can be. It is a kind of trial-and-error process that operates all through life. The child does not know what he is trying to take on, and, at least in the context of cultural forms such as social roles and forms of address, the frames are not so well formed that either the parent or the theorist can describe them in unambiguous terms or can know in any sense their essence over and above their variety. Thus, there is an analogy between what goes on in learning object permanence and learning how to talk. In language games, many have noted how the parent tries to highlight both what he says and what it refers to (e.g., Brown and Hanlon, 1970; Cazden, 1968). So too in hiding games, the experimenter can facilitate the child's search for hidden objects by making certain features and relations of the hiding situation more salient. But in neither case does the child learn a large and unequivocal lesson. In other words, Vygotsky's metaphor is not very different from that of the S-R learning theorists. But the latter approach was both too elementaristic and mechanistic (Overton and Reese, 1973) and did not allow for an actor who at times reflects on what he and others do and tries to frame corrigible and logically incomplete conjectures about what is happening.

What has been said until now might be interpreted as denying the value of thinking of development in terms of stages and as emphasizing environmentalism, focusing primarily on the role of culture and diminishing the importance of constructive activities of the individual actor. That is not the intent here, nor was it Vygotsky's. In analyzing change in the sciences, it is commonplace to speak of "standing on the shoulders of giants" (Merton, 1973). The inventive individual transforms an accepted conception. While we do not understand the process of creativity in the sciences, there is general agreement that the process entails organization and communication. The creative product arises out of the individual taking on the conception and in that process transforming it and making it comprehensible to others (Polanyi, 1964). Moreover whether we focus on such grand matters as science or such small matters as how children solve Piaget's class-inclusion problems, Rommetveit (1977) has pointed out that there is a negotiation between the individual actor and the cultural vicar both about the reality that is being addressed, the referential domain, and the conception of that reality. What is needed is a way of putting the two "parties" to the transaction into perspective. There is a need to find a way of characterizing each which does not attribute too much to the individual and which does not reify provisional conceptions, as Piaget and Chomsky have done with mind and Levy-Strauss has done with social forms.

In touting the idea of "advance organizer," the intention here is to emphasize that "society" sets the stage within which the child comes to "construct" his notion of society. Attempts to capture the organization of the developing child's mind have to take into account the nature of the organization of the cultural forms. We need to complement our notions of the developing actor with notions of the "developmental ecology." Vygotsky did not have such a theory nor does there appear to be one in the offing despite frequent calls for such, e.g., in Bronfenbrenner (1977).

Vygotsky's analysis of play, however, and his analyses of difficulties posed for communication by such cultural forms as telephones and writing, point in a direction appropriate to the task. Thus in analyzing play, Vygotsky (1978) emphasized organization more than Piaget and pointedly suggested ways in which the individual works at developing a mental organization that derives from the cultural form. Piaget (1962) viewed play as the activity of the mind when freed of the demand to adapt to situational constraint. It was a kind of free play within which the mental organization could explore its properties and the elements it worked with. Vygotsky's criterion for play was imaginary activity, and the playful activity occurred within the constraints of the imagined activity. He emphasized that play creates "demands on the child to act against immediate impulse" (1978, p. 99). The child in play creates a "proximal zone" within which he can work on the "organizations" that nature and society impose and thereby make them part of his mental organization. In his analysis of the "ecology" of language, he placed great stress on how the nature of the audience determines whether, and about what, the child can speak and write. The child on the telephone and the child who writes are faced with varying degrees of difficulty with respect to imagining both the domain of reference and the nature of the individual it will be shared with. Vygotsky emphasized that writing poses more than the problem of learning orthography for the well-spoken child. In his analysis of the task demands of a linguistic situation like writing, Vygotsky, like Piaget, placed heavy weight on the difficulties of taking the role of the other. It would appear that in our analyses of how thought and language develop, we need to join with Vygotsky, Asch (1952), and G.H. Mead (1934), in placing more focus on the nature of the "ecology" within which such activities occur. We think and talk about events, but we do this with regard to an audience which both influences the domain of reference and serves to validate and share in our view of events.

ACKNOWLEDGMENTS
The preparation of this paper was supported by Research Grant 5R01 HD10252 from the National Institute of Child Health and Human Development. I want to thank Rick Schuberth for his helpful comments.

Discussion

Kuhl asked if it was not important to pay attention to what the baby might be doing as he attempted to solve object permanence tasks, rather than what she/he was not doing. If one examined the problem from a visual tracking standpoint, one could consider the situation as one of competing perceptions. There was not merely one event to which the baby had to pay attention in the task, but many, all of them quite powerful perceptually. The baby's attention to the objects could be deflected in a number of ways as these events took place. She felt it would be possible to take a psychophysical approach to the object permanence task by examining developmental changes in visual tracking of selected objects in the presence and absence of other, competing visual objects and events. The development of attention to a particular object and the tendency to ignore other, competing objects might show dramatic changes over time. These abilities might interact during the typical object-permanence testing situation. This would be a very functional approach, but perhaps one should defer judgment of the presence of inferential reasoning as a major entity until basic research on these component factors was undertaken.

Gratch said that in any standard procedure, when a result was obtained with an infant, one had no idea as to how that result had been obtained. He felt that that was the essence of the difficulty expressed by Bloom and her colleagues in accepting object permanence scales.

Kuhl then asked if anyone did observe eye movements in the object permanence testing situation. Gratch replied that by gross observation, infants showed different patterns of eye movements during the delay interval in the procedure he had described. Some were distracted and appeared to forget about the hidden object. Others appeared to look back and forth from one possible hiding place to another, as if unable to decide where to search. It might well be that such different patterns of eye movements were correlated with different outcomes or could help to explain them.

Kagan remarked that Gratch's demonstrations had clearly pointed to factors in addition to memory that must account for the errors made by children in the object permanence task. But he wanted Gratch to comment further on the finding that, by changing a toy and making it perceptually more interesting, the probability of the child's making an error could be greatly reduced. This finding was partially inconsistent with the traditional Piagetian interpretation of the A-cup, B-cup error. Gratch had said that there was some truth to the Piagetian explanation. Why, then, didn't the children continue to make that particular A-B error when the toy was made more interesting?

Gratch replied that the toy change did not introduce a major reduction in error. He had wished merely, in mentioning the toy change, to indicate that there were many contextual effects which might be introduced experimentally. He did not believe that it was sufficient in asking questions about object permanence to vary the contexts in which the child performed the task. It was important also to have a theory of the mind, a theory of cognitive development, one that dealt with the thought processes of the child. If the problem was essentially transformed into one of variations in a display, then the only theory that could be tested was one of visual perceptual capabilities, a theory like Gibson's or Bower's. It would not be possible to ask questions about higher mental operations by such means.

Tronick raised a question about the varieties of ways in which hidden object problems could be solved. Was Gratch referring to alternate pathways to the Stage 6-mind in the child. Had he observed such differences among children? Gratch replied that unfortunately he had not studied the solving of invisible displacement problems in young children, which would be necessary to a complete account of the development of representational thinking, that is, of the Stage 6-mind.

Wolff asked Gratch if it would not follow from his insightful critique of the "good Piaget" and the "bad Piaget," that the bad Piaget was attributable not to the master but to his followers, the Piagetians? Could it not be that these workers had indeed misinterpreted Piaget's writing and that their errors had come to be identified with Piaget erroneously? Gratch said that, sadly, he could not see it that way. If one were to take the standardization of scales for measuring mental development as an example, Piaget himself had favored the development of such scales. He had not actually developed them himself, but had approved their development by his students, Casati and Lézine (1968) and others.

Gratch felt, however, that standardized presentation of interesting situations to young children need not always be counter-productive. Depending upon one's question and the ages of the children included, it might be possible to use a standard situation as a starting point and to develop from it other ways of approaching the same question. There was no doubt, however, as Piaget himself had pointed out, that a practice effect would be found if standard situations were presented repeatedly. But such effects could, in turn, be made objects of study, in the manner in which Vygotsky and Luria had counselled that repetitions of tests be treated. In talking about "proximal zones of development," these investigators had tried to distinguish between the child who profits from his failure and the child who does not, in terms of shifts from adult-controlled to self-controlled behavior. The danger of practice effects arises from treating the subsequent success as an index of the achievement of a certain state of mind. It should, instead, be treated as an occasion for exploring the way in which the child achieved success, recognizing that there might be a variety of paths to both success and failure.

Discussion of Cognitive Development in Relation to Language

Jerome Kagan

Department of Psychology and Social Relations, Harvard University, Cambridge, Massachusetts

The status of amateur in the field of developmental psycholinguistics confers the rare advantage of the freedom to be wrong without excessive embarrassment. In this spirit I will try to relate the papers in this section to three important themata which dominate modern studies of cognitive development.

The first of these themata concerns the choice between general constructs and those that are specific to problem situations. Intelligence, memory, achievement, and hostility, for example, are general constructs not constrained by context. Comprehension vocabulary, memory for locations, hostility to an older brother, by contrast, are specific constructs which take into account incentives, materials, and targets. If psychologists take embryology as a useful model then the arguments for specificity seem persuasive. For example, in embryogenesis the tendons, cartilage, and muscles for a particular joint develop independently. If morphological structures show such independence in ontogeny it seems likely that language, memory, and perception also grow independently.

The second theme involves connectivity in growth. The premise of connectivity holds that for some invariant sequences the earlier structure is incorporated into the later one. That assumption is likely to be correct for some sequences, but clearly not for all. Biology provides a useful model. In the development of the central nervous system a class of glial cells, called trellis cells, is always present prior to the migration of neurons to their final destination. The trellis cells form a handrail, as it were, for the neurons migrating from the neural tube to their final locations in the brain. But when the migration is complete, the trellis cells disappear; they are not a structural part of the next stage. It seems likely that there are many examples where a psychological structure or process precedes, but is not part of, a subsequent structure. As a psychologist trained in the early 1950's, it was not possible for me to question the notion that cognitive systems were connected. I took from my mentors and their reading assignments the articulated Western presupposition of cumulative development, connectedness, and continuity. I saw these as empirical propositions rather than philosophical presuppositions. After 20 years of failing to find commanding support for these premises, I became receptive to the position that some aspects of development may have less connected sequences. I have found it refreshing to assume less connectivity and continuity in development; this frame has provided me with a new perspective on my own work.

The third theme, which is epistemological, is concerned with the balance between *a priori* and *a posteriori* constructs. Some psychologists begin their investigative work with idealized constructs and gather data in accord with those ideas; others gather data with less conceptual guidance (although always with some) and invent constructs in order to interpret coherences in the data. I believe that, at the moment, psychologists in the field of cognitive science too often begin with constructs and use the inductive mode less frequently than they should. They first ask about the definitions of constructs—What is a sign? What is a word?—and devote much time to worrying about these definitions when it is not clear that the construct is the most useful one to explain any set of data.

Lois Bloom notes that investigators in developmental psycholinguistics often use categories taken from adult speech and apply them to early child language. But, as Bloom notes, these categories may be inappropriate to the psychology of the young child. As more sophisticated theorists have noted, the young child is often trying to express excitement, to share interests or to acquire information, and uses whatever linguistic forms he has available in order to accomplish these goals. The imposition of formal linguistic categories on these functions may not be helpful and, on occasion, may be misleading.

Let me now consider the Fischer and Corrigan paper in the light of this preliminary discussion. I applaud their emphasis on specificity, but argue with their brief for connectivity. I believe there is less connectivity than they propose. Although development in the first 3 years of life is strongly sequential, many new competences seem to appear quite suddenly, without an obvious connection to past structures or behaviors.

With respect to constructs Fischer and Corrigan are trying to develop a novel set of ideas which have a great deal of attractiveness. One important claim is that the child frequently operates at his or her optimal level. If this hypothesis means that during the first 3 years of life the child will display the competences that he possesses I am afraid I disagree. In one of our recent studies, children between 13 and 29 months played with a set of toys in a laboratory setting designed as a playroom. After the child had played for 10 minutes the female observer, who had been in the room talking to the mother, came to the child and displayed 3 different actions which were at the edge of the child's comprehension. In one of the actions she picked up some animals and said, "I have some animals here and they are going for a walk. But it is raining and so we must cover them." The experimenter then said to the child, "Now it's your turn to play," and she returned to the couch where she had been conversing with the mother. Children 18 months of age and older showed behaviors indicative of distress. They might cry, fret, cling to the mother, or ask to go home. But minutes later, when the child's level of apprehension had subsided a little, some spontaneously imitated some fragments of the model's action. These data suggest that, as early as 18 months, children show anxiety over possible failure when invited to operate at their optimal level. I do not believe the child ever operates at a level approaching his true ability. There is always a gap between his competence and his performance. Although I believe one can arrange situations that narrow that gap and provoke more competent performance, there are probably domains at every age in which children fail to operate at their highest level of skill.

A second implication in the Fischer and Corrigan paper is the suggestion that thought develops out of action—an idea central to Piagetian theory. I do not deny the relevance of action for cognitive development but acceptance of this idea as a general and primary principle of cognitive growth seems to me to be inconsistent with many phenomena observed in young children. Let me share an example with you that concerns the child's sense of the aesthetic. A two-year-old child playing with a set of toys found 2 dolls—one large and one small—and a large toy bed. The child put the large doll on the large bed and then became upset because there was no small bed for the other doll. After minutes of serious search, she found a small stove. Even though it was not a bed the child accepted this object as a bed, put the smaller doll on it, and then smiled. This behavior seems to be generated by a standard the child held which indicated that objects and their settings should be of similar size. I find it difficult to explain this standard and others as coming from prior action sequences. It seems to me, rather, that the child is generating ideal schemes and standards and seeks to match his or her behavior to those self-generated standards. I believe this process does not arise simply as a consequence of action with objects.

A second example from our work suggests that in the middle of the second year, children appreciate that unfamiliar names must apply to unfamiliar objects. An examiner places in front of the child 3 objects whose names the child knows—for example, a cat, a car, and a cup. She then says to the child, "Give me the car." If the child responds correctly and it appears that he understands the game the examiner removes this first set of objects and puts down a new trio consisting of 2 new familiar objects and one unfamiliar one which is an irregular shape made of wood. The examiner then asks, "Give me the iboon." Most children give the examiner the unfamiliar wooden form. This phenomena is as clear in Cambridge children as it is in children growing up in islands belonging to the Fiji chain. How can we account for the fact that children seem to believe that the unfamiliar word names the unfamiliar form? (The child could have failed to respond at all.) It seems that the child makes the inference that since the nonsense word is not the name for the two familiar objects it must be the name for the unfamiliar one. I do not see how this competence could have arisen out of a particular set of interactions.

Third, Fischer and Corrigan suggest that language development may be accounted for by the same skill theory that they wish to apply to cognitive development. This position seems, on the surface, to be inconsistent with the earlier plea for specificity. To demand that the same rules apply to both domains is to regress to a global view of cognition. My reading of the psycholinguistic literature leads me to resist this suggestion.

We have recently completed a study of two longitudinal samples of children on which we gathered data related to language, play, memory for locations, and inference. The relation between mean length of utterance, the primary index of speech development, and memory for locations, imitation of adults, symbolic play with toys, and inference was very low. The independence of speech and the other cognitive functions seems reasonable; language, memory for locations, and symbolic play have their own specific developmental course. I was therefore surprised to hear Fischer and Corrigan say, "The developmental course for language skills is similar in outline and process to that of other sets of skills." I would have expected their principle of specificity to have led them to a different conclusion.

Let me now turn to Gratch's thoughtful paper which provokes considerable assent. Gratch makes 4 major points. The first is that the infant perceives the world in a way that is different from that of the older child. This statement matches our intuitions, even though intuition is often a poor guide to validity. Second, Gratch, with Fischer and Corrigan, favors specificity, arguing that different aspects of cognitive function are "loosely coupled."

Gratch's last two observations are that there is less order in the infant mind than Piaget has implied and that ideas precede language. Most developmental psychologists and psycholinguists would probably agree with the last suggestion. One-year-old children behave as if they possess categories for animals, food, and clothing even though they are not speaking and may not comprehend some linguistic exemplars of these categories. Middle class children 13 to 14 months old have a relatively large comprehension vocabulary, months before they will speak intelligibly. Two children in our longitudinal study understood many more verbs than nouns on a vocabulary recognition test, even though 90% of their speaking vocabulary was composed of nouns.

Finally, I would like to make a plea for more empirical work in which constructs follow data. We should first ask what competences grow together and invent our names after the coherences have been discovered. In the longitudinal studies I have referred to, we have found a coherence among a set of behaviors that emerge between 17 and 23 months of age. These are:

1. Children appear to appreciate the difference between right and wrong and between good and bad events.
2. They smile when they attain a goal in which they have invested effort. We call these mastery smiles.
3. They begin to direct the behavior of adults. They might tell their mother to move to a new chair or push a telephone at her face indicating that they want her to talk in it.
4. They show the distress following the modeling of behavior. We believe they show this anxiety because they are aware of the fact that they cannot imitate the behaviors modeled for them.
5. Typically, following the display of the above 4 behaviors they begin to describe their own actions in language. They might say *fix* as they turn a cover, or *up* as they climb on a chair.

We did not anticipate this coherence. It is not unreasonable to suggest that the 4- or 5-month era before the second birthday may be a time when a special form of self-awareness is developing. This descriptive phrase, *self-awareness,* is not original and is similar to phrases used by nineteenth century observers to account for similar phenomena. But given the Zeitgeist in modern developmental theory such a phrase would not have occurred to me in the absence of these data. Of course I am aware of the premises that are hidden in the selection of the summary phrase *self-awareness.* Tiedemann said the child developed *Eigenliebe* (love of self) during this period. The Utku Eskimo of Hudson Bay believes the child develops *ihuma* (reason) during this same time. Each of these phrases has different connotations for empirical work. If the coherent phenomena geneticists call mutation had been named replacement, alteration, or even damage, different experiments might have been performed. Self-awareness is a popular idea in the West; hence, the scholar's mind leaps to these words quickly. Had these data been discovered by a seventeenth century Chinese observer, it is likely that a different term would have been selected.

I believe that at this particular moment in the study of human development it is useful to gather richly detailed corpora on the growing child in order to detect the coherences in change and to invent constructs, *after the fact,* to name or explain those changes. Like early Renaissance science, some components of developmental psychology are committed to concepts which have their origins in history and sentiment. Progress is likely to be accelerated if we heed Francis Bacon's plea to be somewhat suspicious of *a priori* ideas, even though the historical bases for Bacon's suggestion are quite different from those that dominate contemporary behavioral science. I do not favor a chronic avoidance of inventive *a priori* theorizing. Scientists must continue to make wise guesses as to words that might unite real phenomena and guide the gathering of information. But a mood of self-criticism is likely to be helpful during this temporary period of theoretical barrenness.

Discussion

Chapman asked what maturational changes could enable self-awareness. Kagan said he wished he could find a neurophysiologist interested in this problem. He believed, however, that complex competencies such as self-awareness which appeared to be psychologically determined, were as inevitable as standing, running, or walking.

The following discussion focused almost entirely on connectivity. Fischer remarked that development was likely to be both connective and non-connective. He took representation as a case in point. Piaget believed that representation grew out of action. It was a new scheme and provided a simplifying organization, not merely a greater complexity. Another organizing principle which provided simplification emerged at 12 to 13 years of age when the child became capable of abstraction.

Fogel stated that, in his view, the issue of connectivity was a central one. In his own studies of the ontogeny of gestures (Fogel, this volume, Chapter 2), there did not seem to be any very clear connection between the way in which infants used particular gestures at a few months of age and the way in which they were used in adult life. But, although there was no observable connectivity on the surface, it was still necessary for the developmental scientist to look for the reasons behind these changes of expression. It might be a myth that such reasons could be uncovered in the life cycle of a single developing organism. It concerned him that there might be no discoverable connectivity, no clear connective reason for moving from one stage to the next within the individual. It might be that the connections derived from an evolutionary principle particular to the species. In other words, the movement from one stage to another might have been determined by a long-term phylogenetic selection process rather than by an ontogenetic process. Embryologists had postulated for some time that evolution does not act on specific structures to achieve adaptation, but acts on the entire life cycle. The order in which structures or behaviors appeared in development was just as much a part of evolutionary selection as the particular nature of the structure or behavior itself. Given that the end product must be a creature designed to be optimally adapted to its environment, and also that a set of principles of economy of design must be adhered to with respect to the systems that could be built into this organism, the best solution must incorporate a small number of motor systems that could be used and reused for different functions at different points in the life cycle. Thus, if one observed a gesture and found it being used differently at 3 months of age than at 2 years or at 20 years, then it might be that there was no connectivity at all that one could hope to find within the individual's life cycle. It might just be that, over the course of human evolution, that particular gesture evolved and was adapted to a number of different contexts having no ontogenetic relationships with one another.

Bloom suggested that there might be ontogenetic connections, not in relation to a chronologic time line, but rather at a sub-assembly level within a single stage or time period. Perhaps the mistake was in thinking of connectivity for a discreet behavior as it appeared over time. The more important connections might be of a number of different behaviors with one another at a single point in time, perhaps taking place simultaneously. Thus, a particular gesture at 2 months might not be connected to that same gesture at 2 years or 20 years. It might instead become connected with some other aspect of development at 2 years and again with others at 20 years. She thought that such sub-assemblies of behavior might be consonant with Fischer's model of skill development.

Fogel replied that that view of development was probably correct. At each stage in life there was a separate organization of behaviors with different subsystems working together. He still thought, however, that scientists might be deluding themselves, subscribing to our present-day myth, if they believed that by means of working out the grammar of individual stages they could eventually find a clear connective link between them.

Leavitt argued that just because there was a lawful and orderly progression of behaviors, it was not mandated that that progression was biological in nature. It could be that the progression was socially motivated, related to parental behavior or the type of educational system in place. He drew attention to the possibility that there were connections of several different orders operating in very different ways. Connections might then be very complicated and might even be random in some cases. Much genetic change in the human, for example, was probably due to random drift. If that were the case for specific anatomic structures, it could also be that the anatomic structures would mandate random behaviors. The developmental psychologist might then focus upon these behaviors. Stern commented that although there was a strong tendency for developmentalists to fixate upon Piagetian theory, Piaget himself was influenced by Wallon, a French theorist, who had written about tensions between systems within the organism and its environment. Wallon was very sensitive to the problems of connectivity which Fogel had brought up.

Stark asked Fogel if he was implying that if, say, a pointing gesture did not happen to emerge in the 2-month-old because of some adventitious effect, that it would not even matter. The pointing behavior would still be connected properly with other behaviors at 2 years of age. Fogel said he suspected that this was the case. He referred to Gratch's comment on the rapid changes taking place in all aspects of development at 18 months of age. There did not seem to be any relationship between what went before and what followed after in this period of change. Fogel was reminded also of the studies of the neonatal walking reflex. Some investigators (for example, Bower, 1974; Zelazo, Zelazo, and Kolb, 1972) had tried to accelerate voluntary walking by practicing the walking reflex in the infant, but the results had been equivocal. Some studies indicated that walking emerged earlier in the practiced infants than in those who were not practiced. But by the time the subjects of these experiments were 3 years of age, there was no difference at all between the practiced and the unpracticed infants with respect to their walking.

Kagan reminded the participants of a famous experiment by Carmichael (1926), who had been motivated by the view of development as cumulative to study the salamader larva, the ambystoma. These larvae go through some minor motor movements before they begin to swim. It was assumed that the minor movements were necessary to the development of swimming behavior. Carmichael, however, anesthetized the embryo until that time in the developmental cycle when they normally would swim. He then pumped the anesthetic out of the tank. The ambystoma immediately began to swim. All the minor motor movements were unnecessary for that response.

Fischer argued that, although the movements were unnecessary, the development of the anatomic substrate which permitted the movements to occur *was* necessary. He related his comments to the development of the neural crest. That development did have necessary anatomic precursors. Kagan said that, of course, maturation of the nervous system was necessary. The point was, that although development of the motor cortex of the salamander was necessary for swimming, its expression in form of minor motor movements was not. Fischer argued that the capacity was there, it was capacities that became combined with one another. No one was contending that the finger movements were used for the same purpose in the infant and the adult. Some combinations of movements were present in the infant, others in the adult. He felt that we should be able to say how one combination was transformed into another.

Gratch proposed a somewhat different model. He referred to Gottlieb's study of the duckling embryo (1976). In order for imprinting to take place, it was necessary for the unhatched duckling to experience self-produced vocalization. The embryo, prior to hatching, penetrates the airspace in the egg and then hears the sounds it emits. If, under certain experimental conditions, the duckling is prevented from vocalizing, then it later shows no preference for maternal calls and fails to become imprinted upon the mother. Clearly, this cycle of events was different from the development of swimming in the ambystoma. Experience did play a role in the development of the duckling embryo.

Kagan pointed out that this was a very good example of Fischer's proposition. He ventured to rephrase it thus—nature has both kinds of developmental phenomena, those that are connected and those that are not. Therefore, when we observe an emerging phenomenon, we should not immediately assume that it is connected and ask what are its precursors, but rather we should ask whether it is connected to previous phenomena or not? Bloom pointed out that just because one could not find the connectiveness, that would not necessarily mean that it was not present.

Stern suggested that it might not be worthwhile to derive general principles for connectivity. In specific cases the question might be important. But for many behaviors the nature of connectivity, if it existed, could be very hard to establish. This was true of all of the sensitive-period phenomena, as for example, in Marler's work on bird song (1970) referred to in an earlier discussion. Clearly antecedent phenomena were important in such cases, yet it would be very hard to specify the connectivity. In general, depending upon the system or modality being considered—motor or sensory, phenomena might be disconnected in some cases, connected in others, and, in addition, the connectivity might vary greatly from one case to another. It might be dangerous at this time to attempt an all-inclusive position with respect to such diverse phenomena.

B. Language Development in Relation to Cognition

What Children Say and What They Know: Exploring the Relations between Product and Process in the Development of Early Words and Early Concepts

Lois Bloom, Karin Lifter and John Broughton

Department of Psychology, Teachers College, Columbia University, New York, New York

The developmental relation between language and cognition in the preschool years is an issue of some importance in the child language literature. The present paper begins with a review of the relevant literature as background; goes on to discuss two methodological issues that have surfaced in the context of the contemporary research into early language and thought; and then concludes with a presentation of some preliminary results of research in progress that explores the relation between product and process in the development of early words and early concepts.

Background

The convergence of early language and cognition has been approached empirically from several directions. First, there have been studies of children's language that retrospectively identified correspondences in sensorimotor development (e.g., Bloom, 1970, 1973; Brown, 1973; Edwards, 1973); and that looked first at children's play behaviors and then identified correspondences in early language (Sinclair, 1970). Second, subsequent studies have attempted to use independent measures of both cognitive and language development (e.g., Bates et al., 1977; Corrigan, 1976; Ingram, 1978; Menn and Haselkorn, 1977; Miller et al., 1980; Zachry, 1972).

The first group of studies were descriptive studies of children's language in the period when children say only one word at a time and progress to their first word combinations. A major result of these studies was an account of the semantics of early child speech with the identification of a relatively small set of relational meanings that has proven to be remarkably consistent among children in different cultures. When children say single-word utterances and then early sentences, they talk about *objects:* the fact that objects exist, disappear, and recur; they talk about *actions:* the fact that persons move and act on objects; and they talk about *locations:* the fact that objects change in their locations relative to one another in different contexts (Bloom, 1970, 1973; Brown, 1973; Schlesinger, 1971).

Once the regularities among the meanings of children's words and sentences were identified, it was easy to see a connection between the semantics of early language and the description of children's sensorimotor intelligence in the first 2 years that has been described by Piaget (1954, 1960) and others. The culmination of sensorimotor development comes with the child's awareness of object permanence—the knowledge that objects exist in space and time even though the child can no longer see them or act on them. Moreover, two factors that predominate in leading the child to awareness of object permanence are movement and location (Gratch et al., 1974; Harris, 1975; Piaget, 1954). The facts of sensorimotor intelligence were thus logically relevant for attempts to explain the semantics of early language—the fact that early words and sentences are "about" objects, and action and location relations with respect to objects (Bloom, 1973; Brown, 1973; Edwards, 1973; Sinclair, 1970).

There were at least two specific connections made between progress in language learning and progress in sensorimotor development in the child's second year. First, different kinds of words can be identified in this period: substantive words that refer to objects (either single instance objects such as "Mama" and "blanket," and object class names such as "cookie" and "dog"), and function words that refer more generally to the transformation or relational properties of different objects (such as "more," "gone," "this," etc.). Sinclair (1970) described function words as representing the "organizing activity" of the child who is forming basic action patterns or schemas with respect to objects in general early in the sensorimotor period, whereas "denominational utterances" or object names represent the later developing knowledge of particular objects. The development of knowledge of objects in general together with knowledge of particular objects form the essence of sensorimotor intelligence.

In the longitudinal data from the single subject described in Bloom (1973), there was a developmental difference between substantive and function words and this difference was consistent with Sinclair's account. The words that this child used most frequently in the first half of the second year were the functional, relational, operational terms that included "there," "more," "away," "gone," "up," and "uhoh" and the names of particular persons and objects. Although the names of classes of objects were used from the beginning (e.g., "juice," "car," "ball"), such substantive words were not used more frequently than the functional words and person names until the second half of the second year. The first specific tie between sensorimotor development and early child language was in this identification of the different kinds of words used in the single-word utterance period with different aspects of sensorimotor intelligence. Knowledge about objects develops gradually in the second year of life, and gradual changes occur in the kinds of words that children learn and use in the period.

A second implication was the importance of Stage 6 in sensorimotor intelligence and the child's development of object permanence for the acquisition and use of names of many different objects. It was hypothesized that one cannot know a *word* such as "dog" unless one also knows something about *objects* in general, and *dogs* in particular. Establishing a conceptual relation between a word and an object requires mental representation of an object that is independent of the action and location schemas in which the child encounters the object. One of the most consistent observations in child language is the clear and often precipitous increase in vocabulary size and volubility at about 16–20 months. The two developments—gradual change in the use of different kinds of words, with the subsequent precipitous increase in the use of object words in particular—coincide with the development of sensorimotor Stage 6 and appear to be evidence of the achievement of mental representation that underlies the conceptual relations between words and objects.

This first approach to understanding the convergence of early language and cognition was essentially inferential and speculative: The conceptual antecedents of language were presumed from the evidence of children's language and play behaviors. However, in order to understand the relation of cognitive development to language, it is necessary to obtain evidence of cognitive development that is not itself dependent on the very behavior that one seeks to explain. Thus, the early studies provided a heuristic for a second approach to explain early language with two methods of analysis: correspondence or correlation between development of linguistic and nonlinguistic behaviors. Correspondences between sensorimotor development and language behaviors were examined by, for example, Ingram, 1978; Menn and Haselkorn, 1977; Miller et al., 1980; and Zachry, 1972, 1978. The correlation method was used to test the relationship between language behavior and independent measures of children's sensorimotor functioning by, for example, Bates et al., 1977; Corrigan, 1976; and Miller et al., 1980.

Correspondence Studies

Ingram (1978) used the behavioral data reported by Piaget and other case study diarists to assemble a chronology of language and cognitive behaviors. Using Piaget's indices of stage related behaviors, he classified the children's activities according to sensorimotor stages and observed how the children's language behaviors co-occurred. That is, cognitive behaviors were classified according to stages, and arranged chronologically along with the language behaviors that occurred at the same time. The results were that first words, which were context bound and variable in their use, appeared in Stage 5: the single-word utterance period, along with the gradual increase in vocabulary, corresponded to Stage 6; and the first multi-word utterances and first reference to past events emerged during the early representational period. Thus, this analysis provided evidence of a general relation between language and sensorimotor development. Ingram pointed out, however, that this relation is only general for two major reasons: Stage 6 is very long (9 months) and poorly defined, and the transition to early representation is unclear. Although he did not provide the relevant analysis of the kinds of words the children used, in the diary data he presents, person names and names for single instance objects predominated in the early vocabularies of Piaget's children, and function words predominated in the early vocabularies of the other children.

Menn and Haselkorn (1977), on the other hand, reported a longitudinal study in which they observed one child weekly from 12 to 20 months, and described his language in terms of the words he used and how they were used. Several hours of his language behaviors were recorded at each observation. Four of the Uzgiris and Hunt (1975) scales were administered during 7 observation sessions over the course of the study: object permanence, means-ends, development of operational causality, and construction of objects in space. Menn and Haselkorn categorized the child's early words into categories of action words and object words, a distinction that corresponds to the categories of function words and substantive words described by Bloom (1973), and observed the developmental course of action and object words.

One result of the Menn and Haselkorn study was that action words developed to symbol status, which the authors defined as generalization of the word to new instances, before object words, a result that is in accord with the observation by Bloom (1973) that function words predominated early in the single-word utterance period in the language development of one child and in the early diary studies as well. In addition, Menn and Haselkorn reported certain correspondences between scale performance and the developmental course of particular words as well as categories of words. Some action words achieved symbol status at the same observation that Stage 6 of the object permanence scale was achieved. All the child's action words were used symbolically at the same time that Stage 6 was achieved in all the subscales, suggesting a close relationship between action words and later developments in the sensorimotor period as measured by the ordinal scales. Although the child's symbolic use of action words corresponds with Stage 6 achievement in all the subscales, object words were not yet used symbolically, thus there was a developmental lag between Stage 6 object permanence and the symbolic status of object words. Such a developmental lag may be missed in cross-sectional studies, especially since, as is well known, children differ in time of onset of word use and their rates of development.

Correlation Studies

Corrigan (1976) studied 3 infants longitudinally in the second year and administered an expanded version of the Uzgiris and Hunt ordinal scale of object permanence. There were 21 items in the scale which provided object permanence scores. These object permanence scores were correlated with mean utterance length which was computed by counting single words as 1.0 and "non-lexical vocalizations" as .5. Given the individual differences in the extent to which infants engage in non-lexical vocalizing (see, for example, Kagan, 1979; Stark, in press), such a language measure could distort the results. There was no general correlation between the two scores when age was partialled out, although there was an increase in utterance length at about the time of entry into Stage 6, and an increase in total vocabulary at the "object permanence attainment session." Corrigan also tested the hypothesis that function forms occur more frequently than substantive forms before "object permanence attainment" by comparing the frequencies of the two kinds of words before the last item in the scale was passed. She failed to find significant differences in the frequencies of the two kinds of words.

Since Corrigan reported only scores and correlations to test the above hypotheses, it is not possible to evaluate her findings fully. A simple correlation (or no correlation) between length of utterance and performance on contrived tasks of object hiding and search is less informative than more qualitative descriptions of the developmental relation between the two behaviors would be. The failure to find frequency differences between substantive and function words before object permanence may be due to the fact that the *relative* use of these classes of words is variable either before or within the time period covered by Stage 6. That is, substantive words most probably increase in frequency during Stage 6 so that differences between earlier and later Stage 6, or between Stage 5 and Stage 6, would be concealed if only the cumulative frequencies throughout the period up to the end of Stage 6 were compared. It is also not clear whether Corrigan counted person names (or single instance object names) as substantive words; since these are among the most frequently occurring early words (Bloom, 1973; Leopold, 1939; Nelson, 1973), the relevant relationship between substantive and function words would be obscured if they were not considered separately. It is also the case that Corrigan's language samples were relatively small: the observations were only 30 minutes long and the scales were also administered during this time.

In the study reported by Bates et al. (1977), 25 infants (12 from Rome, Italy, and 13 from Boulder, Colorado) were studied longitudinally from 9 to 13 months of age. Each child was visited 4 times. There were three sources of data: (1) dichotomous scores obtained from mother interviews, with detailed questions about social, sensorimotor, communication, and play behaviors; (2) frequency scores obtained from observation with video records, observation checklists, and narrative descriptions; and (3) standardized cognitive measures which consisted of the Uzgiris and Hunt Scales of object permanence, spatial relations, means-end relations, imitation, schemes for relating to objects and operational causality. The interview and observation data were coded and categorized. Thirty-three measures of communicative and cognitive development were generated for pairwise correlations within and across the 4 observation sessions. Individual data were not reported. As the authors themselves pointed out, there was great variability among the measures. For instance, the parent interviews were not all consistent in the behaviors reported; frequency scores obtained through video observations were different from other observation frequencies, etc.

There are certain methodological problems in the Bates et al. study which need to be taken into account in evaluating their results. To begin with, there was considerable overlap between the observation and the interview sources in the kinds of measures taken. For example, measures of combinatorial play and symbolic play were determined from both the observations and the interviews; thus, there was considerable redundancy in the correlation matrix because several measures of the *same* behaviors were included. In addition, the measures derived from within a source of data were not independent from one another which further compounds the redundancy in the matrix. For example, the two language measures—"frequency of referential speech" and "number of referential words"—cannot be considered to be independent. Further, the individual scales of sensorimotor development are not independent of one another either theoretically or empirically, as will be discussed below, which also contributes to the redundancy in the correlation matrix.

One way to control for redundancy within a correlation matrix is to use adequate numbers of observations for each of the variables under study. A rule of thumb for an intercorrelation matrix would be 20 observations for each variable (i.e., observations from 20 children for each variable measured). Thus, Bates et al. would have had to observe 660 children instead of 25 in order to examine the relationship among 33 variables. These problems could also have been reduced by partialling out the other covariables from the pair being correlated. The issue of partial correlations is particularly important in a study with a large degree of redundancy in the correlation matrix. Unfortunately, partial correlations were not computed in the Bates et al. study. Consequently, the patterns of correlation they did find essentially provide no support for either the deep homologies or the local homologies that they claimed to have observed among cognitive and communicative developments.

With these methodological reservations in mind, the major results reported that are relevant to the present study are, first, that object permanence and spatial relations as measured by the standardized scales were poor predictors of language, and the scales of imitation and means-ends relations were good predictors of language production. Bates et al. in agreement with Ingram, concluded that the Stage 5 awareness of means-ends relationships is more important than the Stage 6 awareness of object permanence for language acquisition. Given that means-ends behaviors and object permanence are interdependent on theoretical grounds (Piaget and Inhelder, 1969) the observations that one sensorimotor measure and not another correlates with language is problematic.

One might expect knowledge of objects to be a more important predictor of language behavior in the second year than in the first year of life. However, Bates et al. observed children only in the period from 9 to 13 months of age. In a follow-up study, Bates (1979) observed the same group of children when they were 18 months old. Yet the five-month period during which most of Stage 6 development ordinarily occurs was ignored. The hypotheses regarding the relationship of language to object permanence (Bloom, 1973) were not limited to Stage 5 object permanence. Thus the results of the Bates et al. study provide no support for or against those hypotheses or others concerning the relation between linguistic knowledge and conceptual development.

In general, very superficial measures of language behaviors were used in most of the above studies. Ingram (1978) and Bates et al. (1977) used onset of first words and numbers of words produced and understood; Bates et al. also reported whether words were used referentially; Corrigan used an essentially arbitrary measure of utterance length. While Corrigan did observe children throughout the Stage 6 period, for at least 6 months in the second year, she did not discriminate among language behaviors within the period. Thus, change in the content of the language behaviors could not be evaluated.

There are, finally, two problems with such correlation and correspondence studies that are more serious than any that have been discussed so far. One is difficulty in assessing the relation between infants' performance on such contrived laboratory tasks as the Uzgiris and Hunt scales (or any other standardized scales) and developmental changes in their behaviors with objects in everyday events in the same time period. There may well be the same discrepancy in these cognitive tasks (with distortions that either overestimate or underestimate capability) as has been observed with the use of contrived elicited imitation tasks to measure linguistic development (see Bloom, 1974; Hood and Lightbown, 1978, for data and discussion of this point). Attempts to relate early language and cognitive development have focused on object permanence and Piaget's Stage 6 in sensorimotor development. However, the standardized tasks presented to infants in the attempt to assess their "level" of object permanence may not be the best index of what and how infants learn about objects in general or about particular objects, just as performance on elicited imitation tasks may not be the best index of what children know about language.

Another serious problem, specific to the correlation studies, is the issue of how appropriate the correlation method is for testing the relation between sensorimotor performance and linguistic development. Certain statistical analyses, in particular the simple Pearson product-moment correlation coefficient, may obscure the possibility of observing alternative relationships between two developments. What follows is a discussion of these two issues: the use of the ordinal scales to assess sensorimotor development and the use of the correlation method to test the developmental relations between the domains of language and thought.

The Application of Piaget's Infant Studies for Standardized Assessment

Although there are other instruments, the Uzgiris and Hunt "Ordinal Scales of Psychological Development" (1975) is the most comprehensive attempt so far to operationalize the observations chronicled by Piaget in his "infant books" (1951, 1952, 1954). It is also the instrument that was used in most of the above studies. The purpose of Uzgiris and Hunt was to construct scales with ordinal properties according to the sensorimotor schemata described by Piaget. Uzgiris and Hunt's scales were designed to assess development, and, in particular, to construct a means whereby the developmental effects of different environmental experiences could be examined, which was consistent with Hunt's (1961) emphasis on the role of the early environment in development. However, the notion of constructing scales for this purpose appears to be inconsistent with Piagetian theory.

The instrument consists of 6 scales each claiming to have "psychological unity": (Uzgiris and Hunt, 1975, p. 102)

I The Development of Visual Pursuit and the Permanence Of Objects

II The Development of Means for Achieving Desired Environmental Events

III The Development of Vocal Imitation and the Development of Gestural Imitation

IV The Development of Operational Causality

V The Construction of Object Relations in Space

VI The Development of Schemes for Relating to Objects

Each of these scales is subdivided into 5 groupings representing the transitions between Piaget's stages of the sensorimotor period. Each grouping has from one to 4 tasks, which resemble those used by Piaget. Thus, each scale involves about 15 tasks altogether. Since Uzgiris and Hunt did not equate the tasks with stage level per se, many researchers who have used the scales have inferred stage level scores from comparison with Piaget's original description.

There are certain problems in the construction of the instrument that need to be considered before accepting, unequivocally, the conclusions that have been drawn from its use. Several of these problems are elaborated below.

General Theoretical Issues

Interaction, for Piaget, is a way in which *organism* and *environment*, or more accurately, *subject and object,* are related in the process of knowing through development of the structures (or schemata) of thought. In this interaction, objects and events are actively understood according to present schemata, which is what Piaget calls "assimilation." However, the constant novelty of these successive encounters resists assimilation and leads to the adaptation of schemata, which is what Piaget calls "accommodation." The concept of "structure" has a relation of interdependence with the notion of "interaction," since it is structures that assimilate and accommodate. "Structure" is the fundamental idea in Piaget's theory, as Furth (1969) and Kohlberg (1969) have pointed out (see Broughton, in press). Structures *underlie* specific contents of behavior. Because Uzgiris and Hunt start from the assumption of an empiricist position, they concentrate heavily upon the role of early experience and environmental contact in development. They view Piaget's core notion of "interaction" as a question of gene/environment interaction (1975, pp. 30–31), which is heavily influenced by differing environmental circumstances (e.g., "differing child-rearing practices," pp. 18–19). Thus, Uzgiris and Hunt's application of Piaget's observations in the construction of the scales appears to reflect an underestimation of interaction and hence of the interdependence between interaction and structure.

Related to Uzgiris and Hunt's conceptualization of interaction and the role of the environment in development is their emphasis on the importance of intrinsic motivation and reinforcement in the theoretical rationale that underlies the construction of the scales (1975, pp. 35–41). Appeals to causal notions of motivation or of reinforcement to explain development are actually contrary to, and irreconcilable with, Piaget's basic conception of the organism as spontaneously operating. For Piaget, the organism is built to function, much as the eye is built to see. As the eye requires no further motivation or reward to perform its function, so the organism requires no push to make it active or reinforcement to maintain its activity. In processes of thought, judgments are connected by relations of *implication*. Each is sufficient (though not necessary) reason for the next. Consequently, no pushing, guiding or reinforcing influence is necessary (Mischel, 1971).

Such theoretical issues as these serve to exemplify discrepancies between Piaget's theoretical construction and the more traditional, empiricist treatment apparently favored by Uzgiris and Hunt.

The Testing Approach: Psychometric and Structural-Development Traditions

As Uzgiris and Hunt point out, most scales for the assessment of infant development have been like that of Gesell and Amatruda (1941), in that they are constructed on the assumption of nonlogical sequence in development, with items selected to predict intellectual status at later ages. Furthermore, the items in these traditional psychometric scales are ordered according to the average age at which each is "passed" by a majority of children. An individual child's status is determined by summing successes and failures on the assumption that items are of equal numerical value and therefore compensate exactly for each other.

Uzgiris and Hunt have correctly realized the centrality of universal invariant sequence in Piaget's findings, a prediction that is fundamental to cognitive-structural development theory. However, they have not adopted the conceptions of structure and interaction which imply and guarantee invariant sequence in the Piagetian account. In Piaget's theory, the sequence of development is *logically* invariant, as well as empirically so, and this idea is at the heart of Piaget's approach. Given the terms of the fundamental tenets of his theory, the developmental sequence *could be no other way,* since higher (later) stages are logically dependent upon prior passage through the lower (earlier) ones. Although the Uzgiris and Hunt scales are empirically invariant, they are not necessarily logically invariant. The order of appearance of "behavioral reactions" is treated just like the order of achievements in psychometric tests where their interrelationship is not guaranteed. As a result, there is concentration on the *product* or end-point in the tasks rather than on the *processes* of behavior, and there is no logical certainty in the observed sequence.

When behaviors are defined by their *products,* that is, their end-product or goal as seen by an observer, they are just scored as simple pass/fail on a problem solution task. As a result, no sequence is guaranteed, since only the end-point and not the way in which the task is solved is taken into account in assessment. Within a Piagetian perspective, the same end-point can subserve different functions according to the structures of the child. These structures will be faithfully reflected only in the process of the infant's behavior, the *way* the infant does something or the structure of the action, and not in *what* is achieved (see, also, Sugarman, 1979). What the logic of the developmental sequence reflects and guarantees is that the development of *processes* involved in the infant's behavior, that is, development in the infant's *way* of behaving, is unidirectional and irreversible.

For example, the actual *discovery* of an object concealed by a cloth is an insufficient criterion for saying that the infant has developed the Stage 4 notion of the permanence of objects. The discovery may be accidental, involving the "magical" instrumental flinging away of anything in front of the infant (Stage 3). Thus, grading on this item must take account of how the object is found: whether there are signs that the infant *expects* to find the object underneath, or whether there is surprise if the object that was apparently concealed is not there upon removal of the cloth (Charlesworth, 1966; Moore, 1973). Similarly, the Stage 6 task of finding an object after successive invisible displacements can be solved in alternative ways. Finding the object may be more a function of the child having learned to perform the task as a result of repeated administration, than it is a reflection of object permanence. Furthermore, the infant can search under the screens in the order of hiding, can search only under the last screen, or can search in an undirected manner. Such processes that the child uses to find the object may be a better indication of object permanence level than simply passing the test item.

What the child learns, or rather what develops, are notions about the permanence of objects, and not behavioral *skills* for locating hidden objects. As Piaget (1954) and others have noted, infants do not have stereotyped strategies for such problems as finding hidden objects, nor is search a matter of acquiring "search skills" in the manner suggested by Bruner (1971) and Fischer (in press). Neither cognition nor behavior at successive points in development show the gradual acquisition of such strategies. Nor can development be characterized as simple progressive approximation to a search skill; the initial step on the way to acquiring a skill and the learning of "modules" of the skills would have no functional value in and of themselves. Rather, at any stage in development, the way in which objects are found is qualitatively different, reflecting a completely different "theorizing" about, or structuring of, the world. Each of these little "theories" (stages) logically follows from the conjunction of the previous "theory" (stage) and the experiences which resisted interpretation in terms of that theory. Each leads in the same way to the next.

These "theories" are stages rather than levels in the sense that they are unified and general across *all* tasks, e.g., not just all problems of locating objects, but all situations which involve objects (thus all situations). The level of invariance is not a behavioral one but is rather a cognitive-structural one, in that structures are necessary but not sufficient conditions for behaviors. Piaget has invoked the notion of "décalage" to explain variation in *behaviors* that are due to the differential performance requirements of tasks in different domains. In other words, to do it justice the development of thinking in the infant should be seen by testers as the application of qualitatively different forms of thinking to the same content area (such as the location of objects). This content area will always be a domain that has to be handled by that person, at any point in life. But the *way* that it is handled changes with development. Such a position is to be distinguished from the psychometric view of development as the acquisition of specific skills or information about a domain through familiarity or maturation.

Turning Piaget's Theory Into a Measurement Instrument

In the construction of the instrument, the nature of the informal tests used and elaborated by Piaget in his clinical studies were not fully taken into account by Uzgiris and Hunt. As a result, the instrument shows more characteristics of the psychometric tradition than the Piagetian one; for example, the criteria that were used for the inclusion of scale items were interobserver and test-retest reliability. There is, then, a confusion of theory with measurement. The *construct validity* of the test should depend upon an operationalization of Piaget's account that does not sacrifice fidelity to the theory. Without a distinction between theory and measurement, the instrument cannot logically derive construct validity from the theory. This confounding is common in the developmental literature (Broughton, 1978; Broughton and Zahaykevich, 1980). It is related to, though not identical with, the confusion of competence with performance (Broughton, in press).

The endeavor of constructing a Piagetian test of infant development may be a reasonable goal; however, the problems involved are considerable. Piaget employed a "méthode" that is distinctly "clinique:" a combination of informal experimentation and observation that derives from and is carefully geared to a structural approach to human knowledge. Rigid "control" of situations in the usual experimental sense was eschewed. Piaget's method involved both spontaneous activities of the child and situations which were "set up" by the experimenter. Ambiguities in the observations due to extraneous causes were resolved by systematically varying the situation, and by presenting further tasks to explore the structure underlying particular patterns of behavior.

Systematization for testing may be a very difficult project, since test items must in some sense "elicit" reactions in quite a short time. This is a problem for a Piagetian test since a structuralist approach to development leads us to believe that "reactions" cannot be "elicited." It is clear in Piaget's books that some of his core observations were observations of spontaneous behavior, the generation of which could not be guaranteed by particular "presentations" in the test situation. Thus, it should be remembered that any test instrument will operate with a corpus of items that is very constrained compared to that used by Piaget, since even those "non-spontaneous" situations in which his own manipulations were involved were often fortuitous in revealing his children's cognitive structure. What we read about in the 3 infant books are probably only the most informative events selected from a vast body of informal observation and experimentation.

In addition to the problems of spontaneity and variety of behavior, a further question is whether there is justification for administering such an instrument for assessment as a number of *separate* subscales. The implication of such a format is that, for example, the subscales "Development of Operational Causality" and "Visual Pursuit and the Permanence of Objects" are in some sense separable. Uzgiris and Hunt made this more explicit when they described the scales as "specific branches of development" (1975, p. 101), and suggested that "progress in the various branches of development is somewhat independent'' (p. 138). However, how can this be if cognition is truly *structured* at a general level? Once again, the properties of the measurement instrument (e.g., scores show variability across subscales) are confused with the theoretically prescribed qualities of cognition (e.g., the infant functions predominantly according to a unified structure or theory about the world). Development is not reducible to separate dimensions of measured change. It is a systematic advance involving *logically* interrelated categories of thought. The development of object permanence is not just *important* for the construction of objective space, it *constitutes* that construction. Advance in the one domain *logically* carries with it a correlated advance in the other. This integrity holds particularly for object/space, and causality/time, and presumably less so for other combinations of these categories. Hence more is implied than "some interesting interrelationships among the various branches of development" (Uzgiris and Hunt, 1975, p. 136).

A final issue revolves around the idea of *ordinality*. Ordinality of stage attainment is a crucial prediction from Piagetian theory, in the sense that the theory predicts that the order of *stage* attainment will be invariant over all subjects. As mentioned previously, this order is not behavioral but cognitive-structural. However, in their scale validation, Uzgiris and Hunt used a scalogram analysis which assumes an accretion of behaviors rather than an integration of structures in the Piagetian sense. The theory applies to *structures*, not behaviors (Kohlberg, 1969) and is based upon the logical necessity in the sequence of stages. This is not to say that earlier stages are merely retained in their original form throughout development, uninfluenced by further development, but rather

> "attainments of earlier stages are carried into later ones . . . (where) . . . they are integrated with new elements arising in the later stages." (Inhelder, 1962).

Thus, earlier behaviors are restructured within a new context at each stage, as schemata became coordinated and integrated. Either the same behavior serves a new function at each stage, or else that behavior disappears from the repertoire having become integrated within more differentiated and organized action patterns. Thus, the ordinality of the scales as described by Uzgiris and Hunt, or rather their scalability (since validation was cross-sectional), is *empirical* in nature, based as it is on behaviors, and not *logical*. This is especially so given the emphasis in administering the tasks on whether a behavioral item is passed and not on how the tasks are solved.

To conclude, these criticisms have been applied to the Uzgiris and Hunt instrument since it is the measurement device most often used in studies that looked for correlations and/or correspondences between the domains of language and cognition in development. It appears, however, that the construction of the instrument may have less relevance to Piaget's theory than has been assumed by researchers using the scales to examine progress in sensorimotor development and to compare progress in different developmental domains. Nevertheless, as Uzgiris and Hunt have claimed, their studies have served also to provoke investigation in the area, and the value of this kind of heuristic finding cannot be underestimated. If more attention were paid to the advantages of Piaget's epistemology and psychology, rather than just assimilating his work to the psychometric tradition, and if measurement were differentiated clearly from theory, the kind of investigations that Uzgiris and Hunt and others have pursued would be more fruitful for assessing infant development. The task of constructing cognitive-structural measurement instruments is not itself spurious. It is the particular *way* in which they are constructed that determines their validity.

Correlation Analyses as Tests for Developmental Contingencies

The correlation method was used to test the relationship of one or more aspects of sensorimotor development to language development in a number of studies cited above. An evaluation of the use of the correlation method in these studies requires, first, a consideration of whether the method should be used, and second, if it is to be used, a consideration of how it should be used.

As pointed out by Porges (1979), the selection of an analysis technique limits the research questions that may be answered; consequently, the possibility exists that certain analyses may obscure the observations of specific developmental relations. The investigation of the nature of the developmental relation between linguistic development and conceptual development is very much in the exploratory stage. Whether the relation is dependent, interdependent, or independent is open to question. Thus far, the correlation method has been the one analysis technique that has been used to test the developmental relation between language and sensorimotor development. As it has been generally applied, it is not clear that the method allows for the possibility of determining a directional dependency relation, for exploring the nature of a dependency relation, or for exploring an interdependency relation. It does allow for the possibility of concluding independence. It is not surprising, then, that in the results that have been reported to date the correlation "evidence" has been strongest in support of independence between behaviors in the two domains.

According to Hays (1973), a requirement in a correlation problem is that "there is no clear cut distinction between the two scores as to which is the independent or predictor variable. Both variables are left completely free to take on any value for any observed individual" (p. 619). Theoretically, then, if the correlation between object permanence and language is being measured, levels of language behaviors "more advanced" than levels of object permanence presumably have as much chance of occurring as object permanence levels more advanced than language behaviors. It seems that this assumption precludes the possibility of inferring a directional dependency or causal relation between language and conceptual development. If one theoretical possibility for the dependency relation is that certain language developments await and are dependent upon certain developments in object permanence, then object permanence becomes the predictor variable or the independent variable. As pointed out by Hays (1973), a regression analysis is appropriate when "there is a clear independent variable (fixed) and a dependent variable" (p. 618). Thus, at this stage of research progress, several approaches are required to begin to illuminate the developmental relation, and these approaches are not limited to traditional statistical analyses.

The second question concerns how the correlation method should be used if it is to be used. Several research methodologies have been discussed by Porges (1979) as alternative approaches to the traditional statistical analyses. One alternative to the Pearson product moment correlation coefficient, described by Porges, allows for the possibility of a directional dependency, namely, a *cross-lag panel design*. Such designs are appropriate if it is expected that a causal relationship could exist between two variables. This requires measures from at least two points in time. Causal inference is derived from the correlation of variable X at time 1 with variable Y at time 2, compared with the correlation of variable Y at time 1 with variable X at time 2. According to Porges, "if the preponderant causal structure is from X to Y, the correlation between X_{t1} and Y_{t2} should be greater than the correlation between Y_{t1} and X_{t2}" (p. 758). Bates et al. did in fact incorporate the major thrust of the cross-lag design by computing correlations among all pairs of variables across the 4 observation sessions. Unfortunately, however, the correlations they obtained cannot be interpreted in this context due to the large degree of redundancy in their correlation matrix.

Other factors need to be considered in the application of the traditional correlation coefficient to examine the relationship between two variables sampled over time. One factor concerns the independence of the measures of the variables being correlated. Where there is a large degree of redundancy in the correlation matrix, there is, consequently, a large degree of dependence among the variables. Such a situation requires a partialling out of the factors that covary with the variables being correlated. Without partial correlations, the existence or nonexistence of statistical significance (as in the Bates et al., 1977 study) cannot be evaluated.

Corrigan (1976), on the other hand, did compute partial correlations, and the significant correlations between language development and object permanence that she had observed, disappeared when *age* was partialled out. Given this result Corrigan concluded that there was only a "loose relation" between language and object permanence. However, when only age is partialled out, there is the danger of considering age as an independent variable. According to Wohlwill (1970) age should be viewed "as a dimension along which the behavior changes which are the concern of the developmentalist are to be studied, that is, it is incorporated into the definition of the dependent variable of interest" (p. 51). If the goal of research is to study developmental *functions*, as suggested by Porges (1979) and Wohlwill (1970), rather than *differences*, as in the traditional analysis of variance design, then "the study of changes in behavior as a function of age is analogous to the study of other changes in behavior which occur along a temporal dimension" (Wohlwill, 1970, p. 75). This suggests that an appropriate description of a developmental function requires the identification of an as yet unspecified set of covariables that interact (vary) with one another along a temporal dimension.

Thus, when computing partial correlations, it is also necessary to consider the relative complexity of the factors being partialled. In this regard, age is far from a simple factor, as pointed out by Miller et al. (1980). Miller et al. tested the relation between sensorimotor development and language comprehension using the correlation method. First, all of the correlations among the 5 sensorimotor subscales administered were significant. (This is in contrast to other research studies where correlations among subscales were either low or insignificant, e.g. Bates et al., 1977; Uzgiris and Hunt, 1975). In addition, all of the correlations between comprehension and each of the sensorimotor tasks, as well as age, were significant. A series of multiple linear regression analyses was performed to further examine the relations of age and sensorimotor performance to comprehension. The result was that age was better than sensorimotor performance as a predictor of overall comprehension performance. However, Miller et al. went on to describe age in normal children as "an index of (at least) cognitive and social level, amount of linguistic input, experience with objects, and maturation" (p. 27). Although they rightly identified age with an important set of intersecting covariables, they unfortunately concluded that these factors play "a somewhat independent role" without testing for each of them individually, which underestimates the synergistic effect of such factors over time.

Several of the covariables that presumably interact and influence one another with synergistic effect in language development were specified in Bloom (1976). According to this synergistic, variable model of language development, the facts of language are not learned one at a time; instead aspects of language form, content, and use are learned concurrently. In addition, the facts of language are not learned in an all or nothing way but covary with other factors, including cognitive factors. The model is based, in part, on a study by Bloom, Miller, and Hood (1975) where lexical, grammatical, and discourse factors were observed to influence children's language behaviors as covariables facilitating and/or constraining what children said. Such a developmental model encourages the identification of as many developmental covariables as possible. Moreover, it provides for intraindividual differences in development as the covariables overlap to varying extents at different points on a developmental continuum.

Given such a model of development, the validity of the correlation method to determine the relation between two variables is problematic. Because an accurate correlation measure depends on the partialling out of factors that covary with the factors being correlated, one problem is identifying all the covariables to begin with; another problem is how to operationalize the covariables once they have been identified. Neither of these problems has been solved. Thus a measure of correlation, whether it is statistically significant or insignificant, may be misleading.

Reviewing the State of the Art

Two assumptions have influenced and guided the contemporary research that has explored the relations between developments in language and cognition in infancy. The first assumption is that the psychometric scales that have been devised (in particular the Uzgiris and Hunt scales) to measure objects permanence *equal* the development of object permanence. Thus, in the studies that have been reviewed here, performance on individual items in the subscales is analogous to progress towards achieving object permanence, and passing the items on the scales is interpreted as evidence that a child has acquired object permanence. The second assumption is that achievement in one of two domains of language and cognition should, necessarily, coincide with achievement in the other if a developmental relation between the two domains is to be assumed. That is, passing the items on the scale of object permanence (given that the scales *equal* object permanence) should be coextensive with relevant progress in linguistic behavior in order for a dependency or interdependent relation between them to be assumed.

Both of these assumptions are seriously flawed, on both theoretical and empirical grounds. As indicated above, the scales that purport to measure object permanence do not *equal* object permanence. The scales are questionable to begin with, and do not appear to measure what they are supposed to be measuring. Second, the assumption that progress in language should occur apace with progress in cognitive development ignores the fact that learning language is not isomorphic with cognitive development. To establish that a relation exists between the two does not require that both occur at the same time.

Preliminary Results of Research in Progress

The major purpose of this study is the investigation of the developmental relationship between language and sensorimotor development through examination and comparison of naturally occurring, spontaneous behaviors in the two domains. For this purpose, sensorimotor development has been evaluated through examination of children's object related behaviors that display the reversible activities of search (hiding/finding) and displacements of objects in relation to one another. The rationale for investigation of behaviors that reflect object knowledge came from the results and hypotheses of the child language studies reviewed above. The preliminary results presented here are based upon a detailed investigation of object-related play behaviors in relation to more global aspects of the children's language development.

Rationale

Piaget distinguished between two types of knowledge derived from *actions on objects:* "one that derives from logicomathematical experience and the other that derives from experience with the actual physical reality" (Sinclair, 1970, p. 122). The former, in contrast to the latter, is not relevant to the properties of particular objects but to knowledge of objects in general. Such general object knowledge is derived from action patterns with respect to objects that are unidirectional at first and eventually reversible. Both unidirectional and reversible action patterns emerge during the sensorimotor period. According to Piaget and Inhelder (1969), "reversibility (is) the source of future 'operations' of thought, already functioning at the sensorimotor level as early as the formation of the practical group of displacements (every displacement AB implies a reverse displacement BA) . . . But it is obvious that on the sensorimotor level . . . this reversibility in action . . . is (not) yet complete for lack of mental representation" (p. 20). Thus, the reversible actions of the sensorimotor period can be described as an operational knowledge or an operative activity displayed on the plane of action. These reversible actions are later interiorized into operations which depend upon the development of mental representation.

The development of language as well as development of operational intelligence presupposes the systematic use of representation (see Décarie, 1965, re: language). The systematic use of mental representation for language requires an understanding of *relations,* specifically the relation between a symbol and its referent and the relation between and among symbols. It is proposed that the emergence and development of operative activity and mental representation within the later sensorimotor period and into the early symbolic period can be described through an examination of children's reversible action patterns with respect to objects, specifically the reversible activities of search and the displacements of objects *in relation* to one another (object-object displacements). Some capacity for mental representation of objects or actions with objects can be inferred when a child can search for an object that is out of sight (i.e., the reversible activity of hiding/finding). Some knowledge that objects can be related to one another in systematic ways and can be seen from alternative perspectives may be inferred when a child displaces objects in relation to one another in reversible patterns. Such reversible activities provide the means through which children develop an awareness of the different kinds of *relations* that are possible between constituents. Such relations are appreciated first between objects and the self, then between and among objects, and, ultimately, between and among symbols. It is proposed that the identification and description of the developmental course of behaviors that display the reversible activities of search, and the displacement of objects in relation to one another, will provide more insight into the development of knowledge of objects, and object relations, than the information gained from children's performance on ordinal scales of sensorimotor development.

Subjects

Three mother-child pairs have served as subjects in this longitudinal study. All the children are first-born and their parents are college educated. The project was described to the mothers as an observational study of language and play. Data collection began when the three children were 8, 10, and 12 months of age which was several months before any language had emerged, and continued until each child was speaking in simple sentences (MLU $\geq$ 2.5). The data in this report cover the 10-month period (approximately) from the first observation of each child through the single-word utterance period.

Procedures

The observations took place every 3 to 4 weeks in a furnished laboratory playroom with groups of toys selected according to their manipulative and representational play possibilities. Each mother was only asked to play with her child as she would if she had a free hour; no other instructions were given. The actual observations consisted of videorecording each mother-child pair playing with the toys and having a snack for an uninterrupted period. At the end of each observation, the Uzgiris and Hunt (1975) Scales of Object Permanence Development were administered in order to obtain reference points for comparing the results of this study with other studies where such ordinal scales have been used.

The videorecorded observations were transcribed into written form, with the linguistic and non-linguistic behaviors of both mother and child carefully synchronized. Direction of gaze as well as gestures was noted.

Both the videorecords and the transcriptions were examined repeatedly in conjunction with one another, with different analysts identifying instances of search or object-object displacements. Separate analyses of the two reversible activities were required because of the theoretical mutual dependence between the two. The criteria for search behaviors were as follows: (1) previous discrete physical contact with the object, either earlier in the session, or, as was the case in the later data, in an earlier observation; (2) the object had to be out of sight for a period of time, which could be as short as a few seconds; and (3) the child had to relocate or search for the object in a directed manner as opposed to finding the object fortuitously. The criterion for object-object displacements was an activity involving two or more objects where at least one of the objects was moved in relation to the other (e.g., putting a bead into a box). Inasmuch as the focus of this study was on the child's spontaneous behaviors, the actions that were suggested by the mother or initially demonstrated by her and imitated by the child were distinguished from spontaneous behaviors.

Preliminary Results

From repeated examinations of the behaviors, several different categories of behaviors were identified and described. The earliest search behaviors (at 8 months) involved *relocating* an object either by looking back to, looking back and touching, or looking back to and picking up an object that was previously placed *by the child*. The delay between initial contact and later relocation was at first very brief (a matter of seconds) and increased considerably with development. The child often relocated an object in order to move it to another place. The early search behaviors seemed to be unrelated to any other activities; the child only appeared to be monitoring the environment by moving an object from place to place in relation to the self.

In the later search behaviors, the child relocated particular objects in order to place them in relation to other objects, first where there was a large degree of perceptual support for the relation between objects (e.g., "like" objects or objects that "go" together). In one form of these behaviors, the child relocated instances of like objects. Often, these relocation behaviors were repeated several times as the child individually transferred several instances of like objects (e.g., beads) from one place to another. Such behaviors suggested that the child had some mental representation of the objects at different locations and of the relation between the locations. In the other form of behaviors involving perceptual support, the child searched for parts of objects that belonged together (e.g., the incline and base for a slide). Most often, catching sight of one part of the object precipitated search for the related part(s). These behaviors suggested that the child had a mental representation of a set of particular objects or the parts of an object in relation to one another. Only later did the children relocate particular objects in order to place them in relation to other objects.

With respect to object-object displacements, the focus in the preliminary analyses was on reversible activity at the most global level of *taking apart* and *constructing* relations between objects. In the earliest observations, actions between objects were unidirectional and consisted primarily of taking apart the constituents in a relationship. However, such behaviors did not suggest any understanding of the different relations between the objects. The relationship was "there" in the environment for the child—it was phenomenal. It appeared that the only way to act on one or both of the objects was to take them apart; no other choice of action appeared to be available to the child. Moreover, in some of the earliest taking apart activities, it was not clear that the child even understood that the objects were separate entities (e.g., pulling on a peg person as if trying to lift the whole seesaw).

With development, the children began to put objects in relation to one another, to "construct" relations between objects (e.g., putting a peg person in a box). There was a steady increase in constructing actions relative to taking apart actions from the first observations through the emergence of first words. Some of the constructions appeared to involve "sudden insight" or the child's part (e.g., seeing the lamb, then picking up and playing with the silverware, and then suddenly going back to get the lamb in order to "feed" it).

The constructed relations were subcategorized into "given" and "imposed" relations between objects. A "given" relation was one that was inherent in the presentation of the toys (e.g., nested boxes; persons in a seesaw; the wooden slide). An "imposed" relation was one that was derived from objects that were introduced into the situation separately (e.g., putting beads into a box; putting a doll into a truck; feeding a lamb with a spoon). A steady increase in the construction of imposed relations relative to the construction of given relations was observed. Thus, in general, the early constructions were *re*constructions of given relations, whereas the later constructions were constructions of new or imposed relations. These developments in the children's object related behaviors are schematized in Figure 1.

With respect to the children's language development, the focus in this report is only on language behavior at the most global level of first words (the first use of at least 3 different words) and vocabulary spurt (a precipitous and marked increase in number of different words). The children differed in age of emergence of first words: 2 children were approximately 14 months of age and the third was almost 19 months. The vocabulary spurt did not appear for the early language users until almost 5 months later than the first word sample whereas for the third child, a little more than 2 months elapsed between first words and the vocabulary spurt. Thus, the children differed in onset of first words and of the vocabulary spurt. However, regularities were observed among them in the development of object-object manipulations. When the third child was 14 months old, that child was constructing relations, particularly imposed relations, to the same extent as the early language users. At the time when the children's first words were observed, the construction of imposed relations had increased to at least 31% of all constructed relations for each child.

Implications

It has been possible to identify and describe children's reversible activities that display search and the displacements of objects in relation to one another, and to relate these activities to relatively gross indices of language acquisition. Before she/he began to use language, each child was constructing relations between objects, particularly imposed relations, a substantial part

SEARCH

Relocation of objects placed by the child in relation to self	Relocation of objects that go together in relation to one another	Relocation of unlike objects in relation to one another
Taking apart relations	Constructing given relations	Constructing imposed relations

OBJECT-OBJECT DISPLACEMENTS

Figure 1. Developmental sequence of object-related behaviors.

of the time during their object-object manipulations. Moreover, the children were relocating objects (search) in order to construct relations between objects. To compare the children's object manipulations with language, it is reasonable to infer that in order to learn to use language, the child has to be able to construct a relation between a symbol and its referent. Such a symbol-referent relation is an imposed relation. The preliminary results of this study suggest that in order to learn language, the child has to be able to construct an imposed relation between two objects before she/he learns to construct a relation between a symbol and its referent. Moreover, the children in this study learned to construct imposed relations only after they constructed (or *re*constructed) the given relations.

A thorough analysis (i.e., identification, description, quantification) of the behaviors that display search and object-object displacements in children's object related behaviors prior to and during the single-word utterance period is in progress. The analyses of these behaviors provide a continuous dimension along which to examine product and process in development and provide a broader context than the ordinal scales in which to explore the development of object knowledge, and, subsequently, the early developmental relationship between language and cognition.

ACKNOWLEDGMENTS
The preparation of this paper was supported by Research Grant BNS7807335 from the National Science Foundation to Lois Bloom, and Fellowship MH 07748 from the National Institute of Mental Health to Karin Lifter. We thank Amy Feldman and Susan Belliveau for their help in processing portions of the data; Ruth Gold for conversations on correlation; Robin Chapman, Susan Sugarman, Jacques Voneche, and Robert Wozniak for their thoughtful and extensive comments on an early draft of this manuscript. For their comments and questions that helped to shape the final version of this presentation, we thank Joanne Bitetti Capatides, Kathleen Fiess, Jeremie Hafitz, Margaret Lahey, Susan Merkin, Jo Tackeff, and Janet Wootten.

Discussion

Wolff asked about the nature of the relationship between language and cognition which Bloom and her colleagues were investigating. Piaget made a distinction between two different types of relations among domains, that is, a functional and a structural relationship. Affectivity and cognition, for example, were functionally but not structurally related. With respect to language, Piaget had begged the question. Wolff believed however that there was interpenetration of language and cognition. Which of these types of relation, the structural or functional, did Bloom et al. predict would be found between the two domains? Bloom replied that it would probably partake of both types. However, she and her colleagues were not yet prepared to answer that question. It was part of their inquiry which had come about because of the recent claim in the literature that there was no dependency or relationship between language and cognition. Wolff asked did *they* then assume that there was such a relationship? Bloom answered that the question of interest to them was not whether there was a relationship, but rather how the two domains were related. Leavitt then asked if their methods were really likely to indicate whether the relationship was structural or functional. He thought that it might be impossible on the basis of the studies being conducted to determine which it was.

Wolff asked if the term reversibility, used by Bloom et al., really had any usefulness. He thought it had meaning only in a later period of development in terms of logical operational structures. He wondered if the investigation could not be carried out just as well with the notion of doing and undoing (that is, constructing/taking apart) without introducing the term, reversibility. Lifter replied that Piaget himself had used the term in relation to the sensorimotor period and, in particular, with regard to the displacements of objects. Piaget described reversible activity as emerging during the sensorimotor period and forming the basis of the logical mathematical structures of cognition which are theoretically independent of language. Lifter thought that reversibility, specifically reversible activity, would be useful for conceptualizing the development of object knowledge and in the analysis of children's spontaneous object manipulations. It is assumed that the child's knowledge of objects is displayed through various object displacements; these displacements, in turn, inform the child's construction of the object concept. She did not think the term "reversible activity" was useful in terms of predictive statements about future operational intelligence or the later conceptualization of reversibility theory. Lifter added that reversible activity might have analogous processes in language and cognition; however, whether the relationship between the two domains was functional or structural remained to be determined.

Leavitt asked if the study of spontaneous behavior was likely to yield information that was qualitatively or quantitatively different from the information that would come from the structured tests that have been used. Did Bloom and her colleagues have evidence that this was so? Lifter said that the behaviors scored in these two situations would be different. Bloom pointed out that the matrix used traditionally in the last 10 years in scales for measuring sensorimotor development, especially in the Uzgiris-Hunt Scales, did not enable one to score a process but only a product. Thus, it was only possible to score whether or not the child succeeded in a particular structured test. Leavitt asked why one could not marry a set of structured tests or eliciting procedures to a different scoring system that might permit one to take advantage of the richness of the child's responses. Bloom replied that that would be possible only if the behaviors elicited were not task-dependent. Otherwise it was not clear what one could say about the child's knowledge or lack of it.

Fischer added that in previous studies of language and cognition elicited behaviors had been scored in measuring cognition, and spontaneous behaviors in measuring language. Bloom remarked that this yielded an asymmetrical approach. Chapman pointed out, however, that one of the Uzgiris-Hunt subscales scored spontaneous actions on objects (schemes in object relations subscale). That particular subscale might, therefore, provide a better index, especially if Bloom and her colleagues wished to compare the data contributed from other studies employing the Uzgiris-Hunt Scales with their own. However, the more detailed set of behaviors with objects studied by Bloom et al. and the quantification of these behaviors, had greater developmental significance. It was particularly interesting to see the ratios of taking apart and constructing activities as the children displaced objects in relation to one another. Such activities are not among the schemes listed in the Uzgiris and Hunt Object Relations Subscale.

Ingram stated that he had carried out similar observations with the same orientation. He had concerns, however, about comparisons of the Uzgiris-Hunt Scale results with those obtained from observation of spontaneous behaviors. The scales predicted earlier occurrences of these behaviors than were in fact observed. It seemed to him that the real value of this work, since Bloom et al. had both observations of spontaneous behaviors and the measures of elicited behaviors from the Uzgiris-Hunt Scales, would be to compare the two. Bloom stated that this comparison of spontaneous and elicited behaviors would be possible, although she and her colleagues had originally included the scales only for the purpose of comparison with previous studies.

Fischer remarked that the objections to using elicited behaviors or structured tests on the grounds that they were counter to Piaget's approach were not justified, since Piaget's students had themselves devised similar scales (Laurendeau and Pinard, 1962; Decarie, 1965; Casati and Lézine, 1968). He agreed that it was important to examine spontaneous behavior but Piaget had not required it.

Leavitt said that there seemed to be a straw man being set up in terms of elicited/spontaneous behaviors. Superfluous meanings might be attached to these words. Something was elicited even if it was only by chance in the so-called spontaneous situation. Chapman suggested that it was not Bloom and her colleagues who were setting the straw man but the participants. If she understood the distinction being made, the participants were not talking about elicited versus spontaneous behavior but about the validity of inferences drawn from observations with respect to the child's underlying structures. The really important issue was: what inferences could be drawn from observations of behavior?

Ingram restated the position expressed thus far by saying that Piagetian theory allowed for an interpretation of spontaneous behavior. Piaget intervened and played with his children. Ingram's favorite example was that in which Piaget carried out some testing with a particular child, left for 3 weeks, and upon his return found that this child had lost one of the levels of object permanence! The abilities that had been demonstrated in the first place had probably been the result of a practice effect.

Bloom did not believe that present day investigators should proceed exactly as Piaget himself had done, or should attempt to replicate his observations exactly. The emphasis in her own work and that of her colleagues was clearly on another set of procedures and interests. However, one had to concede the wealth of concepts he had developed with respect to the construction of reality and other developmental phenomena. Fischer did not understand how it was possible to follow Piaget's model and adopt entirely different procedures. Bloom answered that Piaget had arrived at these concepts by manipulations of the environment, but in ways that were not circumscribed. The Uzgiris-Hunt Scales, on the other hand, used highly circumscribed situations.

Wolff said, in defense of Uzgiris, that she was distressed by the manner in which the scales she and Hunt had developed were being used. He felt that, like the WISC-R Scale, the Uzgiris-Hunt Scales could be used in a process analysis and in an intelligent way. If some investigators misused them that was their problem. Bloom answered that some investigators had used the scales in terms of product analysis of cognitive development in relation to language development, and that did concern her. In fact that was the main point of her objections.

Stark brought up the matter of the use of linguistic prestructures by young children as described in Beilin (1975) and others; that is, the use of words and phrases, often learned by rote, which might be used in appropriate situations but without a grasp of the underlying cognitive structures or meaning. She was reminded of an anecdote that Ingram had told about K., who, in an object permanence task, had said, "Where did it go?" She said this before she could solve the object permanence tasks and while still in late Stage 5 or early Stage 6. Bloom pointed out that K. was assumed to be in late Stage 5 or early Stage 6 precisely because she could not solve the relevant tasks. Bloom added that, even in later language learning, it was possible to identify the use of language forms in children that did not have a firm basis in their knowledge of content. The concept of prestructures or pseudostructures in language originated with Sinclair. Piaget used them also in relation to cognitive function. It was important to remember that, because a child used a word or a linguistic structure, that was not ipso facto evidence that the child knew that word or that structure in the sense that she/he could use it with facility in other contexts.

Tronick suggested that a crucial part of learning language, as he understood it, had to do with the relations imposed upon objects. The relationship could then be expressed in language. Could one then respond to Wolff's earlier question "What is social interaction doing?," by saying that the infant first acquires the ability to impose a relationship on the mother, that is, he becomes able to get the mother to respond in certain ways, to do something during an interaction? Could that be a prior step to imposing a relationship on an object? And could it be that that ability then led in turn to language? Was there perhaps a suggested continuity here? Was it the case that for children deprived of that particular kind of relationship with a caregiver, certain abilities in relation to objects would fail to be acquired and that appropriate linguistic expression of these relations would also be impaired?

Bloom replied that she and her colleagues had focused upon the children's displacement of objects, first in relation to the self and later in relation to other objects. However, all of this was certainly taking place within interpersonal contexts and in a social milieu. Although she had not focused upon the social contexts, they were certainly an ongoing aspect of language development; there was no question about that. However, the effect of early social interaction upon the kinds of relations she had studied remained to be assessed.

Early Patterns of Grammatical Development

David Ingram

Department of Linguistics, University of British Columbia, Vancouver, B.C. V6T 1W5, Canada

Introduction

The emergence of the young child's first sentences has held the fascination of investigators since the origins of child language studies, an interest that has weathered shifts in paradigms and voguish concentrations on other dimensions of acquisition. This is not necessarily surprising, however, if one considers that perhaps these early sentence forms, and not the first word, may constitute the most significant contribution to the initiation of verbal communication. Some data suggest, for example, that the mother shifts from baby-talk style to a simplified speech register some point after these utterances appear (e.g., Phillips, 1972). Also, this milestone marks the appearance of the unique human skill of linguistic competence, the ability to formulate grammatical rules of sentence structure characterized by great complexity.

Despite all of this attention, we are still some distance away from obtaining a complete and satisfying understanding of what occurs when the child formulates these first sentences. We can, for instance, say that children begin to put words together some time during the second year of life, after several months of single word speech characterized by slow lexical growth. We can also say that the first sentences appear infrequently in the first few months (e.g., Braine, 1963) and reflect the content of the young child's cognition (Brown, 1973). Most recently we have added observations that children may vary in certain ways in how they accomplish this in terms of rate (Ramer, 1976), phonetic clarity (Peters, 1977), the rate and nature of spontaneous imitation (Bloom, Hood and Lightbown, 1974), and the diversity and type of structures produced (Ramer, 1976; Bloom, Lightbown, and Hood, 1975).

Currently two topics in particular are commanding much of the attention in research on early grammatical speech. One of these, variation, has just been alluded to and focuses, fortunately, not just on the claim that children are different but also on the ways these differences are manifested and how behaviors may cluster together. The other aspect is the role of cognition, and treats issues such as the importance of individual cognitive skills, like mental imagery and imitation, for the young child's formulation of grammatical rules. The motivation behind both of these directions is sensible enough; by determining the extent to which children differ, we learn in turn what it is that is shared by all, even if that should be a set of alternatives. The cognitive comparisons, likewise, should lead to a better understanding of what is particularly unique to the language learning process.

A third aspect of early development, and one that underlies research into variations among children and the role of cognitive development, is that of grammatical productivity and subsequently of the early emergence of rules of grammar. Productivity refers to that property of rules which allows us to create new instances of structure so that, for example, a rule that says put Noun before Verb will place any noun in the lexicon before any verb. Braine (1976) has shown that the development of stricter criteria of productivity results in a less productive early grammar and one that is lexically oriented. These issues are pursued in Ingram (1979) where a strict set of criteria are developed for determining the status of the individual sentences a child produces in terms of the likelihood that they are produced by a rule of grammar. Such research puts us literally back at square one in terms of the writing of grammars for young children's sentences.

This chapter will present a comparison of the early grammatical patterns of two young children acquiring English as a first language. It will discuss the results in relation to the current literature on variation, the role of cognition, and the nature of early rules of grammar. The two subjects were chosen because they were quite different to all outward appearances in their linguistic development and were consequently potential test cases for some observations on variability in development. In relation to cognitive development, they were at very different stages when sentences first appeared, so that a closer look could suggest those aspects most affected by cognition. Lastly, a careful syntactic analysis of their early productive rules of grammar would possibly reveal different strategies in rule formation, or else provide a strong case for the autonomy of syntax from other aspects of development.

Aspects of Grammatical Variation

At the start, it is necessary to describe the parameters on which two children could be said to differ in grammatical development. Here, it is important to distinguish between two general categories of *syntactic* versus *nonsyntactic* parameters of variation. The former refers to those aspects that have to do with the nature of the child's rules, whereas the latter covers aspects regarding the use of language.

Perhaps the best known possible nonsyntactic parameter is that of *rate* of acquisition. It has been documented for some time that children do not acquire language at the same speed, although the topic has received little attention beyond that. It is possible to compare children on different aspects such as rate of sentence use or syntactic development versus rate of lexical growth. A more often studied nonsyntactic parameter is that of *spontaneous imitation,* the phenomenon of a child repeating all or part of an adult utterance immediately after the adult. Here research suggests that some children do this much more than others, and also that they are selective in what they imitate, focusing on words or structures currently being acquired (Bloom, Hood, and Lightbown, 1974) or on the phonological shape of words (Scollon, 1976). A third and potentially vital nonsyntactic aspect of differences is *phonetic clarity*. Some children (perhaps a minority!) are reasonably clear in what they say, and become natural candidates for language acquisition diaries and studies, for example, Adam and Eve in Brown (1973). Other children, however, may speak quite unclearly and can create problems for even trained linguists, for example, Peters (1977). A last parameter to be considered in the present study is *use of babbling*. Assuming that some form of babbling or sound play precedes the use of meaningful speech by young children, it may be that some children stop babbling at the onset of meaningful speech and show discontinuities in development as suggested by Jakobson (1968), whereas others continue to babble as meaningful speech emerges.

While these are 4 potential differences that are obviously noticeable behaviorally, it is not clear what they imply for syntactic acquisition. Rate is an important parameter, yet itself is the product of other processing skills that need to be isolated. Spontaneous imitation is more interesting, because it is possible that children who do and don't imitate will show grammars with different characteristics. Here though, one needs to distinguish between the tendency to imitate spontaneously and the ability to use a long memory span to retain entire sentences or phrases as memorized wholes. This latter kind of long-term imitation and memorization will lead at least superficially to different-looking grammars, and may be related to syntactic parameters. Spontaneous imitation, on the other hand, based on Bloom et al. (1974), reflects attention to what is being learned and may be a feature of learning in general. Phonetic clarity may be related to syntactic development in at least two ways. One, it may be that the attempt to produce longer utterances early on in acquisition (for example, Peters, 1977) may lead the child to be less clear. Thus a child with less clarity may be one who has a different grammatical system. Second, it may be that a child who is not clear affects the mother such that she adjusts her speech to the child, who in turn acquires grammar differently based on this altered model of adult speech. Such a possibility implies considerable environmental influence on grammatical development, a point which is not well supported by current data. Lastly, it is difficult to postulate any relation between use of babbling and grammatical development, unless this had to do with the ability to segment and string together groups of syllables.

The theoretically more interesting aspects of development are those that constitute syntactic parameters, several of which have been discussed in the literature. While the number of these is potentially large, they can be narrowed down by restriction to the earliest multi-word utterances. Some potential syntactic parameters are:

1. Use of presyntactic forms, which are essentially phonetic elements without meaning used in combination with meaningful words (Ramer, 1976);
2. Use of free versus rigid word order (Ramer, 1976);
3. Use of general categories, for example, Agent, Noun, etc. versus lexical items as categories in rules. Lexically based grammars are discussed in Braine (1976), Ervin-Tripp (1977), and Ingram (1979);
4. Use of memorized formulas or sentences versus productive combinations of categories (Peters, 1977; Braine, 1971; 1976);
5. Use of segmentation (the breaking down of longer utterances into their parts) versus combinatorial processing (putting parts together into a whole) to acquire sentence structure (Ingram, 1979);
6. Use of diverse grammatical structures and consequently grammatical rules at onset (Ramer, 1976);
7. Use of nominal versus pronominal forms of reference (Bloom et al., 1975).

When more careful phonetic transcriptions of childrens' language samples was undertaken in recent years, it was noticed that at least some children use brief phonetic elements before words, and that these elements do not appear to be meaningful although their source may be adult grammatical words (Peters, 1977; Ramer, 1976). There is an interpretation problem here, however, since it may be that they are functional either syntactically or semantically, but that it is difficult if not impossible to determine the exact use. It is possible, though, at least to notice how widespread the use of these elements is and whether or not their use correlates with other grammatical parameters. Braine (1976) has suggested that children may vary in their use of rigid or free word order, and data from Ramer (1976) supports this suggestion. Study of this topic, however, is also troubled by problems of interpretation (cf. Howe, 1976) as is that of presyntactic forms.

The parameters numbered 3 through 7 constitute the most revealing possibilities regarding grammatical variation. These parameters deal with the grammatical analysis of fully transcribed and interpreted utterances and the nature of the rules which combine them. As mentioned in Ingram (1979), there are issues about the nature of these categories and rules that need to be addressed. There, it is pointed out that an utterance for a child may reflect a variety of psychological states. For example, the sentence "doggie eat" could be:

1. An unanalyzed whole.
2. An analyzed utterance without productivity, that is, the child knows the word "doggie" and "eat" but has memorized their combination into a sentence.
3. A partially productive utterance produced by a lexically based rule, for example, sentence is Agent and "eat."
4. A productive utterance, that is, one produced by a rule which says that elements of the category Cx to which "doggie" belongs may be combined with elements of category Cy to which "eat" belongs.

Parameters 3 through 7 (p. 330) describe some variations children could show along this scale or productivity. Parameter 3 suggests that some children may use general categories from the beginning, a claim made with no further discussion by Chomsky (1975) for syntactic categories, and one implied in studies on semantic relations (Brown, 1973). Other children may use more lexically based rules and only build up to general categories. Another dimension concerns the use of memorized sentences rather than those produced by rules. It may be that some children prefer to express multifaceted information in learned phrases rather than produce combinatory rules of grammar. Peters (1977) has studied a child who seemed to have such a preference. In her case, the child's language was also characterized by low phonetic clarity. Not only may categories be limited in scope (parameter 3) but rules may be also (parameter 6). Some children may have rules that produce diverse structures, whereas others may be quite limited in this regard. The last parameter above (parameter 7) refers to forms of reference (cf. Bloom, Lightbown, and Hood, 1975), and distinguishes between children who prefer pronouns in their early word combinations and those who prefer nouns.

If children could differ in all of these different ways, we would indeed be faced with tremendous diversity. In the most complete study of this topic to date, Ramer (1976) concludes that two general styles of syntactic acquisition emerge because of the clustering of some of these behaviors. These two styles are summarized in Table 1 in relation to the parameters discussed above. The slower learners, the boys, used presyntactic forms and never varied in the use of word order. Also, they were less diverse in the use of grammatical structures. This suggests that they may have been using more memorized formulas or routines, but no mention is made of them. Since presyntactic forms were used by the boys, it may be also that their speech was phonetically less clear, although this is not measured or discussed, nor is continuity of babbling and speech.

The boys studied by Ramer sound similar to an extent to the child reported on by Peters (1977). This child was very unclear or unintelligible but Peters

Table 1. Summary of Research Data Reported in the Literature[a] on Grammatical Development in Terms of the Occurrence of 11 Parameters of Variation.

Parameters of variation	Investigators				
	Ramer (1976)		Bloom et al. (1975)		Peters (1977)
	(4 girls)	(3 boys)	Gia	Eric	Minh
Nonsyntactic					
1. Rate of acquisition	rapid	slow	(no differences)		
2. Spontaneous imitation					
3. Phonetic clarity	(clear?)	(not clear)		not clear	not clear
4. Use of babbling				yes[b]	
Syntactic					
1. Presyntactic forms	few	many	yes		yes
2. Variable word order	yes	no	(infrequent)		(no?)
3. Type of categories			syntactic	semantic	
4. Memorized sentences			(no)		yes
5. Gestalt processing				(yes?)	yes
6. Diversity of rules	diverse	limited			limited
7. Mode of reference			nominal	pronominal	

[a]Descriptions enclosed in parentheses are those not directly discussed by the authors but apparent from examination of the data.
[b]Based on personal communication cited in Peters (1977) p. 569.

determined after extensive listening that he was using longer sentences as memorized wholes. She labeled this tendency Gestalt development and suggests that some children prefer to learn phrases early rather than just combine individual words. If such were the case in the Ramer data, one would predict that the linguistic structure would be less diverse as it turned out to be. So too, Peters' subject appeared to use what looked like presyntactic devices (p. 564).

Another important study of grammatical variation is that of Bloom, Lightbown, and Hood (1975) in which two boys, Eric and Peter, differed from two girls, Gia and Kathryn, in the use of reference in multi-word speech. Whereas the girls used nouns, the boys used pronouns predominantly, even though nouns still occurred in their single word speech. A second difference was that the girls appeared to learn syntactic categories as well as semantic ones: "The fact that Kathryn and Gia developed action, locative-action, and possessive relations at the same time was interpreted as evidence that they had learned the superordinate grammatical categories sentence-subject . . . predicate-object . . . and predicate-complement" (p. 19). Observations on Eric reported in Bloom's earlier work (Bloom, 1970, pp. 102–106) suggest that his speech was highly unintelligible and characterized by what could be called presyntactic forms, represented by Bloom as /ə/. Kathryn's and Gia's speech also showed these, but apparently not as frequently. Peters (1977) draws a comparison between Eric and Minh, the child she studied, and suggests that they may have had a similar processing strategy. Unfortunately, the data in Ramer does not mention whether or not the slower learning boys also tended toward a pronominal mode of reference. The fact that the two girls used superordinate categories ahead of the boys, however, is comparable to the tendency of the girls reported in Ramer.

The general impression of these comparisons is that one group of children (apparently girls in particular) learn combinatorial syntax quickly with general categories and diverse combinations of them. Their speech is relatively clear and they show few so-called presyntactic devices. Another group (apparently boys) will be slower (in some cases), less clear, and tend toward the use of presyntactic devices that develop into pronominal forms in multi-word speech. When these first appear, however, the diversity of their grammatical contexts is limited.

In Ingram (1979; in press) preliminary observations are given on a girl K and a boy D who differed from each other in several of these parameters. K was quite rapid in acquisition, had clear speech with few cases of presyntactic devices, and appeared on these grounds to be likely to develop like the other girls discussed above. D, however, was slower, though within the normal range, and was phonetically less clear and consequently more unintelligible. He then looked superficially like the boys discussed above. This chapter will present a more detailed comparison of selected samples of language from these two children on the parameters discussed to determine: (1) if their multi-word speech developed in a way predicted by data from previous studies; and (2) if not, which parameters continued to correlate with others and which did not.

The Relation Between Cognition and Early Grammar

Besides considering the variability among children in the construction of early grammars, it is also necessary to consider the influence of cognitive factors on early syntax. Indirect studies and theoretical reflections on this topic have been skeptical in claiming a strong relation between the two. For example, Bloom, Lightbown, and Hood (1975) state: "Knowing about something does not simply translate to being able to talk about it or to understand when others talk about it . . . linguistic development is neither isomorphic with nor a necessary result of cognitive development" (p. 30). Also, as Fischer and Corrigan point out (this volume, Chapter 10) we need to address specific interactions and not global ones.

The issue of the relation between cognitive behaviors as they occur in sensorimotor stages of development and general stages of language acquisition was examined in Ingram (in press, a) by following 3 young children from 6 months of age to one and one-half years of age. Each was visited every 2 weeks during which time cognitive and linguistic skills were assessed.

Based on previous research (cf. Ingram, 1978), it was predicted that the first words, less than a dozen, would appear during sensorimotor stage 5, and that more rapid lexical growth and the onset of syntax would occur later. While 2 of the children followed these predictions on the co-occurrence of linguistic and cognitive skills, one child, K, did not. She appeared to be quite advanced in language, using several words during stage 5 and multi-word utterances well in advance of other representational skills. In that paper it was concluded: "Cognitive limitations appeared to restrict the use and content of language, but not its syntactic processing. It is proposed that the child evidenced specific syntactic mechanisms for the development of a grammar."

The claim that language has a structure of its own and one that can not be reduced to that of cognitive structures, that is, that syntax is autonomous, is one that has been repeated frequently by Chomsky (1977). For example, in his most recent book he states:

> "The important thing, of course, is to determine the deeper principles and the detailed structure of various cognitive systems, their modes of interaction, and the general conditions which each system satisfies. If one finds that these systems are acquired in a uniform manner with very little specific structure, very well. But for the present at least it seems to me that quite different conclusions are indicated." (Chomsky, 1977, p. 84.)

This position argues that there are specific language universals in terms of restrictions on potential categories and the form of rules. These capacities may mature or become available to the child at similar times as certain cognitive skills develop, but they should not be reduced to or considered as the latter.

The data from K were analyzed in part by the procedures outlined in Ingram (1979) that are briefly summarized in the next section. She showed the ability (1) to determine the structure of sentences through segmentation of adult utterances into their parts, and (2) to formulate categories, through the learning of lexical items, that individually included information on their co-occurrence with other lexical items in consistent ways. The ways in which she segmented sentences and grouped lexical items into classes was not isomorphic with general semantic categories and relations like Agent, Action, etc. A description of her utterances in terms of semantic relations revealed something about what K knew about the world, but little about her classification and co-ordination of words. This led to the following further conclusion: "It is suggested that analyses from other children may yield similar results once syntactic grammars are written (with linguistic criteria for co-occurrence and precedence) to replace current approaches based only on semantic taxonomy" (Ingram, in press).

The data collected from K and D in that study are quite suited for the pursuit of this issue. K acquired syntax quite early in stage 6 of sensorimotor development around 1;1, while D, who otherwise advanced similarly to K in cognitive ability, did not acquire syntax until months later around 1;9, well into representational ability. Since the samples are longitudinal, it is possible to match these two children on linguistic measures and compare their grammars. If processes of syntactic development are autonomous as stated by Chomsky, then their grammars could be potentially quite similar. If, on the other hand, the grammars are influenced by cognition, then D's should show a difference, presumably toward greater productivity and generality, since he was more advanced at the time that syntax emerged. K's, though, should consist of many memorized wholes and few productive rules.

A second aspect of the present chapter is to study this particular question. The null hypothesis will be something like the following: when grammars are written on early samples of language from K and D matched on gross language measures, they will show similar processes of segmentation, combination, and categorization. That is, there will be no substantive differences in their grammars. If so, we can conclude that at least for these two children syntax appears to have autonomy to a large degree. If they are not similar, we can conclude either that cognition does have an important role or that the children show alternative syntactic processes. In the latter case the possibilities are more diverse.

The Formulation of Syntactic Grammars for Young Children

Several years ago, it was common to find syntactic grammars written for the first multi-word utterances of young children, for example, McNeill (1966), Bloom (1970). Even when a shift occurred toward more semantic descriptions, questions of syntactic categories and relations still were faced directly (e.g., the discussion in Bloom, 1973, Chapter 5). This has changed, however, to the extent that most descriptions are essentially semantic taxonomies of those utterances that reach an arbitrary criterion of frequency, usually five. For example, Bloom, Lightbown, and Hood (1975) state in a footnote at the onset of their monograph (p. 4):

"The issue of *formalization* has not been addressed in the present study. Eventually, as data from more children are available, the taxonomic account presented here will need to be formalized with a scheme of semantic-syntactic rules, or grammar, that will represent both the regularities and the systematic variation in child language."

There were several reasons for the shift away from more formal, syntactic grammars. One was that the work on the child's semantics became so fruitful that it attracted a lot of attention. Also, the state of grammatical theory became temporarily quite chaotic, in the sense that a variety of new theories were proposed and defended. For example, the above authors later say (p. 37): "progress in the study of linguistics and linguistic theory has been such that there is no longer a unified theory of generative grammar and no consensus about the kinds of information to be represented by the rules of grammar.'' Thirdly, there were methodological issues that were never resolved about grammar writing that undermined everyone's confidence in the grammars written. To continue with the comments of the above authors: ''There is no way of knowing, at the present time, the form in which such knowledge about linguistic structure is represented in the child's mental grammar'' (p. 33).

In attempting to write grammars, investigators ran into numerous dilemmas. On the one hand, there would be occasional, clearly produced sentences that, when included into the rules of grammar, would make them more powerful than they otherwise seemed. So, too, transcripts often contained only partially intelligible utterances that, if accurately interpreted, could indicate more advanced structures and rules. Continually there was the fear of producing a grammar that either over- or underestimated the child's ability. The concern for formalization itself came from the interest in using the most recent theory of grammar, whatever that might be, for representing the rules.

While Chomsky's theoretical insights have fired an interest in language acquisition studies, and in fact have placed the topic at the center of an explanatory theory of grammar, the practical consequences in terms of advancing our knowledge of the language acquisition process itself have been non-productive. There is one very obvious reason for this. In postulating the existence of language universals of a very restricted kind, he has made the additional assumption (implicitly if not explicitly) that these universals are available to the child from early on, perhaps from the first words. McNeill (1966) provides the classic example of language acquisition research stemming from this assumption. For others, however, who take a more Piagetian view of the origins of structure, the question is no longer whether or not the potential for universals of language is innate, but rather how the child developmentally arrives at or constructs them. For example, if a category such as AUX came to be necessary as a part of universal grammar, it does not necessarily follow that the young child has it available at the time of his earliest grammars or at least we should not assume so until it is behaviorally demonstrated. In Ingram (1979), where this matter is discussed at some length, the following quote from Piaget is included:

> ''It may be objected that the problem is settled in advance [preformation vs. epigenesis:DI], since the various aspects of intellectual behavior are phenotypic reactions and a phenotype is the result of interaction between the genotype and the environment. That is indisputable, but one still needs to explain in detail how, in the field of knowledge as in that of organic epigenesis, this collaboration between the genome and the environment actually works.'' (Piaget, 1971, p. 16).

In terms of grammar writing, this means that the existence of categories (whether semantic or syntactic) or rules should not necessarily be assumed;

but observations should be made of how they occur through the child's interaction with language data. Braine (1963, 1976) has pioneered the use of basic concepts in linguistics to develop criteria for the determination of grammatical rules, although his own use of these has not always been consistent. At its roots, the issue becomes one of developing ways in which one can say, with some degree of confidence, that an utterance has been produced by a grammatical rule and is not a learned phrase. This can be done by looking for co-occurrence, precedence, and semantic consistency. For example, if the child says "eat cookie," we can look to see if "eat" precedes other words, for example, in sentences like "eat pie," "eat apple," with the same meaning.

In Ingram (1979) a method of grammatical description is presented which attempts to determine the form of children's first categories and the productivity of the earliest rules. At the start, it is assumed that all multi-word utterances are memorized wholes unless the data can show otherwise. The procedures for this are discussed later, but basically they consist of the following. First a lexicon is constructed for all the child's words, whether they occur alone or in a longer utterance. A word is then considered *lexically free* if (1) it occurs in isolation, or (2) in at least two different multi-word utterances with varying contexts, for example, "dog" in "see dog" and "dog run." The qualification of varying contexts is important because, if the sentences were "see dog run," "see dog eat," we could only conclude that "see-dog" is a lexically free item since "dog" never occurs without "see." If at least one word in an utterance is lexically free, than the utterance is at least *analytic,* that is, the child knows its parts. The fact that an utterance is analytic is still not proof it has been produced by a rule (although rules proposed for analytic utterances have relatively more potential reality than those proposed for non-analytic ones).

Next, words that occur in more than one multi-word utterance are observed to see if they occur in at least two utterances with (1) consistent meaning, (2) consistent word order, and (3) co-occurrence. For example, Allison in Bloom (1973) at 22 months of age used "there" in isolation and in the utterances "there cookie," "there baby cup," and "there baby." "There" meets all three of these conditions and therefore is weakly *grammatically free*. The word "open" occurred in isolation and in the following utterances: "baby open door," "mommy open," "open can," and "open box." "Open" is strongly grammatically free in that it takes both preceding words (Agents?) and following words (Affected Objects?). A word needs to show two environments of grammatical freedom for it to be strongly grammatically free. An intermediate case is provided by the word "eat" in Allison's data. It occurred in isolation and in the following utterances: "baby eat," "baby eat cookie(s)," "eat cookie(s)," "eat mommy cookie," "mommy eat cookie," and "no eat." Since both "baby" and "mommy" precede "eat," it is grammatically free for the preceding position. There is no co-occurrence after "eat," however, with only "cookie" occurring. It is not grammatically free in this position (based on the available data) so is listed as "eat-cookie" where each part may occur in isolation since they are both analytic.

Words that are grammatically free can then be compared to determine the categories in the child's data. For Allison, the words "baby," "mommy," and "man" all meet criteria as Agents. In this step by step manner, one can observe the gradual construction of categories by the child. A further examination of those utterances composed of grammatically free words allows for the postulation of grammatical rules.

By the use of explicit criteria such as these, using a lexically based analysis, it is possible to study at least the earliest data from children to see if productive grammatical categories and rules exist and, if so, to determine their characteristics. This methodology consists of the application of basic concepts in linguistics, and is used for the analysis of selected data from K and D to provide information on the issues of variation and the influence of cognition.

Subjects and Procedure

Two young children K (female) and D (male) were observed longitudinally from the middle of their first year until the end of their second year, as part of a study designed to compare linguistic and cognitive development (cf. Ingram, in press). K was a first-born child who spent most of her time alone with her mother. Very concerned with her child's language development, the mother verbalized with K often and read books to her frequently as well as insisting on verbal responses such as "hello" and "goodbye." D was a second-born child, the author's son, who lived in a more casual verbal environment where language was not as actively singled out for his attention. D did not spend as much isolated time with his mother since she worked part-time and her presence was often accompanied by that of the first-born girl and her friends. It appeared that K's mother was more referential while D's was more expressive in the sense of Nelson's use of these terms (1973).

Each child was scheduled for a visit every two weeks for approximately 30 minutes. This schedule was occasionally altered due to sickness and vacations, but a regular series of visits was maintained. At each visit, the child's cognitive development was assessed (cf. Ingram, in press, for details), and a spontaneous language sample was taken. At the end of one year of observations, these two aspects of development were compared, with the child's cognitive growth placed into Piagetian sensorimotor stages and the child's language described in gross language measures (see Table 2).

The milestones from D were typical of other children, based on comparisons discussed in Ingram (1978). K, however, was quite different, showing early and rapid attainment of language milestones. With an interest in comparing D's later language to K's, language samples continued to be collected

Table 2. Summary of Cognitive and Linguistic Development of D and K in Terms of Sensorimotor Stages and General Language Milestones (taken from Ingram (in press).

D	Sensorimotor stages	K
	Stage 4	
0;9-0;11		0;9-0;11
Acquired no words but babbled frequently. Appeared to understand "no."		Acquired around 12 words, such as "byebye," "ta," "duck," "mama." Waves when hears "byebye."
	Stage 5	
1;0-1;4		1;0-1;2
Favorite babblings are [dadi] [mami]. Seems to use "ha" as a greeting. No other words are spoken.		Has acquired over 50 words, and sample at 1;1(10) showed 17 multiword utterances.
	Late stage 5, early stage 6	
1;5		1;2-1;3
Says "hi" and also "mami" when wants something. Seems to understand "Daniel" and "no."		Noticeable increase in spontaneous and imitated phrases. Some of the former are "there's a cow," "change the baby," "drop it down."
	Stage 6	
1;6-1;7		1;4-1;6
Acquired 6 or more words at beginning, and starts to show more rapid vocabulary growth. By middle of 1;7 has around 20 words such as "banana," "baby."		Multi-word use increased rapidly, and relational patterns emerged. A sample at 1;5(20) showed an MLU of 1.99; one at 1;6(12) showed an MLU of 2.42.

from D after the end of the original study until his language was comparable to that of K, around 1;7. It took over 6 months before this comparability was reached.

All language samples were transcribed using the guidelines discussed in Ingram (in press) as adapted from Scollon (1976). Briefly, the child's utterances are first placed into a phonetic transcription without attempts to interpret the child's intended meaning. After two listenings, a third listening is done at which time interpretations are assigned and utterances are divided into those that are: totally intelligible, partially intelligible, questionable (when doubt exists regarding the interpretation), unintelligible, and babbled. The last was determined on the basis of rhythmic intonation contour, repeated syllables, and communicative intent.

To analyze the early emergence of syntax, 28 language samples were selected for detailed analysis (see Table 3). The data divided itself into 4 stages. The first of these, the Babbling Sessions, were evident only in D's speech. These sessions show a dominance of babbling with virtually no adult-like utterances produced. There is little babbling data on K because she moved so quickly into meaningful speech. The Holophrastic Sessions represent periods of 2 to 3 months when each child used and developed a small number of single-word vocalizations. During the latter part of what

Table 3. Summary of Information on Ages, MLU, and Sample Size for K and D Across 4 Stages of Acquisition.

Stages	Child	Age range	Samples	MLU	Total tokens	Mean sample size
Babbling sessions:	D	0;9(25)-1;5(2)	5	—	193	39
Holophrastic sessions:	K	0;10(22)-1;0(3)	4	1.0	227	57
	D	1;6(6)-1;7(26)	6	1.0	1,152	192
Onset of multi-	K	1;0(26)-1;3(2)	4	1.0-1.1	1,264	316
word utterances:	D	1;8(22)-1;9(24)	4	1.1	1,198	300
Growth of multi-	K	1;4(8)-1;7(17)	5	1.2-2.4	1,735	347
word utterances:	D	1;10(18)-2;0(29)	5	1.4-1.6	1,460	292

could be called the holophrastic stage, both children began to use some multi-word utterances, although the dominant vocalizations were still single words. These sessions have been separated out for separate analysis and are labeled Onset of Multi-Word Utterances in Table 3. Lastly, both children showed rapid growth in multi-word utterances with an eventual predominance of these over single-word productions.

The analysis of these data is currently in progress. For this chapter, 10 samples have been selected for a preliminary analysis (see Table 4). Since Ramer (1976) has found that presyntactic forms occur during the emergence of syntactic speech, the corpora for Time II on Table 4 were selected for their analysis. A presyntactic form is an utterance that is partially intelligible consisting of an intelligible word preceded by an unintelligible sequence of one or two syllables, for example, "[ina] book." A second type is reduplicative constructions where the child repeats a word with no apparent extra meaning applied to the repetition.

For the purpose of the grammatical analysis, the intelligible utterances in each sample are separated into single-word types and syntactic (that is, multi-word) types in the manner introduced by Bloom et al. (1974). The selection of the samples in Table 4 were influenced by two factors. One, since D's language contained more babbling and unintelligible utterances than K's, his samples needed to be larger in the early comparisons to find comparable numbers of syntactic types. Second, the samples were matched on the ratio of single-word types to syntactic types, and subsequently placed into the three time periods shown. Since the number of syntactic types is small for both children at Time II, the two samples are combined for the grammatical analysis. The data were analyzed for (1) words which showed either weak or strong grammatical freedom, and (2) those syntactic types which consisted of grammatically free words. (See Appendix A for a de-

Table 4. Ages, Total Tokens, Single-Word Types, and Multi-Word Types from 10
Language Samples for D and K, Divided into 3 Time Periods.

	K				D		
Age	Total tokens	Single-word types	Syntactic types	Age	Total tokens	Single-word types	Syntactic types
			I Holophrastic sessions				
0;11(6)	39	10	0	1;6(25)	120	10	2
			II Onset of multi-word utterances				
1;1(10)	220	30	16	1;8(22)	485	18	10
1;2(15)	199	22	5	1;9(23)	398	23	6
			III Growth of multi-word utterances				
1;5(2)	148	31	26	1;10(18)	294	30	26
1;6(12)	179	49	83	1;11(18)	380	31	40

scription of the procedure of the analysis). These words and sentences were
examined to determine the nature of the child's early categories and rules
of combination.

Results

Nonsyntactic Parameters

K and D varied considerably on all 4 parameters of nonsyntactic variation
(Table 5). In terms of rate, it was already noted that K was faster than D
in terms of the output of words and multi-word sentences. As for spontaneous
imitations, K was consistent in her pattern, which is reported in more detail
elsewhere (Ingram, in press). She showed a rapid increase in the use of
spontaneous imitation during Time II, that is, during the end of the holophrastic period when the first multi-word utterances appeared. Once multi-
word speech became dominant, however, it dropped out. The shift was so
noticeable that it was evident to those observing K before any measures
were made. D, however, showed a different pattern. He began to imitate
spontaneously during the same period, but did not do it as much as K; yet
he continued and even increased his use of imitation during the sessions of
rapid syntactic development. In a sample taken at 2;0 (18), for example, the
proportion of imitation types was .30.

The difference between the children in terms of their proportions of totally
intelligible utterances is striking. Even from the earliest samples, K's speech
was relatively high in intelligibility. One contributing factor was pronunci-
ation in that K more clearly segmented her words and articulated her speech
sounds. Also, though K consistently used her speech forms in clear contexts
making it easy to identify intended meanings, not only was D less clear

Table 5. Comparison of K and D on 4 Parameters of Nonsyntactic Variation.

			Parameters		
Times	Child	Age at onset	Spontaneous[a] imitation	Intelligible utterances[b]	Babbled utterances[c]
I. Holophrastic	D	1;6	.08	.33	.13
sessions:	K	0;10	0	.41	0
II. Onset of multi-word	D	1;8	.18	.16	.17
utterances:	K	1;0	.25	.81	0
III. Growth of multi-word	D	1;10	.15	.46	.08
utterances:	K	1;4	.03	.84	0

[a]Proportion of utterance types that were imitated.
[b]Proportion of total non-babbled utterances that were totally intelligible.
[c]Proportion of total utterances that were babbled.

articulatorily, but he also seemed less motivated with respect to intended meanings. This difference was particularly striking in that he was older than K when matched with her linguistically, and consequently knew more things to talk about. Instead, his samples were full of nonintentional babbling, and if his intentional utterances were not understood by those with him, this seemed to cause him little frustration. Even when multi-word speech was dominant, only about half of his utterances were totally intelligible. The even lower intelligibility of his utterances during Time II was the result of his growing use of presyntactic forms. Several of the utterances were of this type (see next section) and were classified as only partially intelligible as a result.

Lastly, D continued to babble even into the multi-word period whereas K stopped babbling quite early. There was some sampling bias deserving of consideration that may have influenced these data. Since D was being observed by his parent in the home, it is possible that he was more comfortable with the setting and more apt to babble. Also, some of his sessions had parts where he was left alone and babbling ensued. K, on the other hand, was visited by an outsider who engaged in active conversation with her. Even though these factors influenced inevitably the amount of babbling observed, there are reasons to believe that the distinction between these two children with respect to babbling is valid. First, K was visited so often by the experimenter that they soon became quite familiar with one another. When left to her own devices while the adults conversed during her sessions, she would talk to herself in words instead of engaging in making sounds without meaning for the apparent pleasure of it. When asked about babbling, her mother responded that K, when left alone, would have conversations with herself using identifiable words rather than sound play. D, on the other hand, even when reading a book, would break into a series of babbled utterances.

Syntactic Parameters: Presyntactic Forms

Using Ramer's measure of percentage of presyntactic utterances out of the total number (presyntactic and syntactic) of utterances, D used 47 presyntactic utterances out of 73 utterances for 64% at Time II. K, however, used only 3 out of 66 utterances for 4%. Clearly, K's speech was not characterized by presyntactic utterances at this time, nor in subsequent samples. D's, however, was full of them. Some examples are: "[də] cookie;" "[u꞉] banana;" "[æ] DoDo" (term for his blanket); "[E?] Do Do;" "[ei] DoDo;" "[dae] Dodo;" "[a] bottle;" "[hei] bottle;" "[er] bottle." The use of these continued for D, although the phonetic forms became more stable. At 1;11(18), for example, [ənə] occurred before twelve different words such as "doggie," "duck," and "cat." It appeared to be a designative form of some kind, possibly from "it's-a," but it was not possible to ascertain the form from its phonetic shape.

Grammatical Categories and Rules

Time I

In these samples each child only showed 10 single-word types, and only D had productions that received multi-word interpretations. The single-word types are listed in each child's lexicon as lexically free forms which can be used in the analysis of later samples. The three multi-word types for D were "want cookie," want this," and "thank you." "Want" satisfies the criteria for lexical freedom and grammatical freedom. Its lexical entry is [__N] where N refers to an emerging nominal category consisting of "this" and "cookie" both of which occurred as single-word utterances and are therefore lexically free. There is no evidence of lexical freedom for the words in "thank you," so it would be entered lexically as "thank-you," where the dash indicates that the words only occur with each other. It is re-analyzed as a single-word type.

Time II

More syntactic types occurred during this time as the children began their entry into multi-word speech. The syntactic types used by both children are given in Table 6. Parentheses encircle words that are not lexically free and a dash marks cases where one of the words has to occur with the other if used in a multi-word utterance. For example, K's sentence "(can't) have-this" indicates that "can't" only occurs in this sentence in the data, and that "have-this" functions as a structural unit because at least one of its parts, in this case "have," never occurs without the other.

For K only two words met the criterion for grammatical freedom—"hi" and "this," although neither pattern occurred very widely. For D, the words that showed grammatical freedom were "a" and "bottle."

Table 6. Syntactic Types Shown for D and K at Time II. Parentheses Enclose Words That Are Not Lexically Free. Dash Indicates Co-Occurrence Restrictions.

K 1;1(10)	D 1;8(22,26)
(A) baby.	A bottle.
Baby's (crying).	Broke-it.
(Can't) have-this.	Here (the) bottle.
Daniel (okay)?	Hi daddy.
Have-this.	Horse doggie.
Hi birdie.	(I) broke-it.
Hi (ya).	It a bottle.
How-are-you?	Kitty cat.
(K) have-this.	Oh a doggie.
(Let) play-(something)-else.	Poor-daddy.
Oh baby.	Thank-you.
Play-else.	That hat?
(Pussy) cat.	That monkey.
(Read) this.	Want a bottle.
Take-off.	Want bottle.
Tata (please).	Want (my cars).
Thank-you.	Want (push).
	What that?

Grammatically Free Forms, Time II

K		D	
"hi" [__N]	"this" [V__]	"a" [__N]	"bottle" [Dem__]
"hi birdie"	"(can't) have-this"	"a bottle"	"here (the) bottle"
"hi (ya)"	"have-this"	"it a bottle"	"it a bottle"
	(K) have-this"	"oh a doggie"	
	"(read) this"	"want a bottle"	
		"that" [__N]	"want" [__N]
		"that hat?"	"want a bottle"
		"that monkey"	"want bottle"
			"want (my cars)"
			"want cookie" (I)

K's sentences showed very little evidence of an emerging grammar at this stage. She appeared aware of the lexical structure of some of her sentences, but two of these words showed signs of emerging co-occurrence, and these were not frequent. D's data showed more patterning, but it too was only emerging. There were two patterns in that development: (1) a Dem-N one where "here," "it," and "that" (and possibly "a") were moving toward a category that could be used to designate or predicate identity to nominal-like elements. However, only "that" and "bottle" had yet to reach criterion; (2) "want"-N, a pattern that first appeared at Time I and continued to develop at Time II.

Time III: First Samples

Table 7 shows the syntactic types used by K and D at 1;5(2) and 1;10(18) respectively. Again, words that were not lexically free were placed in parentheses. Both single word and syntactic types from the previous samples were carried over and used in these decisions.

For K, a small number of categories were beginning to emerge. "It" was combining with "this" (and possibly "that") as a category of pronouns occurring after verbs. It seemed, in fact, that K was learning verbs in the context of this productive category.

K's Grammatically Free Forms, Time III 1;5(2)

1. Pronoun "this;" "it" [V__]
   "have-this" (II) "(call) it"   "K (got) it"   "wanna get it"
   "(read) this" (II) "(cut) it"   "(put) it (on)"
   "want this"   "(drop) it"   "(show) it D"
2. "want" or "wanna" [__Pro/N]
   "want a toy?"   "want (the) book?"
   "wanna toy?"   "want this?"

Table 7. Syntactic Types for D and K at Time III, Ages 1;5(2) and 1;10(18).

K	D
And K.	A little boat.
And this one.	Cat there.
(Call) it.	Doggies here.
Choo-choo-train.	Boat here.
(Cut) it.	Give-you the book.
(Drop) it.	(Got) a (lot of) those.
(I) right-here.	It's a (boy).
It's-gone.	It's a (robot).
K (got) it.	It's cat.
(Push) cup.	It's a (balloon).
(Put) it (on).	Little box there.
(Show) it D.	(More) doggies there.
Take-off.	No book.
(That's) a girl.	Oh cars.
There's cup.	Oh doggie.
This one.	Sit-down.
(Turn) that.	This a bucket.
Want a toy?	That flowers.
Wanna toy?	There's a boat there.
Wanna-get?	Those little boat.
Wanna-get it?	(Touch) it.
Want (the) book?	What those?
Want this?	What's that?
What's-that?	What this?
What's-that one?	Where-going?
(Where) it (go)?	Where (is) the boat?

Two further limited categories were "one" in "this one" and "what's-that one?," and "and" in "and K" and "and this one." The emerging category of "want" had the opposite function of Pronoun as it was used as a context for the use of nouns.

D had also continued in the development of his two categories of Dem or Pro and Noun, although the "want" pattern did not recur.

D's Grammatically Free Forms, Time III 1;10(18)

1. Deictic Pronoun [__N]   [(Adj)N__]
   "that"   "it's"   "here"   "there"
                     "it's a (boy)" "doggies here"   "cat there"
   "that hat?" (II) "it's a (robot)" "boat here"   "little box there"
   "that monkey"   "it's cat"   "(more) doggies
   (II)   there"
   "that flowers"   "it's a ballon"   "there's a boat
                                                         there"
                     "it a bottle" (II)

2. "what" or "what's" [__Pro]   3. Noun [__Loc]
   "what's those?"   "boat here"
   "what's that?"   "there's a boat there"
   "what that?" (II)   "(more) doggies there"
   "what this?"   "doggies here"

4. "I" [__V N]   "my" [__N]
   "I like-sheep"   "my sheep"
   "I see-duck"   "my bear"
   "ooh I see- a-duck"

His acquisition of verbal elements was lacking and only began sporadically in the next samples.

K's development at 1:6(12) had become extensive in that her sentences were longer and she began to develop very rapidly. Below is a selection from her more widespread categories.

Some of K's Grammatically Free Forms, Time III 1;6 (12)

1. Object Pronoun "it" [V__]   2. Subject Pronoun "I" [__V]
   "want open it"   "I play"
   "I wind it"   "I open"
   "man do it"   "I touch"
   "want hold it"   "I shut this"
   "Danny do it"   "I do it"
   etc.   etc.

3. Verb Particle [V(Pro)__] [Dem__]

         "off"   "on"

"I shut it off"   "that's off"   "I want put this on"   "it's on"

"want take off?" "it's off"   "I want that on"   "that's on"

"how'd ya get it off?"

4. "want" [__N]   [__V N]

"want the button"   "want open it"

"want some toys?"   "want get a toy?"

"want some more block"   "want hold that"

5. Object Pronoun "it" [V__]   6. Adjective "little" [__N]

"(broke) it" (II)   "a little boat"

"(touch) it"   "little box there"

The largest category was for the pronouns "that," "it's," "here," and "there." These were used in consistent and recurring patterns to designate a variety of nouns. These variations also showed up in the question forms. "Want" had dropped out and did not re-appear in the next few samples. It apparently was used in Time II in the narrow context of requesting his bottle. Both children are developing pronominal and nominal categories, but in semantically distinct structures.

Time III: Second Samples

In the last sample for K at 1;6(12), she started to develop more productive structures and larger categories. D on the other hand continued to use the limited ones that had appeared in the previous sample. Two new grammatically free forms occurred "I" and "my," but their use was not widespread.

Grammatically Free Forms for D, Time III, 1;11(18)

1. Deictic Pronoun [__N]

"that"   "it's" or [I nə]   "here"   "there"

"that sock" "it's doggie"   "here the (trees)" "there's a duck"

"that (milk)" "it's duck"   "here a car"   "there a sheep"

              "it's cat"   "there's a doggie"

              "etc. (14 types)"   "there little water"

                                     "there a duck"

                                     "there's a boat"

2. "what" [__Pro/PP]

"what those?"   "what's in there?"

"what's that?"   "what's in that block?"

"what's this one?"   "what's in that one?"

K had acquired a variety of verb structures to use with the pronouns "it" and "I." These two pronouns at this stage did not yet belong to larger categories although the object form was combining with "that," "this," and "that/this one" into a object pronoun category. The use of "want" was widespread and suggested a lexical rule that could take broader categories, for example, emerging noun phrases and verb phrases. The noun phrases were nouns limited to occasional articles and quantifiers like "some more." Though a detailed analysis is beyond the scope of this chapter, the forms presented give an idea of K's early pronominal and verbal constructions.

Conclusions

Individual Variation

The closer analysis of the nonsyntactic parameters of K and D showed that the initial impressions were correct and that the language of these two children was outwardly quite different. K was a child who was speaking clearly, with little babbling, and acquiring language at a rapid pace. D, on the other hand, was much slower, babbling often and using much less intelligible speech. Both shared the feature of using spontaneous imitation, but K's use of this dropped out once syntax moved more rapidly while D continued the use of imitation on into syntax.

The differences between the two continued through the analysis of presyntactic devices, which occurred only in D's speech. The occurrence of these devices however, also correlated with the child's level of intelligibility. D's language was generally difficult to interpret and the occurrence of these devices may have resulted from the adult's difficulties rather than from a difference in the child's approach to grammar. This is supported to the extent that the children differed much less on the other syntactic parameters. The first sentences for K and D at Time II showed little evidence for a productive syntax or for general grammatical categories. The one apparent difference at that time was that D's sentences appeared more analytic and less memorized wholes, although the data did not separate them widely in this regard. Later analyses showed both children acquiring limited pronominal categories that provided contexts for the acquisition of other vocabulary. They talked about different things, in the sense of semantic relations, but the nature of the emergence of the categories was similar in that they were limited in membership and focused on pronouns. The early rules used these categories for combinations, as well as lexical rules like K's rule for use of words with "want." There is little evidence until late Time III for K of sentences entirely composed of productive categories. The children's syntactic acquisition does not vary as drastically as their use of language, that is, how they talk and what they select to talk about.

In comparison to the data from other studies, some predictions are supported and others are not. The two styles described by Ramer cannot be identified with as many parameters as attempted in the review at the beginning of the chapter. While nonsyntactically K looked like the girls in Ramer's study, she did not show broad categories and high productivity at the onset. Even when her language consisted of multi-word utterances her diversity of structures was limited and focused on pronominal forms. The remaining characterization is that fast language learners speak clearly, use few presyntactic devices (probably an artifact of the clarity of their language), and do not continue to babble once multi-word speech begins. Since both children showed a pronominal preference, we cannot relate this parameter to the nonsyntactic ones, nor argue that the emergence of pronominal forms is related to the use of presyntactic devices.

The description of what a slow learner does also is limited based on these results. It was noted that Peter's subject used Gestalt learning and was unclear phonetically. K also used Gestalt learning to the extent that many of her longer first sentences looked like memorized wholes, and yet she learned quickly and spoke clearly. It appears that one could argue that the use of the pronominal mode results in more limited diversity of structure, although this limitation is not evident on a time dimension but is one of MLU.

Most generally, much of the diversity evident between these two children was probably due to non-linguistic factors such as interest in communication, sound play, and need to be understood. On the syntactic dimension, their development was more comparable. With only two subjects described with the method used, it is of course impossible to argue that more cautious grammatical analyses will show children to be more similar to one another than the literature has suggested. The next step is to apply this method of analysis to children such as the girls in Ramer's study who did appear to use early and widespread productive language.

Language and Cognition

There is little evidence from this analysis that the additional months of cognitive development for D affected his linguistic development very much. His sentences were somewhat more analytic, yet his categories were no broader than K's nor were his rules more productive. Analysis of later samples would be necessary to see if there were any changes in this regard. The data suggest, however, that the processes necessary to segment adult speech and identify contexts of co-occurrence both within sentences and across words are available to the child early in his cognitive development.

The effects that cognitive factors may have had on the language of K and D were probably on aspects not analyzed in the data. For example, the impression from examing the texts is that D was better at turn-taking and referring to absent events, and he was also more apt to use language play (Davison, 1974). These kinds of factors seem more influenced by cognition and parental speech. Lieven (1978), for example, has observed in a study of the dialogue of three mother-child dyads that while syntax was similar across children, their conversational skills varied greatly. The results here suggest that cognitive influences need to be sought in pragmatic and semantic aspects rather than those of syntax.

Grammatical Categories and Rules

The onset and acquisition of categories in D's and K's samples indicate that children only gradually acquire categories and the rules which relate them. Children learn to pair sound and meaning in context, and to segment adult speech in the form of sentences into their immediate constituents. The earliest sentences were either memorized wholes or analytic, but little evidence suggested rule productivity. The children learned to use certain words with certain others, and stored this information as part of their mental lexicon. Later, as words began to share contexts, broader categories were gradually built up based on their shared properties. It is proposed that through this gradual procedure children eventually acquired the categories of the adult language (cf. Schlesinger [1977] for an elaboration of this point).

Future research of this sort should reveal whether other children begin with greater rule productivity and greater use of early categories. Certainly, it should not be surprising that children rely a gret deal on memory and lexical information. Why should a child have a rule in the first place, except as an efficient last resort to deal with an abundance of memorized information? Recent linguistic theoretical research has also turned to the lexicon as an important aspect of language (Bresnan, 1979), and has argued that such descriptions are psychologically more valid (Halle, Bresnan, and Miller, 1978). It is hoped that the further elaboration of the kinds of criteria discussed in this chapter and the revision of our sampling procedures to seek out gaps in the grammar will lead to a greater understanding of the mental grammars of young children.

Appendix

An Outline of the Procedure Used in the Grammatical Analysis of D and K

1. Audio recordings were made of the speech of each child under naturalistic circumstances (c.f. Ingram, in press).
2. Samples were transcribed using the steps described in Ingram (in press, a). Basically, the child's utterances were phonetically transcribed twice, and then in the third listening transliterations were made. Transliterations are morpheme by morpheme translations into English orthography, e.g., [dɔi] "dog eat." Uncertain transliterations were placed in angle brackets, e.g., "<dog> eat," indicating uncertainty as to whether or not the child meant to say "dog." Uninterpretable parts of the child's utterance were

shown in empty square brackets, e.g., "[   ] cat." The phonetic elements could be entered within the brackets if necessary for comparisons with other unintelligible sequences.

3. The child's utterances were identified as either: imitation, babbling, totally intelligible, partially intelligible, questionable, unintelligible, and non-linguistic (e.g., grunts, laughs).

4. The child's intelligible utterances were used to construct a Lexicon that showed if a word occurred alone or in a sentence, and if the latter, the sentences in which it occurred, e.g., "cookie" in Allison IV in Bloom (1973) would be:

alone	*not alone*	*sentences*
"cookie" (6x)	"cookie"	"Allison cookie"
		"baby eat cookie"
		"baby cookie"
		"chocolate chip cookie"
		"eat cookie"
		"eat mommy cookie"

5. Each word was examined to see if it was *lexically free,* i.e., if it occurred alone or in varying contexts. If it was not free, it was placed in parentheses in the Lexicon. Inflected or contracted and uninflected forms of a word were considered as if one word.

6. Each word that was lexically free was then examined to see if it was *grammatically free.* The latter was the case if it occurred in two or more utterances in which (a) the meaning was consistent, (b) the position was consistent, and (c) co-occurrence took place, i.e., the items with which it occurred varied.

7. On a separate page, single-word types were listed alphabetically, followed by an alphabetical listing of lexically free types which did not occur in isolation. Next an alphabetical list was made for all syntactic types.

8. Syntactic types were identified according to their analytic structure. In each sentence, words that are not lexically free are placed in parentheses and combinations where one word must occur with another are shown in dashes, e.g., "(dog) run" indicates that "dog" only occurred in the data in this utterance, and "eat-cookie" indicates that one of the words always co-occurs with the other in multi-word utterances.

9. Words that are grammatically free were then listed separately along with the sentences in which they occur. The grammatical context of these words was recorded, e.g., "it cat," "it dog" would have "it" as [__N], and overlaps between items were grouped as emerging grammatical categories. When utterances occurred where the words in them were grammatically free, rules were written. Associative patterns (Braine, 1976) are

those where a lexical item is grammatically free, but none of its co-occurring words are. Productive patterns are those where co-occurring categories are all grammatically free.

Discussion

Bloom opened the discussion by complimenting Ingram on the criteria he had developed for determining patterns of early grammatical development. She thought that his system had considerable appeal and deserved respect. However, she had been surprised by Ingram's conclusion; that cognitive influences should be sought in the pragmatic and semantic aspects of language rather than in its syntactic aspects. She thought that Ingram would have concluded from the data he had presented that there was such a thing as autonomous syntax and that children learned syntactic rules from the beginning of multi-word speech. Everyone agreed that the first word combinations used by children were not necessarily rule-governed but that very soon a grammar did emerge, an organization of what the child knew about word combinations.

Ingram then clarified his conclusions. During the onset of multi-word speech there was a time (which he had referred to as Time II), lasting 2 or 3 months, during which his 2 subjects produced a very small number of multi-word utterances and did not appear to have rule-based grammar. After that time, as more multi-word utterances were used (in the period he had referred to as Time III), a grammar began to appear, but it was limited with respect to the scope of the categories that were developed and the diversity of the different structures that were used.

Bloom pressed Ingram to sum up this time line with the statement that there were rules of grammar at Time III. Ingram was more cautious. He said that rules appeared in that period, but he could not yet say at what point exactly they appeared. He would, instead, state the case as follows: There are words that the child acquires. There are sentences that he is producing which may provide evidence that he really knows the different parts of those sentences. There are also aspects of word use that suggest that the child can combine a given word with more than one other word. Once sentences do appear that have *all* of these characteristics, one could probably write rules for word combinations and say that there are rules governing each combination.

Bloom then asked about the relationship of grammatical development in Ingram's subjects to sensorimotor stages in their cognitive development. She suggested that, if one matched the information provided in Tables 2 and 3 in Ingram's paper, it appeared that, while multi-word utterances came in late Stage 5 for subject, K (at Time II), only one of these utterances ("Hi, birdie") showed any evidence of having a combinatorial rule according to Ingram's criteria. It was not until Time III that either child had a productive grammatical rule. In other words, they did not begin to use productive rules until they were in Stage 6. Ingram qualified this general statement. Although his subject, K, had been comparable to other children in the sense that most of the multi-word utterances she produced in Stage 5 were found upon detailed analysis not to be rule-governed, nevertheless she did show some limited productivity in late Stage 5 and early Stage 6. She was using language at that time far in advance of any other Stage 5 child reported in the literature thus far. In addition, although D's grammatical development had been very similar to K's with respect to the sequences followed, it was not sufficiently precise to say that both were at Stage 6 when they first broached true multi-word speech. D did not begin to develop limited grammatical categories and rules until he was quite far advanced in Stage 6 and in the development of representational thinking. He was engaging in combinatorial play and referring to past events in single word speech before a rule system appeared. He was even calling something that wasn't a cookie a cookie as a joke and laughing at adults when they went along with him and made the same ridiculous error. K was not doing any of these things when her grammatical development reached Time III. Bloom asked what Stage 6 behaviors K was showing at Time III. Ingram thought she was just beginning to engage in play focused upon herself, such as pretending to wash herself. D was certainly much more advanced in cognitive development at the same period of grammatical development. Thus, one might conclude that it was possible for the child to acquire syntax fairly early in Stage 6, when the only symbolic functions he or she demonstrated besides language were very simple ones. Alternatively, one might conclude that symbolic function, in spite of all of its diversity, was not highly predictive of the emergence of syntax.

Chapman suggested that D's one-word utterances reflected a different semantic content than K's and might be better matched to his cognitive development at the time of their appearance (in Time I) than K's one-word utterances. Ingram did not think that that was entirely true. It was not only that they were naming different things, but also that K developed a wish expression ("want cookie;" "want go get this") while D did not. He used such expressions once or twice but there was no evidence of further use of the word "want" resulting in a productive category for another 8 months. In that sense the children talked about different things, but if their single words were categorized according to almost any taxonomy, there were still only a small number of things talked about at Time I by either child.

Wolff then asked Ingram to elaborate his provocative statement to the effect that children form rules as a last resort. Did Ingram intend the statement to refer to all kinds of behavior or only to language? Ingram said he was thinking specifically in terms of the language system. Why do rules exist in the first place? Why did we not simply learn a series of sign-symbol relationships that would allow us to say all we want to say. If one wished to say "I want a cookie" why not develop a single vocalization that means

"I want a cookie" and another vocalization for "I want an apple" or even "I want another apple." The reason that that did not happen was that we had many thousands of things to say and we needed a systematic way to say them. This need, he suggested, was the origin of rules. The same types of need could be talked about in relation to Piagetian tasks. If one put a subject in an experimental situation where he had to push one of two buttons to receive a token many times over, such that one button yielded a 25% hit rate and the other a 75% hit rate, the subject tended to perform randomly. If, however, the reinforcer was changed to dollars, the subject quickly acquired a rule enabling him to get the most money, that is, he hit the 75% hit-rate button 100% of the time. Whenever there was too much information to deal with piecemeal and there was motivation to work out a system, rules or strategies were constructed.

Wolff said, if he understood Ingram correctly, because of the limitations in motor skill acquisition, too many items would have to be learned to make the more cumbersome system possible. Ingram said that he was not invoking limitation of motor skill as an explanation. But, Wolff went on to make the point that in any modality, if one didn't make rules, life would be altogether too difficult. It was not that one made a personal choice in the matter. Instead, one could argue from an evolutionary point of view that the capacity to make rules was built into the genome, if not into the gene. Ingram agreed that he had had something like this in mind. Bloom suggested that if that were true, strong universals of language must be present.

Ingram cautioned at this point against assuming that rules were present from the beginning ontogenetically. Even if there were universal categories in language, as Chomsky had proposed, such as nouns, noun phrases, and the auxiliaries commonly used in definitive grammars, there was no reason to assume that these categories were present in the child's system from the very beginning. His own data on early categories and on the nature of early rules provided very scanty evidence for their existence from the beginnings of speech. His data, on the other hand, might suggest a recapitulation of phylogeny. The child grew up into the use of categories. He found out from the language spoken in his environment what these universal categories were and brought them into play. Ingram planned to write grammars for child speech for the next few years. Perhaps then he might have some confidence in descriptions of categories and rules used by children. He was very much afraid that linguists would begin to produce large numbers of papers on child grammar from 2½ to 3 years of age, with categories such as aux, noun phrase, verb phrase, and transformations being indicated from a very superficial study of child speech. The danger was that an adult system would be imposed on utterances like "wanna eat cookie" when there was no evidence in the corpus of child data that the categories of that system were really appropriate. Like Piaget, he believed that adult-like categories existed at some point in development, but the interesting question for him as an observer of developmental change was: When did they come in and how?

Fischer asked about the cognitive behaviors Ingram had studied in assigning the children to sensorimotor stages. Ingram explained that the cognitive analysis had been performed a number of years ago and reported in Ingram (1978). What he had done was to cull the three Piaget works dealing with the sensorimotor period for developmental data. The data were assigned to appropriate stages and entered in a chronological order within each stage. He and two of his colleagues studied this material intensively and trained themselves to observe children and to interpret their spontaneous behaviors in terms of Piaget's system. They worked independently, entering the observed behaviors in chronological order in diary form. Later, Ingram and his colleagues compared all of their observations and findings and discussed them with one another. They then assigned each of the agreed-upon behaviors to developmental stages. Some of the behaviors noted were contributed by the parents' report. For example, one day the bathroom door in K's house was closed, and upon asking why, the investigators were told that K was putting her toys in the toilet all the time. That was a clearly interpretable activity. She was putting things inside of other things. Ingram felt fairly confident that their procedure was a reliable one and was roughly correct and valid, although it certainly called for individualistic skills on the part of the observers.

Fischer asked if one Stage 5 behavior was enough to place a child in Stage 5. Ingram said that, as in Piaget's records, there was a gradual clustering of Stage 5 behaviors, then suddenly every behavior would be at that level. Subsequently, early Stage 6 behaviors would begin to appear.

Fischer commented that the procedures appeared to be much more useful than others that had been tried. Ingram agreed. There would have to be a clustering of stage behaviors before a child was credited with having reached a new stage. Also, because they had examined so many behaviors, he and his colleagues had found a spread more like that in Piaget's own data.

Stark asked about the acquisition of phonological rules. Were they not present from the beginning of multi-word speech? Didn't children have a phonological rule system even before syntactic rules were acquired? Ingram answered that that might be true to some extent. In Ingram (1981), he had presented a great deal of evidence on the acquisition of the first 25 to 30 words. He had not discussed the acquisition of phonological oppositions in that work. These oppositions were needed when the child's vocabulary began to increase, otherwise too many different words would sound exactly alike to the adult. Stark asked if Ingram's two subjects, according to his criteria, were using phonological oppositions before they were using syntactic rules. Ingram replied that he had not studied that question specifically. However, it was his belief that a detailed phonological analysis would show early oppositions just emerging at the time of onset of multi-word speech. Stark asked if he was referring to Time II or Time III multi-word speech.

Ingram said that he had grouped his data to some extent. Also, the term multi-word utterance was merely an enabling term. It was only as a result of the subsequent analysis that the emergence of rules could be determined. However, it was some considerable time before oppositional categories appeared in the phonological system of the child and usually not until she/he had a vocabulary of 50 words or more. Tronick asked if the constraints determining their appearance were of memory and, if so, why the child could remember and understand many more than 50 words at that time. Ingram stated that it was not memory constraints that determined the appearance of phonological oppositions. Their appearance was related to vocabulary size. It was not possible to say /ba/ 50 different ways to indicate 50 different lexical items and be understood. It was necessary to introduce a /pa/ or a /ma/ also. Tronick suggested that the child could have such oppositions without their being rule-governed, given that the child's memory was fairly substantial at that point. Whether one talked about phonological oppositions or multi-word utterances, he would guess that the child could learn several hundred items. Ingram explained that memory was not the limiting factor, but articulatory skill, which was forced to evolve. The child at one year of age could not articulate well and his motor speech timing was poor, but lexical diversity forced the child to change his productions in order to include a sufficient number of lexical items in his speech and still be understood by others.

Chapman asked, what then forced the child to move from two-word combinations to multi-word speech? Ingram felt he had no insight into that problem. Leavitt suggested that, as other systems were developing, the child's wants, needs, and tensions were becoming correspondingly complex. These, and the demands of the environment, might pressure the child to develop better ways of saying things.

Trorick said he would agree with that statement in some ways, but why, when the child had 50 words and 10 multi-word combinations, did he begin to generate rules? His memory capacity would allow him to go on generating more multi-word combinations without pressure for rules. Wolff objected to the words "pressure" and "force" and said he preferred the word "want" in this context. He reminded the participants of Papoušek's (1967) studies. Papoušek had shown that, in learning to turn their heads to the left or the right to suck milk, avoid quinine water, and so on, infants not only learned the task and the contingencies attached to it, but also managed to get the investigator to present him with new problems. It might be a romantic notion, but there were certainly some reasons to assume that young children enjoyed problem solving, and might seek new ways to apply the capacity to form rules and to organize events according to a rule system at their own developmental level, whatever that might be. Ingram said he agreed with that point of view totally.

Chapman then referred to further examples of this kind of behavior in the period of successive one-word utterances. Bloom (1970, 1973) and Greenfield and Smith (1976) had all described episodes in which the young child obviously wanted to comment on 2 or more different aspects of a situation, but simply was unable to put them together in a single multi-word utterance. He had to make do with 2 or 3 separate one-word utterances. These examples suggested that we should not ignore the problems of motor planning for speech production which faced the young child in the evolution of multi-word speech. Wolff pointed out that Chapman was inferring that there might be limitations in the rules that the child could discover. However, Ingram was making a different statement, namely, when the child's previous devices gave out he had to find a more complicated device enabling him to proceed or, alternatively, that there might be a disposition in the child to discover or to seek out rules.

Bloom returned to Chapman's comment. In her own data (1970, 1973) she had observed children producing successive single-word utterances, for example, "Baby," "cookie," and "Mommy." In the situation where there was very strong evidence that the child appreciated the conceptual relations among herself as an agent and the objects which she was about to place in a particular relationship with one another, she had the lexical items, the ability to say them in reference to herself, and the 2 objects. What she had failed to induce at that point was the linguistic rule for assembling the 3 parts into a whole sentence. She was reminded of Braine's (1976) discussion of groping patterns. The child had the words and the ideas but was literally groping for a way to put them together. Within a month, she was able to do just that, to say "baby eat cookie," "eat mommy cookie," and others, and there was distributional evidence that her combinations were rule-governed. Ingram had shown, however, that the children he studied were capable of the motor planning involved in producing so-called multi-word utterances, but they were not able to use these utterances productively, to the extent that the words were not grammatically or lexically free. The term multi-word utterance was really a misnomer in this instance, because many of the child's utterances were holistic phrases and should be treated as single-word entities. Thus, like adults, children might have different degrees of articulatory facility, but articulatory skill was to some extent independent of the ability to derive linguistic rules.

Bloom felt that Ingram's analysis was very persuasive. But, with all due respect to his careful estimates of stage-related behaviors, she was not certain how confident he could be that a child was in late Stage 5 or early Stage 6. She was not convinced that K, at Stage 5 had used syntax, particularly in the light of Ingram's criteria for syntax. She concluded that when these 2 children, K and D, began to show evidence of productive syntax, they were not so very different from one another cognitively and they both had some degree of representational ability.

Cognitive Development and Language Comprehension in 10- to 21-Month-Olds

Robin S. Chapman

Department of Communicative Disorders, University of Wisconsin, Madison, Wisconsin

Introduction

Early language comprehension is the topic of this chapter: Its course of development, the possible roles of cognition in influencing that course, and the possible roles of the mother in making the child's apparent comprehension in everyday interaction appear better than it is. The data come from 48 children, 4 at each month of age from 10 to 21 months, and their mothers that Jon Miller, myself, and our students have studied. Cognitive assessments, comprehension assessments, free speech samples, and vocabulary diaries were obtained for each child. Data from the first 3 sources form the basis for the collaborative work reported here.

The discussion will begin with cognition, taking up issues of method in passing, and proceed to comprehension; thence to the issues of cognition's role in comprehension development, and finally to the roles of mother and child variables in determining comprehension in the natural context.

Cognitive Assessment

The sensorimotor tasks used in assessing the 48 10- to 21-month-olds whose comprehension was studied (Miller et al., 1980) were adapted from 4 existing instruments: the Uzgiris and Hunt scales (Uzgiris and Hunt, 1975); the Albert Einstein Scale of Sensorimotor Development (Corman and Escalona, 1969, unpublished); an observational assessment system (Chatelanat and Schoggen, 1975); and Mehrabian and Williams' scale (Mehrabian and Williams, 1971). Two items of differing difficulty were chosen at each stage level (III through VI) for 4 subscales defined by Uzgiris and Hunt: object permanence, means-ends, causality, and space. A fifth subscale, schemes in relation to objects, was defined by the highest stage level of scored schemes observed and their frequency. Brief descriptions of the items and their sources are given in Table 1. Omitted are the Stage III items, which were never administered; and imitation items that were administered for a portion of the study with few responses from the children.

Items from the first 4 subscales were administered beginning at the level where the child was estimated to be functioning. All subscale items at that level were tested twice before moving up or down a subscale to establish basal and ceiling performances, at which point testing on a subscale stopped. Thus every child did not receive every item. The schemes in relation to objects' score was based on two 10-minute observation periods in which the child played with objects with no intervention from the mother. The videotapes were transcribed for all behaviors; those listed in Table 1 were scored, and the fraction of scored behaviors at the highest stage level observed was computed and used in determining the score.

Cognitive Results

In the course of carrying out the sensorimotor assessment, we learned what every other researcher in that area has learned (see Table 2; Uzgiris, 1976; Corrigan, in press): namely, that performance across the subscales can be variable; that some subscales appear to be harder than others; that exact specification of the test procedures would be necessary to interpret a claim that a child was, for example, Stage IV. Ingram's (1978) reconstruction of Piaget's diary observations on his 3 children makes clear that observed behaviors similarly show a mixture of stage levels; indeed, rereading of Piaget makes the point clearly as well. It becomes clear that one focal issue of this conference—that of continuous versus discontinuous cognitive development—is a debate to be joined at the level of theory rather than of observed behavior.

Others (Fischer and Corrigan, this volume, Chapter 10) and Gratch (this volume, Chapter 11) have taken up that theoretical debate. Here are pursued two methodological points about sensorimotor assessment that are important to the interpretation of studies assessing cognitive prerequisites to various aspects of language acquisition. These points concern: (1) what the effect of requiring two out of two, rather than one out of two, passes on an item would be; and (2) what counts as Stage IV performance on the object permanence tasks.

Effects of Differing Pass Criteria

Following Uzgiris and Hunt (1975), the children in this study were given credit for passing an item if they passed at least one of the two administrations. For assessment purposes, however, it is useful to know what the effect of a more stringent pass criterion, 2 out of 2, might have been. The number of children passing one administration of an item but not the other ranged from 0 to 6, for all but one item. These numbers can be interpreted with respect to the number of children actually receiving the item twice (0 to 25% scored discrepantly); this comparison overestimates the degree of change, since children not receiving the item were assumed likely to pass or fail both. With reference to all 48 children, 0 to 12% of the item scores were discrepant; this estimate, of course, errs in the opposite direction.

One item (Causality 7), discovery of a novel mechanism, was clearly affected by the scoring criterion: 17 children (50% of those tested) passed one administration but not the other; 15 of those passed the first but not the second administration. Apparently the spontaneous search for and activation of the toy wind-up mechanism is a function of its novelty: having figured it out, children did not repeat themselves. Investigators wanting to administer this item multiple times, then, should change the toy on each trial.

Evidence for Stage VI Levels on the Object Permanence Task

Many studies examining cognitive prerequisites to language acquisition have used versions of the Uzgiris and Hunt (1975) object permanence subscale as an index of cognitive functioning (for example, Benedict, 1976; Corrigan, 1976, 1978; Bates et al., 1977). None of these studies of children in the 9- to 16-month range has found a correspondence of word use, gesture use, or word comprehension with the achievement of Stage VI levels of object permanence; that is, with the solution of an invisible displacement task in which the object's transfer from one location to another must be inferred, rather than watched.

What is curious about all these studies—and about the Uzgiris and Hunt (1975) data as well—is how young the children are at the ages at which they pass the invisible displacement tasks traditionally taken as evidence for Stage VI functioning: 11 to 13 months of age (50% pass) in Uzgiris and Hunt's (1975) study and 10 to 12 months in Miller et al. (1980), in contrast to Piaget's report for 18 months.

Piaget (1954, pp. 91–92) makes clear that practice on the search task can lead to success on invisible displacement items at Stage V levels of functioning. It would appear that the administration of easier items in the usual testing format has provided just that: practice on searching for the object and finding it through removal of a screen. When the hiding place is novel in the context of the test session, for example, the experimenter's hand, the age at which 50% pass jumps to 15 to 20 months in the Miller et al. data, an age consistent with 50% pass levels on other Stage VI tasks.

The failure to find language correspondence with Stage VI levels of object permanence in the previously mentioned studies, then, may simply reflect a failure to operationalize Stage VI attainment properly. Observational

Table 1. Sensorimotor Items Used in Testing Children.

Subscale	Stage	Item score and items	Sources[b]	Approx. age/50% pass[d]
Object permanence	IV	3. Finds object that one vertical screen is moved over	E	< 10 mo.
	V	4. Finds object visibly hidden under one screen	E, UH, CS, MW	< 10 mo.
		5. Finds object visibly hidden under one of two screens	E, UH	< 10 mo.
		6. Finds object visibly hidden under one and then another screen	UH, CS, MW	< 10 mo.
	[a]	7. Finds object invisibly hidden under one screen	UH	< 10 mo.
	[a]	8. Finds object invisibly displaced under three screens	UH	12 mo.
	VI	9. Finds object invisibly displaced under three screens and kept in hand	P	15-20 mo.
Means-ends	IV	3. Moves to object out of reach	UH, CS	< 10 mo.
	V	4. Lets go of one object to reach for another	UH	< 10 mo.
		5. Uses string to get object	UH, CS	< 10 mo.
		6. Pulls support to get toy	E, UH	< 10 mo.
	VI	7. Solves the matchbox problem	P	15-19 mo.
		8. Climbs on stool to get toy	CS	18-21 mo.
Causality	IV	3. Pushes away an interfering hand	P	< 10 mo.
	V	4. Attempts to reinitiate familiar game during pause	UH	10 mo.
		5. Gets adult to activate mechanical toy	UH	12-13 mo.
		6. Puts object in position to roll down incline	P	15 mo.
	VI	7. Discovers how to activate mechanical toy	UH	14-16 mo.
		8. Looks for source of a thrown object	P	18-21 mo.

Space

IV	3.	Fails to build a two-block tower after demonstration	UH	<10 mo.
	4.	Reverses direction of looking to find object circled behind him	E	< 10 mo.
V	5.	Stacks two rings on pole after demonstration	E	10-13 mo.
	6.	Rotates container to get toys out	E, UH	12-14 mo.
VI	7.	Goes around simple barrier to get toy	E	15 mo.
	8.	Comes out of and goes around cul-de-sac to get toy	E	16 mo.

Schemes in relation to objects[c]

II	0.	Holds; mouths, looks while holding objects	UH	
III	1. Infrequent	Hits with hand; bangs; hits two objects together; shakes or waves; pushes; pats against face	UH	
	2. Frequent		UH	
IV	3. Infrequent	Throws; examines; manipulates physical properties (spins, crumples, squeezes, drops) puts on/takes off; shows	UH	< 10 mo.
	4. Frequent			< 10 mo.
V	5. Infrequent	Spatial combinations (encloses or puts in proximity); manipulates physical properties (stacks/knocks over; puts in/dumps); functional use (eats with, brushes, etc.) points; gives or puts in lap.	UH	< 10 mo.
	6. Frequent			12-14 mo.
VI	7. Infrequent	Uses one object to stand for another; pretend elaboration of routine actions; groups or makes collections	UH, P	
	8. Frequent			15-20 mo.

[a]Originally interpreted as Stage VI.

[b]Sources: E = Einstein Scales; UH = Uzgiris and Hunt Scales, CS = Chatelant and Schoggen; MW = Mehrabian and Williams; P = Piaget.

[c]Scored by highest stage scheme observed. If schemes at the highest stage accounted for more than 33% of the total scored actions, the higher score at that stage was given.

[d]In the present study.

(Source: Miller, Chapman, Branston, and Reichle, 1980).

Table 2. Percentage of 12 Children in Each Age Group Passing Each Sensorimotor Item.[a]

Subscale	Stage	Item	Age group			
			10-12	13-15	16-18	19-21
Object permanence	IV	3	100%	(100%)	(100%)	(100%)
		4	100%	(100%)	(100%)	(100%)
	V	5	92%	92%	100%	(100%)
		6	75%	100%	91%	(100%)
	[b]	7	67%	83%	100%	100%
	[b]	8	17%	83%	100%	83%
	VI	9	(8%)	17%	33%	42%
Means-ends	IV	3	100%	(100%)	(100%)	(100%)
		4	100%	(100%)	(100%)	(100%)
	V	5	100%	100%	100%	100%
		6	100%	100%	100%	100%
	VI	7	8%	42%	25%	75%
		8	0%	0%	33%	33%
Causality	IV	3	100%	(100%)	(100%)	(100%)
		4	75%	(100%)	(100%)	(100%)
	V	5	17%	75%	100%	100%
		6	17%	42%	92%	92%
	VI	7	0%	58%	83%	92%
		8	0%	17%	33%	50%
Space	IV	3	100%	100%	(100%)	(100%)
		4	75%	100%	(100%)	(100%)
	V	5	50%	83%	100%	(100%)
		6	25%	50%	100%	(100%)
	VI	7	(17%)	(25%)	100%	100%
		8	(8%)	(17%)	92%	75%
Schemes	IV	3	8%	0%	0%	0%
		4	0%	0%	0%	0%
	V	5	67%	42%	0%	0%
		6	8%	17%	50%	25%
	VI	7	17%	42%	50%	75%
		8	0%	0%	0%	0%

[a]Parenthesized entries indicate that passes or failures were assumed for a majority of the group.
[b]Redefined as Stage V.

(Source: Miller, Chapman, Branston, and Reichle, 1980.)

studies, a redefinition of Stage VI object permanence performance, or a change in test procedure are needed to test the hypotheses that representational thought, as indexed by evidence of object permanence, is necessary to early word use or comprehension. Ingram's work (this volume Chapter 13), in which sensorimotor stage is inferred from observation, offers evidence that multi-word utterances can be found in a Stage V child's production.

Data from this study of cognitive prerequisites to comprehension will be presented following a description of the comprehension testing and results.

Comprehension Assessment

Number of Words

The selection of comprehension items was made on the basis of the developmental changes in comprehension demonstrated by prior work with children in each age range. One parameter of importance was the number of words which the child had to understand in the sentence before complying: increases from none to one to two to possibly three could be expected (Benedict, 1978; Shipley, Smith, and Gleitman, 1969; Smith, 1972; Huttenlocher, 1974; Larson, 1974; Sachs and Truswell, 1978). To demonstrate lexical comprehension, of course, gestural cues and the usual routines associated with objects had to be ruled out as explanations for the child's behavior.

Word Order

Word order is often the only cue to semantic role when the roles are not clear from the words themselves: for example, "Mommy kisses Daddy" versus "Daddy kisses Mommy." A number of prior studies of children in the 2- to 3-year range, however, had made clear that children of those ages did not use word order as a cue to agent and object relationships (deVilliers and deVilliers, 1973; Wetstone and Friedlander, 1973; Strohner and Nelson, 1974; Chapman and Miller, 1975; Benedict, 1976; Chapman and Kohn, 1978). For that reason, word order manipulations were not introduced for the 10- to 21-month-olds.

Bound Morphemes

Similarly, the experimental literature on comprehension of bound morphemes by preschoolers did not provide any basis for expecting 10- to 21-month-olds to understand the common grammatical inflections of English such as plural, possessive, tense markers, and definite versus indefinite articles (e.g., Carrow, 1968; norms for the Miller-Yoder Test, Owings, 1972; Fraser, Brown, and Bellugi, 1963). The comprehension of the inflection as the sole cue to meaning is late relative to use (Brown, 1973) and comprehension in contexts that provide multiple cues to meaning. For this reason grammatical inflections, too, were excluded from manipulation in the 10- to 21-month test items.

Contextual Limitations on Lexical Comprehension

Visual presence. Huttenlocher (1974), studying 4 children longitudinally, found that comprehension of words for people, pets, and objects was initially limited to the situations in which the referents were present. Only later in the nine- to 18-month period that she studied did children offer evidence of comprehension of referents out of sight by going to look for them.

Game context with gestural support. An even earlier stage of contextually-restricted comprehension has been reported by Reich (1976) and Benedict (1976), in which understanding is limited to a single setting, the full range of gestural as well as lexical cues, and a stereotyped response; that is, communication games. For example, Reich's 8-month-old child crawled to his father's closet when asked, while in the room, "where's Daddy's shoe?"; but he could not identify shoes among other objects. Common communication games—Peek-a-boo, Patticake—and items testing comprehension of present as well as absent objects were included in our test list.

Developmental Sequences in Production

Object and action? Goldin-Meadow, Seligman, and Gelman (1976) reported a progression in two-year-olds' productive vocabularies from a stage consisting mostly of nouns to a later stage in which verb vocabulary was expanded. When communication routines are excluded from consideration (a distinction not made in Nelson's (1973) nor Benedict's (1976) work), this sequence is confirmed in Greenfield and Smith's (1976) and Menn and Haselkorn's (1977) data.

If acquisition sequences in lexical comprehension mirror the later sequences found in production (a point disputed by Bloom, 1974), one might expect an entity stage followed by an action verb stage in comprehension as well; and so we tested comprehension of action verbs as well as nouns at the one-word level. Note that this prediction excludes the comprehension of action verbs in single routine contexts. Action routines may indeed be among the earliest reported examples of comprehension (Greenfield's *peek-a-boo* game, 1972; Benedict, 1976) or production (Bloom's (1973) example of *again,* in a picture-disappearance game; Reich's (1976) *Where's the shoe?* game; Menn and Haselkorn's *down* in a tower-build-up and knock down game).

Sequence in semantic role interpretation? A related prediction, based on Greenfield and Smith's (1976) report of a developmental progression in the semantic roles that their 2 longitudinally-studied children talked about at a one-word stage, is that certain interpretations of the relations among objects in the world become available for the child at later dates than others. Greenfield and Smith (1976) suggest that static object-object relationships such as location and possession are talked about later than agent-action or action-object relations in one-word speech. In the present study, we included items assessing action-object, agent-object, and possessor-possession relationships in order to see if the last was more difficult.

The Possible Effect of Comprehension Strategies

Children's responses to a comprehension test item may be governed by cues other than—or in addition to—the linguistic ones. Chapman (1978) has reviewed evidence for response preferences that may play a role in the child's apparent comprehension: these preferences have been termed "comprehension strategies."

Among the suggested comprehension strategies that children in the intentional sensorimotor period might use are those outlined in Table 3. Responses determined solely by context, and not linguistic content, are predicted for sensorimotor Stage IV. Lexical guides to context-determined responses are predicted in Stage VI, but context is expected to determine the pragmatic force and sentential meaning of an utterance for the child.

To the extent that these strategies play a role in children's responses on a comprehension task, they suggest a number of factors that must be controlled before comprehension can be attributed to the words (or later, structure) of the utterance. For example, gestural and gaze indications of objects mentioned in an utterance must be withheld. In addition, requests for actions that are probable for the object a child is attending to or playing with, must be set aside as evidence of verb comprehension. These probable actions, as indicated by studies of children's play with objects (e.g., Uzgiris and Hunt, 1975; Lézine, 1973) will shift with the child's developmental level and come to include, at Stages V and VI, conventional uses of objects such as eating from a spoon or drinking from a cup and the repetition of spatial combinations

Table 3. Summary of Non-linguistic Response Strategies and Comprehension Strategies Proposed for Children 8 to 24 Months.

Approximate Piagetian stage and age range	Possible strategy
Sensorimotor stage IV (8-12 months) context-determined responses	1. Look at objects that mother looks at 2. Act on objects that you notice 3. Imitate ongoing action
Sensorimotor stage V (12-18 months) lexical guides to context-determined responses	1. Attend to object mentioned 2. Give evidence of notice 3. Do what you usually do in the situation

Sensorimotor Stage VI (18-24 months) lexical comprehension but context determines sentence meaning	1. Locate the objects mentioned and give evidence of notice
	2. Do what you usually do
	  a. Objects into containers
	  b. Conventional use
	3. Act on the objects in the way mentioned
	  a. Child as agent
	  b. Choose handier object as instrument

(Source: Adapted from Chapman, 1978.)

of stacking and knocking over, putting in and taking out, and giving and taking of objects.

Finally, the child's ability to assign agent role to a noun in the utterance must be tested with an agent other than the child himself. Two-year-olds appear to assume, in sentence comprehension tasks, that they should be the ones to carry out the mentioned action (deVilliers and deVilliers, 1973; Shatz, 1978). This child-as-agent strategy would give the child credit for an extra lexical item in comprehension in, for example, the request "John pat the book."

The Comprehension Task

The 8 comprehension items that we decided to test are summarized in Table 4. Testing took place during two 10-minute videotaped test sessions separated by a week. The experimenter asked questions and gave commands, omitting gestural cues, while playing with the child on the floor of the experimental room; the mother was present. A warm-up in which routine communication games (peek-a-boo, patti-cake) were requested began the session.

Table 4. Comprehension Test Items.

Item and examples	Passing response
1. Person name "Where's" (child name)? "Where's Mama?" "Where's" (X)?	Child indicates himself or mother or other known present person in response to question.

2. Object name
"Where's" (X)?
"Go get" (X).
"Give me" (X).
X = words supplied by mother; "shoe,"
    "hat," "diaper," (stuffed animal
    brought from home), "ball," "book,"
    "pencil," "cup," "bottle," "table" or
    "chair"
	Child looks at, gets, shows, or gives the appropriate object among several present in visual field.

3. Absent person or object Item passed from #1 or #2	Child searches for a person or object when it is out of view.

4. Action verb
(V) ("it")
"Wanna" (V) ("it")?
"Can you" (V) ("it")?
 	
V = verbs supplied by mother; "kiss,"
    "tickle," "pat," "hug," "smell," "blow,"
    "eat," "throw," "open," "close,"
    "drink," and "bang" or "hit"
	Child complies by carrying out action. He may already be attending to the object. If so, the requested action cannot be one conventionally associated with the object.

The vocabulary selected for test was drawn from Sachs and Truswell's (1978) and Goldin-Meadow, Seligman, and Gelman's (1976) work, augmented by the mother's report of words that the child understood or used. The experimenter first attempted to establish evidence of comprehension at least twice on the one-word comprehension items (#1–4); evidence of multi-word comprehension (#5–8) was pursued, if relevant single-word comprehension had been established. The general procedure each time was that used by Huttenlocher (1974): first securing the child's attention, usually by calling his name with the exaggerated stress and intonation contour characteristic of mother's speech to language-learning children. Upon eye contact the request was presented in direct and indirect form (e.g., "Where's X?" "Lookit X." "Wanna X?" "Can you X?").

Scoring of the Comprehension Task

Transcripts of the experimenter's requests with accompanying context and the child's response were prepared from the videotapes. The requests in which the experimenter was unintentionally cuing the child with look or gesture were noted and ruled out as test instances. Similarly, any instances

Table 4. (*continued*)

5. Possessor-possession a. "Where's mama's shoe?" "Where's Joshua's shoe?" b. "Where's Mama's chair?" "Where's Joshua's chair?" Person and object names from those passed in #1 and #2.	Child appropriately locates the correct person's object both times, among present people and objects.
6. Action-object "Kiss the shoe." "Can you hug the ball?" "Wanna pat the book?" Verbs and objects are those passed in #2 and #4	Child complies for the appropriate object among several present. He cannot already be attending to the object; action should not be conventionally associated with object
7. Agent (other than child)-action "Horsey eat." "Make the doggie kiss." "Wanna make the horsey eat?" Verbs and objects are those passed in #2 and #4	Child selects toy among several present and demonstrates action with the toy serving as agent. Action should not be probable for the toy.
8. Agent (other than child)-action-object "Horsey kiss the ball." "Can doggie eat the diaper?" Verbs and objects are those passed in #2 and #4.	Child selects appropriate toy and object among those present and demonstrates appropriately. Action not probable for agent or object.

(*Source: Adapted from Miller, Chapman, Branston, and Reichle, 1980.*)

in which the child was already carrying out the request were noted and ruled out; instances in which the child was already attending to the object were also noted. Each child was credited with passing a given comprehension item if at least one unambiguous instance of passing according to the criteria of Table 4 could be found in the 20 minutes; videotaped replay was used to decide scoring instances that were ambiguous from the transcripts. For example, if the child picked up and kissed the ball in response to "Make the horsey kiss the ball," he was given credit for comprehension of *action-object* but not *agent-action-object*. If he had been playing with the ball when given this command and had then kissed it, he would have been credited only with *action verb*.

Comprehension Results

Children's performance on the comprehension task is summarized in Table 5 according to 4 three-month age ranges. The significant (p < .05) post hoc differences revealed by Tukey's HSD test are summarized there; both main effects of age (4) and item (8) as well as their interaction were significant in an analysis of variance (Miller et al., 1980).

Person vs. Object: Role of Familiarity?

Comprehension of person versus object names were significantly better among 10- to 12-month-olds. Differential familiarity, however, is as likely a source of this difference as an animacy distinction.

Table 5. Percentage of Children in Each Age Group Passing a Comprehension Item at Least Once.

	Age group (months) and number of Ss				
Comprehension	10-12 12	13-15 12	16-18 12	19-21 12	All Ss (n = 48)
1. Person name	100%	100%	92%	92%	96%
2. Object name	42%	100%	100%	100%	85%
3. Action verb	8%	33%	75%	83%	50%
4. Possessor-possession	0%	8%	42%	83%	33%
5. Absent person or object	0%	17%	33%	67%	29%
6. Action-object	0%	8%	42%	67%	29%
7. Agent[a]-action	0%	0%	8%	58%	17%
8. Agent[a]-action-object	0%	0%	0%	8%	2%
Average percentage passing	18.7%	33.2%	49.0%	69.8%	42.6%

[a]Other than child. Differences between entries are significant (p < .05) by Tukey's post hoc HSD Test if they exceed: 25.7 for task by age entries; 15.2 for age averages; and 19.0 for task averages.

(Source: Miller, Chapman, Branston, and Reichle, 1980.)

The Decontextualization of Lexical Comprehension

The restriction of early lexical comprehension to referents present to the child's view was confirmed: not until 18 months did 50% of the children begin to pass the *absent person or object* item (younger children were more likely to search for an absent person than an absent object; but again, differential familiarity may be the source of this difference). All children in this study appeared to have already passed the very early stage in which comprehension is further restricted to a routine context.

Action Verbs: A Later Acquisition Stage?

Significant increases in the proportion of children understanding action verbs occurred across the 10- to 18-month range: 50% were passing in the 15- to 16-month groups. By the test of compliance used here, action verbs were clearly understood later than present person and object names, but earlier than absent referents.

A problem in the assessment of action verbs, however, was that the items required the child to understand the lexical item without support from visually present referential context. Comprehension tested in an analogous fashion for object and person names emerges later, in fact, than action verb comprehension. What is needed is an action verb test item analogous to the object recognition tasks, in which the child has only to look at one among several choices depicting actions to indicate his comprehension.

Although action verb vocabulary in non-routine contexts does appear to emerge late relative to nouns in children's productions (Goldin-Meadow, Seligman, and Gelman, 1976) it has not yet been determined whether a similar sequence occurs in comprehension. If there does turn out to be a later stage of action verb acquisition, competing explanations are available.

Input differences? Differential availability of verb and noun vocabulary in utterance final position or in single-word utterance is one mechanism proposed to account for earlier noun acquisition in English-speaking children (for example, Chapman, in press). According to this view, apparent developmental sequences in semantic or syntactic categories should be identifiable in every language with relatively fixed word orders—but should not be identical across languages, to the extent that the linguistic ordering principles differ. Further, the mechanism accounting for the departure of individual children from the apparent developmental sequence of their peers should be the same: corresponding differences should be noted in the distributional characteristics of their mother's speech to them.

This line of argument rests on two assumptions. The first, supported by the present data, is that 10- to 16-month children are able to process only one lexical item in the mother's input. The second assumption is that attention to a lexical item in an utterance is most probable for single-word utterances, which present no word segmentation problems for the child, and for utterance final position, where recency effects on retention can be expected. Shipley, Smith, and Gleitman's (1969) work would support the former assumption. Evidence for the latter comes from Blasdell and Jensen (1970), Slobin and Welch (1971), and Eilers (1975).

Pragmatic differences? To the extent that action verbs are first used in request contexts, the production décalage could also be attributable to the differential availability of context usually associated with requests for action rather than comments on or requests for present objects.

Two words at a time. Comprehension of at least two words in an utterance was shown by at least 50% of the 17-month-old children for the possessor-possession relation; 18-month-olds for action-object relation; and 19- to 20-month-olds for agent (other than child) and action. The overall differences among these items were not significant, although 16- to 18-month-old children differed on the last in comparison to the first two. The items requiring comprehension of 3 words were beyond the scope of all but one of the children tested.

Thus, we do not find evidence in comprehension for an earlier stage of action-object relations and a later stage of object-object relations, a progression that Greenfield and Smith (1976) found in one-word production. Rather, we find evidence of an apparent increase in short-term memory for lexical items across several relations. This should not be surprising, for there is nothing in the words themselves to indicate the semantic relations intended; and cues from grammatical inflections and word order will apparently not be used till much later. The intended relations must be inferred from the situation. Benedict's (1976) work makes plain that children can make mistakes in these situational inferences; for example, giving mommy another shoe rather than pointing to her shoe.

Comprehension and Production Asymmetry

We find a difference then between the two process modes with respect to developmental change in semantic relations correctly inferred in comprehension, as opposed to expressed in production. The very familiarity with a situation required to render a correct decision as to the semantic relations intended by a speaker should militate against those relations becoming the subject of comment. What is worth drawing attention to is what is new (but not necessarily, as Pea (1979) shows clearly, what is informative). What can be successfully understood with respect to semantic relationships is what is old.

Lexical "relatedness" in comprehension? It could even be asked if young children appreciate the fact that the lexical items of an utterance *are* usually related to one another by the semantic or case relations discussed previously. This question is hard to evaluate with requests for compliance or demonstrations because the action format may bias for a related, rather than a separate, interpretation. That is, it is easier to continue an action with minimal change in agent or instrument or object of action. A better test of the child's preference for the related, as opposed to unrelated, interpretation of words is to offer him both interpretations and see which he chooses. For example, (1) a picture of mother kissing child with the dog standing by versus (2) a picture of mother kissing dog with the child standing by could be offered as the alternatives for "kiss doggie." We have no such data on these children, but we do know that by two-and-a-half years, children will overwhelmingly choose the second, related alternative (Chapman et al., in preparation).

Comprehension in the second year of life: lexical processing in context. From the experimental comprehension task emerges a picture of a child with very simple and limited skills in linguistic comprehension during the second year of life. The child understands words rather than sentences: at 10 months, one word at a time, and then only if its referent is present; at 18 months, 2 words at a time, or one word only when the referent is absent. Missing are all the structural cues to the pragmatic or propositional intent of the speaker. Our theories of the role that mother's input plays in the child's language acquisition must be modified to take into account these very stringent limitations on linguistic comprehension. And the mother's typical belief that her one- to two-year-old understands everything said to him requires some careful scrutiny. If her belief is supported at all by evidence from the natural interaction situation, then sources other than linguistic ones must be found to account for the child's improved performance.

Implications for production. These conclusions about the limited, lexical nature of the child's early comprehension of utterances prove helpful in understanding a number of characteristics of children's early productive syntax: that children start out one word at a time (Bloom, 1973); that their two-word combinations are uninflected; that two-word combinations are often creative. The child's very limited window on input would appear to contribute to these characteristics (not, of course, to all: the source of appropriate word order in production remains an unresolved problem). To the extent that these developmentally changing limitations on comprehension are different in older children beginning to learn a first or second language, one might expect their patterns of acquisition to be rather different in their early productive syntax from those reported for young children.

A second important implication of the conclusions about comprehension skill is that the kind and simplicity of syntactic patterns modeled by the mother in the second year of life may be irrelevant facts about input. Individual variation in mother MLU and proportion of complex sentences might not be expected to lead to consequences for the child precisely because he is guaranteed an even simpler one- to two-word input by his limited comprehension skills.

Cognitive Prerequisites to Comprehension?

Finally we come to the question of cognition's role in the development of comprehension. In particular, we have been interested in evaluating claims that cognitive achievements are necessary but not sufficient for linguistic achievements. There are several specific proposals and one general one that can be examined with relevant data from the Miller et al. (1980) study on subscale performance (see Table 6).

Object Permanence in Relation to Comprehension

Does object concept precede word comprehension? One could argue that Stage IV levels of performance on this subscale, indicating the establishment of an object concept, should be prerequisite to instances of word comprehension. It is true that all children who showed word comprehension scored at least Stage IV on the object permanence subscale. Because no child failed to attain Stage IV levels, however, this prediction cannot be adequately evaluated; younger children would be needed.

Does object permanence precede comprehension of absent people and objects? A second prediction specific to the subscale is that attainment of a Stage VI level of object permanence, indicating the capacity for representational thought, should be prerequisite to the decontextualization of lexical comprehension; that is, to the comprehension of words for absent people and objects. If our argument about the Stage V nature of Items 7 and 8 is correct, however, this prediction is not borne out. Some children who failed to continue searching for a toy invisibly displaced and kept in the examiner's hand nevertheless passed the comprehension item. These passes were as likely to involve absent objects as absent people.

Does object permanence precede action verb comprehension? To the extent that the action verb comprehension item was hard because it required the recall of an absent event, we can predict that Stage VI levels of object permanence should similarly be prerequisite to action verb comprehension. The data refute this prediction too, whether traditional or revised stage levels are assigned to items. Some children functioning at Stage V levels on the subscale show comprehension of action verbs.

Do Conventional Actions on Objects Precede Action Verb Comprehension?

Dihoff and Chapman (1977) have argued that conventional actions, typically emerging in Stage V, could be interpreted as the development of action concepts that the child could, with some time delay, learn to associate with lexical items in input. The schemes transcripts were reanalyzed for the occurrence of conventional actions, which occurred as early as 10 months and increased in both number of instances and number of different types of action to a peak, at 18 months, of 19 instances and 4 different actions occurring in 20 minutes on the average. Only 4 children failed to show any conventional uses, but one of these passed the action comprehension item.

The conventional actions on objects could be regarded, of course, as significant not so much for their action quality as for their apparent function as object recognition routines. Bates and her colleagues (1979) have recently taken this view. It seems a sensible one, because the notions of action encoded in the one- to two-year-old's vocabulary (e.g., Bloom, 1973; Nelson, 1973; Bates, 1979) do not match very well the conventional action schemes, whereas the objects that children learn to name early frequently include those objects that they act on in specific, conventional ways.

Does Recognition of Others as Agents Precede Comprehension of Agent (Other Than Self) and Action?

The child's willingness to assign agent roles to others (Item 5 of the Causality Subscale) could be viewed as evidence of the conceptual development prerequisite to assigning agent roles to lexical items that he hears. The data are consistent with this view, although the agent-action item is obviously hard for a variety of reasons.

What is Prerequisite to Two-Term Comprehension?

Specific prerequisites. Finally, we can ask which cognitive items appear to be prerequisite to possessor-possession or agent-action comprehension, the two items marking the onset of two-word comprehension. Of the children who pass these items, at least some score Stage V on every subscale (with the exception of the spatial subscale and the possessor-possession item), despite the general correspondence of the item to Stage VI levels.

The data offer little support for the particular cognitive prerequisites examined. The claims, if they are to be retained, will have to be consigned to the realm of theory; and the obscuring roles of task difficulty and measurement error will have to be acknowledged in the realm of observation.

Cognitive level as a predictor of comprehension score. Here a weaker view of the Cognition Hypothesis was examined: namely, that cognitive level is a good predictor of comprehension performance, and specifically the possibility that it is a better predictor than age. As an index of general cognitive level the choice was made to sum the subscale scores. Sensorimotor score was significantly correlated with comprehension score (.72); so, too, was age (.84). Multiple regression analyses showed, however, that, of the two, only age was significantly related to comprehension score when each predictor was entered second. This finding was interpreted to mean that cognitive level plus other aspects indexed by age—social experience,

Table 6. Percentage of Children at Each Sensorimotor Subscale Item (Highest Passed) Who Pass Each Comprehension Task.

Sensorimotor subscale	Stage	Item	1. Person name	2. Object name	3. Action verb	4. Possessor-possession	5. Absent object or person	6. Action-object	7. Agent-action	8. Agent-action-object	9. Number of Ss for whom is highest passed
Object permanence	IV	4	100	100	0	0	0	0	0	0	1
	V	5	100	100	0	0	0	0	0	0	1
	a	6	100	50	25	0	0	0	0	0	4
	a	7	100	38	25	13	0	13	13	0	8
		8	91	100	48	39	35	30	13	0	21
	VI	9	100	100	91	54	54	54	36	9	11
Means-ends	V	5	100	100	0	0	100	0	0	0	1
	VI	6	96	74	33	19	15	19	19	0	27
		7	100	100	69	46	38	23	46	8	13
		8	86	100	86	71	57	86	71	0	7

Causality

IV	3	100	25	0	0	0	0	0	0	4
	4	100	57	14	0	0	0	0	0	7
V	5	67	100	100	33	0	67	0	0	3
	6	100	75	25	25	25	25	25	0	4
VI	7	100	100	56	28	33	33	17	6	18
	8	92	100	75	75	58	42	42	0	12

Space

IV	3	100	67	0	0	0	0	0	0	3
	4	100	100	40	0	0	0	0	0	5
V	5	100	38	13	0	13	13	0	0	8
	6	83	100	0	0	0	0	0	0	3
VI	7	83	83	67	50	33	50	17	0	5
	8	96	100	74	57	48	43	30	4	22

Schemes

IV	3	100	0	0	0	0	0	0	0	1
	4	—	—	—	—	—	—	—	—	0
V	5	100	62	0	0	8	8	0	0	13
	6	92	100	33	33	25	33	25	0	12
VI	7	96	95	55	55	45	41	23	5	22
	8	—	—	—	—	—	—	—	—	0

[a]Reinterpreted as Stage V.
(Source: Miller, Chapman, Branston, and Reichle, 1980.)

linguistic input, experience with objects, and maturational level—is a better predictor than cognitive level alone.

Support for this point of view comes from a clinical study of 26 developmentally delayed children functioning at the sensorimotor level (Miller, Chapman, and Bedrosian, 1978). In this group, chronological age indexed length of experience but not cognitive level. Cognitive measures provided a better predictor of upper bound measures of language functioning. That is, all but one child were functioning at (or below) the level predicted by cognitive measures; none, of course, was functioning at the level predicted by chronological age. It was concluded that general cognitive level, as indexed by performance across a variety of sensorimotor tasks, can be a useful guide to level of language comprehension in developmentally disabled populations; but that in establishing expectations among normal children, age gives an even better basis of prediction. Again, the need to make explicit the role of experience in the development of comprehension arises.

Comprehension in Context: Mothers' Requests

To begin making the role of non-linguistic experience explicit, a series of studies has been initiated examining the same 48 children's apparent comprehension in a more natural setting: namely, 10 minutes of videotaped free play with their mothers. For mothers' requests to attend to objects, the following questions were asked: What additional gestural or lexical cues does the mother provide, and which of them are associated with differential success rates? Do children actually use the comprehension strategies predicted on the basis of their sensorimotor schemes and experimental task performances?

The requests of 48 mothers to attend to objects ("see the car") in 10 minutes of videotaped free play with their 10- to 21-month-old children are being analyzed (Chapman, Klee, and Miller, in preparation). Other requests to act on objects ("push the car") or requests for information ("where's the car?") will be examined in later studies. Interaction sequences in which the mother persisted in asking the child to look at an object either directly ("look it") or indirectly ("let's look at the doggie") were identified. Following Shatz and Graves' (1976) terminology, these sequences are called cycles. Cycles were coded as successes (the child looked), failures (the child ignored the request), or pseudosuccesses (the child was already looking).

Each requesting utterance within a cycle was coded for the accompanying gesture, if any; spoken reference to the object by name, pronominally, or not at all; and inclusion of the child's name in the utterance. Shatz and Graves' (1976) list of 8 gestures accompanying mothers' request for action were expanded to a set of 19 gestures (on the basis of our videotaped attention requests). Children's responses were coded for each utterance within the cycle as (1) inattentive or noncompliant; or one of 4 compliant categories; namely (2) gazing at object; (3) examining it; (4) carrying out a conventional action with the object (for example, drinking from cup); (5) other actions on object (for example, banging).

Changes with Developmental Level in Requests to Attend to Objects?

Cycles requesting attention to objects averaged 10.25 per session in the 10- to 12-month age group and 6 to 7 per session in the other groups. The changes were not significantly related to the child's age, cognitive level, or comprehension score (see Table 7). The proportion of cycles ending in success, failure, or pseudosuccess did not alter significantly with age, cognitive level, or comprehension score. Fully one third of the cycles were pseudosuccesses; of the remaining cycles, 86% were successes. Mothers generally succeeded in getting children to look at objects. Indeed, over half of the mothers never failed to get their child to attend to an object; and 42% never required more than one request to achieve their goal. Mean number of requests per cycle did decrease with child age, from an average of 1.5 for 10- to 12-month-olds (SD = .36) to an average of 1.16 for 19- to 21-month-olds (SD = .18).

Individual Differences in Mother-Child Dyads?

It might be hypothesized that the variation that exists in success rates is linked to individual differences in the mother's request patterns as well as differences in children. The lack of variation in success rate or mean length of successful cycles with child age, sensorimotor level, or lexical comprehension score suggests that many mothers have already found ways, by 10 months, of successfully directing their children's attention. Their skills in this arena did not appear to change over the 10- to 21-month period. What might be the differences in the relatively more and less successful mothers?

Sensitivity to child? One possibility is that less successful mothers are less finely-tuned to their children: less sensitive to the child's ongoing activity, and hence less likely to choose a propitious time to make their requests. In terms of the measures in this study, indices of insensitivity might include: (1) pseudorequests to attend, in which the child was already looking at the object that the mother asked him to attend to; and (2) the sheer number of requests to attend to objects. High rates could be regarded as intrusive on the child's activities. Number of pseudorequests and number of all requests to attend cycles should, on this hypothesis, be positively related to each other but negatively related to the number of successful request cycles. Mean length of successful request cycles should be negatively related to number of successful cycles and positively related to number of pseudorequest cycles and total number of cycles.

Or talkativeness? From Table 7, however, it is apparent that the predicted relationships do not hold. For example, number of total request cycles and

Table 7. Pearson Product-Moment Correlations of Children's Age, Cognitive Score, and Comprehension Score, in Relation to Cycles of Mothers' Requests to Attend to Objects (n = 48).

Variable	1.	2.	3.	4.	5.	6.	7.	8.	9.	10.	Mean	S.D.
1. Age											15.5	3.49
2. Sensorimotor total	.86[a]										33.21	4.95
3. Comprehension score	.84[a]	.72[a]									3.44	1.92
4. Number of request cycles	−.23	−.17	−.10								7.67	5.46
5. Mean length of cycle	−.37[a]	−.29[a]	−.21	.44[a]							1.30	.34
6. Mean length of successful cycles	−.22	−.18	−.05	.36[a]	.93[a]						1.42	.53
7. Number of request utterances	−.32[a]	−.29[a]	−.18	.89[a]	.71[a]	.60[a]					11.90	10.35
8. Number of successful cycles	−.26	−.16	−.22	.80[a]	.48[a]	.35[a]	.82[a]				4.02	2.93
9. Number of failed cycles	−.21	−.28	−.09	.47[a]	.34[a]	.27	.52[a]	.37[a]			.77	1.04
10. Number of pseudo-request cycles	−.09	−.05	−.06	.80[a]	.20	.20	.58[a]	.33[a]	.14		2.88	3.27
11. Total mother utterances in 10 minutes	−.22	−.28	−.09	.43[a]	.41[a]	.39[a]	.48[a]	.18	.33[a]	.45[a]	166.81	53.52

[a] df = 46; f < .05, r > .288.

(Source: Chapman, Klee, and Miller, in preparation.)

number of pseudorequest cycles are not negatively, but positively, related to number of success cycles; failure and pseudocycles are unrelated; and failure and success cycles are positively, rather than negatively, related. The explanation of the significant correlations obtained appears to be that some mothers talk more than others; and that talkativeness leads to increases in all of the response categories except the number of successful cycles.

Attention-Directing Cues

A second approach to explaining the variation in number and length of successful cycles is to examine the cues that mothers provide in requesting attention. If presence or absence of the cue predicts performance on an individual utterance, then the frequency with which the cue is provided by mothers should show a distribution along a continuum of success and failure. Two categories of cueing are reported here: gestural accompaniment to the utterance, and use of the object name in the request. The analyses are only preliminary, but the following general facts about cue distribution emerge.

Accompanying gestures. Gestures accompanied almost every request, whether the request occurred before (true) or after (pseudo) the child was looking at the object. The most frequently occurring mother gestures are tabulated separately for true and pseudorequests in Table 8. The frequent accompanying gestures—showing or offering the object, acting on it or moving it—appear equally effective in getting children to look at the object. The mother rarely failed to indicate the object gesturally; and the child rarely failed to see her gestural indication when she spoke.

Interestingly, the frequent gesture categories for both true and pseudorequests have in common the fact that the mother is actually in contact with and moving the object. In the free play situation, the mother has a choice of drawing attention to objects distal to or proximal from herself. Overwhelmingly, the mother chose to request attention to nearby objects. Further, she had a choice of drawing attention to the object itself (for example, through showing it; placing it in the child's view, touching, or pointing); or an event involving it (for example, acting upon object, new spatial combination). These alternatives, as indicated by her accompanying gestures, occurred equally often.

The probable reason for mothers' successes in getting children to attend to objects becomes clearer. Given that the child will turn toward the mother when she speaks, he will see an object, usually a moving object, and he is likely to look at it. It does not appear to be the case that only certain gestures of communicative significance in themselves (for example, pointing or showing) control the child's attention to objects. Rather, we can hypothesize that vocal and subsequent visual change attract his attention.

Mention of object names. What about mention of the object's name in the request? Does the presence of the lexical cue enhance the probability

Table 8. Distribution of Gestures Accompanying True and Pseudo-request Utterances, With Distribution of Child Response to True Requests.

Accompanying gesture	Percent response to each true request type			Percent of request type accompanied by each gesture	
	Look	Act	Ignore	True	Pseudo
Demonstrate action with object	83%	2%	15%	21%	47%
Hold object up to be seen	88%	2%	10%	20%	8%
Place object in new location	84%	3%	13%	13%	5%
Place object in front of child	79%	5%	15%	8%	9%
Extend object to child	67%	17%	17%	7%	9%
Take object from child	67%	0	33%	2%	5%
Touch object (don't move it)	75%	8%	17%	5%	3%
Point to object	60%	10%	30%	4%	3%
Infrequent gestures[a]	30%	10%	60%	4%	6%
Physically maneuver child toward object	—	—	—	—	5%
Mother's gesture not seen by child (excluded from above categories)	10%	0%	90%	16%	—

[a]Infrequent categories included tapping on object, touching child with hand or object, making a noise with the object, looking at object only, looking at child only, and no gesture. No occurrences were noted of tapping one object against another, or pointing or touching the object and then a new location.

(Source: Chapman, Klee, and Miller, in preparation.)

of looking at the object? If so, it would be expected that success in getting the child to attend to objects would be associated with increasing comprehension score and age, which presumably covary with increasing size of nominal comprehension vocabulary. This association, however, was not observed. Further, only 18% of the utterance requests contained the object's name, as opposed to pronominal or omitted mention of the object.

Mothers' use of the object's name in their requests to attend to objects was distributed unimodally. There were too few instances in which object mention co-occurred with no gesture to examine the effect of lexical cueing in the absence of gesture.

Why Do Mothers Not Name Objects in Requesting Attention?

The infrequency of object name mention across the mothers in this study is surprising on two counts.

Individual variation in referential style? The first is from the perspective of individual variation in input style. Nelson (1973) has characterized mothers as differing in referential or expressive style. In the mother, one might suppose that this style would be reflected both in the extent to which nominal vocabulary is modeled and in the extent to which names are demanded. In the child, the difference is operationalized in terms of whether more than 50% of the first 50 words in his spoken vocabulary are general nominals; if so, the child is classified as referential. Mothers' style, Nelson (1973) argued, could be matched or mismatched to their children's patterns, accelerating or retarding spoken vocabulary acquisition as a consequence.

Our data suggest, however, that referential style in the mother, if it exists, does not extend to differential mention of object name in requests to attend to objects. It may be that some mothers follow up requests to attend to objects with the object name, or in older children with a request for the object name—this is the pattern reported for one mother's book-reading episodes with her son (Ninio and Bruner, 1978). Ninio and Bruner's data also show, however, that mother labeling is an activity relatively specific to the book-reading game; in that case, referential mothers may be better conceptualized as book-reading mothers.

Mothers as optimal language teachers? The second perspective from which the lack of object mention is surprising is that of the mother as Supermom, providing an optimal environment for her child's language learning. In the requests for attention to objects, particularly in those that are pseudorequests because the child is already attending, she has an ideal vehicle for pairing the object's name with appropriately attended-to referents. These could serve as vocabulary-teaching trials, in contrasts to the common testing trials provided by "Where's the X?" or "What's that?" interchanges. The mother is no more likely to mention the object name in pseudorequest contexts, however, than in true request contexts. Motivated by common discourse conventions of reference, she omits the lexical information redundant with deictic gesture: "Look it," instead of "Look at the car." She may, of course, go on to label the object or her demonstrated action in a subsequent utterance; we have only examined utterances falling into the category of requests for attention in these data. But she has missed at least one teaching opportunity.

Comprehension in Context: Mothers' Requests for Action

Mothers' requests for action (and action on objects) are also being analyzed in the 10-minute videotaped free play samples (Chapman, Klee, and Miller, in preparation). Sequences in which the mother persisted in the same request were identified, following Shatz and Graves (1976), as cycles. These stretches could have other speech acts embedded in them (e.g., requests for attention or information) as long as no change in topic occurred. The number of utterances requesting action within the cycle was used as a measure of its length. Cycle outcome was coded as either successful (the child complied), failure (the child did not), pseudosuccess (the child was already performing the requested action), or switched (the mother performed the requested action).

Each utterance requesting action was also coded for the child's response: compliance, carrying out some other action, refusing, watching the mother perform the action, looking, or no behavioral change. The gestures accompanying requests were coded according to 24 categories, including those categories used in coding requests to attend to objects; if the child did not see the gesture this was noted.

Developmental Change and Individual Differences in Mothers' Requests for Action

Frequency of action requests. Of the average number of mother utterances in the 10-minute sample, 13.7% were categorized as requests for action; 23.4 utterances, on the average, or 13.1 cycles requesting action (see Table 9). These measures were not significantly correlated with age, sensorimotor

Table 9. Means, Standard Deviations, and Pearson Product-Moment Correlations of Measures of Request for Action with Age, Sensorimotor Score, and Comprehension Score.

Variable	1.	2.	3.	4.	5.	6.	7.	8.	9.
1. Age									
2. Sensorimotor score	$.86^a$								
3. Comprehension score	$.85^a$	$.72^a$							
4. No. of utterances requesting action	$-.11$	$-.14$	$-.04$						
5. No. of request for action cycles	$-.02$	$-.04$	$.02$	$-.92^a$					
6. Mean length of cycles	$-.27$	$-.31^a$	$-.17$	$.51^a$	$.19$				
7. No. of successful cycles	$.17$	$.18$	$.15$	$.73^a$	$.80^a$	$.13$			
8. No. of failed cycles	$-.11$	$-.13$	$-.08$	$.85^a$	$.83^a$	$.32^a$	$.55^a$		
9. No. of pseudocycles-child already doing	$-.11$	$-.12$	$-.04$	$.32^a$	$.42^a$	$.11$	$.17$	$.21$	
10. No. of switched cycles-mother complies	$-.10$	$-.14$	$-.07$	$.45^a$	$.58^a$	$.02$	$.28$	$.24$	$.20$
11. Mean length of successful cycles	$-.19$	$-.23$	$-.15$	$.34^a$	$.21$	$.60^a$	$.24$	$.22$	$-.14$
12. Mean length of failed cycles	$-.24$	$-.29^a$	$-.14$	$.28$	$.10$	$.58^a$	$-.08$	$.19$	$.03$
13. Mean length of pseudo cycles	$-.03$	$-.06$	$.12$	$.37^a$	$.38^a$	$.05$	$.13$	$.27$	$.64^a$
14. Mean length of switched cycles	$.06$	$.10$	$-.03$	$.24$	$.19$	$.33^a$	$.28$	$.10$	$-.08$
15. Percent successful cycles	$.43^a$	$.37^a$	$.34^a$	$.06$	$.07$	$-.05$	$.55^a$	$-.13$	$-.15$
16. Percent failed cycles	$-.30^a$	$-.27$	$-.28$	$.24$	$.18$	$.23$	$-.10$	$.63$	$-.11$
17. Percent pseudocycles	$-.06$	$-.06$	$.08$	$-.13$	$-.08$	$-.29^a$	$-.18$	$-.18$	$.76^a$
18. Percent switched cycles	$-.08$	$-.06$	$-.11$	$-.22$	$-.20$	$.02$	$-.33^a$	$-.39$	$-.21$
19. Percent utterances requesting action	$.05$	$.04$	$.05$	$.84^a$	$.75^a$	$.54^a$	$.62^a$	$.77^a$	$.05$
20. Total number utterances	$-.22$	$-.28$	$-.09$	$.61^a$	$.62^a$	$.15$	$.43^a$	$.48^a$	$.52^a$

^{a}df = 46; f < .05; 2-tailed.

(*Source: Chapman, Klee, and Miller, in preparation.*)

score, or comprehension score. The variation in frequency that exists, then, is unrelated to the children's changing characteristics.

Talkativeness as an individual difference among mothers. The variation among mothers in frequency of requesting action appears to be related primarily to an individual mother characteristic of talkativeness. The total number of mother utterances correlates significantly with number of request utterances and cycles and number of each cycle outcome. It is unrelated, however, to the mother's insistence on a particular request (mean cycle length measures).

Mother's persistence in relation to child's cognitive level. Mean cycle length (1.74 requests) decreased significantly with an increase in sensori-

10.	11.	12.	13.	14.	15.	16.	17.	18.	19.	Mean	S.D.
										15.50	3.49
										33.21	4.95
										3.44	1.92
										23.38	16.35
										13.08	7.51
										1.74	.44
										3.44	3.04
										4.90	3.64
										1.21	1.41
										3.27	2.30
.05										1.82	1.02
.10	.15									1.82	.97
.19	.01	.03								.78	.75
−.17	.10	−.12	.06							1.44	.78
−.21	.21	−.29^a	−.19	.01						25.6	16.5
−.22	.08	.23	−.04	−.05	−.52^a					35.7	17.0
.17	−.35	−.02	.52^a	−.28	−.18	−.16				9.8	11.3
.57^a	−.11	.03	−.14	.29^a	−.34	−.41^a	−.29^a			26.9	16.5
.33^a	.36^a	.32^a	.19	.29^a	.06	.29^a	−.30^a	−.18		13.7	7.30
.40^a	.21	.05	.43^a	.06	−.04	.10	.14	−.13	.15	166.81	53.52

motor score; adding in age or comprehension score as predictors with sensorimotor score did not significantly increase the multiple correlation with mean cycle length. When the mean length of each cycle type is considered, only mean length of the failed cycles (1.82) continues to be significantly (and negatively) related to sensorimotor score: the mother has a tendency to abandon her request earlier with a child scoring at higher sensorimotor levels. She persists just as long, on the average, as she persists for the cycles ending in success.

Children's Responses to Requests for Action

Low success rates. A striking fact about the outcomes of mothers' requests for action, as opposed to their requests that the child attend to objects, is their infrequent success. Request for action cycles end in success only a quarter of the time; mothers' abandon another 36% of their attempts; and they themselves carry out the requested action another quarter of the time. Pseudorequests in which the child was already carrying out the action account for 10% of the cycle outcomes. We see again, then, that more than a third of the cycles have some appearance of satisfactory outcome attributable solely to mother.

Developmental change in percent success and failure. The percent request cycles ending in success and failure are significantly related to indices of the child's developmental level. Step-wise multiple regression analyses with age, sensorimotor score, and comprehension score as the potential predictors of percent success indicated that age alone was a significant predictor, accounting for 19% of the variance; the addition of comprehension score to the equation did not significantly increase R^2. Similar analyses for percent failed cycles again showed age to be the only significant predictor, accounting for 9% of the variance. Table 10 summarizes mean percent success and failure cycles by 3-month-age ranges: the percent of request for action cycles ending in success more than doubles over the 10- to 21-month period.

Mothers' gestures as cues to meaning? There is still substantial variation in individual children's probability of success to explain. Can any of it be

Table 10. Means and Standard Deviations by Age Group (each n = 12) for Percent Successful and Percent Failed Request for Action Cycles.

Variable		Age group			
		10-12	13-15	16-18	19-21
Percent successful cycles:	Mean	15.0%	26.4%	24.9%	36.3%
	SD	11.0	17.2	8.6	20.7
Percent failure cycles:	Mean	45.7%	31.1%	37.7%	28.3%
	SD	13.2	13.8	17.3	19.3

(Source: Chapman, Klee, and Miller, in preparation.)

traced to variation in the provision of gestural cues by mothers? The categories of gesture or no gesture accompanying mothers' request for action utterances of all types are summarized in Table 11 for the 70% of the instances in which the child saw the gesture. Also shown is the distribution of children's responses.

Mothers accompany their requesting utterances with gestures almost 90% of the time that the child sees them. When the child is looking and they fail to do so, however, compliance is no less likely than average.

Of the 303 request utterances excluded from Table 11, 14% were instances in which the child or mother was off-camera at the time. Of the remaining 261 utterances on which the mother's accompanying action was not in the child's view, 84% were instances in which the mother provided no gesture at all. Thus here, too, we have evidence of the power of movement to attract the child's visual attention. What most gestures do not appear to do, however, is to give the child additional cues as to the action he should take.

The mother does try. Demonstrations of the requested action are the single most frequent gesture category, but the probability of imitation (that is, compliance) by the child is small. Two gestures accompanying requests—offering and giving objects—have relatively better compliance rates. It is probable that the requests accompanying these two gestures frequently have the same communicative significance as the gesture ("take this").

Gestures as a preparatory channel for requests. Most of the gesture categories accompanying mothers' requests are not associated with increased compliance. Gesture and utterance are successful, however, in getting the child to attend to the mother and the objects she is interacting with. It was assumed that the associated gesture might have unambiguous communicative value and that what was communicated might be the same content as the spoken request; but there is no necessity that gesture and request match in communicative intent. Indeed, the requests implicit in mothers' gestures to look at her or an object, to take it, to come to her, may be preparatory to the co-occurring spoken request, rather than a gestural paraphrase. This is a question that it will be important to pursue in analyzing the data further.

Lexical comprehension required for compliance with action request? For comprehension of the action request itself then, the child may have to rely on lexical comprehension, often of action verbs, or his comprehension strategies. He would be expected to fare poorly for most of the period if there was only lexical comprehension to guide him.

Evidence For and Against Proposed Comprehension Strategies in the Interaction Data

To what extent do the comprehension strategies previously proposed actually seem to determine children's responses in interaction with their

Table 11. Distribution of Gestures Accompanying 762 Mothers' Utterances Requesting Action to 48 10 to 21-Month-Olds, Broken Down by Child's Response to the Utterance.[b]

Gesture accompanying Request for action utterance	Percent child response to each gesture type							Percent of total requests for action
	Comply	Other act	Refuse	Looks at object	Looks at mother	Mother acts	Child ignores	
Demonstrate requested action (with object)	13%	6%	0%	10%	3%	67%	1%	26%
Extend object to child	38%	18%	1%	27%	5%	2%	9%	10%
Look at child; no other gesture	21%	22%	1%	19%	10%	2%	24%	10%
Extend hand or arms to child	24%	22%	17%	7%	13%	0%	17%	7%
Hold object up to be seen	15%	15%	2%	43%	4%	2%	17%	6%
Take object from child (to demonstrate action)	2%	9%	0%	14%	0%	67%	7%	6%
Physically maneuver child toward referent	14%	33%	12%	2%	0%	12%	26%	6%
Give object to child	43%	23%	0%	20%	0%	0%	13%	4%
Infrequent gestures[a]	21%	14%	4%	19%	10%	10%	22%	25%
Totals	20%	15%	3%	17%	6%	25%	14%	100%

[a]Sixteen categories occurred less than 4% of the time; pointing to object, touch object, tapping on object, tapping one object against another, placing object in front of child, pointing to an object followed by a new location, touching an object and then a new location, placing object in a new location, demonstrating other action (with object), looking at object with no other gesture, touching child with hand or object, making a noise with object, motioning to child with hand, head shake "no," touching or moving objects unrelated to the request, or no gesture at all.

[b]Excluded are those requests (30% of the complete total) for which the child did not see the mother's gesture. Compliance rates on the scorable excluded requests were 16%.

(Source: Chapman, Klee, and Miller, in preparation.)

mothers? The data on mothers' requests for attention and action made it possible to evaluate some of those proposed strategies in a preliminary way for the 48 children.

Strategies Proposed for the 8- to 12-Month Child

Three strategies were proposed for the 8- to 12-month sensorimotor Stage IV child (Table 3): (1) looking at objects the mother looks at, (2) acting on objects that are noticed, and (3) imitating ongoing actions.

Look at objects the mother looks at? Despite experimental demonstrations that 8- to 12-month-olds can follow the mothers' line of regard (Scaife, as reported in Bruner, 1975), these children almost never were asked to attend to or act on objects without some accompanying gesture in addition to or in place of looking. In the very few cases in which the mother indicated the object to which she was requesting attention simply by looking, the children failed to attend. These mothers did not use looking alone or in combination with referential mention to indicate objects; had they done so, the evidence does not suggest that children would have used looking as a deictic cue to the object.

Imitate ongoing action? If children had imitated the mothers' actions, they would have copied the many gestures with which she accompanied her requests to attend to objects; but action of any kind is infrequent in response to the requests. So, too, are successes in complying when the mother demonstrates the appropriate action; but compliance under those circumstances is infrequent too (13%).

There is little evidence, then, to suggest that immediate imitation of the mother's action plays an important role in bringing about compliance with requests. Nor did our experience in attempting to elicit imitations in the sensorimotor assessment sessions suggest that spontaneous imitations occurred very frequently. Many of the children assessed imitated none of the gestures or vocalizations presented, unless they themselves had begun the sequence (a Stage III level response). One speculates that either motivation to imitate is lacking without a history of game-like interaction—or that there may be a few children who do imitate and many who don't.

Act on objects that you notice? If children had made frequent use of the strategy of acting on any object noticed, then they should have been likely to act on those objects to which the mothers drew their attention. Overwhelmingly, however, they looked at, rather than acted upon, those objects. This was true even, for example, when the object was placed in front of the child (5% acting versus 79% looking).

When asked to act, however, other actions were almost as likely as the requested action; so, too, was simply looking at the object. What triggered the child's acting as opposed to just looking appeared to be the mother's provision of the object. In Table 11, for example, high looking and low action rates accompany mothers' demonstrations, showing of objects and removals of objects. High action and low looking rates accompany their extensions of object to the child, maneuvering of child toward referent, or giving of object to child. This same argument can be extended to explain low rates of action in response to mothers' requests to attend to objects. Recall that the gestures inventoried for mothers' requests for attention to objects indicated that the object was usually in her possession. These results suggest three strategies at work in the present data: *Take objects that are offered* (extended or given); *Act on objects in your possession;* and *Act on objects in the way mentioned.* Whether these strategies are in part developmentally ordered, as the late lexical comprehension of verbs suggests that they should be, is currently being investigated. The 3 strategies proposed for Stage IV did not appear to play a role in the 48 children's behavior, possibly reflecting the fact that all but one child were functioning cognitively at Stages V and VI, rather than at Stage IV levels. Alternatively, the finding may mean that these 3 strategies are never frequent in occurrence.

Strategies Proposed for the 12- to 18-Month-Old

Two of the 3 strategies (Table 3) proposed for the 12- to 18-month-old, sensorimotor Stage V child can be partially evaluated in these data: (1) *Attend to the object mentioned,* and (2) *Do what you usually do in the situation.*

Attend to the object mentioned? As previously pointed out, mothers mentioned the object's name in only 18% of the requests to attend to object and rarely failed to accompany the request with an action on the object (demonstrating, showing, moving, placing in front of child, extending or taking it from the child, touching it). What these children appeared to be doing, then, was to *Look at the object being moved.* Lexical comprehension was infrequently of use and was almost never required to interpret mother's request to attend to objects.

Do what you usually do? The more limited claim that can presently be made for action strategies are the 3 previously offered: *Take objects offered, Act on objects in your possession,* and *Act on the object in the way mentioned.* Whether the first 2 are conventionally associated with routine games or with conventional object uses cannot be assessed on the bases of these preliminary analyses.

Strategies Proposed for the 18- to 24-Month-Old

Acton objects in the way mentioned? Only one of the Stage VI strategies proposed can be evaluated at present: there is evidence that children act on objects in the way mentioned. The particular lexical cues associated with success and failure have yet to be examined.

Summary of Mother and Child Strategies

Children's strategies. In natural interaction with mothers, the children consistently (1) *Looked at objects moved,* (2) *Took objects offered,* (3) *Acted on objects in their possession,* (4) *Acted on objects in the way mentioned* subsequent to mothers' requests. Only the last required lexical comprehension, and its frequency increased with age.

Mother strategies in interaction? The mothers of 10- to 21-month-olds had a rather stable pragmatic style that was. simple but not finely tuned to their children's linguistic skills or compliance rates. Frequency of requests for attention and action changed little with the striking changes in linguistic comprehension skill, sensorimotor level, and of course age, in that child. Requests for attention almost always succeeded, eventually. Requests for action, however, were successful only a quarter of the time.

Mothers' successes in getting children to attend to objects occurred because they drew the children's attention to them nonverbally. The gestures served in an indiscriminate fashion to attract the child's attention to the mother and the objects she was manipulating. In addition, mothers succeeded about a third of the time because they requested attention when they already had it. This appeared to happen not because some mothers were insensitive to their children's behavior, but rather because they wanted the child to notice what they were doing with the object. Mothers requested that children carry out actions that they were already carrying out much less frequently—10% of the time.

Mothers' limited success in getting children to carry out requested actions on objects was attributable to the fact that they did not always make the object easily available to the child. When they did, they were at least likely to get action of some kind.`

Paradox resolved. Thus the paradox posed by the child's limited comprehension skills, on the one hand, and the mother's impression that he understands everything, on the other, has a resolution. There is little evidence in the natural interaction data for. linguistic comprehension skill beyond that suggested by the experimental data; but there is much evidence for the child's responsiveness, from 10 months on, to the combined effects of movement and utterance addressed to him. This responsiveness to the mother's combination of speech and gesture may prove an important early indicator of the developing communication skills of the child.

ACKNOWLEDGMENTS
Preparation of this chapter was supported by a Grant (Project No. 100613) from the Graduate School of the University of Wisconsin. The critical comment and substantive analyses of Dr. Jon F. Miller and Thomas Klee are gratefully acknowledged.

Discussion

Bloom felt that one of the most important points about Chapman's paper was the clear demonstration that comprehension and production of language are not in a symmetrical relation with one another. These were two very different processes, with different requirements and different conditions under which they might occur. They also seemed to develop in different ways. Attempts to tease out the nature of the asymmetry had only just begun. Chapman had described it in the following terms: When a child understands, then by necessity that understanding must occur in relation to what the child already knows, to what is already given. One cannot expect a young child to understand a statement which is unrelated to ongoing events or to previous experience. The obverse of that statement was that in production, children typically talked about relatively new information.

Stern was not clear about this distinction. Was it not true that the novel aspects and the given or usual aspects of a situation were all encoded in the head? How, then, were they really different? Chapman replied that there was a conceptual basis for both in the head. What was different was that children often chose to talk about a different set of the concepts available to them, the ones they ordinarily inferred from others' speech.

Eilers added that in production the child had the support of the situational context. He was not being placed in an arbitrary situation, for example, in relation to pictures in a book. In some sense, she felt intuitively that the experimental comprehension tasks Chapman was describing were not quite fair to the child. Chapman explained that that was exactly what the children's mothers told her. It was for precisely this reason that she had analyzed what children actually did in natural interactions with their mothers.

Tronick raised a theoretical issue at this point. It had been said in relation to cognitive development that a task-related behavior did not provide an explanation at a deeper level with respect to the development of the child. New schemes or structures should be in the mind of the child and should not require environmental support for their demonstration. It seemed to him that Chapman's work provided a non-biologic explanation for the growth of comprehension, if the organism could act in certain ways only in a given context and with environmental support. Tronick offered an example from a quite different area of study. In Bower's demonstrations of infant reaching, he had shown that it was only when the very young infant was provided with a particular kind of support, so that she could maintain a posture which she would be incapable of maintaining without help, that she demonstrated appropriate reaching behaviors. Was the context important in this case or not? Could the infant reach or not? Was there something in the infant's mind that permitted her to reach under these particular conditions? Or was the reaching an artifact of a particular posture?

Returning to the matter of comprehension, it seemed to him that in some ways Chapman had made the task of determining the comprehension of the child more difficult, not less—but that was not a trivial finding. Chapman had demonstrated that there was a mutuality between the structures or functions inherent in the child and the environment in which she was placed. We often tended to forget that relationship. We behaved as if we wanted to set it apart or to polarize it, and to objectify the child.

Chapman agreed that it was important to strip away the natural supporting context in order to find out if, in fact, the child would respond on the basis of lexical cues alone. It was then possible to vary the situation in a number of ways so as to determine what lexical cues were sufficient or necessary. That was not yet the end of the story. Once the investigator knew something about the lexical and syntactic cues that the child was capable of processing at different points of time, she must still go back and ask, what, in fact, was actually happening in natural interaction? What was the child's comprehension in terms of compliance under those conditions? And what additional contextual cues were available to her? Could you determine, by experimental manipulation of those cues, which of them are controlling the child's response? Chapman did not believe that any single study gave an entire picture of the child's comprehension system. It was being built up out of these pieces. Bloom reminded her of Tronick's point that, in the natural situation, the pieces were never presented to the child in isolation but always as a whole. In order to evaluate the parts of the puzzle, it *was* necessary to tease them apart and evaluate them separately; no one disputed that. The point was, could one do that realistically?

Stark suggested that for older children, at least, the context could be quite ambiguous with respect to the support offered and, in such cases, lexical and syntactic cues would become increasingly more important for comprehension. Thus, it was important to assess comprehension in relation to different amounts of environmental support. Chapman agreed.

Wolff asked for clarification; where was comprehension if it was not in the child's head? Stern said that was the essence of his question also. Tronick attempted an answer because he felt that Chapman's study exemplified a common problem that still had not been resolved. It was the basis of the empiricism-nativism controversy. Did the organization of the infant's behavior come entirely from the environment, that is, was nothing in the infant's head except a mirror image, or did the organization come entirely from the infant's maturation and was there no role for the environment except one of priming the system and getting it going? Fischer added one had to have a context in which to carry out behavior, and if that were so, then the context must influence behavior.

Gratch, however, felt that varying context in order to study behavior, for example, comprehension behavior, could be overdone. There was ultimately no limit to the variations that might be introduced experimentally. The result of these was overload. No psychological theory could make sense of the data. Gratch felt that Vygotsky's approach, like Chapman's, was to study a common human behavior like writing or reading, talking or listening, and to analyze in some general way the nature of the tasks involved. But when too many different variables were introduced then one could lose sight of the question of importance. It was important to keep essential human behavior in mind when introducing alternative ways of eliciting that behavior.

Bloom returned to Tronick's question which she, too, thought was an important one. In part, the attempt to assess a child's comprehension was one of finding out what was in the child's head with respect to language. The assumption was that the child's knowledge was in the head. That knowledge had by necessity to interact with context in order that behaviors of production and comprehension might be manifested. The mystery that everyone was trying to unravel had to do with what the child's competencies were that made performance possible. One way in which to get at that question was to strip away the contamination of context and try to sample language in its purest form. What was it that a child could understand, given that the supporting context had been stripped away? The answer might be, as Eilers had suggested, that that was an unreasonable task, because, in fact, language never operated in a vacuum or completely cut off from what happened in the context.

Chapman answered that it was only fair to say that the experiments discussed had always retained certain aspects of the natural context. The situation was one of free play except that there were no gestural complements. Intonation and structural characteristics of natural speech to children were employed. If one found that stripping away gestural support then led to apparent loss of comprehension—that is, a failure to comply—relative to appropriate performance in the natural interaction contexts, one could conclude that gestural components were necessary to compliance.

When one moved beyond the level of determining cues that played a role in the child's compliance, one could draw theoretical inferences about the child's state of linguistic comprehension. At this level, theorists—including the discussants present—often disagreed as to the amount and kind of evidence necessary to support the claim. In Bloom (1974), Ingram (1974), Chapman (1978), and Rees and Shulman (1978) could be found more extensive discussions of what investigators mean by "language comprehension." Clearly, for some, the notion meant "concept derived in a context by any means possible;" while for others, including Chapman, it meant "concept derived from the linguistic input with no additional support of immediate context or knowledge of event probabilities." The debate was not about assigning the word "comprehension" in the first instance, but rather about calling it "language comprehension."

Summary

Language Development in Relation to Cognition

Lois Bloom

Department of Psychology, Teacher's College, Columbia University, New York

The developmental relationship between language and cognition may be formalized in different ways. According to one approach, the two domains develop in parallel because both derive more or less independently from the same structure, that is, the symbolic function. Most of the correlation studies based upon this approach have assumed a one-to-one correspondence between language and cognition. Two domains are regarded as co-extensive, so that progress in one domain is parallel to progress in the other.

An alternative conceptualization of the relationship is a serial one in which the domains of cognition and language are causally related. Thus, language development depends upon cognitive development and advances in cognition must occur before advances in linguistic capabilities appear.

While there is evidence in the literature that lends support to both of these approaches, it is likely that the relationship between cognition and language is neither parallel nor serial but rather interdependent or overlapping. Thus, developments in the two domains may or may not co-occur, but they will always influence and transform one another across the first years of life. In addition, the ways in which they influence one another may vary considerably across this developmental period.

Consideration of such an integration model of the relation between the domains of language and cognition brings us to one of the basic themes of this conference—that of individual variation. It seems to me that the overlapping model I have proposed is better able than other models to account for the kinds of individual variation that we encounter in both cognitive and linguistic development. If both domains are developing together and at the same time influencing one another, then we would predict that variation would be introduced. As children come into contact with objects and persons, and also are exposed to language which mediates in many respects not only between persons, but also between objects and persons, we may expect differences among the behaviors of different children.

For a long time, developmental psychologists did not admit to individual variation in development. In the 1930's and the 1940's, there was a drive to generalize across large numbers of children and to search for the developmental milestones that account for the language development of children in general. Developmental milestones are essentially an account of how children are similar to one another.

Similarly, in more recent times, in linguistic theory as well as in the literature on child language, investigators were concerned with demonstrations of similarity among children. Chomsky (1965), Greenberg (1963), and others emphasized the importance of linguistic universals and, as a consequence, it was assumed that the regularity and the commonality among children learning language were more important, and certainly more relevant to accounts of linguistic universals, than the differences among them. Thus, studies of child language in different cultures were concerned with universals of language learning.

Over the past 10 years, however, studies of child language such as Ingram's and my own have been concerned with individual children on a longitudinal basis. When investigators began to observe individual children they found that there were differences among them as they followed alternative paths to similar goals. This finding immediately raised an important question, namely, what is the nature of the individual differences? Is it that individuals are entirely different from one another, or is it that they fall at different points along a continuum of behaviors? Thus, for example, in our own research and in the research of others as well, some children have been observed to use predominantly pronouns while others combine nouns with verbs in their first two-word utterances. Does this mean that we have two entirely different groups of children? When we examine the children described as being different, it turns out that they are not different from one another in all respects. Every child does not present a totally different picture. Rather, it seems that there are always 2 or 3 parameters on which children differ, but that children also tend to form clusters with respect to these parameters. Thus, investigators are beginning to identify subgroups of children, each subgroup having a different developmental pattern. However, it may be that there is a normal distribution with respect to each of the parameters of interest and that investigators are merely sampling children at different points along a given distribution.

The question, "What is the source of individual variation?" is a critically important one and deserves a great deal of thought. It is critically important not only for understanding development but also for understanding pathology. One of the sources of individual variation is that there is more plasticity in the developing organism than we were formerly willing to acknowledge. The organism is capable biologically and maturationally of operating in different ways and of taking alternative developmental paths. For example, Fraiberg's (1974) blind children were able to arrive at notions of object permanence even though they could not see to locate objects. The plasticity of the individual organism, moreover, tends toward variety in the population as a whole. As a result, different adults are likely to create different environments for their children. Thus, we have a plastic organism that is interacting during the developmental period with environments that differ in specifiable ways. The result, again, is variation. It is almost by definition that the organism will have capacities for alternative developmental courses.

What, then, are these divergent paths? We have been struggling with this question for the last 10 years. But we have uncovered more data about the end-points reached by different children than answers that would explain the variation in the routes by which they achieve them. We need, of course, to define the end-points, but we also need to identify more clearly the alternative paths that are being followed to these end-points. It seems to me that a common assumption that may be leading us astray in this endeavor is that the final end-point, namely, mature language, is the same for all children. I do not believe that that is correct. All adults in our community are speakers of English but among them, for example, even among the speakers at this conference, there is a greater facility in speaking in some adults than in others. In other situations and contexts outside of this conference, different rules of grammar may obtain and different degrees of facility with those rules will certainly be found. Carol Chomsky's data (1969) suggested that certain rules of grammar may never be learned by some speakers. Thus, individual variation among children must be considered within the context of the variation that exists among adult speakers of the language. We do not have a homogeneous group of speakers in adulthood, so that we cannot assume homogeneity with respect to the end-point of linguistic development.

Finally, just as it is misleading to think of the adult target language as a unitary phenomenon, so, too, it may be misleading to think of stages of development of language or of cognition as being homogeneous or consistent across individuals, or even within one individual. As Ingram has pointed out (this volume, Chapter 13) there is an overlap between stages in Piaget's own data. We cannot assume that a child who shows Stage V behaviors cognitively in a given context is the same as another child in Stage V in that same context. We cannot even assume that a Stage V child on one day is equal to that same child on another. It is important to avoid stereotyping, so that we do not reify stages or levels of linguistic or cognitive development at the expense of a proper regard for the differences among individuals. Careful study of these differences may well be essential to the proper understanding of both linguistic and cognitive development.

Bibliography:
Section III

Asch, S.E. (1952) *Social Psychology*. New York: Prentice-Hall.

Ausubel, D.P. (1968) *Educational Psychology: A Cognitive View*. New York: Holt, Rinehart, and Winston.

Bates, E. (1979) *The Emergence of Symbols: Communication and Cognition in Infancy*. New York: Academic Press.

Bates, E., Benigni, L., Bretherton, I., Camaioni, L., and Volterra, V. (1977) Cognition and communication from 9–13 months: A correlational study program on cognitive and perceptual factors in human development. Report No. 12. Institute for the Study of Intellectual Behavior, University of Colorado: Boulder, Colorado (April).

Bates, E., Camaioni, L.., and Volterra, V. (1975) The acquisition of performatives prior to speech. *Merrill Palmer Quarterly* 21:205–226.

Beilin, H. (1971) The development of physical concepts. In T. Mischel (Ed.), *Cognitive Development and Epistemology*. New York: Academic Press.

Beilin, H. (1975) *Studies in the Cognitive Basis of Language Development*. New York: Academic Press.

Benedict, H. (1976) Language comprehension in 10- to 16-month-old infants. Unpublished Ph.D. dissertation, Yale University.

Benedict, H. (1978) Language comprehension in 9–15-month-old children. In R. Campbell and P. Smith (Eds.), *Recent Advances in the Psychology of Language: Language Development and Mother-Child Interaction*. New York: Plenum Press.

Bertenthal, B. and Fisher, K.W. (in press) Toward an understanding of early representation. In Proceedings of the 9th Annual Conference on Piagetian Theory and the Helping Professions. Los Angeles: University of Southern California.

Bertenthal, B. and Fischer, K.W. (1978) The development of self-recognition in the infant. *Developmental Psychology* 14:44–50.

Blasdell, R. and Jensen, P. (1970) Stress and word position as determinants of imitation in first language learners. *Journal of Speech and Hearing Research* 13:193–202.

Bloom, L. (1970) *Language Development: Form and Function in Emerging Grammars*. Cambridge, Mass.: M.I.T. Press.

Bloom, L. (1973) *One Word at a Time: The Use of Single-word Utterances before Syntax*. The Hague: Mouton.

Bloom, L. (1974) Talking, understanding and thinking: Developmental relationship between receptive and expressive language. In R.L. Schiefelbusch and L. Lloyd (Eds.), *Language Perspectives—Acquisition, Retardation and Intervention*. Baltimore: University Park Press.

Bloom, L. (1975) Language development. In F.D. Horowitz (Ed.), *Review of Child Development Research, Volume 4*, Chicago: University of Chicago Press.

Bloom, L. (1976) An integrative perspective on language development. Keynote Address, Eighth Annual Forum on Child Language Research, Stanford University. In *Papers and Reports on Child Language Development*, Department of Linguistics, Stanford University.

Bloom, L., Hood, L., and Lightbown, P. (1974) Imitation in language development: If, when and why. *Cognitive Psychology* 6:380–420.

Bloom, L., Lightbown, P., and Hood, L. (1975) Structure and variation in child language. *Monographs of the Society for Research in Child Development* 40, no. 2. (serial no. 160).

Bloom, L., Miller, P., and Hood, L. (1975) Variation and reduction as aspects of competence in child language. In A. Pick (Ed.), *Minnesota Symposia on Child Psychology, Volume 9*. Minneapolis: The University of Minnesota Press.

Bower, T.G.R. (1974) *Development in Infancy*. San Francisco: Freeman.

Bower, T.G.R. (1977) *A Primer of Infant Development*. San Francisco: Freeman.

Bowerman, M. (1976) Semantic factors in the acquisition of rules for word use and sentence construction. In D.M. Morehead and A.E. Morehead (Eds.), *Normal and Deficient Child Language*. Baltimore: University Park Press.

Braine, M. (1963) The ontogeny of English phrase structure: The first phase. *Language* 39:1–13.

Braine, M.D.S. (1971) On two types of models of the internalization of grammars. In D.I. Slobin (Ed.), *The Ontogenesis of Grammar*. New York: Academic Press.

Braine, M.D.S. (1976) Children's first word combinations. *Monographs of the Society for Research in Child Development* 41 (1, Serial No. 164).

Bremner, G. (1978) Egocentric versus allocentric coding in nine-month-old infants: Factors influencing the choice of code. *Developmental Psychology* 14:346–355.

Bresnan, J. (1978) A realistic transformational grammar. In M. Halle, J. Bresnan, and G. Miller (Eds.), *Linguistic Theory and Psychological Reality*. Cambridge, Mass.: MIT Press.

Bronfenbrenner, U. (1977) Toward an experimental ecology of human development. *American Psychologist* 32:513–531.

Broughton, J. (1978) The cognitive-developmental approach to morality. *Journal of Moral Education* 1:81–96.

Broughton, J. and Zahaykevich, M. (1980) Personality and ideology in ego development. In V. Trinh van Thao and J. Gabel (Eds.), *La Dialectique dans les Sciences Sociales*. Paris: Anthropos.

Broughton, J.M. (in press) Piaget's structural developmental psychology, part II, *Human Development*.

Brown, R. (1958) *Words and Things*. Glencoe, Ill.: Free Press.

Brown, R. (1973) A First Language: *The Early Stages*. Cambridge, Massachusetts: Harvard University Press.

Brown, R. (1979) Cognitive categories. Paper presented at University of Houston Symposium (May 4–5).

Brown, R. and Hanlon, C. (1970) Derivational complexity and order of acquisition in child speech. In J.R. Hayes (Ed.), *Cognition and the Development of Language*. New York: Wiley Press.

Bruner, J. (1971) The growth and structure of skill. In K.J. Connolly (Ed.), *Mechanism of Motor Skill Development*. New York: Academic Press.

Bruner, J. (1975) The ontogenesis of speech acts. *Journal of Child Language* 2:1–19.

Bruner, J. (1978) From communication to language: A psychological perspective. In I. Markova (Ed.), *The Social Context of Language*. New York: Wiley Press.

Bullock, D.H. (1979) Social Coordination and Children's Learning of Property Words. Unpublished doctoral dissertation, Stanford University.

Butterworth, G. (1975) Object identity in infancy: The interaction of spatial location codes in determining search errors. *Child Development* 46:866–870.

Butterworth, G. (1979) Logical competence in infancy: Object percept or object concept? Paper presented to the biennial meeting of the Society for the Research in Child Development, San Francisco (March).

Campbell, D.T. (1973) Ostensive instances and entativity in language learning. In W. Gray and N.D. Rizzo (Eds.), *Unity Through Diversity: A Festschrift for Ludwig von Bertalanffy*. New York: Gordon and Breach.

Campbell, D.T. (1977) Descriptive epistemology: Psychological, sociological, and evolutionary. Preliminary draft of the William James Lectures, Harvard University (Spring).

Carey, S. (1973) Cognitive competence. In K. Connolly and J. Bruner (Eds.), *The Growth of Competence*. London: Academic Press.

Carmichael, L. (1926) The development of behavior in vertebrates experimentally removed from the influence of external stimulation. *Psychological Review* 33:51–58.

Carrow, E. (1968) The development of auditory comprehension of language structure in children. *Journal of Speech and Hearing Disorders* 33:105–108.

Case, R. (1978) Intellectual development from birth to adulthood: a Neo-Piagetian interpretation. In R.S. Sigler (Ed.), *Children's Thinking: What Develops?* Hillsdale, N.J.: Lawrence Erlbaum.

Casati, I. and Lézine, I. (1968) *The Stages of Sensorimotor Intelligence*. Unpublished manuscript, Center of Applied Psychology, Paris. (E.V. Ristow, trans.)

Cazden, C.B. (1968) The acquisition of noun and verb inflections. *Child Development* 39:433–448.

Chapman, R.S. (1978) Comprehension strategies in children. In J.F. Kavanagh and W. Strange (Eds.), *Speech and Language in the Laboratory, School, and Clinic*. Cambridge, Mass.: MIT Press.

Chapman, R.S. (in press) Mother-child interaction in the second year of life: Its role in language development. In R. Schiefelbusch and D. Bricker (Eds.), *Early Language: Acquisition and Intervention*. Baltimore: University Park Press.

Chapman, R.S., Klee, T., and Miller, J.F. (in preparation) The development of pragmatic comprehension skills in 10- to 21-month-olds: Responses to request for attention and action.

Chapman, R.S. and Kohn, L.L. (1978) Comprehension strategies in two- and three-year-olds: Animate agents or probable events? *Journal of Speech and Hearing Research* 21:746–761.

Chapman, R.S., Leavitt, L., Miller, J.F., and Stevenson, M. (in preparation) Mother and child variables as predictors of language functioning in two-and-a-half and three-year-olds.

Chapman, R.S. and Miller, J.F. (1975) Word order in early two- and three-word utterances: Does production precede comprehension? *Journal of Speech and Hearing Research* 18:355–371.

Charlesworth, W.R. (1966) The development of the object concept. Paper read at the American Scientific Association, New York.

Chatelanat, G. and Schoggen, M. (1975) An observation system of assessment of spontaneous infant behavior. Unpublished manuscript, George Peabody College.

Chomsky, C. (1969) *The Acquisition of Syntax in Children from 5 to 10*. Cambridge: MIT Press.

Chomsky, N. (1965) *Aspects of the Theory of Syntax*. Cambridge: MIT Press.

Chomsky, N. (1975) *Reflections on Language*. New York: Pantheon.

Chomsky, N. (1977) *Language and Responsibility*. New York: Pantheon.

Cole, M. and Bruner, J.S. (1971) Cultural differences and inferences about psychological processes. *American Psychologist* 26:867–876.

Corman, H.H. and Escalona, S. (unpublished) *Albert Einstein Scales for Sensorimotor Development*. Albert Einstein College of Medicine, New York, New York.

Corman, H.H. and Escalona, S. (1969) Stages of sensorimotor development: A replication study. *Merrill-Palmer Quarterly* 15:351–361.

Corrigan, R. (1976) The relationship between object permanence and language development: How much and how strong? Paper presented at the Stanford Child Language Research Forum, Stanford University (April).

Corrigan, R. (1977) Patterns of individual communication and cognitive development (Doctoral dissertation, University of Denver, 1976). *Dissertation Abstracts International* 37:5393B.

Corrigan, R. (1978) Language development as related to Stage 6 object permanence development. *Journal of Child Language* 5:173–190.

Corrigan, R. (1979) Cognitive correlates of language: Differential criteria yield differential results. *Child Development* 50:617–631.

Corrigan, R. (in press) The use of repetition to facilitate spontaneous language acquisition. *Journal of Psycholinguistic Research*.

Dasen, P., Inhelder, B., Lavalee, M., and Retschitzki, J. (1978) *Naissance de L'intelligence chez L'enfant Baoule de Cote d'Ivoire*. Berne: Huber.

Davison, A. (1974) Linguistic play and language acquisition. *Papers and Reports on Child Language Development* 8:179–187.

Decarie, Th.G. (1965) *Intelligence and Affectivity in Early Childhood*. New York: International Universities Press. (E.P. Brandt and L.W. Brandt, trans.)

deVilliers, J. and deVilliers, P. (1973) Development of the use of word order in comprehension. *Journal of Psycholinguistic Research* 2:331–342.

Dihoff, R.E. and Chapman, R.S. (1977) First words: Their origins in action. Stanford University: *Papers and Reports on Child Language Development* 13:1–7.

Dore, J. (1974) A pragmatic description of early language development. *Journal of Psycholinguistic Research* 3:343–350.

Dore, J. (1978) Conditions for the acquisition of speech acts. In I. Markova (Ed.), *The Social Context of Language*. New York: Wiley Press.

Dore, J., Franklin, M., Miller, R., and Ramer, A. (1976) Transitional phenomena in early language acquisition. *Journal of Child Language* 3:13–28.

Edwards, D. (1973) Sensorimotor intelligence and semantic relations in early child grammar. *Cognition* 2:395–434.

Eilers, R.E. (1975) Suprasegmental and grammatical control over telegraphic speech in young children. *Journal of Psycholinguistic Research* 4:277–239.

Elkind, D. (1978) *The Child's Reality: Three Developmental Themes*. Hillsdale, N.J.: Lawrence Erlbaum.

Epstein, H.T. (1974a) Phrenoblysis: Special brain and mind growth periods. I. Human brain and skill development. *Developmental Psychobiology* 7:207–216.

Epstein, H.T. (1974b) Phrenoblysis: Special brain and mind growth periods. II. Human mental development. *Developmental Psychobiology* 7:217–224.

Ervin-Tripp, S. (1977) From conversation to syntax. *Papers and Reports on Child Language Development* 13:K1–K21.

Feldman, C.F. and Toulmin, S. (1975) Logic and the theory of mind. *Nebraska Symposium on Motivation* 23:409–476.

Fischer, K.W. (1974) Cognitive development as problem solving: The meaning of decalage in seriation tasks. *Proceedings of the Fifth Annual Conference on Structural Learning*. ONRC Technical Report (June 30).

Fischer, K.W. (1979) Towards a method for assessing continuities and discontinuities in behavioral development. Paper presented at the Fifth Biennial Conference of the International Society for the Study of Behavioral Development, Lund, Sweden (June).

Fischer, K.W. (in press) A theory of cognitive development: The control and construction of hierarchies of skills. *Psychological Review*.

Fischer, K.W. and Lazerson, A. (in press) *Human development*. New York: Worth.

Fischer, K.W. and Roberts, R.J., Jr. (1979) Development of classification skills in preschool children. Manuscript submitted for publication.

Flavell, J.H. (1972) An analysis of cognitive-developmental sequences. *Genetic Psychology Monographs* 86:279–350.

Fraiberg, S. (1974) Blind infants and their mothers: An examination of the sign system. In M. Lewis and L. Rosenblum (Eds.), *The Effect of the Infant on its Caregiver*. New York: Wiley.

Fraser, C., Brown, R., and Bellugi, U. (1963) Control of grammar in imitation, comprehension, and production. *Journal of Verbal Learning and Verbal Behavior* 2:121–135.

Furth, H. (1969) *Piaget and Knowledge*. Englewood Cliffs, N.J.: Prentice Hall.

Gesell, A. and Amatruda, C. (1941) *Developmental Diagnosis: Normal and Abnormal Child Development, Clinical Methods and Practical Applications*. New York: Hoeber.

Gibson, E.J. (1969) *Principles of Perceptual Learning and Development*. New York: Appleton.

Gibson, E.J. (1977) The ecological optics of infancy: The differentiation of invariants given by optical motion. Unpublished Presidential Address, Division 3, American Psychological Association, San Francisco (August 29).

Gibson, J.J. (1979) *The Ecological Approach to Visual Perceptions*. Boston: Houghton-Mifflin.

Goldin-Meadow, S., Seligman, M., and Gelman, R. (1976) Language in the two-year-old. *Cognition* 4:189–202.

Gottlieb, G. (1976) Conception of prenatal development. *Psychological Review* 83:215–234.

Gratch, G. (1964) Response alternation in children: A developmental study of orientations to uncertainty. *Vita Humana* 7:49–60.

Gratch, G., Apple, K.J., Evans, W.F., LeCompte, G.K., and Wright, N.A. (1974) Piaget's Stage IV object concept error: Evidence of forgetting or object conception? *Child Development* 45:71–77.

Gratch, G. and Landers, W.F. (1971) Stage IV of Piaget's theory of object concepts: A longitudinal study. *Child Development* 42:359–372.

Greenberg, J.H. (1963) (Ed.) *Universals of Language*. Cambridge: MIT Press.

Greenfield, P. (1972) Playing peek-a-boo with a four-month-old: A study of the role of speech and nonspeech sounds in the formation of a visual schema. *Journal of Psychology* 82:278–298.

Greenfield, P., Nelson, K., and Saltzman, E. (1972) The development of rulebound strategies for manipulating seriated cups; A parallel between action and grammar. *Cognitive Psychology* 3:291–310.

Greenfield, P. and Smith, J. (1976) *The Structure of Communication in Early Language Development*. New York: Academic Press.

Halle, M., Bresnan, J., and Miller, G. (Eds.) (1978) *Linguistic Theory and Psychological Reality*. Cambridge, Mass.: MIT Press.

Hand, H. (1979) The development of children's understanding of opposites in their behavior: How children develop the capacity to rationalize their niceness and meanness. Paper presented at the Biennial Meeting of the Society for Research in Child Development, San Francisco (March).

Harris, P. (1973) Perseverative errors in search by young infants. *Child Development* 44:28–33.

Harris, P.L. (1975) Development of search and object permanence during infancy. *Psychological Bulletin* 82:332–344.

Hays, W. (1973) *Statistics for the Social Sciences*. New York: Holt, Rinehart, and Winston, Inc.

Hood, L. and Lightbown, P. (1978) What children do when asked to "say what I say." *Allied Health and Behavioral Sciences* 1:195–219.

Horn, J.L. and Donaldson, G. (1976) On the myth of intellectual decline in adulthood. *American Psychologist* 31:701–719.

Howe, C. (1976) The meanings of two-word utterances in the speech of young children. *Journal of Child Language* 3:29–47.

Hunt, J. McV. (1961) *Intelligence and Experience*. New York: Ronald.

Hunter, W.F. (1913) The delayed reaction in animals and children. *Behavioral Monographs* 2:No. 1 (Serial No. 6).

Huttenlocher, J. (1974) The origins of language comprehension. In R.L. Solso (Ed.), *Theories of Cognitive Psychology*. Potomac, MD: Lawrence Erlbaum.

Ingram, D. (1974) Issues in understanding, comprehension and production. Paper presented at the American Speech and Hearing Association Convention. Las Vegas.

Ingram, D. (1975) Language development during the sensorimotor period. Paper presented at the Third International Child Language Symposium, London (September).

Ingram, D. (1978) Sensorimotor intelligence and language development. In A. Lock (Ed.), *Action, Gesture, and Symbol*. London: Academic Press.

Ingram, D. (1979) The psychological reality of grammatical rules in children's language. Paper presented at the University of Washington (February).

Ingram, D. (in press) The transition from early symbols to syntax. In R. Schiefelbusch (Ed.), *Early Language: Acquisition and Intervention*. Baltimore, Md.: University Park Press.

Ingram, D. (1981) *Procedures for the Phonological Analysis of Children's Language*. Baltimore: University Park Press.

Inhelder, B. (1962) In W. Kessen and C. Kuhlman (Eds.), *Thought in the Young Child. Monographs of the Society for Research in Child Development* 27.

Inhelder, B. and Piaget, J. (1964) *The Early Growth of Logic in the Child* (G.A. Lunzer and D. Papert, trans.). New York: Harper & Row. (Originally published, 1959).

Jackson, E., Campos, J.J., and Fischer, K.W. (1978) The question of *décalage* between object permanence and person permanence. *Developmental Psychology* 14:1–10.

Jakobson, R. (1968) *Child Language, Aphasia, and Phonological Universals*. The Hague: Mouton.

Kagan, J. (1979) Overview: Perspectives on human infancy. In J.D. Osofsky (Ed.), *Handbook of Infant Development*. New York: Wiley Press.

Kagan, J., Kearsley, R.B., and Zelazo, P.R. (1978) *Infancy, Its Place in Human Development*. Cambridge, Mass.: Harvard University Press.

Kohlberg, L. (1968) Early education—a cognitive developmental view. *Child Development* 39:1013.

Kohlberg, L. (1969) Stage and sequence. In D. Goslin (Ed.), *Handbook of Socialization*. Chicago: Rand McNally.

Köhler, W. (1959) *The Mentality of Apes*. New York: Vintage.

Larson, V.L. (1974) Comprehension of telegraphic and expanded utterances by mentally retarded and normal children. Unpublished doctoral dissertation, University of Wisconsin-Madison.

Laurendeau, M. and Pinard, A. (1962) *Causal thinking in the child: A genetic and experimental approach.* New York: International Universities Press.

Laurendeau. M. and Pinard, A. (1969) "Stage" in Piaget's cognitive developmental theory. In D. Elkind and J. Flavell (Eds.), *Studies in Cognitive Development.* London: Oxford University Press.

LeCompte, G.K. and Gratch, G. (1972) Violation of a rule as a method of diagnosing infants' level of object concept. *Child Development* 43:385–396.

Leopold, W. (1939) *Speech Development of a Bilingual Child* (4 volumes). Evanston, Ill.: Northwestern University Press.

Lézine, J. (1973) The transition from sensorimotor to earliest symbolic function in early development. *Early Development* 51:221–228.

Lieven, E. (1978) Turn taking and pragmatics: Two issues in early child language. In R. Campbell and P. Smith (Eds.) *Recent Advances in the Psychology of Language.* New York: Plenum Press.

Lucas, T.C. and Uzgiris, I.C. (1977) Spatial factors in the development of the object concept. *Developmental Psychology* 13:492–500.

MacWhinney, B. (1978) The acquisition of morphophonology. *Monographs of the Society for Research in Child Development* 43 (1–2, Serial No. 174).

MacWhinney, B. (in press) Levels of syntactic acquisition. In S. Kuczaj (Ed.), *Language Development: Syntax and Semantics.* Hillsdale, N.J.: Lawrence Erlbaum.

McCall, R., Eichorn, D., and Hogarty, P. (1977) Transitions in early mental development. *Monographs of the Society for Research in Child Development* 42 (3, Serial No. 171).

McNeill, D. (1966) Developmental psycholinguistics. In F. Smith and G. Miller (Eds.), *The Genesis of Language.* Cambridge, Mass.: MIT Press.

McNeill, D. (1978) Speech and thought. In I. Markova (Ed.), *The Social Context of Language.* New York: Wiley Press.

Maratsos, M. and Chalkley, M.A. (1980) The internal language of children's syntax: The ontogenesis and representation of syntactic categories. In K. Nelson (Ed.), *Children's Language Volume II.* New York: Gardner Press.

Marler, P. (1970) A comparative approach to vocal development: Song learning in the white crown sparrow. *Journal Comparative Physiology and Psychology* 71:1–25.

Mead, G.H. (1934) *Mind, Self, and Society.* Chicago: University of Chicago Press.

Mehrabian, A. and Williams, M. (1971) Piagetian measure of cognitive development for children up to age two. *Journal of Psycholinguistic Research* 1:113–124.

Menn, L. and Haselkorn, S. (1977) Now you see it, now you don't: Tracing the development of communicative competence. Unpublished paper, Boston University.

Merton, R. (1973) *The Sociology of Science.* Chicago: University of Chicago Press.

Michotte, A. (1955) Perception and Cognition. *Acta Psychologica* 11:69–91.

Miller, J.F., Chapman, R., and Bedrosian, J. (1978) The relationship between etiology, cognitive development, and communicative performance. *New Zealand Speech Therapist's Journal* (November).

Miller, J.F., Chapman, R.S., Branston, M.E., and Reichle, J. (1980) Language comprehension in sensorimotor Stages V and VI. *Journal of Speech and Hearing Research.*

Mischel, T. (1971) Piaget—Cognitive conflict and the motivation of thought. In T. Mischel (Ed.), *Cognitive Psychology and Epistemology.* New York: Academic Press.

Moore, M.K. (1973) The genesis of object permanence. Unpublished doctoral dissertation. Harvard University.

Neisser, U. (1976) *Cognition and Reality*. San Francisco: Freeman.

Nelson, K. (1973) Structure and strategy in learning to talk. *Monographs of the Society for Research in Child Development* 38 (1–2, Serial No. 149).

Ninio, A. and Bruner, J. (1978) The achievement and antecedents of labeling. *Journal of Child Language* 5:1–16.

Nisbett, R.A. (1969) *Social Change and History*. New York: Oxford University Press.

Overton, W.F. and Reese, H.W. (1973) Models of development: Methodological implications. In J.R. Nesselrode and H.W. Reese (Eds.), *Life Span Developmental Psychology*. New York: Academic Press.

Owings, N. (1972) Internal reliability and item analysis of the Miller-Yoder Test of Grammatical Comprehension. Master's thesis, University of Wisconsin.

Papoušek, H. (1967) Conditioning during early postnatal development. In Y. Brackbill and G.G. Thompson (Eds.), *Behavior in Infancy and Early Childhood*. New York: Free Press.

Pea, R.D. (1978) Early negation: The development from relating internal states to comments on the external world. Paper presented at Third Annual Boston University Conference on Language Development, Boston (September).

Peters, A. (1977) Language learning strategies. *Language* 53:560–573.

Philips, J. (1972) Syntax and vocabulary of mother's speech to young children: Age and sex comparisons. *Child Development* 44:182–185.

Piaget, J. (1951) *Play, Dreams, and Imitation in Childhood*. New York: W.W. Norton and Co., Inc.

Piaget, J. (1941) Le mechanisme du developpement mental et les lois du groupement des operations. *Archives de Psychologie*, Geneve, 28:215–285.

Piaget, J. (1952) *The Origins of Intelligence in Children*. New York: W.W. Norton and Co., Inc.

Piaget, J. (1954) *The Construction of Reality in the Child*. New York: Basic Books.

Piaget, J. (1960) *The Psychology of Intelligence*. Paterson, N.J.: Littlefield Adams.

Piaget, J. (1962) *Play, Dreams, and Imitation*. New York: Norton.

Piaget, J. (1971) *Biology and Knowledge*. Chicago: University of Chicago Press.

Piaget, J. and Grize, J.-B. (1971) *Essai de Logique Operatoire*. Paris: Dunod.

Piaget, J., Grize, J.-B., Szeminska, A., and Vinh Bang. (1968) Epistemologie at psychologie de la fonction. *Etudes d'Epistemologie Genetique* 23.

Piaget, J. and Inhelder, B. (1969) *The Psychology of the Child*. New York: Basic Books.

Polanyi, M. (1964) *Personal Knowledge*. New York: Harper Torchback.

Porges, S.W. (1979) Developmental designs for infancy research. In J.D. Osofsky (Ed.), *Handbook of Infant Development*. New York: Wiley Press.

Premack, D. and Woodruff, G. (1978) Does the chimpanzee have a theory of mind? *The Behavioral and Brain Sciences* 1:515–526.

Ramer, A. (1976) Syntactic styles in emerging grammars. *Journal of Child Language* 3:49–62.

Ramsay, D.S. (1977) Object word spurt, handedness, and object permanence in the infant (Doctoral dissertation, University of Denver, 1977). *Dissertation Abstracts International*.

Ramsay, D.S. and Campos, J.J. (1978) The onset of representation and entry into Stage 6 of object permanence. *Developmental Psychology* 14:79–86.

Rees, N. and Shulman, M. (1978) I don't understand what you mean by comprehension. *Journal of Speech and Hearing Disorders* 43:208–219.

Reich, P. (1976) The early acquisition of word meaning. *Journal of Child Language* 3:117–123.

Rommetveit, R. (1977) Psychology, language, and thought: Three lectures given at Cornell University, November, unpublished manuscript, University of Oslo.

Rosch, R. (1973) On the internal structure of perceptual and semantic categories. In T.E. Moore (Ed.), *Cognitive Development and the Acquisition of Language*. New York: Academic Press.

Rotman, B. (1978) Jean Piaget: *Psychologist of the Real*. Ithaca, New York: Cornell University Press.

Sachs, J. and Truswell, L. (1978) Comprehension of two-word instructions by children in the one-word stage. *Journal of Child Language* 5:17–24.

Savage-Rumbaugh, E.S. (1979) Symbolic communication: Its origins and early development in the chimpanzee. In D. Wolf and H. Gardner (Eds.), *Early Symbolization*. San Francisco: Jossey-Bass.

Savage-Rumbaugh, E.S., Rumbaugh, D.M., and Boysen, S. (1978) Linguistically mediated tool use and exchange by chimpanzees (Pan troglodytes). *The Behavioral and Brain Sciences* 1:539–554.

Schaie, K.W. and Parham, I.A. (1977) Cohort-sequential analyses of adult intellectual development. *Developmental Psychology* 13:649–653.

Schlesinger, I.M. (1971) Production of utterances and language acquisition. In D. Slobin (Ed.), *The Ontogenesis of Grammar*. New York: Academic Press.

Schlesinger, I.M. (1977) The role of cognitive development and linguistic input in language acquisition. *Journal of Child Language* 4:153–169.

Schrier, A.M., Harlow, H.F., and Stollnitz, F. (Eds.) (1965) *Behavior of Nonhuman Primates, Volume 1*. New York: Academic Press.

Scollon, R. (1976) *Conversations with a One-Year-Old*. Honolulu: University Press of Hawaii.

Shatz, M. (1977) The relationship between cognitive processes and the development of communication skills. *Nebraska Symposium on Motivation* 25:1–42.

Shatz, M. (1978) Children's comprehension of their mothers' question-directives. *Journal of Child Language* 5:39–46.

Shatz, M. and Graves, Z. (1976) The role of maternal gesturing in language acquisition: Do actions speak louder than words? Paper presented at Boston University Conference on Language Development (October).

Shipley, E., Smith, C., and Gleitman, L. (1969) A study on the acquisition of language: Free responses to commands. *Language* 45:322–342.

Sinclair, H. (1970) The transition from sensorimotor behavior to symbolic activity. *Interchange* 1:119–129.

Slobin, D.I. and Welch, C.A. (1971) Elicited imitation as a research tool in developmental psycholinguistics. In C.S. Laratelli (Ed.), *Language Training in Early Childhood Education*. Campagne-Urbana, Ill.: University of Illinois Press.

Smith, L.L. (1972) Comprehension performance of oral deaf and normal hearing children at three stages of language development. Unpublished doctoral dissertation, University of Wisconsin-Madison.

Smith, M.E. (1926) An investigation of the development of the sentence and the extent of vocabulary in children. *University of Iowa Studies in Child Welfare* 3:No. 5.

Stark, R.E. (in press) Phonatory development of normal and hearing impaired children. In *Proceedings of the Conference on the Speech of the Hearing Impaired: Research Training and Personnel Preparation*. Washington, D.C.: Alexander Graham Bell Association for the Deaf.

Stone, C.A. and Day, M.C. (in press) Competence and performance models and the characterization of formal operational skills. *Human Development*.

Strohner, H. and Nelson, K. (1974) The young child's development of sentence comprehension: Influence of event probability, nonverbal context, syntactic form, and strategies. *Child Development* 45:567–576.

Sugarman, S. (1979) Product and process in the evaluation of early preschool intelligence. *The Quarterly Newsletter of the Laboratory of Comparative Human Cognition* 1:17–22.

Sugarman-Bell, S. (1978) Some organizational aspects of pre-verbal communication. In I. Markova (Ed.), *The Social Context of Language*. New York: Wiley Press.

Uzgiris, I.C. (1976) Organization of sensorimotor intelligence. In M. Lewis (Ed.), *Origins of Intelligence: Infancy and Early Childhood*. New York: Plenum Press.

Uzgiris, I.C. and Hunt, J. McV. (1975) *Assessment in Infancy: Ordinal Scales of Psychological Development*. Urbana, Ill.: University of Illinois Press.

Vygotsky, L.S. (1962) *Thought and Language*. Cambridge, Mass.: M.I.T. Press.

Vygotsky, L.S. (1978) *Mind in Society: The Development of Higher Psychological Processes*. Cambridge, Mass.: Harvard University Press.

Watson, M.W. (1978) A developmental sequence of social role concepts in preschool children (Doctoral dissertation, University of Denver, 1977). *Dissertation Abstracts International* 38:4546B.

Watson, M.W. and Fischer, K.W. (1977) A developmental sequence of agent use in late infancy. *Child Development* 48:828–835.

Watson, M.W. and Fischer, K.W. (1979a) Development of social roles in preschool children. Manuscript submitted for publication.

Watson, M.W. and Fischer, K.W. (1979b) A relation between play and cognitive development. Manuscript submitted for publication.

Weir, R. (1962) *Language in the Crib*. The Hague: Mouton.

Wertheimer, M. (1959) *Productive Thinking*. New York: Greenwood House.

Wertsch, J.V. (1979) From social interaction to higher psychological process: A clarification and application of Vygotsky's theory. *Human Development* 22:1–22.

Wetstone, H. and Friedlander, B. (1973) The effect of word order on young children's responses to simple questions and commands. *Child Development* 44:734–740.

Wohlwill, J.F. (1970) The age variable in psychological research. *Psychological Review* 77:49–64.

Zachry, W. (1972) The relation of language development to sensorimotor level in second-year infants. Unpublished doctoral dissertation, Memphis State University.

Zachry, W. (1978) Ordinality and interdependence of representation and language development in infancy. *Child Development* 49:681–687.

Zelazo, P.R., Zelazo, N.A., and Koll, S. (1972) "Walking" in the newborn. *Science* 176:314–315.

SECTION IV:
Implications for the Handicapped Child

Introduction

In this section of the text, the implications of current thinking about normal language development for the child who is delayed or disordered in language are considered. First, the effects of biologic (hearing impairment) and sociologic (sociocultural deprivation) differences upon language are described. Secondly, the problems of screening for language impairment early in life are discussed in relation to notions of delay, dissociation and deviancy of language development. Finally, in a summary chapter, delay and deviancy in language development are discussed in relation to the model of content, form, and use of language proposed by Bloom and Lahey (1978). In this chapter, the relationship of the materials in the three previous sections of the text to language impairment is considered. In addition, these materials are summarized in the light of the major themes of the conference on which the text was based; namely, individual differences and continuity or connectedness of development versus discontinuity or disconnectedness. Methodological problems that were discussed during the conference are also reviewed.

Language Development in Handicapped Children: Biosocial Determinants

Janet B. Hardy and Doris W. Welcher

The Department of Pediatrics, The Johns Hopkins University School of Medicine, Baltimore, Maryland

The acquisition of language and of its associated communication skills of reading, writing, and computation is probably the most difficult and complex developmental task confronting an individual. It is a task which is more complex, more difficult, and more critically important in a highly developed technological society than in primitive groups of hunters and gatherers.

The first author brings to this conference a background of pediatrics which includes neonatal and adolescent medicine with special emphasis on the developmental aspects. To this base has been added an overlay of epidemiology and an interest in behavioral and social science. It provides the advantage of a broad perspective, and the obvious limitation of no depth in the language area, an area of critical importance in the long-range development of the individual. The second author is a psychologist. Perhaps this presentation can serve to provide a general frame of reference for the more technical and more specific contributions of other participants.

It is the authors' belief that one should not divorce consideration of language development from consideration of the development of communication skills in general. Language is but one of the outputs of a complex neurosensory mechanism, analogous to a sophisticated computer (Figure 1). It will not be described in any detail, but it is helpful to consider several parallels: (1) The brain, like any good computer, has "input" channels, auditory, visual, and kinesthetic. These are linked by neural pathways with central processing units which, in turn, are linked together and with output channels. An important feature is the capability for monitoring and changing output. (2) The "better" and more complex the quality of the "computer," the better its performance and the wider the range of its output. (3) The

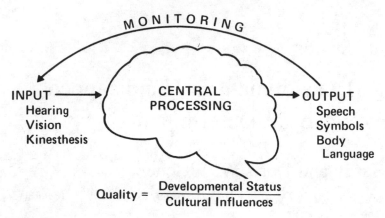

Figure 1.

intactness of the system, that is, its state of repair, is a matter of concern. Obviously, mechanical deficits in one or more areas (in this instance, anatomical, physiological, and/or biochemical) can cause malfunction of the whole system. (4) Another consideration of great importance is the quality of "input" to this communication system. The programming feeds in the raw material with which the central processing units must work; it plays a vital role in language learning. A time-worn saying among computer people states "garbage in-garbage out."

This analogy has been sufficiently belabored. Let us turn now to a superficial examination of the development of the communication system. Figure 2 shows, in schematic fashion, the determinants of an individual's de-

Figure 2.

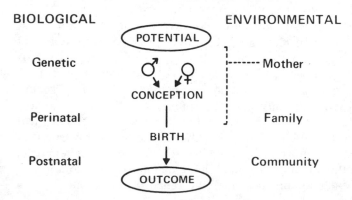

velopment. One must remember that the potential for development, both physical and cognitive, is established at conception, by the union of the genetic material from each parent. As growth and development progress, this potential may be nurtured or it may be reduced by interactions between the developing person and the many adverse environmental factors to which she/he may be exposed. During intrauterine life, the environmental influences are reduced to biological terms and are mediated through the mother. Birth is potentially traumatic, both mechanically and biochemically, and the brain is particularly vulnerable. After birth, both biological and psychosocial environmental influences directly affect the developing child. The biological influences tend to affect the quality and integrity of the communication system. The psychosocial environmental influences tend to affect the quality of the programming and input. The ultimate functional, developmental end result depends upon the balance between positive and negative effects on the child.

Table 1 provides a list of biological influences which may affect development. The reader's attention is directed particularly to infection. Some prenatal viral infections such as rubella may cause mechanical brain damage by the infection and death of vital cells during organogenesis. Infection somewhat later in intrauterine life may lead only to more qualitative types of deficits resulting from the smaller size and number of cells in the brain and other organs resulting from the generalized infectious process (Hardy, 1973).

There is increasing evidence that nutritional factors during fetal and early postnatal life have important developmental implications (Winick, 1969). Adequate maternal nutrition is related to infant birthweight (Weiss and Jackson, 1969). Birthweight correlates with later intellectual development. In our experience, an almost linear relationship exists between an infant's weight at birth and later intellectual functioning measured at 4 and 7 years (Hardy and Mellits, 1976). When birthweight is appropriate for gestational age, the larger the baby at birth, the higher the average IQ score in later life (Figure 3). This pattern pertains to both black and white children.

Let us turn now to consideration of environmental influences on development in general and language in particular. Table 2 summarizes some environmental factors which, in conjunction with genetic and other possible biological hazards, will determine the adequacy of the overall early language development. Because young children tend to be sheltered within the family with limited outside contacts, the quality of their immediate environment is

Table 1. Biological Influences on Child Development.

Genetic	Toxic
Nutritional	Traumatic
Infectious	Neoplastic

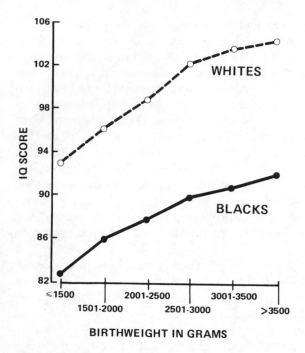

Figure 3. Relationship between birthweight and IQ score at age 7 years (Wechsler Intelligence Scale for Children) for infants born after 36 weeks gestation.

critical. Important is the educational and socio-economic level of the immediate caretakers; remember they provide the language models and the child speaks as he hears. The coping ability and the quality of parenting are other important influences. The quality of the parenting and the parent/child relationship are of paramount importance in the stimulation of communication skills in infants.

The relationship between the informal, instructional role of parents and children's cognitive and academic achievements has been suggested by many studies. Freeberg and Payne (1967), Hess (1970), Deutsch (1973), Leichter

Table 2. Environmental Influences on Child Development.

Family structure and stability
Quality of parenting
Education and information
Coping ability of parents
Resources:
  Socio-economic
  Helping networks
  Community services

(1974), and Rutter (1979) have conducted reviews of this literature from the perspective of early development.

Both Carew (1975) and Clarke-Stewart (1973) carried out longitudinal studies of the relationship between maternal behaviors and early development. They made extensive home observations. Carew studied white middle and working-class children and Clarke-Stewart investigated black and white working-class children. Carew studied children between ages 12 to 35 months, while Clarke-Stewart studied children between the ages of 9 and 18 months.

Carew reports that the amount of early joint reciprocal interaction of mother and child, prior to 30 months, correlated .76 with the child's performance on the Stanford Binet Intelligence Scale at 36 months. Furthermore, the child's solitary play activities prior to 30 months did not contribute to the Stanford Binet scores. This early interaction, which predicted high cognitive performance among some children later in their development, accounted for only a very small percentage of observed time, about 5% for higher IQ children by comparison to 2% for lower IQ children, at 12–15 months (Bayley Scales), and 13% in higher IQ children by comparison to 7% in lower IQ children at 30–33 months. Carew noted that the quality of the solitary play of the higher IQ children was distinctly better, as judged from observations, than that of the lower IQ children by 30–33 months, but not before that age. The early maternal style was described by Carew as participatory, not merely supportive or facilitative. Mothers of higher IQ children literally created the intellectual content of their children's play activities by guiding them, expanding their language skills, and entertaining them in the process.

Clarke-Stewart's observations lend support to the above findings. Observers coded an array of discrete behaviors, rather than predetermined categories of behaviors, as in the Carew study. These data were then factored. A correlation of .67 between the first maternal and child factors, optimal care and infant competence, was found. That is, a mother who was judged warm, contingently responsive, stimulating and enriching, from both visual and verbal perspectives, in relation to the infant, appeared to produce an intellectually competent, secure child as judged from behaviors within and outside of the home environment. The best single predictor of the child's overall competence score was the amount of maternal verbal stimulation, not necessarily, however, the verbalizations involved in direct responses to childhood vocalizations.

Having described in simplistic fashion our concept of the determinants of child development, some illustrative examples will be presented.

Biologically Compromised Children: Language Development

The first set of examples attest to the importance of both the integrity of the communication system and the quality and quantity of the input to that system. These comments are based on clinical observations made during the 8 to 10-year, prospective, longitudinal, and multidisciplinary follow-up of approximately 300 children in the Johns Hopkins Rubella Study. These children were born in the wake of the pandemic of rubella which struck the United States in 1963–1965. They came from a wide range of socio-economic levels. Over 60% had hearing deficits, 29% had serious intellectual deficits, and only 5% had IQ scores of 110 or higher (Hardy, 1971). Many had a variety of other rubella-related problems, including small body size, cardiac defects, and visual handicaps. As the children proceeded through the elementary school years, it was apparent that a high proportion of those with normal intelligence and normal hearing and vision had academic problems consistent with a diagnosis of Minimal Brain Dysfunction (MBD).

Let us consider the language function of some of the children with moderate to severe auditory deficits. Figure 4 shows a typical audiogram. It should be pointed out that these problems were recognized very early, during the first few months in most instances, and remediation was also begun very

Figure 4. Audiogram of a child in the Johns Hopkins Rubella Study.

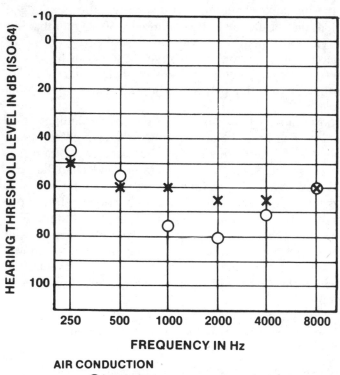

early. Most hearing problems were bilateral and binaural aids were provided in most cases. Parents were urged to stimulate language development, but no outreach services were provided. However, the children were entered early into special preschool programs where training could be provided. When they were of appropriate age, the children were, for the most part, enrolled in special educational programs.

Here then was a group of children who had problems in communication which could be attributed to difficulty in one or more of the following areas: receiving sound signals; transmission of signals along neural pathways; central processing, storage, and retrieval of information; possibly also in the initiation of output and finally in monitoring that output.

How did these handicapped children fare with respect to language development? None had entirely normal development in terms of rate or richness. The outcome appeared to depend on two sets of factors: one, biological, including the nature of the deficit and the basic intellectual capability of the child, and the other, environmental, that is, the quality of the parenting, available resources and the parents' ability to cope.

Comparing children of apparently similar degrees of intellectual ability and similar degrees of hearing handicap, those who learned language had parents who were highly motivated with respect to language stimulation, kept the hearing aids in repair, and obtained special preschool education for their children. Those who did not learn language and who had to depend primarily on signing and gestures were, for the most part, those whose parents did not appreciate the necessity for, or could not provide, the things listed above. Thus, outcome can be influenced by the quality and quantity of input.

Socially Compromised Children: Language Development

The second set of examples comes from two sources. The first source is the Johns Hopkins Child Development Study (JHCDS) (Hardy, 1971a); the second is the experience gained in an ongoing Adolescent Pregnancy Program. This set is concerned with the language development of children of adolescent mothers (that is, mothers of 17 years or below when pregnant). These children, in general, appear to be delayed in language development.

The JHCDS has yielded many years of prospective, longitudinal and multidisciplinary experience in the follow-up of adolescent mothers and their children. Among 4570 pregnancies in the Johns Hopkins Child Development Study, 702 were to adolescent mothers of 17 years and below. The mothers in the study were of lower-middle and lower class backgrounds; 77% were black. However, there was little socio-economic difference between the black and white families and their children attended the same urban schools. No intervention of any sort was provided. The study was observational and directed primarily toward developing an understanding of the etiology of neurological and intellectual handicaps. All children and their families were followed to the age of 8 years. A representative subsample of approximately 10% was followed for 12 years after birth.

As the various outcome categories were examined, it became clear that the children of adolescents were disproportionately represented among those with perinatal and infant mortality, low birthweight, defective and borderline intellectual function, inadequate academic achievement, and school failure. These findings persisted even when race and parity were controlled. Thus, the children of adolescents were found to be at higher risk academically than the children of older mothers (Hardy et al., 1978).

In the current Johns Hopkins Adolescent Program, comprehensive services are provided during the prenatal and delivery periods to some 350 adolescent mothers per year. Approximately one-half of these mother/child pairs are entered into a follow-up program, where comprehensive services are continued for both mother and child for 3 years. In addition to routine health supervision and well-baby care, family planning services and education are emphasized and intensive instruction, both group and individual, in parenting, child care, adolescent and child development, nutrition, safety, etc. is provided. Prior deficits in maternal information and the information gains from the educational program have been documented (Stanley, in press).

The program has attained many of its objectives, for example: (1) improved health for mothers and babies; (2) markedly lower rates of repeated pregnancy (7.5% in one year as compared with 25% nationally and 40% for black adolescents); (3) greatly improved educational attainment, with 85% in school or graduated; and (4) reduced welfare dependency. However, problem areas remain to be resolved.

Psychological screenings of both mother and baby are routine in the program. Some of the results are provided in the following tables and figures. The mothers range in age from about 13 to 18 years, with an average age of about 16 years. Their average grade placement is 9.4, although their actual achievement using the Wide Range Achievement Test (WRAT) is much lower. Figure 5 shows the distribution of the WRAT scores attained by 246 young mothers. It is quite clear that the great majority are performing academically in the lower ranges, that is, below 90. The average reading level is about 6th grade.

Figure 6 shows the distribution of receptive language scores obtained by the mothers using the Peabody Picture Vocabulary Test (Dunn, 1959). Granted that this test has cultural bias, it is used on the basis that middle-class language is current coinage in the important areas of education and employment. People who cannot make full use of middle-class language are very apt to be at a considerable disadvantage regardless of their basic intellectual competence. As can be seen from the depressed scores, these mothers are generally disadvantaged in language.

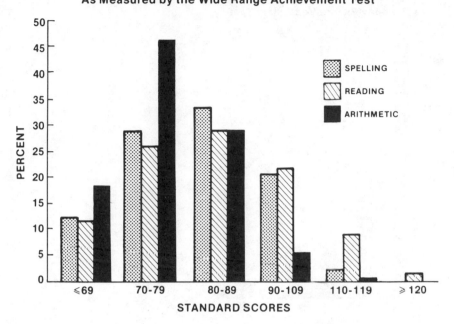

Figure 5.

Table 3 shows the level of self-esteem of the young mothers as measured by the Coopersmith Inventory of Self-Esteem. Contrary to many reports, these mothers do not show generally low levels of self-esteem. The lowest average subscale scores are with respect to their feelings about school. Our goal is to build on the strengths of the young mothers, that is, the strong feeling of self-esteem, in administering the educational program.

These mothers are adolescents, who are often impatient, oriented to the present with difficulty in planning for the future. They have little knowledge of child development or child care and generally have inadequate role models for their own behavior. Without help they are generally poor parents. These young mothers provide the critical, early environmental influences for their children. However, with help, they do an adequate job of parenting.

Let us now turn to the children. They are screened developmentally by a psychologist at 12, 24, and 36 months of age. Development overall is generally quite advanced at 12 months as may be seen in Table 4. Table 5 provides more detail of the infants' performance as compared with a standard normative population. Even at this age, that is, 12 months, language devel-

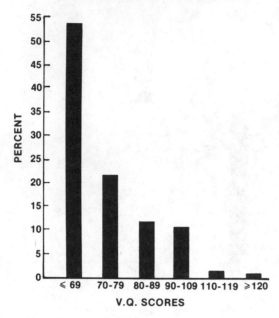

**ADOLESCENT MOTHERS IN
FOLLOW-UP PROGRAM**
Distribution of Receptive Language Scores
as Measured by
The Peabody Picture Vocabulary Test

Figure 6.

Table 3. Adolescent Mothers in Follow-up Program.

Coopersmith Inventory of Self-Esteem (n = 244)			
Total Raw Score	**Classification**	**Number**	**Percent**
84	Above average	43	17.6
59-83	Average	153	62.7
58	Below average	48	19.7

Mean total score: 70.49
Standard deviation: 15.26

Coopersmith Subscales (n = 244)			
	Self	**Home**	**Social**	**School**
---	---	---	---	---
Mean	18.67	5.18	6.63	4.86
SD	8.13	2.06	1.43	1.74

Table 4. Classification of Children of Adolescent Mothers on the One Year Developmental Examination (n = 186).

Classification	Gross Motor		Fine Motor		Adaptive		Language	
	N	%	N	%	N	%	N	%
Average	179	96.24	162	87.10	176	94.62	129	69.35
Suspect					10	5.38	57	30.65
Moderate delay	7	3.76	24	12.90				

opment in terms of vocalizations, imitative behavior and words seems delayed; 31.3% were rated as suspect in this area. By age 2 years (Table 6), the distributionof overall developmental performance has shifted downward, with only 5% achieving above average scores. At age 3 years (Table 7), a still larger proportion is performing in the dull, normal, and borderline ranges.

Table 5. Performance of 12-Month-Old Children of Adolescent Mothers on the Bayley Scales of Mental and Motor Development, 1969 (n = 186).

Item description	Percent passing on each item	Normal age range and point at which 50% passed
Adaptive subscale		6 8 10 12 14 16 18
Object Permanence		
Uncovering and securing cube	100	
Unwrapping the tissue	96	
Imitating		
Pat-a-cake	84	
Bringing hands to midline	93	
Stacking cubes	91	
Places cube in cup	94	
Receptive language subscale		
Response to verbal request	75	
Places cube in cup with verbal request	66	
Gives toy on request	64	
Inhibits on command	72	
Gross motor subscale		
Locomotion		
Walks alone	81	
Walks with support	98	
Pulls to stand	81	
Fine motor subscale		
Preferred hand—neat pincer	87	
Opposite hand	78	

Key: Initial   Mean   Limit
        Age   Age   Age

Table 6. Two-Year Developmental Examination (Binet and Cattell) (n = 56).

Classification	Number	Percent
Above average (≥ 110)	3	5.36
Average (90-109)	37	66.07
Dull normal (80-89)	5	8.93
Borderline (70-79)	1	1.78
Deficit (≤ 69)	0	

(n = 46)[a]
Mean IQ: 98.71
SD: 9.62
[a]10 inadequate examinations; child either sleepy or too tired for adequate testing; 17.8%.

At both ages, 2 and 3 years, language development is on the average delayed, with greater degrees of delay exhibited at 3 years than at 2. This is the age period (1½ to 3½ years) in which, typically, differences in average IQ performance emerge between children of higher and lower socio-economic background (Golden and Birns, 1976). During this age period, in particular, differences favoring higher socio-economic status children and white children become evident.

Mother/child interaction appears to be a critical factor. Many of the adolescent mothers are impatient with their babies. They talk to their children but mainly in terms of demands—"Do this," "No," "Don't do that." They do not give the babies adequate time to answer back verbally, nor do they reinforce language performance. This is not to imply that they are bad mothers overall, but they do not, for the most part, encourage language development and their own impoverished language provides a poor model for the infant's learning. Talking to a baby is often a very novel idea to many of them.

Table 7. Three-Year Developmental Examination (n = 34).

Classification	Number	Percent
Above average (≥ 110)	1	2.94
Average (90-109)	18	52.94
Dull normal (80-89)	7	20.59
Borderline (70-79)	4	11.76
Deficit (≤ 69)	2	5.88
Inadequate	2	5.88

(n = 32)[a]
Mean IQ: 98.71
SD: 9.62
[a]2 inadequate examinations.

It is very rewarding to find that these young mothers, when provided with information, role models, and understanding of development, can change. Once the staff of the program became aware of the problem, they all began to emphasize language stimulation in educational efforts and improvements are being seen. However, clinical observations require documentation and testing; proper controls must be studied.

Studies have been reported which demonstrate that intervention programs can effect positive changes in the verbal and cognitive skills of both mother and child. Bronfenbrenner (1975) and Goodson and Hess (1976) have reviewed evaluations of parent education programs and have concluded that the literature to date suggests that home-based, moderately structured parent programs produced the most striking short and long-term gains for children, using intelligence and achievement test performances as criteria of effectiveness. Goodson and Hess noted that neither curriculum content per se, nor degree of specificity in tutoring the parent were related to these gains. They suggested that such programs may achieve their effect because they positively impact parental attitudes and parent/child interaction. That is, some parents seemed to have a greater sense of control over their own lives and more flexible attitudes towards the child's development; these parents used a more elaborate language style, and were judged to be more involved and responsible in interactions with their children.

Infant development and mother/child interactions, in black infants from lower socio-economic communities whose mothers were enrolled in a center-based parent group program, were studied in the New Orleans Parent/Child Development Center. Evaluation of children began at age 4 months and continued through 36 months. Results from a study of 2 enrollments of mother/child pairs were initially reported (Andrews, et al., 1975).

In both enrollments, the researchers observed differences between program and serial control mothers in an unstructured interaction (waiting room situation) with their infants, prior to any emergent cognitive test differences in the infants. Mothers' behaviors differed across the 2 groups by the time the infants reached 22 months in the first enrollment, but as early as 12 months in the second.

In both enrollments, maternal behaviors in the program and in the serial control groups began to diverge along social and affective dimensions. Observers judged program mothers to be significantly more sensitive, accepting, cooperative, and responsive by the time the child reached 22–24 months. Specific ratings at 15-second intervals of amount of positive interactive maternal behaviors such as giving affection, asking the child questions, general conversation, labeling, and extending, etc. were also significantly greater for program mothers. The results demonstrated that it was not maternal language per se, but the social-affective context of the language and the parents' ability to give the child a chance to respond which differentiated program mothers from controls. Results also suggested that changes in maternal interactive style must precede, or at least parallel, any positive changes in the children.

An additional observation in our own program is that the infants who are enrolled with their mothers in the Parent/Child Centers in the Baltimore Public Schools have far superior language levels at ages 2 and 3 years than those who are not so fortunate. These centers provide child care in the school during school hours. Mothers are shown how to parent their children and language acquisition is stressed for both mother and child.

In conclusion, we would like to advance the following premises: (1) language acquisition may be delayed as the result of both biological and environmental influences (handicaps), acting independently or in concert; (2) biological deficits in communication, in an otherwise competent child, can be, to a large extent, compensated for by appropriate medical care and environmental stimulation from parents and educators; (3) environmental deficits, in terms of inadequate parenting and education, can also be compensated for by appropriate intervention and parent education but, for optimal results, parenting must be adequate from a very early age; (4) adolescent motherhood is often a handicap; (5) adequate parenting and language stimulation is especially important to the language development of the communicatively handicapped infant. It can make the difference between attaining oral communication skills or being able only to sign; and (6) delayed language development in early infancy may be a sufficient handicap to impede cognitive development in general, and to retard academic achievement from the very beginning of the school experience. It is the authors' belief that the "great society" programs did not reach back early enough. Head Start is helpful, but it should begin earlier. Training for more effective, responsible and more stimulating parenthood should be provided for both boys and girls in junior high and high school grades. Parents are the primary teachers of language; it is important that they have the training necessary for this critical task.

Discussion

Lifter was particularly interested in Hardy's thesis that language delay might impede cognitive development in the children of adolescent mothers. She felt it might be an important illustration of the mutual dependence and interaction of language and cognition. Thus, if good language models were provided, cognitive development might be enriched. This notion was based on the premise that, once the child learns something about the language spoken in his environment, he may use it to interact with others and thus learn more about his environment. Hardy replied that the thought processes of children who were not exposed to good language models did appear to be adversely affected. She had given concept formation tests to 4-year-old children from the inner city in the course of the Collaborative Perinatal Project and had observed that poor scores on these tests in otherwise normal children appeared to be related to low language scores.

Chapman suggested that screening measures for assessment of the emotional quality of mother-child interaction and of the level of parenting skill might be as important as language screening measures in identifying children at risk for a communication disorder. Hardy then described a case which dramatically illustrated the need for such assessments. She described a 14-year-old mother who was functioning at a low level in terms of IQ scores and who had poor models of parenting in her own home. Her baby was intact neurologically and appeared to have a normal intellectual potential. The mother sat with the baby on her lap, but turned away from her at all times. She entertained herself at one point by trying to pull out the baby's eyelashes, until restrained from doing so. She was obviously unhappy with the baby. The baby was failing to thrive and was also withdrawn, not interacting socially with anyone. A team of educators and a social worker visited this young mother's home and undertook to teach her how to interact with her baby. In a few months, a satisfactory relationship had been achieved between the mother and baby, and they seemed attached to one another and much happier.

Ingram suggested that, in these studies, two different factors were being confused that should probably be considered separately. First, there were cultural dimensions to be considered. Some years ago it was believed that in other cultures, mothers would relate to their infants just as middle-class Americans did. That wasn't the case at all. Blount (1971) had found in his studies of the Luo culture in Africa that these parents never talked to their children. It was the older siblings who did so. If there was a concern about the child's exposure to language,then one could not identify the practice of one culture as providing a "good" model or that of another as providing a "bad" one. Apparently, if a mother did not talk much to her baby, he would still learn language. We were in danger of imposing our middle-class standards, with their high emphasis upon verbal abilities and intellectual achievement, upon other cultures for whom they were inappropriate. On the other hand, Hardy was also describing another very different set of problems, those stemming from a lack of emotional involvement of a young mother with her child. These problems clearly did require intervention.

Hardy agreed. However, she felt that in the United States, minority group children and children from poverty-stricken homes did have to compete for jobs and for educational opportunities in a society dominated by middle-class English. The only relief which she could see for the resulting inequities and chaotic social situation was by means of imposing middle-class English, at least as a second language, upon all children early.

Ingram pointed out that around the world in many cultures children became bilingual, even trilingual. It appeared to be a natural consequence of exposure to more than one language. We did not think of Southern United States English speakers as having difficulties because they were exposed to standard American English also. Why should minority group children have difficulty learning standard English? There was no explanation at a purely linguistic level. The phenomenon was a paradox.

Chapman agreed that, when language acquisition was studied in a culturally unbiased way in minority groups, for example, in black families, it did look normal. But some of the children in these groups were truly language impaired. Thus, it was important to have appropriate, culturally adjusted measures of language development. Otherwise, it would be impossible to decide whether a minority group child was delayed in acquiring the language modeled in his own home or not. Stark mentioned that such measures were being developed under the auspices of an NIH Contract, *Evaluation of Procedures for Screening Preschool Children for Signs of Impaired Language Development* (Project NS-6-2353 from the National Institute of Neurological Diseases Communicative Disorders and Stroke).

Leavitt then stressed the point that Ingram had raised with respect to cultural values. He thought that there were many reasons, social, political, and economic, why minority group children might fail in school, even if they had a complex and rich, but nonstandard language. These children might appear to have "poor" language, but only in relation to some arbitrary nonlinguistic standard. Such arbitrary standards were difficult to deal with in planning intervention. It was important in intervention programs to include nutrition and health care. No one would quarrel with those provisions, but changing the natural patterns of mother-infant interaction was another matter. Here it was important to exercise great care. Otherwise, there might be unintended harmful effects relating to the disruption of natural behavior, as well as beneficial effects. Hardy agreed that not enough was known about such effects.

Fogel pointed out that, in the case of adolescent mothers, more than a cultural issue was involved. Adolescent mothers were not adult in their attitudes and could not take on adult roles. Perhaps society was adopting a parental role toward these mothers through intervention programs. If so, it might be better to work through the parents of the adolescents.

Hardy pointed out that 51% of the mothers of pregnant adolescents in her program had themselves had their first pregnancy in adolescence. Leavitt said that teen-age pregnancy had become a pathologic phenomenon in our society because social forces made it so. There was no reason why it should necessarily be pathologic. Adolescent pregnancies were considered to be normal in other societies, as Margaret Mead had shown. But in our society the children of adolescent mothers were failing, so clearly for us these pregnancies were a problem.

Fogel objected to the use of the term "pathological." In New Guinea, the whole culture was oriented around adolescent births and the extended family was involved in raising the children. The adolescent mothers in our society did not have the support of an extended family. They were often left to take full responsibility for their children at a time when they were immature and focused upon their own needs. They didn't have a social support system. Hardy said that 20 years ago in Baltimore, they did have the support of an extended family. But now the grandmothers had joined the work force and were not always available to help raise the children of their teen-age daughters. Furthermore, these grandmothers were not about to leave their jobs in order to do so.

Early Language Development:
Clinical Application of the Language and Auditory Milestone Scale

Arnold J. Capute, Frederick B. Palmer,
Bruce K. Shapiro, Renee C. Wachtel, and
Pasquale J. Accardo

The Johns Hopkins Univerity School of Medicine; The John F. Kennedy Institute, Baltimore, Maryland

The subspecialty of Developmental Pediatrics focuses upon the spectrum of developmental disabilities and their detection, diagnosis, and habilitation. This spectrum consists of 3 main diagnostic categories: cerebral palsy, mental retardation, and communicative disorders (central and peripheral). Although much of the developmental pediatricians' efforts are directed toward habilitation, it should be noted that no well-controlled outcome studies conclusively demonstrate a positive effect on development for any habilitation strategy. Such studies are essential and should be a major goal for the 1980's. However, before such studies can be undertaken, effective methods of early detection and diagnosis in the developing infant must be devised. Attention to prelinguistic and language development in infancy should provide the framework for such early assessment of communication.

It is important for the practicing pediatrician and allied health personnel who evaluate children with developmental disabilities to appreciate the special significance of language development.

1. Language is the best predictor of future intellectual endowment. Its assessment should be the basis of cognitive assessment in the infant and young child.
2. Language is the common denominator for the early detection of developmental disabilities. Comparison of language development to progress in other developmental areas can yield important diagnostic information.

Milestone data should be assessed within the framework of two prominent developmental phenomena: deviancy and dissociation. Deviancy refers to the nonsequential appearance of milestones within a developmental field and is valuable as an early indicator of abnormality. Dissociation refers to different rates of progress in separate developmental fields. Observation of dissociation is helpful in establishing the specific diagnosis.

For example, in early infancy, a dissociation between language and problem solving skills with problem solving being significantly better developed, places the infant at high risk for a communicative disorder. This communicative disorder may be a peripheral hearing loss (perhaps of high frequency) requiring careful audiologic assessment for detection. Alternatively, it may be a central communicative disorder and reflect an auditory processing abnormality which later may manifest as a learning disability. This is particularly important as learning disabilities represent the most common developmental disability (as much as 10% of the population). Early appreciation of language abnormalities allows the professional to identify children at high risk for subsequent learning disability.

If the child possesses a language/motor dissociation with motor skills significantly behind, he is at high risk for motor delay and possible cerebral palsy. For example, consider the child at 18 months of age who has a vocabulary of 12 words (Developmental Level [DL], 18 months) and mature jargoning (DL, 18 months) but is not sitting without support (DL, 8 months).

Infant and child development, particularly prelinguistic auditory and language development, is not generally taught in medical schools; in fact, the great majority of pediatric training programs do not focus upon this area. There is an urgent need for pediatricians and other professionals to recognize that auditory and language milestones exist and can readily be obtained from the parents, particularly the mother, if the professional understands and can interpret them. These milestones represent the end product of the integration of a number of prelinguistic and linguistic skills.

A series of milestones has been collated from various sources for use in the language evaluation of handicapped and suspect children at the John F. Kennedy Institute for the habilitation of the handicapped (Capute and Biehl, 1973). These have been recently revised (Capute and Accardo, 1978). The works of Gesell and Amatruda (1941), Cattell (1940), Bayley (1969), Illingworth (1962, 1970), and particularly Sheridan (1968), as well as others (Lillywhite, 1958, 1970; Knobloch, 1966; Mecham, 1971; Northern and Downs, 1974) have been of great help in developing this language assessment tool. As one will note from Table 1, there are language milestones for each month of life for the first 12 months and several for the second year with particular emphasis on the 15th, 18th, 21st, and 24th month.

By one month of age, usually within the first week of life, the alerting response (sound recognition) appears and can be detected by a motor response on the part of the infant (for example, blinking, moving a body part,

Table 1. Linguistic and Auditory Milestones.

Language milestone	Months of age
1. Alerting	1
2. Social smile	1 1/2
3. Cooing	3
4. Orient to voice	4
5. Orient to bell (I)	5
6. "Ah-goo"	5
7. Razzing	5
8. Babbling	6
9. Orient to bell (II)	7
10. "Dada/mama" (inappropriately)	8
11. Gesture	9
12. Orient to bell (III)	10
13. "Dada/mama" (Appropriately)	10
14. One word	11
15. One-step command (with gesture)	12
16. Two words	12
17. Three words	14
18. One-step command (without gestures)	15
19. Four-six words	15
20. Immature jargoning	15
21. Seven-twenty words	18
22. Mature jargoning	18
23. One body part	18
24. Three body parts	21
25. Two-word combinations	21
26. Five body parts	23
27. Fifty words	24
28. Two word sentences (noun/pronoun inappropriately and verb)	24
29. Pronouns (I, me, you, etc., inappropriately)	24

Moro response) or by an increase or decrease in the heart or respiratory rates. The social smile is truly a language milestone and not a social one, since it appears at the 46th month post conceptional week (fourth to sixth week of life) (Bower, 1974) and is not influenced by environmental stimulation. Cooing, the production of long vowels, appears at the third month of life. The orienting response, which is the turning of the head towards mother's voice, comes in at 4 months. In addition, there are 3 other orienting responses elicited by ringing a bell above and to one side of the child's head: the 5-month response (I) in which the infant looks only laterally toward the bell; the 7-month response (II) in which the infant turns in a 90° fashion toward the sound and then up toward the bell; and finally the 9½ to 10-month response (III) in which the infant turns directly toward the bell. Gesture language, "playing pat-a-cake" or "waving bye-bye" is a 9-month response. "Dada" used inappropriately usually appears before "mama" even though a father or father figure is not present in the family. "Dada" and "mama" used appropriately are heard at about 10 months of age with a first word appearing at 11 months. The ability to follow a one-step command accompanied by gesture is seen at 12 months of age and without gesture augmentation at 15 months. At this time, 4 to 6 words are evident, generally coupled with immature jargoning. It is important to explain jargoning in terms understandable to parents. Immature jargoning is an attempt at sentence formation using unintelligible speech-like sounds with proper inflection and cadence. To the parents it may be suggestive of a foreign language. At 18 months, there is a 7 to 20 word vocabulary along with mature jargoning, jargon with an occasional interspersed recognizable word. Recognition of one body part appears at 18 months, 3 body parts at 21 months, and 5 body parts at 23 months. By 21 months of age, a two-word phrase appears. At 2 years of age, a child has at least a 50-word vocabulary and uses two-word sentences. Pronouns (I, me, and you) are used inappropriately at this time.

Table 2 indicates sample questions to ask of the parents. These particular milestones were selected because they could be easily put into question form for parents to answer with a good degree of accuracy. In addition, it was felt that they might be good predictors of language development, once sub-

Table 2. Questions for Obtaining Accurate Parental Reporting of Language Items in Table 1.

1. When did your infant first recognize the presence of sound by blinking, startling, moving any part of the body, etc.?
2. When did your infant smile at you when you talked to him or stroked his face?
3. When did your infant produce long vowel sounds in a musical fashion?
4. When did your infant turn to you when you spoke to him? (Rule out any visual clues.)
6. When did your infant first say "Ah-goo?"
7. When did your infant first give you the "raspberry?" (Demonstrate).
8. When did your infant first babble? (Demonstrate).
10. When did your infant first wave bye-bye or play pat-a-cake?
11. When did your infant first say "dada" and "mama" but inappropriately?
13. When did your infant first begin to use "dada" or "mama" appropriately?
14. When did your infant say his first word other than "dada" and "mama?"
15. When did your infant begin to follow simple commands such as "Give me _____" or "Bring me _____" accompanied by a gesture?
16, 17, 19, 21, 27. How large is your child's vocabulary?
18. When was your infant able to follow simple commands without any accompanying gesture?
20. When did your infant begin to jargon—to run unintelligible "words" together in an attempt to make a "sentence"—or speak as if in a foreign language?
22. When did your child's jargoning begin to include several intelligible words?
23, 24, 25. How many body parts can your child point to when named? Which ones?
26. When did your child start to put two words together? (Demonstrate).
28. When did your child start to combine a noun or pronoun with a verb?
29. When did your child use three pronouns but inappropriately?

jected to clinical studies using the normal and developmentally disabled populations.

Because these milestones were generated from a variety of different populations at different times by different observers, further standardization may be necessary, particularly if patterns of deviancy and dissociation are emphasized rather than just delay in milestone emergence. Such data is being collected on normal and handicapped children at The John F. Kennedy Institute. It is anticipated that a questionnaire will evolve which can easily be answered by parents with some assistance by a professional.

Tables 3, 4, 5, and 6 summarize the findings of our first 86 Bayley-normal, white, middle-class children. Parents were questioned regarding individual milestones at sequential pediatric well child visits. Several points are worthy of mention. First, the individual milestones are occurring in sequential fashion. Second, range of variation of each milestone is rather narrow for this small sample. If this consistent, sequential appearance of milestones persists throughout the entire sample of 400 children, the recording of such data should be a good measure of early language development. When refined, the scale can serve as a tool for the early detection and diagnosis of communicative disorders and mental retardation.

It should also be noted that these milestones are divided into receptive (language understanding) and expressive (language production) skills. Therefore, a receptive/expressive dissociation, as frequently seen in communicative disorders, can be more easily recognized.

In addition to the language milestones presented, the practicing pediatrician and other professionals should become familiar with the articulation milestones (Templin, 1956; Poole, 1934). In the past, since articulation skills do not fully mature until 6 or 7 years of age, speech therapy was not usually initiated until this age was reached. Thus, if a child had a language age of 2 or 3 years, administering formal articulation therapy would not be indicated and could even cause frustration to the child, parents, and therapist. In this case, language stimulation would be more appropriate than speech therapy.

Table 3. Receptive Prelinguistic Milestones (0-12 Months).

Milestone	Mean (Age in months)	Standard deviation (months)
Alerting	1.15[a]	1.54[a]
Orienting (voice)	3.64	1.20
Orienting (bell)	6.08	1.84
One step command (+ gesture)	11.41	1.78
One step command (− gesture)	13.82	2.36

[a]Weeks.

Table 4. Expressive Prelinguistic Milestones (0-12 Months).

Milestone	Mean (Age in months)	Standard deviation (months)
Social smile	4.90[a]	1.90[a]
Cooing	6.14[a]	2.33[a]
Ah-goo	3.29	1.29
Razzing	4.21	1.58
Babbling	5.83	1.54
Gesture	8.45	1.39
Mama/dada (inapp)	8.72	1.77
Dada (app)	11.09	2.98
Mama (app)	11.33	2.76
One word	11.15	2.41

[a]Weeks.

However, by fully appreciating the existence of these articulation milestones, in a child with a language age of 4 to 5 years, speech therapy can be administered in a limited fashion as long as the therapist clearly defines the child's current developmental level. Until further research is performed, these articulation milestones can be used as additional markers for deviant or delayed language development.

Clinically, the pediatrician is able to roughly ascertain the articulation age at which the child is functioning by asking the following question of the parents: "At what age was Johnny understood by the immediate family (father, mother, siblings)?" The majority of children at 2 years of age are understood by extended family members (uncles, aunts, cousin, etc.). These are valuable clues to the clinician although only a rough approximation of articulation ability. Today, we realize that children with language disabilities frequently have both language delay and misarticulations.

Early identification is a necessary prelude to early intervention for developmentally disabled children. The valid assessment of intervention strategies will depend on the accuracy of early diagnostic tools. Careful attention to prelinguistic and language milestones can provide such a tool.

ACKNOWLEDGMENTS
The participation of Harvey P. Katz, M.D. and the staff of the Columbia Medical Plan and Leroy Bernstein, M.D. is gratefully acknowledged. This work was supported in part by research project #MC-R-240392-01-0 and Project #917, Maternal and Child Health Service, U.S. Department of Health and Human Services.

Discussion

Lifter said she realized that pediatricians had to have screening tools that would enable them to make decisions quickly as to the hearing, speech, and language status of young children. She could see that, for such a purpose,

Table 5. Receptive Language Milestones (12-24 Months).

Milestone	Mean (Age in months)	Standard deviation (months)
One step command (+ gesture)	11.41	1.78
One step command (− gesture)	13.82	2.36
Five body parts	16.36	2.44
Eight body parts	18.53	2.71

a list of language milestones might provide a useful index. She thought it was important, however, in arriving at milestones, to make sure that behaviors that occur regularly in all normal children were included, and that behaviors that were subject to marked individual differences were not. Some measures might be more robust than others. If babbling, for example, were to be included, it was important to realize that there was a wide range of variability of babbling in normal children. It might be very easy to misjudge the child based on whether or not he babbled. Similarly, it would be all too easy to misjudge a child based on the onset of first words, where considerable variation had been observed. Instead, it would be more useful to evaluate the child's language in terms of the kinds of early words used, their frequency of use, and persistence over time (see Bloom, Lifter, and Broughton [this volume, Chapter 12] for examples of single-word utterances). A more useful milestone than age of onset of first words might be the marked spurt in vocabulary growth taking place several months after the first words appear. That rapid increase in number of words used by children has been observed by many researchers and is quite clear and unmistakable. Still another measure that is sometimes used by clinicians is that of imitation. But some children imitated a great deal and others not at all (see Bloom, Hood, and Lightbown, (1974), for analyses and discussion of spontaneous versus imi-

Table 6. Expressive Language Milestones (12-24 Months).

Milestone	Mean (Age in months)	Standard deviation (months)
One word	11.15	2.41
Two words	12.34	2.18
Three words	13.03	2.04
4-6 words	14.32	2.40
Immature jargoning	12.15	2.05
Mature jargoning	16.38	3.03
7-20 words	16.44	3.19
Two-word combination	18.87	2.58
50 words	20.41	2.90
Two word sentences (N + V)	20.67	2.62
Three pronouns (I, me you, inapp.)	23.07	1.19

tative speech as well as variation across children in extent of imitation). It would be possible to arrive at a position where children who imitated a lot were regarded, quite erroneously, as being more advanced in language development and more sophisticated than those who did not imitate. It was important to be aware of such normal individual differences. Lifter thought that careful observation of the child might be as useful as the administration of scales, even if the aim were merely to screen for abnormal or delayed language.

In response, Capute emphasized the narrow range of variability in age of attainment of milestones in his cohort. He reiterated that careful and precise questioning of parents could minimize this variability.

Kent suggested that with the accumulating data based on infant vocalization, it might be helpful to prepare a tape recording with examples of vocalizations that were typical of different age levels or stages of development. That tape could be played to the mother who would then be asked if she ever had heard these vocalizations from her own baby. That might be much easier for mothers than responding to verbal descriptions of infant vocal behavior. Some vocal behaviors were harder to describe than others. Stark pointed out that Capute's verbal description of what were probably vocal play sounds, for example, as "Ah-goo" might be confused with cooing by the mother. The parent's response might be more reliable if tape recordings were provided.

Ingram suggested that, instead of establishing milestones related to chronologic age, the pediatrician might find it more useful to look for bizarre vocal or linguistic behaviors that would be pathognomic of a speech or language disorder. He could not think of any unusual behaviors in grammatical development that could be used in this way as warning signs. However, phonology, he believed, did provide such an example, in that the child that was able to make word-initial consonants quite well but who could never produce consonants properly at the end of a word, might be at risk. That kind of difficulty might be an easy thing to look for. A check-list of such unusual behaviors might be as useful in screening for speech and language disorders as a list of milestones. Capute said he thought that the onset of first words before the child used "mama" or "dada" discriminatively in babbling was a useful warning sign. This order of events was out of sequence (deviant) and might be the earliest marker predicting a language disorder. Chapman thought it would be important to document any instances of milestone behaviors which were not observed at all in a given child. Stark suggested, as an example of such an unusual characteristic, the absence of any consonants in early vocalizations. Capute answered that it was important to describe some of the measures being suggested by the participants for detection of language delay in children more clearly for the benefit of the pediatrician. He suggested that the participants should consider publishing their findings in pediatric journals as well as their own discipline's journals.

Aspects of Language Behavior in Infancy and Early Childhood: Summary and Implications

Rachel E. Stark

Department of Neurology, Johns Hopkins University, Baltimore, Maryland

The clinician often seeks to apply information about normal development to the treatment of language disorders in children. The conclusions that may be drawn from the materials assembled in this text may not, at first sight, offer encouragement to this endeavor. The caution was given that, while satisfactory mother-infant interaction may be important for the child's development overall, there are many different styles of interaction. Intervention aimed at "improving" the quality of verbal interaction may violate the cultural norms for the society to which a given mother-child pair belongs, and may thus be misguided. It was stated that, while there are instruments for detecting gross delays in speech production skills and language comprehension in young children, the development of speech perception and speech production is still not well understood. There are, as yet, no reliable procedures for measuring speech perception abilities in infants and young children. Finally, although it has long been assumed that language development in the normal child is closely related to cognitive level, and that a disparity in level of verbal and nonverbal abilities must be therefore indicative of abnormality, the studies presented in the text raised questions about this basic assumption.

A more careful study of the contributions to this text and of the discussions to which they gave rise suggests, however, that they may help us in our attempts to reach a coherent view of normal language development. However incomplete, they may also provide us with fresh insights with respect to manifestations of language disorder in children. In this final chapter, the material from the text will be summarized from these points of view.

First, let us consider the section that deals with questions about language and cognition. For professionals concerned with early language behavior, this topic is, perhaps, the most familiar of those included in the text. In this section, the investigators concerned with cognitive development expressed their dissatisfaction with Piagetian theory and described new attempts to account for cognitive development in the sensorimotor period. Yet at the same time, those concerned with early language development, in examining the relationship between the acquisition of grammar and language comprehension and of cognitive abilities, determined the cognitive abilities on the basis of Piagetian constructs and of strict interpretation of Piagetian theory. It may be instructive to review each of these somewhat contradictory approaches in relation to the other.

Fischer and Corrigan first expressed themselves as unable to reconcile the variability which they observed among children in performance on sensorimotor tasks with the schemes and structures of Piagetian theory (this volume, Chapter 10). Like Bruner (1975), they account for developmental changes by invoking theories of skill development. Skills are more basic than schemes and are specific to a given area of development. Lower level skills may form separate modules and components and may be combined within higher level skills. In this process they may be integrated and transformed as well as conjoined with one another. According to Fischer and Corrigan, different sets of skills are important for language development and for cognitive development. However, the processes of transformation, combination, and integration are essentially the same for both domains, as is the essential nature of the levels attained (sensorimotor, referential, and abstract). In the Fischer-Corrigan account, levels relate to rates of change in skills. There are cyclical changes over time, such that periods of relatively low rates of change (within a level) alternate with periods of relatively high rates (that are associated with achievement of a new level). Thus, there are major statistical shifts in development associated with changes of level. It might be hypothesized that these shifts coincide with periods of accelerated growth within the central nervous system.

Other investigators have, instead, explored new approaches to mental development (Gratch, this volume Chapter 11). Theories of mental development maintain that the child is always, by nature, attempting to solve problems and to form and to test hypotheses about the nature of the phenomena he encounters. Indeed it has been suggested that he will do so merely for the sake of the satisfaction that such activity affords him (Papoušek, 1969). The logical structures in the mind of the developing child may enable him to simplify the tasks at hand by perceptualization of cognitive information. Problems may then be solved with less conscious effort. In language development also, the child appears to form hypotheses about phonological and syntactic rule systems, and to derive these systems unconsciously.

Gratch, like Fischer and Corrigan, dealt with specific abilities but he tried to avoid imposing adult modes of thinking or adult schemes upon the child.

He regards the mind of the child as less orderly than such schemes imply and he emphasizes the ecology of development and the importance of "advance organizers," that is, situations in which the infant or young child shows only some of the aspects of a mature behavior but is responded to by adults as if he had acquired that behavior fully. Thus, a framework is provided within which the learning of that specific behavior is greatly facilitated.

Kagan, on the other hand, stressed the neurological maturation of the organism (see Discussion of Cognitive Development in Relation to Language, this volume). New structures are formed in the mind of the child as maturation takes place, in response to "environmental challenge." He also suggested that it is important, in studying the behavior of young children, not to constrain one's observations by setting up *a priori* constructs, but to be open to new interpretations of data and new constructs. He maintained that the language of children should not be studied in terms of models of adult language.

In the studies of language development, the children's cognitive level was assessed by observation of spontaneous behaviors which were rated according to the Piagetian stages in the sensorimotor period; or in terms of performance on scales deriving from Piaget's account of sensorimotor development. In Ingram's study (Chapter 13) and that of Bloom and her colleagues (Chapter 12), samples of language behavior were recorded for later analysis. In Chapman's (Chapter 14), language comprehension was assessed in a more structured manner. In all 3 studies, the children's verbal behaviors were compared with their level of cognitive functioning. The results from the Bloom, Lifter, and Broughton study are not yet available, but those reported by Ingram suggest that there is considerable variation among normal children with respect to the level of grammatical development achieved in Stages 5 and 6 of the sensorimotor period. Multi-word utterances were found in one child's productions in late Stage 5, but in another's not until late in Stage 6. Chapman's results, like those reported earlier by Miller et al. (1980) indicated that, while cognitive level, as measured by a variety of instruments, was a good predictor of performance on the comprehension tasks, it was not as good a predictor as age. A variety of factors indexed by age, for example, social experience, linguistic input, experience with objects, and maturational level, contributed significantly to the prediction of comprehension, in addition to cognitive level.

Chapman also reported that the mothers of the children in her studies believed that the children understood everything that was said to them. Thus, they grossly overestimated their children's comprehension. By continuing to provide them with input on that basis, and by engaging them in many exchanges, the mothers may have provided the best possible support for the children's growth of comprehension. Thus, the mother's belief that the child understands her, and her skill in contributing to their exchanges may also be factors influencing the child's level of comprehension.

Two of these studies, in common with others that have been criticized on a number of grounds (Corrigan, 1978; Sinclair, 1970), suggest that the form of language and nonverbal cognitive abilities develop somewhat independently of one another. If these findings are confirmed in further studies, they may not, after all, be very surprising. The development of language form may depend upon the ability to process speech input and to generate motor programs for speech output as well as upon a grasp of meaning relations. The child will not be able to map these meaning relations by means of word order or grammatical rules on to sentences, if he has difficulty in recognizing words spoken within sentences or cannot yet name objects or actions. It is further possible that the development of content in language may be constrained to some extent by the child's ability to deal with its form.

It has been suggested that acquisition of the social, communicative uses of language is also related to level of cognitive development (Bates et al., 1977; Halliday, 1973; Dore, 1973). The studies reported in the first section of this volume suggest that the ability to establish these relationships begins to develop very early in life. Infants (from middle-class American and British families at least) participate actively in exchanges with those who care for them. These early exchanges have as their content expressions of affect; the infant's ability to regulate them appears in the first months of life. The early development of facial expressiveness and of the ability to vocalize pleasure as well as discomfort enables the infant to be responsive to the mother and to influence her behavior. The relative maturity of the oculomotor system provides the infant with some degree of control over his gaze behavior. Ultimately the infant learns to use all of these skills to control the mother's behavior to some extent.

The degree of control does suggest that there is a cognitive component to the infant's participation in mother/infant exchanges as well as in later communicative exchanges. So, too, does the infant's reaction to certain discrepancies that may be introduced into the interactive situation. Infants become distressed when they see the mother's nodding, smiling, talking face, but hear a voice apparently emanating from that face that is not the mother's but that of a stranger (Carpenter, 1973). They also become distressed if the speech they hear matches the mother's face, but comes from an unexpected direction, that is, from a speaker to one side when the mother's face is directly in front of them (Aronson and Rosenblum, 1973); and as reported in this volume (Tronick, Chapter 1), if the mother adopts an unnatural "still-face." It should also be noted, however, that infants are not disturbed by certain oddities, for example, the presence of 3 mother images instead of one only (Bower, 1974). In response to unusual liveliness on the part of the mother, they are not distressed but show pleasure and respond to her as they do towards objects, as if she were a marionette.

Successful mother-infant interaction may be extremely important for attachment and for the identification of the infant with the mother. It has also been suggested (Tronick, this volume, Chapter 1; Hardy, this volume, Chapter 15) that the exercise of some degree of control over the regulation of social exchanges may be a necessary precursor to gaining control over inanimate objects and over the environment in general. This position appears to be consistent with that of Bruner (1975), who suggests that the joint regulation of activity in relation to objects is important for the learning of speech acts and possibly of language forms as well. Wolff reminds us, however, that we should be careful not to insist that early mother-infant interaction is a prerequisite to linguistic development (see discussion on Social Development and Communicative Behavior this volume). It has been shown, for example, that infants in other cultures may interact with adults much less, or quite differently, and still show normal cognitive-linguistic abilities as adults (Blount, 1971). The different experiences of social interaction of children in different cultures may lead to different styles of communication but not to differences in language structure or in grammatical development.

Initially, the success of mother-infant exchanges may depend upon the mother's ability to maintain them. She assumes the greater part of the responsibility for interaction in the first weeks of life, commenting upon the behaviors of the infant that are poorly controlled or even reflexive, for example, coughing or sneezing, as though they were produced with communicative intent. By attributing such intent to the infant, the mother may facilitate his development of communication skills. The infant responds to the mother as if he actually understood what she has said to him or as if he actually were greeting her or taking leave of her. Her willingness to credit him with these intentions and her responsiveness to them may help the infant to learn about social uses of language. Similarly, by attributing greater comprehension of language to the young child than he actually possesses, the mother, as we have seen, may facilitate the growth of comprehension.

It seems possible, however, that the ability to establish relationships with people may also depend upon factors other than cognitive level or the mother's skill in communication. These factors may include the temperament and emerging personality of the infant.

Individual Differences

In early studies of language acquisition, the emphasis at first was upon the milestones observed in all normal children, and upon the progressive changes in spontaneous utterances and in comprehension that all children showed in common. More recently the emphasis has shifted. Individual differences among children have been described with respect to language output (Ingram 1974; this volume, Chapter 13; Bloom et al., 1975). Considerable variation in the integration of content, form, and use in expressive language appears to be present in normal children. No attempt has been made thus far to account for this variation. It could be hypothesized that the individual differences in the degree of mastery over the dimensions of language that young children manifest are related primarily to their level of cognitive development, and to the language models to which they are exposed (Hardy, this volume, Chapter 15). The work of Nelson (1973), Ingram (in press), and Dore (1975), however, suggests that there may be differences among children from similar environments and of similar cognitive levels in the strategies they employ in acquiring language. It is possible that these differences are related to level of functioning in component or language-related skills.

This notion derives from the study of a relatively small group of children who are normal-hearing and of normal nonverbal intelligence but who experience a great deal of difficulty in acquiring the forms of language. It has been shown that the difficulties experienced by these children are related to basic auditory rate-processing deficits and/or motor sequencing deficits (Tallal and Piercy, 1973, 1974; Stark and Tallal, 1980, 1981). This relationship is not necessarily a causal one. There may be a continuum with respect to speech motor and auditory perception abilities, such that the normal-hearing child who is language delayed is at the low end on one or other (or both) of these continua. Or there may be qualitative differences among children, such that children with severe language delay be classified quite differently from their peers, that is, as belonging to a different population, characterized by abnormal motor or perceptual abilities.

Thus far, as Rees (1975; 1981) pointed out, auditory perceptual capabilities have not been tested in large groups of children who were not first selected on the basis of their language abilities. It will be important to find out to what extent perception of the most important aspects of the speech signal, and speech motor abilities, are related to measures of receptive and expressive language ability in unselected groups of children.

As yet there are no measures of speech perception nor of speech motor programming (other than screening instruments) that may be used in assessment of individual infants or of preschool children. Approaches to the generation of such measures are reviewed in this text by Kuhl (Chapter 8) and Eilers (Chapter 9) in the area of speech perception, and by Netsell (Chapter 6) who proposes a "speech motor age" for assessment of speech production. Such measures are currently being developed by Stark and Resnick (in preparation).

It is interesting to note that the measures of speech perception that have been developed in experimental work with groups of normal infants make use of responses appropriate to the cognitive level of the subjects. These measures can consequently be used only with infants in a given age range. However, when tasks that are within the cognitive capacity of infants in a given age range are administered, some still respond inconsistently and are less accurate than others (Kuhl, personal communication). These infants appear to be generally less attentive than their peers. It is possible, however, that their inattention is related to some extent to difficulty in discriminating and categorizing the stimuli presented to them. Basic mechanisms such as temporal ordering of stimuli (Hirsh, 1959; Hirsh and Sherrick, 1961; Pisoni, 1977), temporal resolution (Patterson and Green, 1971; Resnick and Feth, 1975), backward masking (Pickett, 1959; Elliott, 1962), and central masking (Danaher, Osberger and Pickett, 1973) might be affected in children who continue to have difficulty in attending to speech. Alternatively, the ability to restructure and reorganize perceptual information may be delayed in some children. Since no model for the development of mechanisms of this kind has been proposed, there has been no attempt to study individual differences in children from this point of view.

The ability of preschool and school-age children to discriminate and identify speech stimuli in more adult-like tasks appears to improve with age (Simon and Fourcin, 1978; Tallal and Stark, in press). However, children of normal intelligence at a given age level still appear to show a great deal of individual variation in their ability to categorize certain speech stimuli. Aspects of the speech signal that may be most difficult for infants and preschool children to process are the reduced length of a syllable to be discriminated when it is embedded in a series of syllables (for example, pataka versus patata), brief duration of vowel formant transitions, and high-frequency noise bands in consonants such as /s/ and /š/.

The procedures that are used to elicit speech production in infants and young children also change with the age of the child. For infants who are not yet speaking, a screening instrument based upon milestones described in the literature has been proposed by Capute et al. (this volume, Chapter 16). Procedures for use with infants that are based upon more recent linguistic and acoustic findings are suggested by Oller (1978) and Stark (1980), and have been applied to developmentally disabled children (Smith and Oller, 1980). Kent and Netsell (this volume, Chapters 5 and 6) emphasize the need to take into account the anatomic and neurophysiologic development of the infant's vocal tract in preparing such instruments. Speech motor skills in preschool and school-age children have also been studied from an acoustic and linguistic point of view (Eguchi and Hirsh, 1969; Smith, 1978). These studies indicate that children show changes with age in timing and sequencing of speech motor gestures, and in the degree of variability in their performance. But when procedures are administered that are within the cognitive capacity of subjects in a given age range, their performance may vary considerably. The performance of normal infants and of young children of the same age may show variation in sequencing and timing: that of the older child, in recall of speech motor gestures.

Differences in auditory processing and sequencing abilities; or differences in the acquisition or sequencing of speech movements, optimal rate of speech movements, or in the ability to recall the motor plan for production of words or multi-word utterances, might well affect the acquisition of the forms of language in children of normal intelligence. Thus, all of these factors potentially affect the integration of content and form in the language of children.

It could also be proposed that differences among children in communicative skill and in learning the uses of language in context are related primarily to differences in level of cognitive functioning, or, alternatively to the kinds of models that have been presented to the child in his immediate family. It is possible that individual differences are also related to the child's own style of interaction. Individual differences in interactive style are present even in infancy and are not all attributable to differences in cognitive functioning. Factors such as temperament and responsiveness of the infant (which may be subject to dynamic processes and therefore more subject to change than perceptual and motor skills) may also influence the infant's skill in mother-infant exchanges. Lack of success in such exchanges, as manifested by withdrawal, resistance to body contact, excessive crying, or limited non-cry vocalization, may be found in potentially normal infants; for example, those whose mothers label them as "difficult" (see Leavitt, Discussion of Early Forms of Language, this volume). In their most extreme forms, lack of responsiveness and of eye contact may be considered pathological, as in the case of autistic infants, in whom abnormality of functioning of the central nervous system may be implicated. But even less severely affected children who are unusually apprehensive in the presence of strange adults or children, or who prefer not to be held or touched, may be excluded from social peer groups as they grow older. Some of them, perhaps those of lower nonverbal intelligence, may be at increased risk for a communicative disorder.

It is not clear at present whether pathological lack of social contact is a separate entity, unrelated to milder disorders, or whether the interactive abilities of infants are normally distributed, so that extreme withdrawal represents one end of a continuum and extreme social responsiveness or manipulativeness, another. It may be, however, that differences along such a continuum affect the development of control over use of language in children of normal intelligence.

In summary, individual differences in the strategies that children employ in learning language may be related to differences in level of component (auditory and speech motor) abilities, or in temperament and style of interaction. Clearly, a child with a basic perceptual or motor deficit must adopt different strategies from the normal child in acquiring language. In the most extreme case, that of the deaf child, sign language may be adopted. The child with an auditory processing deficit might rely more heavily than a normal child on steady state (as opposed to rapidly changing) portions of the speech signal in listening, or upon recognition of single words in comprehension. It is also possible that children functioning in the normal range with respect to perceptual and motor abilities adopt different strategies; these strategies may be determined by the overall pattern of their component perceptual and motor abilities.

The strategies adopted by a given child in language learning may also be determined by his temperament and affectivity. A child who has difficulty in relating to others may learn language more readily from a caregiver who understands his needs and allows him to remain at a sufficient distance. But children who are considered normal may also vary in their ability to respond to others, and may become more expressive or more object-oriented in their approach to language learning according to their style of interaction.

Individual differences in social-interactive aspects of development, and also in perceptual and motor skills subserving language, may have different effects in different developmental stages. Such questions should be considered, however, in relation to the ongoing debate about connectivity versus discontinuity of development. It is generally agreed that there are different stages or levels of development in all domains. These levels or stages may be differentiated from one another by means of certain landmark or milestone behaviors. There is disagreement, however, as to whether there are necessary relations between the structures and the abilities achieved in one stage, and those of succeeding stages.

It does not seem necessary to propose that all skills will show developmental change at the same time. The infant's preoccupation with one skill may preempt practice of another. It has been suggested, for example, that the effort to gain control over balance and posture in walking may demand so much concentration on the part of the infant that vocal development is temporarily inhibited (McCarthy, 1954; Netsell, this volume, Chapter 6). Differences in schedules of skill development may also reflect different schedules of maturation across regions of the cortex or subcortical structures. Such differences are implied in the notion of horizontal décalage invoked by Piaget, who emphasized the differences in performance requirements that are present across developmental domains. Individual differences among children might, at all events, relate to variation in rates of dendritic growth across those areas of the central nervous system that are most important for the development of language.

Continuity Versus Discontinuity

Some investigators believe that, in development, new skills are built upon others that were acquired previously. Other investigators, like Kagan, point out that this hypothesis requires proof and that the burden of proof may rest with its proponents. It is equally possible that new structures may not have prerequisites or necessary antecedents. Their acquisition may, instead, represent true discontinuities in development. Kagan suggests that, although a given behavior may always precede another in development, the first behavior does not necessarily become integrated within the second.

The continuity/discontinuity debate is exemplified in the views of development of vocal behavior and speech production that are expressed in this volume. Oller (1978, 1980) proposes a view consistent with the Fischer-Corrigan skill theory. New components of vocal behavior are added in successive stages of development as the infant's vocalizations become more speech-like. Stark (1980) proposes that there is a progressive reordering and restructuring of components of vocal behavior as it develops. Both views imply that discontinuities of development are more apparent than real. Kent (this volume, Chapter 5) suggests, however, that there are real discontinuities of vocal development which relate to changes in the anatomical structure of the vocal tract. Limitations upon vocal behavior are imposed upon the young infant by reason of the very limited space available within the mouth for maneuvering its movable structures. When the larynx begins to descend and the downward and forward growth of the facial skeleton begins to take place, these limitations are partially removed and new vocal behaviors become possible.

If these anatomical changes alone determined vocal behavior, it might be difficult to defend a theory suggesting that vocal behaviors in the first 3 months of life are incorporated in those of the second. But clearly, as Kent and Netsell both point out, neurophysiologic changes are also involved. Goldstein (1980), in a recent thesis, has suggested that the newborn infant may not make full use of the limited vocal tract available to him in his soundmaking. The rhesus monkey, whose vocal tract resembles that of the newborn infant, shows a similar failure to exploit the vowel space that its vocal tract should make available (Lieberman, 1968).

These findings suggest that neurophysiologic effects upon soundmaking are present from the beginning. These effects may account for many developmental changes in vocalization and may be of greater importance than anatomical changes under certain circumstances. If the vocal behaviors that are present in early infancy persist in humans whose vocal tract shows normal growth, but whose neurophysiological and cognitive development is grossly retarded, then these latter factors might be considered as having greater importance for vocal development than anatomical constraints. It is not yet known, however, to what extent primitive reflexive behaviors of the vocal tract, like those of the extremities and of the head and body as a whole, become integrated within the higher-level reactions and movements of babbling and speech that come under voluntary control; or whether these reflexive behaviors reappear in persons who suffer degenerative diseases of the central nervous system.

It was pointed out by Fogel (Chapter 2) and Capute et al. (Chapter 7) that certain components of primitive reflex behaviors appear to mimic mature motor behaviors. They might be thought of as too-early appearances of the mature behaviors. Reflexive walking is a familiar example (McGraw, 1954; Zelazo and Kolb, 1972). Fogel described the appearance in the first months of life of hand configurations, such as those of finger pointing and finger spreading, which later take on communicative significance in older children and adults. It was suggested by Oller that some of these hand configurations may form the substrate for the basic key gestures of sign language. Yet the infant gestures go unnoticed, even by the most observant of mothers, in an interactive situation. Capute pointed out that the infant's gestures were likely to be expressions of primitive reflex mechanisms. They must come under the control of higher centers and become integrated within other motor programs before they can be executed smoothly and in relation to a variety of arm positions and independently of postural reactions, that is, before they find mature expression (Twitchell, 1965; Trevarthan, 1975). However, the possibility that primitive reflex behaviors may mimic or prefigure adult communicative behavior is of considerable interest. Such phenomena may provide special examples of continuity of development.

It is possible that similar phenomena are present in perceptual development. It has been observed, for example, that although very young infants are capable of demonstrating categorical perception in discrimination test procedures that involve high amplitude sucking responses, preschool children, responding in identification and discrimination decision-making tasks, do not demonstrate clear categorical perception. It appears that identification and discrimination of phonemes in the older child has to be mastered afresh in a new (linguistic) context, even though the child may be making use of lower-level component capabilities in performing these tasks.

Issues of connectivity and discontinuity must be considered in relation to the development of subsystems which *do* become integrated with one another. For example, two separate gestural systems subserving language may be acquired and integrated with one another in the first years of life. One, that is in place very early in life, has to do with expressions of affect and of attitude; it includes posture, facial expression, and the rate and extent of movement with which hand gestures are made. This system also includes the acquisition of a personal space. These aspects of nonverbal communication may be modified early in life but they do not become encoded verbally (Stern, this volume, Chapter 3). They may reveal the speaker's feelings and attitudes to a perceptive listener, even when the speaker attempts to conceal them, but they have the great virtue of being deniable. The second nonverbal system is made up of gestures that convey communicative intention, those of pointing, reaching, grasping, and pushing away. However, this system, as we have seen, is also present in fragmentary form in the first months of life. It develops throughout early infancy and childhood and the communicative intent of component gestures does become encoded verbally. This system also provides the referential aspects of meaning to the user of sign language. The infant learns to respond to these two nonverbal communicative systems as well as to use them himself.

It was also pointed out, in the introduction to Section II, that there may also be two vocal systems subserving language: one, a prosodic system that may be used to mark phrase boundaries and syntactic features, to indicate stress and emphasis and to provide special nuances of meaning, but which also conveys the feelings and attitudes of the speaker (aspects of communication which may be denicd); the other, a phonetic system which primarily serves the referential aspects of language. The two systems appear to become progressively integrated with one another throughout the preschool years. But, as in the case of the gestural systems, the elements of both the more expressive and the more referential vocal system may be present in the first months of life. In this period, it is the expressive, affective vocal system (crying, cooing, laughing) that is responded to by the caregiver; the primitive elements of the phonetic system, which may be manifested as brief and very faint vegetative noises that are present only in the young infant, are not remarked upon by the mother. The prosodic and phonetic systems of language provide the structure for comprehension of language as well as its expression.

There may also be aspects of development that are marked by discontinuity or disconnectedness. The findings obtained thus far with respect to the vocal and nonvocal, verbal and nonverbal, aspects of communication suggest that two major types of processes may underlie both cognitive and language development. One of these process types may be the successive integration, coordination, and transforming of lower level perceptual and motor skills; these skills become increasingly important for the development of language and thought as they come under higher centers of control. The other may be the development of logical, hierarchical rule systems and their generalization to new occasions; it is these systems that put the component perceptual and motor skills to use in the development of thought and language. The two types of processes, the development of component skills and the generation of logical systems, cannot be separated in the behavior of the normal child. It could be, however, that there is a demonstrable connectivity of development with respect to the component skills, but that the development of higher level cognitive systems shows disconnectedness and is marked by discovery and new directions.

It is noteworthy that the component perceptual and motor skills subserving language take a long time to develop in the normal child. It has been suggested that this long period of maturation allows for the progressive development of lower level skills before they must be encumbered with the higher level tasks of associating sound and meaning, and movement and meaning. In fact, as they develop, these component skills probably do become associated with very simple general or expressive meanings in the infant. They are still quite immature, however, at the time when single-words or even multi-word

In addition, as Leavitt points out (see Discussion of the Early Forms of Language, this volume) it is important to take into account the effects of labeling children as having SLD. Parents and teachers all too frequently adopt a didactic approach in speaking to these children and thus do not provide them with supportive or rewarding communicative contexts.

It may be significant, with respect to the debate over etiology of language delay, that children with SLD do not form a homogeneous group (Stark and Tallal, in press). Different patterns of deficit, that is, different profiles of ability in terms of measures of speech articulation and of receptive and expressive language, are found among them. Receptive language, however, may only *appear* to be much better than expressive language. This impression may be obtained because the SLD child, like the younger normal child, relies a great deal on single-word understanding and upon the probability that the words of a sentence are related in ways that he can predict from his knowledge of the relations between ongoing aspects of a situation. Thus, he may score within the normal range on tests that permit him to use these abilities. When these strategies do not serve, for example, when nonredundant instructions are given in the classroom, or when the topic of conversation changes suddenly and the content of an utterance cannot readily be predicted, the SLD child may not have sufficient knowledge of grammatical relations to arrive at the intended meaning. Communication tasks which present nonredundant material, providing little contextual support, however, enable the tester to assess difficulties in the grasp of syntax. When it is measured in this more stringent fashion, the superiority of receptive over expressive language functioning may still be present. That is, the difference is a real one rather than an artifact of the test employed.

These differences, taken together with the asymmetrical relationship between comprehension and expression of language in normal infants, suggest that different processes may be involved in different types of SLD. In other words different patterns of delay or deficit in auditory rate processing and sequencing, in sequencing of volitional oral movements, and in acquiring linguistic rules may be found among SLD children. Recent findings (Stark and Tallal, 1980) do, indeed, suggest that the level of receptive language may be significantly correlated with measures of auditory perception in children with SLD. The measures of auditory perception include those employing speech-like stimuli, that is, of synthesized consonant vowel syllables in which rapidly changing vowel formant transitions provide cues to identification. The results of the Stark-Tallal study also show that auditory processing abilities increase with age in normal and in SLD children. Receptive language and auditory processing may not develop in relation to one another in SLD children. Language comprehension, however, may be related to overall ability in these children as well as to their changing auditory capacities.

utterances are first acquired. Thus, the opportunity remains for them to be progressively modified as they are put to use in the developing cognitive-linguistic rule systems. It may be important for this development that maturation of those areas of the cerebral cortex, usually in the left hemisphere, that have been identified as primary and secondary association areas subserving language are the last to mature, at least with respect to myelination. Certain structures such as the inferior parietal lobule (Chase, 1972) where the mixing of auditory, visual, and somesthetic perceptions is mediated mature much later than others. It may be as a result of this slow development of a variety of component skills, and the slow maturation of primary and secondary association areas of the cortex, that a greater degree of complexity of communication is possible for the human than for the non-human primate.

Methodological Considerations

Methodological problems were discussed in all 3 sections of the text that dealt with normal development. In the first section, the need for a hierarchical model of mother/infant interaction was stressed (see Wolff, Discussion of Social Development and Communication, this volume). It was strongly suggested that statistical approaches to the data should be based upon such a model rather than upon Markovian chain processes. It might be difficult to propose a hierarchical model, however. Except in feeding, the goals of mother and infant may not be specifiable in the earliest interactions, and they may vary from one mother infant dyad to another. As a result, it is difficult to suggest the effects that reduced or unsatisfactory interactions might have upon later language acquisition. It is possible, however, to describe abnormal responses of the infant in an interactive situation. Information of this kind may have prognostic value.

In Section II, the methodological problems involved in assessing speech perception in infants were given most attention. Experimental procedures and statistical design both present problems. Transfer of learning (Kuhl, this volume, Chapter 8) and up-down staircase (Aslin et al., 1979) procedures and pseudorandom presentation of control and experimental trials (Eilers, this volume, Chapter 9) are all presently in use and may yield differing results. Statistical problems are dealt with by Eilers, and, elsewhere, by Aslin and Pisoni (1980). Perhaps because there is still preoccupation with these problems, no model for the development of speech perception abilities in children has, as yet, been proposed. Methodological problems in studies of speech production in infants have received less attention. They have to do with the sampling of vocalizations and the manner in which vocalizations are described (Oller, this volume, Chapter 4; Stark, 1980).

In Section III, the methodological problems discussed had to do with the relative merits of spontaneous versus structured assessments of cognitive functioning. The value of assimilating Piagetian constructs to a psychometric tradition was questioned. The effects of apparently minor changes in the testing situation upon the performance of the child were shown to be important and sometimes surprising. Such problems have increasingly motivated psychologists to search for a new theory of cognitive development. The studies of language development that were reported, although adhering to a Piagetian point of view, were all concerned with amassing data that describes the performance of children in considerable detail, and without adherence to *a priori* constructs.

Implications for the Handicapped Child

It was suggested by Capute et al. (this volume, Chapter 16) that language is the best single predictor of future intelligence in young children. It is frequently found that children delayed in language are delayed in cognitive development also, and that those accelerated in language are accelerated in cognitive development. Obvious exceptions, as far as spoken language is concerned, are found in the intelligent child with severe hearing loss or severe neuromuscular problems involving the speech mechanism. But in children who do not have peripheral disorders of hearing or of movement, marked discrepancies in ability in the domains of language and cognition may still be found. Capute et al. refer to this phenomenon as one of dissociation. Where nonverbal intelligence is normal and language is not, others have preferred the term "language delay" because the language forms used by the affected children are most frequently like those normally found in much younger children (Morehead and Ingram, 1973; but see Menyuk [1964] for a different view, namely, that the utterances of these children are qualitatively different from those of normal children). Language abilities may also be superior to nonverbal abilities, but this discrepancy does not receive attention from educators or clinicians and is not considered pathological.

In addition, in children who are low in both verbal and nonverbal functioning, a number of unusual types of language disorder may be found. These disorders are characterized by severe mismatch in level of performance across both verbal and nonverbal tests. The language of these children is not like that of much younger normal children. Clinicians and investigators alike would agree that they are deviant in their language development. The observation that there is a nonsequential appearance of language milestones in these children (Capute et al., this volume, Chapter 16) is an interesting and insightful one, although traditionally such a statement has not been used in definitions of deviant language in children.

Specific Language Deficit

Specific language delay or deficit (SLD) in children may be characterized by delay in acquisition of language form. In children with specific language

delay, nonverbal intelligence on standardized testing is within the normal range but performance on language tests is not. Hearing is normal and there is no primary emotional or behavioral disorder. Benton (1964) suggests that these children have neurologic deficits or lesions. In our experience (Stark and Tallal, in press), however, most children presenting with language delay in childhood do not show classical "hard signs" suggestive of neurologic impairment and do not have a medical history suggestive of neurologic lesion. (Those children who do have such a history are likely to present deviant rather than delayed language.) The SLD children often show reduced spoken language, a reluctance to speak, and a lack of interest in listening. Their employment of language form in expressive output may be more stereotypic and less creative than that of younger children. Similarily, in comprehension, they may have difficulty in understanding metaphors or analogies unless these are expressed in simple forms. These differences also appear to depe... upon a primary delay in the acquisition of the form of language.

Children with specific language deficits may show a preference f... ities that do not involve language. The topics that interest them... topics that interest other children of their chronologic age. Th... satisfactory relations with their peers, especially if they excel... may also, however, experience frustration and become emo... over their difficulty in communicating verbally, in speak... ing, especially if they are not placed in a supportive ed... The language disorder, however, is not primarily c... uses of language; social problems arise because o... the level of spoken language that is possible... expectations and demands that teachers and... These demands are based upon the chil... obvious nonverbal abilities. In the mos... language may enable them to commu...

Among those working with spec... there is considerable debate wit... held by some that SLD reflect... (Morehead and Ingram, 197... primarily to auditory rate... senson, 1972; Tallal an... mately, with the natur... of that which is tak... one hand, develo... also the contribu... of representation an... and rule derivation are c... level skills are thought of a... kinds of abilities in relation to

Stark and Tallal (1980) have, in addition, shown that the level of expressive language in SLD children may be significantly related to persisting speech articulation deficits and possibly to deficits in rate and in sequencing of movements of the articulators also. Additional studies suggest that naming difficulties are likely to be present in children with expressive language deficits; and that factors associated with nonverbal intelligence are quite highly correlated with expressive language in SLD children also.

In summary, there are SLD children who have deficits in receptive *and* expressive language, and there are SLD children in whom deficits in expressive language only are present. These language deficits vary in degree or severity. Grammatical development may be delayed because of more primary deficits in lower level speech processing; alternatively, difficulty or delay in organizing auditory input and/or speech motor output within a rule-governed system may give rise to deficits in phonologic and/or syntactic development. The terms "lower level" and "higher level" are used only in relation to a psychological description of language, however, and not to specific cortical or subcortical structures that might be involved.

Deviant Language

Children with deviant language do not simply show a delay in acquisition of the form of language but present instead less well understood deficits and sometimes bizarre language behaviors. A few children with deviant language have normal or near-normal nonverbal intelligence. These children may have a history of head trauma or other neurologic lesion in infancy or early childhood. They may properly be referred to as developmentally dysphasic (Benton, 1964). Some of them may show symptoms of "word deafness;" others may show disordered syntax in their output, producing long strings of content words and few function words. As a result many of their utterances are ambiguous, even for those who know the situational context in which they are produced.

The term deviant is used to refer to gross mismatches in the level of a child's ability to manage the form, use *and* content of language, and/or to the inability to integrate the three dimensions of language. In addition, receptive and expressive language abilities may be poorly matched in children with deviant language, with expressive abilities sometimes being apparently much superior to receptive abilities.

Children with deviant language form an even more heterogeneous group than those who have SLD. Many are found to be functioning below the normal range in nonverbal intelligence as well as in verbal intelligence on the WPPSI or WISC-R Scales. Children with deviant language may also show an uneven profile of subtest scores on the Performance Scale of the WPPSI or WISC-R. They may also present marked differences in level of performance on tests of component, perceptual, and motor skills, as well as across the domains of language and cognition.

Other children with deviant language development appear to have auditory and speech motor abilities that are superior to their nonverbal cognitive functioning; still others have verbal and nonverbal cognitive abilities that are superior to their ability to interact with people or to communicate. Many of these children are highly imitative. They may be able to produce a limited set of long and fairly complex sentences without error, even though they do not understand the sentences. In this, they are not like normal children, who will rephrase a sentence in an imitation task in such a way that the new version matches their own grammatical ability and reflects their comprehension of the sentence (Menyuk, 1969). Children with deviant language may produce these stock sentences in appropriate situational contexts and may even be capable of manipulating aspects of syntax within them. They may, for example, have control over the use of pronouns or verb forms in the limited set of utterances they produce. At the same time it may be observed that the content of their output is very different from that of a normal child at the same level of cognitive development.

A 12-year-old boy exemplifying this type of deviant language produced sentences in appropriate situational contexts and with minimal prompting, such as, "May I have the pinball machine (or other toy) please?" This child could not, however, encode simple object relations in his spontaneous utterances. His comprehension of language was estimated to be at the two-year level. Another child, an 8-year-old, showed a less severe disorder of this kind. He could name colors and shapes (including trapezoid and rhomboid shapes) accurately but he could not encode agent-action meaning relations, or locative or possessive relations. An example of this child's spontaneous speech, produced as a monologue while looking at a wall decoration, went as follows: "That's orange and gold and brown. Very good J. You said that correctly. That's a Thanksgiving turkey."

These children, and others with similar patterns of disability, show very little spontaneous, communicative use of language. Their comprehension of language may be much lower than would be expected from the grammatical level of the sentences they learn to produce by imitation. The forms of language which such children are capable of using in structured situations, forms that are learned by rote and used semi-appropriately, create a false impression of their intellectual interests and abilities. This impression may be confirmed by the presence of "splinter" skills, such as those of visual form matching. Teachers, therapists, and even parents may exacerbate the problems of these children by continuing to demand well-formed utterances from them, at a level of linguistic skill that is poorly matched with their overall cognitive skills. These adults may never engage the affected children in play activities that are appropriate to their level of cognitive functioning and their language comprehension. When such activities are initiated, these utterances are first acquired. Thus, the opportunity remains for them to be progressively modified as they are put to use in the developing cognitive-linguistic rule systems. It may be important for this development that maturation of those areas of the cerebral cortex, usually in the left hemisphere, that have been identified as primary and secondary association areas subserving language are the last to mature, at least with respect to myelination. Certain structures such as the inferior parietal lobule (Chase, 1972) where the mixing of auditory, visual, and somesthetic perceptions is mediated mature much later than others. It may be as a result of this slow development of a variety of component skills, and the slow maturation of primary and secondary association areas of the cortex, that a greater degree of complexity of communication is possible for the human than for the non-human primate.

Methodological Considerations

Methodological problems were discussed in all 3 sections of the text that dealt with normal development. In the first section, the need for a hierarchical model of mother/infant interaction was stressed (see Wolff, Discussion of Social Development and Communication, this volume). It was strongly suggested that statistical approaches to the data should be based upon such a model rather than upon Markovian chain processes. It might be difficult to propose a hierarchical model, however. Except in feeding, the goals of mother and infant may not be specifiable in the earliest interactions, and they may vary from one mother infant dyad to another. As a result, it is difficult to suggest the effects that reduced or unsatisfactory interactions might have upon later language acquisition. It is possible, however, to describe abnormal responses of the infant in an interactive situation. Information of this kind may have prognostic value.

In Section II, the methodological problems involved in assessing speech perception in infants were given most attention. Experimental procedures and statistical design both present problems. Transfer of learning (Kuhl, this volume, Chapter 8) and up-down staircase (Aslin et al., 1979) procedures and pseudorandom presentation of control and experimental trials (Eilers, this volume, Chapter 9) are all presently in use and may yield differing results. Statistical problems are dealt with by Eilers, and, elsewhere, by Aslin and Pisoni (1980). Perhaps because there is still preoccupation with these problems, no model for the development of speech perception abilities in children has, as yet, been proposed. Methodological problems in studies of speech production in infants have received less attention. They have to do with the sampling of vocalizations and the manner in which vocalizations are described (Oller, this volume, Chapter 4; Stark, 1980).

In Section III, the methodological problems discussed had to do with the relative merits of spontaneous versus structured assessments of cognitive functioning. The value of assimilating Piagetian constructs to a psychometric tradition was questioned. The effects of apparently minor changes in the testing situation upon the performance of the child were shown to be important and sometimes surprising. Such problems have increasingly motivated psychologists to search for a new theory of cognitive development. The studies of language development that were reported, although adhering to a Piagetian point of view, were all concerned with amassing data that describes the performance of children in considerable detail, and without adherence to *a priori* constructs.

Implications for the Handicapped Child

It was suggested by Capute et al. (this volume, Chapter 16) that language is the best single predictor of future intelligence in young children. It is frequently found that children delayed in language are delayed in cognitive development also, and that those accelerated in language are accelerated in cognitive development. Obvious exceptions, as far as spoken language is concerned, are found in the intelligent child with severe hearing loss or severe neuromuscular problems involving the speech mechanism. But in children who do not have peripheral disorders of hearing or of movement, marked discrepancies in ability in the domains of language and cognition may still be found. Capute et al. refer to this phenomenon as one of dissociation. Where nonverbal intelligence is normal and language is not, others have preferred the term "language delay" because the language forms used by the affected children are most frequently like those normally found in much younger children (Morehead and Ingram, 1973; but see Menyuk [1964] for a different view, namely, that the utterances of these children are qualitatively different from those of normal children). Language abilities may also be superior to nonverbal abilities, but this discrepancy does not receive attention from educators or clinicians and is not considered pathological.

In addition, in children who are low in both verbal and nonverbal functioning, a number of unusual types of language disorder may be found. These disorders are characterized by severe mismatch in level of performance across both verbal and nonverbal tests. The language of these children is not like that of much younger normal children. Clinicians and investigators alike would agree that they are deviant in their language development. The observation that there is a nonsequential appearance of language milestones in these children (Capute et al., this volume, Chapter 16) is an interesting and insightful one, although traditionally such a statement has not been used in definitions of deviant language in children.

Specific Language Deficit

Specific language delay or deficit (SLD) in children may be characterized by delay in acquisition of language form. In children with specific language delay, nonverbal intelligence on standardized testing is within the normal range but performance on language tests is not. Hearing is normal and there is no primary emotional or behavioral disorder. Benton (1964) suggests that these children have neurologic deficits or lesions. In our experience (Stark and Tallal, in press), however, most children presenting with language delay in childhood do not show classical "hard signs" suggestive of neurologic impairment and do not have a medical history suggestive of neurologic lesion. (Those children who do have such a history are likely to present deviant rather than delayed language.) The SLD children often show reduced spoken language, a reluctance to speak, and a lack of interest in listening. Their employment of language form in expressive output may be more stereotypic and less creative than that of younger children. Similarily, in comprehension, they may have difficulty in understanding metaphors or analogies unless these are expressed in simple forms. These differences also appear to depend upon a primary delay in the acquisition of the form of language.

Children with specific language deficits may show a preference for activities that do not involve language. The topics that interest them will be the topics that interest other children of their chronologic age. They may have satisfactory relations with their peers, especially if they excel in sports. They may also, however, experience frustration and become emotionally disturbed over their difficulty in communicating verbally, in speaking and understanding, especially if they are not placed in a supportive educational environment. The language disorder, however, is not primarily one of learning the social uses of language; social problems arise because of the discrepancy between the level of spoken language that is possible for these children and the expectations and demands that teachers and parents may place upon them. These demands are based upon the children's chronologic age and their obvious nonverbal abilities. In the most severe cases, the teaching of sign language may enable them to communicate effectively.

Among those working with specific language deficit (SLD) in children, there is considerable debate with respect to the underlying etiology. It is held by some that SLD reflects a subtle cognitive, representational deficit (Morehead and Ingram, 1973; Rees, 1975), and by others that it relates primarily to auditory rate processing and auditory sequencing deficits (Eisenson, 1972; Tallal and Piercy, 1973, 1974). This debate has to do, ultimately, with the nature of language development in children. It is reminiscent of that which is taking place in the area of cognitive development. On the one hand, development of, and deficit in, component skills is stressed and also the contribution of these skills, or lack of it, to higher level processes of representation and abstraction; on the other hand, symbolic processing and rule derivation are considered to be primary and deficits found in lower level skills are thought of as incidental. In fact, it is necessary to study both kinds of abilities in relation to SLD in children.

In addition, as Leavitt points out (see Discussion of the Early Forms of Language, this volume) it is important to take into account the effects of labeling children as having SLD. Parents and teachers all too frequently adopt a didactic approach in speaking to these children and thus do not provide them with supportive or rewarding communicative contexts.

It may be significant, with respect to the debate over etiology of language delay, that children with SLD do not form a homogeneous group (Stark and Tallal, in press). Different patterns of deficit, that is, different profiles of ability in terms of measures of speech articulation and of receptive and expressive language, are found among them. Receptive language, however, may only *appear* to be much better than expressive language. This impression may be obtained because the SLD child, like the younger normal child, relies a great deal on single-word understanding and upon the probability that the words of a sentence are related in ways that he can predict from his knowledge of the relations between ongoing aspects of a situation. Thus, he may score within the normal range on tests that permit him to use these abilities. When these strategies do not serve, for example, when nonredundant instructions are given in the classroom, or when the topic of conversation changes suddenly and the content of an utterance cannot readily be predicted, the SLD child may not have sufficient knowledge of grammatical relations to arrive at the intended meaning. Communication tasks which present nonredundant material, providing little contextual support, however, enable the tester to assess difficulties in the grasp of syntax. When it is measured in this more stringent fashion, the superiority of receptive over expressive language functioning may still be present. That is, the difference may be a real one rather than an artifact of the test employed.

These differences, taken together with the asymmetrical relationship between comprehension and expression of language in normal infants, suggest that different processes may be involved in different types of SLD. In other words, different patterns of delay or deficit in auditory rate processing and auditory sequencing, in sequencing of volitional oral movements, and in abstracting linguistic rules may be found among SLD children. Recent findings (Stark and Tallal, 1980) do, indeed, suggest that the level of receptive language may be significantly correlated with measures of auditory perception in children with SLD. The measures of auditory perception include discrimination of speech-like stimuli, that is, of synthesized consonant vowel (CV) syllables in which rapidly changing vowel formant transitions provide the essential cues to identification. The results of the Stark-Tallal study also suggest that auditory processing abilities increase with age in normal and language delayed children. Receptive language and auditory processing abilities may tend to develop in relation to one another in SLD children. Improvement in language comprehension, however, may be related to overall intelligence in these children as well as to their changing auditory capabilities.

Stark and Tallal (1980) have, in addition, shown that the level of expressive language in SLD children may be significantly related to persisting speech articulation deficits and possibly to deficits in rate and in sequencing of movements of the articulators also. Additional studies suggest that naming difficulties are likely to be present in children with expressive language deficits; and that factors associated with nonverbal intelligence are quite highly correlated with expressive language in SLD children also.

In summary, there are SLD children who have deficits in receptive *and* expressive language, and there are SLD children in whom deficits in expressive language only are present. These language deficits vary in degree or severity. Grammatical development may be delayed because of more primary deficits in lower level speech processing; alternatively, difficulty or delay in organizing auditory input and/or speech motor output within a rule-governed system may give rise to deficits in phonologic and/or syntactic development. The terms "lower level" and "higher level" are used only in relation to a psychological description of language, however, and not to specific cortical or subcortical structures that might be involved.

Deviant Language

Children with deviant language do not simply show a delay in acquisition of the form of language but present instead less well understood deficits and sometimes bizarre language behaviors. A few children with deviant language have normal or near-normal nonverbal intelligence. These children may have a history of head trauma or other neurologic lesion in infancy or early childhood. They may properly be referred to as developmentally dysphasic (Benton, 1964). Some of them may show symptoms of "word deafness;" others may show disordered syntax in their output, producing long strings of content words and few function words. As a result many of their utterances are ambiguous, even for those who know the situational context in which they are produced.

The term deviant is used to refer to gross mismatches in the level of a child's ability to manage the form, use *and* content of language, and/or to the inability to integrate the three dimensions of language. In addition, receptive and expressive language abilities may be poorly matched in children with deviant language, with expressive abilities sometimes being apparently much superior to receptive abilities.

Children with deviant language form an even more heterogeneous group than those who have SLD. Many are found to be functioning below the normal range in nonverbal intelligence as well as in verbal intelligence on the WPPSI or WISC-R Scales. Children with deviant language may also show an uneven profile of subtest scores on the Performance Scale of the WPPSI or WISC-R. They may also present marked differences in level of performance on tests of component, perceptual, and motor skills, as well as across the domains of language and cognition.

Other children with deviant language development appear to have auditory and speech motor abilities that are superior to their nonverbal cognitive functioning; still others have verbal and nonverbal cognitive abilities that are superior to their ability to interact with people or to communicate. Many of these children are highly imitative. They may be able to produce a limited set of long and fairly complex sentences without error, even though they do not understand the sentences. In this, they are not like normal children, who will rephrase a sentence in an imitation task in such a way that the new version matches their own grammatical ability and reflects their comprehension of the sentence (Menyuk, 1969). Children with deviant language may produce these stock sentences in appropriate situational contexts and may even be capable of manipulating aspects of syntax within them. They may, for example, have control over the use of pronouns or verb forms in the limited set of utterances they produce. At the same time it may be observed that the content of their output is very different from that of a normal child at the same level of cognitive development.

A 12-year-old boy exemplifying this type of deviant language produced sentences in appropriate situational contexts and with minimal prompting, such as, "May I have the pinball machine (or other toy) please?" This child could not, however, encode simple object relations in his spontaneous utterances. His comprehension of language was estimated to be at the two-year level. Another child, an 8-year-old, showed a less severe disorder of this kind. He could name colors and shapes (including trapezoid and rhomboid shapes) accurately but he could not encode agent-action meaning relations, or locative or possessive relations. An example of this child's spontaneous speech, produced as a monologue while looking at a wall decoration, went as follows: "That's orange and gold and brown. Very good J. You said that correctly. That's a Thanksgiving turkey."

These children, and others with similar patterns of disability, show very little spontaneous, communicative use of language. Their comprehension of language may be much lower than would be expected from the grammatical level of the sentences they learn to produce by imitation. The forms of language which such children are capable of using in structured situations, forms that are learned by rote and used semi-appropriately, create a false impression of their intellectual interests and abilities. This impression may be confirmed by the presence of "splinter" skills, such as those of visual form matching. Teachers, therapists, and even parents may exacerbate the problems of these children by continuing to demand well-formed utterances from them, at a level of linguistic skill that is poorly matched with their overall cognitive skills. These adults may never engage the affected children in play activities that are appropriate to their level of cognitive functioning and their language comprehension. When such activities are initiated, these children may understand the speech addressed to them quite differently from before. They may begin to offer spontaneous comments and to make requests using forms that are consonant with their cognitive level. J., for example, would say "no more tweety bird," spontaneously and interactively in a game where farm animals could be made to disappear behind a screen, with much more enjoyment than attended his more formal, rote-learned speech.

Other children with deviant language appear to have a primary difficulty in interacting with both adults and children. If this difficulty is sufficiently severe, the children, who may be labeled as autistic or autistic-like, are likely to have severe deficits in both receptive and expressive language. Defects of articulation are less common in these children than in children with SLD or developmental aphasia (Rutter and Schopler, 1978). Many of them are below normal in intellectual functioning. They have been characterized as showing lack of eye contact and as engaging in a number of stereotypic patterns of behavior, among other symptoms (L. Wing, 1964; J.K. Wing, 1969). Echolalia is quite common among those who are able to speak and some produce a variety of language forms learned from television commercials. Such children also appear to have relatively good auditory perceptual and speech motor skills at least for imitative production of the phonetic aspects of speech. They may even learn to produce a number of rote-learned phrases in semi-appropriate contexts. It has been reported, however, that the prosodic aspects of their speech output are distorted and that they have difficulty in making use of the prosodic patterns of speech addressed to them in language comprehension (Simmons and Baltaxe, 1975). Pronoun use is also frequently deviant, for example, in the utterance, "What would you like P.? Would P. like a cookie? Yes P. wants cookie," produced by a child, P., who accepted and ate the cookie he was understood to be requesting. Still other children with deviant language may be able to read and write and may learn to interact with a computer in programmed learning sequences.

Language Intervention

It might be assumed from the foregoing that, if all dimensions of language are related to cognitive level in the normal child, then the goal of intervention should be to bring these dimensions, content, form, and use, into closer alignment with nonverbal intelligence in the language impaired child and at the same time to integrate them with one another. Such a goal would imply that, while improved language might enhance the language impaired child's overall cognitive development, the child's intellectual potential should ultimately limit the progress that may be made in both language and in cognition.

It is widely believed that cognitive development may also be facilitated or improved. Enrichment of the environment is most often proposed for this purpose (Bronfenbrenner, 1975). However, this belief is usually qualified, either explicitly or implicitly. It is assumed that the child's cognitive potential will ultimately limit the effects of an enrichment program. Such limitations are not always taken into account in planning language intervention programs for the handicapped child, particularly in the case of those who show significant mental retardation. Instead, the notion that speech and language delay or deficit can be ameliorated by special intervention techniques has become so prevalent that these techniques are often implemented without question.

Before language intervention begins, the child's verbal abilities and nonverbal intelligence should be carefully measured. His skill in communicating with others should also be assessed. In children who show unusual or deviant spoken language or lack of integration of form, content, and use in language comprehension, profiles of cognitive and language abilities should be studied. Nonverbal intelligence should not be estimated only on the basis of isolated or "splinter" skills, such as matching of geometric shapes or performance on the block design subtest of the WISC-R. Attempts should be made to determine the child's response to activities that are at a lower cognitive level than estimated from isolated skills. Component perceptual and motor skills, including speech articulation skills and the prosody and fluency of speech, should also be estimated. The child's responses to the prosody of speech, that is, to rhythmic patterning of speech and to its intonation contour should be assessed, as well as his responses to the phonetic aspect of speech. His responses to language learning programs, where there are no demands for interpersonal skills, should be documented.

If it becomes apparent that both language and cognition are delayed in a given child but commensurate with one another, and the child is communicating satisfactorily with others, then a language intervention program may not be indicated. Instead, the child might be provided with language stimulation designed to help him achieve his optimum level in all areas. If, however, language is delayed in relation to cognition or if a wide scatter of verbal and nonverbal skills is found to be present, language intervention may be indicated.

The belief is frequently expressed that the earlier language intervention is initiated, the better the outcome is likely to be. This assumption will be a difficult one to test. However, it suggests that early indications of communication disorder should be specified and used in screening instruments to identify infants and young children who may be at risk for such a disorder. At present the following indications might be considered in infancy and early childhood for this purpose:

1. Excessive crying in infancy, especially after 3 months of age; failure to quiet to familiar voice.
2. Lack of crying in an infant or crying that is perceived as abnormal.
3. Lack of eye contact and/or of smiling after 3 months of age.

4. Lack of vocalization in response to smiling adults from 3 to 6 months of age, especially when the adults talk to the baby, then wait for a reply.
5. Expressions of dislike of being held in an infant.
6. Failure to produce consonant sounds in the first year of life.
7. Delayed appearance of cooing, laughing, play with sounds, reduplicated babbling, and other speech production milestones.
8. Failure to indicate communicative intention nonverbally by one year of age.
9. Failure to respond to environmental sounds.
10. Difficulty in localizing a sound source correctly after 9–12 months.
11. Failure to respond to voices of family members, for example, when they return after an absence, in the second 6 months of life.
12. Failure to respond in interactive peek-a-boo and patty-cake games by one year of age.
13. Failure to indicate one or two familiar objects when these are named, at the beginning of the second year.
14. Report that a child does not understand what is said to him, "takes no notice" of what is said to him, or takes "a long time to catch on" when he is spoken to, at the end of the second year.
15. Delayed appearance of single-words, of the expected rapid increase in vocabulary some time thereafter, or of multi-word utterances in the second and third year.

As soon as it is feasible, more detailed assessment of auditory sensitivity, auditory perception, speech motor skills, speech production, phonological, semantic, and syntactic development, ability to maintain discourse and to use language in context should be assessed in children thought to be at risk for a communication disorder. Nonverbal cognitive functioning should be assessed by means of careful observation of spontaneous behavior as well as more structured developmental scales.

In conclusion, it is suggested that a detailed assessment of abilities should be carried out in children suspected of language delay or of deviant language behavior. This assessment should include measurement of cognitive functioning or, in older children, of nonverbal intelligence as well as of language and language-related abilities. This assessment should always precede intervention. The measurements and the description of the child's disorder should be cast in terms of the 3 dimensions of language that have been dealt with in this text namely, content, form and use. These dimensions and their interaction may be much more complex than has previously been supposed; they may interact with one another from the beginning of life. Nevertheless, it is suggested that this model will continue to be a productive one for studies of both language development and language disorders in children for some time to come.

Bibliography:
Section IV

Aronson, E. and Rosenbloom, S. (1973) Space perception in early infancy: Perception within a common auditory—visual space. *Science* 172:1161–1163.

Andrews, S., Blumenthal, J., Bache, W., and Wiener, G. (1975) *Parents as Early Childhood Educators: The New Orleans Models.* Paper presented at the Biennial Meeting of the Society for Research in Child Development.

Aslin, R.N. and Pisoni, D.B. (1980) Effects of early linguistic experience on speech discrimination by infants. A critique of Eilers, Gavin, and Wilson (1979). *Child Development* 51:107–112.

Aslin, R.N., Hennessy, B., Pisoni, D., and Perey, A. (1979) Individual infants' discrimination of voice onset time: Evidence for three modes of voicing. Paper presented at the Biennial Meeting of the Society for Research in Child Development.

Bates, E., Benigni, L., Bretherton, I., Camaioni, L., and Volterra, V. (1977) From gesture to first word: On cognitive and social prerequisites. In M. Lewis and L. Rosenblum (Eds.), *Interaction, Conversation and the Development of Language.* New York: Wiley.

Bates, E., Benigni, L., Bretherton, I., Cameroni, L., and Volterra, V. (1977) From gesture to first word: On cognitive and social prerequisites. In M. Lewis and L. Rosenblum (Eds.), *Interaction, Conversation and the Development of Language.* New York: Wiley.

Bayley, N. (1969) *Bayley Scales of Infant Development.* New York: The Psychological Corporation.

Benton, A. (1964) Developmental aphasia and brain damage. *Cortex* 1:40–52.

Bloom, L. and Lahey, M. (1978) *Language Development and Language Disorders.* New York: Wiley.

Bloom, L., Hood, L., and Lightbown, P. (1974) Imitation in language development: If, when, and why. *Cognitive Psychology* 6:380–420.

Bloom, L., Lightbown, P., and Hood, L. (1975) Structure and variation in child language. *Monographs of the Society for Research in Child Development* 40 (no. 2, serial #160).

Bower, T.G.R. (1974) *Development in Infancy.* San Francisco: W.H. Freeman and Co.

Bronfenbrenner, U. (1975) Is early intervention effective? In *Influences on Human Development*. U. Bronfenbrenner (Ed.) (2nd edition). Hinsdale, Illinois: Dryden Press, pp. 329–354.

Bruner, J. (1975) The ontogenesis of speech acts. *Journal of Child Language* 2:1–19.

Capute, A.J. (1975) Developmental disabilities: An overview. *Dental Clinics of North America* 18:557–577.

Capute, A.J. and Biehl, R.F. (1973) Functional developmental evaluation; prerequisite to habilitation. *Pediatric Clinics of North America* 20:3–26.

Capute, A.J. and Accardo, P.J. (1978) Linguistic and auditory milestones during the first two years of life. *Clinical Pediatrics* 17:847–853.

Carew, J. (1975) Predicting IQ from the young child's everyday experience. Paper presented at the Symposium "Soziale Bedingungen fur die Entwicklung der Lernfahigheit" in Bad Homburg, Germany. (An earlier version of this paper was also presented at the Biennial Meeting of the Society for Research in Child Development.)

Carpenter, G.C. (1973) Differential response to mother and stranger within the first month of life. *Bulletin of the British Psychological Society* 26:138.

Cattell, P. (1940) *The Measurement of Intelligence of Infants and Young Children*. New York: The Psychological Corporation.

Chase, R. (1972) Neurological aspects of language disorders in children. In J.V. Irwin and M. Marge (Eds.), *Principles of Childhood Language Disabilities*. New York: Appleton Century Crofts.

Clarke-Stewart, K.A. (1973) Interactions between mothers and their young children: Characteristics and consequences. *Monographs of the Society for Research in Child Development* 38 (6–7, Serial #153).

Corrigan, R. (1978) Language development as related to Stage 6 object permanence development. *Journal of Child Language* 5:173–190.

Danaher, E.M., Osberger, M.J., and Pickett, J.M. (1973) Discrimination of formant frequency transitions in synthetic vowels. *Journal of Speech and Hearing Research* 16:439–451.

Deutsch, C. (1973) Social class and child development. In B. Caldwell and H. Ricciuti (Eds.), *Review of Child Development Research, Vol. 3*. Chicago: University of Chicago Press, pp. 233–282.

Dore, J. (1974) A pragmatic description of early language development. *Journal of Psycholinguistic Research* 3:343–350.

Dunn, L.M. (1959) *Peabody Picture Vocabulary Test*. Circle Pines, Minnesota: American Guidance Service.

Eguchi, S. and Hirsh, I. (1969) Development of speech sounds in children. *Acta Otolaryngologica*. Supplement 257, Uppsala, Sweden.

Eisenson, J. (1972) *Aphasia in Children*. New York: Harper and Row.

Elliott, L. (1962) Backward masking: Monotic and diotic conditions. *Journal of the Acoustical Society of America* 34:1108–1115.

Freeberg, N. and Payne, D. (1967) Parental influence on cognitive development in early childhood: A Review. *Child Development* 38:65–89.

Gesell, A. and Amatruda, C. (1941) *Developmental Diagnosis*. New York: Paul Hoeber, Inc.

Golden, M. and Birns, B. (1976) Social class and infant intelligence. In M. Lewis (Ed.), *Origins of Intelligence*. New York: Plenum Press, pp. 299–352.

Goldstein, U. (1980) An articulatory model of the vocal tracts of growing children. Unpublished doctoral dissertation, MIT.

Goodson, B. and Hess, R.D. (1976) *The effects of parent training programs on child performance and parent behavior*. Unpublished manuscript, Stanford University.

Halliday, M.A.K. (1973) *Exploration in the Functions of Language*. London: Edward Arnold.

Hardy, J.B. (1971) Rubella as a teratogen. In *Birth Defects: An Original Article Series, Vol. 7, No. 1.*

Hardy, J.B. (Ed.) (1971a) The Johns Hopkins Collaborative Perinatal Project Symposium, March 30, 1970. Factors affecting the growth and development of children. Monograph of collected reprints from proceedings published in *The Johns Hopkins Medical Journal*.

Hardy, J.B. (1973) Fetal consequences of maternal viral infections in pregnancy. *Archives of Otolaryngology* 98:218–227.

Hardy, J.B. and Mellits, E.D. (1976) Relationship of low birthweight to maternal characteristics of age, parity, education and body size. In D.M. Reed and F.J. Stanley (Eds.), *The Epidemiology of Prematurity*. Proceedings of a working conference held at NICHD/NIH, Bethesda, Maryland.

Hardy, J.B., Welcher, D.W., Stanley, J., and Dallas, J.R. (1978) The long-range outcome of adolescent pregnancy. *Clinical Obstetrics and Gynecology* 21:1215–1232.

Hess, R.D. (1970) Social class and ethnic influences upon socialization. In P. Mussen (Ed.), *Manual of Child Psychology*. New York: Wiley.

Hirsh, I. (1959) Auditory perception of temporal order. *Journal of the Acoustical Society of America* 57:1547–1551.

Hirsh, I. and Sherrick, C.E. (1961) Perceived order in different sensory modalities. *Journal of Esperimental Psychology* 62:423–432.

Illingworth, R.S. (1962) An introduction to developmental assessment in the first year, *Little Club Clinics in Developmental Medicine*, No. 3. London: The National Spastics Society Medical Education and Information Unit in Association with William Heinemann Medical Books, Ltd.

Illingworth, R.S. (1970) *Development of the Infant and Young Child, Normal and Abnormal*. Baltimore: Williams & Wilkins.

Ingram, D. (in press) The transition from early symbols to syntax. In R. Schiefelbusch (Ed.), *Early Language Intervention*. Baltimore: University Park Press.

Knobloch, H., Pasamanick, B., and Sherad, E.S., Jr. (1966) A developmental screening inventory for infants. *Pediatrics* 38:1095–1108.

Leichter, H. (1974) *The Family as Educator*. New York: Teachers College Press.

Lieberman, P. (1968) Primate vocalizations and human linguistic ability. *Journal of the Acoustical Society of America* 44:1574–1584.

Lillywhite, H.S. (1958) Doctor's manual of speech disorder. *Journal of the American Medical Association* 167:850–858.

Lillywhite, H.S., Young, N.B., and Olmsted, R.W. (1970) *Pediatrician's Handbook of Communication Disorders*. Philadelphia: Lea & Febiger.

McCarthy, D. (1954) Language development in children. In L. Carmichael (Ed.), *Manual of Child Psychology*. New York: Wiley.

McGraw, M.B. (1954) Maturation of behavior. In L. Carmichael (Ed.), *Manual of Child Psychology*. New York: Wiley.

Mecham, M.J. (1971) *Verbal Language Development Scale*. Circle Pines, Minnesota: American Guidance Service.

Menyuk, P. (1964) Comparison of grammar of children with functionally deviant and normal speech. *Journal of Speech and Hearing Research* 7:109–121.

Menyuk, P. (1969) *Sentences Children Use*. Cambridge, Mass.: MIT Press.

Miller, J.F., Chapman, R.S., Branston, M.E., and Reichle, J. (1980) Language comprehension in sensorimotor Stages V and VI. *Journal of Speech and Hearing Research* 23:284–311.

Morehead, D.M. and Ingram, D. (1973) The development of base syntax in normal and linguistically deviant children. *Journal of Speech and Hearing Research* 16:330–352.

Nelson, K. (1973) Structure and strategy in learning to talk. *Monographs of the Society for Research in Child Development* 38 (1–2, Serial #149).

Northern, J. and Downs, M. (1974) *Hearing in Children*. Baltimore: William & Wilkins.

Oller, D.K. (1978) Infant vocalizations and the development of speech. *Allied Health and Behavioral Sciences* 1:523–549.

Oller, D.K. (1980) The emergence of the sounds of speech in infancy. In G. Yeni-Komshian, C.A. Ferguson, and J. Kavanagh (Eds.), *Child Phonology: Vol. I Production*. New York: Academic Press.

Papoušek, H. (1969) Individual variability in learned responses in human infants. In R.J. Robinson (Ed.), *Brain and Early Behavior*. London: Academic Press.

Patterson, J.H. and Green, D.M. (1971) Masking of transient signals having identical energy spectra. *Audiology* 10:85–96.

Pickett, J.M. (1959) Backward masking. *Journal of the Acoustical Society of America* 31:1613–1615.

Pisoni, D. (1977) Identification and discrimination of the relative onset time of two component tones: Implications for voicing perception in stops. *Journal of the Acoustical Society of America* 61:1352–1361.

Poole, I. (1934) Genetic development of articulation of consonant sounds in speech. *Elementary English Review, Vol. 159*.

Rees, N.S. (1975) Auditory processing factors in language disorders: The view from Procrustes bed. *Journal of Speech and Hearing Disorders* 39:305–315.

Rees, N.S. (1981) Saying more than we know: Is auditory processing a meaningful concept? In R. Keith (Ed.), *Central Auditory and Language Disorders in Children*. Houston: College Press.

Resnick, S.B. and Feth, L.L. (1975) Discriminability of time-reversed click pairs: Intensity effects. *Journal of the Acoustical Society of America* 57:1493–1499.

Rutter, M. (1979) Maternal deprivation 1972–1978: New findings, new concepts, new approaches. *Child Development* 50:283–305.

Rutter, M. and Schopler, E. (1978) *Autism: A Reappraisal of Concepts and Treatment*. New York: Plenum Press.

Sheridan, M.D. (1968) *Developmental Progress of Infants and Young Children*. London: Her Majesty's Stationary Office.

Simon, C. and Fourcin, A. (1978) Cross-language study of speech-pattern learning. *Journal of the Acoustical Society of America* 63:925–935.

Simmons, J. and Baltaxe, C.L. (1975) Language patterns of autistic children who have reached adolescence. *Journal of Autism and Childhood Schizophrenia* 5:333–351.

Sinclair, H. (1970) The transition from sensory motor behavior to symbolic activity. *Interchange* 1:119–129.

Smith, B.L. (1978) Temporal aspects of English speech production: A developmental perspective. *Journal of Phonetics* 6:37–67.

Smith, B.L. and Oller, D.K. (1980) A comparative study of pre-meaningful vocalizations produced by normal and Down syndrome infants (in preparation).

Stanley, J. (in press) *Effect of Parenting Education*. Proceedings of the "Symposium of Adolescent Pregnancy: Management and Prevention, An Investment in Future," held October 3–5, 1979.

Stark, R.E. (1980) Stages of speech development in the first year of life. In Grace H. Yeni-Komshian, C.A. Ferguson, and J. Kavanagh (Eds.), *Child Phonology: Production Vol. I.* New York: Academic Press.

Stark, R.E. and Resnich, S.B. (in preparation) Measurement of prespeech skills in young children. Research Grant MCR409 from Maternal and Child Health.

Stark, R.E. and Tallal, P. (1980) Sensory and perceptual functioning of young children with and without delayed language development. Final Report, NINCDS Contract NS-5-2323.

Stark, R.E. and Tallal, P. (1981) Perceptual and motor deficits in language impaired children. In R. Keith (Ed.), *Central Auditory and Language Disorders in Children*. Houston: College Press.

Stark, R.E. and Tallal, P. (in press) Selection of children with specific language deficits. *Journal of Speech and Hearing Disorders*.

Tallal, P. and Piercy, M. (1973) Defects of nonverbal auditory processing in children with development aphasia. *Nature* 242:468–469.

Tallal, P. and Stark, R.E. (in press) A re-examination of some nonverbal perceptual abilities of language impaired and normal children as a function of age and sensory modality. *Journal of Hearing and Speech Research*.

Templin, M.C. (1956) The study of articulation and language development during the early school years. In S. Smith and G.A. Miller (Eds.), *The Genesis of Language*. Cambridge: MIT Press.

Trevarthan, C. (1975) Growth of visuomotor coordination in infants. *Journal of Human Movement Studies* 1:57.

Twitchell, T.E. (1965) The automatic grasping responses of infants. *Neuropsychologia* 3:247–259.

Weiss, E. and Jackson, E.C. (1969) Maternal factors affecting birthweight. In *Perinatal Factors Affecting Human Development*. Washington, D.C.: Pan American Health Organization, Scientific Publication No. 185, pp. 54–59.

Winick, M. (1969) Malnutrition and brain development. *Journal of Pediatrics* 74:667–679.

Wing, J.K. (1969) (Ed.) *Early Childhood Autism: Clinical, Educational and Social Aspects*. New York: Pergamon Press.

Wing, L. (1964) *Autistic Children*. London: National Association for Mental Health and Society for Autistic Children.

Zelazo, P.R., Zelazo, N.A., and Kolb, S. (1972) "Walking" in the newborn. *Science* 176:314–315.

Author Index

Subject Index